SURVIVAL ON THE MARGINS

SURVIVAL ON THE MARGINS

Polish Jewish Refugees in the Wartime Soviet Union

ELIYANA R. ADLER

HARVARD UNIVERSITY PRESS

Cambridge, Massachusetts & London, England

2020

Library of Congress Cataloging-in-Publication Data

Names: Adler, Eliyana R., author.
Title: Survival on the margins : Polish Jewish refugees in the wartime
    Soviet Union / Eliyana R. Adler.
Description: Cambridge, Massachusetts : Harvard University Press, 2020. |
    Includes bibliographical references and index.
Identifiers: LCCN 2020027130 | ISBN 9780674988026 (hardcover)
Subjects: LCSH: Jews, Polish—Refugees—Soviet Union. | World War,
    1939–1945—Refugees—Soviet Union. | Holocaust, Jewish (1939–1945) |
    Return migration—Poland—History—20th century.
Classification: LCC D809.P6 A34 2020 | DDC 940.53/180869140947—dc23
LC record available at https://lccn.loc.gov/2020027130

And I,

fugitive from under that black pall

am homeless still,

a wanderer,

nomad, with no guide,

a leper

scarred by adversity and pain.

—ROKHL KORN

FOR THE WANDERERS

Contents

Note on Transliteration and Translation

In transliterating foreign words, I use the standard Library of Congress system for Russian and the modified one (lacking diacritics) for Hebrew. The YIVO transliteration system is employed for Yiddish. Proper names of people and of places introduce some additional challenges. I have endeavored to transliterate people's names according to the language in which they wrote. Thus, the biblical name Rachel might appear as Rokhl in a Yiddish document, Rahel in Hebrew, and Rachela in Polish. With people who published in more than one language, I have chosen the language they were most associated with or the most common spelling of their name. When appropriate, I have relied upon the *YIVO Encyclopedia of Jews in Eastern Europe* for the proper spelling of the names of prominent East European Jews. However, at times a less consistent form of the name has been employed because it is more widely known: thus, Peretz Markish instead of Perets Markish.

In an attempt to avoid both politics and anachronism, I spell place names according to their chronological appearance in the narrative. Thus, if someone was born in a Polish city before the war, it will be spelled as it was then (Kowel, Białystok). However, if someone else traveled through that same city while it was under Soviet rule, a transliteration of the Russian name will be used (Kovel, Bialystok). Parenthetical notations list previous and current names in alphabetical order. The Yiddish alternative is offered only when it differs significantly from the others. The only exceptions are names given in direct quotations or when dealing with cities with an accepted English form (Warsaw, Kiev).

Although these same standards apply to cities and regions within the old borders of the USSR, I have often followed the lead of the Polish Jewish refugees in referring to Central Asian areas. The Uzbek Soviet Socialist Republic was not an independent country at the time of study. Yet, those who passed through there invariably describe having lived in Uzbekistan. For clarity, I will use the standard name of Soviet regions rather than the Russian adjectival forms (i.e., Altai and not Altaiskaia).

Translations are my own, except when cited from English-language or translated sources.

SOVIET AND GERMAN DIVISION OF POLAND AND THE BALTIC STATES, 1939-1940

UNION OF SOVIET SOCIALIST REPUBLICS, CIRCA 1940

SFSR Soviet Federal Socialist Republic

SSR Soviet Socialist Republic

Svalbard

SWEDEN

Barents Sea

FINLAND

• Murmansk

Tallinn

LATVIAN SSR

Riga ESTONIAN SSR

LITHUANIAN SSR

KARELO-FINNISH SSR

Vilnius

• Grodno

Leningrad

Arkhangelsk

Warsaw

BELORUSSIAN SSR

Minsk

• Smolensk

VOLOGDA OBLAST

Kotlas •

KOMI ASSR

Yaroslavl

• Syktyvkar

UKRAINIAN SSR

Moscow

Gorky • Yoshkar-Ola • Kirov

MOLOTOV OBLAST

• Chernovits • Kiev

MOLDAVIAN SSR

MARI ASSR

• Berezniki

Toryal •

UDMURT ASSR

Kharkòv •

Kremenchug

URAL MOUNTAINS

Molotov •

Kherson • Voroshilovgrad •

CRIMEAN ASSR

• Stalino

VOLGA GERMAN ASSR

Saratov

Kuibyshev

• Sverdlovsk

R

Rostov • Kachalino •

Black Sea

Volga

• Buzuluk

Chelyabinsk •

Stalingrad

CHKALOV OBLAST

Magnitogorsk •

• Omsk

Tomsk •

Astrakhan •

Novosibirsk •

KE

GEORGIAN SSR

• Barnau

Staliniri •

Caspian Sea

ALTAI KRAI

Tbilisi

KAZAKH SSR

Yerevan

Aral Sea

Semipalatinsk •

ARMENIAN SSR

AZERBAIJAN SSR

Baku

UZBEK SSR

Alma-Ata

TURKMEN SSR

Tashkent

Ashkabad

Frunze

KIRGHIZ SSR

IRAN

Stalinabad

TAJIK SSR

RCTIC OCEAN

*Bering
Sea*

C OCEAN

N

YAKUT ASSR

•Yakutsk

Magadan
•

*Sea of
Okhotsk*

N S F S R

Sakhalin

Irkutsk
•

JAPAN

*Sea of
Japan*

MONGOLIA

500 miles

0

1000 km

A

*Yellow
Sea*

CENTRAL ASIAN REPUBLICS AND KAZAKHSTAN, 1940s

POLAND, 1946

	Polish territory annexed by the USSR
	German territory annexed by Poland
	Other territory annexed by the USSR
–·–·–	Poland border in 1946

Baltic Sea

Rīga

LATVIAN SSR

LITHUANIAN SSR

Kaunas

Vilnius

KALININGRÅD
OBLAST
Kaliningrad

N

SZCZECIN

•Gdańsk

GDAŃSK

OLSZTYN

Olsztyn •

•Grodno

•Szczecin

POMERANIA

•Bydgoscz

BIAŁYSTOK

Białystok •

BELO-
RUSSIAN
SSR

Odra

POZNAŃ

Poznań •

Vistula

WARSAW

Bug

U.S.S.R.

⊚Berlin

Odra

•Radzyń

⊚Warsaw

Biała Podlaska

Warta

•Łódź

ŁÓDŹ

Tomaszów
(Mazowiecki)

Ryki•

LUBLIN

WROCŁAW

Zgorzelec

•Wrocław

•Lubań

Wałbrzych

•Dzierżoniów

Ziębice•

SILESIA

POLAND

•Częstochowa

KIELCE

•Kielce

•Lublin

Hrubieszów

Zamość

Elbe

⊚Prague

•Katowice

Bielsko
•

•Kraków

KRAKÓW

RZESZÓW

•Rzeszów

San

•Lvov

UKRAINIAN
SSR

C Z E C H O S L O V A K I A

Danube

AUSTRIA

0   100 miles

200 km

SURVIVAL ON THE MARGINS

Introduction

On the Other Side

> Now the number of carts that pass through the street filled
> with people bound for the Other Side, increases from day
> to day. None of the tenants can sit home anymore, business
> and work are at a standstill, the remaining household
> possessions are sold, and everyone dreams only about going
> to the Other Side.
>
> —PERETZ OPOCZYNSKI

IN "HOUSE NO. 21," Peretz Opoczynski used his building and its residents as a microcosm for Warsaw Jewish society in the early weeks and months of the Second World War. Throughout the piece, filed with the underground archive of the Warsaw Ghetto in 1941, Opoczynski's neighbors continuously discuss whether and when they should flee east: "By now this has become the sole topic of conversation in the tenement: in front of the gate, in sitting rooms by day and in beds by night."[1] In Opoczynski's original, the Polish Jews use the vague but laden Yiddish term *yener zayt* to refer to the Polish territory newly occupied by the USSR.[2] In a culture in which certain topics were best left unsaid, *yener zayt* allowed Yiddish speakers to gesture toward unspeakable concepts—such as death, prison, or Soviet territory—without naming them. Although Yiddish lacks capital letters, Robert Wolf's translation renders it the "Other Side," capturing the portentous connotation. Also contained within the term is the sense of the unknown. Even as they rehash rumors and pass around letters, the Jews in German-occupied Poland have very little idea what is going on across the newly established border in the Soviet zone.

1

Moreover, the Other Side provides a compelling metaphor to conceptualize the survival of as many as two hundred thousand Polish Jews, the bulk of the survivors of the largest Jewish community in Europe, deep in Soviet territory. Their choice to flee east—and subsequent choices—placed them outside the reach of the Nazi genocide. Yet it also placed them in a sort of netherworld of history and memory; on the *other side* of the stories we tell about the Holocaust and the Second World War. This book aims to recover and reintegrate their stories.

During the fall of 1939, following the dual invasions of Poland, well over 100,000 Polish Jews chose to flee from the areas conquered by the Nazis to those newly under Soviet control. Although they did not know it at the time, this decision effectively changed the trajectory of their lives. Unlike the Polish Jews who stayed behind, and soon faced ghettoization and death at the hands of Adolf Hitler's forces, those who fled to Soviet territory came under Joseph Stalin's fist. They were deported to labor installations in Kazakhstan and Siberia, amnestied to Central Asia, and later repatriated to Communist Poland. The decision to flee placed them not only beyond the reach of the Holocaust but also beyond the scope of Holocaust scholarship and memory. In a 1959 article for *Yad Washem Studies,* historian Meir Korzen reflected on this absence:

> The Holocaust that swept the Jewish communities of Poland and other countries during the Nazi reign has almost completely diverted the attention of contemporary Jewish historiography from another dramatic and interesting episode in the history of the Jews during the Second World War—that of the Jewish refugees in the Soviet Union.[3]

Just over a decade after the end of the war, Korzen was already concerned about the eclipse of one Jewish war story in favor of another. His article primarily focuses on telling the story of the Polish Jewish refugees. Even in 1959, Korzen felt the need to familiarize his readers with the war experiences of Polish Jewish refugees. He ends with a plea for further research and recommends distributing questionnaires to learn more about the experiences of the forgotten survivors.

Although I do not believe that anyone ever followed Korzen's recommendation, fortunately the former refugees themselves have written and recorded numerous testimonies and memoirs about their experiences in the Soviet Union during the war. As Nora Levin has pointed out, "The history of the deported Jews remains to be written, but a number of survivors have recounted their experiences."[4] This book seeks to fill that gap, using auto-biographical accounts and other available primary sources to present the story of Polish Jews in the Soviet Union and reflect on its marginal status in historical scholarship. Scholars generally agree that the majority of Polish Jews who survived World War II did so in the USSR, although the exact number of these survivors remains contested. Polish survivors, in turn, formed the majority of Jewish displaced persons (DPs) after the war and established many of the historical commissions and commemorative practices that set the stage for how the Jewish tragedy would come to be constructed and understood. How, then, is it possible that one chapter of that story was almost entirely displaced by another?

While scholars and survivors are aware of the Polish Jewish refugees, their stories of survival remain peripheral to the study of the Holocaust. Historians, on the whole, have noted their existence only when they exited, and then reentered, the more central story of the Nazi genocide against the Jews. For example, Saul Friedländer's masterful work on the Holocaust refers to the Polish Jews who fled to the USSR only in passing. He contrasts the deteriorating conditions in the German-occupied areas of Poland with the conditions experienced by Polish Jews under Soviet occupation:

> While the German grip over the Jewish population of the Warthegau and the General Government was tightening, in the Soviet-occupied zone of Poland, the 1.2 million local Jews and the approximately 300,000 to 350,000 Jewish refugees from the western part of the country were getting acquainted with the heavy hand of Stalinism.[5]

Refugees who stayed in the newly acquired Soviet territories reappear later in Friedländer's account, as they were murdered during the 1941 German invasion. Yet those who were deported into the Soviet interior disappear from the narrative entirely.

In his important work on postwar DPs, Zeev Mankowitz notes the return of the refugees, and even their large numbers, but focuses on the Holocaust survivors among the Surviving Remnant (She'erit Hapletah).

> It turns out that by the end of 1946 fully two-thirds of *She'erith Hapleitah* were repatriates who had not been personally and directly caught up in the Nazi policies of terror, torture and killing. They had endured harsh, and for some, fatal years of exile; in most cases they lost their families from whom they were separated and, on their return, found their homes occupied by

others, their property stolen or confiscated and facing a world that had turned alien and implacably hostile. Their situation, nonetheless, was very different from those who had survived the horrors of the Shoah and their demographic structure, most particularly, was strikingly dissimilar to the founding nucleus of *She'erith Hapleitah*.[6]

After this key insight, however, Mankowitz, like other scholars of the survivor community, tends to treat the Surviving Remnant as if it were a group composed exclusively of those who survived under Nazi occupation.

Scholarship on the emigration of DPs abroad also tends to obscure the Polish Jewish refugees. Dina Porat has noted that "in 1951, one out of every two Israelis was a newcomer, and practically one out of four was a survivor. According to recent research, 25 per cent of the fighting forces in the War of Independence and 15 per cent of the casualties were survivors."[7] She acknowledges that no one was keeping track of the many new arrivals and their previous experiences. Even these approximate percentages, therefore, must assume the identities of the survivors based on where they came from. In these examples and many others the refugees are subsumed within the survivor population.

Indeed, Polish Jewish refugees who survived in the Soviet Union frequently disappear into larger or more prominent historical trends. Whether or not they count as Holocaust survivors, the "survivor" nomenclature used in many historical accounts does not effectively distinguish them as a subgroup. Throughout this book, therefore, I will refer to them by a number of names. Most often they will be called refugees or Polish Jewish refugees. Fleeing from western Poland inaugurated their wartime journey. Moreover, their status as refugees often lasted well beyond the war. Additionally, both at the time in official documents and later in historical treatments, they were often categorized as refugees. Although, as Olga Medvedeva-Nathoo points out, even this single term can have multiple meanings with the Russian (*bezhenets*) connoting constant movement and the Polish (*uchodźca*) suggesting one who has completed the act of leaving.[8]

Elsewhere they will also be referred to as Polish citizens, former Polish citizens, deportees, and repatriates, although each of these designations can also be confusing. Certainly they considered themselves to be Polish citizens, despite the fact that Poland no longer existed and the Soviet authorities tried, at various points, to force them to accept Soviet citizenship. Deportation, when applied to the Second World War, typically brings to mind

German cattle cars instead of Soviet freight wagons. And the term *repatriation,* although used in all of the documentation at the time, elides the fact that many Polish citizens who "returned" had to leave behind their homes and property in the annexed Soviet territories and move into regions that had been part of Germany before the war. Atina Grossmann has pointed to the irony of these Central European Jews being called Westerners (*zapadniki*) in the Soviet Union and then Asiatics back in Poland after the war.[9] Allied administrators of DP camps often referred to them as infiltrees. In narrating the postwar period I will also make use of the term *flight survivors* even though it is not in wide usage.[10] The lack of a simple appellation for this population illustrates the marginalization of their story, but also the ways in which that story touches on so many others.

My own engagement with this topic developed gradually. It began with individual, almost unbelievable stories. The relatively popular, and highly evocative, memoiristic novels—or novelistic memoirs—of Chaim Grade and Esther Hautzig tell remarkable tales of deportation or flight from Vilna and survival in exotic locales.[11] I also heard several fragments of stories from friends and acquaintances: the Polish Jewish father born in Magnitogorsk, the Ashkenazi rabbi who celebrated his bar mitzvah in Bukhara, the many Polish Jews who describe their own and their parents' survival in Siberia. It took a long time for me to realize that these experiences were ultimately all part of one larger story of the war and its displacements, and even longer to appreciate that I would be the one to tell it.

In the first chapter of his groundbreaking book *Neighbors,* Jan Gross describes the passage of five years between his introduction to the primary document that formed the basis for his project and his willingness to accept its validity.[12] While this project does not require nearly as much suspension of disbelief or painful reckoning, my awareness of the story that I would tell also dawned slowly. Only once I understood that these stories of survival were part of the larger story of the Holocaust and World War II did I begin to conduct research to find out more.

Yosef Litvak, both a survivor of the experience and a historian, published the only full-length treatment of the Polish Jewish refugees in the Soviet Union in Hebrew in 1988.[13] The book was never translated and is now fairly difficult to obtain. Litvak's work is remarkably thorough, making use of all the archival documents available at the time. Although he does include references to autobiographies, he is chiefly concerned with explaining the ongoing political shifts in Soviet policy that dictated the refugees' status. This is a tremendously complicated area, and one where the documents are not forthcoming. Litvak does an excellent job coaxing a narrative out of diplomatic, memoiristic, philanthropic, and other sources.

This work differs from Litvak's not so much in its access to sources but in its approach and focus. Some new documents have been released, and others discovered, since his pioneering study, but not as many as one might hope after the passage of thirty years. In the Soviet Union the Polish Jewish refugees were primarily overseen by the state security services. Unfortunately, neither the Russian Federation nor most of the other successor states to the Soviet Union have been willing to grant access to these records. This reticence stems, of course, from concerns about other potentially damaging information in their archives rather than any particular interest in this relatively minor tale. Somewhat ironically, the endurance of a surviving remnant of Polish Jewry under Soviet stewardship could provide a relatively positive angle on Soviet policies. I have even tried to argue this point with archivists in the former Soviet Union, to no avail.

However, the memoirs and testimonies that ground this study reflect on many realms of life that even the most thorough and voluminous government documents can never reveal. And while these accounts are certainly subjective, it is not necessarily true that archival material provides a more objective point of view. All documents contain bias, as do documentary repositories and their staffs. In Kate Brown's rendering, "archivists and historians know that documents can be inaccurate, obscurantist, aspirational, and sometimes just plain false, written to deceive. Historians are discovering that archives are not inert repositories, but contain their own narratives that are active in framing and determining the past."[14]

This may be even more true for Soviet sources, as Sonja Luehrmann explains: "In the case of Soviet documents, their relationship to what one might think of as social reality is further complicated by the fact that documentation of life in the USSR was never intended to be neutral or objective but to participate in transforming the reality it described."[15] Indeed, according to one group of scholars engaged in the use of oral histories to study life in the Soviet Union, "It is sometimes said, and is almost true, that 'for us the documents are subjective, and the only thing which might be objective are the memories.'"[16]

Additionally, as Joanna Michlic has noted, our sources determine the questions we can ask.[17] The present work is a social history, focused on the day-to-day existence of the refugees during the course of the war. How did they live? With whom did they live? What characterized their relations with various other groups of locals, evacuees, and deportees? This book is also concerned with the many difficult choices, large and small, that the refugees had to make during the war years. These are the sorts of questions that can only be explored via autobiographical sources.

Allowing the voices of the former refugees to guide the narrative has necessarily determined its direction. As much as possible, this book follows their lead. As a result, it at times differs from previous scholarship and may defy expectations regarding its approach to periodization, chronology, content, focus, and perspective. For example, readers might expect the discussion on deportation and the experience of forced labor to primarily address the latter. The deportees spent at most two months in passage, whereas all spent roughly a year engaged in heavy labor. However, in their own oral and written testimonies, at least as much space is devoted to the shocking experience of deportation as to the exile itself. Deportation was a pivotal period of transition for the Polish Jewish refugees, who discuss its various stages at length and in detail. Chapter 3 defers to their priorities, split between the experience of reaching the labor camps and what they found upon arrival.

The subject of philanthropy, addressed in Chapter 4, also illustrates how adopting the refugees' perspective shapes the resulting account. Aid to the refugees from a variety of governmental, semigovernmental, and nongovernmental actors is one of the few areas for which ample archival records exist. Previous scholars, including Yehuda Bauer, Atina Grossmann, Shlomo Kless, Yosef Litvak, and Keith Sword, have prepared excellent work on the tremendously complicated political, bureaucratic, geographic, and other obstacles involved in providing material aid to the refugees during the war.[18] Yet the refugees themselves evince surprisingly little interest in this topic. Materials received from the American Jewish Joint Distribution Committee and the Polish government-in-exile merit only cursory mention in their written and oral recollections, while packages from family members and friends loom large. The narrative thus focuses primarily on the impact of receiving items from loved ones within and outside the USSR.

People often ask me how much the refugees deep in Soviet territory knew about the Holocaust in Poland. This is another area where the testimonies defy expectation. Although we now know that information about the genocide appeared in Soviet news outlets and was available to the refugees, they overwhelmingly describe grasping the destruction only upon return to Poland. Of course, these narratives need not be contradictory. People can and do absorb individual facts without comprehending the bigger picture. Chapter 5 examines the ways in which news reached the refugees, as well as the experience of repatriation. While engaging with scholarly conversations to contextualize the refugees' access to information, it also endeavors to follow the lead of the testimonies themselves, acknowledging the ways in which the surviving refugees chose to frame their apprehension of the Holocaust.

In order to provide the fullest possible picture of refugee life in the Soviet Union during the war, I also seek to reflect the varied experiences of different groups within the larger community of exiled Polish Jews: older and younger refugees, men and women, religious and secular Jews, Polish and Yiddish speakers, those who came alone and those who traveled in family groups, and those of different levels of education and professional background. Testimonies produced during the war and immediately afterward are often short and unemotional. Some of the very first memoirs were produced by professional writers. Examining newer publications, as well as the wealth of oral testimonies, allows for a more diverse and representative sample.

For the sake of clarity, the book's narrative structure privileges what would become the most common path for Polish Jewish refugees: flight from Poland, resettlement in newly annexed Soviet territory, deportation to the interior, amnesty to Central Asia, repatriation to Poland, and then emigration to the West. However, there were also multiple junctures along the way where discrete groups of refugees forged different paths. For example, some refugees who fled to Soviet territory in 1939 stayed only long enough to reach unoccupied Lithuania. Although most were still there when the Soviet Union invaded in 1940, a few were fortunate enough to get visas allowing them to reach Shanghai or other ports outside Europe. At another pivotal moment, in 1942, several thousand refugees, including hundreds of orphans, managed to evacuate the Soviet Union via Iran with the Polish Army. I endeavor to include these alternative routes throughout the narrative.

This book also seeks to engage with the genre of testimonial literature more broadly and contribute to the growing scholarly conversation about the use of testimonies in historical research on the Holocaust. A sophisticated theoretical and methodological discussion on how to read and interpret testimonies has begun to influence the field of Holocaust studies. Nevertheless, concerns remain about the subjectivity of testimonial sources. In addition, some may hesitate to embrace these sources because of certain taboos about the Holocaust and survivors. It is my contention that the marginalized testimonies of Polish Jews who survived in the Soviet Union can shed light on the practice of reading Holocaust testimonies more broadly.[19]

Zoë Waxman's *Writing the Holocaust* is one of many scholarly works that has influenced my approach to reading testimonies. Waxman insists that Holocaust testimony is "contingent upon and mediated by" its own history, a claim that she develops through close reading of primarily published and translated Holocaust testimonies. Moreover, she highlights the heterogeneity of Holocaust experiences, as evidenced by these testimonies: "The Holocaust was not just one event, but many different events, witnessed by many different people, over a time span of several years and covering an expansive geographical area."[20] These claims are highly relevant to the testimonial literature of the Polish Jewish refugee experience in the Soviet Union.

Noah Shenker's application of these insights to testimony collection institutions, including the Fortunoff Video Archive for Holocaust Testimonies, the United States Holocaust Memorial Museum, and the Visual History Archive of the Shoah Foundation, has been similarly enlightening:

> The labor of testimony is not simply a matter of retrieving the past, but also of recording the ways by which one reenacts that past. Interviewers, archivists, and those who access these sources encounter the challenge of engaging how testimony is generated and performed as part of a mutual, contingent process—one that is embedded in both personal and institutional practices and which does not reveal a static or infallible notion of memory.[21]

As Shenker's study reveals, the findings of all testimonial collection efforts are profoundly influenced by their circumstances: the location, timing, goals, and methods of each project all play a role in the outcome, as do the personnel involved.

The three major institutions in Shenker's study, along with Yad Vashem in Israel, all collected testimonies from survivors of flight into the Soviet Union. Yet the inclusion of these survivors was somewhat accidental. Each of these organizations has a mandate to document experiences of the Holocaust. While each has also conducted interviews with refugees from the Holocaust who left at various points, this is not their primary purpose. The Central Jewish Historical Commission, convened in 1944 in Lublin, also included interviews with Polish Jewish refugees, albeit for different reasons.

The underground archive of the Warsaw Ghetto and the Polish government-in-exile, on the other hand, purposely sought out these witnesses in the midst of the war for their testimonial projects. Politics played a major role in defining the projects of these groups.

Published and unpublished memoirs and autobiographies, while less directly mediated by historical or political institutions, are still very much the products of their time and culture. Texts produced by fervent political or religious activists, including Orthodox Jews and Zionists, might interpret the same events very differently. The Cold War waxed and waned its centrality to the testimonial literature produced in different locations and time periods. More generally, the refugees' individual memories and perceptions of their experiences varied depending on where and when they traveled across a vast geographical spread.

Henry Greenspan's myriad contributions to Holocaust testimony scholarship include highlighting the role of the listener. As Greenspan points out, "Survivors do not recount in a vacuum but always to an actual or imagined audience of listeners." He suggests, for example, that the concept of "survivor guilt" may be more "speakable" than other, deeper agonies. Its ubiquity thus reflects modes of retelling, and of hearing, rather than actual emotions: "For certainly it is easier for us to accommodate the guilty survivor than the utterly abandoned survivor or the rageful, indicting survivor."[22] Certain topics can be broached, while others are only hinted at.

Pascale Rachel Bos has called attention to the cultural processes that shaped witnesses and some of the resulting lacunae: "I suggest that the lens of gender accounts for the fact that similar events and circumstances were sometimes experienced differently, were remembered differently, and are written or spoken differently." Bos also recognizes the broader application of her claims about gender socialization: "The socialization of those involved, the discourses in and through which one is constituted and understands one's self, affect what kinds of narratives one employs to relate one's trauma."[23]

The trauma experienced by the flight survivors was not the same as the trauma experienced by Polish Jews who stayed behind. While the Polish Jews in the unoccupied regions of the USSR endured forced labor, imprisonment, starvation, disease, and the loss of loved ones, they escaped the genocide. Some certainly mention antisemitic incidents in the USSR, but they rarely faced active discrimination and only learned of the Holocaust on their return to Poland after the war. The testimonies produced by the two groups are fundamentally different, although they start and end at the same point. Both groups of Polish Jews confronted the Nazi invasion in 1939, and both reeled from its effects in the aftermath of the war. In between, both groups were dislocated, divested, and disenfranchised by the war. I argue that it is possible to learn from, and to contribute to, the developing scholarly discussion on Holocaust testimony.

This work also benefits from the growing library of secondary research about particular aspects of the Polish Jewish experience in the Soviet Union. Numerous articles have treated perceptions of Jewish and Polish responses to the arrival of Soviet forces in 1939, as well as the reception of Jews in Polish military units during the war.[24] Soviet treatment of the Polish Jewish Bundist leaders Henryk Erlich and Wiktor Alter has also garnered attention, from the time of their disappearance to the present.[25] In addition to Litvak's book, a small but steady stream of articles on subsections of Polish Jewish refugee life in the Soviet Union have appeared since Korzen's plea for research in 1959. Yet the period following the fall of the Soviet Union has seen increased attention to the topic. This is part of a larger scholarly trend of interest in the war and Holocaust in the USSR, occasioned by the opening of Soviet archives, that has inspired a thorough rethinking of paradigms of the Holocaust. As a result, this research relies on insights from colleagues and is in conversation with their findings and publications.[26]

In addition to contributing to a more nuanced picture of the war and Holocaust in the Soviet Union, this work is in dialogue with the emerging scholarly interest in transnational studies of the Holocaust, as well as the field of migration studies. Undoubtedly, Timothy Snyder has made the most visible effort to rethinking national boundaries in approaching the eastern front of the war.[27] And while his research has also proven influential, it represents only one approach. Following the migration of Polish Jewish refugees necessitates expanding the compass of the war and its effects. Like other Polish Jewish victims, they began the war buffeted by the Nazi terror and were left homeless and powerless in the war's aftermath. Yet while these bracketing events associate them with other Polish Jewish survivors of the Holocaust, their forced and voluntary migrations across the steppes require different tools of analysis, maps of the war, and definitions of survival.

*　　*　　*

Several years ago, when I was already deeply engaged in research for this project, an elderly foreign-born Jewish man gingerly handed me his father's handwritten memoirs. He felt it was only safe then, decades after his father's death, to allow the full story of his miraculous survival in the Soviet Union to come to light. "My father was released from the Gulag," the man whispered urgently. I assured him that the Soviets issued a blanket amnesty for all Polish deportees in late 1941 following the Nazi invasion. But the man was too shocked by his own revelation to take mine in. "No one gets *released* from the Gulag," he insisted.

Once again, I tried to explain that his father's story was part of a larger narrative with global geopolitical implications. Yet after spending his entire adult life guarding the shameful secret that his father must have been a collaborator—an informer for the Soviet secret police—and after waiting until all of his relatives had passed away to share the ugly truth, he was no longer capable of recognizing a more benign truth.

This book is thus also a guide for the many children and grandchildren of the Polish Jewish refugees in the USSR. Although most are not burdened with the terrible, hidden stigma the man mentioned above had, many remain confused about the experiences that made their own lives possible. The individual stories of the many survivors, whether in published memoirs, recorded testimonies, personal documents, or retold around kitchen tables, leave many questions unanswered. People often had no idea why they were taken to a particular camp or settlement, why they were then set free, why the Polish or Soviet military accepted or rejected them, or how their repatriation was organized. Sometimes they found answers to these questions based on rumors or hypotheses. Other times they left them unanswered.

Each individual story is unique. Indeed, one of the major benefits of this testimony-based approach to the topic has been access to so many remarkable retellings of trauma and survival under difficult and entirely unexpected circumstances. At times my research has taken the form of an enormous map crisscrossed with lines representing the paths of hundreds of individuals and families across the Soviet Union and beyond. Taken in aggregate, however, and with the addition of the archival documentation available, important trends and trails begin to emerge. While it may never be possible to answer all the outstanding questions, this work should provide the geographical and historical grounding for making sense of many singular tales.

The book is organized in a roughly chronological manner. Chapter 1 narrates the beginning of the war and the decisions that all Polish citizens, but especially Jews, confronted. Should they seek to avoid the German invasion? Where should they go? And once the Soviets invaded from the other side, where were their chances more favorable? As numerous testimonies demonstrate, Polish Jews thought and rethought their decisions throughout the early months of the war, moving back and forth across the newly established border in their imaginations as well as in reality.

Chapter 2 follows the refugees' attempts to establish themselves in the newly annexed regions of the Soviet Union. On the one hand, they faced the increasing strictures of Soviet life. On the other, they benefited from the lack of institutionalized antisemitism in their professional and especially educational careers. Along with daily decisions about where to settle and what paths to pursue, the refugees also had to weigh their long-term prospects when the Soviet government offered them a choice: accept modified Soviet citizenship and move outside the border region, or retain Polish citizenship and return to the German-held areas.

Exhausted by their unstable lifestyle, afraid to give up their Polish citizenship, and reluctant to move outside the most heavily Polish and Jewish parts of the country, many elected to return to their homes across the western border. In actuality, however, the trains they boarded took them east. As a result of their vote of no confidence in the Soviet Union, the refugees were deported as socially unreliable elements to special settlements for reeducation. Chapter 3 chronicles their time as slave laborers in what almost all of them refer to as Siberia. For the Polish Jewish refugees, Siberia was a construct as much as a geographic location. Although some were in fact sent to harvest trees in the far east of the country, many others were put to similar work in the Arctic or assigned agricultural labor in northern Kazakhstan or the Ural Mountains. Told they would never be released, the refugee deportees were as surprised as their guards when word arrived, soon after the German invasion of the Soviet Union in June 1941, that all Polish citizens were to be amnestied.

The amnesty was applied differentially. Some received documents and even money for travel, while others were left entirely to their own devices. Some were released much later, or not at all. Cold, hungry, and unable to return to the war-torn areas where they began, most chose to go south, hoping for better conditions and perhaps even an opportunity to escape. Chapter 4 addresses their living conditions in Central Asia, as well as their relations with Soviet citizens, including other Jews, and with other Polish citizens. During this period, the refugees had a variety of interactions with the Soviet state apparatus and official Polish bodies. They also began to receive letters and charity from abroad.

The end of the war ushered in a period of intense negotiations over the fate of Polish citizens in the USSR, as the Cold War began to chill relations among the Allies. Chapter 5 opens with news of the Holocaust reaching the refugees before turning to the process of repatriation, and its results. While some of the Jewish repatriates stayed in postwar Poland, most decided to leave once more, in the absence of their homes, families, and communities. Many moved to DP camps in Western Europe, along with survivors of the Holocaust in Poland, where they tried to make sense of their war experiences while awaiting refuge in distant locations. The unanimity of purpose among the Jewish DPs, whatever their war experiences, is striking. They commemorated their dead while quickly marrying one another and building up new families. They moved to new countries where they tried to establish new lives while honoring all that was lost.

The Conclusion makes an argument for expanding the definition of survival and rethinking several related historiographies. The Polish Jews who spent the war in the unoccupied regions of the USSR escaped the eliminationist antisemitism of the Nazis, but only barely. And unlike refugees from Nazi Germany who left Europe in the 1930s, they remained within reach of Hitler's armies. Some spent the initial months of the war under Nazi occupation. Others evacuated within Soviet territory as the German forces approached for a second time. After the war, most rejoined the few surviving Polish Jews in entering the DP population and resettling abroad. If the Polish Jews who spent World War II in the far reaches of the Soviet Union are not Holocaust survivors, then we need a new term to describe them. Their experiences are part of the displacement and destruction wrought by the Nazis, and their stories need to be accounted for in the greater narrative of the war and the Holocaust.

The stories of Polish Jewish refugees on the Other Side also suggest that certain national narratives of the war require reexamination. The Soviet invasion and annexation of part of Poland, and subsequent deportation of thousands of Polish citizens, remains a deep wound in Polish society. Jews, along with other Polish citizens, suffered the brutality of the Soviet penal system, yet for them it turned out to be salvation. It may well be that the anomalous nature of this situation has played a role in the marginalization of the story. The experiences of the Polish Jewish refugees in the USSR also challenge some of the orthodoxies of the war, the Cold War, and contemporary periods.

1

Esau or Laban?

Wrestling with the German and Soviet Occupations

> And so one moment decides a person's fate. One runs this
> way, the other that way, and neither of them knows what the
> future holds in store. But what—excuse the expression—can
> the future hold in store for a Jew? I ask. Here it's bad and
> there it's no good.
>
> —BOGDAN WOJDOWSKI

IN THE THIRTY-FIRST chapter of the book of Genesis, God calls upon Jacob to leave the home of Laban, his father-in-law, and return to his homeland. The next few chapters detail Jacob's painstaking efforts to reap some material benefit from his twenty-one years serving Laban, as well as his careful preparations for the inevitable reunion with his brother Esau. The tension in the story is palpable as Jacob attempts to steer between the perfidy of his father-in-law and the threat of violence from his estranged brother. Throughout Jewish history, thinkers have returned to this archetypal story as a way of discussing later dangerous situations and perilous decisions. Already in rabbinic exegesis Laban, and especially Esau, are identified with subsequent enemies of the Jews.[1] This deliberate obfuscation allowed Jews to avoid explicitly naming their adversaries and offered a way to connect their own troubles to those of their illustrious forebears.

In the fall of 1939, the patriarch of the Hendel family in Horodło, Poland, called upon these familiar tropes once again. On the second day of the celebration of the Jewish New Year, September 15, 1939, the Germans reached the town of Horodło and immediately began ransacking Jewish-owned shops. After several chaotic days they pulled out. On Yom Kippur, the Red Army arrived and was greeted by members of the Jewish community wearing prayer shawls. Yet soon they, too, prepared to retreat and invited the local Jews to accompany them across the nearby Bug River to the newly captured Soviet territory. With a heavy heart the Hendel father packed up his family to go with the Soviets.

When asked by other religious Jews how he could possibly risk the spiritual development of his children under the godless communists, Hendel compared himself to his forefather Jacob. Yet whereas Jacob chose to leave Laban for Esau, Hendel preferred his chances under Laban—the Soviets. Hendel understood that their way of life would be under siege in the Soviet Union, but concluded that this was better than struggling for their very lives under Esau—the Germans.[2]

Although their priorities and circumstances varied, ultimately all Jews in the western half of Poland faced versions of this question in the late summer and early fall of 1939. Their country had been partitioned—quickly and painfully—by the Germans and the Soviets, splitting the largest Jewish community in Europe roughly in half. Thousands of Polish Jews, like the Hendels, took to the roads to try to change their fate. Most, however, chose to remain in their homes. Individuals and families faced weeks and months of uncertainty and difficult decisions that began with the Nazi invasion of Poland on September 1, 1939. Polish Jews in 1939 could not have known the import of their choice between Esau and Laban, yet they knew that they faced a decision point and mustered their resources to respond.

"To Jest Koniec"

According to her postwar memoir, in September 1939 Krystyna Chiger's father took her to the window of their Lwów (Rus. Lvov, Ukr. Lviv, Yid. Lemberg) apartment to see the German bombers and announced, "To jest koniec" (This is the end).[3] Whatever exactly he meant by this ominous pronouncement, he was correct that the invasion would suddenly, and irrevocably, alter the future of Poland and its citizens. While the term *blitzkrieg* is most commonly associated with the German invasion of the Soviet Union in the summer of 1941, this new approach to warfare was in fact developed for the invasion of Poland roughly two years earlier. Germany initiated blitzkrieg warfare, according to Omer Bartov, in order to avoid the costly losses and stalemates of the First World War. Bartov describes it as "based on massive, concentrated, and well-coordinated attacks along narrow fronts, leading to encirclements of large enemy forces and aimed at achieving a rapid military and political disintegration of the opponent by undermining both his logistical apparatus and psychological determination at a minimum cost to the attacking force."[4] In Poland, as elsewhere, the approach proved very successful. After entering the country on September 1, 1939, German forces had surrounded the capital, Warsaw, within two weeks.[5]

Although unprovoked, the invasion was not a surprise after Adolf Hitler's bloodless takeovers of Austria and Czechoslovakia—especially given his increasingly belligerent tone toward Poland. The signing of the Molotov-Ribbentrop Pact between Germany and the Soviet Union on August 23, moreover, meant that Hitler could invade Poland without any concern about rousing the sleeping bear to the east.

In the face of this nonaggression pact, and with German troops massing on the border, Poland began clandestinely mobilizing its own forces. Meanwhile, France and the United Kingdom, which had pledged to defend Poland, futiley attempted to avoid war through diplomacy.[6] Even had the Poles been able to muster all of their forces and reserve units, they were ill equipped to take on the Wehrmacht. According to Norman Davies, the Poles had 150 tanks while the Germans wielded twenty-six hundred. The proportion of warplanes was slightly better, with four hundred to the German two thousand, but most of the Polish planes were destroyed in the opening bombing raids before even leaving the ground.[7] Poland was a poor country and no match for Germany's highly trained and heavily armed forces. England and France, despite their sympathy and promises, had not prepared for the campaign to begin so early or proceed so quickly. They were unable to contribute to Poland's defense.

Fighting continued throughout the month, including the siege and heroic defense of Warsaw. The Germans bombed the city mercilessly, and as many as forty thousand civilians may have lost their lives.[8] American photojournalist Julien Bryan, who entered Poland immediately following the invasion and spent much of September in Warsaw, described his emerging awareness of the German military's deliberate targeting of civilians in a book published in 1940:

> It was this ruthlessness against the civilian population that I found hardest to believe. Even when they bombed my own train within a few minutes after

I had crossed the Rumanian border, I explained it as probably an isolated instance. Then I saw similar bombings. I talked with many peasants and refugees and finally with American citizens who had been machine-gunned from a height of no more than one hundred feet.

Then slowly it dawned on me that these were not isolated incidents, but a part of Hitler's plan for terrorizing millions of people.[9]

By the time German forces entered the capital on September 30, the government and military command had long ago fled. Polish government officials entered Romanian territory on September 17. Eventually they established a government-in-exile in Paris, which evacuated to London via Angers after the German invasion of France. En route from the capital, Polish politicians were joined by thousands of civilians.

Fleeing the destruction, these civilians grabbed what they could carry and headed east ahead of the invading forces. Many witnesses recall harrowing scenes along the way. Jan Karski, at the time a second lieutenant in the Polish Army, had been mobilized to Oświęcim, near the German border. He describes his chaotic retreat, on the second day of the war: "We were now no longer an army, a detachment, or a battery, but individuals wandering collectively toward some wholly indefinite goal. We found the highways jammed with hundreds of thousands of refugees, soldiers looking for their commands, and others just drifting with the tide."[10]

In the lightning war, Polish citizens of every ethnic and religious background were bombed in their homes and on the road, chased from their towns by fighting, and terrified by the German forces. Polish Jews, however, had particular cause for concern. In September 1939, Hitler's antisemitism, his treatment of German Jews, his expulsion of Polish Jews, and his fanatical following were already well known. As Anna Landau-Czajka has shown, by 1939 even the conservative, nationalist, and antisemitic Polish press organs were expressing concern about the violence and excess of Nazi anti-Jewish policies.[11]

When asked, decades afterward, whether their families had followed news of the Nazi rise to power in Germany, most Polish Jews interviewed by the Shoah Foundation answered in the affirmative. Shalom Omri, born in Hrubieszów, a small city in the middle of the country, describes his father reading the Warsaw Yiddish daily *Haynt*, which was affiliated with the Zionist movement. They knew about the Nazis' growing strength and effort to push the Jews out of Germany.[12] Moshe Ben-Asher, born in 1912 in

Piotrków Trybunalski, was already working as a ladies' tailor by the 1930s. He followed the deteriorating situation of German Jews in *Haynt* as well as in *Der Moment,* another Yiddish daily.[13]

A number of survivors recall the so-called Polenaktion as a turning point in their awareness of Nazi intentions. On the night of October 28, 1938, roughly seventeen thousand Jews residing in Germany and Austria were pushed across the Polish border. They had previously been Polish citizens, with legal sanction to live in Austria or Germany. Now the Third Reich had rescinded their status, and neither side would take them in. The plight of the homeless refugees, forced to camp out in the no-man's-land between Germany and Poland, gained worldwide attention. While it was soon surpassed in international import by the November Pogrom, instigated against Jews in the Reich after the assassination of a German consular official by the unbalanced son of an expelled Polish Jewish couple, the Polenaktion made a great impression on many Polish Jews at the time. State censorship limited coverage of the event in the general Polish press, but as Jerzy Tomaszewski has demonstrated, Polish Jewish newspapers were allowed to write about the daily difficulties faced by the refugees in Zbąszyń.[14]

Zyga Elton in Warsaw and Shaul Shternfeld in Sosnowiec both remember interacting with Jews expelled from Germany who eventually settled in their communities.[15] Ann Szedlecki, born in 1925, fondly recalls a 1931 visit to her rich aunt and uncle in Berlin. Seven years later, the now impoverished aunt and uncle had to rejoin the rest of the family in Łódź.[16] Boruch Frusztajer remembers a distinguished German Jewish gentleman who stayed with his family for a year, after his expulsion and before his immigration to the United States.[17] Reading about the cruel treatment of the Polish Jews expelled from Germany, and especially talking with them about the alarming surge of state-sponsored antisemitism there, can only have increased the apprehension of Polish Jews regarding the invasion. Both Simon Davidson and Moshe Etzion directly credit their families' knowledge of the expulsion of Polish Jews from Germany with their decision to flee east ahead of the German forces.[18] Etzion recalls breaking the toy German soldiers his refugee relatives had brought him before becoming a refugee himself.[19]

The November Pogrom, dubbed Kristallnacht by the Nazis, and the subsequent incarceration of many German Jewish men in concentration camps, also caught the attention of many Polish Jews. Henry Orenstein, in discussing his family's deliberations, declares, "We had the example of Hitler's treatment of the German Jews to warn us what we could expect;

'Chrystal Night,' when Jewish shops had been smashed, the concentration camps all had been well publicized."[20]

Jews fighting in the Polish Army experienced even more anxiety, especially once retreat began. Even if their names, physical appearance, or comrades did not reveal their background, it was relatively easy for the Germans to check which soldiers were circumcised, and thus unequivocally Jewish. Israel Feldman, mobilized in the run-up to the invasion, soon found himself marching west as a German prisoner of war. Along the way, Jews were asked to step out of the line voluntarily. Although he did not do so, he realized that he had to escape and used a water break to run into the forest.[21]

Compounding the confusion and anxiety in these early weeks of the war was the fact that news was sporadic and unreliable. The German advance was relentless, but many Polish citizens of all backgrounds still held out hope that the Polish Army, with help from the French and British, would rally and repel the invaders. Larry Wenig, in Dynów, a small town in southern Poland, describes his community invoking a rare Ashkenazi folk custom to call upon divine intercession:

> The next morning, September 2, at the Sabbath prayers, the women were admitted to the men's sanctuary, highly unusual except in the most extraordinary circumstances. Their heads covered in shawls, they approached the Torah Ark and beseeched God for help. Their keening voices brought tears and cries from the men. The scintillated prayers of the men swelled and seemed to hurtle against the walls of the synagogue. Surely God would hear their supplications, they hoped.[22]

Not long afterward, the situation took an unexpected turn.

On September 17, Soviet forces attacked Poland from the east. At first, some Polish citizens hoped that the Soviets had arrived to help fight the Germans. In reality, secret protocols attached to the Molotov-Ribbentrop Pact had delineated German and Soviet "spheres of influence" in Poland.[23] In other words, Germany and the Soviet Union—which had controlled parts of Polish territory before the foundation of the Second Polish Republic in the wake of the First World War—had once again partitioned Poland. After the Polish Army had been routed, Soviet forces committed to the invasion with a far more modest offensive than their German allies.[24]

There was still some sporadic fighting, and Polish forces retreating eastward were often captured unaware by the Soviet advance. It is estimated that by the end of the September Campaign, the Germans held 694,000

Polish prisoners of war and the Soviets 240,000.[25] At least seventy thousand Polish troops died in the fighting, while civilian losses were even higher.[26] Of the over thirty-two million Polish citizens before the war, about twenty million wound up in German-occupied regions and twelve million in Soviet ones.[27] The Jewish population of over three million, about 10 percent, was split roughly in half by the invasion. About 1.3 million Jews lived in the eastern regions, and these were augmented with refugees from the west.[28] Ethnic Ukrainians and Belorussians, who had represented approximately 15 and 4.5 percent, respectively, of the prewar Polish population, resided mainly in these eastern areas and thus made up an even higher percentage after the division.[29]

By the end of September, Poland was sufficiently subdued that the Germans and Soviets could negotiate borders and move their respective forces accordingly. In exchange for greater control over the Baltic states, the Soviets ceded the Germans more Polish territory. As of September 28, the Bug River in the north and San River in the south marked the boundary between German and Soviet-controlled areas.[30] It would take several more weeks for the two forces to disentangle on their own sides of the rivers, and even longer to establish effective and regular border controls.

The waning months of 1939 saw the gradual buildup of patrols on both sides of the new border. In addition, the occupying nations began the process of assimilating and annexing what had so recently been Poland. The western, German-held territories were divided into two distinct areas. The northern and western regions closest to Germany—including the formerly free port city of Danzig (Pol. Gdańsk), which the Germans had long coveted—were incorporated directly into the Reich. What was left of the central region of the country was to be administered separately as the General Government. Over time this would become an arena for brutal experimentation, but from the start, Polish citizens in both of the German-administered areas were treated with extreme cruelty. The campaign of terror included roundups of intellectual, spiritual, political and other leaders, and subjugation of the population. Jewish Poles were particular targets for expropriation, humiliation, random violence, and increasing isolation.

In the eastern regions of Poland, the Soviets were establishing their own regime, taking over schools and businesses, and registering the population for internal Soviet passports. In a November plebiscite, the population overwhelmingly, and perforce, voted to join the Union of Soviet Socialist Republics. While there was no official ethnic discrimination in this area, the regime encouraged Belorussian and Ukrainian language, culture, and employment, respectively, in the newly annexed republics of Western Belorussia and Western Ukraine, at the expense of the previous Polish leadership. This led ethnic Poles to lose their jobs and authority in the region. Power dynamics in the area were further destabilized by a series of deportations affecting all ethnic groups and targeting local government officials, landowners, police officers, religious leaders, and others deemed capable of fomenting opposition.

Throughout this period of upheaval, Polish citizens on both sides of the newly established border kept in touch and followed developments on the opposite side. Once the Germans and Soviets had established local government structures, mail service became possible. Even before that, however, it was relatively easy to send and receive messages and packages with human couriers. Before the two regimes settled upon and began policing the borders, crossing the rivers via bridge or boat was fairly straightforward.

Given the rapidity of the invasion, many people happened to be away from home when the hostilities began. University or yeshiva students who had already returned to their studies, for example, often ended up across the border from their parents. Those Polish soldiers fortunate enough not to have been captured or killed had to find a way back to their families. Families on vacation and teenagers at summer camps in the mountains faced a similar challenge. In the early weeks of the war, thousands of Poles streamed across the rivers in both directions, seeking to reunite with family or return to the relative safety of their homes and communities. These returnees brought word of the conditions, and personal messages, from wherever they had originated.

Choice

Jews were not the only Polish citizens who considered flight to the east. Both the Polish government and the military high command left Poland via Romania in mid-September. Members of the banned Polish Communist Party also had good reasons to weigh their options. Communists had ranked with Jews as favorite enemies of the Nazis before the about-face occasioned by the Molotov-Ribbentrop Pact. Additionally, life in the Workers' Paradise held at least a theoretical appeal for them. Some Polish communists did become border crossers. Other ethnic Poles crossed in each direction, but in small numbers that had more to do with family reunification than with expectations of the occupations. Above all for the large Jewish community of Poland, there was a stark difference between oppression in the west and oppression in the east.

All of the over 1.5 million Jews residing in the territory now held by the Germans had to at least contemplate whether to stay or go.[31] To varying degrees, they knew about the legal exclusion, expropriation, and expulsion of Jews in Germany. More immediately, they had their own initial interactions with German forces in Poland. Jews across Nazi-occupied Poland faced public humiliations, forced recruitment onto labor brigades, and random acts of violence from the start, although the frequency and intensity of the violence varied by locale and commander. It took the Nazis some time to organize and implement their anti-Jewish policies, leaving room for local initiative and creative experimentation in the treatment of the sizable Polish Jewish population.

Thus individuals, families, and communities witnessed very different examples of German behavior in those early weeks of the war. Sacher Grünbaum's testimony, recorded in Przemyśl in 1945, describes the German assault on the fifteen hundred Jews of Dynów; after killing over a hundred on the first day of Rosh Hashanah, and burning down the synagogue on the second day, they expelled the entire community on the festival of Sukkot:

> When the Jews had gathered together, they were surrounded by German army and *Gestapo* guards and, accompanied by music of a local orchestra, they were driven toward the San river. Random shots were fired here to frighten the Jews and they were all driven across the river. Since the water was deep and ran swiftly several elderly women drowned in the crossing. That's how the Jews of Dynów, having lost almost all their possessions, left their home town, where for hundreds of years their ancestors had been sharing the life's fortunes with Polish people.[32]

In the small town of Krzeszów, also near the San River, Polish resistance led to German reprisals against the local Jews. Yosef Rozenberg and his family heard the shots. The rabbi's son was forced to dig a grave for his father. According to Rozenberg, "We knew then about the destruction [*khurbn*] that the Germans had caused."[33] In Hrubieszów, on the other hand, there was relatively little violence in the first weeks of the war. Avraham Blander explains that at first it was only the Wehrmacht, and not the Schutzstaffel (SS). Of course they stole from stores, he adds, but the situation only really deteriorated in December.[34] Among the reasons his family did not leave, Martin Kaner, also from Hrubieszów, specifically mentions that the Germans had not yet done anything terrible.[35]

Many eyewitnesses, both those who stayed in German-occupied Poland and those who fled to the Soviet-held side, recall ongoing discussions about this decision. In the words of Tsiporah Horvits, a child survivor, "The issue of flight to Russia was always on the agenda."[36] Zyga Elton writes that he and his friends talked constantly about the pros and cons of leaving.[37] For Moshe, whose testimony was recorded in the Warsaw Ghetto after his return, the question was not whether to cross, but in what way: "But how was one to smuggle himself across the border? This is the question that hung on everyone's lips and was the theme of everyone's conversations in the street and in the kitchens."[38]

Many individuals recall family conferences to discuss options. Gerda Weissmann Klein relates the following scene around her father's sick bed in Bielsko as the war began, and her father requested that his two adolescent children leave:

> "I feel you children should go. Mama just told me that Mr. and Mrs. Ebersohn have asked to take you with them to look for refuge in the interior of Poland. I am sick when you most need my strength. I want you to go, children. I command you to go!" His voice had assumed a tone of authority that I had never heard before. I saw Arthur look up startled at the mention of his girl friend's parents. More than ever he looked like Mama, but somehow he reminded me of Papa as he stood there tall, erect, and determined.
>
> Almost without hesitation, he said, "No! We are going to stay together."
>
> My parents' eyes met. I had the feeling there was relief and pride in their faces.
>
> "I hoped you would say that," Papa said brokenly, "not for my sake, but because I hate to cast out my children to complete uncertainty. I believe that God will keep us together and under the roof of our house."[39]

Sara Selver-Urbach recalls a similar discussion in her home: "We wanted to stay together. My brother thought of going to Wilno on behalf of his Youth Movement, and of taking me with him, but my father was opposed to the idea of sending us, children, into the hostile world; the unity of the family was his uppermost concern."[40]

Staying together could also mean crossing the border as a family. Yankl Saler's father was a socialist involved in the Jewish Labor Bund, and Yankl joined Tsukunft, the youth organization of the Bund. He and his father were tradesmen. Although the Germans, in his description, looked as though they were "dressed for a ball" and the Soviets, embarrassingly, looked even worse than the Polish Army, his family believed that communism was preferable to fascism. When offered the opportunity to leave with the Soviets, the family discussed it and decided to go. Later Yankl and his father came back to retrieve some of their belongings.[41] Yankl's brother Mendel, younger by three years, remembered less about their decision making, but agreed in principle: "We believed [that] in Russia we will be able better to survive. Better than with the Germans."[42]

Other families decided that separation was the best choice available to them. Isabelle Choko describes coming from a warm and tightknit family in Łódź. Although comfortable, they did not have the funds to obtain visas to emigrate before the war started. Following the German invasion, the family gathered to weigh their options. As Choko recalls,

Bela's husband Zygmunt immediately set out on the road toward Russia. He would be the only member of his family to survive. My father was too ill to consider fleeing. Instead he, and my mother, Aunt Bela, her daughter Danusia and I all hurried to Babcia's house, where the family held a long meeting and concluded that Aunt Pola's husband Natas Kowalew should also leave, but that Babcia and the rest of us would stay put.[43]

In some cases, consensus was not possible. Jack Pomerantz narrates growing up as the youngest of eight in a poor family in Radzyń. When the bombing began, his family met in a barn to discuss their options. At twenty-one, he was the only one who wanted to flee. Pomerantz left on his own that night, but by the next month most of his brothers and sisters had joined him in Soviet territory.[44] Helena Starkiewicz's father berated her when she made a second attempt at crossing: "You are escaping and leaving us behind, and you don't care about our fate!"[45]

Many also based their decisions on expectations, or early impressions, of the Germans or the Soviets. Meyer Megdal, in a privately published memoir, says that his mother "kept referring to her recollections of the German front-line soldiers [in World War I]."[46] The image of honorable German soldiers from the previous war was particularly compelling for the older generation. Boris Baum's father told him that Germans had saved him from the Bolsheviks.[47] Shalom Omri's mother understood from her World War I experience that the German forces would never harm women.[48] Chaim Ajzen describes his horror as he watched his grandfather convince his parents that they should stay in their home because the Austrians had been better than the Cossacks during the First World War.[49]

The German forces also looked, in their new crisp uniforms, like representatives of a civilized and well-ordered state. The Soviet troops, per Yankl Saler's comments above, lacked that polish; according to Matla Blander, many of them went barefoot.[50] Aleksandra Alexander, who lived in a town occupied first by the Germans, then the Soviets, and then again by the Germans in the course of September 1939, noted the contrast. The first German troops were polite and friendly to the Jews because they could communicate with them. Then the Red Army arrived. "Their soldiers were undernourished, unfriendly, and they looked dirty," according to Alexander. "People didn't trust the soldiers, and the soldiers didn't like us—the dirty capitalists."[51] The Nazi occupiers soon showed their true designs, she adds, but by then her family had already made their decision.

Reports of the difficulty of crossing and of overcrowding in border areas also acted as a disincentive. Megdal mentions how both influenced his family's decision:

> My immediate family, after a lot of soul searching, decided to remain—
> especially when news reports began reaching us of the deplorable condi-
> tions the refugees in the Russian border towns were subjected to. The towns
> became overcrowded and many of the newcomers were suffering from lack
> of food and no place with a roof over their heads. There were also instances
> where Jews attempting to cross the border were stopped by the Russian
> border guards and sent back.[52]

Many individuals and families articulated their decisions in terms of perceived safety. Matla Blander, who was eleven when the war broke out, remembers her father and older sister arguing about whether to leave with the Soviets. The family was well off, and her father believed that money could buy them out of any difficulties.[53] Josef Scher's father, on the other hand, was convinced that the Germans would target the wealthy. He felt sure that his status as working class would protect his family.[54] Both families used a combination of logic and faith to justify their decisions to stay.

Ultimately, however, all of these reasons are partial and transitory explanations for that which is instinctual: the desire to remain at home, in a known region, among family and friends. In trying to explain the mind-set of the people from his hometown, Avraham Ayzen wrote, "They rehearsed every possible and impossible miracle, just to avoid taking up their walking sticks."[55] Notwithstanding the pull of home, many Polish Jews under Nazi occupation considered crossing, and even tried to cross, to the Soviet-held regions. Despite persuasive reasons to remain where they were, Polish Jews weighed their options and made the best choices that they could in the circumstances.

Demographics and Decision Making

Under attack, the Polish state could not keep track of its citizens. Thousands headed east, ahead of the German troops. Rachel Auerbach, who did not leave Warsaw, describes emerging from the cellar of her building after a night of bombing in early September 1939. She found the streets jammed with young men responding to the government's call to muster in the east, as well as Jews trying to escape the arrival of German forces: "The street looked like a swollen river that had overflown its banks . . . a thick mass of heads, marching feet, backs saddled with rucksacks."[56] Sara Selver-Urbach recalls a similar vision in Łódź: "We stood for one hour, two hours, and they were still marching, a column of people that had no end."[57]

Still within the boundaries of their own nation, many refugees were met by Soviet troops moving westward. At this juncture, and at many points afterward, refugees reversed and returned to their homes. Eventually, once a border had been established, Soviet overseers in the annexed Polish territories would register both the Poles who had lived there previously and the refugees who had arrived following the invasion. This registration was run by the NKVD (Narodnyi Komissariat Vnutrennikh Del, People's Commissariat for Internal Affairs), or security services, and only a small number of their documents have become available. Even full access would offer, at best, a snapshot. Before and after the registration, Jewish refugees continued to move within the newly annexed areas, as well as to and from unoccupied Lithuania and German-occupied Poland.

Hence, the best estimates can offer only an approximation of the movement of population occasioned by the Nazi invasion. Up through the 1990s, those studying Jewish flight from German-occupied Poland assumed numbers ranging from 300,000 to 400,000.[58] Access to some published and archival Soviet figures has caused scholars to significantly lower the estimates of refugees from Nazi-held areas, some to as low as 100,000.[59] Although, as Katherine Jolluck notes, the Soviets' frequent attempts to exclude Belorussians, Jews, and Ukrainians from Polish citizenship, as well as the generally

FIGURE 1.1. Refugees flee German invasion in Lublin, Poland, 1939. Yad Vashem Photo Archive.

chaotic atmosphere, does call their figures into question.[60] Mark Edele and Wanda Warlik offer a compromise between the lower and higher estimates. Settling on a range of figures rather than a single number, they conclude that between 150,000 and 300,000 Polish Jews moved from German to Soviet occupation, and that approximately sixteen hundred of them returned to the German-held areas before the invasion of the Soviet Union in 1941.[61]

What can be said with certainty is that a significant number of Polish Jews left the Nazi areas for the Soviet ones. Moreover, this number became more significant over time because the vast majority of Polish Jews perished in the Nazi genocide. Those who fled to the Soviets were far more likely to survive the war. My own inclination is to assume numbers at the higher end of the scale, with the understanding that many of these refugees crossed back to German-occupied regions over time. Even if it is true that as many as 20 percent of Jews living in western Poland tried living in the eastern territories, however temporarily, it remains the case that most Polish Jews under Nazi occupation stayed in their homes and hoped for the best.

Scholars have tended to agree that it was chiefly young men who crossed into Soviet-annexed territory.[62] This had to do both with the military call-up and with expectations of German behavior. A selective mobilization of Polish soldiers began even before the invasion.[63] With the start of the war it was expanded, but also hindered by the chaotic conditions. Marian Feldman, at age seventeen, was traveling with a friend toward their required registration office when they were suddenly overtaken by the German army. The two young men ran into the woods and walked only by night until they reached Soviet territory with no idea where to go next.[64] For these youth, as well as for many others, separation from their families was temporary and unplanned but had real ramifications.

Other families had the opportunity to make more deliberate decisions. Natan Gross illustrates the role of gender in his family's decision-making process:

> The Steinmetzes, Grunbergs and Grosses, mother's family and father's family, set about drinking coffee, debating, going out, coming in, urging, threatening, deciding yes and then deciding no. The formula "They don't do anything to the women" was established. Men, however, risked repression, and it was better to stay out of the hands of the Germans.[65]

Many other families reached the same conclusion. According to Henry Orenstein, who fled with his father, "Men, we thought, would be in much greater danger from the Nazis than women, who might be subjected to fines and indignities but whose lives wouldn't be at risk."[66]

These expectations were not purely hypothetical. In Dynów, Larry Wenig, an adolescent at the time, recalls the Germans tearing through the town searching for Jewish men on the first day of Rosh Hashanah. Later, word reached the townspeople that some men had been shot in the woods and others taken to forced labor, and "on September 28, my aunt Etka, my father's sister-in-law, came to our house; she came to plead with my mother to let me go with her son, my cousin Shmulik, to cross the river San, perhaps to safety."[67] By this time, Wenig's father and two older brothers had already fled east. Based on a reasoned calculation of the risks, his mother allowed him to go to join them.

If men were perceived to be at greater risk from the German troops, women's perceived vulnerabilities often tied them to home. Zorach Warhaftig had originally planned to flee Warsaw without his wife, due to a difficult pregnancy, but in the end she elected to join him.[68] In the initial chaos of the invasion, Chaim Ajzen's father would not even consider fleeing, due to concerns about his wife and daughter: "Gutka was not yet seven and my mother was not a strong woman."[69] Several testimonies mention entire families fleeing together, only to separate en route. According to Victor Zarnowitz, his mother and grandmother urged him and his brother to continue without them when it became clear that they were slowing the boys down. The women claimed that no one would harm two old women and returned home.[70]

As a result of both military mobilization and predictions about the German occupation, many Polish Jewish families separated in the early weeks of the war—which would lead to immediate and later consequences. Frida Zerubavel, in her Hebrew memoir published in 1941, describes the eerie situation in her building in Warsaw, bereft of men in September 1939. Charged with taking care of her own elderly mother, Zerubavel also had to seek medical help for a neighbor and friend who went into labor. All of the other women in the building were afraid to step outside due to the bombing. Soon Zerubavel, a Zionist activist, was also organizing a communal rotation for cooking, shopping, and cleaning.[71]

Michal Unger provides statistical support with evidence of the gender imbalance in the Łódź Ghetto. According to a census conducted in June 1940, men made up 45.5 percent of the ghetto population and women 54.4 percent. In the age group of twenty to forty-five, women were 57.7 percent of the total.[72] Dalia Ofer's statistics for the Warsaw Jewish population are similar.[73] Both scholars also demonstrate that women in the ghettos were well aware of the burdens that this imbalance placed upon them. Of course, the participation of Jewish men in the September Campaign, and the death and capture of many, created much of this asymmetry.

Edele and Warlik's findings, based on Polish Jewish registrants in Tashkent in 1941, are more directly relevant. They show that of 1,039 Polish Jews who registered at that time, 58 percent were male, 38 percent in their twenties, and 27 percent in their thirties. And yet, the documentation did not require them to specify whether they were refugees from German-occupied Poland or Polish Jews from eastern Poland who had evacuated after the German invasion of the USSR.[74] Indeed, some of the same factors might have led Jews in the newly incorporated Soviet territories to flee the next German invasion in similarly lopsided numbers.

Yet clearly not all, nor even the majority, of the men left. Kitty Hart notes that her brother fled, but her father "could not bring himself to leave my mother, grandmother, and myself."[75] Additionally, some families decided to send all of the young people. Moshe Brener's family heard a rumor that the youth would be treated as a *kaparah,* or "guilt offering," under German occupation. His eldest sister already had a family of her own but he, his brothers, and his younger sister left together in the fall of 1939. He recalls his mother joking darkly as she said goodbye that she had merited to marry off all of her children at once.[76] Helen Zuberman, who fled with her immediate family at the age of fourteen, remembers her grandfather's demurral: "You are young, but I am old and will stay."[77]

Many of these separations were not meant to be permanent. Alexander Donat, a journalist who had written against the Nazis, fled immediately following the invasion. In November, he traveled back to Warsaw to bring his wife and child to join him in Soviet Lutsk (Pol. Łuck), but

> Lena refused to go. She took me on a tour of our beautiful seven-room apartment and talked about how miserable life was in Russia. It was November, already turning cold, and how could we expect to sneak across the frontier with a baby not yet two years old? And what about the seventy-two-year-old aunt who lived with us? And the rest of the family? Lena was sure that the Germans would be vicious, but what could happen to women and children?[78]

Other families were more fortunate. Henry Skorr crossed into Soviet territory only in November, when his life was in danger from the Germans. Nonetheless, he soon returned to bring his family to join him. Skorr's sister crossed back yet again to escort their grandmother to Kovel (Pol. Kowel).[79] Irving Beada worked hard to convince his father to join him in fleeing to the Soviets. Eventually he succeeded, and they were able to join his father's brother in Ukraine. Once they got settled, Beada's father returned to bring his mother and younger siblings to join them.[80] On the other hand, Sally Alban, who looked Polish, helped her father cross; but winter, and then deportation, prevented them from going back to get her mother and younger siblings.[81]

These early separations, voluntary or forced, could lead to the gendering of later decisions and actions. Hanna Davidson Pankowsky writes that after her father and older brother left their home in Łódź to report for military duty, all of their female relatives moved in. Once they heard that her father and brother had reached Bialystok (Pol. Białystok), Hanna's mother had to arrange false papers, transport, and smugglers for the two of them on her own.[82]

In these testimonies, gender and decision making are less predictably correlated. Often, it would seem, entire families met and reached egalitarian consensus on what should be done. In other families, the opinions of certain members are portrayed as having swayed the decision. However, these strong-willed leaders could be men or women, and their verdicts either to go or to stay. Both men and women convinced their families of the benefits of both paths. That said, the testimonial literature more often depicts men as active in pursuing and planning exit strategies, while women more frequently express ties to home and family.

Sally Alban, in her oral history for the Shoah Foundation, states that her father decided the family would be better off under the Soviets. He took her with him across the Bug to set up jobs and living quarters for the rest of the family.[83] Because no other family members provide testimony, we cannot know what the mother or adult children thought of his decision. In Kitty Hart's story, the main actor and decider is also the father. He first decided that the family should not leave, then planned a daring winter escape, only to fail and bring his family back to Bielsko.[84] Marian Feldman describes himself, rather than his father, as the main actor in the drama. Feldman ended up under Soviet control while trying to join his unit of the Polish Army. He liked what he saw in the Soviet zone and decided to go back to Warsaw for his parents and sister. However, Feldman's mother was adamant about not leaving her own elderly parents. Feldman returned on his own, only to meet up with his father and sister, who later heeded his advice. The three spent the remainder of the war together. In his highly unemotional book, Feldman briefly expresses guilt that he was unable to convince his mother to come as well.[85]

Feldman's mother was one of many who refused to leave relatives behind. Adam Boren, who left Warsaw in late October with his father and brother, found out only later that his mother had not wanted to leave her sister alone.[86] After Zvi Faier and his father fled across the border, his father repeatedly sent a wagon to pick up his mother, but she always sent it back empty. When his father returned to get her himself, she continued to refuse, citing the needs of local relatives. Finally, though, he was able to bring his wife and her mother to the Soviet zone.[87]

While these testimonies conform to expected gender norms, they contrast with Marion Kaplan's findings in her now classic work on German Jewry between 1933 and 1945. Examining trauma and dislocation through the lens of gender, Kaplan reveals how the particular assumptions and policies of the Nazis, as well as prewar economic and familial roles among Jews, led to some surprising outcomes. Women, more attuned to the word on the street than their husbands, who relied on official channels for information, were often the first to realize the danger and advocated for emigration. Kaplan also shows that the early anti-Jewish legislation, especially relating to the closure of professional avenues, hit men much harder, sometimes emotionally debilitating them. Women were more prepared to take on menial labor in order to feed their families, with consequences for familial roles.[88]

Of course, the situations of German and Polish Jews are hardly identical. German Jews lived for years through a relatively gradual loss of rights with only occasional violence. They had far more time to consider their options. Polish Jews, on the other hand, faced this fateful choice in the midst of a sudden invasion and occupation. They had, at most, a few months to decide whether to flee areas taken by the Germans for those taken by the Soviets. Although some anti-Jewish action and legislation started immediately, systematic isolation of the Jews occurred more slowly. Ghettoization, for example, began in late 1939, spreading across Poland unevenly in the following months and years. Yet by early 1940, border crossing was nearly impossible. Nonetheless, it is certainly noteworthy that the same sort of gender reversals appears to have been less frequent in the east.

Scholars and survivors have also indicated that communists in particular, and leftists more generally, gravitated more readily to the Soviet sphere of influence.[89] Others have suggested that those with looser religious bonds were more prone to submit to Soviet antireligious policies. Geography also may have played a role: people residing close to the new border might have crossed with more ease and frequency.[90] These Jews were more likely to have connections on the other side and local knowledge about the terrain; they also did not have to undergo the trials of crossing through Nazi-occupied Polish territory. Yet given the lack of quantitative data, and the great variety of experiences within the qualitative data, it is impossible to prove these hypotheses.

In a resolutely anticommunist memoir, Yitzhak Erlichson claims he was originally attracted to what the Soviet Union had to offer: "For me it was not just the wish to escape from Nazi rule, which at that time still had not revealed its bloody teeth in our town, but there was also a deeply felt longing to go to that legendary land where 'all are equal.'"[91] Yankl Saler, whose family was involved in the Jewish Labor Bund, firmly believed that communism was preferable to fascism.[92] Yet for every idealist, there were also pragmatists. Aleksandra Alexander notes her grandfather's attempt to convince her own parents to cross the border with him: "My grandfather said he preferred the dirty Russians even if they were communists, as he didn't trust the blue-eyed, clean-shaven Germans."[93]

Refugees also varied in their degree of religious devotion. While some may have felt at home in the atheistic state and mention nothing about Jewish religious practice in their testimonies, the majority do recall at least a few efforts to observe holidays, burial customs, dietary laws, or other Jewish rituals. A few, like Reb Hendel in the introduction to the chapter, were deeply religious and even used Jewish texts and traditions to justify their decisions. Rabbi Jacob Halpern recalls that on Saturday, September 2, the second day of the war, his father, Rabbi Uszer Szaja Halpern, exhorted his congregation in Kraków to flee the city. The elder Rabbi Halpern told them that it was their religious duty to escape the clutches of Hitler, and the next day he, his family, and most of his parishioners left on foot. By the time they reached Soviet territory, all but his own family had returned to their homes.[94]

The economic status of the refugees was similarly mixed. Sara Selver-Urbach claims that wealthy families were at an advantage in attempting to flee:

> Some families, especially the most affluent, sought to save themselves in various ways, to flee across the border to Russia . . . but we, additionally, lacked the money for bribes and money gifts, without which it was impossible to obtain even the most primitive wagon, not to speak of better means of transportation; fabulous sums were likewise necessary to bribe the frontier-guards.[95]

Certainly, cash could be helpful for arranging transportation and paying for smugglers. Janka Goldberger's family was well enough off to hire a cart to carry the immediate family, their considerable possessions, and a grandmother and disabled uncle to the border.[96] Money could also, however, weigh down a family both figuratively and literally. Klara Samuels's parents converted much of their property into gold, but the time and effort involved in transporting the fortune ultimately meant they were not able to carry out their plan to reach Palestine via Vilna (Lit. Vilnius, Pol. Wilno).[97] Matla Blander, whose family did not cross the border, stated that the poorer families were more likely to leave.[98]

Natalia Aleksiun's research suggests that young Jews originally from eastern Galicia, now within Soviet territory, were particularly inclined to return to their parents' homes when the war began. Having left the area for educational or professional opportunities in other parts of Poland, this group—which included many writers and other intellectuals—retained strong ties and "cultural capital."[99] Yehoshua Gilboa's flight to his family home farther north reflects similar motivations: "I was on the way to Pinsk. Someone like me, with family and a home in the eastern regions was considered lucky. My only thought was to reach home."[100]

A thorough analysis of geography's role in decision making at the start of the war would require juxtaposing prewar settlement patterns with a map of the incidence of flight. Given the impossibility of counting a large mobile population, I can only point to anecdotal evidence. Not surprisingly, urban areas, and Warsaw in particular, are prominent in testimonies and memoirs. With a prewar Jewish population of 350,000, Warsaw dwarfed all other Polish Jewish communities in size. Yet testimonies also refer to attempts to cross the border from cities and towns much closer or much farther away than the capital. It is certainly possible that higher numbers of Jews escaped to the east from specific regions, but this may have as much to do with local conditions as with border proximity. Some scholarship has demonstrated both the tremendous variation in Nazi policies across Poland and the profound influence this had on Jewish life and death.[101]

On the whole, we can conclude that the refugees fleeing east were disproportionately young and male. The numbers may have skewed toward those with progressive politics, unorthodox religious practices, and residence close to the Bug and San Rivers. Significantly, though, these migrants represented a diverse cross-section of Polish Jewish society. Writing in his diary in Warsaw on October 13, 1939, Hebrew teacher Chaim Kaplan captured the diversity and desperation of the refugees:

> Thousands of young people went to Bolshevik Russia on foot, that is to say, to the areas conquered by Russia. They looked upon the Bolsheviks as redeeming Messiahs. Even the wealthy, who would become poor under Bolshevism, preferred the Russians to the Germans. There is plunder on the one hand and plunder on the other, but the Russians plunder one as a citizen and as a man, while the Nazis plunder one as a Jew.[102]

Where Is Our Moses? A Chronology of Crossing

All crossings were challenging, emotionally and physically. Yitzhak Erlichson, in his 1953 memoir, compared the situation to the Exodus from Egypt, but without Moses to part the waters and lead the Children of Israel through.[103]

Yet the experience of passing from one zone to the other also differed diachronically and based on location and luck. This section, in addition to examining the process of flight, will attend to chronology insofar as possible. At times, the testimonies—which were often produced fifty years after the events—mix up months, or do not mention them at all.

Dov Levin identifies four distinct periods of migration between the German invasions of Poland and the USSR. From the outbreak of war until September 17, Poland remained a single country, albeit under attack. From mid-September until the end of October, the new border was still in flux and relatively open. From November 1939 to the spring of 1940, the border was gradually tightened and the flow of migrants ebbed as a result. In the following months, Soviet annexations of Bukhovina and the Baltics led to increased efforts to leave those areas.[104] Yosef Litvak divides the refugees into three groups: those who were already in Soviet territory when the war broke out, those who crossed before November, when it was still relatively easy, and those who crossed afterward, when it was more risky.[105]

While Levin focuses on Jewish migration into Soviet territory in general, and Litvak only on Polish Jewish population movement, both attend to politics and the changing status of the border. During their initial assault on Poland, German troops moved well beyond the dividing line established by the secret protocol of the Molotov-Ribbentrop agreement. That document had divided the German and Soviet zones near Warsaw, in the center of the country.[106] Once the Red Army entered the fray, on September 17, the German forces did retreat. However, troops on the ground are not necessarily privy to high-level negotiations, nor are conditions always amenable to quick and easy transfers. Thus, both Levin and Litvak correctly emphasize that for the first month of the war, there was no real border.

Toward the end of September, with their forces still entwined but the Polish military no longer a threat, the Soviets presented their allies with a new proposal: the Germans would receive a larger share of Polish territory, in return for granting the USSR control over the Baltic states.[107] This would form the basis of the German-Soviet Boundary and Friendship Treaty, signed September 28, 1939. Although the treaty included a detailed accompanying statement about the exact border, it also specified that a joint committee would convene in October to draw the border on a high-resolution map.[108] Crossing remained relatively easy until November, when the two sides began patrolling the agreed-upon border in earnest.

From that point forward, traversing the border required greater ingenuity and luck. Of course, the November weather also made travel considerably more arduous. In addition, access to information and changing circumstances on both sides of the border impacted decisions about whether and how to cross. Betty Rich, for example, describes the gradually worsening situation under German occupation in her memoir. At sixteen she was having little success convincing her parents to flee but had not even considered leaving on her own. Eventually, however, her parents urged her to go: "My campaign to leave had taken a couple of months and finally, near the end of December 1939, my parents said to each other, and to me, that they had no right, in a time of war like this, to hold me back. Maybe this was my fate."[109]

Crossing the border became harder with each passing week. In the months before ghettoization, as the Germans daily snatched Jews for hard labor, a popular witticism in Warsaw stated that it was easier to cross the Bug than to cross Nalewki, the central street of the Jewish neighborhood.[110] Although there is no single story of how Jews crossed into Soviet territory, patterns do emerge in the testimonial literature.

Those who crossed immediately after the German invasion refer to crowded roads and strafing from the Luftwaffe, as well as haste, fear, and confusion. However, the passage itself often goes unremarked upon. Victor Zarnowitz, whose family lived not far from the German frontier, conveys the sense of speed and chaos in his depiction of leaving home:

> Many of the Jewish citizens of Oswiecim awoke that morning and felt the same impulse: flee. The Germans were coming. They were almost here. No time to carefully pack. No time to clearly divide what would be helpful on the roads from what would be a burden. We took random things, often the wrong things. We gathered all the money in the house, and we left.

His description of crossing into Soviet territory is vaguer. After two grueling weeks of travel, he and his brother reached Lwów and kept moving. Not long afterward, they heard the singing of Soviet troops and returned to the city to await them. The Soviets soon began constructing their new order.[111]

For Harry Berkelhammer, memories of the route are also far more vivid than those of arrival. When German forces reached Tarnów, he and his brother jumped on a bicycle and left. Both were of military age and concerned about their safety. They stopped at a nearby village, where they planned to hide out until the danger had passed. Rumors of shooting caused them to once again move east. Berkelhammer describes eating out of people's gardens and traveling day and night with the Germans close behind them. And then one day, to their great relief, they encountered Soviet tanks. The narrative then turns to their new lives in Soviet Lvov.[112]

Many of the Jews who left at the start of the war had no particular destination. They fled *from* rather than *to*. Henry Orenstein's family watched the tide of refugees fleeing through Hrubieszów grow daily. They continually discussed their options and finally, on September 15, joined in. Within days, word of the Soviet invasion upset their careful calculations. They were pleased to be able to return to their home. A couple of weeks later, when the Soviets withdrew to the agreed-upon border, the Orensteins once again agonized over the possibilities. This time they decided that only the men would leave, although they hoped to be able to return soon.[113]

Jews who resided on the western banks of the Bug or San Rivers often experienced consecutive occupations in quick succession and were offered the opportunity to leave with the retreating Soviets. In these areas, past the dividing line of the German-Soviet pact, German forces retreated following the Soviet invasion in mid-September. However, with the establishment of new borders in late September, Soviet troops made room for the Germans to return. On their way out of town, many Soviet units offered to take the Jews with them to safety. Yosef Rozenberg claims that all of the Jews in his native Krzeszów left with the Soviet troops.[114] Leybish Frost, on the other hand, suggests that those who had cooperated with the Soviets in his town were most eager to leave with them and avoid Polish retribution. He adds that the religious Jews did not accept the Soviet offer.[115] While I have not seen any Soviet document officially sanctioning this offer, it recurs frequently enough in the testimonies of Polish Jews from that region that it appears to have been at least an unofficial policy.

During this same period, some Jewish soldiers from western Poland found themselves in Soviet territory when the Polish Army dissolved. Those fortunate enough to avoid capture had to decide whether to return to their families or stay in the Soviet zone. Alexander Donat initially stayed. Then in November, hearing terrible reports of life under the Nazis, he went to bring his wife and child across the border. His wife refused to leave Warsaw but encouraged him to go back to Lutsk, where he would be safer. Donat returned in December, but by January he was concerned that their separation would become permanent and made a final crossing. Due to both the temperature and the border patrols, this one was particularly difficult.[116]

Some still attempted the crossing on their own after border patrols were initiated, but most turned to locals for help. Yosef Goldkorn and his wife left Sosnowiec when the Judenrat began calling up young men for labor in October. As they neared the border, they paid a smuggler for safe passage across the San River. The next day he brought a wagonload of Jews to a German checkpoint. Several members of their party made it across before the line of waiting Jews was attacked by a German officer. The refugees scrambled, and the Goldkorns, with the help of another smuggler, hid in a peasant house nearby. When it was surrounded by German soldiers, Yosef managed to convince them that they were Jews from the eastern side of Poland, trying only to return to their homes. Eventually they were allowed to cross the river.[117]

Chaim Kaplan, writing in his diary in Warsaw in mid-November, summed up the situation: "On the way they are assaulted and robbed. The border guards know that Jewish lives and money are public property and they deal with those who cross in whatever fashion strikes their fancy."[118] Sometimes assault and robbery gave way to more dangerous cruelty. Roza Hirsz and her party endured watching the German border guards take all of their belongings, including the winter coat she was wearing. The guards then gave them permission to cross, but shot at them for sport. Three of their number did not make it to the Soviet side. From Hirsz's perspective, the older Germans were kinder and could often be bribed, but the younger ones used all the prerogatives of their position.[119]

The arbitrariness of the German border guards is also illustrated in the amount of cash that witnesses say they were allowed to retain. An unnamed refugee interviewed in the Warsaw Ghetto recounts being arrested at the Małkinia Station, near the border, and stripped of all of his belongings. The guards left each prisoner with ten złoty before allowing them to approach the river. At that point, a German patrol fell upon them and took each person's last ten złoty.[120] Kaplan recorded in his diary that Jews were permitted to take twenty złoty with them.[121] While it is possible that some of these individuals misremembered the exact numbers, it is equally possible that German guards and local commanders made up new rules as they went.

Refugees increasingly relied on smugglers to help navigate the border guards and, for those Jews who came from other areas of Poland, the unfamiliar borderlands. Most of the smugglers mentioned in testimonial sources were local Poles or Ukrainians, paid for their service. In a few cases, Jews helped other Polish Jews to reach the Soviet side. Sara Bergman was given

FIGURE 1.2. German soldiers search Jews who are leaving German-held territory by crossing the San River into Soviet territory, Tarnobrzeg, September 1939. United States Holocaust Memorial Museum, courtesy of Instytut Pamięci Narodowej, Poland.

false papers and taken across the border by the Polish Underground. In return, she was asked to return and bring other refugees. Bergman explains that young Jewish women who looked and spoke Polish were chosen because Jewish men were circumcised. At the age of seventeen, with instructions and documents from the underground, Bergman crossed the border on her own in both directions several more times. She learned to read the signals of the German guards and had an agreement with the Soviet guards.[122] Other Jews helped their coreligionists in a less organized manner. Eve Silver reports in her oral testimony that her sister took Jewish men to the nearby Bug nightly, including their father and her sister's husband.[123] At seventeen, Mietek Sieradzki and his two friends were taken to the border by friendly Polish girls who lived in the area.[124]

"Whole companies of smugglers were busy transporting people across the border," according to one chronicler in Warsaw.[125] Refugees who could afford to do so hired members of the new professional class living near the border. In this shadow economy, prices and quality varied greatly. Szymon Grajcar describes paying twenty złoty per head for his group of twenty to be rowed across the Bug in the middle of the night. Halfway across, on the third trip, the Polish smuggler demanded an additional ten złoty per person or he would throw them into the water. The refugees eventually convinced him to bring them closer to the shore and swam the final yards.[126] Adam Boren and his party paid only a bottle of vodka for their passage.[127]

While Polish Jews crossed the border at many points, certain routes were particularly popular. As the last stop on the train from Warsaw before the new border, Małkinia appears in numerous testimonies. Those without the funds to hire private transport went to various lengths to disguise themselves, board empty train cars, or rely on German ignorance of the differences between Poles and Jews to take the train as close as they could to Soviet territory. Upon arrival, if they were lucky, they were able to exit with the crowd or make contact with smugglers they had already hired. In many cases, however, they found German guards awaiting them.

Aware of Małkinia's popularity as a crossing place, the Soviets also eventually sought to limit the flow of refugees across the new border. By the late fall of 1939, there were several no-man's-land areas between the two occupying powers, where Jewish refugees, robbed of their possessions by the German guards, awaited mercy from the Soviet ones. One would-be border crosser described homeless refugees building temporary dwellings that brought to mind the "sukes" traditional Jews erect yearly to commemorate the Feast of Tabernacles and the years of wandering in the desert.[128]

Symcha Burstin and his father made their third attempt to cross into Soviet territory slightly later in the season. The Germans met their train in Małkinia, rounded up all of the Jews, and searched them for valuables or cash. Then, while beating them with sticks, the border guards herded them into the neutral zone on the Soviet border. Chanting pro-Soviet slogans, the refugees attempted to push across the border, but a Soviet officer informed them that permission had not yet arrived. After four days in the elements, Burstin saw a Polish smuggler heading a different direction and followed him. He and his father made it into Soviet territory. One anonymous witness interviewed later in the Warsaw Ghetto describes Jews in the no-man's-land coming to the realization that the Soviet guards would never grant them permission, but fully expected some of them to pass when they were not looking.[129]

Frida Zerubavel, after she reached Lvov, reports a similar story from the other side. A friend introduced her to a Soviet Jewish officer, who had encountered an enormous group of Polish Jewish refugees singing "The

Internationale" while he was patrolling the border. He promptly informed them, in Russian, that the border was closed. When they did not budge, assuming they had not understood, he made the same announcement in Yiddish. The group rushed forward, surrounding him with stories of their missing husbands and brothers. Moved by their words, but not wanting to directly disobey orders, the officer eventually continued on his patrol route, so that he would not have to sanction or see the refugees cross the border.[130] The many versions of this story suggest that it was either a common occurrence or a popular tale.

Jan Karski filed a report with the Polish Underground in February 1940, which vividly describes a similar situation in a camp near Bełżec, where the Germans had imprisoned many Jewish families attempting to cross the border in December 1939:

> An enormous proportion walked and slept under the open sky. Very many people [were] without proper clothing or other covering. While one group slept, the other waited its turn, so that outer garments could be lent one another. Those who waited jumped and ran around so as not to freeze. A few hundred people, among them children, women, and old people, run around for hours or jump in place for if they stand still, they will freeze. After a few hours [the groups] change places. [Those who have been waiting] go to sleep, and another few hundred people jump and run, jump and run. All are frozen, in despair, unable to think, hungry. [They are] a herd of harassed beasts—not people. This has been going on for weeks.
>
> I watched this for a whole hour, riveted to the spot, frightened, confused. A nightmare—not real. Blue and red freaks—not people. I shall never forget it. Never in my life have I beheld anything more frightening.[131]

While some German officials stopped, harassed, robbed, and arrested Jews attempting to flee into Soviet territory, others attempted to push entire local Jewish populations across this same border. Although this was never a top-down policy, it occurred in areas close to the border and within the General Government. In these regions especially, German officials experimented with brutal new policies toward Jews and Poles. Some of the worst excesses took place in the Lublin District where, as David Silberklang has demonstrated, conventional explanations for Nazi behavior are insufficient: "Rather, the expulsions and other population movements in the Lublin District were the result of local decisions, usually by SS personnel, and based primarily on antisemitic ideology, together with a variety of other reasons."[132]

One of the worst actions took place in the towns of Chełm and Hrubieszów in early December 1939. On November 30, Jewish men between the ages of sixteen and sixty were told to gather in the town square in Chełm the next morning. The following day, the same decree was promulgated in nearby Hrubieszów. What followed was the first documented death march of the war. Although both towns were relatively close to the Bug River, the four thousand or so men were taken on a circuitous route of over one hundred kilometers in the course of three days. The men were subjected to freezing temperatures, lack of food and water, and a bizarre variety of humiliations; many were simply shot along the way. Toward the end of the ordeal, the remaining men were divided into two groups and forcibly pushed into Soviet territory, amid a hail of bullets from both sides. Some of the several hundred survivors made it into the Soviet zone, while others were caught by Soviet border guards and pushed back into German territory. These poor souls had to find their way home and deliver the dreadful news to the families of the deceased.[133]

This event had the paradoxical effect of both encouraging and discouraging further flight. Jews in the two towns, as well as others who heard about them, were now convinced of the brutality of the Nazi overlords and fearful for their lives. At the same time, the danger of the crossing and aggression by the Soviets gave cause for hesitation. Chaim Zemel was pushed across the Bug by the Germans in Sokol, only to be sent back by the Soviets. During the night, hiding out in a school, he was discovered and beaten by a German patrol; the next day he crossed back into Soviet territory. Finding conditions unbearable, Zemel wrote to his wife that he would be returning. A postcard from her stating "In shtot iz a gehenom" (It is hell in the city) ultimately convinced him to stay.[134]

Even German and Soviet authorities noted and responded to the expulsions. A memorandum by the state secretary of Germany's Ministry of Foreign Affairs from December 5, 1939, warned of scuffles between border units over Jews expelled by the Germans and not accepted by the Soviets.[135] Later that month, Hans Frank, the Governor-General of the General Government, demanded an end to such expulsions: "The complaint made by the Soviet Union is to be taken absolutely seriously; disturbances of the necessary friendly relations between the Soviet Union and Germany by such actions must in all circumstances be avoided."[136]

By the end of 1939 the increased discipline of border patrols on both sides of the rivers made crossing an even greater gamble. After an expensive and dangerous first failed effort, Tsiporah Horvits recalls her father telling his friend, "I . . . have finished fleeing. Whatever happens to the Jews here will happen to us as well."[137] Kitty Hart's brother fled soon after the war started, but the rest of the family remained in Bielsko. As conditions worsened, her father decided that the entire family should cross. In the winter of 1940 he hired a smuggler and moved the family to a village near the Bug. Upon arrival they found other refugees discouraged from crossing by the border patrols on both sides, and word that the border had been closed. The family waited for an opportune moment to launch their attempt. While their cousins made it across, Hart's immediate family was turned back by Soviet shooting.[138]

In closing the section of their narratives about attempts to enter the Soviet zone, witnesses often claim that at a certain point it was too late. In most cases this statement is proffered without proof of its veracity or a clear chronological marker. Shalom Omri says that before the Soviets retreated from their town they offered free passage. Many, including his maternal grandparents, accepted this offer, but Omri's mother was adamant that they stay. After the Germans arrived, brandished their guns, and expropriated the family shop, the family realized that they had made a mistake. Yet by that time, Omri adds, a real border had been established and they could no longer cross.[139]

Yochewed Deutch, in her Shoah Foundation testimony, explains that she and her mother crossed the Bug with Soviet troops, and then came back to get her grandmother. However, Deutch's uncles disagreed with the plan and the resulting family conference lasted until 5:00 a.m., at which point the border was closed. Deutch concedes that some crossed later but says that it was far more dangerous.[140] Although border crossing continued well into 1940, and in some cases into 1941, there is no question that it became more difficult over time. Whether or not stealing across the border was possible, it stands to reason that people needed to close the chapter on crossing and turn to other daily concerns. The literary trope of the closure of the border thus offers a sense of closure to the entire episode.[141]

Yet a small number of Polish Jews continued to move across the border in both directions. In Rachela Tytelman Wygodzki's narrative, crossing the border is portrayed as fairly routine. First Wygodzki's father traveled from Warsaw to the Soviet zone in order to collect debts from clients after losing his business in the bombing. Soon afterward, her older brother Samek went to meet their father in Bialystok. Rachela wanted to join them, as she had obviously Jewish features and was in danger in public. Eventually she convinced her mother and crossed the border with a friend. In the spring of 1940, with the drive to register refugees, they began to reconsider. At this point, Wygodzki's father began looking into smuggling himself and his two older children back into Nazi-occupied Poland. Rather than wait for the appointed day, Samek, a competitive swimmer, swam across the river on his own. Before Rachela and her father could join him, they were deported by the Soviet authorities.[142] After relocating to the Soviet-occupied area, David Azrieli returned to his home in Maków on three separate occasions, including a final trip in the spring of 1940 to escort his mother back home after she came to visit her sons.[143]

The German invasion of the USSR in June 1941 effectively destroyed the border. Some of the Polish Jewish refugees who had avoided deportation into the interior now had the option of returning to their former communities in the western regions of what had been Poland. A sizable number did so, as evidenced by a remarkable set of documents. By the summer of 1941, Emanuel Ringelblum and his collaborators in Oneg Shabbes, the underground Jewish archive of the Warsaw Ghetto, felt that they had gathered sufficient general documentation. They decided to focus on particular communities within the ghetto population, including those who had returned from Soviet territory. For this purpose, they created a questionnaire and sent out interviewers.[144]

The documents they collected highlight the prevalence of return refugees in the Warsaw Ghetto and the variety of their experiences. Abraham Lewin titled one interview he conducted "Fun Varshe keyn Vitebsk un tsurik" (From Warsaw to Vitebsk and back). Dissatisfied with life under the Soviets, he actually left by train on December 31, 1939. By good fortune, guards on both sides of the border were celebrating, and he made it back to Warsaw.[145] A second man, interviewed by Rabbi Shimon Huberband, stayed in the Bialystok Ghetto for two months after the German invasion of the USSR. In mid-September 1941 he was able to escape. On the way to Warsaw, he passed towns entirely emptied of Jews.[146]

Hindsight

With the exception of the Oneg Shabbes interviews, the Polish government-in-exile testimonies, and the diaries, all of the firsthand accounts cited in this chapter were written well after the war. Most witnesses thus write or speak about their choices to stay or go with a retrospective awareness of their import. Alexander Donat chronicles the moment when the Poles surrendered, before the Nazis and Soviets secured the borders:

> Jews had to face the decision: to return to Nazi-occupied Warsaw to join their families, or to remain under Soviet rule. The new Nazi-Soviet border was not too difficult or too dangerous to cross. Wave after wave of refugees from Nazi-held Poland brought terrifying reports of what was happening there. From that side thousands fled Nazi persecution; from the other, thousands returned, overwhelmed by family attachments or possessions. How many lives might have been saved then, at the very beginning of the war, when the Soviet Union opened its gates to refugees from Nazism.[147]

Boris Baum also remembers a moment of decision with regret, more personally expressed. He crossed into Soviet territory in October 1939 with his seventeen-year-old brother and cousins. In November, when it became necessary to register with the authorities, his brother begged to be allowed to return to the rest of their family in Nazi-held territory. Baum took him to the river and watched him cross. In his testimony, he says that he will never be able to forgive himself, and that his brother and parents died in Sobibor.[148] Both Baum and Donat look back with the knowledge that the chances for survival were significantly higher in the Soviet zone. Yet without that knowledge, their families—like most Jews in the western regions of Poland—preferred to stay in their homes.

The minority who fled carry a burden of anguish for having allowed their loved ones to stay behind. A small number of them describe conflicts among family members deciding whether or not to flee, and the subsequent guilt of having survived. Yet most recall a smooth and consensual decision, often one where they had little to no agency. Zyga Elton explains that after his uncle crossed the border and wrote to encourage the family to follow him, Elton's parents urged him and his brother to go.[149] In David Azrieli's story, as narrated by his daughter, he and his mother were more concerned about a German occupation than his father. Immediately following the German invasion, "we gathered around the dining room table and my parents decided that Pinchas [his younger brother] and I should flee from Makow." Traveling with other local boys, they hoped to reach Palestine.[150] The narrative hints at conflict—without showing it—and then resolves it in a way that absolves the younger generation of responsibility.

Tema Abel's account introduces ambivalence regarding the decision to leave others behind. On the one hand, she recrossed the border with her father's grudging permission. She had crossed earlier to find her brother, before returning to consult with her parents. After witnessing conditions under the Germans, she determined to return to the Soviet zone. Although the testimony is in English, Abel quotes her father in Yiddish, as if underlining the veracity of her recollection: "S'iz gekumen a tsayt a kind vil avek forn un ikh hob nit keyn rekht tsu zogn neyn" (The time has come when a child wishes to travel away and I have no right to say no). On the other hand, Abel adds that she refused her thirteen-year-old sister's plea to accompany her, afraid it would be too much responsibility. This decision led to a lifetime of regret.[151]

Moshe Erlich, who left Warsaw after escaping a brutal German slave labor assignment, also quotes his father's last command in Yiddish. Erlich's Hebrew testimony contains only a handful of Yiddish words and only one other direct quotation. According to his account, when he returned home and described what he had experienced, his father's immediate response was, "Moyshe, loyf avek" (Moshe, run away).[152] He left the city on his own, but at the behest of his father. Włodzimierz Szer writes that his mother's insistence that he flee without her "gave me life for a second time."[153]

Chaim Shapiro's moment of decision is notable for its centrality to his narrative. Shapiro and his parents resided in eastern Poland, but after the Soviet takeover they encouraged him to journey to unoccupied Lithuania to continue his yeshiva studies. As a result, the young man was separated from his family during the subsequent German invasion and he did not share their end. The very title of Shapiro's memoir, *Go, My Son: A Young Jewish Refugee's Story of Survival*, absolves him of responsibility for abandoning his family. In the text Shapiro foregrounds his parents' insistence on his return to the yeshiva as proof that they encouraged him to set out on his own.[154]

Despite the added weight given to these early episodes of crossing, they are ultimately passing moments in the memoirs and testimonies. Even for Shapiro, who highlighted the gravity of the moment in his book title, the decision itself is but a fleeting instant. In her oral testimony of surviving the Holocaust in German-occupied Poland, Nechama Tec mentions her father's exploratory trip to the Soviet territories almost as an afterthought, only because this event anchors in time a more significant one: the brutal beating of her mother.[155] In her written memoir, her father's trip is more developed than in the oral testimony, yet it is soon forgotten in the complicated narrative of the family's many sojourns with different Polish families.[156]

On multiple occasions, when I have spoken about or published citations to discussions of flight from well-known memoirs of Holocaust survivors, other scholars have expressed surprise that they never noticed these references. This topic is marginal not only to the memoirs themselves but also to the experience of many readers of these texts. The impact of the events that follow is so great that this relatively insignificant moment passes out of memory. I would argue that despite the potentially contaminating effects of retrospective analysis, this very marginality preserves some of the validity of these postwar testimonial justifications.

Scholars of testimony have argued that certain elements of the Holocaust have become so emblematic that survivors feel a need to include them in their testimonies, as if not doing so will diminish the legitimacy of their recollections. In Zoë Waxman's words, "collective memory obscures the diversity of Holocaust testimonies."[157] Lawrence Langer highlights a recurring episode in which new arrivals at death camps are shown the smoke from the crematoria and cruelly told that it is their loved ones.[158] As Christopher Browning points out, using the ubiquitous sightings of Dr. Josef Mengele as an example, the most problematic testimonies are those "that incorporate iconic Holocaust tropes gained from post-war exposure to widespread representations in documentaries, movies, memoirs, and novels."[159]

If overexposure can contaminate the veracity of memories, perhaps underexposure can contribute to retaining its essential truth. Indeed, Browning suggests that the relative obscurity of the camp he studied ensured that "memories of that experience remain relatively pristine and untouched by iconic tropes."[160] The story of survival in the USSR is so far beyond the pale of normative Holocaust experiences, and even refugee experiences, that those who survived it have not needed to develop answers to recurring questions about their actions or decisions. Nor have they had the opportunity to read or listen to so many other similar testimonies that they have a sense of what is expected of them. In many cases they are not even aware of how many others underwent related experiences. As a result, their memoirs and testimonies, while still subject to the vagaries of memory and mediation of retelling, are less susceptible to the homogenization of collective memory.

Yet the memoirs of those who opted to flee across the border often still hint at lingering anxiety about their decision and its consequences. Ironically, one memoir that is even more mediated than most accounts of these events demonstrates this point most dramatically. The children of survivors have written a number of hybrid Holocaust memoirs using their parents' materials and words.[161] While these dual memoirs—both biographies and autobiographies—are even farther from the raw experiences, their retrospective point of view can shed new light on neglected areas. Suzanna Eibuszyc, writing about her own and her mother's experiences, is able to say plainly what someone of the previous generation might not have been able to: "My mother never forgave herself for leaving Poland to save her own life and abandoning her loved ones to the horrible deaths that followed."[162]

Whether or not they realized it at the time, crossing the border was a major turning point for Jewish refugees. The Polish Jews who chose to move from Esau to Laban had to adapt to life in the totalizing Soviet system. Ida Kaminska, the famous Polish Jewish actress, invokes a sense of being part of a people primed for reinvention in her autobiography. Describing her October 17, 1939, border crossing, she recalls the following scene:

"Who are you?" the Germans asked.

"Actors."

"All Jews are actors," one of the Germans called out. I thought to myself, perhaps he's right.[163]

2

If a Man Did Flee from a Lion, and a Bear Met Him

The Soviet Embrace

From the river Bug—an insane blizzard rages,
With its whipping snow, it wipes out every footstep;
And from the twisted menorahs of the Bialystok synagogues,
They hung the *goles*, like some hanging fiddles.

— PERETZ MARKISH

IN HIS EPIC 1940 poem "To a Jewish Dancer," chronicling the first stirrings of the Holocaust, Peretz Markish, the well-known Soviet Yiddish poet, explicitly mentions the fate of the newly arrived refugees from Nazi-occupied Poland.[1] Invoking the echoes of previous dispersions, or *goles*, and the symbolism of wandering, he paints the current refugees like their ancient ancestors. Yet he also references contemporary events: these wandering Jews have crossed the Bug River, and attempt to find shelter in synagogues in Bialystok (Pol. Białystok). The blizzard they battle is an actual snowstorm and, symbolically, the harrowing conditions of crossing. Their passage to safety in the Workers' Paradise is a painful ending and a new beginning. Here we will examine the experiences of the Polish Jewish refugees, from their arrival in Soviet territory until the 1941 German invasion.

First Impressions

Before turning to the refugees' early encounters with Soviet life, it is necessary to touch upon an issue that remains controversial. While the war experience of Polish Jewish refugees has received relatively little attention in general, the subject of relations between Catholic and Jewish Poles in the Soviet-occupied territories—and more specifically, perceived Jewish responses to the Soviet occupation—has generated more interest than other aspects of this story. In general, I try to let the concerns and observations of the Polish Jewish refugees themselves guide my narrative. In this case, however, their testimonies contain few references to this issue. It was not one that concerned them greatly at the time, nor, apparently, afterward. Yet because this subject has become a point of contention in Polish and Jewish history and memory, it requires some explication.

At its heart, the issue revolves around Polish accusations about Jewish responses to the Soviet invaders and occupiers. As Alexander Brakel explains, the accusation has three distinct yet related parts. First, Jews were said to have enthusiastically welcomed the arrival of Soviet troops in Polish territory. Second, Jews are viewed as having collaborated with the new regime on a larger scale than other groups. And third, Jews were thus beneficiaries of the Soviet system.[2] The subjectivity of these claims should be obvious. Marek Wierzbicki, even as he asserts that Polish Jews welcomed the Soviet troops, has to admit, "Of course, we do not possess any statistical data confirming this view, but numerous Jewish, Polish, and Soviet sources attest to the existence of this phenomenon."[3] Yet, as Joanna Michlic shows, Wierzbicki and other historians use the Jewish sources out of context and ignore the problematic nature of many of the Polish sources: "It reflects a lack of understanding on the part of some scholars of the fundamental difference between historically reconstructed memory and unreflective popular memory."[4]

At the time of the Soviet takeover, Polish assumptions about Jews' leftist leanings and Jewish assumptions about ethnic Poles' antisemitic beliefs already had a long history. Both sets of assumptions are reflected in a 1940 report about the situation in Soviet territory produced by Polish Underground courier Jan Karski for the Polish government-in-exile. On the one hand, he seems to recognize the potential distance between popular sentiments and reality in his carefully worded description of Polish perceptions of Jewish commitments: "The attitude of the Jews toward the Bolsheviks is regarded among the Polish populace as quite positive. It is generally believed that the Jews betrayed Poland and the Poles, that they are basically communists, that they crossed over to the Bolsheviks with flags unfurled." Yet on the previous page, he himself stereotypes Jews and minimizes their exposure to Soviet negative policies: "The Jews are at home here, not only because they do not experience humiliations or persecutions, but [also because] they possess, thanks to their quick-wittedness and ability to adapt to every new situation, a certain power of both a political and an economic nature."[5] Although Karski's report was ostensibly intended to inform and not editorialize, he perpetuates popular ideas tying Jews to communism, as well as less acknowledged biases about Jewish guile. David Engel calls Karski's portrayal "an unwarranted extrapolation from a fundamental kernel of truth."[6]

Polish Jews were already sensitive to these accusations, as illustrated in a testimony recorded in the Warsaw Ghetto in 1942. The anonymous witness, who had fled Warsaw, describes arriving in Łuck (Rus./Ukr. Lutsk) on the afternoon of September 18, 1939. Several hours later, the Red Army marched in. In this account, many young Jews enthusiastically welcomed the Soviets. Yet the witness quickly adds that the local peasants in the villages also greeted the Soviet troops with open arms.[7] Even in the midst of the war, writing from the ghetto for a purely Jewish archival collection effort, this individual felt the need to provide an apologetic account.[8] Concerned about possible misinterpretations of the account, the witness pointed to instances of non-Jewish Polish citizens who were equally pleased to see the arrival of the Red Army.

According to Katherine Jolluck, "Polish attitudes toward Jews, Ukrainians, and Byelorussians only hardened in exile." Using testimonies recorded in 1942 and 1943 by the Polish government-in-exile in Iran, she shows how Soviet repression increased the centrality of national identity among Polish women. But this ethnic and religious solidarity also resulted in the exclusion of national minorities and their plight: "Blind to the injustices that were perpetrated against the minorities in the interwar period, they operate from a strict code of loyalty and obedience." Jolluck also demonstrates how easy it is for people to view traitorous behavior within their own group as exceptional while condemning that same behavior among others as representative.[9]

It stands to reason that many Polish Jews would have greeted the initial Soviet invasion with relief: for a Jew, Soviet troops were preferable to German ones. Yehuda Bauer points out that "the alternative to Soviet occupation was German rule, and by mid-September 1939, Jews realized that German rule meant violent persecution and terrible suffering, although what we now know as the Holocaust was far from people's imagination."[10] Most Jews had never been members of the Polish Communist Party, and wealthy Jews—or religious ones—had particular reasons to fear Soviet policies. But given what was known about both powers, Jews had more reason to fear Nazi hegemony. Additionally, all the national minorities had experienced official discrimination in Poland. Jews and others had reason to welcome Soviet promises of cultural autonomy and affirmative action in employment.

Baruch Milch, in his reconstructed wartime diary, expresses all of these sentiments:

> On September 17, 1939, we heard that the Soviets had crossed the Polish border and were closing in. The news soothed the Jewish population, except for the wealthy, who remembered the Soviet invasion of 1920.
>
> I was not worried. I had had moderate leftist leadings since my teen years, when the authorities would not allow me to study medicine, the profession I loved. Although I had no idea what the new regime might bring—there is a large gap between even a wonderful theory and practice—I was sure the Soviet regime would not be antisemitic and would let me practice my profession. I was a little afraid for my family because they were all merchants, but I thought that since they were all young they could work at anything and make a living. We would do much better here, I was sure, than in the places where Hitler was pursuing and murdering Jews.[11]

Yet to ethnic Poles, for whom the two occupations were equally disastrous, this kind of reasoning appeared not only self-serving but treasonous. In the words of Andrzej Żbikowski, "in the Polish unwritten code universally rejecting the occupation and in the call for at least passive resistance, there was no room for exceptions: who is not with us is against us."[12]

Postwar politics only further complicated these issues, building on the already complex legacy of Polish and Jewish relations in the prewar era and the accusations launched during the Soviet occupation of 1939–1941. If the so-called żydokomuna, the idea of a link between Jews and communism, held sway before the war, it only increased in prominence afterward. Antisemitism and anticommunism have been closely linked in postwar Poland, whether due to the influence of Nazi propaganda, prewar prejudices, awareness of Jewish participation in establishing the Polish People's Republic, or some combination of these factors.

There is a rich scholarly literature about the history of this pernicious allegation. In his provocative 2001 book Jan Gross suggests that guilt over Polish participation in the Holocaust and the Soviet occupation allowed some perpetrators of the 1941 Jedwabne Pogrom to retroactively justify their actions by reading postwar Jewish participation in the communist government back into the first period of Soviet occupation.[13] His claim was met with fierce resistance, some of which was decidedly antisemitic.[14] As Ben-Cion Pinchuk notes, "The attempt to connect the massacre of an entire community, an obvious act of genocide, to the behavior of the victims during the Soviet period is historically false and morally untenable."[15]

Poland today, in the wake of a protracted period of communist rule, is still trying to assimilate what Joanna Michlic has termed the "dark aspects" in its past.[16] The initial period of Soviet oversight remains a highly charged topic, especially with regard to the perceived behavior of national minorities. As Tarik Amar writes in his study of Lviv (Pol. Lwów, Rus. Lvov, Yid. Lemberg), "It bears emphasis that contemporaries could not actually *know* anything about who greeted the Soviets the most. Instead, in an ethnically fissiparous city in a state of emergency, fragmented impressions and rumors combined with prior stereotypes."[17] While the Polish public and scholars continue to scrutinize the responses of Jews to the Soviet invasion in 1939, Polish Jews have evinced interest in other aspects of this rocky period.

After their difficulties crossing the border, Polish Jewish refugees recorded both relief and anxiety at arriving in Soviet territory. "When I reached Bialystok, I felt like a new man suddenly awakened from a nightmarish dream. No hateful swastikas, no arrogant Nazis, no fear, no limitations on movement!"[18] But in leaving behind those terrible threats they had also left their homes, families, jobs, and belongings. Even those with family or work connections in the area, or who had spent time there in the past, were confronted with a new reality. In memoirs and testimonies, they describe the overwhelming crush of other refugees, as well as their dawning awareness of the imperatives of Soviet life.

Most refugees went first to the larger cities within formerly Polish areas. Bialystok and Lvov were inundated with refugees. Indeed, Markish's moving image of refugees retiring their exile on the Bialystok synagogue menorahs is not entirely metaphorical. Thousands of refugees found housing in synagogue buildings. Symcha Burstin considered himself lucky to be one of ten men sharing a small private room in a synagogue in Bialystok. The main hall, in his opinion, was far worse, with crying and filth everywhere.[19] By December, when Ann Szedlecki and her brother arrived in Bialystok, conditions in the unheated and infested synagogue were so dire that her brother wanted to go straight back to Łódź. However, she convinced him to stay.[20]

Cities offered seemingly the best opportunities for housing and employment. Surrounded by so many others in similar positions, refugees established networks of information. Yet relief efforts were hindered by the unexpectedly large influx of refugees, as well as the general upheaval. According to one anonymous refugee, later interviewed in the Warsaw Ghetto, Lvov was overrun with refugees when he arrived on October 3. Moreover, the city provided no organized form of aid for them.[21] Many of the testimonies make no reference to formal aid. Some mention callous responses from locals. A few cite examples of communal or governmental welfare. Shaul Shternfeld mentions the shame of eating in a soup kitchen but does not say who ran it.[22] After a difficult journey from Lublin in early November, Iakov Khonigsman was relieved to find a Jewish communal soup kitchen in Brest (Pol. Brześć, Yid. Brisk).[23]

Dov Levin observes the perversity of Soviet policies abolishing all Jewish communal organizations just as the refugees needed them most.[24] Nonetheless, communal aid continued to function in at least some locales. Emanuel Goldberg, a resident of the town of Svisloch (Bel. Svislach), recalls an elderly refugee who came to their house daily. Goldberg's mother fed him and washed his clothes. In his memoir in the town's memorial book, Goldberg wonders whether the refugee was formally assigned to their family by a clandestine Jewish aid group.[25] When Betty Rich, age sixteen, arrived in Bialystok with a group of other teens, the Jewish community distributed them to communities in smaller towns. Rich was sent to Kuznitsa (Pol. Kuźnica) in late December 1939 or early January 1940, which may help to explain the fairly organized absorption process.[26] By that time the flow of refugees had eased and communities had learned more about how to care for those still arriving. Over time, Soviet offices were established to fill some of the refugees' needs. Zyga Elton, who reached Bialystok in mid-November with his brother, lodged in a synagogue and registered immediately with what he refers to as the Refugee Committee and Labor Exchange.[27]

A refugee referred to only as SL, who was interviewed shortly after the war by the American Jewish Committee, explained that the former officers of the Jewish community in Bialystok had spontaneously formed a Jewish refugee committee with donations from local Jews. Taken over by the state, it then became a general refugee office under the leadership of a Soviet commissar. Under state auspices, it was able to offer access to medical care, as well as fuel and food. However, according to SL, who worked for the committee, the commissar also helped himself to large quantities of the goods.[28] This scandalized the other employees, not yet accustomed to Soviet standards of behavior.

In Lvov a Commission for Assistance to Refugees and the Unemployed operated from October 2 through December 21, 1939. The commission, according to its preserved file, operated soup kitchens, sanitary points, and medical clinics.[29] In Bialystok a similar governmental initiative sought to estimate the number of refugees, as well as to help them find housing.[30] Yet only the earliest testimonies, such as SL's, mention any form of state assistance.[31] It is possible that the aid did not make enough of an impression to bear remembering in later testimonies. Given the surge of refugees and suddenly unemployed locals, it is also probable that the resources were insufficient for the need. Additionally, the fact that the assistance points kept track of recipients' names and addresses may have discouraged some from seeking help.

Whether in larger cities or smaller towns, refugees who had friends or family to stay with certainly had the smoothest transition. Even if temporary, an initial place to stay helped refugees avoid the worst difficulties and indignities of arrival. Irving Badner was fortunate to find his sister and brother-in-law, who had crossed the border earlier and could offer him shelter when he arrived.[32] Mike Weinreich and his father found a warm welcome at the home of first cousins in Graevo (Pol. Grajewo).[33] Prominent Zionist activist Zorach Warhaftig, along with his wife and sister, was greatly aided by his brother-in-law—who not only knew the border area well, but was able to take them to his parents' home in Lutsk.[34] These are among the few witnesses who do not mention overcrowding or discomfort.

Besides overcrowding, the other major theme in refugees' initial responses to the newly Soviet territories is the odd behavior of Soviet troops. Nearly all note the almost frantic spending spree by the Soviet soldiers. The soldiers cleaned out Polish shops, seeking watches—valuable and portable items—in particular. Although they often relayed these stories with humor, the Poles were quite aware that this compulsive buying betrayed chronic shortages. Yet the soldiers, parroting their superiors, responded to questions about the availability of goods with a stock phrase, "u nas vse yest" (we have everything).[35] Baruch Minz provides a particularly tragicomic version of such an interchange: "To every question that we asked, they answered: 'With us you can have everything you desire.' When we asked them in Jewish if they also had 'trouble,' they replied: 'We have lots of it.'"[36] By switching from Russian to Yiddish, comprehensible only to fellow Jews, the Minz family at last got a straight answer from some of the Jews among the Soviet soldiers.

Lithuanian Passage

Even as the refugees and the residents of eastern Poland slowly became accustomed to the Soviet presence, population movement persisted. Refugees continued to arrive in the Soviet zone, while smaller numbers returned to Nazi-held Polish territories. In addition, many Polish Jews sought to reach unoccupied areas. At first, Hungary and Romania appeared to be the most promising possibilities for escape, and indeed, members of the Polish government had taken these routes. Families living near the eastern and southern Polish borders at the beginning of the war remember seeing columns of well-dressed would-be escapees coming through, and cars abandoned by the side of the road when no more fuel was available.

The southern escape route proved very difficult. A. Reisfeld and his father actually did manage to get to Romania, and from there to Palestine. But even with generous sums of money for payments and bribes, his father's decisive and powerful personality, and considerable luck, they did not succeed in saving the whole family: Reisfeld's father was unable to take his wife and daughter with them.[37] Frida Zerubavel, visiting her mother in Warsaw when the war began, was trying to get back to her home in Palestine. After being turned away from the Romanian consulate in Lvov, she determined to cross into Romania illegally and traveled as far as Kolomea (Pol. Kołomyja, Ukr. Kolomyia) near the border. There she found only suspicion and confusion.[38] Zerubavel returned to Lvov, and later crossed into Lithuania instead. Indeed, as word spread that the borders into Hungary and Romania had become impassable, the Baltic states became the next best option. Lithuania, with its accessible border and large and historic Jewish community, was particularly attractive to refugee Jews.

Like Poland, Lithuania became a sovereign nation after the First World War. The Lithuanians were pleased to regain their autonomy, although distressed to find their historical capital Vilnius (Pol. Wilno, Rus. Vilna) given to Poland. As part of the revised agreement between Nazi Germany and the Soviet Union after their joint dismemberment of Poland, the Baltic states fell under the Soviet sphere of influence. On October 10, 1939, the USSR offered control over Vilna, and its surrounding region, to Lithuania in return for a promise of mutual assistance and the right to keep troops in the country.[39] Although well aware that this was a dangerous bargain, the Lithuanian state was gratified to reunite with the Vilnius region. The actual transfer took place on October 28, 1939. The Lithuanian government was eager to increase the power and presence of Lithuanians over that of Poles in the region, and willing to use the Jews—who constituted close to 40 percent of the population in Vilnius—as a bulwark against the ethnic Poles.[40] Lithuania, and especially the Vilnius region, became a destination for Polish Jewish refugees.

Describing those first weeks and months of the war, and the surge of refugees, Herman Kruk, having arrived from Warsaw himself in early October, wrote, "The sea overflowed and flooded Vilna." Kruk also depicted the distress of the war refugees:

> A woman lost her husband, a man searches for his child, children ask about their parents—everything is mixed up, confused, and lost. Here is a woman running wearing only her shirt, covered with a coat—fleeing her burning home. A man on a bicycle: in front of him a child, in back of him a little dog—all his remaining property. . . .
>
> Lubliners ask Plotskers, Plotskers seek among the refugees from Warsaw, people from Łódź crawl up to those from Kalisz—a confusion, a tangle of such dreadful loneliness, of such scared madness—the war tremors of Hitler's invasion![41]

Until the Lithuanians and Soviets established firm borders, passage into the area was relatively uncomplicated. By the end of 1939, guards patrolled both sides. However, many who tried to cross said that the Soviets were far more concerned about those leaving than the Lithuanians were about new arrivals. By early 1940 both sides watched the border more carefully and crossing became dangerous. Frida Zerubavel tried to cross into Lithuania on a cold, dark January night, but was arrested by a Soviet border guard after her guide left her and she got lost. The next morning, she and fifty other prisoners were marched twenty-four kilometers to a larger police station, interrogated, divested of all of their cash, and then set free. With the help of local peasants, she arrived in Vilnius the following night.[42]

Shaul Shternfeld was not so lucky. The second time he was caught trying to cross the Lithuanian border, a Soviet Jewish agent from the NKVD (Narodnyi Komissariat Vnutrennikh Del, People's Commissariat for Internal Affairs) explained to him in Yiddish that he could not afford to get caught a third time. Shternfeld had to return to Lvov.[43] Leib Novik did not receive a warning. Apprehended trying to steal into Lithuania around New Year's Day 1940, he was imprisoned and interrogated for six months. In July he was sentenced to five years of hard labor and taken to an isolated work camp in the Komi Autonomous Soviet Socialist Republic (ASSR).[44] Soviet guards arrested Klara Samuels's whole family at the border, but only her father was transferred to a prison in Baranovichi (Bel. Baranavichy, Pol. Baranowicze). "We did not know it," writes Samuels, "but at that moment our hope of escaping the horrors of the Holocaust ended."[45]

By early 1940, as more and more European countries either fell to or joined forces with the Germans, only a handful of countries in the region— among them Estonia, Latvia, and Lithuania—were controlled by neither the Nazis nor the Soviets. This made them particularly popular destinations for those sure to be persecuted by both totalitarian states, including many members of Zionist parties and Orthodox religious groups. Szlomo Zdrojo- wicz, in a testimony recorded after his fortuitous evacuation to Iran, claims that rabbis granted Orthodox Jews permission to travel even on the Sab- bath in order to escape the "Bolsheviks."[46] Polish Jews holding emigration documents for other countries also flocked to Lithuania, as it seemed to offer their final opportunity for escape. Other Polish Jews had no hope of escaping Europe but dreamed of greater safety and security. Zekharia Chesno, whose family resided in Kaunas (Rus. Kovno) after fleeing Germany, remembers taking in a family of Polish Jewish refugees they met at synagogue.[47] Dina Porat has called Lithuania, during this brief period, both "shelter and exit."[48]

Porat estimates, based largely on Zionist sources, that between thirteen and fourteen thousand Polish Jews arrived in Lithuania as refugees.[49] Sarunas Liekis's research finds 18,311 refugees, 6,860 of whom were Jewish, in the Vilnius district alone by December 1939.[50] Most Jewish refugees came first to Vilnius, which had until recently been a Polish city and had a large Jewish community. It became necessary to redistribute the refugees after January 1940, when the Lithuanian government called for the depar- ture of all who had arrived in the city after its annexation.[51]

For the more than two thousand yeshiva students who came to Vilnius as refugees, the redistribution was organized by Rabbi Hayim Ozer Grodzenski. Reb Khayim Oyzer, as he was known, was a towering figure famous as much for his philanthropic and communal activities as for his legal rulings. Although already ailing, he devoted great care to seeing that Torah study carried on in Lithuania, after both the Germans and the Soviets had put a stop to it in the formerly Polish areas under their control.

Menachem Mendl Grossman, who attended a large and well-respected yeshiva in Kamieniec (Bel. Kamyenyets, Rus. Kamenets) before the war, states in his testimony that it was a great relief to wind up under the Soviets and not the Nazis in 1939. But soon the authorities closed down the yeshiva. When a letter arrived from Rabbi Grodzenski urging them to relocate to Vilnius, the assistant director of the yeshiva, Rabbi Reuven Grozovsky, prepared to leave. However, the older rabbi in charge of the yeshiva elected to stay with his community. The students split up, with Grossman joining Rabbi Grozovsky and one hundred other students first in Vilnius and then in Raseiniai (Yid. Raseyn, Raseiniai District). There they received material support from the American Jewish Joint Distribution Committee (JDC) and continued their studies.[52] Simcha Shafran, age fourteen at the time, followed his yeshiva from Bialystok to Vilnius. They were then relocated to Biržai (Yid. Birzh, Biržai District), where the local Jewish community supported them with "eating days."[53]

Zionist activists also attempted to get to Lithuania during this period. When the war started in September 1939, many leaders of Zionist groups in Poland were still traveling back from the World Zionist Conference held in Geneva in August. The breakdown of communication meant that many young activists, especially those on *hakhsharot* (agricultural training farms), had to make decisions entirely on their own. Several groups of young Zionists set off east ahead of the Germans. They settled temporarily in what became Soviet territory, but soon discovered that their ideas were not welcome there. Lithuania appeared to offer them not only an escape from Nazi and Soviet terror but the possibility of leaving for Palestine. Approximately two thousand such pioneers fled to Lithuania, with an additional five hundred from the right-wing Betar movement.[54]

Rachela Zilberberg, along with her husband and other members of their Zionist training camp near Kraków, managed to reach Vilnius at the end of November 1939. They stayed there through Passover of 1940, receiving aid from the Joint (as the JDC was colloquially known), and then moved to the shtetl of Virbalis (Yid. Virbaln, Vilkaviškis District). Later that summer they had to relocate farther from the German border and settled in Anykščiai (Yid. Aniksht, Utena District). Zilberberg found the Jews in Vilnius aloof, citing a joke from the period that Vilna's Jews were threatening their daughters with marriage to refugees if they misbehaved. Yet she had only praise for the Jews in the two small towns who took them in and helped them find work.[55]

From the time of the invasion in September through the period of Lithuania's independence, the Lithuanian Jewish community, with help from organizations at home and abroad, provided aid to Jews in need, and especially the refugees. The Society for Safeguarding the Health of the Jewish Population (Towarzystwo Ochrony Zdrowia Ludności Żydowskiej, TOZ), a Polish Jewish organization already functioning in Polish areas such as Vilnius, opened soup kitchens and health stations, and distributed food and clothing from the start.[56] TOZ accepted material aid from the JDC in order to maintain these vital functions. Although the German- and Soviet-occupied areas of Poland also experienced great need, it was more and more difficult to deliver aid to these areas. Jewish philanthropies thus focused much of their attention on Lithuania. The JDC was particularly active, while trying to work with locals.[57]

A JDC memorandum of November 1939 describes the horrific circumstances faced by Polish Jews expelled by the Germans and not accepted by the Lithuanians, as well as the help they received from Lithuanian Jews:

> It is impossible to overemphasize the devotion and sacrifice of these small Jewish communities. In a town [of] fifty Jewish families every home had seven or eight refugees who were being housed and fed. An underground railway system fully comparable to anything I have ever read about in Civil War stories was in full operation.[58]

In addition to closely monitoring the situation through local contacts and official representatives, the Joint sent over seven hundred thousand dollars of aid to the area in the next year.[59] Other organizations, such as the Vaad Hatzala, created expressly to rescue Orthodox rabbis and yeshiva students, were also involved in charitable work.[60] Liekis notes that Jews were far more successful at raising funds to help their refugees than either the Lithuanians or the Poles.[61]

While some Polish Jews sought to reestablish life in neutral Lithuania, others saw it chiefly as a way out of Europe. This was particularly true for Zionists. The Jewish Agency, in Palestine, granted Zorach Warhaftig, a lawyer and Zionist activist from Warsaw, permission to establish the Palestine Commission in Lithuania. Moving to Kaunas in order to be closer to representatives of foreign powers, he attempted to negotiate with British and Lithuanian authorities about immigration certificates and safe passage. The work of Warhaftig and his colleagues, as he describes in his postwar memoir, was hampered by the low number of certificates available, the challenge of deciding who should receive priority, and the difficulty and expense of travel. In the end, they were able to save about five hundred people with 303 permits. They also helped hundreds of other certificate holders,

Palestinian citizens, and Polish Jews with other documents find their way out of the war zone.[62]

Of course, there were many whom the Palestine Commission could not help. Complaints about favoritism and the commission's criteria circulated both at the time and afterward.[63] Warhaftig tries to address some of these in his memoir, concluding, "The fact is that all rescue work must be selective."[64] Even for those lucky enough to obtain certificates, there was no guarantee of safe passage. Dov Lederman's father went ahead to Vilnius and procured certificates for the whole family. Meanwhile, his mother managed to smuggle her two children from Warsaw to Bialystok and awaited word from her husband. Unfortunately, he was caught by Soviet guards trying to cross the Lithuanian border and imprisoned. The family reunited only after the war.[65]

Frida Zerubavel, a Palestinian citizen who had left her husband and small son behind to visit her mother in Warsaw in August 1939, was one of the fortunate ones. After traveling through several cities held by the Soviets following rumors of exit routes, she eventually made it to Lithuania and passed through the bureaucratic hoops required to receive permission to leave. Zerubavel and the other Palestinian citizens were taken through Latvia, Sweden, Denmark (where they picked up a youth Aliyah group), the Netherlands, Belgium, and France. There were close calls and high tensions on the way, but she made it back to Tel Aviv.[66]

Most people realized that it was only a matter of time before the Soviets expanded their control over the Baltic states. Zerubavel mentions anti-Zionists, and even one Polish Catholic woman she knew, fearfully queuing for a way out of Europe: "Even she, the Christian woman, believed in the dream of the certificate."[67] Indeed, in June 1940, Soviet forces moved into Lithuania. Zekharia Chesno describes the clock ticking on his father's elaborate and expensive arrangements to procure certificates to Palestine. The family joked darkly that two more weeks of exile could hardly matter after two thousand years, but in fact Soviet tanks put an end to their plans. Chesno writes, "And here begins the tragi-comic story. If not for this story, everything would have ended differently."[68]

Soviet rule in the Baltic states signaled major changes for both citizens and refugees. Rapid sovietization, which included nationalization and deportations, began immediately. Jewish religious, cultural, and political life, formerly allowed to thrive in Lithuania, was quickly curtailed.[69] Although most contemporary observers assumed that emigration was no longer a possibility, in fact the Soviets made an unexpected exception for those refugees already in possession of the proper documents. However, many refugees were too terrified by the likelihood that registering for emigration would lead to their arrest to take advantage of this unlikely opening. The Soviets were not known for allowing free transit either in or out of their domains, and historians have struggled to make sense of this interlude. Dov Levin suggests that the Soviets were concerned about international opinion at that point, and that it offered them the opportunity of sneaking out some spies.[70] According to Porat, the refugees were considered an obstacle to sovietization. Additionally, plans to make the area more ethnically homogeneous would be aided by allowing some of the Jews to leave.[71]

Whatever the reasons, emigration continued after the annexation in August 1940. Nonetheless, as Soviet control increased and the war cut off exit routes across Europe, possibilities for escape dwindled. In April 1941 emigration ended entirely.[72] As the gates gradually closed, refugees sought fiercely to find ways out. They approached consuls, paid exorbitant fees from their own savings as well as subsidies from the JDC, and wrote to anyone they thought could help their causes. In December 1940, Chaim Lilienheim wrote from Vilnius to Zorach Warhaftig, who was by then in Japan. Lilienheim, a refugee from Warsaw, had at last procured permission to immigrate to Mexico with his wife. "Now my voyage is pending on getting the Japanese transit visa and the object of my letter is to beg you to obtain it for me."[73] Although the files do not contain a resolution to Lilienheim's case, several thousand refugees did manage to leave Soviet Lithuania before April 1941, many through Japan.[74]

Yisrael Gerber, a Polish yeshiva student before the war, fled to Lithuania to avoid the Soviets in 1939. He was fortunate to receive papers to immigrate to the United States. Through a series of what he terms miracles, he made it as far as Shanghai before the conditions of war made it impossible to travel farther.[75] Masha Leon and her mother Zelda followed a similar route, but after a year in Japan, they boarded a boat bound for Seattle before the bombing on Pearl Harbor and spent the remainder of the war in Canada. They only reunited with Leon's father, Mordechai Bernstein, who had been arrested by the Soviets, well after the war.[76]

All of these positive stories should not obscure the fact that the vast majority of Lithuanian Jews, as well as the majority of Polish Jewish refugees among them, stayed on. Sovietization was more rapid in the Baltics than in the Polish territories, but followed along the same lines. Deportation happened later. Just like the Polish Jews, Lithuanian Jews adapted to the new regime until the German invasion in June 1941. On the morning of the invasion, before his own self-evacuation, Chaim Grade recalls promising himself, "I shall not become a refugee and curse the day I left my home, as the refugees from Poland are doing."[77]

Refugee Life and the Family

Although many considered escaping to Lithuania, most refugees in the formerly eastern Polish territories decided to stay where they were. Crossing the border was risky, and most—having just begun to settle into housing and routines—were reluctant to take to the road once again. Some also foresaw that Lithuania, too, would eventually be subject to Soviet takeover. Instead they worked to make the most of the rapidly changing circumstances. In the words of Israel Feldman, a refugee from Łódź, "Life was about as 'normal' as it can get. We were escaping something. We were not in the city of our birth, the city we grew up in, but life was good."[78]

After the chaos of the first weeks of the invasions, life in Soviet territory began to settle into regular patterns. A priority, and a challenge, was to find stable housing. Camping out in synagogues, or even with relatives or friends, was not generally a long-term solution. But the influx of refugees and the arrival of Soviet officials led to a shortage of housing.[79] As Sheila Fitzpatrick has shown, housing shortages were already a regular feature of Soviet life.[80] One refugee, interviewed in the Warsaw Ghetto in 1942, claimed that local Jews in Vitebsk used the promise of a room as dowry to convince refugees from Poland to marry their daughters.[81]

Szymon Grajcar arrived in Brest in November 1939 with a group of relatives from Ryki. He says that, after they had slept for a week in a courthouse, a Russian official brought them to a storage shed that the landlord had been forced to make available. They stayed there until they were deported the following summer.[82] The Halpern family from Kraków reached a relative's house in Brody, only to discover that it had been requisitioned by the new authorities. The relative and his family had been moved to the top floor of a synagogue.[83] Helen Zuberman, with her parents and brother, moved into an abandoned grocery store that had no plumbing.[84]

It was easier to find suitable accommodations away from the larger cities and the border. Yocheved Zamari's family stayed initially with relatives near the border. When their home became too crowded, they moved into a partially built structure nearby. Finally, they accepted the Soviet offer to move to the interior and settled in Poltava with other relatives.[85] The Saler family, along with many others from Hrubieszów, settled in the town of Vladimir-Volynskii (Pol. Włodzimierz Wołyński, Ukr. Volodymyr-Volynskyi, Yid. Ludmir), not far from the Bug River.[86] After securing a room for the family, the father returned to Hrubieszów with a cart to pick up their belongings, including a sewing machine. This allowed him to continue in his profession as a tailor.[87]

Finding work was the next concern of the refugees. Even those who brought cash or other valuables could not live on them indefinitely, and most of the refugees had very little to spare. Certain skills were more easily transferable than others. An anonymous refugee, interviewed in the Warsaw Ghetto, originally registered with the work committee in Bialystok. When they had no offers for him after two weeks, he moved to the smaller city of Sokolka (Pol. Sokółka), and immediately obtained a position as a bookkeeper in a government office. He boasts that when he relocated to Pinsk in the spring of 1940 he found work as a bookkeeper in a factory within two hours.[88] A painter, Israel Feldman, also seems to have had no trouble obtaining jobs wherever he moved.[89] Mikhael Berlovitch, a building engineer, and his wife, a dentist, both secured employment in Rovno (Pol. Równe, Ukr. Rivne). On paper, their salaries were generous. In reality, they discovered that their workplaces lacked amenities and proper tools, and their salaries often were not paid in full.[90]

Others had a more difficult time finding employment in their fields of expertise. Adam Boren's father felt that he needed to hide his capitalist background and took a job as a laborer in a fruit cooperative. Because he had access to salt used for pickling, he could also sell the excess to supplement his income.[91] Khanina Teitel and his family fled on the sixth day of the war. Teitel's father had owned a brewery in Poland but was unable to find work in Kovel (Pol. Kowel). After several months of living off their savings, the family wanted only to return to the German-held areas.[92]

The unemployed, and those whose salaries were insufficient for their needs, sometimes turned to the black or gray markets. Harry Berkelhammer and his two brothers shared a room in Lvov, where they made a living selling flint and headache medication on the black market.[93] Although Shmuel Burshtein's father found work as a tailor, three of his children (ages fifteen, nine, and seven) supplemented the family income by trading on the black market.[94] Nachman Elbojm made enough with his black market smuggling

FIGURE 2.1. Refugee Hershek Stapler carries kerosene lamps to sell on the black market in Lvov, ca. 1941. United States Holocaust Memorial Museum, courtesy of Helen Sendyk.

in Baranovichi to send money home to his mother in Warsaw.[95] According to Adam Boren,

> On the local black market, townspeople and refugees like us sold their possessions to the Russians, who bought almost anything being offered, even if it was old-broken watches, old clothing, and Jewish prayer shawls that were sewn into shirts. Lingerie and nightgowns were bought for the Soviet women. Later, we saw them wearing them on the streets and we were all amazed. Was this the worker's paradise they kept telling us about?[96]

Often refugees moved multiple times in search of better opportunities. After failing to find housing or work in Bialystok, Zyga Elton and his friends tried their luck in Grodno. There Elton found a job digging, but the work proved too difficult. They relocated to Lvov, where they lived in an old school building and sold cigarettes on the street until the police forced them to leave the city. At their next stop, in Berezhani (Pol. Brzeżany, Ukr. Berezhany), Elton was fortunate to enter a teacher's college, which gave him housing and a stipend.[97] Chawa Kestenbojm, whose husband was a prisoner of war, originally traveled east with her two children in order to stay with her mother in Podvolochisk (Pol. Podwołoczyska, Ukr. Pidvolochysk). When the family home and business were nationalized, she returned to Lvov. Subsequently, her mother was able to get her house back. Kestenbojm and her children returned, and the family survived by renting out rooms to other refugees.[98]

In this case, as in many others, the presence of close relatives in the Soviet-held territories proved invaluable. Natalia Aleksiun has identified a reverse stream of Jewish intellectuals who left Galicia in the interwar period to pursue educational or professional opportunities, only to return once the war began. They already understood the local environment and knew that they could count on help from their families.[99] Refugees originally from other Soviet-occupied areas had similar experiences. Yaffa Margulies-Shnitzer explains that her parents in Tarnopol, "thinking that we might arrive destitute from Warsaw, had prepared an extensive stock of things for us, in addition to food, new blankets, linens, fabric for clothes, leather for shoes, and even a bicycle for my son. It was like arriving from Nazi hell into paradise."[100] In addition, the combination of professional skills, leftist leanings, and family connections often helped these return migrants to find work.[101]

For the remainder of the refugees, without family to welcome them home, the older generation often had a more difficult time adjusting than the youth. Education was free in the Soviet Union, and, as several of the refugees noted, there were no anti-Jewish quotas.[102] This proved particularly advantageous for older students, who, due to the *numerus clausus* and financial burden, had often had to give up on the hope of higher education in Poland. Bernard Ginsburg's younger siblings enrolled in school, while his teenaged sister entered a pedagogical training program in Lutsk. Ginsburg himself found satisfying work as a photojournalist.[103] David Azrieli, age seventeen when the war broke out, describes a relatively carefree period after crossing into Soviet territory. He attended school and enjoyed living with his brothers. His only concern was his mother back in German territory, whom he visited several times.[104] After crossing the border, Marian Feldman was able to finish high school in Lutsk and enter a polytechnic institute in Lvov.[105] Moshe Erlich's boss in the coal mine discovered his violin virtuosity and helped him enroll in a music conservatory.[106] Malka Rozenblat was offered a place in an art school in Moscow. As she did not know anyone there, she received permission to study art in Bialystok. However, she left for Lithuania after experiencing extreme hunger as a result of her meager stipend.[107]

Some younger children also remarked on their changed circumstances. In the words of Bob Golan, "joining the Pioneers made me feel as if the other students and I shared a common bond. And indeed, in this communist country I experienced no religious discrimination and no name-calling. What a drastic change from the Polish schools! In spite of my constant hunger, I started to feel good about this new country." Golan, however, contrasts his own attitude with that of his parents. He recalls his family's arrival at the home of relatives in Liuboml (Pol. Luboml) as a sort of vacation, but he also remembers his parents' agitation and anxiety.[108] Even children who were less enthusiastic, or faced linguistic challenges, generally acclimated. Klara Samuels, living in Bialystok, was not initially impressed with the teachers or the requirement to learn Belorussian, but came to enjoy studying the Russian language.[109] Yosef Rozenberg, who had previously studied only in Yiddish at a religious school, found the transition to Russian and Ukrainian in Poltava daunting, but he made friends and soon looked forward to attending school.[110] Mike Weinreich missed his mother, who had stayed behind in Warsaw, but loved his cousins' rural home in Graevo. He and his father stayed there for a year until they were required to move farther from the border. Their new home, in the town of Kletsk (Pol. Kleck), was also an adventure for this city boy.[111]

Yet even as they explored their new environments with interest, many children had to take on new roles. As with other migratory populations, children's greater linguistic and cultural elasticity led adults to place greater demands upon them. Yehudis Patash, at twelve, and her younger sister, at ten, took over black market trading for the family because their father was terrified of getting caught and arrested.[112] Klara Samuels, whose father was imprisoned and whose wealthy mother had never had to fend for herself, noted that while their relationship appeared traditional in public, in reality it was Klara, at thirteen, who took charge of their lives.[113]

These vignettes also highlight the side effects of family separation. Families split up for many reasons. Sometimes a father, brother, or husband was mobilized and was killed, imprisoned, or otherwise separated from his loved ones. Often families sent their young men, all men, or all youth out of harm's way temporarily. Locating separated family members in the new Soviet territories was an especially difficult task, because refugees were often on the move in search of work and housing. According to Frida Zerubavel, the walls of the cafés in Bialystok were plastered with notes in Polish and Yiddish from friends and family trying to find one another.[114]

Want ads in *Der Bialystoker Shtern,* the only Yiddish newspaper allowed to function in the annexed territories, also feature family members endeavoring to find one another.[115] In January 1940 a woman wrote from German-occupied Łódź asking anyone with information about her husband, Volf Salet, to contact her.[116] In February Shmuel Morgenshtern requested help finding his brother Henokh.[117] Those fortunate enough to locate their loved ones then had to decide how and where to reunite. Should the refugees return to their homes under German occupation now that the fighting had stopped, or should the relatives who stayed behind attempt to escape to the Soviet side? The memoirs and testimonies contain every possible answer to this question. In many cases the decision-making process was ongoing, with letters passing back and forth and various plans considered, adopted, revised, rejected, and reconsidered.

Marian Feldman, at age seventeen, was mobilized in September 1939. He and a friend left Warsaw on bicycles to join the Polish Army. Instead of meeting their unit, they met up with the Red Army. Finding favorable conditions under the Soviets, Feldman cycled back to Warsaw in order to bring his parents and sister. His father, sure that only men would be in danger, was eager to join him, but his mother refused to leave her own elderly parents. Feldman returned to Lutsk, followed by his father and sister.[118] His efforts thus resulted in a partial family reunion, but also, inadvertently, further isolated the most vulnerable members of the family.

Like Feldman, Alexander Donat originally left his family in order to defend his country. He also fell under Soviet control and returned home to Warsaw in order to bring his family to safety. According to Donat's account, his wife convinced him to return to Lutsk until conditions improved, assuring him that she and their son would be fine. Donat, however, could not bear the separation. In December, he made a second and final trip back to Warsaw. Reflecting on the flow of refugees, he wrote, "From that side thousands fled Nazi persecution; from the other, thousands returned, overwhelmed by family attachments or possessions."[119]

Sovietization on the Polish Jewish Street

On October 22, 1939, the Soviet government began the formal process of incorporating the Polish territories it had occupied. In what Tarik Amar terms an exercise in "hypervirtual democracy," residents of the region were offered the opportunity to request annexation into the USSR.[120] Forgoing the plebiscite was not an option, as the authorities made clear: in addition to a propaganda blitz, the Soviet government gave voters the day off from work, offered transportation for the infirm, and provided clear instructions on how to vote.[121] The population overwhelmingly approved the initiative, as was to be expected in Soviet elections.[122] Subsequently the Supreme Soviet—in response to popular demand—approved the annexation of Western Ukraine and Western Belorussia on November 1 and 2, respectively. By the end of November all permanent residents of the regions automatically became Soviet citizens. This same legislation also enabled refugees from western Poland to acquire Soviet citizenship.[123]

Immediately after their arrival, the Soviets began establishing their own governmental and other systems in the newly conquered areas. Both refugees and permanent residents were affected by the spread of Soviet policies and responded in a variety of ways. Polish citizens of this region had a unique perspective on the process of sovietization. Many Poles were aware of the revolutionary changes that had taken place in the USSR since its inception, but they did not know the details of their implementation. Even for communist activists in Poland, the Soviet Union remained a bit of a black box. Most had spent far more time in Polish prisons than in the USSR. After the Comintern dissolved the Polish Communist Party in August 1938, even that stream of communication dried up. Thus, Polish citizens' encounters with Soviet norms and policies were sudden, and their views, when untainted by later Cold War biases, offer a fresh point of view.

When the Bolsheviks first began to introduce their policies into the Soviet Union after the October Revolution in 1917, they were hindered by the ongoing Civil War, as well as the experimental nature of their enterprise. Armed with a rich theoretical literature, they had little practical experience. But by the time that the Soviet Union invaded Poland in 1939, it had developed a system of governance and cultural patterns. These would, according to Marxist ideology, eventually be exported to the world at large. Yet, as Amar points out, for all its internationalist rhetoric, the USSR was remarkably closed prior to 1939.[124] The occupied territories thus provided a staging ground for implementing Soviet policies: official Soviet administration and law, as well as the soft infrastructure of Soviet life.

Several scholars have written about this process of sovietization. Tracing the evolution of totalitarian control over the formerly Polish territories and their population, Jan Gross concludes that for ethnic Poles, during the period between 1939 and 1941 "the Soviet actions, relatively speaking, would prove far more injurious than those of the Nazis." Even Polish Jews agreed, Gross suggests, when they opted for repatriation rather than Soviet citizenship. And yet he also admits that the terror Poles of all backgrounds experienced in the Soviet Union was no worse than the day-to-day experiences of ordinary Soviet citizens. In this way, the Stalinist state distinguished itself from Nazi Germany and other occupation regimes.[125]

Ben-Cion Pinchuk divides the period of Soviet control, 1939–1941, into two phases. The first, transitional, phase was relatively benign and included an effort to win the support of the local population. From the summer of 1940 on, however, the Soviets began to employ harsher measures to achieve their goals. Still, Pinchuk notes that his framework is not universally applicable; for example, he suggests that Soviet cultural and political policies initially attempted to displace ethnic Poles, and only belatedly sought to co-opt them. As Pinchuk points out, at times there were also stark differences between policies and local realities: "There was a gap between planning and execution, particularly in view of the chaos that reigned in the territories and the size of the area and complexity of its problems."[126] This insight is particularly relevant to the lived experiences of refugees and residents. While general chronologies are useful, they do not always conform to the experiences of individuals. Moreover, retrospective measures of state intervention were not legible to the refugees at the time. They saw the world changing around them and registered even seemingly minor impositions as significant.

As civilian authorities replaced the occupation army, Polish citizens began to notice the proliferation of lines. According to a report filed in Palestine in March 1940 by Moshe Kleinbaum (Sneh): "Millions of human beings are standing entire days in lines in order to get some bread and herring. That is the prevailing picture of daily life in the Soviet zone in Poland."[127] Looking back on her experience in the Soviet Union, Yaffa Margulies-Shnitzer offered an explanation: "the local supply of flour was quite ample for the entire city, it was a kind of 'famine psychosis' on the part of the Soviet administrators that created the atmosphere of shortage."[128] One witness, interviewed in the Warsaw Ghetto after his return from the Soviet territories, complained that the refugees suffered the most from the incessant lines. In his view, locals knew the bakers and storekeepers personally and were able to count on their relationships to receive goods. Soviet officials simply bypassed the lines and demanded special privileges. Only the refugees had to devote excessive time and effort to meeting their most basic needs.[129] While this may have been true in certain cases, it was certainly an exaggeration. Soviet reliance on lines for social control resulted in a general transformation of day-to-day life, as Dov Levin has noted: "Social life was displaced from the home and the café to the street and the queue."[130]

While lines really were integral to Soviet life, they had existed in Poland as well. Yet the frequency of references to lines, like those of Red Army soldiers purchasing multiple watches, and Soviet women buying nightgowns to wear as dresses, became signifiers of Soviet difference—and of Polish superiority. These tropes appear in so many testimonies that they represent more than coincidental observations. Ola Hnatiuk cites the nightgown story as a form of revenge, but in many cases, it is related with good humor.[131] Caricaturing Soviet practices helped Polish citizens to retain their separate identity.

The linguistic patterns surrounding the many lines fascinated and frustrated those who came under Soviet hegemony. Janka Goldberger noted that nothing could be "purchased" in shops; it was only "given" (*dayut*). At first, she believed that the Russian language lacked the capacity for active speech. Only later, as she learned Russian better, did she come to understand that the passive rhetorical structure encapsulated an important aspect of Soviet society.[132] Hanna Davidson Pankowsky observed the irony of using the Russian word *dayut,* in that one both had to pay and wait in line for hours.[133]

Refugees and others accustomed to life in a democratic country also had trouble adjusting to the place of Soviet premier Joseph Stalin in the Soviet pantheon. According to Chaim Shapiro,

> Soon the people became annoyed by the incessant quotations attributed to Stalin, as if he were an infallible being. Worse yet, they were irritated by the phraseology used by Party members and propagandists whenever they made any reference to Stalin. It sounded as though the words had been plagiarized from the prayer books: "the great Stalin," "the mighty leader," "the sunshine of the world," "the wisdom of the human race," "the hope of the universe," "the teacher and leader of mankind."[134]

Even more caustically, a former refugee interviewed in the Warsaw Ghetto claimed, "It seems [to me] that in the Jewish prayer service [*davenen*] one does not find as many praises for the Master of the Universe."[135]

Just as Soviet citizens used humor to indicate their skepticism and ambivalence about their regime, so too did the Polish Jews cultivate a set of shared jokes.[136] One common theme was the reinterpretation of Soviet slogans. Krystyna Chiger remembers her father saying, "They call themselves our liberators, because they liberate us from everything."[137] In his 1943 testimony for the Polish government-in-exile, Aharon Fish offered a variant of this same joke: "The Bolsheviks really did come to free them, but to free them from bread, family and shoes."[138] Adopting a similar format, Zorach Warhaftig wrote, "Though rescued from the death penalty, we have been sentenced to life imprisonment."[139]

Other jokes were more conceptual, relying on the audience's knowledge of the Soviet reality. Referencing the all-encompassing bureaucracy and overreliance on official documents, one refugee cited a witticism about a man caught trying to cross into Soviet territory. When asked to prove that he was not a smuggler, he produced a written analysis of his urine sample— showing definitively that he was not carrying any suspicious items.[140] Boruch Frusztajer recalled a popular joke about proving that one was *not* a goat, which reflected on the near impossibility of providing satisfactory evidence that one was not disloyal.[141]

Other recurring themes included the scarcity of consumer goods and the special access granted to Soviet officials. Baruch Milch recorded a humorous urban myth about shortages in his diary:

> The story circulated about a Ukrainian who had managed to obtain only one pair of patent leather pumps and stopped and kissed them as he left the store. Someone from Tarnopol saw him and asked, "Are you nuts? Why are you kissing shoes?"
>
> "Mister," he said, if you'd lived under the Bolsheviks for twenty years, you'd kiss shoes too."[142]

In another such story, Soviet soldiers arrive at the nearly empty shop of two elderly Jews and ask for textiles. When the old man tells them that they have none, one soldier asks about a bit of fabric on a shelf. In his Ukrainian dialect, this comes out: "A yento chto?" (What about Yenta?"), instead of the Russian "Eto chto?" (What is that?). This prompts the man to wearily tell his sleeping wife Yenta that they want to buy her as well.[143] Refugees and other Polish citizens laughed, and complained, but also set about accustoming themselves to Soviet life.

In the annexed territories, cultural life was both encouraged and circumscribed by the new regime. Yiddish writers, artists, and performers—like Belorussian and Ukrainian, and (less so) Polish ones—could seek state employment and take advantage of the benefits given to workers in the cultural sphere. A writer from Łódź sleeping rough in Bialystok in late October was thrilled to see an announcement in the Yiddish paper *Der Bialystoker Shtern* for a new Yiddish writer's club. He registered right away and moved into his own room in December.[144] But what seemed relatively straightforward to this Polish Jewish refugee was in fact more convoluted. Gennady Estraikh explains that of the 226 writers who registered, only sixty-six were deemed sufficiently loyal to be granted spots.[145] In addition, accommodations were not ideal. Frida Zerubavel visited this same writers' house, looking for a better living space than the one she rented in the room of an elderly woman. When she saw that the rooms in the house had no furniture and that people were sleeping in their coats, she elected to stay where she was.[146]

In addition to dealing with the challenges of daily life, the writers and artists had to learn how to perform in an acceptable idiom. In many cases they could count on Soviet Yiddish writers to explain the unwritten rules. Praise for the Soviet Union as their savior was, not surprisingly, required. However, writers and artists were also forced to scorn Poland and forbidden from writing about German treatment of Polish Jews.[147] In the words of Moyshe (Mojsze) Broderzon, "A Jewish newspaper in a Jewish city, several kilometers from the German murder inferno, refused to devote one line or even one word to the gruesome experiences of Jews on the other side of the border, in Poland where Jewish blood is being spilled with abandon."[148] Soviet Yiddish writers were also themselves still traumatized and confused from the recent purges and cultural shifts, as Estraikh has shown.[149] Nonetheless, Soviet Yiddish writers visited their Polish colleagues in Lvov and Bialystok and tried to guide them. Hersh Smolar, for example, recalls Soviet Yiddish poet Zelig Akselrod kicking him under the table to get him to stop asking too many questions of a visiting dignitary.[150]

While newspaper articles about these visits were universally positive, memoirs are more ambivalent. Yet even these accounts, written outside the USSR and thus not subject to censorship, as Estraikh also notes, are clearly influenced by the knowledge that many of these same Soviet Yiddish writers were executed by the state after the war. It is hard to criticize cultural figures for not being more welcoming or forthcoming when they were later killed for even these meager efforts. Joseph Rubinstein's *Megilath Russland,* a memoir in verse, includes a lengthy and sensitive portrayal of the writer Dovid Bergelson, with whom he stayed on a visit to Moscow. Leyb Kvitko also receives sympathetic treatment. Rubinstein is less impressed with Peretz Markish and theater impresario Solomon Mikhoels, but does not dwell on their characters. Silence and silencing are major themes in this section of his book.[151] Itzhak Yasanowicz notes that many Soviet Yiddish writers visited the Polish Yiddish writers for their own purposes, for a "breath of Warsaw and Vilna," but that later on, when the refugees were truly in need, only Kvitko came to their aid. Playing on the well-known statement in Ethics of the Fathers 3:21, he writes that Kvitko cared for their "kemah" (flour—i.e., sustenance) and "Torah" (i.e., creative work).[152]

Tania Fuks, a journalist by profession, actually published her autobiography before the 1952 trial and murder of the Soviet Yiddish writers. She was dismissive of Itsik Fefer's visit to Lvov, while writing movingly of that of Peretz Markish. During his visit, Markish gave several well-attended public lectures and then became ill. After his recovery he read aloud, presumably privately, his poem "To a Jewish Dancer," which is quoted in this chapter's epigraph. The poem, never published in the USSR or during Markish's lifetime, was a powerful meditation on Jewish history, from the book of Lamentations to the Nazi oppression of Polish Jews.[153] In Fuks's words, "Only once in my life have I heard such a reading. It was a concert, a musical symphony: the Jewish dancer danced and to the rhythm of her steps came visions, generations, performances of the entire history of the martyrology of a people, of its rising and its falling."[154]

Pinchuk concludes that "the Jewish literati were probably the most important single vehicle used to spread Soviet ideology among the new Jewish citizens."[155] Yet, as is clear from Markish's poem, influences were mutual. As Yehoshua Gilboa notes, not only writers but also other Soviet Jews were impressed by the Jewish culture that had thrived in what they had learned was backward and antisemitic Poland.[156] Moreover, it is unlikely that Pinchuk's assessment of the literati holds equally true for all of the refugees and former Polish citizens. Jewish writers of Polish literature, for example, had to contend with the Soviet policy of limiting Polish influence in the newly annexed territories. The Soviet government made a concerted effort not only to control the content of Polish literature, as it did with Yiddish literature, but also to diminish Polish literary output altogether.

Yet, as Bogdan Czaykowski shows, Polish literary efforts were not completely stifled. *Czerwony Sztandar,* the party line newspaper started in Lvov, employed a number of Polish writers, including some Jews. Even as some leading Polish literary figures were arrested in early 1940, others were kept in place. Czaykowski suggests that the Soviets retained some of these leaders as a safety measure, given the possibility that it might soon require Polish support against the Germans. The government also loosened strictures on Polish writing toward the end of 1940, as this possibility increased.[157] Mieczysław Inglot demonstrates the complexities of these changing policies, in his study of the state's attempts to coopt the legacy of the important literary figure Adam Mickiewicz.[158]

Some writers opted to work in journalism or children's books, which they hoped would be less ideologically fraught than expressive literature. Chone Szmeruk demonstrates how the influx of Polish Jewish writers revived both genres, which had previously been in steep decline.[159] In the new territories, the Soviets allowed one official organ each in Polish and Yiddish. Polish Jewish writers found employment at both *Czerwony Sztandar* and *Der Bialystoker Shtern.*[160] Both were overseen by Soviet writers and censors. They served primarily to teach Polish and Yiddish speakers about Soviet life and expectations, as well as to announce upcoming events. These newspapers are filled with profiles of important Soviet leaders, preparations for Soviet holidays and periodic elections, and articles about improvements since the Soviet takeover.

Those who worked at Soviet newspapers had to remain vigilant about ideological shifts. Aharon Fish, a printer by trade, obtained a relatively good position as a typesetter at the Soviet newspaper *Oktiabr* in Minsk. He was promoted after his supervisor was sent to Siberia for printing the phrase "refugees from Poland" instead of "unemployed Poles." Fish himself left within weeks, terrified of allowing a similar mistake to slip through.[161] Bernard Ginsburg, a photojournalist, was hired by *Radianska Volyn* soon after he reached Lutsk. Both he and his work were highly respected, and he even sent his photos to other Soviet papers. This proved helpful when his editor attacked one of his photos for showing "naturalism" instead of "Soviet realism."[162]

Ida Kaminska, star of the Warsaw Yiddish stage, was invited to establish a state Yiddish theater in Lvov soon after her arrival. In her memoir she mentions fairly breezily that politics and egos could be sensitive, while providing no details.[163] Fortunately the local Polish paper, *Czerwony Sztandar,* regularly included theater news. In December the writer Aleksander Wat set the tone in an article on the new Soviet theaters in the city: "The theaters of Lvov stand on the eve of decisive change."[164] Like Kaminska, Wat was also a refugee from Poland—although much more associated with Polish than with Jewish culture. He profiled the upcoming seasons of the Polish, Ukrainian, and Yiddish theaters, but also reminded them of their responsibilities. As recipients of the state's largesse, they had to expand their audiences, train a new generation of artists, and "play a major role in the education of the masses."

Kaminska endeavored to heed the new directives. In December the theater opened the Yiddish version of *Uncle Tom's Cabin,* a sentimental indictment of the excesses of capitalism sure to please the authorities.[165] By January she had introduced *Her Son,* a tragedy about a Hungarian revolutionary.[166] P. Stark's review later that month was highly enthusiastic; he lauded Kaminska for her role as the suffering mother, and assured readers that the play was also well received by the proletariat.[167] However, Stark's review of Kaminska's next effort was considerably less laudatory. He perceived her adaptation of the Spanish court drama *Owcze Źródło* (known in English as *The Dog in the Manger* or *The Gardener's Dog*) by Lope de Vega as an unconvincing illustration of feudalism. The peasants, in particular, lacked verisimilitude. Nonetheless, he concluded, the theater collective was still young and developing.[168] Kaminska continued to introduce shows aimed at pleasing her audience and the new regime, and many of the productions remained in her repertoire in Communist Poland after the war.[169]

Shimon (Szymon) Dzigan and Israel Schumacher (Szumacher), a popular Polish Jewish comedy duo, faced similar challenges. In his bittersweet memoir, Dzigan tells of a meeting with a Soviet bureaucrat in Bialystok soon after their arrival. They were told that humor was different in the USSR and that every show must end with "Long Live Stalin." When Schumacher jokingly suggested "God Save the Tsar" as an alternative, he received a stone-faced reply, reinforcing the necessity of adjustments to their program.[170] Alongside poet and theater director Moyshe Broderzon, with whom they had worked previously in Łódź, Dzigan and Schumacher established the Yidisher Melukhe Miniatur Teatr in February 1940.[171] They performed successfully throughout the Soviet Union, in between periods of incarceration, and many refugees remember seeing them in Bialystok and other cities.[172]

Soviet policy reshaped other cultural institutions as well. In her memoir, Frida Zerubavel mentions visiting a library soon after her arrival in Bialystok in the fall of 1939. She was disheartened to find it closed for inventory checking, which she understood to mean that the new authorities were deciding which books to remove from the shelves.[173] On the other hand, according to one refugee interviewed after returning to Warsaw, the Soviets established Yiddish lending libraries in even the tiniest of shtetlach. At these libraries, one could find approved reading material by Sholom Aleichem, Peretz Markish, I. L. Peretz, and others.[174]

Schools had to adapt both their language and curricula. In order to destroy Polish hegemony in the area, and to woo national minorities, the reopened schools taught not only Russian but also Belorussian, Ukrainian, or Yiddish. Hebrew, due to its association with both religion and Zionism, could not be taught. According to one memoirist from the Warsaw Ghetto, who had previously worked as a teacher in Lvov, this led to chaos. Teachers, even if they knew the requisite languages, had no access to educational materials in those languages. Students knew mainly Polish and were unprepared for an overnight switch to a new language.[175] Parents often complained. According to Zerubavel, Jewish parents in particular wanted their children to learn a more useful language such as Polish, or at least Russian, rather than Yiddish.[176] Later, schools in Lvov had to transition entirely to Ukrainian. Teachers who could not readily adopt the new language found themselves unemployed.[177]

The files of the Lvov Regional Department of Education reflect the ambition of the new administration. Toward the end of 1939, the office received, created, and filed reports and charts on the Polish school system, trying to categorize its many institutions.[178] It also sought to register all of the qualified teachers, both employed and unemployed, and all of the students.[179] But even as they tried to make sense of the prior situation, the Soviet functionaries also began creating new pedagogical institutes, textbooks, and educational plans for expanding the use of the Ukrainian language.[180]

As a result, regulations proliferated. By 1940 all teachers had to be Soviet citizens. Soviet administrators took over the schools, demanding detailed lesson plans and regular attendance at committee meetings. According to an anonymous apt observer from the Warsaw Ghetto, all subjects—including languages—were taught through the prism of revolution. Teachers had to include the proper content, such as the efforts and successes of the Communist Party in those foreign lands. Ironically, children of all ages studied Stalin's constitution and its guarantee of the free practice of religion, and at the same time were exposed to creative and sophisticated antireligious propaganda. Older students studied anti-Zionist teachings as well.[181]

Abraham Kreusler originally worked as a German teacher at a Russian high school in Bialystok. Soon, however, he became disillusioned with the philosophy of education and discipline. Frustrated by the hierarchies and lack of accountability, he escaped to a teacher's college.[182] Enforcement and oversight were more heavy-handed in the cities. Yosef Halperin, sent to teach in a small Belorussian village, received little direct supervision, or even direction. Several months after the school year began, he traveled on his own initiative to visit another school and solicit advice from a more experienced teacher. When directives arrived from his superiors, he tried to honor them within the confines of the peasant community in which he lived. At his yearly evaluation, he was asked about his decisions to start school after the harvest and hold a party instead of regular classes on Christmas. Halperin writes that the official ultimately accepted his justifications and praised his progress.[183]

Children, on the whole, accepted the changes more readily than did their elders. Boruch Frusztajer remembers being informed, at the age of nine, of the death of God, along with other antireligious propaganda.[184] Hanna Davidson Pankowsky's introduction to atheism came through a modified version of a pedagogical trick long used in traditional Jewish education.[185] Initiation into the heder, since at least medieval times, involved the magical appearance of honey cake or other treats to teach the child to associate studying God's word with sweetness.[186] In the Soviet version, Jewish children were encouraged to pray to God for candy. When it did not rain down upon them, they were told instead to ask their teachers for candy, a request that was readily granted. In this way, students were taught the inanity and inefficacy of praying to an imaginary deity.

The school system endeavored to socialize new Soviet citizens into their proper roles and duties through all aspects of the curriculum, including extracurricular activities such as clubs, youth groups, wall newspapers, and mandatory volunteer projects.[187] Some testimonies mention pressure to join the Komsomol or other activities, but it is not accidental that most portray the schools' antireligious efforts so vividly. Beyond language of instruction, this was the Soviet regime's most radical and undisguised change to the education system.

Indeed, inculcating atheism was central to the Soviet educational project. According to a January 1940 article in the education section of *Der*

Bialystoker Shtern, "The antireligious spirit in the school, this means—that this philosophy must penetrate every lesson, every task, every contact between the pupil and the teacher."[188] Adults were also targeted with antireligious messages. An article from earlier that month, "Dos shtetl oyf-gelebt" (The shtetl revived), interwove examples of recent improvements in Jewish life in a village with disdainful reminders of the old-fashioned mores that had previously held sway. "A mere three months ago the shtetl was known only for houses of study and prayer houses."[189]

Efforts to destroy the perceived power of religion went well beyond the pages of newspapers. The practice of Judaism was never outlawed, nor, as several eyewitnesses carefully point out, was Judaism treated differently than other religions. Instead the Soviets used the policies that had proved effective on their own population to disincentivize involvement in any religious group: indoctrination of young people in schools and youth groups, economic measures against the holdings of religious organizations, labor laws that made professional clergy and religious functionaries obsolete, and supervision—or sometimes, arrest and punishment—of religious leaders engaging in any activities deemed unacceptable.

Sometimes the administration created structural obstacles to religious worship. The official day off from both work and school in the Soviet Union was Sunday, which complicated Sabbath worship for Jews. A couple of witnesses note that artels, or collective craft workshops, had the option of choosing their own day to close. Those with a majority of Jewish members often chose Saturday, but this option was available to relatively few.[190] Ahron Blenkitni belonged to a shoemakers' artel in the shtetl of Glubokoe (Bel. Hly-bokaye, Pol. Głębokie, Yid. Glubok). He notes that some fervent Jews avoided working on the Sabbath and mentions one more flexible man who said his prayers, ate the festive meals, and also worked.[191] Jewish holidays were also difficult to keep. One former refugee interviewed in the Warsaw Ghetto observed that a law penalizing tardiness to work, issued on June 26, 1940, was yet another blow to the religiously observant. Those who wished to pray a full morning service on the Sabbath and holidays risked severe punishment.[192]

Soviet officials also sought to monitor ongoing religious activities. One report, prepared for the security services in Baranovichi in February 1941, opens with an unsympathetic portrait of the Jewish community, followed by the names and addresses of all rabbis, prayer houses, religious functionaries, religious schools, teachers in religious schools, Orthodox organizations, and their staff members. Betraying the report's reliance on inside informants, one document lists "anti-Soviet" rhetoric uttered by various rabbis, including, "They don't even give out enough bread."[193] Whether or not they knew that they were being monitored this closely, rabbis, cantors, ritual slaughterers, and mohels who chose to stay in the Soviet zone certainly knew that they had to keep a low profile.

As Dov Levin shows, authorities frequently used pressure, rather than direct intervention, to discourage organized religion. Synagogues and rabbis received inflated tax bills.[194] Other religious functionaries often had an easier time hiding their activities. According to his son Shmuel's 1943 testimony in Palestine, Moshe Labin had served as a ritual slaughterer in their hometown of Tarnobrzeg. As a religious Jew with eight children, he had not wanted to travel to Soviet territory, but after the Germans expelled the local Jews, he had little choice. Once in Lvov, he continued in his profession while the children worked on the black market. With care, they managed to survive until their deportation.[195] A religious refugee from Warsaw wrote about the compromises the situation required. He and his colleagues fasted on Yom Kippur, but had to work and could only complete the prayer service in the evening. Couples married in the Soviet bureau, but then went home to discharge the traditional Jewish wedding ceremony, in his retelling.[196]

These deliberate antireligious policies, along with the deterrents embedded in Soviet society, made the practice of Judaism progressively more difficult—especially for the youth. The state understood that religious life was most effectively quashed by starving it of new adherents. A local Jew in Sokoli (Pol. Sokoły) remarked that within a few months, only older men attended synagogue.[197] Shmuel Labin remembered his father's lament, soon after their arrival in Lvov: "I don't know which is worse: the German troubles or the Russians making them [his children] into goyim."[198] In his memoir, Chaim Shapiro describes passing through a former synagogue: "Suddenly a strange thought occurred to me: since this building has been confiscated by the Communists and is to be converted into a movie theater or a factory, God forbid, then one might say that God Himself is also a refugee now!"[199]

To underscore the totality of the Soviet transformation of Jewish life, Ben-Cion Pinchuk avers that, especially in the smaller towns, the destruction of traditional Judaism actually led to physical changes: "Secularization and the diminished influence of the synagogue and religion on the life-style of the Jews also had their effect on the external appearance of the shtetl." His account mourns the changes in these towns, including the substitution of

Soviet holidays and symbols for Jewish ones, the replacement of Jewish elites with Soviet *nomenklatura,* and the denuding of the marketplace and Jewish structures.[200] Yaffa Margulies-Shnitzer, a refugee from Warsaw who returned to her hometown of Tarnopol (Ukr. Tarnopil) with a Soviet passport, essentially agrees: "Tarnopol, on the eve of the Nazi conquest was utterly unlike its former self."[201]

Those who became Soviet citizens, either by choice or by force, were most likely to become involved in Soviet politics. Emanuel Goldberg, a resident of the town of Svisloch in the Soviet zone, described his political activism in his town's memorial book: "The hope for a better life in a more just society, was so great, that one needed and wanted to be optimistic, and one naturally tried evading the disturbing reality which was becoming increasingly apparent."[202] Because of his political leanings (he had been a communist activist before the war) and his pedagogical background, Goldberg initially joined a committee restructuring the local schools. This brought him to the attention of the new Soviet authorities, who subsequently encouraged him to fill a variety of other roles, including informing on his peers. While the Soviets recruited primarily Belorussians and Ukrainians for high-visibility political positions, some Jews were elected to political office, including the Yiddish poet Rokhl Korn.

All residents of the new Soviet territories had to affirm Soviet might and right—at school, on the street, in public festivals and commemorations, and at their places of employment. Yuli Margolin gave a particularly evocative account of his participation in the Polish section of the Writers' Association:

> I have never been in such a humiliating and absurd situation. Each day we have a meeting. I sit in the front row and they look at me. I hear propaganda, nonsense and lies. Whenever they mention Stalin my supervisor starts clapping and everyone present follows suit. I also clap, and I feel like a court jester. I do not want to translate Mayakovsky, but I have no choice. I do not want to clap, but I am forced to. I do not want Lwow to be a Soviet city, but a hundred times a day I say the opposite. All my life I have been myself and an honest person, and now I am playing the fool. I have become a scoundrel.[203]

Margolin eventually returned to the German-held territories. This option existed primarily for refugees.

Economically, the difference between refugees and local residents was also significant. Refugees had already decided to leave their jobs and financial holdings behind. Some came with cash reserves or products to sell, while others arrived with only the shirts on their backs; all expected to have to make a new start. Residents of eastern Poland sought to stay in their own homes and professions while the world changed around them. Locals found their lives and livelihoods transformed by nationalizations, appropriations, currency manipulation, agricultural redistribution and collectivization, the decline of private enterprise, and the formation of cooperatives. Keith Sword notes wryly that the Germans worked hard to destroy their part of Poland, while the Soviets did so effortlessly, simply by introducing their own economic policies.[204] But as Tarik Amar explains, even contemporary Soviet administrators realized that the pace was too extreme. The haste of the expropriations led to mass unemployment, hunger, homelessness, and crime.[205]

Of course, these policies affected different population groups in different ways. Pinchuk points out that the Jewish occupational structure, reliant on petty trades, was especially at odds with Soviet goals.[206] The wealthy, and property, business, or factory owners, had the most to lose. Ethnic Poles in professional, and especially governmental, roles were often replaced with Belorussians, Jews, or Ukrainians.

Naturally, the background and experiences of witnesses influenced their perspectives. A young refugee from Warsaw, interviewed later in the ghetto, remarked laconically, "The economic situation for the nonproletarian population changed very radically." With greater enthusiasm, he added, "The standard of living of the working population changed for the better. People saw opportunities and were content everywhere."[207] His views reflect a youthful, progressive, and optimistic attitude. Chawa Kestenbojm, to the contrary, was fortunate to retain one room for her family of five within her requisitioned house in Lvov, and to obtain work in the nationalized sausage factory that had formerly belonged to her husband's family. For someone from the formerly privileged class, the situation looked much less rosy.[208]

Yet even workers had mixed reactions to the economic changes. The artels did bring regular work to many artisans and previously semiemployed laborers. Ann Benjamin-Goldberg's father, who had eked out a living as a tailor in Poland, joined an artel and began to receive regular paychecks when their town became Soviet.[209] Women, in particular, had greater opportunities under the Soviet regime. At age sixteen, Betty Rich fled Łódź for Kuznitsa, where she began working on a sleeper train. Until loneliness set in, she was thrilled with the independence that the job afforded her.[210] Many witnesses, male and female, mention the shock of seeing Soviet women laboring alongside men.[211] As Katherine Jolluck observes, many Poles, who had a more conservative worldview, saw this as backward rather than progressive.[212] Some workers were also troubled by the low pay, poor conditions, and political demands of their jobs. Although all workers had to attend meetings, serve on committees, issue proclamations, and mark Soviet holidays, those working outside the cultural sphere experienced fewer ideological demands.

Soviet authorities also relied on the methods of the NKVD to monitor the refugees. In January and February 1940, for instance, a Belorussian bureau report on a meeting of over thirty "Polish Hasids" drew the NKVD's attention due to purported anti-Soviet agitation. The NKVD also tracked several hundred refugees believed to be German spies. A number of these people had been members of the Polish Communist Party. One refugee fell under suspicion merely because he arrived in Soviet territory carrying a German-language topographical map. In addition, NKVD agents closely watched "fascist counter-revolutionaries," including activists in the Jewish Labor Bund and Revisionist Zionists.[213]

Authorities engaged in an ongoing battle against what they referred to as "speculation." In the Soviet lexicon, speculation referred both to small-scale black market activities and to organized smuggling rings that brought in consumer goods from across the border. Jews and other Poles were involved in both of these pursuits, and it is sometimes difficult to ascertain, from the reports and arrests, whether the targets were professional criminals or merely unemployed refugees. In a testimony to the underground archive in the Warsaw Ghetto, a former resident of the town of Rutki (Pol. Rutki-Kossaki) alleged that even the shoemakers employed in the state collective had to make private sales in order to earn enough to live. Others made their living by traveling to Bialystok for goods and selling them in the town and surrounding villages.[214]

Newspaper articles touted Soviet efforts to eradicate speculation, at once raising popular awareness of such activities and offering veiled threats to speculators. In October 1939 *Czerwony Sztandar* equated speculators with saboteurs, noting the state's increased penalties against both groups. The names of the individuals arrested were primarily Jewish, although no mention was made of their ethnicity.[215] Soon "Walka ze spekulacja" (The struggle against speculation) became a recurring column, always including the names of those arrested.[216] The Yiddish newspaper also frequently included pieces about speculation. For example, one article from January 1940 described the successful trial of a currency speculator.[217]

In May 1940, the prosecutor for the Lvov region brought charges against three men for speculation. The men were accused of stealing items from their artel to sell at inflated prices. From the documents available, it is difficult to ascertain whether theirs was a profitable business venture or mere skimming off the top for minor gain. As is true for many cases in the file, the prosecutor and accused all have identifiably Jewish names. However, neither the background nor the civic status of the accused is noted.[218] A report filed with the Grodno region's NKVD covering the first half of 1940 also contains a list of accused speculators with a disproportionate number of Jewish names, but little other information.[219]

Refugees and residents were equally likely to come to the attention of the NKVD for their religious and political leanings or activities. However, accusations of speculation and spying were most frequently leveled against refugees. Due to their often complicated family situations, they were more prone to be crossing and recrossing the border. Although some refugees, as well as residents, undoubtedly tried to make a profit from the situation, many turned to illegal forms of trade just to meet their basic needs. Evgenii Rozenblat points out that the NKVD noted the suspect class background and criminal tendencies of the refugees without taking stock of their appalling poverty.[220]

Solving the Refugee Problem

Soviet authorities seemed to view the arrival of the first refugees from western Poland as benign and temporary. In September 1939 sporadic fighting was still taking place and borders were relatively open. It was reasonable to expect that the frightened masses would return to their homes when hostilities ended and firmer borders were established. However, the flow of refugees continued. By October, Soviet border guards began to detain some border crossers, and patrol their borders, leading to the proliferation of homeless and hungry people in the no-man's-land between the two powers. Yet without clear instructions from above, guards also sanctioned a great many who stole across the rivers and into Soviet territory. Testimonies show that crossing remained possible through 1939, and even into the new year.

Nonetheless, the state paid increased attention to the refugee situation as it became clear that they were not returning. Rozenblat's study of Soviet attitudes toward refugees in Western Belorussia has equal bearing on the whole region. He divides the period between the 1939 Soviet invasion and the 1941 German invasion of eastern Poland into three phases: cordial and loyal, indecisive and correct, and demanding and harsh.[221] Early on, he explains, the Soviet authorities were fairly welcoming, or at least noncommittal toward the refugees. After observing that the refugees did not plan to return to their homes, the government initiated experimental measures to standardize their status. Only belatedly, once these measures had proven ineffective, did they resort to severe responses. Rozenblat's rubric helpfully shows that the Soviet authorities did not begin with an overarching refugee policy but developed policies along the way as the longevity of the refugee problem became apparent.

The government's first formal attempt to deal with the refugees, beyond some aid and oversight, involved encouraging them to disperse and take jobs outside the former Polish areas. In Western Belorussia, a special commission was established to coordinate with authorities in the eastern regions.[222] The employment drive lasted from November 1939 through February 1940. Refugees were recruited to relocate to the eastern regions of Belorussia and Ukraine, and take jobs in industry, building, and mining in particular. The plan thus had the potential to simultaneously diminish overcrowding in the annexed territories and bring needed laborers to unfilled positions in underpopulated areas. It also appeared to offer a solution to the refugees' employment problems. Witnessing the terrible conditions in which many refugees lived, Frida Zerubavel could not understand why they did not accept work in the interior. Someone explained to her that the refugees did not want to risk losing contact with family members on both sides of the new border.[223] Having already relocated at least once, many were also loath to pick up and move again.

Nonetheless, some refugees viewed the offer of labor as an opportunity. One refugee from Warsaw, who returned and produced a testimony after the German invasion of the Soviet Union, recalls singing with friends as they awaited transport to their new jobs. After they passed into old Soviet territory, an elderly man working at a bathhouse warned them about the hunger they would soon face. They dismissed his warning, assuming the older man was simply unable to adjust to the Soviet reality and still "dreaming about fish and wine on the Sabbath." Soon they found themselves both working and sleeping in a factory, where they were paid 170–180 rubles per month instead of the one thousand they had been promised. The only way to survive was to work overtime and attempt to cheat the system in various ways.[224]

In a Hebrew memoir published well after the war, David Brandshpigel remembers the confusion of arriving in Magnitogorsk with his family. Theirs was the first group of refugees to arrive, and they were originally placed in a school building. Having been promised the opportunity to work in their own fields, they stood in line and attempted to pantomime their specialties to the Russian-speaking official in charge of labor distribution. Everyone, however, received assignments in the building trades. David's father, a cobbler, went to work in construction. His mother, a housewife, had to make bricks to receive her rations. The work proved difficult for the Brandshpigels, and they determined to leave.[225] Dora Drescher and her family stayed briefly with relatives after crossing into Soviet territory. Not finding a place of their own, they signed up for labor and were taken to a kolkhoz (collective farm) in Poltava. The entire family had to engage in arduous agricultural work, including Dora, who was not yet fifteen. They left the kolkhoz within a few months, arriving in Lutsk before Passover of 1940.[226]

Despite the involvement of the special commissions and supervision from various regional authorities, local officials were often both unprepared and unwilling to receive refugees in their midst. Dmitrii Tolochko chronicles these conditions in Belorussia: "Providing employment for refugees in the western *oblasti* of the BSSR was difficult due to the total lack of congruence between the training and interests of the refugees and the labor requirements of the local administrations."[227] Tolochko also shows that the refugees' obvious dismay over local conditions, in a vicious circle, led the authorities there to dislike and distrust them even more.

A comparable dynamic played out among the refugees. As some began to leave, others who were wavering felt encouraged to leave as well. These escapees then spread their tales of woe among refugees who had not gone to the interior, which made them far less likely to sign up. Shaul Shternfeld stopped considering work in the interior after he ran into an acquaintance who had returned from the Donbas in terrible physical shape.[228] Dovid Feinzeig's homeless relatives were sent to Magnitogorsk when they volunteered. "Later on, when we were in Bialystok," he writes, "we received letters from them, and although they were afraid to write anything negative about their situation since the letters were censored, we discerned from between the lines that the government's promises of a life of comfort had been unfounded."[229]

In both the testimonial and historical literature, the plan to resettle refugees in the interior has generally been portrayed as a failure. Certainly, the number of refugees who resettled did not live up to Soviet expectations—although it is also not clear that work sites could have handled larger numbers. Nonetheless, this was an important chapter in the Soviet odyssey of the minority who went. Citing figures provided by the Soviet press, Dov Levin states that forty thousand refugees volunteered over the course of the program.[230] Despite this impressive figure, however, as Rozenblat shows, the subsequent return of approximately 20 percent led to frustration among the planners.[231]

While the first volunteers often faced difficulties with their transport and reception, over time the process began to work more smoothly. A document produced in early February 1940 in Voroshilovgrad (Ukr. Luhansk) outlined all of the preparations necessary for the arrival of Polish refugee workers, including guidelines for work allocation as well as educational initiatives. As of February 15, all children were to be placed in school. Those under school age had to be provided with nursery programs. Local officials were also directed to provide adults with appropriate political instruction.[232]

This hands-on approach paid off in the experiences of later arrivals. Yosef and Mania Goldkorn, after wandering around the annexed territories homeless for a time, received not only free transportation but a sum of money upon signing up for labor in the interior. Their arrival in the Pervomaiskii (Ukr. Pervomayskiy) region was heralded by a Pioneer choir, a patriotic meeting, and a welcome feast. They were then taken to clean barracks and given two days of rest before training began.[233] This did not diminish the long hours and difficult work conditions to come, but it did create a good first impression and show the level of organization and planning involved in the program. Ann Szedlecki and her brother, who had been staying in an unheated synagogue in Bialystok, were gratified to receive both food and housing while they awaited transport after signing up for the program.[234]

The propaganda campaign also became more sophisticated with time. Both the Polish and Yiddish newspapers in the annexed territories featured announcements regarding the program, as well as letters purportedly written by satisfied volunteers. Two letters published in February 1940, at the height of the recruiting drive, demonstrate the tactics of such propaganda campaigns. *Der Bialystoker Shtern* published "Mir zeynen gliklech!" (We are fortunate), Dovid Brenner's detailed description of his family's arrival in Magnitogorsk. He mentions the comfortable conditions on the train,

FIGURE 2.2. "We are Fortunate!," *Der Bialystoker Shtern* 22, February 4, 1940, which discusses the great benefits of volunteering for labor in the interior. The National Library of Israel Collection.

the special care offered to children and the elderly, the warm welcome (including speeches and an orchestra), the well-equipped rooms, and the warm work clothes given to each refugee. The article ends not with a depiction of labor, but an articulation of his current status: "I, with my wife, child, and mother-in-law, [we] are all happy."[235]

Czerwony Sztandar's "List z Donbasu" (Letter from Donbas) is presented as a letter from correspondent Markus Zwerling to his mother. In it he conveniently mentions his monthly paycheck (between 350 and 400 rubles) and the fact that he has access to generous and healthy meals for a mere nine rubles daily. His lodging, he adds, is provided for free. He also reminds her that the Soviet constitution guarantees work for every citizen.[236] It is certainly not accidental that these two letters explicitly address some of the frequently raised concerns and complaints about labor in the interior. By focusing on the benefits of life in the interior, the letter writers sought to allay fears and encourage registration.

In her study of Bialystok, Sara Bender maintains that the propaganda was so effective that twenty thousand refugees signed up in one week—although many would soon return to the former Polish areas.[237] Among those who volunteered for labor in the interior was Simon Davidson. His transport, which included the film director Aleksander Ford, arrived first in Vitebsk. The authorities there did not want them, however, and he was then sent to Orsha. He soon secured work as a bookkeeper and sent for his wife and daughter, still in German-occupied Łódź. Although food was scarce and the local people treated the refugees with disdain, he found the work and lodging acceptable. When other refugees began to consider escaping, he tried to convince them that they were far better off than they had been back home, and no worse off than Soviet citizens.[238]

Despite the modest successes of the resettlement program, most refugees remained in the annexed territories. The newspaper propaganda pieces that appeared in February 1940 were part of one last concerted effort to increase the participation in this voluntary program. By this time, Soviet power was well established. The permanent residents of Western Belorussia and Ukraine had all received citizenship and internal passports. Economic, political, educational, cultural, and other Soviet norms were in place. Yet the refugees, with their low rates of employment, high rates of speculation, and unregulated mobility, remained a problem. Therefore, even as they promoted labor in the interior, the Soviet authorities were also preparing a more drastic solution to the refugee situation.

On February 5, 1940, an announcement in *Der Bialystoker Shtern* called upon all refugees to register with the authorities.[239] Refugees soon learned that they faced an ultimatum: they could accept Soviet citizenship or agree to return to their homes in German-occupied Poland. Moreover, the Soviet government offered only a modified form of citizenship, in an effort to compel dispersal. The so-called passportization drive stipulated that refugees could only register for Soviet passports with a paragraph 11 status, which disbarred their holders from residing within one hundred kilometers of the border.[240] The stipulation effectively required refugees to relocate once again, this time outside their comfort zone with other Polish Jews.

The passportization drive forced refugees, many of whom were already second-guessing their original choice to cross into Soviet territory, to make yet another decision in relatively little time. It would appear that most refugees from western and central Poland registered to return there. In their testimonies and memoirs, the former refugees assert that nearly all of them arrived at this decision. While it does seem that the majority elected to return to the Nazis, the numbers were probably not as overwhelming as they submit. Mordechai Altshuler estimates that sixty-five thousand Polish Jewish refugees accepted Soviet citizenship.[241] The assertion of virtual unanimity may itself be part of a justification for this startling choice. Given what they knew about the Germans from their own experiences and from correspondence with friends and relatives left behind, why would they have voluntarily subjected themselves to German control? And why did they believe that the Germans would be willing to accept thousands of additional Jews into their territories? As it turns out, the memoirs and testimonies deal with the former question at length, and barely touch upon the latter.

According to an anonymous chronicler from the Warsaw Ghetto, refugees attempted to return to German-held territory chiefly because they either felt unable to adjust to Soviet norms or they wished to reunite with family.[242] This is largely borne out by refugee testimonies. Upon his escape from labor in the interior, one refugee stated simply, "Everyone is thinking about the same thing: how to get home."[243] Without waiting for registration, some refugees began their own trek back to Polish territory under German occupation. From his vantage point in Warsaw in May 1940, diarist Chaim Kaplan wrote,

> Just as we witnessed the exodus from Poland earlier we are now witnessing the exodus from Russia. They return out of the frying pan into the fire. They exchange garlic for onions. They flee from one prison to another. They do not fear the cruelty, the hatred, and all the various activities in which the Nazis are expert.[244]

Many refugees expressed specific concerns about the requirement to move away from the border. Using the language of Jewish law to illustrate his distaste for paragraph 11, one refugee described the modified Soviet passport as "kosher" but with a "pasul" (i.e., a defect rendering a ritual object unfit for use).[245] In some cases, paragraph 11 led to additional complications for those who took the new passports. Several testimonies refer to families split apart when some members received permission to stay in place and others had to move.[246] Polish Jewish refugees also testified to their anxiety about losing the right to reclaim Polish citizenship after the war—and thus possibly becoming trapped in the USSR.

At the same time, many refugees had left behind close relatives and were feeling the pain of separation. Betty Rich, at sixteen, had crossed the border with other teens. As posters announcing mandatory registration began to appear, she received a postcard from her mother, begging her to return home. Consumed with guilt, she signed up to do so, stating in her memoir, "We forgot what the Nazis stood for—time and distance can accomplish a lot."[247]

In addition to forgetting "what the Nazis stood for," many refugees registered to return based on feelings of nostalgia and an unrealistic sense of the changes that had taken place in German-held territory. Journalist Tania Fuks recalls her bewilderment at seeing acquaintances in line to sign up for return to the Nazis. Yet in the end, she also understood their rationale:

> People had their reasons. The majority of the refugees there were men who had fled in the first days of the war and left behind wives and children. In their minds their homes remained the same as when they left them: complete, warm, pure, and here they existed in loneliness, filth, and hunger, most of them had no work or insufficient work. There wife and child, there at least a roof over their head, a shirt on their back. They did not grasp that their homes there were already no longer homes.[248]

While many refugees discuss how and why they elected to return to their homes, relatively few engage with the question of why the Germans would have willingly accepted them back. German forces had encouraged, and sometimes even compelled, Jews to flee the regions of Poland they conquered. As the refugees learned through letters from home, the Germans had subsequently forced the remaining Polish Jews into ghettos. It is difficult to imagine what would have induced them to readmit thousands of additional Polish Jews after they had already crammed over one million into vastly overcrowded holding areas.

Refugees may have been encouraged by the fact that Germany and the Soviet Union had already engaged in a limited population exchange. The Germans had welcomed a number of ethnic Germans from Soviet territory, and in turn sent some Belorussians and Ukrainians to the Soviets.[249] Additionally, the Soviet authorities created a system of registration that appeared to be official and neutral. The fact that so few of the refugees refer to any pressure, hints, or threats at the point of registration provides convincing evidence that the lower-level bureaucrats charged with interacting with the public also had no idea that it was all a performance.

While it is unclear exactly when the decision was made, the Soviet government had already decided to deport the refugees who signed up for repatriation. They knew that the German authorities would not readmit the Jews they had managed to expel. They probably did not know that so many of the refugees would refuse their offer of citizenship. From the perspective of the Soviet state, it was a generous offer. In his autobiography, Nikita Khrushchev, then the head of the Communist Party in Ukraine, records his dismay on hearing that Polish Jews were standing in long lines and even bribing German officials in order to leave the USSR.[250]

Scholars have sought to understand the logic behind both the Soviet registration effort and the refugees' collective decision to leave. Litvak concludes that passportization was the government's final test for the refugees—and they failed.[251] According to Gross, "The registration saga shows that from the very beginning, Jewish support for Soviet rule derived to a significant degree from seeing it as the lesser evil, and that in relatively short time this judgment was reevaluated by large masses of Jews."[252] Elsewhere Gross calls the decision by the majority of Jews to register to leave an act of "resistance." He believes that the Soviet government recognized it as such, although Polish historiography has never agreed on this point.[253] Andrzej Żbikowski prefers disillusionment to nationalism as an explanation.[254]

Only a small number of Polish Jewish refugees describe registration as something other than a choice that they had to make. Chana Gelernter claims that Soviet citizenship was thrust upon her.[255] Shaul Shternfeld, who moved around multiple times, seems to have avoided registration until he was arrested in June 1940.[256] Given the large and widespread population of refugees, some local officials may have misinterpreted the registration directive, some refugees may have slipped through the cracks, and some refugees may have registered to leave without knowing what they had signed up for. For most refugees the decision was difficult and important. In the words of Yosef Halperin, "They are asking us to choose between the Garden of Eden of death and permanent incarceration."[257]

Many testimonials describe refugees' indecision and uncertainty in considering registration. Zyga Elton and his friends originally signed up for citizenship. After meeting some recent escapees from voluntary labor in a coal mine, however, they decided to join them in registering to return to their homes. While waiting in line to register, the young men had another change of heart and switched into a line for labor in the interior.[258] Victor Zarnowitz and his brother Tadek proved unable to make any decision at all:

We were being urged to choose a direction. The decision felt crucial and life changing, as indeed it was. We had no facts. Sentimentally, we wanted to go home, to our mother and grandmother. Tadek and I still felt very attached to our former way of life and we had a strong intuitive feeling that applying for Soviet citizenship meant abandoning all of this. On the other hand, we also still shared great fears of the Nazis . . . Stalin or Hitler. East or west. We had no way to choose. There was no right answer. We were paralyzed. We procrastinated. In the end, we did nothing. We didn't register for repatriation or apply for a passport. For months, we sat and waited. And looking back, that turned out to be the best decision.[259]

Short-Lived Soviet Citizenship

The majority of Jewish refugees from western Poland rejected modified Soviet passports and registered to return to their homes under German control. The remainder of this book will follow their trajectories deep into Soviet territory. However, a significant portion of the refugees did accept Soviet citizenship. In most ways, they became like the Jews who had resided in the annexed territories before 1939, on whom Soviet citizenship had been imposed. Some of these local Jews also faced deportation, but most remained in their homes. These Jews appeared to be the lucky ones, remaining in relative safety and comfort as the deportation proceeded.

One former child refugee related to me the lengths to which his mother went in order to avoid Soviet deportation. When the roundups began, she sent her husband, a rabbi and thus in greater danger, from Brody to Lvov. She and their two children moved from one relative to another, never spending two nights in one location. It was only when her youngest, at age seven, regressed to bed-wetting from the anxiety of constant motion, that she allowed the Soviets to catch up with them.[260] Other Polish Jews expressed relief that they had successfully avoided deportation. Yaffa Margulies-Shnitzer and her family watched as other well-off Jews in Tarnopol were either deported or forced to relocate farther from the border. She and her husband, as returnees from Warsaw with new passports, should have been part of this group—along with her parents, property and business owners. Margulies-Schnitzer credits their good fortune to her and her husband's respectable proletariat jobs as teachers, and her father's good reputation in the area.[261]

Just as the pull of family caused many refugees to sign up to return to the German-held areas, family could be a reason to stay under Soviet control. As one witness wrote about his own community, "A small portion, those who found for themselves a place to stay among relatives, accepted passports and automatically became citizens."[262] Yocheved Zamari, at eleven, was too young to understand the adults' deliberations, but she felt the warm embrace of her mother's relatives in Poltava. In her oral testimony, she says simply that they stayed on until the Germans came.[263] Eva Gregoratos writes that as soon as the war started in 1939, her parents locked up their store and house and went to live with her father's parents in Nowa Mysz (Bel. Novaya Mysh, Rus. Mysh Nova, Yid. Mush). Soon they rented their own place nearby, she started school, and her parents started work. When offered Soviet citizenship, her parents accepted.[264]

Polish Jewish refugees in certain professions may have also stayed in higher percentages. Many writers and actors employed by the state had compelling reasons to remain in Western Belorussia and Western Ukraine.[265] The same appears to be true for refugees who became involved in politics. In a longitudinal study of Polish Jewish communists before, during, and after the war, Jaff Schatz observes that those who had managed to avoid arrest welcomed Soviet citizenship.[266] Anecdotal evidence suggests that refugees who had close and reliable family, steady and rewarding work, or a hand in the new regime were more likely to consider staying in the region. Hersh Smolar, a writer and communist activist before the war, became the editor of *Der Bialystoker Shtern*. Initially he had high hopes of building Soviet Yiddish culture. Although he later wrote that those hopes were soon dashed, he stayed on in Western Belorussia.[267]

Refugees who had opted for labor in the interior and stayed there also avoided deportation. Unlike the refugees and residents in the former Polish territories, who were surrounded almost entirely by other former Polish citizens, these individuals had the opportunity to interact with other Soviet citizens and, therefore, to learn considerably more about Soviet life, history, and culture. Yosef Goldkorn became close with the local librarian in the coal mining settlement in the Donbas to which he and his wife Mania had been sent. From the librarian he learned about the horrors of collectivization in the area. When Goldkorn feared arrest after an altercation with his supervisor about the poor working conditions, the librarian helpfully informed him that if he had not been picked up in two days, he was safe. After the Goldkorns relocated to Voroshilovgrad due to Mania's pregnancy, an anxious landlord warned them that their frequent gatherings at the apartment had the authorities asking questions.[268] Such interactions helped the refugees begin to understand the land in which they now lived.

A refugee from Warsaw who worked first in Vitebsk and subsequently in Minsk later recorded his impressions of life in the interior. He learned from peers and colleagues about their relatively poor level of education, the recent purges, and ways to game the system in order to survive. He also noted details about Jewish life in the Soviet Union. There were, he said, no synagogues left in Vitebsk. Yet people still gathered on the Jewish holidays, and two kosher butchers and several rabbis functioned clandestinely. The older generation continued to speak Yiddish, but the youth went to Russian schools and spoke only Russian. He claimed that few Jews married non-Jews.[269] Ahron Blenkitni, also working in the interior, wrote that the local Jews did not believe his stories about German atrocities in Poland. They were convinced by the propaganda published in the regrettably named Soviet Yiddish newspaper *Der emes* (The Truth). However, when his wife gave birth to their son, the Jews in the small town provided not only a prayer quorum for the circumcision but even liquor. Nonetheless, feeling far from home, they named the child Gershom (Hebrew for "stranger there").[270]

Those who stayed in the former Polish areas with new passports, or labored in the eastern regions of Belorussia and Ukraine, often tried to help their deported friends and relatives. Many memoirs and testimonies describe the frantic scenes at railway stations as trains full of Polish Jews sat on the rails before deportation. Families provided aid at this juncture as well as afterward.[271] While David Azrieli's brothers registered to return to Maków, he elected to stay and accept Soviet citizenship. Azrieli thus had to leave Bialystok and settle in a smaller town close to the old Soviet border. He was lonely, but found housing and work, and was able to send care packages to his family members suffering in work settlements.[272]

As much as possible, Polish Jews who became Soviet citizens endeavored to keep in touch with friends and relatives who had been deported, as well as those who remained under German occupation. However, they also got on with their lives. In the absence of news from the west, most were not greatly concerned by the threat of war. One exception was Simon Davidson. As a Bundist with relatives in the USSR, he was skeptical of Soviet propaganda and tried to keep a low profile. Davidson volunteered for work in the interior partly to evade notice. In Orsha, he was able to bring his family from the German-held areas and find steady employment. Yet rumors from the border disturbed him, and Davidson got permission to transfer to Gorky

(Rus. Nizhny Novgorod) in May 1941. However, the family chose to stay through the end of the school year and were thus still in danger when the Germans invaded. Davidson, his wife, and two children left everything behind and fled east, eventually settling on a kolkhoz in Yoshkar-Ola in the Mari ASSR.[273]

Zyga Elton, on the other hand, had no such premonitions. He states, in fact, that he experienced the censored radio news as relaxing.[274] After registering for work in the interior, then for a passport, and subsequently for return to western Poland, Elton had finally settled down at a teachers' college in Berezhani. He received a stipend and housing, played sports, and benefited from some excellent professors. Elton completed his studies in June 1941 and tried to volunteer for the Red Army as it retreated through town. Michael Sherwood, who also finished school in June, recalls the scene in his memoir: "On the streets of Sambor, I saw groups of Jews gathering together and whispering the latest news. In their eyes I saw the despair of 2,000 years."[275]

The memoir of David Brandshpigel illustrates just how suddenly disaster struck some unsuspecting refugees. After suffering from hunger in Bialystok, his family volunteered for labor in the interior and accepted transport to Magnitogorsk. There he made friends, learned Russian, and enjoyed the school and local library. His parents, however, were miserable and ill from the hard labor. They made plans to join David's uncle in Orsha, Belorussia. In March 1941, having received permission to relocate, David's father Hayim traveled to Orsha. After several months with his brother, he was able to rent and furnish an apartment. On June 17 the family bid farewell to their friends in Magnitogorsk and boarded a westward train. They arrived on June 20 to a warm welcome. On June 22 their relatives took them on a tour of town. That afternoon, the bombing started. Abandoning all their careful plans, the family fled by train and by foot, sleeping in cemeteries and forests, often under fire. They were fortunate to make it back to Magnitogorsk.[276]

Others chose not to self-evacuate or were unable to do so. Yosef Halperin, who had moved repeatedly after entering Soviet territory in late 1939, accepted Soviet citizenship and took a job as a teacher in a small Belorussian village. Although barely out of school himself, he brought energy and commitment to his work. He found favor with both the local families and his superiors; relationships that would serve him well later. Halperin writes that when the Germans invaded, he did not want to leave his girlfriend or his nearby cousins. Additionally, he had heard rumors that the border into the old Soviet territories was closed.[277] Halperin received protection from the residents of the village, who decided as a group to hide his identity. Soon, however, he felt it would be safer to relocate, and returned to his wandering.

Scholarship has long maintained that the modified passports held by refugees who had accepted Soviet citizenship hindered them after the invasion.[278] This was certainly true in some cases. Leybish Frost alleges that residents of Hrubieszów who took Soviet citizenship and resettled in Tuchin (Ukr. Tuchyn) were all blocked at the old Soviet border.[279] However, this was not a firm policy. In fact, it seems likely that it was not a policy at all, but that certain local commanders interpreted paragraph 11 to mean that the former refugees could not enter the Soviet interior.[280] Others mention no such issues on their escape routes.

Some refugees actually moved west instead of east after the German invasion of the USSR. Henry Orenstein and his father had originally settled in Vladimir-Volynskii, across the Bug from their hometown of Hrubieszów. After taking Soviet passports, they had to move one hundred kilometers farther east. Isolated from news and convinced by Soviet propaganda about the Red Army, they stayed there even as the invasion began.[281] Only when German forces began massacring helpless Jewish civilians did they make the counterintuitive decision to migrate westward. In October, after several months of close calls and fortuitous help along the way, they managed to briefly reunite with the rest of the family in their home. Like other victims of the Holocaust, Orenstein endured terrible suffering and crushing losses in the coming years. Unlike most, he survived.

Klara Samuels and her parents also took advantage of the dissolution of the border to move back to central Poland after the German invasion. Recognizing the absurdity of her parents paying German soldiers for transport and registering with the Gestapo in order to enter the Warsaw Ghetto, Samuels writes, "To me, this is symbolic of precisely the kind of confluence of circumstances that was necessary for survival."[282] Adam Boren and his father and brother were not so lucky. After paying smugglers to get them out of the Bialystok Ghetto and back to Warsaw, they were caught and imprisoned. Boren remembers hearing his brother's and father's executions while hiding in a shed on the prison grounds.[283] Later he managed to reach his mother in the Warsaw Ghetto, but did not have the heart to tell her, in her weakened state, about her son's and husband's deaths. Boren stayed with his mother through the beginning of the Warsaw Ghetto Uprising, when her bunker was bombed while he was on patrol. After enduring several camps and two death marches, Boren was the only member of his family to survive.

During the war the Soviets claimed that they had evacuated Jews from the front lines following the 1941 invasion. This claim was then frequently repeated in scholarship. It is now clear that this was not true. Some Jews were evacuated because of their military, professional, or Communist Party affiliations, or their particular areas of expertise, but there was no coordinated effort to move Jews out of the areas taken by the Germans. Nor could there have been, in the initial chaos of the invasion. Yet even afterward, as the genocidal aims of the Germans became more evident, the Soviet Union prioritized military and industrial concerns over humanitarian ones.[284] Only when the invaders neared the largest centers of population did the state begin a mass civilian evacuation, with no ethnic preference.[285] The minority of Jews who left the western territories ahead of the Nazi forces did so on their own initiative.

Why did more Polish Jews not perceive the danger and move farther from the border before the 1941 invasion? At the very least, once the invasion commenced, why did so many fail to flee the German advance? First of all, they had limited access to information. Soviet newspapers—in Polish, Russian, Yiddish, and other languages—carried news of Axis victories in western and southern Europe, but it was not front-page news. "The newspaper," as Ben-Cion Pinchuk notes, "was merely another organ of the regime, itself suspected and under supervision, and designed to extol the virtues and praise the greatness of Stalin and the socialist state."[286] Even the Jewish papers were silent on the anti-Jewish policies of the Germans, with whom the Soviets had a nonaggression pact until the surprise invasion.

Jewish residents of Western Ukraine and Western Belorussia did read about German actions before 1939, in the press in Poland. They received regular, albeit censored, letters from relatives in ghettos. They even had occasion to interact with more recent refugees, who brought eyewitness testimony of German cruelty. Yet most of these residents still stayed in place, whether due to inertia, hope, or the difficulty or impossibility of travel.[287]

This is not the place to narrate the conditions of life and death for Jews in the areas taken by the Germans in 1941, a story that has received both scholarly and popular attention since the fall of the Soviet Union. Yehuda Bauer points out that Jews in these regions experienced "a disaster in two stages," as the terror of the Soviet occupation left them atomized in the face of the German onslaught.[288] Additionally, many Soviet policies, especially in the economic and political spheres, had exacerbated interethnic tensions and led to increased local collaboration.[289] Most of the Jews in the areas that had been eastern Poland died in what Father Patrick Desbois has termed "the Holocaust by bullets," as opposed to the better-known death camps.[290] Yitzhak Arad estimates that of Polish Jews who remained in the annexed territories, approximately 5 percent survived.[291]

The choice to accept Soviet citizenship, over a year before the invasion, doomed these Jews to an almost certain death. The testimonial literature is haunted by the knowledge that these "lucky" ones, who avoided the horror of Soviet deportation, were later murdered at the hands of the Germans. All of the testimonies of those deported remark on the supreme irony of their survival. Boruch Frusztajer called his father's decision to register for repatriation "the right decision for the wrong reason." This contingency of fate is perhaps best captured in a verse from Amos 5:19: "As if a man did flee from a lion, and a bear met him; or went into the house, and leaned his hand on the wall, and a snake bit him."

3

Jewish Luck

Deportation to Siberia

> My mother remarked: "We are so lucky it is not winter."
> "You are full of Jewish luck these days," my father answered
> irritably.
>
> —JANKA GOLDBERGER

IN EASTERN EUROPEAN Jewish folklore, the concept of "Jewish luck" contains layers of meaning. On the simplest level, it is bad luck. In what Max Weinreich points out is probably a misinterpretation of a Talmudic warning against reliance on astrology, a Yiddish proverb declares that Jews have no luck (*mazal*, from the Hebrew, also means "constellations"). Non-Jews, on the other hand, have superior luck.[1] Yet an alternate—and not entirely incompatible—meaning expressed in this brief exchange recalled by Polish Jewish refugee Janka Goldberger is that while fortune does not appear at first to smile upon the Jews, in the end everything works out for them. The title of the 1925 Soviet film *Evreiskoye schast'e* (Yidishe glikn, or Jewish Luck), based on stories from the popular Yiddish writer Sholom Aleichem, reflects this ironic interpretation. It would be difficult to find a set of historical circumstances more constitutive of Jewish luck than the bizarre fact that Joseph Stalin's deportation of a selection of Polish Jews effectively saved them from Adolf Hitler's murderous reign.

Goldberger was a child when the war began. Her charming memoir, written decades later, retains the perspective of youth. As Goldberger states, "The worlds of adults, and of eleven-year-old children are remote from each other. We were completely preoccupied with our own affairs, and only vaguely aware of the hardships with which our parents had to put up, though I do not think we were more egotistic than other children." Yet Goldberger, even as a youth, was also a keen observer. She recalls, for example, that her father woke her up as their deportation train crossed the mighty Volga River.[2] Indeed, the ordeal of the train to the east, and especially the moment of realization that they were leaving "European Russia," figures prominently in many of the memoirs and oral testimonies. Crossing the Volga meant, for many Central Europeans, leaving civilization as they knew it for unknown territory—which they called Siberia—regardless of cartographical distinctions.

Arrests and Deportations

The deportation of Polish Jewish refugees from the border areas into the Soviet interior can only be understood within the context of other deportations of Polish citizens, as well as within the greater context of Soviet population transfers. When the Bolsheviks gained control of what became the Soviet Union, they inherited a penal system based on the threat and reality of internal exile. Owing to its enormous land mass—and outdated political system—the Tsarist regime had relied on Siberian banishment and what we now call ethnic cleansing to control political enemies and populations deemed dangerous. Despite their own bitter experiences of incarceration and forced resettlement in the interior, the new Soviet leaders kept the system in place and expanded it considerably.[3]

According to Pavel Polian, all forced migrations serve both political and pragmatic purposes.[4] In other words, what is publicly constructed as justifiable punishment also benefits the powers that be. The accrual of reward, often economic, in turn stimulates authorities' desire for more. As Kate Brown puts it,

> One of the sadder ironies of the period is that Soviet leaders, trying furiously to build socialism in the shortest breadth of time, colonized their own country, conquered and defeated their own cause, and turned directly down the path of their worst nightmare, toward a capitalist exploitation of labor, raw, unmasked, and profusely described in the pages of *Das Kapital*.[5]

Polian uses the term "geographies of unreliability" to demonstrate how the Soviet system moved inexorably from applying social criteria to ethnic ones in its pursuit of suspected opponents.[6] This phenomenon is evident in the case of Ukraine—where collectivization and *dekulakization* (the repression and deportation of wealthier peasants) turned into the Holodomor—and elsewhere.[7] In her evocative chronicle of "resettlements" in the Kresy (the Polish Ukrainian borderland region), Brown explains this transformation:

> It is not that the men in the Communist Party leadership made up the accusations against Poles and Germans expressly to subjugate and persecute. It seems they believed in their taxonomies and came to trust an ethnic predisposition to treachery because they were seduced by their own statistical representation of reality.[8]

By the time of the so-called Great Purges (1937–1938), the Soviet leadership had turned against itself, murdering and deporting the elite and the military brass along with millions of others.[9]

Thus, well before the annexation of the Polish lands, the Soviet Union had developed and implemented a vast infrastructure of judicial, penal, transportation, and labor systems capable of absorbing millions of people. According to Lynne Viola,

> In 1941, there were some 4 million inmates in the various domains of the Gulag: 1.5 million in labor camps, 429,000 in labor colonies, 488,000 in prisons, and another 1.5 million in special settlements. In 1939/40, forced deportations from the Baltic countries and Poland had restocked the special settlements with new generations of exiles.[10]

The incarceration of Polish citizens began with prisoners of war (POWs); spread to include some border crossers; grew rapidly to target certain professional, social, economic, and political groups; and culminated in the deportation of the refugees. After annexing the Baltic states, the Soviets implemented the same system even more rapidly, with the refugees leaving the area just as the German forces moved in.

Polish experiences in the USSR must also be framed by the deportations of other national groups, which continued even after the German invasion in 1941. Even as the Soviets rapidly retreated from the German advance, they managed to carry out unprecedented population transfers. As Yaacov Ro'i notes, the repercussions of these deportations continue to this day.[11] Moreover, Alexander Statiev calls this moment the tipping point, from justifications for deportation based on class to justifications based on ethnicity: "With the beginning of the German invasion, the ethnic factor finally replaced class affiliation as the primary blacklisting criterion."[12] While the treatment of other national groups is beyond the scope of this book, it is worth noting that Polish citizens of all backgrounds joined their diverse Soviet peers in prisons and camps as early as 1939.

The speed of the invasion of Poland in September 1939 meant that hundreds of thousands of soldiers fell into enemy hands. The Germans captured close to seven hundred thousand Polish prisoners of war. Yet Polish authorities still urged men of fighting age to move east and muster for defense. Thus, several hundred thousand more Polish fighters turned up under Soviet control following their invasion on September 17.[13] With their superior knowledge of the language and the region, some of these managed to escape. Others, especially enlisted men and officers of low rank, were released due to lack of space once it was clear they posed no threat.[14] Grzegorz Hryciuk has found that of the 139,000 captives held by the Soviets in 1939, by December forty thousand had been sent to the German side of the border and another forty thousand released. The thirty-nine thousand who remained in Soviet custody were confined in POW camps.[15] Notably, many of these were in the Smolensk region, but others were in the newly occupied territories.[16] Based on a study of documents of the NKVD (Narodnyi Komissariat Vnutrennikh Del, People's Commissariat for Internal Affairs), Natalia Lebedeva adds that an additional 1,057 officers, who had not been taken prisoner during the September Campaign, were arrested in December.[17]

Herman Taube, originally from Łódź, was working with a medical unit of the Polish Army in September 1939. His unit had retreated east and was operating out of a church when Soviet soldiers arrived. The following night the Soviets arrested the doctor and two officers from the unit. The next day the soldiers were marched to a hospital in Vladimir-Volynskii (Pol. Włodzimierz Wołyński, Ukr. Volodymyr-Volynskyi, Yid. Ludmir). In his oral testimony Taube explains that some of the soldiers escaped and returned to their homes, but as a Jew, he did not want to risk entering German captivity. Several days later, the remaining prisoners were sent to work on a *sovkhoz* (Soviet farm) near Kremenchug (Ukr. Kremenchuk). Apparently they were not particularly well guarded, as Taube, still wearing half his uniform, managed to leave.[18]

The logic behind Soviet decisions is not always clear.[19] Some high-value prisoners, such as General Władysław Anders, were transferred early to Moscow and repeatedly tortured for information. Joseph Czapski, a Polish officer who met Anders immediately after his release from the Lubianka Prison in 1941, mentions he was still walking with a cane due to his injuries.[20] Yet other high-ranking officers were left behind in the squalid POW camps. In April 1940 some officers, including Captain Czapski, were sent from the separate Polish POW camps to general Soviet labor camps. A small portion of this group, presumably those considered to be the most amenable to Soviet ideology or to other incentives, was then brought to Moscow to discuss forming a Polish unit of the Red Army. Among these was Lieutenant Colonel Zygmunt Berling, who later served as the general of this unit.[21]

After his amnesty in late 1941, Czapski became obsessed with investigating why he and a few others had been transferred in 1940 and what had happened to the comrades they left behind in the camps in Kozielsk, Ostashkov, and Starobielsk. He ran a bureau of the Polish Army under British command dedicated to listing and finding the missing Polish officers and, in his 1951 memoir *The Inhuman Land,* chronicles his slowly dawning realization that something sinister had taken place. By 1943 the entire world knew that the Soviets had shot thousands of Polish officers in the forests of Katyn in the spring of 1940, although full details emerged only later. The Katyn Massacre remains deeply important to Polish national identity today.[22] At the time, however, Polish citizens only knew that many of their soldiers were imprisoned. Even after the details came to light—and despite the fact that Jewish victims were among the murdered soldiers— this particular massacre receives relatively little attention in the testimonial literature of the Polish Jewish refugees.

Maria Hadow, the non-Jewish wife of a young non-Jewish officer, notes in her memoir that her husband Antoni sent her postcards from his camp for several months. He even managed to smuggle out a few more substantive letters. When both forms of communication ceased, she had a foreboding dream, but she would not know the truth for several years.[23] The same was true for the Steinberg family. After fleeing Jarosław for Peremyshliany (Pol. Przemyślany, Ukr. Peremyshlianyu, Yid. Primishlan), they discovered that Baruch Steinberg, the chief rabbi of the Polish Army and the father's brother, had been captured in flight to Romania along with much of the officer corps. For a while they maintained contact, and were even allowed to send packages, but then the responses mysteriously ended.[24] As Natalia Aleksiun has noted, Rabbi Steinberg was a symbol of the Polish Jewish "brotherhood-in-arms" during his lifetime, and especially after his murder at Katyn was discovered.[25]

Other Polish citizens encountered the penal system when they or their friends or relatives were arrested for illegal border crossing. Thousands of

Polish Jews entered the Soviet zone in the early weeks of the war, often even with the collusion of Red Army soldiers. As the borders were settled, and especially after the annexation in November 1939, crossing became dangerous from both sides. The arrest of border crossers had an arbitrary quality. Yitzhak Erlichson describes being arrested for not having documents when he arrived in Lvov in September 1939. Accused of being a British spy, he spent months in jail, where he endured torture, disease, and malnutrition.[26] Helena Starkiewicz was caught crossing the border in October and sent to a prison in Lvov. She spent time in several other prisons before receiving a three-year sentence and transport to a Soviet prison camp in Mariinsk (Kemerovo Oblast).[27] Their stories are unusual only in that they were arrested so early.

The following cases are more typical. German soldiers pushed Moshe Kaner across the Bug River as part of the terrible death march of Jews from Chełm and Hrubieszów in December 1939.[28] He made it back to his family only to find that it was no longer safe for him at home. Kaner was caught while trying to reenter Soviet territory to reach his relatives in Vladimir-Volynskii. From there he was transferred to a larger jail in Russia and then to a work camp in the Karelia region for a three-year sentence.[29] Maria Rudnicka received the same sentence for crossing the border in February 1940. Several months later, she arrived in a camp amid a series of Gulag installations around the village of Dolinka in Kazakhstan.[30]

Attempts to reach Lithuania could also lead to incarceration. Klara Samuels and her family were all arrested near the Lithuanian border. After several days, she and her mother were released, but her father was sent to Baranovichi (Bel. Baranavichy, Pol. Baranowicze) to stand trial. For the next fourteen months, Klara and her mother struggled to survive in Slonim (Pol. Słonim), while also sending packages with encoded messages to her father. Klara's father was not deported, and she and her mother accepted Soviet citizenship in order to stay near him. They were reunited after the German invasion, when the Soviet jailers unlocked the cells before fleeing.[31] This was particularly fortunate, as NKVD troops elsewhere shot thousands of prisoners before retreating.[32]

Leib Novik, a journalist from Warsaw, could not find work in Bialystok and attempted to get to Vilnius (Pol. Wilno, Rus. Vilna) around New Year's Day 1940. Arrested en route, he spent months under interrogation before receiving a sentence of five years. In his 1942 testimony Novik claimed that his camp near the White Sea was so distant from civilization that it did not even have a name.[33] Under similar circumstances, Garri Urban was caught trying to make his way to Romania in late November 1939. He felt he would not be safe back in Warsaw and was no longer comfortable in Lvov. Despite the presence of Soviet border guards and the freezing temperatures, Urban attempted to cross the Prut River. According to his memoir, he was shot before he even reached the water. After interrogations in several prisons, Urban was sentenced to five years of hard labor and sent to a camp near Kandalaksha in the Murmansk Oblast.[34]

When picked up trying to cross a border, sometimes refugees simply disappeared. David Azrieli, for example, lost track of his younger brother Pinchas after he was arrested in Bialystok. Azrieli assumes Pinchas was sent to a camp but does not have any further information.[35] In July 1942 Ester Luft of Jerusalem wrote to the Polish government-in-exile seeking information about her brother Szulim Wallach, arrested in Lvov by the NKVD and not heard from since.[36] The files of the Polish government in London, as well as Jewish newspapers after the war, contain numerous requests for information of this type.

Some of the arrested refugees managed to avoid sentencing, thanks to luck, connections, or simply the mood of the officers in charge on a given day. When Israel Feldman's wife Lonia was captured while trying to reach him in Lvov in October 1939, the NKVD called him in for questioning. Apparently his answers were satisfying, as Lonia was freed.[37] This, however, was not a typical case. Once arrested, most refugees were absorbed quickly into the Soviets' enormous and highly developed system of incarceration.

This system also soon incorporated other categories of prisoners from the Polish population. In addition to POWs and border crossers, the NKVD began to pick up prominent political and intellectual leaders as well as accused criminals. While less distinguished lawyers, priests, rabbis, and local politicians faced deportation, these more famous individuals entered the prison system. The fact that Polish prisoners both entered the system for different reasons and faced diverse fates within it makes it difficult to count them. Grzegorz Hryciuk estimates there were 110,000 Polish prisoners, of whom over 20 percent were Jews.[38]

Aleksander Wat, a well-known Polish writer of Jewish background, was arrested in January 1940. Conditions in the Soviet prisons were meant to be cruel, but they were made even more dire by overcrowding. All of the memoirs and testimonies mention the unreasonable number of prisoners per room. Wat described twenty-eight people occupying eleven square meters for over nine months.[39] "I learned that the capacity of a prison cell is limit-less," wrote Yehoshua Gilboa.[40] Many texts also refer to the lack of adequate food, hygiene, exercise, and medical resources. Some prisoners faced phys-ical torture, while others endured psychological torture.

Most of the firsthand testimonies come from men, and indeed the au-thorities were more suspicious of men and arrested more of them. The few texts produced by women show that conditions were similar, with a few ad-ditional challenges. Helen Starkiewicz, a nurse by training, discusses the challenges female prisoners faced in trying to maintain hygiene during men-struation.[41] Jane Lipski, arrested later during the war, discovered she was pregnant while incarcerated. After giving birth without any anesthetic, she was transferred to a cell for mothers and infants. All struggled with nursing their babies and protecting them from disease.[42] Men sometimes tried to care for teenage brothers or sons in prison, but never had infants with them.

Those who had been communists, or fellow travelers, often found the re-alities of Soviet life particularly appalling. Moshe Grossman, with the as-perity of this hard-won knowledge, describes the Soviet prison system as a necessary rite of passage:

> It is a vast university. I shall not exaggerate when I declare that it is one of
> the most important, instructive and useful schools of life. I hope they will
> cease to be, I hope that there will be no more "students" in them, that is my
> deepest dream and longing. But if you want to know all stages and levels of
> life, if you wish to recognize and know what the reality of life is, if you want
> to know Russia and the Soviet order, you have to be in the prisons there.[43]

For the Polish Jewish prisoners who faced charges instead of instanta-neous deportation, arrest ignited a loss of faith in the communist system for some, confusion and pain for all, and a surprising amount of mixing and bonding with other Polish citizens. Although this was certainly not a goal of their jailers, incarcerated Poles of different ethnic, religious, educational, professional, and social backgrounds often experienced greater integration and camaraderie than they had at any time previously in their lives. In the words of Leib Novik, "Relations in prison between Jews and Poles were brotherly."[44]

Many write with wonderment about their interactions with other pris-oners, and especially the famous or unlikely people they met. Arrested for refusing to vote, Edmund Finkler was assigned to a cell with, among others, Senator Stanisław Głąbiński, of the antisemitic National Democracy movement, and Mojżesz Schorr, an important Warsaw rabbi, scholar, and political leader.[45] Finkler claims that the two high-profile men not only got along but even shared a bed. When Schorr was taken away, Głąbiński's new bedmate was the Bund leader Wiktor Alter. All of them, according to Finkler, were beaten severely.[46] He is one of several witnesses who claim to have met either Alter or his fellow Bund leader Henryk Erlich in a Soviet prison. The two did spend time in several prisons before their deaths, and it is certainly plausible that other prisoners interacted with them. At the very least, the existence of these stories illustrates the sense of Polish fellowship that developed in the Soviet prisons. Yitzhak Erlichson cites evening discussions between a Polish general and three rabbis as a highlight of his time in prison.[47]

Reflections about prison life also describe the rituals of prison society and cultural endeavors. Most cells had an official or unofficial leader; he or she might assign beds or chores, or might intervene in fights. Hierarchies in prison echoed those outside, but incorporated respect for certain skills. Both chess acumen and the ability to recall and recount literature, for example, could raise a prisoner's status.[48] All of these relationships, however, were fragile by their very nature. Each day brought new arrivals to a cell, as well as departures. The inmates tried to guess whether a missing cellmate had been moved to another cell, another prison, or deported east for "reeducation," but they had no way of really knowing.

Not everyone who was arrested faced deportation, and not everyone deported spent time in jail first. Yet many Polish citizens experienced arrest and deportation as part of the same continuum of Soviet oppression. In his attempt to create a typology of the entire system of forced relocation, Terry Martin writes,

> Deportation and incarceration, then, served different but complementary purposes. Deportation served primarily to remove a suspected population category from a given territory, and to do so without the effort of distinguishing more or less guilty individuals; incarceration served both to remove and punish individuals as well as to intimidate those not arrested (the terror function).[49]

Like arrests, deportations began as soon as the new regime established itself. Historians typically describe four waves of deportation of Polish citizens in Soviet territories between 1939 and 1941. This useful framework will be employed here as well, although it is important to note that there were exceptions: some members of the targeted groups evaded capture, while other people were deported with the wrong group, or for the wrong reason, or at different times.

Keith Sword thus refers to the four waves of deportation as "peaks" amid a general flow of Polish citizens to the east. Following the spate of individual arrests in the fall, the first peak came in February 1940 when Polish military colonists, forestry workers, and state employees were packed into frigid railway wagons and deported into the interior. The next group, in April, included members of the intelligentsia, political leaders, the wealthy, and families of POWs and other prisoners. Both of these deportations targeted all former and current Polish citizens, but given the makeup of the population, residents of the annexed territories and ethnic Poles predominated. In June 1940, refugees who had not accepted Soviet citizenship had their turn. This group, of course, was primarily Jews from western Poland. In June 1941, just before the German invasion, Poles of all backgrounds were swept up in the Baltic states, along with citizens of Estonia, Latvia, and Lithuania. The Soviets also used this opportunity to pick up some Poles in Western Belorussia and Western Ukraine who had managed to avoid deportation previously.[50] Summing up the entire process, Katherine Jolluck writes, "The deportation resulted from the occupying power's desire to rid the territory of eastern Poland of all elements it suspected would be disloyal to the new regime or counterrevolutionary."[51]

Piotr Wróbel concludes that the deportation of Polish citizens in 1939 and 1940 contained elements of class warfare and ethnic cleansing. He is certainly correct that Polish culture was targeted by Soviet policies in the incorporated areas. The use of ethnic cleansing techniques against ethnic Poles both before and after this period also lends weight to his argument.[52] Nonetheless, the inclusion of significant numbers of Belorussians, Ukrainians, and especially Jews among the deportees would seem to weaken this interpretation. Additionally, it is difficult to draw a straight line between policies in different periods, given that, as Wróbel himself notes, "Soviet policies toward the nations of the USSR in general and toward the Polish people in particular were inconsistent, ambiguous, and ambivalent."[53]

Throughout the war, as well as afterward, the Polish government-in-exile believed that over one million of its citizens had been deported by the Soviets. Poles in London sought to publicize the fate of their compatriots unjustly incarcerated, organizing this information into charts, maps, and lists.

Polish government records show that 52 percent of deportees were ethnic Poles, 30 percent were Jews, and 18 percent were Belorussians and Ukrainians.[54] Since the fall of communism, a number of scholars have sought to revise these figures using available Soviet sources.[55] Access to these sources, however, remains incomplete.

Updated figures suggest that there were slightly fewer than 320,000 Polish deportees spread out among the four waves in groups of approximately 140,000, 61,000, 79,000, and 40,000.[56] The third deportation included mainly Jewish refugees and the others had smaller numbers of Jews among the other Polish citizens. Hryciuk and others rely on a 1941 document listing 64,533 Jews, or 84.56 percent, in the third deportation group. Overall he counts 69,000 Polish Jewish deportees, or 21.9 percent of the total.[57] Mark Edele and Wanda Warlik, in view of the insufficient data, provide a range of 68,000–71,000 Polish Jews deported by the Soviets.[58]

All of these imprisoned, arrested, and deported Polish citizens entered the Gulag system under the auspices of the NKVD.[59] They lost their freedom and had to labor for survival. They lived in isolation with their modes of expression greatly curtailed. However, just as the timing and methods of seizure differed, so too did the types of confinement impact greatly on the experiences of the prisoners. Polish officers, captured mainly in September 1939, were held primarily in separate Polish POW camps. A small number spent time in Soviet prisons as well. Those arrested for crossing the border or as political prisoners typically spent most of their period of incarceration in Soviet prisons. Some describe cells filled primarily with other Polish citizens at the outset, while a few joined the population of Soviet prisoners immediately and all did so after sentencing to labor camps. The Polish deportees of February 1940 included many men on their own. Even when entire families were deported, the men were often separated from the women and children. All were sent to special settlements (*spetsposelki*), a somewhat amorphous category of internal exile. For the men this often meant isolated encampments adjacent to forests, mines, rivers, or factories. The families, and women and children, were generally sent to communal farms in northern Kazakhstan or the Ural Mountains, like the next group of deportees in April. The June 1940 deportation, including most of the Polish Jewish refugees, alighted in isolated special settlements in the Arctic, northern Kazakhstan, Siberia, and the Urals for the most part.[60] Table 3.1 shows a breakdown of deportation destinations for this group based on Soviet figures. Baltic citizens and Poles deported with them in June 1941

TABLE 3.1 Destinations and Numbers of June 1940 Deportation

Destination	Families	Individuals
Altai Krai	1,115	4,085
Arkhangelsk Oblast	4,016	12,309
Vologda Oblast	1,599	4,816
Gorky Oblast	291	901
Irkutsk Oblast	547	2,370
Komi ASSR	2,778	9,035
Mari ASSR	2,020	5,831
Molotov Oblast	523	1,542
Novosibirsk Oblast	6,921	21,840
Omsk Oblast	500	1,278
Sverdlovsk Oblast	2,728	8,186
Chelyabinsk Oblast	203	538
Yakutsk Oblast	1,211	3,523
Total	**24,772**	**77,710**

Source: "Memorandum of the Chief of the Department of Labor Settlements of the GULAG M. V. Konradov to the Commissar of Internal Affairs of the USSR L. P. Beria regarding the Reception and Settlement of Refugees from the Ukrainian SSR and Belarusian SSR," August 19, 1940, in *Istorii stanalinskogo gulaga,* ed. Iu. N. Afans'ev and V. P. Kozlov, vol. 5, *Spetspereselentsy v SSSR,* ed. T. V. Tsarevskaia-Daikina, (Moscow: ROSSPEN, 2004), 300–301.

were sent to all of these types of labor installations, as well as to communities in the Soviet Far East.

As this book focuses principally on refugees from German-occupied Poland, we will concentrate on their experiences in Soviet special settlements. However, refugees were also swept up with other waves of deportation, and at times the deported Poles mixed together. For this reason, the narrative will also explore similarities and differences in their ordeals. I will endeavor to use the appellation specific to each place of incarceration, at times using broader terms, such as *labor installation,* to encompass all of the types. The refugees themselves sometimes use Russian terms in their testimonies, but more frequently describe having lived in labor camps.

The Knock at the Door in the Middle of the Night

Polish Jewish refugees at first knew little about the day-to-day terror in the USSR, although those who had followed the press closely in the late 1930s remembered the purges and show trials of prominent figures. The imprisonment, and subsequent release, of military personnel was to be expected and did not raise undue concerns. Refugees only began to worry as they heard about the arrests of some of their compatriots at the borders and as they saw various social groups subsequently targeted for arrest and deportation. The first to be alarmed were those whose political, religious, economic, or professional backgrounds clashed with Soviet conventions.

Menachem Begin, at that time head of the youth wing of the Revisionist Zionist Party, relates the dread of awaiting arrest. Like many Zionist leaders, he had fled, together with his wife, to Vilna to avoid German and Soviet persecution. Several months after the Soviet takeover of Lithuania, Begin received an official summons, which he ignored. Soon a trio of observers appeared outside his house. For ten days, they watched the house and followed him whenever he went out. As Begin explains, "Therefore, I am telling nothing but the truth when I say that when the fateful day came and the agents of the Russian Intelligence arrived to take me on my long journey, I felt no anxiety. On the contrary, my principal emotion was one of intense relief."[61] Matwiej Bernstein, a Bundist who met Begin in prison, watched his comrades' arrests before his own turn came in August 1940.[62]

Marian Pretzel, whose father owned a small business in Lwów before the war, writes of the anxiety his parents experienced after the Soviet arrival:

> Almost every night, month after month, we heard trucks driving along the streets below. As long as they kept on driving, we knew we were safe; but sometimes they stopped and then we began to worry. My mother packed four cases with our clothes and put them next to our beds.[63]

Although the new regime did nationalize Pretzel's father's piano store, their holdings were not large enough to trigger further action.

Any Polish citizen who had been involved in politics, was a religious leader, owned significant property, or had a military commission began to expect the knock at the door. Soviet security services usually arrived in the middle of the night, as they had done with the infamous Black Marias during the purges. Working at night not only masked the scope and breadth of their projects, but also helped them to avoid traffic, communication, and prying eyes. Additionally, most people could be found at home in the early hours of the morning.

While certain groups dreaded the arrival of the secret police, others thought they were above suspicion. They feared for their wealthier or more prominent friends and neighbors but did not expect to be affected themselves. Refugees had predominated among those arrested for crossing the border illegally and most likely among the Polish Jews arrested for speculation. They were also represented among the Polish citizens deported for their occupational or political backgrounds. They had no reason, however, to expect the mass roundup of all refugees who had registered to return to German-occupied Poland in June 1940.

The majority of the refugees had, in the spring of 1940, elected to register for return to the German-held areas rather than accept modified Soviet passports. Thus, they anticipated travel west at some unspecified time. On occasion, the Soviet authorities used this expectation to facilitate deportation by convincing the hapless refugees they were heading home at last. When the trucks arrived to take Frumie Cohen and her family to the train station, her mother was frantic, as Frumie's older sister was at sleep-away camp. At the train station she told the officer in charge that the entire family would rather stay in the Soviet Union than risk losing their daughter. They were deeply relieved when the officer allowed the father to fetch the child, still believing they were on their way back to Kraków.[64] Other refugees had no such illusions, but by the time the NKVD arrived, they had no choice but to follow orders.

For each of the mass deportations, the Soviet authorities planned ahead and worked systematically. They prepared organized lists of names and addresses for each household. NKVD officers worked in teams, often with local civilian partners, to help identify the individuals sought. The teams spread out across the designated areas simultaneously, decreasing the chances of one party being able to warn another. Each individual or family was given a time limit and a weight limit for packing. They were then transported to the train station for the journey.

Although official documents outline exacting procedures, accounts of the reality differ widely. Either memory has distorted details, or individual NKVD agents used their own discretion. Probably both are true. One set of instructions for deportations from the Baltic states dated October 11, 1939, describes the process in detail. Coordinating with local officials, authorities created operational groups with distinct roles: some members were assigned to watch the entrances and exits of homes, others to conduct a search and check documents. Household members were to be informed of their impending deportation to "other regions" of the USSR and allowed to pack one hundred kilograms of clothing and household items. When heads of households were to be separated from their families, they were encouraged to pack separately, but not told why. The family's items were then to be placed on waiting carts, to be followed by the family on foot and under guard. At the train station, all goods and people were to be loaded in an orderly manner with no more than twenty-five persons per car.[65]

Although this document was intended specifically for the deportations that took place during the first Soviet incursion into the Baltic states, the same basic rubric appears to have guided deportations from all of the newly annexed territories. A set of instructions from December 29, 1939, for the deportation of Polish military colonists also specifies twenty-five passengers per train car, each of whom will receive one hot drink and eight hundred grams of bread daily. In this case the luggage limit is five hundred kilograms per family.[66]

Many deported Polish citizens recall the arrival of a small group to oversee their removal. At midnight on June 28, 1940, one officer and two civilians woke up Dora Werker, her husband, and two teenage children in Zolotchev (Pol. Złoczów, Ukr. Zolochiv). After their documents were checked, they were allowed to pack fifty kilograms of baggage and transported to the train station. According to Werker, the civilian told them they would be sent to the German territories.[67] Rabbi Avraham Steinberg mentions in his oral testimony that the guards who picked up his family were Jewish and known to his grandfather, who was a local. Nonetheless, they would not answer the family's pleas or questions.[68] It makes sense that some guards were chosen from the local population, given their facility with the landscape and the languages.[69]

The guidelines seem to suggest not disclosing final destinations to the deportees. In fact, even the guards themselves did not know where any individual or group was to be sent within the vast web of Soviet deportation camps and special settlements. Nonetheless, the refugees and residents often believed they knew where they were going. Some assumed they were traveling back to German-occupied Poland. Moshe Gliksberg's father was pleased when he heard that his family would be transported back to the city of Lida (Bel. Lida, Pol. Lyda), where they had lived before accepting passports and being forced to move farther from the border. The train did indeed travel to Lida, but there they were locked in the wagons while other refugees joined their transport into the unknown.[70]

Looking back on this moment, with the benefit of hindsight, many of the deportees lamented their lack of foresight. Rachela Tytelman Wygodzki and her father had been desperately trying to get back to Warsaw. On the summer evening when they were deported, she writes, her father was too upset to think of packing winter clothes.[71] Others were more fortunate—or ingenious. Janka Goldberger's father handed a bottle of vodka to the officer in charge of rounding them up: "He gratefully accepted and told us that we did not need to hurry too much about packing. This probably saved our health if not our lives. We packed everything, including ski-clothes, and sheets of leather Father had sent from the factory."[72]

Timely deliveries from friends and family helped some deportees to acquire much-needed items after their hurried departures. Menahem Ben-Moshe's family was arrested with hundreds of others on June 30, 1940. According to his account in the Sanok *yizkor-bukh,* "Every Jew in Galicia heard about our plight and so the train yards filled with people bringing us food and other items."[73] This was particularly fortuitous for Yisrael Orlansky, who voluntarily joined his father on the deportation train. Neither had been at home during the arrest, and so they had nothing with them. Happily, while the train waited at the station, Orlansky's brother and sisters brought them useful items from home.[74]

As numerous testimonies relate, deportation often broke up families. Like many other witnesses, Orlansky breaks chronology at this point in his narrative to emphasize that this was his family's last interaction together. He describes his father's unsuccessful efforts to locate his wife and children, or even any information about their deaths, after the war. Ultimately Orlansky's father had to create artificial dates on which to commemorate them.[75] Whether or not nuclear families were separated depended on the circumstances and timing of the deportation. While most refugee families were allowed to stay together, deportation separated them from other relatives. When Esther Hautzig's uncle came to check on the family as they were packing for deportation, her mother told the Soviet guard she did not know him, in order to save him from their fate—thus determining his.[76] As they spread out across the Soviet Union family members struggled to keep in touch and help one another.

Geography Lessons

The experience of transit was highly significant for many refugees. Almost all of the testimonies and memoirs describe bewildering train trips into the Soviet interior that ushered in their new status as prisoners. It is perhaps for this reason, as well as for the many new and baffling experiences on the way, that transit figures so prominently in their retellings.[77]

The first step of each journey was the trip to the train station, which deportees made either on foot or in trucks and carts. On arrival, they encountered masses of other confused and terrified Polish citizens—and began to recognize the scale of the forced removal. As quickly as possible, in order to avoid escape, Soviet personnel forced the hapless deportees into train cars. Families were inevitably, if inadvertently, separated in the process. Twenty-year-old Harry Berkelhammer, who had made a new life with his two older brothers in Lvov, lost sight of them at the station. As he was shoved into a freight car with sixty other people, the guards promised that all of the wagons were headed to the same location. Yet upon arrival, he still could not find his brothers. Berkelhammer describes the next months as the loneliest in his life. Mercifully, his brothers eventually found him and brought him to their place of settlement.[78]

Despite the regulations that limited the number of people per train wagon, and the careful lists prepared by the NKVD, the train stations were chaotic, and the wagons overcrowded. Many witnesses recall the disorientation and embarrassment of being crammed together with so many strangers. Baggage contributed to the lack of space, but at least provided seating. Some of the wagons had been outfitted with crude bunks. Others had no furnishing whatsoever. Shalom Omri relates that with fifty to sixty people per train car, there was barely room for everyone to lie down.[79] Sally Alban recalls lying on straw, "like cattle."[80]

As per Soviet custom, in many cases a *starosta,* or elder, was selected from each wagon. These individuals, usually middle-aged men who spoke some Russian, were charged with allocating food and water and communicating with the guards. Szymon Grajcar, although only in his twenties, filled this role because he had mastered Russian.[81] This position is typically mentioned by those who held it, or by members of their families. Other witnesses are far more likely to describe the anarchy and tumult than any system of organization.

At least some deportees began the journey with enough to eat, having packed food or received parcels from relatives at the train station. Samuel Honig recalls people helping one another and sharing what they had early on. When their reserves ran out, they had to rely on the meager rations provided.[82] David Shadkhanovich, deported from Lithuania in June 1941, reports that most of the prisoners on his train tossed their first delivery of porridge out the window; it tasted terrible and they all still had food from home. Only when they saw local peasants eagerly picking up the rejected meal did they begin to realize the level of hunger in the countryside. In order to conserve their own stock, they too began to eat the gruel.

Shalom Omri states that everyone received four hundred grams of bread with hot water in the mornings and soup in the afternoons. However, many deportees describe a more arbitrary distribution.[83] According to Ruzena Berler, her transport received soup only on the fifth day of travel.[84] Symcha Burstin mentions irregular deliveries, which included salted herring but no water. He adds that this was particularly difficult for the pregnant women.[85] Sporadic access to sustenance was also dangerous for nursing mothers. Berler says she became hysterical when her three-month-old daughter would no longer nurse. Other women on her wagon forced another passenger to share her powdered milk so that the baby would not die.[86] Dorothy Zanker Abend, traveling with a six-week-old child, marvels that her baby survived after her milk dried up. Occasionally she was able to buy cow's milk from peasants at train stations. Other times she dipped her bread ration into water to feed her infant son.[87]

Witnesses rarely fail to mention the *kipiatok*, the free hot water dispenser available at every train station in the Soviet Union. Shadkhanovich even recalls that, with his slow and imperfect knowledge of Russian, he mistakenly thought *kipiatok* must mean "station."[88] For those who kept strictly kosher, like Menachem Mendl Grossman and the yeshiva students traveling with him, the *kipiatok* was literally lifesaving. When they refused to eat the soup, their guard threatened dire punishment. Seeing they would not relent, however, he allowed them access to hot water in order to survive.[89] Others relied on the hot water to supplement their food or attempt to wash themselves.

The lack of proper toilets provoked great concern among the Polish deportees. They traveled not in passenger cars but in wagons built for freight or animals, which had no bathrooms. Usually, a bucket or mere hole in the train car's floor was expected to suffice. All deportees were appalled, but women arguably suffered the most discomfort. In Włodzimierz Szer's car, the women, many of whom already knew one another, hung sheets around the bucket to provide a modicum of privacy.[90] When the trains pulled up at small stations or along the tracks, the passengers were sometimes allowed to relieve themselves underneath. In Yankl Saler's retelling, men and women initially avoided seeing one another by going on different sides of the cars, but eventually they lost their inhibitions.[91] Some people, however, never overcame their reticence. In July 1940, Pearl Minz wrote in her diary that it had been nineteen days since she had moved her bowels and she was in agony.[92]

Lice proliferated in the filthy and overcrowded trains, causing irritation, mortification, and disease. Helen Zuberman says that after a month of travel, all of the passengers were covered with enormous lice. Some had already contracted typhoid.[93] Lice were an interminable problem in the USSR more generally, and one of the most common temporary treatments was steaming in the *banya,* or Russian bathhouse. Most of the trains stopped at least once to allow the people to wash and to delouse their clothing at public bathhouses. After days or weeks of travel, the deportees urgently wanted to bathe but were often shocked and confused by Soviet practices. Poles were unaccustomed to public baths, even separate-sex ones. Janka Goldberger, still a child, averred, "I had never had to undress in front of strangers before and clung onto my knickers for dear life."[94] Even more disconcerting was the presence of the bathhouse staff, as Yitzchok Perlov discusses with biting humor in his memoir:

> I do not know whether it is a law of the Soviet Union or just a custom in defiance of the law, but it was a fact that the attendant in every women's bathhouse was a man, while in every men's bathhouse the attendant was a woman. She moved about among the naked males as though they were a herd of oxen; she wore a pair of high rubber boots, distributing the footlockers, basins, and whisk brooms. She collected the left-over pieces of soap and bummed a *makhorka* smoke.
>
> Well, I do not know what effect this lady would have had on you, gentle reader, but I was very ill at ease when I had to present myself mother-naked to a fully clothed representative of the opposite sex who, moreover, was well armored in a leather jacket and a large apron supported by long rubber shoulder straps.[95]

The *banya* was a standard feature of all Soviet settlements, providing an efficient, inexpensive, and relatively hygienic way to maintain public health and comfort. The Polish Jewish deportees would soon look forward to their weekly visits, but the first time stayed in their memories.

Despite these halfhearted efforts in the name of nutrition and cleanliness, health rapidly declined on the trains, where passengers also lacked access to medical supplies. The young and the elderly were particularly vulnerable. In the words of Leon Klajman, "We became accustomed to the screams of the children."[96] In her diary, Pearl Minz mentions stopping along the way for burials.[97] A colleague who preferred not to use her name told me that the only story her parents would share about their time in the Soviet Union was of her father's heroic effort to find a Jewish cemetery for his father-in-law's body. The older man had died on the deportation train, and his son-in-law traveled by train and on foot—without official permission and with a corpse—until he could lay it to rest as proscribed by Jewish law.[98]

The cruelty of the conditions shocked deportees, who despaired of surviving the ordeal. As Tarik Amar puts it, "Locked into cattle cars in freezing temperatures, victims faced a lethal threat, complicating fine distinctions between murderous intent and murderous neglect."[99] His reference to "freezing temperatures" on the trains reflects his focus on ethnic Poles, deported primarily in the winter months of 1939–1940, whereas most Polish Jews were deported in June 1940. Their accounts thus emphasize the extreme heat. Interestingly, however, deportees very rarely referred to Soviet antisemitism. Some describe difficult relations between Polish Jews and non-Jews, but the Soviet forces that ripped them from their temporary homes are rarely, if ever, imagined as anti-Jewish. The deportees understood, correctly, that their treatment was no worse than that received by other Polish citizens, and by Soviet citizens as well.

The first Polish Jews captured or arrested in the winter months of 1939–1940 were incarcerated mainly with non-Jews. Menachem Begin, after his arrest, interrogation, and sentencing in Lithuania, traveled northeast with Poles and Lithuanians. He was the only Jew in his train car and remembers the varied responses to the German invasion of the USSR. At the camp, however, they were all in the minority among Soviet prisoners.[100]

On March 2, 1940, the NKVD issued a set of instructions for deporting the families of the men previously taken, as well as the refugees from Polish territory. Like previous directives, it included regulations for the treatment of the prisoners en route. In this case, each echelon would include a doctor and other medical professionals.[101] As had been the case previously, such regulations remained more theoretical than actual. In April, Soviet forces began deportation of the wives, children, and sometimes elderly parents, of the Polish men taken earlier. Ruzena Berler was six months pregnant when her husband, a lawyer and Zionist activist, was arrested. The Soviet authorities came for her in April 1940, and her three-month-old daughter

Olga was the youngest of the many children on her wagon; at Berler's insistence, the guards agreed to install a small heating stove in the wagon.[102] Chawa Kestenbojm's husband, an engineer in the Polish Army, had been captured in Hungary in September 1939. In April 1940, the NKVD arrested her along with her two children. In her testimony delivered to the Polish government-in-exile in 1943, Kestenbojm explains that her entire wagon was filled with the wives and children of soldiers.[103] Both Berler and Kestenbojm emphasize the significance of gender in their testimonies, focusing on their experiences as women traveling with other mothers and children. Neither refers to interethnic relations, or her own Jewish identity, during the period of transport.

Dina Gabel's memoir, on the other hand, is infused with references to religious practice and identity. Gabel's family lived in Soviet-occupied Lida, where her father was a rabbi and business owner. He was arrested in January 1940. One Friday night in April, the NKVD arrived for Gabel and her mother. Gabel's mother insisted on observing the remainder of the Sabbath scrupulously in the train car. The holiday of Passover arrived while they were still traveling east. Gabel traded their bread ration for additional water, which allowed them to survive the week without eating leavened products. She writes that the Polish women in their wagon did not understand her mother's faith.[104] It is clear that she and her mother saw themselves primarily as Jews rather than as fellow Polish women.

Unlike Berler, Kestenbojm, and Gabel, most of the Polish Jewish deportees left with their families and predominantly with other Jews. The final major wave of deportation from the annexed Polish lands, in June 1940, was intended to solve the refugee problem. When Symcha Burstin describes an overall sense of camaraderie in his wagon, despite petty quarrels, he reflects not only his own positive attitude but also the reality that his train was almost entirely filled with people like himself: Polish Jewish refugees.[105]

In memoirs, witnesses often describe their journeys in terms of the miles or kilometers traveled. Many include maps of their routes.[106] Few, however, had access to this information at the time. They could merely count the days and the number of conveyances taken to reach their destination. Such details appear regularly in their accounts. Burstin described twenty-eight days of train travel to Kotlas, where he and his father were loaded into barges with the other deportees. They traveled up the river for two days, then used carts to travel for two more days to a small settlement in the forest. Later, they discovered that this settlement was only six kilometers from a village. The NKVD had planned the final leg of the trip to make them believe they were all alone in the wilderness.[107]

In many cases, at some point during the journey, guards began to leave the doors of the train cars unlocked. They also occasionally allowed deportees to disembark and explore local areas. This improved immediate conditions, enabling regular access to fresh air, as well as periodic opportunities to barter with locals and to take care of personal hygiene at stations. At the same time, unlocked doors signaled their distance from centers of population. As deportees realized, the guards' growing disinterest suggested escape was no longer even possible.

Several testimonies describe deportees inadvertently left behind at stations along the way. There was no train schedule, and the prisoners were not told how long they had at a given stop. Ann Szedlecki's brother Shoel missed their train at one station, but was able to catch up and rejoin her soon afterward.[108] Olga Kochanska, a Polish American woman deported in a predominantly Jewish group, mentions that her train left behind a mother and also picked up a lone child from a previous transport at one station.[109] Like Kochanska, many witnesses describe this particular trauma as having happened to an unnamed individual. It is hard to know whether this signals the circulation of rumors rather than eyewitness experiences. Certainly, all of the deportees were anxious about this possibility.

The long trip into the unknown also introduced the deportees to the vast expanse of Soviet domains. As Dina Gabel reports, "When we passed the Ural Mountains, the natural border between Europe and Asia, one of the women in our car remarked, 'I feel like I'm going to my own funeral.'"[110] The remark of this anonymous witness, remembered and relayed decades later, reflects a deep-seated fear of Siberia, a bourgeoisie European sensibility about the other, and also a certain wonderment. Bob Golan registers his sense of awe, in a more positive reflection on the mountains: "In spite of our misery, we also had moments of joy. The scenery in the Ural Mountains was absolutely breathtaking."[111] Szymon Grajcar, however, recalls a wealthy man in his train car banging his head against the wall and screaming about white bears.[112] Leon Klajman wrote of sensing the "taste of being sent to Siberia" as he passed through the mountains.[113]

While Gabel calls the Ural Mountains a "natural border between Europe and Asia," this border was certainly more invented than real. As Kate Brown points out, all of the other continents are divided by oceans.[114] The mountains are real enough, but the arbitrary decision to bifurcate the contiguous landmass into two distinct continents is the product of political processes.[115] Nor is Siberia easy to define. Yuri Slezkine writes, "Siberia has not been a single administrative unit since the 1820s. It has no history of independent political existence, no claim to a separate ethnic identity, and no clear borders."[116] Nonetheless, the mountain range remains a widely accepted border and crossing it was a highly symbolic part of the journey for these bourgeois Central Europeans.

Many of the Polish deportees—even those few who had lived in more rural areas—had never seen anything like the Soviet landscape. Janka Goldberger remembers that her father woke her up in the middle of the night to see the Volga River out of the wagon's small window:

> I did not know that rivers could be so wide. The bridge seemed to go into nowhere. Whether this was the pale greyness of the very early morning, or the actual distance, I could not tell. All was grey, the water, the sky and the bridge were like a black and white film with the wheels of the train providing the background music. I was sorry when the crossing ended.[117]

Her father wanted her to see the majesty of the river, but he also saw the Volga as a line of demarcation. For the Polish deportees, the foreignness of this landscape indicated the end of the civilization they knew and the start of something else. Many referred to the new environment as Siberia, regardless of exact cartographic distinctions.

Siberia, in other words, is a constructed space.[118] Drawing on scholarship in geography and other fields, historians have begun to differentiate place, which can be located on a map, from space, the social apprehension of place.[119] The deportees knew about Siberia, having heard stories of exiles sent there under the tsars and the communists. The nightmare of deportation became, to a great degree, synonymous with the imagined space of Siberia.

Helen Zuberman, in her interview for the Shoah Foundation in 1998, describes Polish students at her Russian school disappearing one-by-one. She was told they had been sent to Siberia. When her own turn came, Zuberman says they were first taken to their "Siberia," a settlement outside Novosibirsk, and subsequently transferred to the Urals, outside Sverdlovsk (Rus. Yekaterinburg). Yet she continues to refer to this second location as Siberia as well.[120]

Many of the refugees deported north instead of east, to the Arkhangelsk and Murmansk regions, use the name Siberia to describe their general state of being. For Khanina Teitel, Yemtsa (Arkhangelsk Oblast), deep in the Arctic, was Siberia. This terminology was not merely a verbal shortcut, a way for witnesses to inform ignorant American interviewers of their plight without having to explain themselves; Teitel recorded his testimony, including this description of Siberia, in 1943 for the Polish government.[121] The section of Roza Buchman's testimony about her time in Vologda, a region north and slightly east of Moscow, is "Sybir."[122] Her testimony was also recorded in 1943, for the Polish Ministry of Information. As Abraham Bichler stated in his description of Asino (Omsk Oblast), "To us, it was the end of the earth. If there is such a thing as hell, this was it."[123]

Of course, many deportees really did land in indisputably Siberian territories. At the same time, the semimythical cultural images of Siberia and the harsh realities of forced labor also allowed deportees to create a shared experience of "Siberia" that overlapped—but was not entirely contiguous—with the geographic region. Slezkine notes a similar phenomenon in the nineteenth-century writings of political exile Alexander Herzen: "His place of confinement might be on the wrong side of the Urals, but if Siberia was a metaphor for a land of pristine snow violated by St. Petersburg's agents, then Viatka too was in Siberia."[124]

Many of the maps included in published memoirs, in addition to informing readers of unfamiliar locations and showing the great distances the authors traversed, also graphically represent their feelings of exile and isolation. Similarly, many memoirs and testimonies state that their journey's terminus was at the end of the tracks. Maintaining that their camp was past the final terminus of the railway line signaled their sense of being entirely cut off from the world. As with recollections of having either caught or missed the last train to the border in their efforts to flee, the perception may be more significant than the reality.

In a poem written in the USSR and published in Argentina in 1949, Avrom Zak, as Magdalena Ruta writes, tied his own feelings of exile on the banks of the Chib'iu River in the Komi Autonomous Soviet Socialist Republic (ASSR) to those of his ancient forebears:

> Tshibiu, Tshibiu!
> Your wild zigzags

Across the boundless taiga
Have entangled my life,
Have caught up my days and nights
In nightmares.

. . . .

For hours I sit by your
Dark waters,
And listen to their quiet murmur,
I hear a sob,
The voice of generations,
The weeping of generations:
"On the banks of Babylon"[125]

Camp Life

After weeks on the road, the deportees reached their destinations. Those who had been deported as refugees typically arrived in uninhabited and undeveloped areas. Sometimes the barracks bore signs of the recent departure of other deported peoples. Often there were no buildings at all, and the first job of the new arrivals was to prepare their own dwellings. Deep in the taiga of the USSR's northern and eastern regions, the deportees had access to few resources beyond wood for building and fires. The forests would sustain their livelihoods and provide them with nutrition but are often described in their testimonies as symbolic of danger and distance. As town and city dwellers, they had both practical and cultural reasons to fear the wilderness. Bob Golan writes of his group of refugees' arrival on the banks of a river in Siberia with only mosquitoes for company: "My parents picked a spot next to one of the bonfires, joining a group of hollow-eyed people staring into space. What were their thoughts? What would the future bring? How long were we going to be here?"[126]

Many of the deportees recall hearing some version of this speech when they arrived at their destinations: "'Here you will spend the rest of your life,' he announced. 'You can forget your Poland. The conditions will be hard, but you will get used to them. If you don't, you will die.'"[127] In Russian, the word for death in this construction was not the polite term used for humans (*umeret'*), but one typically used for animals (*sdokhnut'*). Some witnesses thus translate it as "die like a dog" or "croak":

"Most of you will survive, because you will get used to it, but if not, you will die like dogs. Long live Lenin, Marx, Engels and Father Stalin." We were to learn that every public speech had to end with the invocation of all communist saints. It was a convention, like 'amen' at the end of a prayer, except that everybody had to clap.[128]

The frequency with which some version of this welcome speech is mentioned suggests that it really was common to the ethos of the special settlements. In many cases, deportees also remember being told that attempting to escape was futile due to wolves, bears, or simply their extreme isolation. Some, like Moshe Etzion, illustrate this isolation by specifying that their locations were not fenced or closed off in any way.[129]

Upon arrival, the deportees either moved into existing barracks or began to build them from scratch. Commenting on the absurdity of expecting shoemakers and housewives to construct their own camp, Yosef Shvarts compared their situation to the primordial nothingness that preceded God's miraculous creation ex nihilo in the Jewish tradition: "Small town Jews and we had to start there the wonders of Creation [*mayse breyshis*]."[130] Even when available, housing was typically very primitive. Etzion's unfenced labor installation, outside Sverdlovsk, contained a school, an administrative building, a store, and barracks for the forty-five families. Each of the wooden barracks had two rooms with a single large stove in the middle; each family received one room.[131] Moshe Bunem Gliksberg and his family were sent to a special settlement in the Kotlas area, which also had barracks—but not enough for the number of prisoners. In his 1943 testimony for the Polish government-in-exile, Gliksberg wrote that the Poles would not let the Jews move in and the Soviet authorities had to move the Jews to another location nearby.[132]

The camps and special settlements were built around labor, and all deportees were expected to work. Many questioned the logic of this system, including Helen Starkiewicz, a nurse deported to a clinic outside Novosibirsk: "I could not understand what the Russians wanted with all these thousands of Polish citizens—they had to be fed, and the returns from starving workers were minimal."[133] In a report about the problems of absorbing the deportees prepared by the Party apparatus in Kazakhstan in 1940, the director of one collective farm to which Polish deportees had been sent is quoted complaining to his superiors that he had "absolutely no need of these people."[134] Scholars of the Soviet Gulag continue to weigh the relative

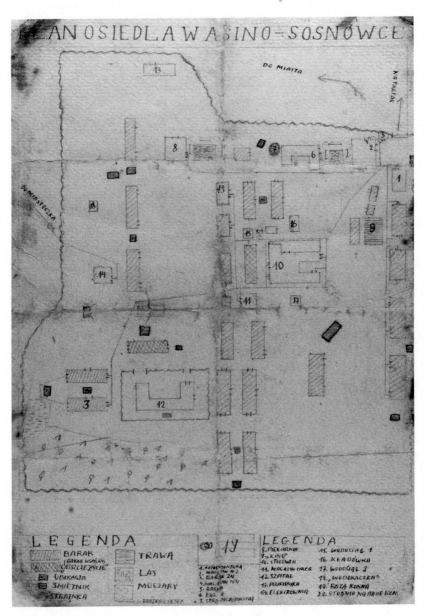

FIGURE 3.1. Map produced by Emil Landau, age thirteen, of the Asino camp he and his family lived and worked in after their deportation, c. 1941. Yad Vashem Archives.

importance of punishment, reeducation, and labor in the vast network of camps.[135]

The expectation that women labor alongside men came as a shock to the deportees. Both traditional Jewish culture and Polish culture emphasized separate gender roles, and the Soviets' more egalitarian ideal provoked consternation. Shmuel Zifberfeyn, arrested for avoiding deportation and thus sent to a Soviet rather than a Polish camp, wondered at seeing female political and criminal prisoners laboring in conditions akin to his own: as he put it in his testimony, "mercy be upon them."[136] In her testimony to the Polish government, Maria Rudnicka includes women's labor under a section entitled "Demoralization."[137]

For the Soviets, however, this was normal. The motto "Kto ne rabotayet, tot ne yest" (Whoever does not work, does not eat) was proclaimed in all of the camps. Azriel Regenbogen is one of many Polish Jewish deportees to recall this warning, along with the promise that they would never be allowed to leave, as among the first formal pronouncements of his settlement's NKVD commandant. After a couple of days to adjust, Regenboigen, his wife, and the older of his two daughters had to start work in the forest.[138] Yankl Saler and his family also began work soon after arriving at a labor installation in the Vologda Oblast. The men were given double-handed saws and axes and expected to cut down trees. The women cut branches from the felled trees to power the tractors that transported the trees to the river.[139]

Yet for many families this was simply not possible. The Labins, religious Jews from Tarnobrzeg, traveled with their eight children. Upon reaching their special settlement in the Molotov (Rus. Perm) Oblast, the older children all volunteered for work in the forest so their weak father could stay home. The mother had to take care of the younger children and prepare meals. At age thirteen, Shmuel, who left his testimony with the Polish government in Palestine in 1943, could not complete the expected workload and was in great pain. Eventually Shmuel and two of his older siblings managed to secure less arduous work, so only his eldest brother Shalom had to cut down trees. Shmuel was later caught bringing potatoes into the settlement to sell, and subsequently sent back to forestry work. His brief testimony primarily details his family's arduous efforts to earn enough to feed ten people.[140]

Both work output and food intake were strictly quantified in the labor installations. Each worker, depending on age, sex, and type of labor, had a set quota, referred to as a norm. Generally, full rations were only available to those who completed their daily norm. Leib Novik and his fellow prisoners were put to work extending the railroad in the Kotlas region. Their daily norms depended on whether they were clearing trees, moving sand, or laying rails, but Novik claims they were always impossible to achieve. They worked from four o'clock in the morning until seven in the evening, and received three hundred grams of bread in the morning and another three hundred grams plus soup in the evenings.[141] Z. Elsan was expected to produce eight cubic meters of lumber per day in their special settlement near Arkhangelsk, but she could only complete one. As a thirteen-year-old, she received four hundred grams of bread, whereas adults got eight hundred.[142]

Very few of the Polish Jews, men or women, were physically or technically prepared for hard labor. This led to exhaustion and weakness, and also to accidents. In his testimony, Shmuel Burshtein writes that his father recognized a Polish officer among the deportees on their train but did not tell the guards. This proved useful, as the officer had forestry experience and was able to train the other laborers. Even so, one healthy young man from Warsaw died instantly when a tree fell on him.[143] Chava Chaya Frenkel's father injured himself while building temporary structures—before the real work even started.[144]

While all of the deportees toiled and suffered, the worst work was generally meted out to the prisoners. They were also often sent to the most distant locations. Jozef Zgudnicki, arrested and sentenced to five years' labor for crossing the border, describes thirty-seven straight days of work in the forest upon his arrival at a labor camp near Arkhangelsk. He adds that no one could fulfill the norm and thus all went hungry. The only bright note was that the terrible conditions created solidarity among the Polish citizens. Later, Zgudnicki was taken to another camp in the Urals where laborers had to stand in the cold mud all day while working.[145] Sentenced as a Polish officer, Edmund Finkler spent time in many Soviet prison camps. In one, prisoners were expected to work fourteen-hour days on two hundred grams of bread with water. At his final camp near the Bering Sea, according to Finkler, laborers worked in the ice for eighteen hours per day and received three hundred grams of bread and soup that sometimes contained fish.[146]

At the other extreme, those who were deported before the refugees—mainly women, children, and older people—often were sent to collective farms or special settlements in northern Kazakhstan and the Urals. The work there was generally less strenuous and more varied, although the conditions were still very difficult. Deported in April along with other family members of Polish officers, Ruzena Berler and her baby arrived in a village in the Urals. The women moved into a school building and took turns watching the children, making clay bricks, and cleaning out stables.[147] Chawa Kestenbojm's transport, which included 120 Polish and four Jewish families of Polish officers, had to work on a collective farm in the Semipalatinsk Oblast. Expected to labor outside from seven in the morning to eight in the evening, as well as to walk several kilometers each way, Kestenbojm soon became ill.[148]

Those able to obtain work indoors generally fared better. Emma Lewinowna's father, a doctor, was already treating patients on the deportation train in June 1940. At their special settlement in Asino, he continued in his profession. Lewinowna herself worked in the cafeteria and was able to bring home soup. Between their privileged positions and packages from Radom, they were fairly comfortable.[149] Moshe Etzion's father and mother, through their older son's clever maneuvering, obtained work guarding the bakery at night and cleaning the administration building. Neither job was overly strenuous, and both offered opportunities to obtain extra food.[150] Office work, however, had potential pitfalls. Rojza Lauterbach's husband earned an enviable indoor position because he spoke Russian. However, he was later accused of sabotage for submitting a form without a signature and was sent to Altai for sentencing. To their great joy, he received a pay cut instead of a prison term.[151]

Environmental factors played a key role in shaping deportees' experience of hard labor. According to nearly all of the witnesses, insects in the Soviet interior were both larger and more pervasive than elsewhere. Lice, mosquitoes, and bed bugs receive particular attention in their accounts. The summer flies that bit Frumie Cohen were large enough to leave scars.[152] Rojza Lauterbach states it was impossible to sleep because the "bugs were countless."[153] Chava Chaya Frenkel remembers terrible mosquitoes attacking everyone but her mother in the taiga.[154] Dora Drescher recalls swarms of flies and mosquitoes, as well as the unpleasant smell of the ever-present bed bugs.[155] In a short story written in Poland after the war, Kalman Segal wrote that in his camp, the prisoners pitied the voracious lice: "We placed bets as to who would snuff it first—us or them."[156]

The climate also presented grave challenges. Many of the deportees illustrate the severity of the cold by citing the temperature at which they were no longer expected to work. Claims range from −45 to −70 degrees. Whether or not they remembered these numbers accurately, and whether or not the

NKVD staff honored their threats, deportees clearly were expected to work outside even in the dead of Siberian winter. Descriptions of the snow, ice, and darkness also underline the extremity of the environment. Fortunately, wood was plentiful in most of these work settlements. However, heating the barracks meant someone had to gather and prepare the logs in addition to his or her other duties. Shalom Omri and his roommates in the barracks carried a tree home each day to fuel their stove.[157] Moshe Etzion, a child at the time, earned extra money for his family by cutting up branches to sell for heating wood.[158] Helen Zuberman's parents were not well. In addition to carrying bricks for ten hours each day, she had to gather wood in the evenings for her mother to use for cooking and heating during the day.[159]

Deported in June, few refugees had the foresight to pack for the winter. Even had they done so, their winter clothing would have been inadequate for the extreme cold and punishing labor. Many recount their difficulties trying to obtain suitable gear for outdoor labor. After wearing through their shoes, some, like Sally Alban, learned to make straw or bark *lapti* to cover their feet.[160] Daniella Bell, who had been a small child in their Siberian labor installation, remembers the cold and hunger, and wearing rags on her feet.[161] Stuffing rags inside dilapidated shoes was a tried-and-true method of prolonging their usefulness in Russia. Dorothy Zanker Abend recalls putting cloth in her husband's thin boots to help him survive in the forest.[162] In Moshe Ben-Asher's special settlement, in an unspecified location in "Siberia," workers eventually received the *fufaiki* (quilted jackets) and *valenki* (felt boots) preferred by Soviet laborers.[163] Boruch Frusztajer's father managed to barter for *valenki*, but most were not so lucky; a friend lost his toes to frostbite.[164] Frusztajer adds that the *fufaiki* required constant patching in order to hold their stuffing. Khanina Teitel, in his 1943 testimony to the Polish government-in-exile, claims that 60 percent of the Polish citizens in his family's special settlement in the Arkhangelsk Oblast left without pieces of their fingers or noses.[165]

Furthermore, the meager camp diet left deportees constantly hungry and without all of the vitamins necessary for health. Diana Ackerman's family, deported to the Altai region, was fortunate to be close enough to a Russian settlement to exchange their possessions for food. The daily bread ration was insufficient for the family, but they were able to survive by trading clothing and shoes for cabbages and potatoes.[166] Emilia Koustova has written about the importance of objects from home for deportees for emotional and practical reasons.[167] Some of the refugees recall objects of emotional import, especially religious articles or books; nearly all of them derived material benefit from selling and trading their western products.

They also discovered other ways to increase their intake of calories and vitamins. Moshe Etzion's older brother, frequently the hero in his testimony, was able to earn milk for the family by serving as a shepherd for their Russian neighbors.[168] Moshe Ben-Asher supplemented his daily ration—four hundred grams of bread and a bowl of kasha—with mushrooms and berries he found in the forest.[169] Berries provided crucial nutrients, and many deportees recall gathering them in the summer to save for the winter. In Boruch Frusztajer's settlement east of Irkutsk, deportees also learned to preserve certain edible nettles.[170]

Packages from relatives also supplemented their meager diets. Despite their incarceration, deportees were frequently allowed to receive mail. Of course, many of the letters and parcels sent never reached their intended recipients due to prisoner transfers, postal errors, censorship, or theft. Most of the packages that reached the deportees came from relatives in the formerly Polish regions of the USSR. These family members had either resided in eastern Poland before the war or taken Soviet citizenship after annexation and thus avoided deportation. At this juncture they appeared to be the lucky ones and endeavored to help their benighted friends and family struggling to survive in Stalin's prisons, labor camps, and special settlements.

David Azrieli's brothers and their friends all signed up to return to their homes in the German-held area, but he had enjoyed both the education and the experimental nature of their time in Lvov and took a Soviet passport. After moving farther from the border region, Azrieli found a job at a flour mill. He was able to send packages to his brother Ephraim, who had been deported east.[171] Yosef Rozenberg remembers that the packages his family received from Western Ukraine helped them to survive.[172]

Packages also passed between labor installations. Dina Stahl, in her 1943 testimony to the Polish government-in-exile, claims that her immediate family of four would not have survived in their special settlement in Asino without packages from her grandparents, who lived in a nearby labor installation with better access to food.[173] Even more remarkably, some of the deportees were in such dire straits that they relied upon their relatives under German occupation. In April 1941, Helena Starkiewicz, who had been arrested and tried for crossing the border over a year before, was moved to a camp outside of Mariinsk. She was able to reestablish contact with her parents back in Hrubieszów, who soon began sending her packages.[174]

In Omsk, Harry Berkelhammer and his brother were pleased to receive underwear from their parents in Brzesko.[175]

Despite these impressive efforts, the health of the deportees continued to deteriorate. Dov Lederman, a child in exile, recalls itching boils on his skin due to lack of vitamins.[176] Janka Goldberger's memoir reflects on the ability of children to adjust to anything, but also describes skin sores that did not heal.[177] Naftali Zylbersztejn, in a labor camp in the far north, complained that it became difficult to eat as his teeth fell out due to vitamin deficiency.[178] Another common result of malnutrition was the loss of night vision. Variously called night blindness and chicken blindness, it terrified many of the deportees. Referring to the physical state of himself and his fellow prisoners, Yehoshua Gilboa quoted in his memoir from Isaiah 1:6: "From the sole of the feet even unto the head there is no soundness in it but wounds, and bruises, and festering sores; they have not been pressed, neither bound up, neither mollified with oil."[179]

Access to medical care was determined partly by the size and location of the labor installation, and partly by whether or not a medical professional happened to be among the deportees. In her memoir, Ruth Hohberg reports that there was no clinic in their village in the Yakutsk region. Fortunately, however, one of the deportees happened to be a doctor.[180] When there was no doctor or nurse available, families and communities had to administer to their own needs as well as they could. As an older and experienced woman, Pearl Minz became the de facto midwife in the distant northern settlement to which her family was sent.[181] When Frumie Cohen split open her forehead, no medicine or stitches were available. For frostbite and fever, Cohen remembers her older sister being treated with the traditional remedy of *bankes* (cupping). The closest hospital, in Tomsk, could only be reached by dogsled, and their medical needs were not sufficient for the trip.[182]

Lack of access to medical care led to many tragic situations. In her 1943 testimony for the Polish government, Yehudis Patash described her mother's physical deterioration in their special settlement in Arkhangelsk Oblast. After Passover 1941, Yehudis received permission to fetch the *feldsher* (medic) from a neighboring labor installation. He agreed the situation was grave but could offer no real help. Yehudis then walked ten kilometers to a settlement that had a Polish doctor. After hearing about her mother's symptoms, he provided her with a note to put the older woman in a hospital. Back in the settlement, the officer in charge acknowledged the note but would not provide transportation. Yehudis finally found a horse, and other children helped her to load her mother onto it. She began the journey toward the city, but her mother died on the way. After burying her mother, Yehudis—at twelve the eldest daughter in the exiled family—became the *balebusta* (mistress of the house).[183]

Occasionally, instances of injury and disease attracted the attention of the authorities. Leib Novik states that a medical commission visited his camp in the far north, as dysentery and other ailments caused many in his group of 280 men to fall ill and die. As a result, two hundred of them, including Novik, were sent to a hospital to recover. There they had better food, but no medicine. Novik recalls that after he returned to work, night blindness led to many dangers in the evening hours.[184] In his prison camp near the Arctic Circle, Garri Urban, a doctor, was eventually promoted to health inspector. He tried to help his fellow prisoners, but determined that graft throughout the distribution system meant there would never be sufficient food to keep them all alive.[185]

Every testimony includes at least some reference to deaths in the labor installations. David Shmietanke, originally from Jadów, fled with his family to Bialystok, from whence he was deported to a special settlement near Novosibirsk. Later they were moved farther east. Due to the grueling conditions, Shmietanke buried both his wife and his eldest child within the first year. He was left alone with a baby.[186] Some testimonies even try to quantify the scale of death. Edmund Finkler writes that 30 percent of the prisoners with whom he arrived in Magadan never left.[187] Naftali Zylbersztejn claims that half of his cohort of 360 prisoners died within the first six months.[188] Both of these men had been arrested, as well as deported, so it is likely their camps were crueler than most. Citing Soviet sources, Natalia Lebedeva shows that just over 5 percent of the deportees in the first wave had died by the time of their amnesty, whereas Jolluck shows a figure of 7.4 percent, with 2.3 percent for the third deportation.[189] Compiling the sources available, scholars have offered estimated mortality rates for deported Polish citizens ranging from 8 to 10 percent overall.[190]

Despite the prevalence of death, the testimonies and memoirs—especially the earlier and shorter ones—contain little emotional reflection. They outline the conditions, describe the particulars, list their losses, and then move on to the results. Even in later discussions of this period, the former refugees rarely refer to their feelings. It is as if the appalling conditions, grueling labor, and bitter cold numbed their emotions or did not allow them the luxury of personal expression.

The conditions in different settlements varied based on local leadership. Labor installations were governed by the idiosyncratic dictates of individual officials, and cruel or venal commandants could make life truly miserable. However, most of the ill treatment resulted from ingrained Soviet power structures and was not related to the background of the prisoners. All prisoners were treated terribly, but antisemitism was not a policy of Soviet camps. Of course, there were some antisemitic NKVD staff. In his 1943 testimony for the Polish government, Yosef Rozenberg describes an ethnic German commandant at his camp near Sverdlovsk, who hated Jews and gave them no mercy. Later, however, this man got in trouble and was removed. The new director increased morale and survival rates by giving the workers opportunities to earn extra money.[191] Shaul Shternfeld was arrested for refusing to register and thus exiled with prisoners rather than other refugees. He describes a sadistic camp leader who happened to be Jewish. Two musical brothers brought tears to the officer's eyes with their version of the nostalgic Yiddish classic "Yidishe Mame," but he continued to treat the prisoners as subhuman. He was eventually removed when too many of his charges died.[192] In her testimony for the Polish government-in-exile, Z. Elsan wrote that the commandant in her family's special settlement in the Arkhangelsk area disliked Jews, but hated Poles more.[193] In Dora Werker's labor installation past Irkutsk, on the other hand, Polish prisoners were allowed to visit the nearest market. Jews were not, because the commandant believed they were all engaged in speculation.[194]

Several of the testimonies refer to strikes by the Polish deportees. Without access to NKVD records, it is difficult to ascertain the frequency or extent of these demonstrations. Irving Beada claims that after several days of inhuman labor in the forests of the Tomsk region, his father and a number of other men organized a strike for better conditions. The guards brought in reinforcements, forced everyone back to work, and arrested twenty men, including Beada's father. Their families lived in fear, as terrible rumors circulated in the absence of any word from the arrested men. A few months later, however, the arrested men returned.[195] Dina Stahl's family was fortunate: her father found work as a locksmith and her grandparents sent packages from a nearby settlement. Others at their location in "Siberia" went hungry, and eventually held a strike, according to her 1943 testimony.[196] In

Yosef Rozenberg's special settlement in the Asino area, the Jewish families demonstrated for more food after thirty children died of hunger.[197]

Conditions differed among the special settlements, and all the more so between them and other types of Gulag installations, but all of the deported Polish citizens suffered tremendously during their months of incarceration. In later testimonies they struggle to find the words to describe their lives during this period. One lawyer from Kraków, cited in a 1943 Polish report, fell back upon the idiom of Jewish tradition to depict the laborers' trials:

> We dress like on Purim,
> Eat as on Yom Kippur,
> And work like in Egypt.[198]

Any Jew reading his words would easily recognize his references. He compared the bizarre collection of patched remnants of clothing to costumes on the masquerade holiday of Purim. References to fasting on the Day of Atonement, and to Egypt as the crucible of biblical slavery and redemption, are even more readily recognizable. Such cultural references provided a convenient shorthand for depicting difficult events, and a framework for assimilating them.

Culture and Religion

Despite the harsh conditions in labor installations, cultural and religious life were not entirely suppressed by the authorities. Although the practice of religion was sanctioned only infrequently, labor installations—with some variation—often provided space for cultural life among the deportees. Szymon Grajcar, deported to the far north, used his interview with the Shoah Foundation to describe the extreme weather and difficult work. Only when asked directly about Jewish life did he mention that he and his fellow prisoners held periodic recitals and had a dramatic circle. These activities seem to have been authorized: Grajcar mentions films brought in by boat from Syktyvkar on Sundays and dances in the *stolovaia* (canteen).[199] Samuel Honig, deported to the Mari ASSR, enjoyed a "culture club."[200] Rivka Agron was a child when her family arrived at a special settlement outside Sverdlovsk. In her retelling, a self-appointed committee of communist deportees negotiated with the guards to be allowed to organize Yiddish song nights and plays.[201] Helen Zuberman also recalls group singing on holidays, but always under supervision.[202] A club building served as the cultural center in Emma Lewinowna's special settlement east of Tomsk. She writes that a Soviet act or film came through periodically. Propaganda events also took place here.[203]

Less formally, Abraham Bichler recalls what he terms a "krasni ugolog" [sic], or "red corner," in his special settlement outside Redva in the Sverdlovsk region. In traditional peasant culture, a corner of the home was reserved as a place of honor for the family icon. Soviet authorities appropriated and reinterpreted this practice as a place to honor Soviet leaders. In addition to serving as the visual focus of the room, the red corner at Bichler's deportation site also provided a space for recreational activities. He describes spontaneous gatherings for music and singing, and notes that despite their poverty, the Russian people displayed a great love of life.[204]

Organized cultural activities took place alongside more spontaneous and unauthorized ones. While the authorities never allowed overt political organizing, they sometimes permitted small get-togethers with less obviously subversive content. In Mordechai Altshuler's special settlement, the young people gathered outside on certain winter evenings to sing songs from their Zionist youth groups.[205] At a sixteenth birthday party for one of the young women in her barrack, Olga Kochanska and her neighbors sang Polish songs, including the national anthem.[206]

Some of the camps and settlements provided schooling for the children. According to Shmuel Burshtein, one month after their arrival in the Mari ASSR, children fourteen and younger were invited to attend a school in the Mari village five kilometers away. Fifteen-year-old Burshtein lied about his age in order to avoid work, but he had soon mastered the curriculum and was sent back to the forest.[207] At a settlement outside Sverdlovsk, Rivka Agron and her fellow deportees also found themselves ahead of the locals in school. After the settlement residents finished building huts, a committee—established by the communists among the deportees—requested the establishment of a school. When it was completed, children came from other labor installations as well as local villages. In her oral testimony for the Shoah Foundation, Agron says that the Russian teachers were impressed by how much the Polish children knew but still gave them bad grades. Nonetheless, she was pleased to be in school because she had been bored before.[208]

Bob Golan was also happy to be back in school. Although he did not enjoy the propaganda, history fascinated him. Snow arrived early in their tiny settlement outside Asino, and Golan soon relied on homemade skis to get to school. Sometimes whiteout conditions meant he could not go at all.[209] The closest high school to Włodzimierz Szer's special settlement in the Sverdlovsk area was twenty-five kilometers away, but his father insisted he continue his education, even if it meant long walks and boarding in town over the winter due to weather conditions and wolves.[210] After several months working in an isolated special settlement past the Volga, Azriel Regenbogen heard that his wife's relatives had more favorable conditions in Krasnouralsk (Sverdlovsk Oblast). He wrote an ultimately successful letter to Soviet foreign minister Vyacheslav Molotov, in which he requested permission to move and emphasized that his two daughters wished to continue their education.[211]

Due to the location of the settlements or intransigence of their leaders, other deported children had no access to formal education. Diana Ackerman simply states that there was no school in their special settlement in the Altai region. She does not explain how they were close enough to Russian settlements to engage in barter, but not to attend school.[212] Boruch Frusztajer also notes that there was no school in his distant Siberian settlement, and no one had the energy or resources to tutor the children.[213] Other children were fortunate enough to receive informal education from family members. Adina Lahav's father, as a sign of his belief in a better future, had her keep up her Yiddish by writing in her diary daily. She described her old life, as well as current conditions. Every day after laboring in the forest, Lahav's father took off his work clothes and read her diary entry out loud to her mother.[214] Avraham Steinberg's older brother became ill working in the forest in the Sverdlovsk area. While he recuperated in bed without medical care, he taught young Avraham the parts of the Bible he had memorized. Steinberg adds that other children also received a clandestine religious education.[215]

Many Polish Jews endeavored to retain aspects of their religious traditions in exile. For Orthodox Jews, observance was central to an interwoven structure of law, faith, and praxis. For non-Orthodox Jews, religious practices remained part of their culture and identity. Holidays and life cycle rituals were particularly resonant. The fall High Holy Days were the first major test for most of the Polish Jewish deportees, who left in June and arrived in July or August. Should they refuse to work on their most sacred days? Should they attempt to gather for communal prayer? The answers to these questions depended on the social makeup of different groups of deportees, as well as conditions in their settlements.

In prison camps, communal observance of Jewish holidays was out of the question. However, some individuals found their own ways of marking them. Yehoshua Gilboa notes that one prisoner insisted on fasting on Yom Kippur for the first time since his bar mitzvah. According to Gilboa, when asked about his new embrace of religion, he replied:

> I can go hungry when the NKVD wants me to so why can't I go hungry when I want to? It's my way of protesting; or else it's a demonstration of a personal ambition. Maybe it comes from a vague longing. I myself don't know for what.[216]

Lack of access to Jewish calendars hindered observance of the holidays particularly for those deportees in settlements where Jews were in the minority. Warsaw journalist Leib Novik, who recorded a testimony in 1943 in Palestine, wrote about a friend in his labor camp in the Kotlas region trying to keep track of days so that they could mark the Jewish new year together. After they were moved to a new camp, he discovered that his calculations had been off by two days.[217] In Gilboa's prison camp, one man was a "walking Jewish calendar," informing the other Polish Jews about upcoming holidays and calculating personal days of mourning on request.[218]

Only those deported as refugees, located in special settlements primarily with other Polish Jews, could observe the communal aspects of the fall holidays. Moshe Zolenfreind, a teenager, was punished for not working on Rosh Hashanah by being assigned to a harder work crew and forced to go to the forest on Yom Kippur. Unexpectedly, the guard on duty allowed them to pray together, on the condition they pray on his behalf as well.[219] Shlomo Gevirtz, age fifty-five in 1940, claimed that only older men like himself formed a prayer quorum on Rosh Hashanah. The younger men had to work, except for a few from Hasidic homes. Nonetheless, the NKVD officer interrupted their services and arrested Gevirtz, whom he determined was the leader. Later some of the younger men were also arrested. After pleading that they were new to the Soviet system and did not know the rules, they received a pay cut instead of jail time.[220]

Some of the deportees claim to have attempted to use the Soviets' own logic against them. According to the children in the Hendel family, their father and several other observant Jews made a formal proposal to their officer regarding Yom Kippur. If only those who worked would be fed, per the stated motto, they requested to forgo their rations in return for not having to work on the Day of Atonement. The officer allowed them to pray in the evening but said they had to work on the day of the holiday. The Hendels' father still refused to work but was fortunate enough to get a doctor's release for the day.[221] Gitla Rabinowicz's father, a rabbi, was similarly unsuccessful in his interpretation of Soviet law. Before Rosh Hashanah, the commandant warned him that the freedom of religion granted in Stalin's constitution only referred to individual observance, not gatherings for prayer. Rabbi Rabinowicz countered that if others chose to join him while he prayed, he would not deny their religious freedom by asking them to leave. Gitla adds that ultimately the commandant won the argument: her father was arrested after thirty people came to pray on Rosh Hashanah. Even though he was soon released, far fewer joined him in prayer ten days later on Yom Kippur.[222]

Even in settlements where it was easier to observe the holidays, obtaining the necessary ritual objects was a challenge. Ludwik Pechster's sister Regina, who was back in Lvov, sent their father a shofar. According to Pechster, this was the first time the Ural forests had heard the unique call of the ram's horn. The children too young to work guarded the barrack during prayer services.[223] Nasan Tvi Baron, a Polish Jewish refugee deported from Lithuania with his yeshiva in June 1941, describes their efforts to obtain a shofar near Novosibirsk. With poor Russian language skills and a drawing, he paid a local Russian to find a ram. The Russian returned first with a cow, but eventually understood and the yeshiva students were able to carve out their shofar in time for the holiday. While they had no prayer books, Baron's brother had written down the special holiday prayers from memory in advance. He sang them to Russian tunes in order to arouse less suspicion.[224]

Like the High Holy Days in the fall, the spring holiday of Passover also united Jews in exile. And while the fall holidays brought memories of home, the themes of Pesach were particularly well attuned to the deportees' current situation. In the words of Abraham Bichler:

> The seder in Siberia in a slave labor camp was not a celebration of joy and freedom. On the contrary, we saw ourselves as our forefathers in Egypt. They were slaves to Pharaoh, and we were slaves to Stalin and the Communists. They waited for redemption and freedom, and so did we. G-d heard their outcry and sent Moses; our outcry had not yet been heard. We were still waiting for our Moses. We felt that we could write our own Haggadah.[225]

Juda Ari Wohlgemuth essentially did write his own Haggadah, or text for the Passover seder. In 1942 he recorded a lengthy liturgical poem in honor of Pesach. Lacking paper, he wrote it in a prayer book his friend E. Kopfstein had managed to bring to Novosibirsk:

Thus sat our parties reclining in cells,
Telling the tales of our people's departure from Egypt
and giving voice to the spirit of Freedom in the midst of our constraint.

Most of the poem describes how Wohlgemuth and his compatriots collected the ritual foods for the seder.[226]

Some of the Polish Jews were fortunate enough to receive shipments of matzah from relatives who had avoided deportation. Moshe Bunem Gliksberg's sister was out of town when the rest of the family was deported from Ive (Bel. Iwye, Pol. Iwje). Although the family begged the NKVD commander to wait for her return, they were forced to leave her behind. Once the family sent her a telegram with their whereabouts, she began to send them regular shipments of cash and goods. For Pesach of 1941, she sent thirty kilograms of matzah, raisins for wine, and *shmalts* (chicken fat). The family also managed to gather potatoes for a meal that made Gliksberg and the younger children wish the whole year could be Passover.[227] Jacob Halpern's aunt, back in the former Polish areas, was only able to send eight small pieces of matzah to her family. Halpern said that his father, a rabbi, consumed only these and water over the weeklong holiday.[228]

A couple of the deportees report having found a way to make matzah. Pearl Minz's family was so deep in Siberia that there was relatively little supervision. Her diary entry for April 10, 1941, mentions that the snow continued, they had made matzah, and other people received packages.[229] Most of the deportees, however, had to observe the holiday without this central ritual food. The Patash family was already starving by Passover of 1941. Yehudis reports that her father tried to fast on the first day of the holiday but almost collapsed. That evening he ate bread with tears streaming down his cheeks.[230] Some managed to avoid leavening by trading their bread rations for other staples, such as potatoes, during the holiday.[231]

While major holidays were important to Polish Jews of many social, religious, and political commitments, observing the Sabbath was a concern primarily of Orthodox Jews. Yisrael Orlansky had been deported with his father, who felt very strongly about Sabbath observance. To avoid work in the forest, the elder Orlansky registered himself as older than his actual age and Yisrael as younger. As a result, Yisrael did not have to work at all. His father was given a position in a factory, where non-Jewish workers agreed to cover for him on Saturdays. In his video testimony decades later, Orlansky recalls how difficult it was to abstain from eating his bread ration every Friday so that he and his father could combine their rations to have the customary two loaves for each of the Sabbath meals.[232]

Menachem Mendl Grossman, along with his yeshiva and their rabbi, arrived in an isolated settlement that had formerly housed deported Volga Germans. As a collective, they voted to take their day off on Saturdays instead of Sundays. Together with frequent gifts to the officer in charge, this worked for a while. After an inspection visit, however, they were forced to go out to the forest on Saturdays. They contrived to avoid forbidden labor by producing extra on Fridays and hiding it. On Saturdays they prayed together in the woods, far from the ears of their overseers, and then presented their cached output.[233] Not all Orthodox Jews had this good fortune; some had no choice but to work.

Unlike the weekly Sabbath, life cycle events took place sporadically. They were also often consequential to Polish Jews of diverse backgrounds. When Bob Golan turned thirteen in a special settlement outside Asino, his mother took him to the barrack of a rabbi in their group. The rabbi taught him to say a few words in Hebrew and wrapped his head and arm in tefillin. That was his bar mitzvah and, Golan adds, the extent of his religious practice while in the USSR.[234] Bronia Proshker was deported with her sister to Siberia. After she was injured at work, Jacob Zisfain, another Polish Jewish deportee, helped her and then suggested they marry. In her oral testimony, she describes the event as a "little bit wedding." She had no dress, but Jacob provided candy for the few guests and a deported rabbi wrote the *ketubah* (wedding contract) from memory.[235]

Deportees also held funerals in the labor installations. While Jewish law and custom are fairly vague regarding the nature of funerals, the proper treatment and burial of the dead is of immense import. Jechiel Tennenblum had been arrested trying to obtain travel documents to leave the USSR. In August 1940 he reached an unnamed camp where most of the two thousand or so inhabitants were Jews. Tennenblum writes that conditions were terrible and 150 died within the first six months. He adds that several religious Jews took it upon themselves to bury all of the dead in a traditional manner.[236] Shmuel Burshtein recalls that the refugees in his village all participated in the burials of a Jewish man killed by a falling tree and a Polish woman who died of sickness. The local Mari people allowed them to use their cemetery at no cost. The Jews placed their dead at a slight distance and made a wooden headstone with writing in both Russian and Yiddish.[237]

Cultural and religious practices helped to connect deported Polish Jews to their past lives and commitments, as well as to other like-minded individuals. Simply feeling like part of a community, even temporarily, could prove very meaningful for deportees so far from their homes. Most of the former refugees write or speak about these experiences as points of light within the darkness. Religious activities appear to have been especially memorable, perhaps because these activities channeled the refugees' previous lives. In the memoirs and testimonies, references to religious commemoration appear far more frequently than references to cultural or educational involvement.

Occasionally, memoirs and testimonies reference the more subversive potential of unsupervised group activities. Włodzimierz Szer, whose father was a loyal Bundist, describes a community of similarly committed individuals in a special settlement in the Urals as practicing "anti-state Socialism."[238] Dina Gabel, a fervently Orthodox Jew who frequently both sought out and provided Jewish community while in exile, articulates the same phenomenon among religious Jews:

> The authorities didn't know that real communism was being practiced in our tent more effectively, with justice and discipline, than they had ever managed with their propaganda and terror. Above all, ours was without sacrifice and casualties. Had they been in the practice of learning anything, they could have learned something from us.[239]

Amnesty

When they arrived in the camps and special settlements, many of the deportees were informed that they would never be released. Indeed, Soviet deportation policy did not generally allow for return or release. However, the Polish population was once again treated differently from other deported groups. Stalin clearly had designs on Polish territory and wanted to reduce Polish influence there. Yet he did not deport the Poles en masse, and even allowed them some cultural life in the annexed territories and in their places of exile. This tension—between a desire to destroy Polish autonomy on the one hand, and to co-opt parts of the Polish population on the other—continued throughout the war and into the postwar period. It is particularly evident in the evolution of the unlikely—and in many ways unfulfilled—amnesty agreement.[240]

On June 22, 1941, less than two years after signing the Molotov-Ribbentrop Pact, Germany and its Axis partners launched Operation Barbarossa and invaded the Soviet Union. Their blitzkrieg strategy, honed in Poland and western Europe, was remarkably successful. Within weeks, the Germans had captured all of the former Polish lands and moved across the old Soviet border. Despite repeated warnings, and a generally paranoid character, Stalin had not prepared for a German attack. The USSR rapidly lost an enormous amount of territory and endured a staggering number of human casualties. Moreover, it had little leverage to negotiate alliances with Hitler's other enemies.

The United Kingdom, the last country standing against Germany in Europe, reached out to the Soviet leadership immediately following the invasion. In order to form a coalition to defeat Hitler, Prime Minister Winston Churchill had to contain his own strongly anticommunist views in these negotiations. However, he was not willing to abandon Poland entirely. Great Britain had entered the war due to the German invasion of Poland, and Poland's government-in-exile was camped out in London. The British encouraged Stalin to reach some reconciliation with the Poles. The subsequent agreement between the Polish and Soviet governments, known as the Sikorski-Maisky Pact, was signed on July 30, 1941, with significant British pressure on both parties. The pact offered a blanket amnesty to Polish citizens incarcerated in the USSR and guaranteed the formation of a Polish army to aid in the fight against Germany. To the dismay of many Poles at the time, and in the years to come, it did not explicitly recognize the borders of the interwar Polish state as inviolable.[241]

While Poles around the world reacted, both positively and negatively, to these compromises, the Polish citizens in the far reaches of the Soviet Union heard news of the war and their amnesty only gradually. Some recall large meetings to disseminate the news. In the special settlement where Yehudis Patash and her family lived, the assembly was initially told that a war had started. Authorities informed the residents that they would have to work harder, with fewer rations, in order to help the troops. News of the amnesty reached them only several weeks later.[242] Many do not describe the revelation, focusing instead on its repercussions. Victor Zarnowitz notes that once the war started, there was no choice but to support the Soviets. He and his fellow inmates in Arkhangelsk wanted to fight but were mostly too weak to even travel.[243]

While news of the war and the amnesty reached some labor installations almost immediately, others waited months for the information to arrive. Janka Goldberger writes that her family learned of the war and the amnesty only in the early autumn. Additionally, according to her report, they were told that they would have to accept Soviet citizenship in order to leave the special settlement.[244] Alan Elsner, in a book about the survival experiences of his father and uncle, claims that their amnesty in November came just in time. Their labor camp had so little food that the inmates were dying of starvation.[245] Prisoners in Shaul Shternfeld's prison camp near Karelia found out about the invasion when they had to be evacuated, but rumors of the amnesty and Polish army only arrived in December 1941. The following month, Jews from western Poland were taken to a separate location. They did not receive their amnesty until June 1942.[246]

Some Polish citizens heard the news even later than this, and a few appear not to have heard it at all. Even with the NKVD's impressive record keeping, it was not easy to locate and notify all of the Poles deported across the Soviet Union's vast expanse. As German victories mounted, Soviet camp personnel also had little incentive to free their inmates. Doing so could mean the closure of the installations and the possibility that staff might be sent to the front. Nevertheless, over time, most of the Polish citizens in Soviet prisons, camps, and special settlements received their amnesty. A Soviet political prisoner in Magadan, the very heart of the Gulag archipelago, recalled in her memoir the day on which the six former members of the Polish Sejm received news of their amnesty and a summons to report to the chief procurator. The camp leadership offered to provide Polina Gertsenberg with more respectable clothing, but she insisted on leaving the labor camp in the same patched uniform she had worked in there.[247]

The situation of Polish Jews deported from the Baltic states—chiefly Lithuania—was somewhat different. As we have seen, deportations from Estonia, Latvia, and Lithuania took place later than those from the former Polish territories. Therefore, the Polish citizens in this group spent considerably less time as prisoners. Maria Mandelbrot's husband Lejb, a journalist, fled Warsaw in August 1939. Maria stayed, but soon found the German persecution too much to bear. In the fall she traveled to Bialystok, and then on to Lida. Smugglers helped her to reach her husband in Vilna. The Mandelbrots moved to Kovno when the Soviets arrived, but the NKVD caught up with them in June 1941. After two weeks of travel, the men were taken off the train, leading to harrowing scenes of separation. Maria spent several months working in a brick factory in the Altai region before her amnesty. Afterward, she moved around Central Asia and eventually contacted her husband through the Polish delegate's office.[248]

After the war, Polish Jewish deportees could not help but reflect on their "Jewish luck." This retrospective awareness of their narrow escape from the Holocaust was all the more poignant for those deported on the very eve of the invasion. Esther Hautzig writes that her mother was haunted by her refusal to acknowledge her own brother when he came to see them off in Vilna in June 1941.[249] Her well-meaning effort to shield him from the misery of being deported with them meant that he was murdered within a matter of months.

Additionally, Polish citizens deported from the Baltic states—whether Jewish or non-Jewish—had the unusual experience of leaving behind the Estonian, Latvian, and Lithuanian citizens when the amnesty came. Aharon Fish, in a transit camp on his way south after his amnesty, recalls seeing Lithuanian Jews, including a surprising number of the elderly, being led north.[250] Although the Baltic states had representation in England, these smaller countries also had weaker relationships with the Allied nations and less influential diaspora communities than the Poles. They were not able to negotiate equivalent treatment for their own deported citizens in the USSR. In response to a call for help for interned Latvians, an internal British memo from 1941 states simply that there is no benefit to be gained from intervention.[251]

Thus, while Polish citizens regained their freedom in late 1941, former citizens of the Baltic states, who had been granted automatic Soviet citizenship, remained in custody long after the war ended. In fact, most of them were released from their exile only in 1956, in the period known as the Thaw, following Stalin's death.[252] Even then, many were not allowed to return to their former hometowns. Instead they were forced to settle in smaller villages or in other regions. As Violeta Davoliūtė has noted, the specifically Jewish experience of this deportation has been largely forgotten.[253] Of the 17,500 Lithuanians deported in June 1941, about seventeen hundred were Jews, roughly commensurate with their percentage of the population.[254] For Estonian, Latvian, and Lithuanian nationals, the Soviet deportations have been viewed as—at best—a form of cultural genocide. For Jews, however, despite the duration, it was also a miraculous escape.[255] Rachel Rachlin, who spent sixteen years in Siberia with her husband Israel and their growing family, reflects on this:

> Only much later did we realize that our deportation actually was our salvation. If we had remained in Lithuania with Israel's relatives and all the other Jews, we would hardly have been able to avoid sharing their fate. The wilds of Siberia and all the ordeals we were to go through in the course of the following years were to save us from certain death. It is true that the object of our deportation was not to prevent us from falling into the hands of the Germans, but the course of history nevertheless caused this to become its paradoxical consequence.[256]

4

City of Want

Survival in Central Asia

Do they want for bread here too?

—ALEXANDER NEVEROV

AFTER THE AMNESTY, the Uzbek capital of Tashkent became a popular destination for Polish Jewish refugees. Many were motivated, at least in part, by the image of the city presented in Alexander Neverov's popular Soviet children's book, *Tashkent, City of Bread*. In this 1923 classic, a plucky youngster travels to Uzbekistan in order to get the grain seeds his peasant family so desperately needs. Although the book is filled with hunger and pain—including the moment of disillusionment when the protagonist finally reaches Tashkent cited above—it is ultimately a story of hope, in which a resilient youth overcomes all odds to help his family.[1] Translated into both Polish and Yiddish, the book left a strong impression on many of its readers.[2] But this sense of possibility was belied by actual wartime conditions. Yitzchok Perlov was one of many who traveled to Tashkent, encouraged by the book's hopeful narrative. His memoir, however, mocks the hope it engendered with a chapter titled "Tashkent—The City of Want." In it, Perlov describes the bleak reality of his time in the city:

It was past midnight when I arrived in Tashkent.

The plaza before the station was a billowing, raging, sea of humanity. Half of Russia had been evacuated to Central Asia, and there were also hundreds of thousands from Poland, Lithuania, Latvia, Estonia, Romania.

Not all of them desired to remain in Tashkent. Many were waiting for trains, just stopping over till they could continue their journey to other cities of Central Asia. For days and weeks they tarried thus, on the alert for an opportunity to get themselves into a train. Meanwhile, they squatted there on the plaza, in the small park, under the open sky. They subsisted on a ration of boiled water and dried bread. For nursing infants, they cooked cereals over fires of twigs and splinters of wood. The resulting porridge was smoky and black as soot. In these open-air "homes" people were sick, made love, and laundered their shirts.

As with refugees all over the world, denizens of the underworld also congregated here, headed by swaggering youngsters from Odessa. They didn't operate furtively. Things were grabbed out of one's hands, brazenly, during the day. Only lesser pilferers skulked at night. At daybreak one could hear the stifled wailing of people who had been robbed.[3]

Perlov's tragicomic evocation of the train station in Tashkent reflects many of the themes found in other memoirs. Arrival in the fabled City of Bread, and in other Central Asian destinations, was a bitter disappointment—especially after the initial euphoria of the amnesty.

The formal amnesty between Poland's government-in-exile and the Soviet Union was but the first of several policy shifts that would significantly impact the lives of the Polish Jewish refugees deep in the Soviet interior. Polish and Soviet officials engaged in an ongoing tug-of-war over land, people, and publicity, which often directly—if unthinkingly—impacted the refugees. The war, Soviet norms, and interactions with a host of other players, including the Polish government-in-exile and relief organizations abroad, also influenced their experiences of finding refuge in Kazakhstan, Central Asia, and other destinations far outside their previous lives and expectations.

The amnesty agreements granted the Polish government-in-exile the right to organize both a military and aid operations in the USSR. The formation of the Polish II Corps, known as Anders Army after its commander, Władysław Anders, was of particular import for the Polish authorities. It would allow them to contribute to the fight against German expansionism, to evacuate a portion of Polish citizens from the USSR, and to have a greater say in determining the future of Poland. Immediately after his amnesty from prison, Anders went to work trying to find all of the other Polish officers and recruiting among the depleted Polish citizens emerging from the special settlements and labor camps. Despite not being able to locate most of his most experienced comrades, Anders built up a general staff and enough soldiers to undertake training and prepare for evacuation. They traveled to

Iran in two main groups in the spring and summer of 1942. During this same period, Polish authorities outside the USSR worked assiduously with organizations around the world to provide aid for Polish authorities inside the USSR (the Delegatura) to distribute. The Soviets, having agreed to these provisions under duress, created all sorts of obstacles to their implementation until the German publication of the discovery of the graves of the missing Polish officers, murdered by the NKVD (Narodnyi Komissariat Vnutrennikh Del, People's Commissariat for Internal Affairs) in and around Katyn, put an end to all cooperation in April 1943.

Soviet attempts to hinder Polish progress and intervene in postwar politics included trying to expand Soviet citizenship. Residents of the annexed Polish territories had already received it automatically. In November 1941 the Soviets began to mobilize ethnically Belorussian, Jewish, and Ukrainian Polish citizens into labor battalions of the Red Army. When the Polish government-in-exile protested, the Soviets countered by putting forward a narrow interpretation of Polish citizenship to include only ethnic Poles.[4] Going even further, in January 1943, the Soviet government announced that anyone in Soviet territory as of the annexation (November 1–2, 1939) was automatically a Soviet citizen, further enraging the Poles abroad.[5] A passportization drive accompanied this move. Finally, following the break with the London Poles, in the summer of 1943 the Soviets began recruiting for a Polish division of the Red Army. For the purposes of clarity, the Kosciuszko Division (later, the Polish First Army) under General Zygmunt Berling will be referred to as Berling's Army and the Polish government-in-exile's forces as the Anders Army.

While historiography presents a fairly clear and chronological development as the refugees passed through their amnesty and endured the various phases of Soviet interference, the refugees' reflections suggest a more tangled and entangled experience. Rather than writing or speaking about a set of distinct Soviet policies or separate interactions with Polish authorities, they more frequently discuss how Soviet policies as a whole, or the sum of Polish interactions, affected them. This chapter attempts to mirror their constructions of this part of their wartime experience by focusing on themes rather than following a strictly chronological path. It begins with the variety of choices and journeys that brought them together, before looking at the struggles that characterized their first year or so outside the special settlements. Further sections examine their exposure to Soviet life and peoples, their confrontations with official Soviet policies and programs, gendered and sexual aspects of their time, Polish and Jewish relations, and relief and communication from outside the USSR.

Devious Paths

The German invasion of the USSR put millions of people in motion, including evacuees, troops, prisoners of war, and deportees. Indeed, Lewis Siegelbaum and Leslie Page Moch suggest broadening the definition of migration to include all of these related voluntary and involuntary phenomena within the Soviet Union.[6] Mark Edele prefers displacement as an explanatory framework for the mass movements.[7] The Polish citizens, and the Jewish refugees among them, were just a small fraction of this mobile population. Their story must be contextualized within this general upheaval, especially since amnesty pushed the Polish Jews from the relative isolation of the labor installations to encounters with many Soviet ethnic, social, and political groups. First they had to decide where to go and how to get there.

The timing and the conditions of the amnesty differed by location. Aharon Fish, released from a prison camp, was told that he would be sent to Syktyvkar in the Komi Autonomous Soviet Socialist Republic (ASSR). When he and several of the other young Polish men expressed their desire to travel to Buzuluk (Orenburg Oblast) to join Anders Army, they were denied permission. Even a strike did not change the position of the camp officials, so the young men determined to accept transport to Syktyvkar and then arrange further travel from there.[8] Zeev F., interviewed in Iran after being evacuated with his orphanage, maintained that his family was punished for his father's religious activism in their deportation settlement. When the other Polish citizens received their amnesty, his family had to stay behind. They were later allowed to leave the camp, but only to move to the nearest small town.[9]

Several of the refugees describe being dispatched directly from their work camps or special settlements to collective farms nearby or farther afield. Z. Elsan claims that the Poles from her special settlement were sent to Kazakhstan and the Jews to the Ural Mountains. When her family complained that the kolkhoz had no work, food, or even housing for them, they were sent to a second, and then a third.[10] When Khanina Teitel and his family arrived at the kolkhoz to which they had been sent with two hundred other refugees, the Uzbeks who worked there were not expecting them. The Polish citizens, Jewish and non-Jewish, were given a small amount of flour and placed in empty tents.[11]

Symcha Burstin recalls being set free—but without money, documents, or transport. Fortunately, Burstin's father had made connections while in the nearby prison. He was able to get a truck and driver to take them to the nearest rail station. The incident stuck with Burstin because after refusing to help him—a sixteen-year-old alone while his father was imprisoned—some of the other refugees nevertheless had the temerity to approach them for a ride.[12] When Shaul Shternfeld and his fellow Polish citizens were freed in June 1942 they received permission to settle anywhere in the USSR outside the major urban areas. However, without money or tickets, most relocated to the nearest town of Solikamsk, in the Molotov region, at least until they could earn enough to move farther.[13]

Leib Novik, on the other hand, amnestied from a prison camp in September 1941, writes that each of the Polish citizens received 130 rubles and documents granting them permission to travel. The NKVD tried to interest them in joining the Red Army, but when they declined, allowed them to proceed toward Anders Army.[14] The amnestied Polish citizens in Shmuel Labin's camp were told they would receive fifteen rubles per day to cover travel expenses to wherever they wanted to go. In the end, his family of ten got a lump sum of 350 rubles.[15] According to Natalia Lebedeva's research in Soviet sources, Levrentii Beria, at the head of the NKVD, canceled an earlier order to provide the amnestied Poles with funds and passes for travel at the end of August 1941.[16] Like the amnesty itself, it seems that before and after this ruling, local implementation varied.

Once amnestied, most Polish Jewish deportees converged on Kazakhstan and the Central Asian republics, traveling by whatever means possible.[17] Some made the journey over the course of weeks or months, with stops along the way. According to Samuel Honig's published memoir, the decision to travel south was self-evident. Journeying farther north or east held little attraction, while the war blocked any possibility of traveling west toward their home.[18] Ruth Hohberg, a child at the time, writes that news of the amnesty did not reach their isolated village outside Yakutsk until October. By that time, her mother was terribly cold, and they went south in search of warmth.[19]

Deportees hoped that the climate in Central Asia would not only be more comfortable but would also provide better access to nutrients. Many Polish Jews mention the common association of Tashkent with bread, mocked by Perlov in his memoir. More broadly, they had good reason to believe that the sunny conditions and longer growing season would translate into a more robust and diverse diet. Herman Taube, in an oral testimony recorded for the United States Holocaust Memorial Museum, misremembering either the book or his recollection of it, recalls that he traveled to Uzbekistan because he had read a book about bread and oranges in Tashkent.[20] Chava Chaya Frenkel states in her oral testimony that everyone wanted to go south. Her family would have liked to disembark in Alma-Ata (Kaz. Almaty), known as the City of Apples, but there were too many refugees there already and they had to stay on the train.[21]

Some of the Zionists among the refugees mention that Central Asia was an attractive destination because of its greater proximity to Palestine. Jacob Halpern was too young to make decisions about moving, but recalls that everyone wanted to be closer to the Land of Israel, and thus traveled to Uzbekistan.[22] In his testimony for the Sanok *yizkor-bukh,* Azriel Regenbogen notes that his family decided to travel south because they found the climate attractive, not yet realizing that warmth breeds disease. They also liked the idea of slipping across the border.[23] Shlomo Kless, both a historian and a former refugee himself, claims that there actually were some attempts. His research shows that Zionist activists who tried to cross the border uncovered only NKVD traps.[24]

Over time the rumored presence of other Polish Jews became the major reason for squatting in railroad stations over thousands of miles. Most of the refugees went south in the hopes of finding friends, relatives, *landslayt* (those from the same town), or at least other people who shared their languages and culture. Their journeys often took weeks, as the troop trains had first priority and civilians sat on the rails for days. Along the way, they collected bits and pieces of information about their far-flung relations from fellow travelers.

Miriam Bar had been separated from her husband Pavel during deportation. Many people in her small Siberian settlement decided to stay, but she went south to search for him. On the way she learned that Tashkent was the major evacuation center, but also that no one could enter without a special *komandirovka* (official authorization). Bar exited the train at the station after Tashkent and came back on foot to inquire about her husband.[25] Some did not even get that close to their desired destinations. Margot S., interviewed for a McGill University testimony project, said that she and her father, evacuating from the far north, wanted to reach Asia, but all of the trains were full. They made it as far as Kirov, still in Russia, where their documents were stolen. The authorities then sent them to a nearby kolkhoz.[26]

Most of the testimonies and memoirs spend less time describing this train trip than they did their original deportation. After all, they were leaving places of incarceration and were more familiar with Soviet modes of travel. At the same time, they often did not have a clear destination. They did not know where they would be allowed to settle, how to locate their relations, or how they would support themselves. Their hope and anxiety are captured in this excerpt from a postwar poem by the former refugee Herman Taube, which also provides the title of this section:

> Now my roving daydreams take me
> back to the spring of my life.
> Autumn travels lead me to the
> Devious paths of my stormy youth.[27]

Like the testimonies and memoirs, Taube's poem reflects on the mobility of the former deportees. Despite Soviet efforts to control and corral the refugee population, Polish Jews moved continuously in search of separated family members, professional or educational opportunities, and better living conditions. Keith Sword has noted that the Soviets had no real plan for the amnestied Poles. The decision to send some to collective farms was reactive and poorly managed.[28] The refugees' ongoing mobility challenges assumptions about authoritarian discipline in the USSR.

While most of the amnestied Polish Jews traveled south from their labor installations, a minority stayed in the regions to which they had been deported. In some cases, this was because news of the amnesty and army recruitment had not reached them. Others, however, made the decision to leave their special settlements but stay in the same areas. They would experience many of the same challenges as those who relocated, including hunger, sexual harassment, forced mobilization, and interactions with Catholic Poles and various Soviet ethnic groups. Yet there were also some unique aspects to their time in exile, as well as distinct paths by which some other groups of Polish Jews reached Central Asia.

Pearl Minz and her family came from Krosno, crossing the San River in September 1939. They resettled in Sambor (Ukr. Sambir) from whence they were deported in June 1940. After ten weeks of travel deep into Siberian territory, they arrived at an empty settlement in the region of Yakutsk. They were fifty kilometers from the nearest village. The next year was terribly difficult, but the Minz family survived. In June 1941 they heard about the German invasion. By August other groups of deportees and evacuees began to arrive in the area. Rumors of possible amnesty reached them at the same time. In late September they were at last free to leave. Yet most of the refugees, including the Minzes, were unable to prepare themselves in time to leave a few days later on the last boat before the river froze.

Pearl Minz's diary entries throughout the fall and winter describe groups of refugees leaving via raft, truck, or sled, as well as much discussion of where to go. Finally, in February 1942 the Minz family raised the funds for a harrowing trip of over one month and one thousand kilometers to Yakutsk. Like Polish Jewish refugees farther south, they faced pressure to take passports and difficulties with the Soviet authorities. They also formed a community with others like themselves and found work. Their distance from the centers of the country made news hard to come by. On November 7, 1943, Minz records the rare occasion of reading a newspaper from Moscow.[29]

Unlike the Minzes, Simcha Shafran and his group of yeshiva students arrived in Siberia only in 1941, having been deported from Biržai, Lithuania, just before the German invasion. The relative isolation proved useful for the displaced yeshiva. In their small settlement they managed to observe the major Jewish holidays, keep kosher, and meet for both study and prayer. "In Siberia," according to Shafran, "we learned what prayer really means."[30] They stayed until repatriation.

Although they faced real hardships, the deportees who remained in the far north avoided some of the diseases and hunger that plagued those in the overcrowded southern areas of refuge. Some, like Ann Szedlecki, reflected on this after the fact:

> Chance and choice matter too. My group was part of a tiny number of Jews who volunteered to work in Siberia, rather than being part of a roundup or deportation. We were part of an even smaller minority who didn't head back home once we realized the hardships of Siberia. Was it luck? Or was it what we Jews call a nes, a miracle?[31]

While most of the deported Polish Jews chose to leave their places of incarceration, many who left would later second-guess their decisions. Janka Goldberger, in her postwar memoir, wrote that her father had a good job in Siberia and had recommended that the family stay after their amnesty: "In retrospect, he may have been right. It would have been better to have stayed, but we wanted warmth, and were not blessed with clairvoyance."[32]

While many of the Polish Jews released from labor installations traveled south, some Polish Jews who had escaped deportation from Western Belorussia and Western Ukraine were evacuating to the east, ahead of the Germans. This group included both refugees from western Poland who had elected to take Soviet citizenship and stay in the annexed territories, and residents of those territories who had not fit the criteria for deportation.[33] It is not possible even to estimate the number who successfully escaped eastward, but certainly it was very small. Most Polish Jewish residents of the annexed territories, including the refugees who had chosen to accept Soviet citizenship and join them, were murdered during the German occupation.[34]

After crossing into Soviet territory from Hrubieszów, Yankl Saler and his family had signed up for labor in the interior, believing they would be sent to Berdichev (Ukr. Berdychiv), where they had an aunt. Instead, the train took them north toward Vologda. After several months of forced labor, they contacted their aunt and determined that they would join her. They sold their belongings and bartered in order to bribe guards and pay their passage. The family settled comfortably in Berdichev, finding housing, work, and schools. They continued to receive letters from Hrubieszów and knew they had made the right decision in leaving. When the bombing suddenly started in the summer of 1941, the Salers did not hesitate to evacuate. Yankl, remembering a book he had read, suggested to his father that they go to Tashkent. Upon arrival, however, they found it overcrowded and traveled on to Leninsk (Uzb. Asaka) in the Fergana Valley.[35]

Eva Gregoratos was at summer camp and had just celebrated her eleventh birthday when the Germans invaded. Nearly two years earlier, her family had fled from Łódź to join her father's parents in Mysh Nova (Bel. Novaya Mysh, Pol. Nowa Mysz, Yid. Mush). They settled in the nearest city of Baranovichi and accepted Soviet citizenship. On June 23, 1941, Gregoratos's aunt and uncle, who happened to be in the area, picked her up from camp.[36] Soviet soldiers would not let them return to Baranovichi, so they fled east. Gregoratos spent the war in Tajikistan with her aunt, uncle, and other relatives. She never saw her parents again.

In some cases, entire summer camps evacuated ahead of the German armies, and without their families. Lena Jedwab Rozenberg, from Bialystok, had become a Soviet citizen automatically along with her family. When the Germans invaded in June 1941, she was at a Pioneer camp in Lithuania. As it was not possible to return the children to their homes, the staff evacuated all of them eastward for their own safety. Lena, age sixteen at the time, recorded her angst in a diary entry, written in October from a kolkhoz in the Udmurt Autonomous Soviet Socialist Republic (ASSR):

> The accursed war has taken away my home, my parents, teachers, friends! It's landed me deep in the Soviet Union, in order to take away my ideals, my country, my goal in life. Fate has spared my life so that I could suffer, so that I could see everything that is sacred to me go to ruin. I am becoming a shadow of myself!

In December she noted with sympathy the visit of a Lithuanian Jewish man looking for his son. Sadly, the son was not in their group of evacuated children and the father had to continue his search.[37] A file in the papers of the Social Welfare Department of the Polish government-in-exile is devoted entirely to correspondence from parents searching for their children and from orphanages looking for parents.[38]

This harried self-evacuation was traumatic for many. Yosef Goldkorn describes fevered dreams of his flight from Sosnowiec in 1939, on the night before he and his wife Mania planned to flee Voroshilovgrad (Ukr. Luhansk) two years later. They had volunteered to work in the area, but then left the coal mines after Mania became pregnant. In October 1941, with German planes closing in, they boarded an eastbound train with their nine-month-old daughter Klara. When the train stopped after 150 kilometers, Klara was having difficulty breathing. A *feldsher* (medic) on the train diagnosed diphtheria, and the other passengers ostracized them. By the time they reached a hospital, Klara had died, and Mania was dangerously ill.[39]

Some of the Polish Jews even had to confront German advances a third time. After considerable hesitation, Abraham Kreusler left Warsaw with his wife and daughter in October 1939. Following a brief stop in Bialystok, Kreusler found work teaching German in Stanislav (Ukr. Ivano-Frankivsk). The family accepted Soviet citizenship and stayed there until 1941. That summer, as the Germans approached, they faced a familiar decision:

> Some were overcome with a kind of fatalistic indifference, by the paralyzing conviction that there was no way to escape the Nazis, no power capable of withstanding them, and thus the sooner the end came the better. Others were helped in their decisions by a chance word. Ours was our daughter, Lucy, who tipped the scales of our irresolution. She listened quietly to our

deliberations and vacillating opinions. She knew what was at stake and why some chose to die. But she did not want to give up all hope.[40]

Strengthened by their daughter's resolve, the family boarded a train for Stalingrad (Rus. Volgograd). Kreusler soon obtained a teaching position in the provincial town of Kachalino. They moved to a nearby collective farm peopled mainly by Don Cossacks, and once again began learning the culture and customs of new neighbors. As the front continued to advance, however, the Kreuslers' neighbors grew progressively less tolerant of refugees and Jews. Kreusler writes, "How efficacious Nazi propaganda was, how fertile the soil was on which its poisonous seeds fell, could be seen in the area of Stalingrad."[41] When they could wait no longer, the family crossed the Volga River under fire. In September 1942 they reached Belovodskoye (Kirghiz SSR), where they settled in safety.

In their places of refuge, the Polish Jews moving east to outrun the Germans mixed with those moving south to escape the harsh conditions of the labor installations. In the coming years they would confront similar challenges. This narrative thus expands to include Polish Jews who had shed their refugee status by accepting Soviet citizenship, or who became citizens automatically due to their residence in eastern Poland. In much larger numbers, Soviet citizens were also on the move. Over sixteen million Soviets left their homes during this period. Some fled the fighting on their own, while others participated in organized evacuations. Most of them converged in Central Asia.[42] Entire industries and institutions fled the violence, in addition to ordinary citizens; eventually, the government also took flight. As one journalist working for the Polish delegation to the USSR described, "It was a migration on a gigantic scale, recalling ancient times. The mass of Polish Jews who took part in it were probably reminded of their ancestors in Babylon."[43] This mass migration put an enormous strain on an already relatively weak infrastructure, guaranteeing that the cities of bread and apples would disappoint.

The First Year

All of the Polish Jews arriving in Central Asia depict their first year as dire, beginning with the initial shock of the overcrowded and unsafe train stations. Aharon Fish, on his own and not yet twenty when amnestied, headed south in the hopes of reaching the Anders Army. He describes Tashkent as equally crowded as Bialystok in 1939, but with the addition of rampant thievery. Fish slept in a park there for eight days before he was picked up by the authorities and sent to a kolkhoz. Upon discovering that everyone on the kolkhoz was starving, he left for Bukhara. Once again, the influx of refugees and evacuees meant that no work was available. For a couple of months, Fish got by working on the black market. After his landlord informed on him, however, he had to flee. Fish briefly worked on a kolkhoz in the region of Karakol (also known as Przhevalsk, Kirghiz SSR), before hunger made him move on once more.[44]

The constant hunger that Fish describes during his unplanned travels is echoed by other Polish Jews in the southern Soviet Union. Starvation was particularly acute on the communal farms. Comedic actor Shimon Dzigan reflected on this irony, citing a popular joke of the time: "What's the difference between a kolkhoz and *kol-nidre* [the prayer that ushers in the Jewish holy day of Yom Kippur, on which Jews traditionally do not partake of food]? When you say *kol-nidre,* you don't eat for a day. When you say kolkhoz, you don't eat for a year."[45]

Like Fish, many of the refugees also passed through Tashkent. Few were allowed to stay. Miriam Bar entered the city illegally, hoping that the sheer concentration of refugees would yield information about her husband. Her brief memoir, *Lelot Tashkent* (The Tashkent nights), reflects the day-to-day misery of a homeless, stateless, illegal refugee just trying to survive. Bar spent her days visiting offices across the city, hoping to obtain documents that would allow her to work and find housing or information about her husband. She spent her nights dodging thieves and the NKVD and trying to catch occasional moments of sleep. Eventually she developed a rotation, sleeping some nights in a student dormitory, some in the hut of a watchman out on his rounds, some in public waiting rooms, and some in the beds of acquaintances who could occasionally make room for her. Bar eventually received a letter from her husband and was able to evacuate with Anders Army. The conclusion of her story is sudden, even anticlimactic.[46]

Weakened by their time in the labor camps and bewildered by the rules of Soviet conduct, the refugees were ill equipped to handle the challenges of their new circumstances. At the same time, the Soviet Union itself had been laid low by the war. The phenomenal losses of the military in the west meant that more and more people were descending on an underdeveloped area of the country with no capacity to feed and house them, at a time when the government had little to offer. Soviet citizens—armed with connections, a hard-earned knowledge of the system, and proper paperwork—were better able to obtain necessities. As John Barber and Mark Harrison note, they were also accustomed to deprivation.[47] Notwithstanding this, Soviet citizens certainly suffered in the turbulent conditions of evacuation.[48] The refugees, lacking cultural capital and documentation, fell through the ever-widening cracks.

The results were devastating. Yehudis Patash lost her mother to disease and lack of medical care in the special settlement. Then, on the way to Tashkent, her father became ill and could not walk the ten kilometers to their assigned kolkhoz. She stayed with him in a teahouse while her older brother took their three younger siblings on ahead. Patash's father died during the night. In the morning, local people, undoubtedly concerned about contagion, took his body away. But Patash could not communicate with the Uzbek people and was distraught not to be able to offer her father a Jewish burial. A month after her arrival on the kolkhoz, Patash's older brother became ill. It took her over a week to figure out how to get him medical care, and he died two days after reaching the hospital. When she arrived, no one would tell her where his body had been laid to rest.

At fourteen, Patash became the chief breadwinner for her three orphaned siblings. She and Bela, two years younger, worked through the winter, but then came down with typhus. In order to avoid the spread of the disease, the kolkhoz sent them to a hospital in Tashkent, but made no provisions for their younger siblings. Avrom and Tsvi resorted to begging, which, Patash points out in her testimony, was illegal. She had to go back to work immediately upon her release from the hospital. That summer all four of them worked on the communal farm. Patash then found out about a Polish orphanage that would ultimately provide their salvation.[49] As Patash's tale makes clear, her family had no advocates and frequently were not even able to make their needs understood.

All of the refugees' postwar recollections mention struggles to survive relentless hunger and the ravages of disease during their first year in Central Asia. In his interview for the Shoah Foundation, Symcha Burstin says that it is impossible to even imagine the level of hunger on the kolkhoz outside Andizhan (Uzbek SSR) where he and his father lived and worked. Rations were continually cut until they received a mere one hundred grams of flour per day. People resorted to eating the skins from produce crushed for oil and fried cutlets made of grass. While the grass cakes were edible, he adds, they did nothing to sate the hunger.[50] On their kolkhoz outside Leninsk,

Yankl Saler describes his previously dignified mother fighting a stray dog for a piece of stale bread on the ground. Soon afterward, the refugees on their communal farm all contracted malaria from bathing in the river.[51]

The refugees mention typhus and dysentery most frequently, but they were also plagued by malaria, typhoid, tuberculosis, and cholera. All of these diseases thrive in overcrowded and unsanitary environments. In 1942, when Boris Baum met the woman who would become his wife, she was begging on the street in Bukhara. Her father and brother had already died serving in the Red Army. Then she and her mother contracted typhus and her mother died.[52] Baum helped her, and they married several months later. Shimon Dzigan was also fortunate to get support from others. In 1943, Dzigan was suffering from dysentery in a prison camp. Knowing his erstwhile popularity with the Polish Jewish masses as a prewar entertainer, he had word of his condition smuggled out to the nearby refugee community. Immediately, nutritious food began to arrive to see him through.[53]

Moshe Grossman had more difficulty finding help. When he could no longer work, the doctor on his kolkhoz sent him to a hospital with pneumonia and typhus. However, neither the first nor the second hospital he managed to reach were accepting typhus cases. He slept in a teahouse and dragged himself to a larger city the next day. In Samarkand, the first hospitals he reached were too full to take new patients. Finally, he gained admittance to a hospital run by a Jewish doctor from Odessa. Grossman credits the doctor's background for allowing him and other Polish Jews to get medical attention. Yet not everyone in the hospital appreciated her admitting the refugee Jews. According to Grossman, one nurse complained, "Those Jews have a nasty habit. They grab everything first, even the typhus."[54]

Herman Taube saw the medical crises of his fellow refugees from a different perspective. Trained as a medic in Poland, Taube continued his work in the Polish Army in 1939, and later in several different locations in the USSR before joining Berling's Army. After his amnesty, Taube worked at a malaria clinic in a farming village.[55] In his autobiographical novel, Taube describes the constant supply shortages, the dedicated medical staff, and the misery of the refugee population. Due to corruption, suspicion, and lack of resources, they were largely abandoned by the local authorities. Even those whose family members served in the military did not receive food. Taube tried to organize the refugees, in addition to treating their medical needs, but ultimately many of them ended up in the new section of the cemetery nicknamed Gan Eden Boulevard.[56]

FIGURE 4.1. Necha Ajzen and her daughters Chaika, Mania, Malka, and Ethel, refugees from Chełm, and an unknown associate, pose at the grave of her husband and their father, who died in Gorky in 1943. United States Holocaust Memorial Museum, courtesy of Ester Ajzen Lewin.

Due to deaths and dislocations, roles and responsibilities often changed within refugee families. Rivka Agron's mother had died when she was an infant. At the age of nine she fled Poland along with her father and several older siblings. While they were in the special settlement outside Sverdlovsk (Rus. Yekaterinburg), her father stayed home to take care of her while her brothers and sister worked in the forest. After the amnesty their roles switched. Agron's older sister, who had been in charge of feeding the family, married an evacuated Polish Jewish dentist. Her father, meanwhile, was prematurely old from his suffering. In her interview, Agron says that she was angry with her sister and resented having to care for her ailing father. She was only twelve years old. After their father died, Agron's brothers expected her to continue running the household. Instead she placed herself in an orphanage so that she could continue her education.[57] Having been forced into the role of an adult, she had become accustomed to making her own decisions.

As family members suffered from hunger and disease, women frequently had to move outside their typical gender roles. Sarah K.'s husband volunteered for Anders Army after amnesty, but he died of typhus in the recruitment camp. She and her younger brother tried to take care of one another in northern Kazakhstan that terrible winter. He lost his vision temporarily due to malnutrition, and afterward was drafted into Berling's Army. Sarah K., pregnant and alone, had to proceed on her own. She fulfilled typical nurturing roles for her husband and brother, and later her son, but without the protection she might have expected in return. Ultimately, she made her way back to Poland with her child.[58]

In a memoir largely dedicated to the bravery and ingenuity of his mother, Dov Lederman suggests that this adoption of unaccustomed roles occurred in the religious sphere as well. Lederman's father had fled Warsaw to Vilnius (Pol. Wilno, Rus. Vilna) soon after the war began. He managed to procure certificates for Palestine for the family but was arrested while trying to reach them in Bialystok. Although Lederman, his younger sister, and both parents survived, and even maintained contact, they did not reunite until after the war. Lederman's pious mother thus oversaw all of her children's physical and spiritual needs for over six years. He notes that the situation was similar for the many other refugee Jewish households headed by women.[59]

The desperation of the first year in Central Asia did eventually pass. In her memoir, Sarah K. mentions having the relative leisure to pursue religious education and practice and also points to a gradual improvement in conditions. In Sarah K.'s case, the turning point was the decision to move from Atbasar (Kazakh SSR), where she and her brother had settled after the amnesty, to the larger city and refugee center of Akmolinsk (Kaz. Nur-Sultan). There they found better jobs and greater access to goods, services, and cultural events. Not long afterward, good news from the front improved their emotional well-being as well.[60] Symcha Burstin and his father also benefited from voluntary relocation. When conditions on the kolkhoz became unbearable, they explored opportunities first in Andizhan, and then in Khanabad (Uzbek SSR). There they both secured work. Symcha was even able to advance in his position when his boss offered to send him on a six-week course for certification as a surveyor.[61]

Both of these cases reflect the refugees' growing mastery of Soviet conditions. When first refused entry into larger urban centers and sent to collective farms, most of the refugees assumed that they had to stay there.

Initially they may also have believed—not unreasonably—that food would be more plentiful in a farming community. However, they soon learned that the army had requisitioned all of the produce. While the locals might have held back enough to feed their families, the newcomers lacked the knowledge and connections to survive in such conditions. Their testimonies and memoirs reflect a developing realization that they had to take matters into their own hands.

At the same time the Soviet Union—after the initial shock of the invasion and the chaos of rapid retreat—gradually put systems in place to better police and provision the burgeoning population in Central Asia. In her work on evacuation, Rebecca Manley chronicles how lack of information, the fear and venality of local officials, and policies designed to privilege industrial production over human lives combined to create havoc in the early months of the war.[62] Yet although these problems remained, and new ones developed, the state was eventually able to bring in more personnel and institutions to meet the basic needs of its populace. A ration system was in place by November 1941.[63] Although mostly outside the official categories, Polish Jews nonetheless experienced some benefits from greater stabilization. Additionally, goods and cash from the Polish government-in-exile eased the material straits of at least some of the Polish exiles.

Some of the testimonies frame the Soviet victory at Stalingrad in early 1943 as a critical juncture. In retrospect, the battle is often called a turning point—if not *the* turning point—of the war: the moment when the Soviets halted their retreat and began their slow advance toward Berlin. Although no one at the time knew exactly what it meant, it was certainly celebrated as a major triumph. Even when conditions did not improve materially, some, like Abraham Kreusler, mention that they felt more hopeful after Stalingrad.[64] The refugees continued to experience hunger, disease, overcrowding, and unemployment throughout their time in the Soviet Union. Yet after that first desperate year or so in Central Asia, key changes—including their gradual adjustment to the conditions, relocations to better environments, increasingly available systems of support, and good news from the front—led to a perception of improvement. Certainly, the refugees experienced these improvements in a haphazard and uneven manner. After describing those initial months or year of abject suffering, most of the testimonies turn to describing the lives they built during their period of exile.

Life in Exile

Mobility continued to define the lives of many of the refugees. While most eventually settled in one location, others were continually on the move, chasing rumors of better conditions, family, and friends. A goldsmith from Warsaw interviewed by the American Jewish Committee (AJC) after the war relates that he was unable to leave his special settlement in the Komi ASSR after the amnesty because the administration gave them neither back pay nor transport. He left with a group of eight refugees only in April 1942. Within the next year, they stayed and worked on three different collective farms in the Kirov Oblast, each time finding the work intolerable. In the winter they were sent to work in the forest again. When his first child was born, he managed to get his family to the district capital of Loino. There he worked in a blacksmith shop and his wife worked in a tailor shop. The family finally settled into a relatively stable position in 1944.[65]

The quest for food, work, and lodging intertwined. Ration cards were tied to employment. Often housing—or at least a residence permit—was as well. Even when it was not, many owners did not want a tenant without a steady income. Some places of employment offered daily meals or other perks, licit or not, that helped people to get by. Sally Alban's husband Samuel was a tailor, which proved useful for them. In 1943 they left the kolkhoz where they had been living and working. In Dzhambul (Kaz. Taraz) Samuel found work in his field. Sally supplemented their income by selling items he made outside of work on the black market. The local people paid in produce, and she was even able to buy him a small sewing machine. However, they feared losing Samuel to a labor brigade, after her father and his brother had already died. In early 1944 they decided to register for factory work in Alma-Ata. The Albans were thrilled that the factory provided housing, the nicest they had experienced in the Soviet Union, and stayed there until repatriation.[66]

A refugee originally from Sompolno, Poland, and recorded only as H. when interviewed shortly after the war, arrived in Sverdlovsk in the winter of 1941–1942 after a difficult experience on a kolkhoz. The evacuation center offered him work in a military ski factory, but without a residence permit or ration card. A Soviet Jewish woman managed to get him a ration card for bread, but it was not enough, and he moved on to Tashkent for news of his sister. For H., aligning food, housing, and work proved challenging. After trying several other urban areas, he spent some time on a different kolkhoz, only to contract typhus. Unexpectedly, his most stable period was the two years he served in a labor battalion of the Red Army. Although he lived in a communal tent, he had access to steady nourishment and work.[67]

Housing could only be scarce, with the enormous influx of evacuees. In Tashkent alone, according to Paul Stronski, a prewar population of 600,000 grew to 750,000 in 1942 and over one million by 1944. He adds, "The evacuation process also revealed hierarchies of the Soviet social and economic system."[68] Polish citizens languished at the bottom of this hierarchy. When they managed to secure the paperwork and funds, and find willing landlords, they typically lived in the homes of Soviet families. The conditions of war, including the high cost of commodities and the drafting of many primary wage earners, made boarders a necessity for many locals. This, in turn, led to some strange bedfellows.

In the northern Kazakh town where Janka Goldberger and her parents settled, Polish refugees lived in the homes of deported Mordvin peasants— chiefly women and children.[69] It is likely that neither group had encountered the other previously. Esther Hautzig's peasant landlady in Rubtsovsk, a village in the Altai region, did not believe that Esther and her family could actually be Jews.[70] Yosef and Mania Goldkorn settled in Uralsk (Kaz. Oral) with a Don Cossack woman. Although historically Cossacks and Jews had difficult relations, this woman had lived through collectivization and was sympathetic to the homeless refugees. She even insisted that they stay after her husband returned home wounded from the front, believing that he had been saved from death because she had taken them in.[71]

Some refugees managed to live on their own, although this was also frequently a cultural experience. Rivka Agron describes the clay houses in Bukhara as straight out of the "Aggadah" (exegetical literature, i.e., ancient Jewish history).[72] Frumie Cohen's family, also in Bukhara, was given a room in a large courtyard and told that it had once belonged to a concubine of the emir. It had an outdoor oven and no plumbing.[73] In Andizhan, Irene Rogers's family shared a *kibitka* (a traditional round felt tent) with another refugee family.[74] Dina Gabel was able to purchase an *izba*, or summer log cabin, for herself and her mother in Tokushi (Kazakh SSR).[75] Many refugees comment on the large stoves that dominated most of the homes in Central Asia and served for cooking, heating, and sleeping.

Although there was rarely enough food on the collective farms, leaving a kolkhoz meant providing entirely for oneself. Some refugees were fortunate enough to have trained in professions useful within the wartime economy.

Herman Taube was looking for food in a garbage can in Andizhan when a woman asked about his status and background. Finding out that he was a trained medic, she brought him to the local health department. Desperate for medical professionals, the staff fed him and sent him to work at a malaria station in a nearby farming community.

Sometimes unskilled factory work was the best option, especially when food or other accommodations were available. After her release from a hospital, Eva Blatt worked for a while in a shoe factory in Uzbekistan. With associated lodgings and a canteen that served soup and bread, it was a very attractive position.[76] A capmaker by profession, referred to as SL by his AJC interviewer, held a number of unsatisfactory jobs before he attained a position in a food cooperative in the Fergana region. In addition to his salary, he was paid generously to overlook the director's various schemes for skimming and selling produce on the side.[77]

Refugees also relied on the black market to survive. Dov Lederman's mother had a regular job in their settlement in the Komi ASSR but used her sewing skills to barter for difficult-to-obtain food and clothing.[78] In Dzhambul, Chava Chaya Frenkel's mother supported their family at first by selling her clothing on the black market. She later made a deal with a Soviet Jewish baker to sell her excess loaves and split the profit. Frenkel's father was physically weak and hid out in order to avoid mobilization. The family survived thanks to her mother's illegal enterprises.[79] Roma Eibuszyc, in her joint memoir with her daughter, discusses both the ubiquity and the anxiety of this way of life:

> As our involvement in the black market expanded, we met more people from Poland. Every one of them was involved in some form of illegal trade. But we still had to look behind our backs at all times, living in constant fear of arrest and jail and the knowledge that at any moment the Russian authorities could send our men to the front lines. There was no relaxing. Nobody knew what the next hour might bring.[80]

While the majority of the refugees relied on the black market just to make ends meet, a smaller number established more lucrative ventures. Harry Berkelhammer and his brothers moved to Karabulak (Kazakh SSR) to work in an evacuated sugar factory. While he worked in the blacksmith shop and made extra tools after hours, they also paid off a night watchman in order to steal sugar and alcohol. As a result, the brothers lived very comfortably.[81]

Many refugees had to work below their former status. Yet young adults sometimes had access to education or training that helped them to rise above their previous status. Ann Benjamin-Goldberg came from a working-class home in eastern Poland. In her testimony for the Shoah Foundation, she specifies that she would have never been able to get a higher education in Poland. After her flight east, however, she was accepted into a medical training program. Her life there was not easy. She had to work and stand in line for hours in order to barely feed herself. Yet she was able to complete her medical education after the war and become a doctor.[82] Lena Rozenberg's family in Bialystok was poor. She suffered along with the other children with whom she was evacuated to the Udmurt ASSR. Yet after her graduation from the children's home, she was able to go to Moscow to continue her studies.[83]

At home, at work, and at school, the Polish Jewish refugees had the opportunity to interact with many different peoples. During the war, Central Asia was home to local indigenous groups, Soviet peoples who had been deported to the area, and millions of evacuees from the capitals and western regions of the USSR. In their testimonies the refugees mention this diversity of ethnic and religious groups with a range of emotions, including curiosity, camaraderie, sympathy, fear, and feelings of superiority. Overall, however, relations between the Polish Jews and their neighbors remained fairly distant. Their testimonies display concern and closeness primarily toward their own families. Beyond that inner circle, they relied upon Polish Jews with whom they had a political, regional, religious, professional, or other connection. At times these relationships even replaced the familial, especially for those deeply engaged in political movements before the war. Activists in the Jewish Labor Bund and various Zionist organizations often looked out for one another as members of the same tribe.[84] More broadly, Polish Jews in general constituted their primary social world. Jews from Poland, even those from different regions, generations, and backgrounds, shared certain fundamental commonalities and were most comfortable with one another.

Outside that social core the refugees expressed the greatest interest in Ashkenazi Soviet Jews, who had an identical history and grandparents born in the same shtetlach as their own, yet were separated by twenty years of a revolutionary ideology. Many of the refugees evinced fascination with the committed communists in particular. Others sought out vestiges of traditional Jewish practice in their coreligionists. Shaul Shternfeld found both extremes in one family he met in Kazan (Tatar ASSR). The parents were involved in the local Jewish community and invited him for Friday night dinner. Shternfeld contrasts their easy conviviality with the slogans and zealotry of their son, a Party member who had married a Chuvash woman.[85]

Most frequently, the Polish Jews commented upon the Yiddish spoken by Soviet Jews. The shared language allowed Polish and Soviet Jews to bridge their cultural divide, offering comfort and a certain conversational intimacy.[86] Full conversations were, of course, the most satisfying, but even a word could make a difference. Yehoshua Gilboa, in a memoir published in 1968, recalls an anonymous guard wishing him "Goot Shabbes" [*sic*] (a good Sabbath) one Saturday.[87] The momentary greeting stayed with him. And yet, as Natalie Belsky has demonstrated, there remained important cultural and political differences between the evacuees and the refugees.[88]

The divide was even greater with non-Ashkenazi Jewish populations. Betty Rich describes a warm welcome from the Georgian Jews in Staliniri (Geo. Tskhinvali, Oss. Tskhinval), but adds that they did not share a common language.[89] Reports on interactions with other Jews are mixed. Few refugees who passed through Uzbekistan fail to mention the Bukharan Jews there, but even those who visited their synagogues or received their help did not form lasting relationships. Of the Bukharan rabbi who conducted her wedding ceremony in June 1944, Tema Abel reports only that he spoke a "different Yiddish."[90] In acknowledging that his hybridized language was also fundamentally Jewish, she simultaneously both recognizes him as a Jew and explains their lack of communication.

Of course, some individuals formed meaningful connections with neighbors or colleagues. All mention receiving help from a variety of acquaintances. Yet language and culture limited their social interactions. This was particularly true with regard to the autochthonous peoples, whom they often viewed from a great distance. Abraham Bichler's depiction of local customs in Turkestan (Kaz. Turkistan) demonstrates the anthropological lens that many Central Europeans brought to Central Asia:

> It was almost as if we were living in the days of the Bible. Their garments were similar to what we are accustomed to seeing in movies portraying biblical life, and so was their behavior. The men, regardless of where they went, carried large staffs on their backs, with their hands wrapped around them. The married women covered their faces with veils.[91]

Nor is Bichler's affront at the roles of women unusual. Many of the refugees, oblivious to their own culturally determined gender codes, commented disapprovingly on the way that women were treated in the Central Asian cultures they viewed from the outside.

And it was not only the adult Polish Jews whose social worlds revolved primarily around those most like themselves. This was true even of children, who one might expect to be less aware of distinctions between people. Esther Hautzig is unusual in describing herself as becoming more like the other children while exiled in a village in the Altai region. While her father had been mobilized, and her mother was determined to leave, Esther was engaged in school and the social world of young adolescents in the village.[92] Janka Goldberger's experience was more common. In addition to the usual pressures of adolescence, she felt the added burden of coming from a different and distrusted ethnic group. Goldberger claimed to be Polish to avoid antisemitism at her school in Kazakhstan. She describes one friend, a Russian Jew, with whom she could speak openly about politics. She was most sad to leave him behind when she returned to Poland.[93]

Hanna Davidson Pankowsky's school in Toryal (Mari ASSR) was a learning experience in many ways. She was academically ahead of her class, which included local Mari children who spoke little Russian as well as evacuees from elsewhere in the Soviet Union. Everyone was hungry, but she saw that children whose parents were Party members had more to eat. Pankowsky was disappointed with the level of education, explaining in her memoir that many of the better teachers had been drafted, and was surprised at the teaching of military skills. She writes that the other children appreciated her help with schoolwork but did not befriend her. When the family relocated to the capital city of Yoshkar-Ola, she became friendly with a Jewish evacuee from Odessa. This, too, proved complicated, when the girl's family asked about Pankowsky's father's background.[94] Simon Davidson, a Bundist with roots and family in Soviet territory, made a great effort to hide both of these facts throughout his time in the USSR.[95]

Notwithstanding some social separation, few refugees write of experiencing overt antisemitism from Soviet citizens—this despite the widely recognized increase in antisemitism in the USSR during the war. Many scholars have discussed this phenomenon. Zeev Levin has chronicled the arrival of both Jews and antisemitism in areas where neither had been present before the war.[96] In trying to explain the change, Oleg Leibovich describes it as a confluence of grassroots leanings and official developments.[97]

Sheila Fitzpatrick has raised the intriguing possibility that the visible presence of Polish and other Jewish refugees in the interior—combined with the presence of Jewish evacuees—created the impression that Jews were shirking their military duties.[98]

An unusually high number of refugees interviewed by the AJC in the late 1940s refer to incidents of antisemitism. While it is certainly possible that this is related to the timing of their interviews, so close to the experience, I find it more plausible that this had to do with the direct questions of the interviewer. Rachel Erlich, who compiled the material in 1949, comes across as deeply concerned with Soviet antisemitism in her summaries of the interviews.[99] Also, the descriptions are vague rather than personal. Many of the refugees recall wounded Soviet soldiers bringing anti-Jewish sentiments with them from the front without referencing individual incidents.[100] Antisemitism existed, and was on the rise, but it was not a major concern of the Polish Jews.

While struggling to survive in Central Asia, the Polish Jewish refugees were still able to maintain some normality in their own lives. Paradoxically, the very chaos that made survival so precarious also created a temporary window of opportunity for cultural and religious practice. Given reduced authoritarian control in the region, Soviet citizens—and those passing through—had more freedom in the private realm. In the words of Barber and Harrison, "War greatly exacerbated the problems of translating Moscow's will into action at the local level."[101]

These sorts of cultural experiences often do not appear in the testimonial accounts. Once they left, the former refugees were far more likely to describe the difficulties they faced and the overall desperation they felt. And yet, there were breaks in the monotony. In her diary, Pearl Minz mentions several cultural events organized by Polish refugees in Yakutsk. An entry from August 1942 proudly states that Minz's daughter had performed at an evening celebration. The following December, Pearl recorded a melancholy get-together with fellow Poles.[102] Dr. R., formerly of Lvov, reached Tashkent in 1943. In his postwar testimony for the AJC, he recalled attending several cultural events there, including a memorial service run by Rabbi Nurok of Riga. He also noted the presence of traveling troupes of Polish Jewish entertainers included the well-known star of the Yiddish stage, Ida Kaminska.[103] In her memoir, Kaminska writes powerfully about the experience of entertaining other refugees in Central Asia: "When I appeared on stage, I witnessed a moving demonstration. Everyone stood, applauded, and wept. All of us onstage wept, too. Here stood audience and actors facing one another, homeless, persecuted, thousands of miles from our homes, where most of us had left our dearest kin."[104] These events—in Polish and Yiddish—were public and sanctioned by the authorities. Religious events were unsanctioned, but they appear far more frequently in postwar recollections. Not only for Orthodox Jews, but for many other individuals as well, such episodes were outstanding enough to warrant documentation years later.

Observant Jews who had found it impossible to honor the Sabbath in a traditional manner during their period of forced labor were often able to remedy this situation after the amnesty. A lucky few obtained positions that did not require work on Saturday. Some others managed to negotiate an accommodation with their supervisors or colleagues that allowed them to rest on the Sabbath. For most refugees, however, the only way to guarantee Sabbath observance was to work outside the official, legal structure. This meant forgoing a ration card and risking imprisonment, but it also offered flexibility.

Dina Gabel came from a pious family, in what had been the eastern Polish city of Lida. She and her sickly mother had been deported separately from her father and lost track of him. After amnesty, Gabel obtained work in an artel in Tokushi. With generous gifts of vodka, she convinced her boss to allow her to work at home on Saturdays so long as she completed her assigned norm. Gabel would stay up all night after the Sabbath and arrive at work on Sunday exhausted, but with her finished product. However, after her boss was transferred, she was unable to work out a similar deal with his replacement. Not long afterward, Gabel left her job and entered the dangerous and semilegal area of private enterprise.[105]

As they had in the labor installations, the refugees also faced the challenge of preparing for Jewish holidays. For the holiday of Sukkot, Rabbi Simcha Shafran and the other religious Jews with him in Siberia convinced an anti-Soviet peasant to let them use his shed as their temporary dwelling. Rabbi Yitzhak Meir Safronovitch's father despaired of describing horseradish to a vendor before Passover. He told the man that he did not know the Russian word, but that Jews call it *khreyn.* Happily, the word was a cognate: the man responded that he would be happy to sell him some *khren.*[106]

Well before the springtime holiday of Pesach, many families began collecting the flour needed to prepare matzah. When Chava Chaya Frenkel's family in Dzhambul heard that the government was trading flour for gold, her mother brought in all of her jewelry.[107] Finding a suitable place to pre-

FIGURE 4.2. Polish Jews in the USSR bake matzah for Passover, 1943. Yad Vashem Photo Archive.

pare and bake matzah could also prove challenging. Safronovitch's father had to assure his landlady that the Jews had been using the same method for two thousand years and it would not damage her oven.[108]

Those who observed Jewish holidays and customs were not necessarily Orthodox or regularly practicing Jews. Menachem Mendl Grossman, a former yeshiva student well known for his level of Jewish practice and knowledge, recalls being summoned to help an old army sergeant assemble a minyan, or prayer quorum, in order to say the prayer of mourning for the sergeant's mother. Grossman describes finding the sergeant, who now served as the chef in an Anders Army camp, sitting on a low bucket without his shoes on. Knowing enough about traditional Jewish practice to sit shiva and wish to say kaddish, he relied on Grossman to bring together the minyan and lead the prayer services.[109] A man who had served in the Polish Army and worked in a nonkosher kitchen could hardly have been Orthodox, but he chose to mark the life cycle ritual in a traditional manner.

Most religious practice took place within families or small groups of Polish Jews. Less frequently it involved Soviet Jews as well. Chaim Shapiro, an observant Jew who traveled often during his time in the USSR, had several occasions to share his religious knowledge. While working on a kolkhoz near Kzyl-Orda (Kaz. Kyzlorda), Shapiro met an evacuated Soviet Jew from Minsk who asked him to lead the High Holy Days services he was organizing. The Soviet Jews provided a Torah scroll and the congregation. Shapiro, a Polish rabbinical student, knew the prayers.[110] J.S., a Polish citizen who had fled Lithuania with his wife in 1941, portrayed a unified Jewish community in Ushtobe, Kazakhstan, during the war. In his interview with the AJC in 1947, he said that refugee Jews from Bessarabia, Poland, and Russia practiced their religion together with two synagogues, a ritual slaughterer, and a mohel from Kiev.[111]

Some of the former refugees suggested, in their postwar reminiscences, that their Jewish knowledge and practice proved inspiring for the Soviet Jews. "Russian Jews in Djambul [*sic*] gained confidence from the example of the Polish Jews who observed Jewish customs," according to Traitman, interviewed by the AJC after the war.[112] Demonstrating causality is not possible, but certainly the presence of observant Jews, and the lessening of antireligious strictures, made religious practice easier.

Official Contact

The breakdown of strict government oversight was not the only reason that the practice of Judaism became somewhat easier during this time. In a bid to increase enthusiasm for the Soviet war effort both at home and abroad, the Soviet state introduced some new policies. For domestic consumption, the government proactively relaxed its antireligious stance and encouraged Russian nationalism. As Shimon Redlich notes, this tactical reconciliation with the Orthodox Church meant that Jews and Muslims "were also granted certain concessions." For an international audience, the state mobilized front organizations to contact related interest groups outside the USSR and boost their support for the Soviets' existential struggle. The Jewish Anti-Fascist Committee (JAFC) was one of these organizations.[113]

Histories of Soviet Jews during the Second World War tend to feature the JAFC prominently. Although the committee began as essentially a mechanism for the delivery of propaganda, it evolved into a Jewish cultural organization and clearinghouse for war news, complete with its own press organ. *Eynikayt* (Unity), first issued in the summer of 1942, quickly sold out its initial run of ten thousand copies and proved popular abroad as well. Letters, and missing persons announcements, poured in from Soviet Jews.[114] As Arkadi Zeltser has shown, the editors of *Eynikayt* ascertained that extolling Soviet Jewish war heroes was a safe way to combat antisemitism without leading to accusations of nationalism.[115] The rise and fall of the JAFC, including the pivotal visit of its chairman Solomon Mikhoels and the Yiddish poet Itsik Fefer to the United States in 1943, are significant to the fate of Soviet Jewry during and after the war.[116]

On the whole, the JAFC appears far less in the recollections of the Polish Jews. Only a small number record seeing copies of *Eynikayt* or attending any of the featured events. Even fewer had occasion to meet any of the major players. Some Polish Yiddish writers, who had distinguished themselves for their communist credentials after the annexation, and who were fortunate enough to escape the 1941 German invasion, did contribute to *Eynikayt*. In an issue from October 1942, Ber Mark, a writer who fled from Warsaw and would later play an active role in postwar Jewish life in Poland, wrote a short article about Jewish refugees winning recognition for their superior agricultural work.[117] In November 1942 the Polish Yiddish poet Binem Heller published an angry poem about the Holocaust in Poland.[118] Most Polish Jewish refugees, however, could not even obtain copies of *Eynikayt*, let alone publish within its pages.

In Fergana, Yiddish poet Rokhl Korn submitted some poems to *Eynikayt* but only rarely got ahold of a copy. In a 1942 letter she complained of a lack of Jewish books despite the concentration of Jews.[119] Two Polish Jewish refugees, interviewed by the AJC soon after their arrival in the United States in 1947, mention thwarted desires to read the Yiddish newspaper. One found it too expensive. The other, residing in Ushtobe, said that the few Yiddish books or periodicals that reached his town were generally sold as paper to wrap fish or roll cigarettes before he could obtain them.[120] Had they been able to acquire *Eynikayt*, they may well have not been able to recognize themselves within it.

In keeping with its mission, the newspaper was primarily devoted to coverage of the war: reports on its progress, articles about heroic battles and partisan resistance, poetry, evocative essays, and patriotic exhortations. A smaller portion of the newspaper dealt with the home front, including the experience of evacuation. With millions of Soviet citizens displaced from their homes, the Polish refugees were a minor concern and appeared rarely. When they did appear, as in Mark's article, they frequently did so in patriotic and positive guise.

One important area of overlap between Polish Jewish and Soviet Jewish narratives of the war is the tragic case of Wiktor Alter and Henryk Erlich, the prewar leaders of the socialist Jewish Labor Bund. In 1939 Alter and Erlich fled east and were arrested almost immediately. They spent two years in Soviet prisons and were released after the 1941 invasion. Jumping into the war effort, they met with Polish, Soviet, and other officials. The prison experience appears not to have diminished their willingness to work with and for the Soviets, nor, unfortunately, to have enhanced their understanding of how to do so safely. In December 1941 Alter and Erlich were arrested again. Pleas for their release came from Soviet allies abroad, the Polish government-in-exile, and even prominent voices among Polish communists in the USSR. Yet not long after the victory at Stalingrad, word reached the West that they had been executed.[121]

The cause, and the demise, of these two prominent Polish Jewish leaders attracted great attention at the time, both in and outside the USSR. It has remained a source of fascination and is one of the few topics relating to the Polish Jews in the Soviet Union that has received significant scholarly attention. Several Polish Jews who spent time in Soviet prisons mention crossing paths with one or the other of them in their testimonies, which probably has as much to do with postwar questions about their fate as with their renown at the time. Erlich and Alter were victims of the Soviet regime, yet also retained their belief in its power to do good. At the time of their second arrest, they were negotiating both with the Poles about creating a Jewish army division and with the Soviets about forming what would become the JAFC.[122]

Most Polish Jews had fewer opportunities to interact with the Soviet state. On the whole, after their amnesty, they avoided Soviet officialdom. At certain junctures, however, this was not possible. Obtaining work, housing, and ration cards meant registering with the local authorities. Olga Medvedeva-Nathoo's portrayal of one refugee woman's struggles in the Kirghiz SSR provides a penetrating analysis of the mutual misunderstandings between a single Polish Jew and the Soviet authorities with whom she interacted. While her diary reports official obstacles, insensitivity, and graft as she worked tirelessly to keep her baby alive, Soviet bureaucrats saw her as lacking initiative.[123]

Unwanted official contact came when the NKVD approached Polish Jews to serve as informers within their communities and when Polish Jews were targeted for forced or coerced Soviet citizenship and mobilization in the Red Army. For the newly appointed Polish ambassador, Stanisław Kot, the Soviet policy of forcing amnestied Belorussians, Jews, and Ukrainians from Poland to serve in labor battalions of the Red Army beginning in November 1941 was a major breach of the letter and spirit of the Sikorski-Maisky Pact and a threat to Poland's future. Kot immediately lodged complaints about individual Polish Jews forced to serve in the Red Army, as well as about the policy as a whole.[124] He continued to spar over these issues with his Soviet counterpart, Andrey Vyshinsky, at the People's Commissariat of Foreign Affairs, throughout his brief tenure in the USSR. In July 1942 the Polish embassy in Kuibyshev (Rus. Samara) sent a reply to one Simcha Sztern regarding their efforts to have him released from a labor brigade.[125]

Such high-level diplomatic dealings, however, remained opaque to the Polish Jewish refugees. When faced with mobilization to the Soviet forces, most did not know either their rights or the political struggle being waged on their behalf. They knew only the terror of service in labor battalions. The *trudovaiia armiia* (labor army) allowed the Red Army—stretched thin and in great need of recruits and manpower—to benefit from the work of less reliable elements of the population. Prisoners, or members of suspect ethnic or national groups, were forced to endure brutal labor behind the lines to aid the military.[126] Polish Belorussians, Ukrainians, and especially Jews, as the largest minority group among the deportees and evacuees, were often assigned to these hated units.

It would appear that Jack Pomerantz accepted Soviet citizenship in 1940, as he was not deported with other refugees from western Poland. On June 22, 1941, he was on a train headed south, on his way to invite some of his siblings—who had also fled their home in Radzyń—to attend his wedding to a young woman he had met in Brest. Separated from both his fiancée and his siblings by the new invasion, Pomerantz escaped eastward once again. He had difficulty finding and keeping work and moved around Kazakhstan numerous times. Finally, he was picked up and sent to Irkutsk to join a division of the labor army. Pomerantz writes that he and the other recruits lost their strength and health, with impossible quotas and insufficient food. Eventually he ran away, so as not to die of disease and starvation.[127]

Marian Feldman claims that the Soviets would not let him join Anders Army, but took note of his name to find him later. Like Pomerantz he was a refugee, but not a deportee, and thus likely accepted Soviet citizenship in 1940. In the spring of 1943, he was mobilized into a labor brigade, where he found the conditions terrible. Feldman writes that he was turned away from Berling's Army in May 1943, along with other Jews, but finally allowed to join in the winter of 1944. Although his level of education allowed him to rise in the ranks and fulfill important tasks, Feldman felt that his status as a Jew held him back from promotion.[128]

The passportization drive in 1943 also pitted Poles against the Soviet state. Interestingly, though, it receives less attention than either the labor army or the first passportization drive in 1940 in the memoirs and testimonies. This may be partly because its consequences carried less weight, and partly because the dispersion of the refugee population made it more difficult to reach them all. As Albert Kaganovitch has shown, this directive was interpreted and enforced in different ways across the vast areas where Polish citizens resided.[129]

That said, however, the NKVD passportization drive did make it all the way to the Polish refugee community in Yakutsk in March 1943. In her diary, Pearl Minz recorded that her son Bunek, along with a few Zionists, were jailed for refusing Soviet passports. Her husband was working outside the town, but she and her daughter Nuska became Soviet citizens. In April, after Bunek had been released, she began to worry about whether she and Nuska would be allowed to return to Poland after the war. She also complained that taking Soviet passports had brought them no new rights and only more surveillance.[130] Sara Bergman (née Barasz), in Syktyvkar in 1942, was also afraid that taking the proffered passport would affect her postwar status. She went to jail briefly, but Shalom Bergman—the man who would become her husband—persuaded her that survival was more important than symbolism.[131]

Individuals who took a stand on these issues, like Bunek and Barasz, were the exception rather than the rule. Aleksander Wat, a writer of Jewish origins and fellow traveler of the Soviet Union before the war, saw a different side of Soviet communism following his arrest in Lvov in January 1940. After amnesty, and reunion with his wife and son, Wat settled in Ili, Kazakhstan, as the Polish delegate. According to his wife Polina's addendum to his memoir, he led the local Poles, the majority of whom were devout Jews, in a campaign to refuse Soviet citizenship. Arrested and subjected to NKVD intimidation techniques, most of them, including Polina, gave in. Wat, however, was steadfast in his refusal.[132] Marci Shore calls this Wat's greatest moment of clarity and leadership, in a life otherwise characterized by ideological ambivalence.[133]

In a diplomatic post sent from Moscow to London in March 1943, Kot's replacement, Polish ambassador Tadeusz Romer, reported that Emil Sommerstein, formerly in the Sejm and now very ill, had been sentenced to a five-year prison term for his rejection of Soviet citizenship. He assured his colleagues that the embassy had intervened in support of Sommerstein and asked them to inform the Jewish press in the United Kingdom and the United States about his state, as well as their efforts.[134] Sommerstein had served in the Polish parliament from 1922 to 1927, and again from 1929 to 1939. He was a well-known Zionist and Jewish leader in interwar Poland, which helps to explain his treatment in the USSR and the attention given to his case abroad.[135]

Not everyone tried to avoid Soviet officialdom and military service. Some Polish Jews volunteered to serve in the Red Army, especially after the break between the Poles and the Soviets in 1943 and the formation of a Polish division within the Red Army. As Klemens Nussbaum has pointed out, the Soviet government's decision to establish the Kosciuszko Division was chiefly a political move. After their victory at Stalingrad and the evacuation of Anders Army, it was time to plan for the liberation of Poland. Yet for many of the refugees, the opportunity to fight back against the Nazis trumped ideological concerns. Jewish communists were heavily represented among the political commissars, but Jews also served as officers, medical staff, and enlisted men and women.[136]

Like many other Polish Jews, Hersz Bimko joined Berling's Army only after being turned away from Anders Army, although he adds that the food and uniforms were also better.[137] Jack Pomerantz—who had run away from a labor unit—later joined Berling's Army and became a driver. He and his unit fought all the way to Berlin.[138] In a letter to the JAFC, the young Polish Jewish refugee and later eminent professor of Yiddish literature, Chone Shmeruk, lamented his fate in a labor battalion and barred entry into Berling's Army: "From the time that I learned about the fall of the Warsaw ghetto and the heroic fight of its inmates, I have not been able to remain calm until I obtain the opportunity to personally participate in the liberation of all people from Hitler's yoke."[139] Shmeruk advocated creating a Jewish division in the Red Army.

The idea of a separate Jewish unit surfaced a number of different times in relation to various Allied armies.[140] Erlich and Alter had been pursuing this at the time of their second arrest. Polish Jews who had experienced antisemitism in recruitment or acceptance into military units saw this as a potential solution. While antisemitism was a major issue in Anders Army, it occurred in the Red Army as well. M.K., a refugee from Warsaw interviewed by the AJC after the war, was drafted into a labor brigade. He volunteered to go to the front, where he heard complaints from his fellow soldiers that Jews were avoiding their military duty. Later he served as a bodyguard for a high-ranking commissar, who admitted to him that he had taken a non-Jewish surname to hide his origins. After he heard about the formation of Berling's Army, M.K. signed up under a Polish name. In the ranks he met many other Jews who had masked their identities in order to be accepted.[141]

The Kosciuszko Division of the Red Army, under General Berling, had to gain legitimacy as a Polish force. Thus, although the troops were subject to communist propaganda, they also celebrated Catholic holidays. In this case, taking Polish names was not so much due to active antisemitism as to a more passive belief that Jews could not be real Poles.[142] When I. Lieberman joined in 1944, the district commander told him to take a Polish name, although Lieberman demurs that with his physical appearance, no one would have taken him for an ethnic Pole.[143]

Ruzena Berler was one of the few female Polish Jews to sign on, although she served in the Czech, rather than the Polish, division of the Red Army. A doctor and the wife of a Zionist activist, Berler had been deported to northern Kazakhstan along with her baby and the wives and children of imprisoned Polish officers in April 1940. After the amnesty, when other women's husbands came to pick them up, she realized that her husband had most likely died and that she was on her own. When a Czech colleague invited her to join him in the new military unit in formation, she accepted. Between her medical credentials and taking his Czech name, she was able to use the westward momentum of the unit to make her way out of the Soviet Union.[144]

While some Polish Jews demonstrated their heroism and patriotism through military service, and others through holding on to their Polish citizenship and identity, many include a scene of refusing to bow to official Soviet pressure to supply information to the NKVD as an important moment in their stories. A few also recall the terrible emotional and legal consequences of betrayal by those they believed were their friends. Yet almost none want to admit to caving in to the threats or blandishments of the state and exposing their fellows. Bernard Ginsburg is unusual in confessing in his memoir to have even spoken to the NKVD. Yet he assures his readers that, despite being entrapped and interrogated, he not only refused to inform on a family that helped him earlier but even managed to let them know that they were under observation.[145]

Like other totalitarian states, the Soviet Union developed a sophisticated system of internal surveillance that relied from the start on the cooperation, or co-optation, of a portion of the population. Although the Polish citizens had been subject to NKVD supervision since their arrival in Soviet territory and throughout their period in labor installations, they became more aware of it during this period of their wartime experiences.

Many describe interactions with the NKVD as passing, albeit intensely uncomfortable, encounters. Esther Hautzig writes that her father refused to spy on other Polish refugees for the NKVD.[146] S.L., a refugee from Warsaw interviewed by the AJC in 1948, recalls that the NKVD official on his kolkhoz summoned him to point out the individual(s) negatively influencing the attitude, and thus the productivity, of the refugees. Offered a kerosene stove and chair as incentives, S.L. proclaimed that he was unaware of any such problem. Despite the officer's threats, the incident passed without further repercussions.[147]

Other refugees mention longer-term consequences. Sarah K., interviewed in Israel well after the war, was working at a hospital in northern Kazakhstan in 1942 when the NKVD approached her about becoming an informant. She refused and agreed to sign a document to that effect. This document was then used to have her fired from her job. Subsequently, she could not obtain other work. In 1946, when other Polish citizens were allowed to return to Poland, Sarah K. was arrested. During her interrogation, the officer opened her file to reveal not only her earlier refusal to cooperate but also statements about her alleged anti-Soviet statements—contributed by others who had informed on her.[148]

Like Sarah K., many of the refugees contrast their own unwillingness to cooperate with the less praiseworthy decisions taken by others in their midst. Betty Rich, not yet twenty years old, was called by the local NKVD to report on black market activity in her community in Staliniri. According to her memoir, she knew that she could never work as an informer but was unsure how to extricate herself from the situation. Eventually, she explains, she was able to call upon the officer's humanity to safely decline. Later, when some friends were arrested, the chief of police interrogated Rich for information about their illegal activities. In her account, she convinced him to "lose" their files, but she was distraught to discover that one member of their own small community of Polish Jewish refugees had denounced the others. To explain her good fortune, Rich notes that the Georgians felt put upon by the system and were willing to cross Soviet authority at times.[149]

After his release from a prison camp, Shaul Shternfeld stayed in the Ural region. He found work in a hospital and made friends with other young refugees, as well as with Soviet citizens, both Jewish and non-Jewish. Shternfeld writes that they knew little about Zionism or religion and this led to interesting conversations. One day his friend Vovka admitted that the NKVD was pressuring him for information about Shternfeld's anti-Soviet rhetoric. Soon afterward, Shternfeld was arrested and accused of counterrevolutionary activities. After some deliberation, according to Shternfeld, he decided to confess to Zionist recruitment, but refused to denounce two of his friends. At his trial in November 1943, he was shocked and saddened to see his old friend Frizer on the stand, apologizing for his own Zionist errors and blaming Shternfeld as the ringleader. Fortunately, the defense was able to call upon Shternfeld's youth and tractability. While Frizer received a ten-year sentence, Shternfeld was only sentenced to five years.[150]

By 1947, with the war well over and news of a new communist government in Poland, Shternfeld requested permission for repatriation. In a subsequent interrogation he was asked to denounce his fellow prisoner, an ethnic Pole by the name of Buklad with whom he was friendly. Despite being told that Buklad was antisemitic and had already denounced him, Shternfeld asserts that he refused to give in to their demands. In 1948 he, Buklad, and other Polish citizens in their prison camp were allowed to return to Poland.[151]

Ann Szedlecki's autobiography also denies personal culpability while admitting that members of her community did cross ethical lines. Szedlecki maintains that she refused to lie when interviewed by the NKVD soon after her brother Shoel's arrest. After his release two years later, starving and sickly, Shoel told her that he believed another Polish Jew in their group of volunteers had denounced him. Despite his sister's care, Shoel died within six months. Szedlecki later wrote, "He was only twenty-three years old, a victim of both the Nazis and the Soviet regime, thanks to a fellow member of our own tribe."[152]

Katherine Jolluck's reading of testimonies from Polish Catholic women yields a slightly different dynamic. According to Jolluck, Polish women were equally staunch in professing their own virtue, but more likely to place the blame on others outside their group. Whereas traitorous Poles were not mentioned or were viewed as exceptional, Jews were frequently viewed as collectively untrustworthy.[153] Edward Jesko demonstrates this sort of thinking in his postwar memoir, when he writes how shocked he and his mother were to see Jews on their deportation train. Having seen the NKVD successfully recruit so many local Jews, they had assumed that all Polish Jews had become informants and would therefore not face deportation themselves.[154]

However they apportion blame, all of the Poles in the Soviet Union proclaim their own and their families' innocence, even though it stands to reason that some must have turned on their fellows. Garri Urban offers a particularly dramatic case of the difficulties inherent in untangling complicity. When offered a job as an informer, Urban—despite already being in trouble with the security services—claims in his memoir to have forcefully refused:

> You know what. I'll leave the thinking to you; you are specialists in destroying people, and turning them into what you want them to be, but you won't succeed with me. You are taking the law into your own hands. I have nothing to fear. I will not agree to any of your dirty propositions.[155]

A decade after publishing his memoir, Urban returned to the former Soviet Union with his son Stuart, a filmmaker. After several trips and talks with numerous officials, they managed to procure at least part of Garri Urban's secret file.

In a 2008 film completed after his father's death, Stuart Urban explores not only the older Urban's sensational adventures but also the possibility of his having collaborated in the wartime Soviet Union. The film is a love letter to a larger-than-life father. For the younger Urban, the evidence of possible collusion is just further proof of his father's mythic status. After his father's death, Stuart went looking for the secret file in his father's papers. He discovered that most of it had been destroyed. What remained, as translated by Stuart's mother, suggested that Garri Urban was both already married and a spy at the time the file had been written. Stuart discusses this possibility with fascination in a conversation with scholar Anne Applebaum, but ultimately there is not enough information to know for sure whether or not Garri was an informer.[156] Like Urban, none of the other former refugees admits to having benefited from denouncing others, although many refer to the phenomenon. In his interview, Jacob Halpern made light of the ubiquity of informers, noting that the individual charged with reporting on his father's clandestine synagogue in Bukhara was at least a generous benefactor when it came time for fund-raising.[157]

Generally speaking, in these enforced interactions with the Soviet state, the refugees were not treated worse than ordinary Soviet citizens. At times their particular civil status meant that they were handled differently. Additionally, they were significantly less prepared for encounters with the NKVD than those who had lived longer in the USSR. Yet, overall, the former Polish citizens faced the same bureaucratic hurdles and day-to-day challenges as the local and evacuated peoples among whom they lived.

The Spectrum of Sexual Interactions

During their time in exile, some of the Polish Jewish refugees were victims of sexual assault or rape. The low social status of the displaced refugees, their lack of familiarity with cultural norms, and the asymmetrical power dynamics in labor camps, places of employment, and the Soviet bureaucracy all contributed to their potential exploitation. As with survivors of the Holocaust, however, these painful and shameful episodes more often appear in the testimonial literature as having happened to unnamed compatriots. As Zoë Waxman notes in her discussion of this reluctance to expose sexual humiliation, "Part of the process of writing a testimony may be to record a story of survival in a way that helps the survivor to carry on with his or her own life within a culture in which gender norms are strong."[158] In Jolluck's study of Polish women in the USSR, fear of rape is ubiquitous, but no one admits to having been a victim of it.[159]

As Joan Ringelheim has noted with regard to oral testimonies by Holocaust survivors, interviewers are often untrained and unprepared to respond to these sorts of revelations when they do occur.[160] For example, hints of the interviewer's discomfort appear in a summary of S. Rotstein's 1947 testimony to the AJC (the original transcript has not been preserved). Of Rotstein's suffering after evacuation, the interviewer wrote, "S.R. also suffered in the kolchoz because she was young and attractive, but she does not want to talk about this in greater detail." Later the interviewer describes Rotstein's experiences after her mother died and she began to work for the railroad: "Again she had trouble because of her age and beauty. She requests not to be asked about it.[161] We will never know exactly what Rotstein endured, nor how and why she raised the topic in her interview, yet the sense of unease in the communication is palpable across the decades. Nevertheless, a few Jewish women do record such incidents.

Ann Szedlecki was only fourteen when she fled Łódź with her older brother Shoel in November 1939. After a month in Bialystok, they volunteered for labor in the interior and were sent to Leninogorsk (Kaz. Ridder). In June 1940 Shoel was arrested. Although he was later released, he died soon afterward, and Ann spent the war years mainly on her own. Her memoir includes her struggles, her successes, and her numerous experiences of exploitation by others. On the train to Kazakhstan in January 1940 she was sexually molested by an adult Polish Jew in their cohort. Later that year, soon after her brother's arrest, a Soviet soldier began to court her; she eventually realized that he was not interested in her, but in gathering incriminating information about her brother. And finally, Szedlecki mentions averting an attempted rape while she was preparing to leave the USSR.[162] Hanna Davidson Pankowsky also references a close call with drunken soldiers after the war ended.[163]

Indeed, incidents of evading assault appear more frequently in the testimonial literature than do incidents of actual assault. After her brother died, Helen Zuberman's mother sent her to register for a ration book. The man at the office was drunk, according to Zuberman, and wanted sexual favors in return for the coveted item. She refused and ran out of the office, but was too ashamed to tell her mother, who soon sent her back. Fortunately, by the time she returned, the man had been drafted and a woman installed in his place.[164] Rachela Wygodzki refers to averted rapes on her kolkhoz in Kazakhstan.[165] Suzanna Eibuszyc relates that her mother had to give up a paying job when her Uzbek boss repeatedly tried to get her alone.[166]

Notably, many of these cases also have a transactional quality. In the scenario described by Zuberman, for example, it does not appear that the Soviet official attacked her. Rather, he offered her an exchange. In her work on Holocaust victims, Anna Hájková draws on the concept of sexual barter. While not denying the pernicious presence of unequal power dynamics and sexual violence, it seeks to also recognize the agency that is sometimes available to even those without power.[167] This is a gendered phenomenon, but not one limited to either sex. Men and women often played different roles, and often report those roles in very different language.

As with sexual assault, most accounts of sexual barter focus on deflection, or they involve unnamed actors. Moshe Grossman writes with pathos of the Polish Jewish women who had to engage in prostitution in the teahouses in Samarkand in order to feed themselves: "They did not need to bargain or talk much. People knew the price already. Only one of the big rolls."[168] In some cases, sexual barter appears in the narratives as a repugnant convention practiced by some other group. Like many Polish Jews, Yitzhak Erlichson was horrified to see women laboring alongside men in the Soviet Union. How, he wondered, did women have the stamina for such work? He found his answer in the example of his neighbor, who, he writes, was able to eat well by selling both sexual favors and stolen items.[169] Similarly, Szlomo Zdrojowicz contrasts the difficulties he and his wife faced in their forest settlement near Novosibirsk with the life of plenty among the women who formed relationships with the NKVD officers.[170] Pearl Minz, the lay midwife in her Siberian settlement, complained more than once in her diary about delivering babies without fathers and about the promiscuous Russian women.[171]

One testimony describes an instance of sexual barter involving the witness's sister, although the story is fairly vague. After the tragic deaths of her parents and baby sister to disease and hunger, Irene Rogers, still a child at the time, was alone with her older sister in Andizhan. Her sister supported them by working on the black market and was arrested one day. According to Rogers's oral testimony for the Shoah Foundation, her sister was hysterical about leaving Irene at home alone and had to "kiss" the NKVD agent in charge to secure her release.[172] More common are stories like that of Jane Lipski recorded in a book of women's testimonies. After her release from prison, Lipski worked as a seamstress in the Komi ASSR. At one point she was offered a more lucrative position but had to pass it up because she was unwilling to barter sex in return.[173]

Examples of men in similar circumstances are less common, due both to gender norms and also the preponderance of men in positions of power. Undoubtedly, men were also less likely to admit to such relationships. One exception is Jack Pomerantz. He and his older brother traversed much of the Soviet Union in the course of the war. At one point, while living with other Polish Jewish refugees in the town of Berezovka (Altai Krai), he was dispatched to get a doctor from the neighboring town. The doctor invited him to spend the night and initiated a sexual relationship. Soon she was supplying him with extra food and medical releases from work. Pomerantz's brother, as well as the other refugees, came to rely on this bounty and encouraged him to stay with her. Pomerantz describes enjoying the attention but feeling trapped in the relationship. Eventually he and his brother left the area.[174]

Pomerantz is unusual in painting himself as the more submissive partner. More prevalent are the stories of men who engage in relationships of exchange without framing them as such. Perhaps the most vivid example is Garri Urban's memoir, which is full of fairly graphic sex scenes with numerous partners. Urban's sexual prowess is part of the character he creates, and he presents these encounters as evidence of his youth, desirability, and virility. Yet his memoir also seems to display an unacknowledged awareness that at least some of the sexual transactions were to his material benefit. As a doctor, he had a fairly privileged position in the labor camp, but not enough to allow him to escape. "After I had been out with the working parties a few times, I realized I had no chance unless I could get help from someone else." In his retelling, he noted his superior's extra uniforms and willing wife almost immediately. He soon made a plan: "Would Volkovitch's wife be willing to help me? Our relationship had by now developed into a very close one, and I felt she would."[175]

After his escape from the camp, Urban—without papers and wearing a uniform that was not his own—made his way to Leningrad (Rus. St. Petersburg) and propositioned an attractive woman in a public place. She took him home, where he stayed for several weeks. In his version of events, that period was filled with wild sex, but it is also clear that she was both hiding and aiding him. At one point he even reflects on this, albeit in a typically unreflective way: "Well, we made love yet again. Every corner of that room had been used for some act of love. I never asked where she got the passport from or what price she paid for it. My situation forced me to accept something which was against my nature—help from a woman."[176] Whether or not the account is completely true, Urban's entire story revolves around his acceptance of help from women. Yet in his own retelling, he was rendering benefits to them.

The transactional situations described thus far were short-term ones and offered tangible advantages to each party. Examining the range of sexual relations in exile requires looking at various types of marriage as well. Arguably, all marriage has a transactional aspect, with the woman's sexual fidelity matched by the man's guarantee of support, but sometimes this is more explicit than others. Additionally, the perspective of the witness greatly affects how different marriages are viewed. Suzanna Eibuszyc's mother, Roma, condemned the tragedy of a Jewish evacuee girl married off to an older Uzbek man in exchange for food for the family. However, Roma also second-guessed her own rejection of a suitor who could have provided support for her family during the war.[177] In his semiautobiographical novel, Herman Taube writes movingly of a young refugee woman, Eva, who realized that Taube was a friend but not a lover. Instead she married the Ukrainian admirer who took such good care of her and her mother.[178] Taube frames her choice as a sign of the difficult decisions people had to make. The reader does not hear from Eva and does not even know if she existed.

A number of the refugees mention contracting fictional marriages of various durations and for a variety of purposes. L. Witkowska, interviewed by the American Jewish Committee after she arrived in the United States in 1948, explained that by the time she was deported from Brest in 1940, word had already spread that those in family units fared better than single people. She and others quickly formed new "families" and avoided being sent to the worst camps. The summary of her interview makes no further mention of her simulated family.[179] After her son was rejected from Anders Army as a Jew, Roza Buchman found a lieutenant she knew who was willing to list her as his wife and her two children as his.[180] With his help, the family was allowed to evacuate from the Soviet Union to Iran and then Palestine. As her testimony was taken in 1943, there is no information about whether Buchman's husband, who had stayed in Radom, survived, nor whether she had further dealings with the Polish officer. Helena Starkiewicz actually married a Polish soldier in order to escape the USSR, but they missed the last transport to Iran. Their fictional marriage developed into an actual marriage and the couple stayed together.[181]

It is difficult to ascertain the level of commitment and intimacy in many of these marriages. Ruzena Berler, a doctor married to a Zionist activist who had been deported separately, was alone in the USSR with her young daughter. Needing a doctor elsewhere, the NKVD transported her from one special settlement to another without any explanation. Several days later, a Czech Komsomol member finally arrived, answered her questions, and helped set her up in the clinic. Later he heard about a Czech army organizing and invited her to join him in volunteering. He even told his colonel that he had a wife and child in Kazakhstan whom he wanted to bring along. According to her testimony, Berler only agreed after she had reason to believe that her husband had died. She adds that upon reaching the army, she and her daughter took his Czech name. Her testimony does not mention this helpful man again. As her unit moved through Chernovits (Ukr. Chernivtsi), Berler met the man who would become her second husband in 1947.[182] Her testimony does not address the nature of her relationship with the man who facilitated her exit from the USSR.

Marriages, or relationships, of convenience also appear in some of the accounts. After their amnesty, Yitzhak Erlichson traveled with a friend, Schultz, from the far reaches of Siberia to a more centrally located kolkhoz. There, the refugees suffered from hunger and cold until Schultz devised a solution for himself:

> He found himself a farm woman whose husband had been called up and he moved in with her into her hut. The woman had two children, and she could not manage with her work on the farm. In addition, she was impressed by the looks of this Polish refugee with his big-city ways, compared to her husband, a village peasant. She soon outfitted him in her husband's underwear and clothes, and cooked him tasty meals. In a word, Schultz had fallen into a honey-pot, and he advised me to do the same. When it came to women there was no shortage, for almost all of the huts had lost their men.[183]

Erlichson's retelling is fairly neutral, although the transactional nature of the relationship is clear. Pearl Minz's testimony, however, is one of several that refer disdainfully to the promiscuous and disloyal Soviet women who cheated on their husbands at the front.[184]

Włodzimierz Szer's account reflects the ambiguity inherent to such arrangements. Szer and his father had fled Warsaw together, at his mother's insistence. They survived hard labor and moved to a town on the Volga, where Włodzimierz continued his high school education. Due to lack of work, however, his father and a group of other Polish Jewish refugees relocated to a kolkhoz in the area. On a winter visit to the communal farm, Szer discovered that his father was living with one of the refugee women, who had left her own husband. Although he could understand that her marriage had been unhappy, and that both were lonely, "I kept thinking about Mom and could not accept this arrangement." Szer temporarily cut off relations with his father, but soon reconciled himself to the situation.[185]

In 1944 Szer's father was arrested. Although contact became more difficult in the years that followed, Szer continued to write to his father and attempted to intervene on his behalf, even after his own repatriation to Poland. Finally, in 1955, Szer received word that his father was alive and had settled in a Siberian exile village after his release from prison in 1949. Szer's father had formed a relationship with a local widow, and they had a child together. "I didn't believe I would ever get out of here," the elder Szer explained.[186] Within nine months, Szer's father joined him in Warsaw. From there he traveled to Israel and then the United States. He left behind his partner and younger son, although he continued to send them money.

Although atypical, the case of Szer's father illustrates the complexities of relationships in a time of war and dislocation. The two intimate relationships that he formed in the Soviet Union appear to have been more about convenience than romance, or even compatibility. According to Szer, his father did not fit in in the Siberian town to which he had been exiled: "Dad was very popular and well liked. Despite that, he wasn't one of them."[187] And when the opportunity arose, he elected to leave them. Discussing intermarriage more generally, one displaced person interviewed in 1948 claimed that mixed marriages were mainly between Jewish men and non-Jewish women. Some, he says, managed to repatriate along with their wives. Others left them behind when they returned to Poland.[188]

While marriages between Jews and Christians were somewhat anomalous, other marriages also involved partners who would have been unlikely to unite in more normal circumstances. In a 1947 interview with the AJC, S. Rotstein, a Soviet Jew, states that she married a Polish Jewish refugee twelve years her senior only because she needed to care for her brother, who, released from the Red Army, was missing his feet. At the time of the interview, she was miserable with her husband.[189] Joseph Berger's memoir, which chronicles his experiences as the child of flight survivors, gives the impression that his parents married and stayed together primarily out of necessity. They were from different parts of Poland, with different backgrounds and temperaments.[190]

Bronia Zisfain was deported with her sister to a special settlement where men and women worked together. When she was injured, one man helped her, and even shared his food with her. In her concise account, he soon decided that they should be together. They had a small wedding, complete with a rabbi, who wrote out the traditional *ketubah* (wedding contract).[191] From her retelling, it is hard to ascertain whether they fell in love, came to rely on each other's help and support, or some combination of the two. Zisfain adds that as of the time of the recording, they had been together for fifty-four years. All of these relationships, from the coercive and exploitative, to the calculated and commercial, to the spontaneous and the voluntary, help us to understand the gendered aspects and opportunities of refugee life.

Polish and Jewish Relations

Relations between Jewish and non-Jewish Poles exiled in the USSR were constantly in flux, conditioned by prewar history and memory, as well as by the experiences of war, sovietization, and deportation. As the war progressed, dramatic changes in the diplomatic positions of the Polish government-in-exile and the Soviet Union complicated their negotiations and influenced how both governments viewed the Polish Jewish population. This section examines the exiled Polish Jews' perspectives on their interactions with non-Jewish Poles in the USSR, contextualized by developments in the Soviet Union and abroad.

As the interwar Polish state gradually shifted toward an exclusive form of ethno-nationalism, Jews found themselves increasingly outside the body politic.[192] In what has been viewed as both a cause and an effect, some Jews moved farther to the left during this period, leading to a popular association between Jews and communism. This association, the so-called *żydokomuna,* encouraged some Polish non-Jews to see only Jews as having welcomed the Soviet invasion in 1939. Soviet policies in the annexed territories further exacerbated these tensions. However, the experience of deportation often led to improved relations between groups of Polish citizens.

Most of the Polish Jewish refugees and deportees report positive interactions with other Polish citizens during their period of enforced labor. Torn from their homes and families, they faced the harsh conditions together and often helped one another. This collaboration was important for both Jews and non-Jews, given that one or the other was always a clear minority in any given deportation group. Olga Kochanska was among the only non-Jews deported to a special settlement in northern Kazakhstan, as she explained to a writer upon her arrival in the United States in 1941. She speaks of warm relations on the deportation train, where, "under the pressure of misery shared together, the formality of Polish bourgeois conventions broke down." This warmth continued through bittersweet goodbyes when her American passport finally arrived.[193] In Dora Werker's camp past Irkutsk, the 450 deportees included only fifteen Jewish families. Werker writes that the antisemitic Soviet commandant would not allow Jews to leave the camp to go to the nearest market town, but Poles in their barracks bought and sold on their behalf.[194]

While amnesty certainly led to new social and residential patterns, other circumstances also impacted interactions between the two groups. The amnesty agreements between the Polish government-in-exile and the Soviet Union included provisions for the establishment of a Polish army and the appointment of Polish delegates to track Polish citizens and provide them with aid.[195] These provisions provoked ongoing conflict between Polish and Soviet representatives and affected relations between Polish Jews and non-Jews.

Polish authorities in London and the USSR understood the purpose and potential of the emergent Polish military in fundamentally different ways from Polish Jews in exile. The Jews saw themselves as full-fledged Polish citizens with every right to join the army and evacuate from the Soviet Union. Some imagined the army chiefly as a convenient way to escape the terrible conditions. Others were eager to join the fight against Nazism. The Polish government and its representatives, however, prioritized forging an effective fighting force and aiding as many Poles as possible. Both of these goals—from their point of view—mitigated against accepting Jews into the armed services. While they decried Soviet efforts to appropriate Polish Jews when these efforts might have deleterious long-term effects on Poland, as in the case of the passportization drive, their primary loyalty was to ethnic Poles.

That Jews remained peripheral to the purview of the state is evident in correspondence at all levels of the government, but particularly pernicious with regard to the armed forces. The stereotype that Jews made poor soldiers was widespread enough that Joseph Stalin was able to entrap General Władysław Anders, the commander of the Polish forces, into saying so at a state dinner in late 1941, according to Polish ambassador Stanisław Kot. Kot understood that this admission had been cleverly managed to delegitimize Polish complaints about Soviet treatment of Polish Jews. Anders was understandably concerned about the hundreds of missing officers but also believed there were too many Jews joining the army. He and others assumed this was a result of the Soviets preferentially releasing Jews, whereas in fact it had more to do with Jews being overrepresented among the deportees and self-evacuees.[196]

Anders responded by limiting Jewish recruitment and dismissing some of the Jewish soldiers already accepted. However, Ambassador Kot and other representatives of the Polish government-in-exile tried to curtail his efforts. They were concerned about international opinion as complaints mounted from Jews abroad. They also worried about the future of the Polish state, given Soviet claims on Polish territory and citizens. This concern swelled after the Soviets began changing their definitions of Polish citizenship and forcing many nonethnic Poles to take Soviet passports and enter the Red Army. As a result, in November 1941 General Anders issued an order promising that all Polish citizens would be treated equally in the armed forces. However, both his own actions and his issuance of a contradictory private order several weeks later seriously undercut the gravity of the statement.[197]

A number of scholars have sought to untangle these threads. Drawing extensively on the Polish government-in-exile's files, as well as previous scholarship, David Engel clearly shows how Soviet manipulation and Polish antisemitism combined to severely limit Jewish recruitment into the Polish forces and evacuation from the Soviet Union.[198] He also demonstrates that, despite complicated ongoing negotiations over Polish citizenship, and questionable behavior on both sides, "it was the Poles, not the Soviets, who emerged from the evacuation controversy as the villains in Jewish eyes."[199]

Polish Jewish volunteers for Anders Army faced painful obstacles, which they nearly always understood to be the result of Polish discrimination. According to their testimonies and autobiographies, most of the Jews who presented themselves at the recruiting stations for Anders Army were turned away. Those few who were accepted soon encountered difficulties. As Yehoshua Gilboa explains, the reason was all too evident: "They sent me to a medical board in an army camp. Standing before it, I sensed my difficulty at once. The Polish officers and physicians only looked at the lower part of the body in order to determine a volunteer's fitness for service."[200] Michael Sherwood describes trying to cover his circumcision while bathing at the Polish Army camp in Jalal-Abad (Kirghiz SSR). Nonetheless, he soon faced insults and had difficulty obtaining food. Sherwood writes that when the rest of the unit evacuated, the three Jews were left behind.[201]

I. Lib (Lieberman), interviewed by the AJC after the war, was initially pleased by the conditions at the Polish Army camp in Guzar (Uzb. Guzor). Soon afterward, however, he describes a "pogrom" wherein Polish soldiers attacked the Jews in their ranks and stole their new English blankets and uniforms. He and his friends left for their own safety.[202] In a testimony recorded for the Jewish Historical Institute in Warsaw in 1965, Abraham

Frydman does not mention any difficulty joining Anders Army. But when the Polish forces were divided into train wagons for evacuation, the wagons holding the Jewish soldiers were left behind at the station.[203]

As word of these problems spread, Polish Jews came to expect such treatment. David Azrieli explains that he was surprised to be accepted into the army. He had presented himself mainly to get documentation of his rejection, which he thought might prove useful later. However, Azrieli was in relatively good physical shape: he had accepted Soviet citizenship in 1940, and therefore avoided the trials of forced labor. In fact, he was one of the best athletes in his unit. Nevertheless, he and the other three Jews in his unit faced daily humiliations. Azrieli notes that the antisemitism in the Polish Army turned him gradually from Polish patriotism toward Zionism.[204] Mikhael Berlovitch maintained his Polish nationalism, explaining in his testimony that sometimes people who have suffered take out their rage on Jews.[205]

Civilians and women hoping to evacuate faced similar problems. Roza Hirsz was shocked to be rejected as a volunteer. Fluent in several languages, she was the daughter of a Polish patriot who had fought for the nation's independence as far back as 1905. For two thousand rubles she purchased a new passport under the Polish-sounding name Helena Ziminska and managed to reach Palestine in 1943.[206] Celina Goldberg's testimony, recorded in Poland after her return from the Soviet Union in 1945, describes her experience of antisemitism from the top down in the Women's Auxiliary, before the Jews and invalids were left behind during the evacuation.[207] Helena Ajzenberg, although her husband was a missing Polish soldier, had to buy false papers in order to leave the USSR with Anders Army. In her testimony for the Polish government-in-exile, she described the situation for Jewish women in the military as a "true Gehenom [Hell]."[208]

Some Jews, like Ajzenberg, managed to get around the restrictions by creating new identities or relying on well-connected protectors. In a 1947 report based on his own experiences and his work for the Polish government-in-exile, Jerzy Gliksman claims that so many Jews were trying to be counted as Polish that Catholic priests "arranged special courses of Catechism and performed mass baptisms for the neofites in the respective evacuation centers."[209] Leon Klajman states matter-of-factly that he obtained a forged passport, with a different last name, in order to join Anders Army.[210] Dora Werker and her family received help from Polish politician Jan Kwapiński on several occasions after the amnesty. He not only got Werker's

son into the army in Kermine (Uzb. Navoiy), but subsequently had h\
ferred to London.[211] For Szmul Zyfberfajn, it was one Major Dud\
intervened when Jews were being thrown from the evacuation train

In addition to evacuating military personnel and their families, the \
authorities tried to evacuate as many of the Polish orphanages as possible. This humanitarian effort to save Polish children was not authorized by their agreements with the Soviets. The orphanages had been established under the authority of the Polish delegates and were staffed with Polish citizens. Many of the children had one or both parents still living but were left at the orphanages because their families were unable to care for them. After their evacuation to Iran, the small minority of Jewish children generally separated from the other Polish children and received aid from Jewish organizations before traveling to Palestine.[213]

In 1943, fifteen-year-old Shmuel Labin and his three younger siblings arrived in Palestine. All of the children from their Polish orphanage in Tashkent had been taken by truck to Yangiyul, then by train to the Caspian Sea. They then traveled by boat to Bandar-e Pahlavi (Per. Bandar-e Anzali), where they spent several months before receiving transport to Palestine. When interviewed in Tel Aviv by an agent from the Polish government-in-exile, Shmuel stated that his mother walked behind the truck from Tashkent for seven kilometers. He was unsure if she and his two remaining older siblings would be able to survive the starvation and disease raging on the kolkhoz and wondered if they even knew how to reach him.[214]

Labin mentions only good relations with non-Jewish Poles. When his older sister contacted the local Polish delegate for help, she received four hundred rubles and an invitation to enroll any of her siblings under fifteen years of age in the orphanage. Many of the other Jewish children interviewed after their arrival recall antisemitism in the orphanages. Dina Stahl and her brother were dreadfully hungry in the Polish orphanage in which their mother had placed them. "Worst of all," in Stahl's words, "was the way the Christian children called us dirty [parszywych] Jews and taunted us."[215] Z. Elsan's father placed his two youngest children in an orphanage after his wife's death. According to her testimony to the Polish representatives in Palestine, Z. and her younger brother were tortured by the Polish children and denied soup by the administrators. When she reached Teheran, she was treated by an English medical team. Elsan says that the doctor's first response to seeing her was, "Whom have you sent us? Corpses or children?"[216]

Other families sent their children to the orphanages only when it became clear that they were to be evacuated. When Bob Golan's father was turned away from Anders Army, he decided that at least his children should be able to leave the USSR, and he bribed an official to allow his two sons into an orphanage preparing to depart. In his memoir, Golan describes regular meals and clean clothing, but also ill treatment from the Polish non-Jewish children in Iran. He was only too pleased to transfer to a camp run by the Jewish Agency when the opportunity arose.[217] Similarly, when Gitla Rabinowicz's father was not accepted as a military chaplain, he arranged to have his children enter orphanages. Gitla was blond and able to pass as a Pole. Her brothers, however, had to enter a different orphanage, and they reunited only in Iran.[218]

While they were widespread, reports of antisemitism were not universal among Jews who interacted with the Polish military or orphanages. Some Polish Jews were fortunate enough to fall into a useful category. Given the dearth of officers, military experience was particularly advantageous. In his 1942 testimony, Edmund Finkler, an officer and former legionnaire, states that he faced abuse as a Pole and a Jew while in a Soviet labor camp but joined General Anders's staff in Buzuluk without hindrance. In Teheran he reunited with his wife and two children.[219]

Medical personnel and musicians were also in demand. Emma Lewinowna's father, a doctor from Radom, had taken a job in a Polish hospital outside Tashkent after the amnesty. Although she does not specify the reason, her family was able to leave with the Polish military; she also recalls other Jews not being allowed to evacuate.[220] Likewise, L. Witkowska, a trained nurse, succeeded in joining Anders Army. Witkowska explains that she received help from a Polish officer who told her to hide her Jewishness from the Soviets on the recruiting board and supported her case among the Polish members. She served in Egypt, Iraq, and Scotland.[221]

Beth Holmgren discusses both the reasons Jewish musicians were recruited and their experiences serving.[222] Dawid Zylkiewicz, a jazz musician, did not leave Warsaw right away in September 1939 because he felt that his Polish Music Association card and Polish-sounding last name would protect him. Soon, though, he joined the stream of refugees fleeing eastward. In his testimony for the Polish government-in-exile, Zylkiewicz mentions that the army did not really want Jews, but he was able to join the evacuation nonetheless. He does not explain why he was allowed to do so, but it may certainly have been because of his name or profession.[223]

Joseph Czapski leaves no such questions about Holcman, the young, starving, piano virtuoso from Warsaw he met in Tashkent. As the army captain charged with locating the missing officers, Czapski had high-level access and much autonomy within the Polish military staff. Nonetheless, it was no simple matter to bring the Jewish musician on board. As Czapski recalls,

> The incorporation into our ranks of any new Polish citizen with a non-Polish sounding name met with great difficulties at the hands of the Bolsheviks, and these had, in some way or other, to be circumvented or overcome. There was much antisemitism among us, and this, unfortunately and more irresponsibly, made the task of the Bolsheviks easier.

Once Czapski brought the young man to the base in Yangiyul, and provided him with a piano, his value was immediately recognized. Czapski describes Holcman playing Chopin to a large crowd in the open air when it began to rain, but no one moved. "We listened to these things in precisely the same way the Jews listen to the words of the Prophets," he explains.[224]

There was also some effort to get Polish rabbis out of the USSR. The files of the Polish Ministry of Information and Documentation include several lists of Polish rabbis and their addresses within the Soviet Union.[225] Rabbi Joel Landau explains in his 1943 testimony that the Soviets tried to stop Jews from reaching the Polish forces. However, with the intervention of the ambassador and a bishop, he and his family departed for Iran on August 22, 1942.[226] Zeev F., on the other hand, states in his testimony that although General Anders had promised to evacuate rabbis, he reneged on his promise. While Zeev was able to reach Teheran with an orphanage, his father, already under close surveillance for his religious activism, had to stay behind.[227] Similarly, Chaim Shapiro was turned away from the Anders Army recruiting center in Guzar even though he held a letter arranged by Ludwik Seidenman at the Polish embassy in Kuibyshev. Seidenman had advised the rabbinical student to portray himself as a rabbi but was not surprised when the gambit failed.[228]

A few Polish Jews received permission to leave with the Polish military due to the lobbying efforts of the Yishuv, the Jewish community in Palestine. Soviet authorities allowed the well-known Zionist leader Menachem Begin to leave, despite complaints that other Polish Jews were held back due to their purported citizenship status.[229] Some lesser-known Polish Jews also benefited from the Yishuv's help. Regina Treler, a teacher from Kraków, relates that her husband Emanuel, a lawyer, had originally been turned down by Anders Army. In March 1942, however, they received word that a certificate for their immigration to Palestine was available in Kuibyshev. Despite enduring complications with documents and visas, and seeing other Jews thrown off the transports, they arrived in Palestine in January 1943 via Pahlavi and Baghdad.[230]

Although they are a minority, some Jews who joined the Polish Army and evacuated the Soviet Union do not mention encountering antisemitism. Naftali Zylbersztejn arrived at the military recruiting station in Kermine after recovering from typhus. There he met some acquaintances before traveling to the Caspian Sea for embarkation.[231] If he experienced antisemitism along the way, Zylbersztejn did not choose to record it, nor was it sufficient to keep him from reaching Iran. Jozef Zgudnicki, a lawyer from Kraków, blamed any difficulties Jews had registering for Anders Army on Soviet intervention.[232] Similarly, Chawa Kestenbojm, the wife of a Polish officer and prisoner of war, traveled to Uzbekistan together with her two children and another Jewish officer's wife. According to her report, they were greeted warmly. The Soviets took her off the list for evacuation with the first transport, but she managed to get out soon afterward.[233]

Edward Herzbaum, who fought with Anders Army, did not mention antisemitism in his experience of recruitment or evacuation. On the whole, however, his journal focuses much more on landscape, philosophy, and his inner life than on day-to-day events. He explains, "This is not a diary or a novel; these are mostly unrelated images, as if a poor photographer has taken his snapshots at random, hoping that after he comes back home from holiday, maybe something will show up."[234] Whatever Herzbaum's experiences, the topic of antisemitism seems not to have interested him. He frequently describes his boredom, isolation, and depression, but offers only subtle hints that he was treated differently as a Jew. In December 1942, while training in Khanaquin, Iraq, Herzbaum received a letter from his uncle in Palestine informing him that a cousin was serving in a unit nearby. When he applied for a pass to visit, he was told that non-Catholics could not receive passes during the holidays. While serving in Italy in 1944, Herzbaum asked rhetorically why his application for officer training was not accepted despite his experience.[235]

In contrast, most of the other accounts of Jews who evacuated with Anders Army come from interviews and questionnaires collected by the army and other branches of the Polish government-in-exile in Iran and Palestine. The purpose of these testimonies was chiefly to document the crimes of the

Soviet state toward Polish citizens. And yet, Polish Jews made a point of subverting the process by recording the antisemitism they experienced at the hands of other Polish citizens—and Polish authorities—while in the USSR. After all they had endured, the indignity of facing discrimination from representatives of their own state weighed heavily upon them in 1942 and 1943.

Polish Jewish refugees expressed their outrage not only to the Polish government-in-exile but also to Jewish organizations and individuals abroad. As part of its charm offensive toward the West, the USSR had opened up easier routes of communication. Heavy censorship still existed but reports of Polish antisemitism actually suited Soviet goals very well. Thus, news of such prejudice in the army reached Jewish leaders in the Yishuv, the United Kingdom, and the United States, who in turn passed the news on. In October 1942 Ignacy Szwartzbart, the representative of the Jewish Labor Bund on the Polish National Council in London, announced that he would raise this issue at the upcoming council meeting. According to the Jewish Telegraphic Agency, the Polish government-in-exile responded by promising "to forget the misunderstandings of the past."[236]

The British, who provided both financial backing and a command structure for Anders Army, grew more and more concerned about the conspicuous antisemitism in its ranks. In addition to the public relations situation, they had to deal with the spate of desertions. An estimated three to four thousand Polish Jews escaped from their units during the Polish military's stay in Palestine.[237] While they were welcomed into the Jewish community, their numbers threatened Britain's hold on the volatile region. Smaller numbers of Polish Jews stayed with Anders Army longer, only to attempt to flee the antisemitism and request citizenship when their units reached the United Kingdom. All of this led to a flurry of correspondence between British military and diplomatic offices and the Polish government-in-exile.[238]

Public criticism put the Polish government in a difficult position and was shrewdly exploited by the Soviets. In November 1942 Wanda Wasilewska, a prominent leftist Polish writer who became very close to the Kremlin after her flight into Soviet territory, used the pro-Soviet Polish journal *Nowe Widnokręgi* (New Horizons) to raise further allegations. In one article she details the dismissal of hundreds of Polish Jews from Anders Army just before evacuation. Polish official claims that they did so due to Soviet pressure are dismissed as "imaginary." Wasilewska deftly praises the egalitarian statements issued by Generals Anders and Sikorski while also implying that such rhetoric is insufficient without meaningful action.[239]

Overall, between 1942 and 1943 the Polish government-in-exile succeeded in evacuating almost seventy thousand Polish citizens from the USSR via Iran. In addition to the officially sanctioned soldiers, the Poles managed to sneak out as many as twenty-five thousand civilians, including the staff and children from the orphanages.[240] While Jews were overrepresented among Polish citizens in the USSR during the war, constituting up to 30 percent of the exiles, they were a much smaller proportion of the evacuees. Israel Gutman estimated that Jews were 5 percent of the soldiers and 7 percent of civilians, or about six thousand in all.[241]

The amnesty agreements signed by the Polish and Soviet governments also allowed for a system of social welfare and educational institutions. The establishment of this welfare system, however, contributed to the tense public relations between Polish Jews and representatives of the Polish state. Xavier Pruszynski, a journalist attached to Ambassador Kot's delegation to the USSR, describes the elite among the former prisoners, converging in Moscow:

> In the corridors of the Polish Embassy, in its unfurnished waiting rooms and offices, there are—standing or camping—people whose very appearance recalls the epic of Dante . . . We can find among them ex-premiers of Poland, generals, Polish princes and Jewish socialists, priests and rabbis, peasants and squires, working men and revolutionary poets.

Among them he met Anders, and Erlich and Alter. Most of the refugees, however, did not travel to the capital. Indeed, the capital itself had to evacuate to Kuibyshev soon after the Polish representatives arrived.[242] Some of the Polish Jewish refugees visited the official headquarters there. Most met Polish delegates closer to their places of residence.

To establish the welfare system, the Polish government in London assembled needed items in Iran for shipment into the USSR. These goods were then distributed to regional offices run by embassy-selected staff. The regional offices faced the difficult task of disbursing the supplies, which were never enough. These offices were referred to as the Delegatura in the Polish documents and given a variety of other names—among them, Polish bureaus, Polish delegates, and Polish offices—in the testimonial literature.

As with military recruitment, persistent accusations of unfair treatment of Polish Jews shadowed the welfare system. These accusations reached

Jewish communities and Allied governments abroad, which pressured the Polish government-in-exile to take action. Reliant on financial contributions from these sources, the government-in-exile had to take such allegations seriously. Yet even as some Polish Jews complained of mistreatment, many expressed satisfaction with the aid that reached them. Moshe Grossman describes receiving cash and goods with no hint of antisemitism. According to him, "The relief did something to restore the thousands of suffering and starving refugees. It also gave the courage to hold out."[243] Recrimination was less widespread and damaging to Polish Jewish relations when it came to aid distribution than with military recruitment.

The Safronovitch family, living outside the major urban areas in Uzbekistan, relied heavily on goods from the Polish bureau. Although both parents worked, they found it difficult to get by. Fortunately, they were able to pay their landlady—whose husband and son were serving in the Red Army—in linens, tea, and other foodstuffs delivered from the Delegatura. Shaul Shternfeld, working in a hospital in Berezniki, in the Molotov (Rus. Perm) region, was in an area with fewer refugees and no local delegate. He was thrilled when a package containing a coat and shoes arrived from the Polish office in Kuibyshev. Between those items and his hair growing back in, he writes that he finally "had a human look."[244]

Helena Starkiewicz also secured winter clothing from the local Polish office, but she maintains that a group of young men from a yeshiva in Vilna received nothing. In her privately printed memoir, Starkiewicz characterizes the Delegatura as self-serving and antisemitic.[245] When Ahron Blenkitni approached the Polish representatives soon after arriving in Kazakhstan, they turned him away for having accepted Soviet citizenship. His pleas on behalf of his starving children elicited only the suggestion that he go to the NKVD for help.[246] Although Blenkitni does not explicitly accuse the local Poles of antisemitism in his postwar Yiddish memoir, it is easy to see how some Jews might have taken such a refusal personally. Chana Gelernter, who had been living in a Zionist *hakhsharah* (agricultural training camp) in Lublin before the war, had also accepted Soviet citizenship after her flight eastward. She claims that she was turned away from the Polish delegate's office because she was Jewish. When she returned to the same office with a Polish name, she received both aid and clothing.[247]

Yet others had only positive reports from their efforts to secure aid. Dorothy Zanker Abend and her husband Oscar were amnestied fairly late and traveled in search of a place to live. Their baby son died along the way. After they heard about Anders Army, Oscar went to Krasnovodsk (Turk. Turkmenbashy) to seek entry and Dorothy to the Polish representative in Ashkhabad (Turk. Ashgabat). There she received useful products, including reading material, but the highlight was news of her brother Roman; through another Polish Jewish supplicant she learned that Roman, deported separately, was in the Polish forces in Kermine.[248]

As Abend's case illustrates, the delegates' offices served multiple purposes. In addition to allocating needed goods, they functioned as hubs for information, another commodity in the USSR. Informally, Polish citizens who gathered there to obtain food and clothing could share news of friends, neighbors, and relations. Mikhael Berlovitch and his wife were able to evacuate with Anders Army only because an acquaintance they met at the Polish office told them that their son Meyer was serving in Jalal-Abad.[249] More formally, the delegates provided Polish citizens with replacement documents and advice about navigating Soviet regulations and laws.

As they handed out food and information, the Polish delegates also actively gathered intelligence about the location and condition of Polish citizens in the USSR. This data helped to highlight the areas of greatest concentration, and thus greatest need, in addition to documenting the situation in general. Furthermore, it allowed the delegates to assess whether the Soviets were actually releasing Polish citizens as required by the amnesty agreement. Passed to the Polish embassy and thence to London, this information formed the basis of a data collection system that would be further elaborated in Iran, Palestine, and the other locations through which the Polish forces passed. The Polish Ministry of Information and Documentation established protocols and questionnaires to interview the evacuated Polish citizens about their time in the USSR. In the long term, the information could be used as proof of Soviet mistreatment of Polish citizens. In the shorter term, reports on all sorts of relevant issues could be prepared.

Although this was certainly not the main purpose of the data collection efforts, the Poles also publicized their good works to help discredit accounts of discrimination in the distribution of food and other goods. When the new Polish ambassador, Tadeusz Romer, arrived in the USSR in late 1942, he received a statement declaring that its 387 employees had been able to provide aid to 260,000 Polish citizens, of whom 36.15 percent were Jews.[250] Another report, more widely circulated and even translated into English, detailed the embassy's tremendous relief efforts overall and in particular toward Polish Jews.[251] Other consular memos highlighted the number of Jews employed in the delegates' offices, thereby suggesting that the presence of Jews would automatically decrease discrimination. In response to a complaint received from the Jewish Agency in Palestine, a June 1942 report from Kuibyshev insisted that sixty Jews worked in the Delegatura. Jews were so prevalent, it claimed, that Polish Catholics complained about their presence.[252]

Illustrating the challenges of deciphering the evidence, two of the scholars who have most closely examined interactions between the Polish government-in-exile and Polish Jews disagree over how to interpret this data. Keith Sword is convinced that Jewish participation in aid distribution would have created equitable conditions. David Engel, however, avers that such data is meaningless without more information on the length of the Jews' employment, the scale of the aid provided, and other such details.[253] Testimonial evidence is also mixed. Moshe Ben-Asher (Belzacki) explains that he and his older brother worked for the Polish delegate's office in Tashkent but that their Polish-sounding name allowed them to pass as non-Jews.[254] Dov Lederman claims that because of cronyism his family received very little help. At the same time, however, he notes that his father was actually employed in a food distribution center.[255]

During this period the Polish government-in-exile, through its local delegates, was also able to establish and fund Polish educational institutions. Like the orphanages, the schools functioned in Polish and employed Polish citizens. While some Polish youth had to work, and others attended Soviet schools, some were fortunate enough to live close to a Polish school. In a testimony published in his community's memorial book, Azriel Regenbogen notes that his older daughter completed her Polish high school matriculation exams in Dzhambul. He adds that the schools were on a very high level and his brother-in-law taught in one.[256]

Assuredly, Polish Jews were not the main concern of either the Polish government-in-exile in London, or its branches in Iran, Palestine, the Soviet Union, and elsewhere. Their primary goal was always the re-creation of a Polish state, with its previous borders, at the end of the war. Polish Jews were, however, an ongoing cause of concern and the subject of voluminous correspondence. Several scholars have examined aspects of the exiled government's policies toward the Jewish population. Notably, Engel's studies on the Polish authorities and the Holocaust also address the Polish state's attitude toward Polish Jewish exiles in the Soviet Union. He shows that prewar patterns and expectations consistently foiled attempts to collaborate effectively.[257]

The private memorandums and letters of Poland's official representatives during the war reflect a strong belief that while Polish Jews, as Polish nationals, were responsible for acting honorably toward their homeland, they were at the same time fundamentally outside its purview. Even Kot, neither a career politician nor an antisemite, saw Polish Jews as a separate category, outside the Polish nation. Memorandums express genuine shock that Polish Jews around the world were speaking up about antisemitism in Anders Army at a time when the Poles in London were in grave need of international support. Simultaneously, they question whether Polish Jews even belonged in the Polish forces at all; entirely unaware of the inconsistency of their own statements.

Whether completed during or after the war, testimonies and memoirs regularly complain about antisemitism in mobilization. Accounts of intimidation, violence, withheld food and medical care, and dismissal from the military are fairly convincing, although Soviet intervention must be factored in. It is harder to know how to read the complaints about aid distribution. Many families, for example, did receive aid from the Polish centers but complained that it was insufficient and that others—ethnic Poles—received more. It is difficult to ascertain how much of this was perception and how much reality. Additionally, the system was relatively new and still reaching its full capacity.

The already complicated relations between Polish Jews and the representatives of their home country were further bedeviled, in the midst of the war, by the political schemes of both Stalin and the Polish government-in-exile. Even decades later, it remains difficult to disentangle the narrative threads. How much of the anti-Jewish prejudice that Jews experienced in and around the Polish military was the result of entrenched Polish sentiments, and how much was related to Soviet policies? Certainly both contributed, and most Polish authorities were unwilling, or unable, to recognize and combat their own prejudices. In the aid and educational institutions, it would appear that relations between Polish Jews and non-Jews varied greatly based on local leadership. The degree to which testimonies focus on these issues is conditioned not only by personal experience but by the timing and circumstances of the recording or writing.

Almost from the moment of signing the agreements with the Polish government-in-exile, Soviet authorities tried to limit implementation. The

Polish authorities had to fight for every shipment into the country and every individual evacuated from it. The scarcity of—and conflict over—resources meant that they were never adequate to the needs. Even those who received aid or reached Iran were painfully aware of others less fortunate. In early 1943, as Soviet forces neared victory at Stalingrad, the Soviet government put an end to the whole experiment. They severed diplomatic ties with the Polish government in London, effectively shuttering the entire system of education, aid distribution, recruitment, and information gathering that had been built over the course of a year. In some cases, local delegates were even arrested.[258] It is impossible to know if the allotment would have improved over time. However, the hard work of creating systems to transport and distribute aid, and building educational institutions, was not entirely in vain. To some degree, other groups were able to pick up where the Polish delegates ended.

Relief from Abroad

While a Soviet-Polish organization to be discussed in the next chapter took over educational institutions and administrative functions for Polish citizens, a number of aid groups, including most prominently the American Jewish Joint Distribution Committee (JDC), committed to providing relief. Founded in the wake of the First World War, the JDC was devoted to helping Jews in need around the world, but especially in Central and Eastern Europe. Following the breakup of the old empires into new states, the Joint (as the JDC was colloquially known) was able to continue its work partly because of its strictly apolitical stance. Yet in the late 1930s, as the USSR turned increasingly inward and Stalin began his campaign against outside saboteurs, the Joint was expelled from the USSR. It was a painful ending to a large and successful set of programs helping war refugees through the Joint and new colonists through the JDC's Joint Agricultural Corporation, Agro-Joint.[259]

Nonetheless, the JDC remained active in feeding and educating impoverished Jewish communities in Poland and elsewhere. In addition, it provided financial and logistical support to many European Jews seeking to leave the continent in the 1930s. It also lobbied for Jewish refugees and asylum seekers and supported them around the world. When the war began, the JDC was initially able to smuggle money to Jews in Nazi-occupied Poland. Soon, however, this became impossible. The JDC continued to operate in Lithuania, helping refugees and would-be emigrants before the

Soviet takeover in 1940. As more of Europe fell to the Germans or the Soviets, it became harder to provide direct aid. When offered the opportunity to contribute to the Polish government-in-exile's relief efforts in the Soviet Union, the JDC was keen to participate.

The Polish government-in-exile received contributions from Jewish organizations, Polish émigré organizations, and the US Lend-Lease program. JDC files show the inner workings of the transfer operations, which were complicated by the vast distances and ongoing hostilities. Fortunately, the Joint developed knowledge and relationships in this effort that made it easier to continue its activities once the Polish Delegatura had ceased to function. Additionally, Moscow was paying close attention to the Soviet image abroad. Indeed, it has been suggested that the timing of Itsik Fefer and Solomon Mikhoels's famous trip on behalf of the JAFC in 1943 can be largely explained by concern over the fallout of the Erlich and Alter affair.[260] This trip laid the groundwork for direct cooperation between the Joint and the USSR. After donating several hundred thousand dollars' worth of goods to the Poles and Jews stranded in the USSR through the Delegatura, the JDC used the occasion of Fefer and Mikhoels's visit to push for a new aid package. The break between the Poles and the Soviets had temporarily halted their relief efforts, and the JDC wanted desperately to continue helping the few European Jews they could reach in the midst of the war.

On September 27, 1943, representatives of the JDC met with the two visiting Soviet Jews as well as staff members from the Soviet embassy. According to a confidential memo submitted by J. C. Hyman after the meeting,

> Prof. Mikhoels, in opening the informal discussion, stressed the fact that the Joint and the Agro-Joint were, indeed, well-known in Russia, not only to Russian officials, but to people throughout the country—perhaps even more so than the names of the Joint and Agro-Joint are known in the United States. There was a great feeling of regard and appreciation for the activity conducted by the Joint and the Agro-Joint there, for many years.[261]

A sticking point in the negotiations was the debate over how best to get the aid to those in greatest need, which involved practical questions about how to physically distribute the aid on the ground, as well as philosophical questions about who should receive it. For the Soviets, aid that was earmarked specifically for Jews was a nonstarter. The Joint, however, demanded a commitment to at least send the aid to areas of high Jewish refugee concentration. JDC documents also claim that the JDC received a verbal agreement to allow its representatives to distribute food and other goods inside the Soviet Union. Soviet sources do not mention this agreement, and it was certainly never acted upon.

In the end, the JDC negotiated mainly with the Soviet Red Cross rather than embassy officials or Jewish representatives. Talks were, at times, highly charged, both between these organizations and at JDC committee and board meetings. It seemed to many on the board that the Soviets were asking for a great deal while guaranteeing very little in return. It was also difficult to get accurate information about the situation on the ground, as Paul Baerwald shared in a letter to Judah Magnes in Jerusalem:

> One of the real difficulties, about which we have no first-hand information, is the attitude of the Russian authorities toward the Jewish refugees, in contra-distinction to the non-Jewish Polish refugees. Whether this attitude has any bearing on the distribution of supplies, is a question of which we are not quite sure.[262]

Nevertheless, the JDC funded and ran a large and impressive relief program on behalf of their coreligionists in the USSR. Between 1942 and 1943 the Joint spent well over a million dollars on general aid to the USSR and direct assistance to Jewish refugees through an individual parcel service.[263] The program involved regular communication and cooperation with both the Iranian and Soviet governments. The Joint faced the additional challenge of trying to gain the trust and help of Jewish socialists like those on the Jewish Labor Committee, Orthodox groups like Vaad Hatzala, establishment Jewish organizations like the World Jewish Congress, and a variety of stakeholders in the Yishuv. The dizzyingly transnational nature of the JDC's work during this period has already been pointed out by others, including Atina Grossmann:

> Parcels sent from Teheran to Tashkent, addressed and packed by Polish and German Jewish refugees in Iran, funded by Jews in New York and Tel Aviv, acquired in part with the help of the Bombay Jewish Relief Association, transported by Red Army trucks and ships, and sanctioned by delicate negotiations among the JDC, the Jewish Agency, the Soviet Union, Great Britain, and Iran helped to sustain from 65–80 percent of all Polish Jews (altogether perhaps 10 percent of the 3.3–3.5 million Jews residing in prewar Poland) who managed to survive World War II.[264]

FIGURE 4.3. Packages of clothing collected by the American Jewish Joint Distribution Committee in Palestine, as well as small personal parcels, to be shipped via Iraq into Iran and from there to refugees in the USSR, July 1943. American Jewish Joint Distribution Committee Archives.

Although her estimation of the results is perhaps exaggerated, she is certainly correct to highlight the scope of the work.

Yet despite these efforts, it was not possible to reach all, or even most, of the refugees in need. While the Joint archives are full of heartfelt fundraising letters, backroom negotiations, and lists of funds and goods to be distributed, this is rarely reflected in the testimonial sources of the recipients. By 1943, when the Joint began direct delivery, most of the Polish Jewish refugees report that life got easier, but they mention the JDC only very rarely. Frumie Cohen had her first chocolate in a Joint package. Later, a second package arrived with sardines and tuna. She remembers gobbling up her portion while her more mature sister saved hers for their parents. Frumie and her parents came down with food poisoning, while her sister felt fine.[265] Avraham Steinberg states that his father, a well-respected rabbi in Samarkand, served on a committee charged with dividing up the relief that arrived from the Joint. Steinberg says that this was a thankless job, and led to complaints and personal attacks, but that the aid did make a difference for the refugees.[266] The most enthusiastic evaluation I have found comes from Marian Feldman, who was mobilized into the Red Army in 1943. During this period, he was very concerned about his sister, left alone on a kolkhoz. Her boyfriend had already been killed fighting for the Soviet Union. Fortunately, in addition to money that Feldman sent from his stipend, she received some packages from the Joint. According to him, these helped her to get by during this difficult time.[267]

Beyond these examples, however, very few of the memoirs or testimonies mention the Joint's help at that juncture. Far more frequently they recall packages sent from relatives or more exclusive international organizations. For several years, Dina Gabel had either gone without matzah for Passover or baked them clandestinely. In 1944 she saw boxes of Manischewitz matzah on sale on the black market in Tokushi, courtesy of the Joint. Yet far more valuable, in her mind, were the packages she began to receive later that year from Vaad Hatzala, the Orthodox organization operating out of New York. They contained American tea, which fetched a high price when traded for flour from the local Kazakhs.[268]

Dorothy Zanker Abend was still in a special settlement in the Vologda region with her husband and infant when she received a package from her parents in the United States. It contained a can of Crisco and boots for her baby. As she states in her interview with the Shoah Foundation, it was a "true treasure." Mietek Sieradzki and his father received packages from his uncle in Tel Aviv while they were struggling to survive near Dzhambul. According to Sieradzki, "The arrival of a food parcel, which our family, like many others, received from time to time, was a great event in our lives and a godsend for us."[269]

These packages from smaller organizations and family members, which began arriving in 1943, were actually also a result of the Joint's efforts—a fact often lost on the refugees. Although the Joint had originally initiated a general relief program, sending bulk products to areas within the Soviet Union, it transitioned over time to a more targeted parcel program. As the JDC, Vaad Hatzala, the World Jewish Congress, *landsmanshaftn* (hometown associations), Zionist parties, and other Jewish organizations became involved, they collected addresses for individual families of Polish Jewish refugees. These lists were passed around and also augmented by and shared with relatives abroad. As a result, individual packages became more common.

Given how frequently the refugees moved after their amnesty, it is remarkable that so many of the packages from abroad reached their desired recipients. All of the organizations had to pool their information, beginning with the names and addresses collected by the Polish government-in-exile. Soon before their expulsion in 1943, the Consular Legal Department of the Polish embassy in Kuibyshev prepared a list of all of the Polish citizens to whom the Jewish Agency had sent certificates for Palestine. Rabbi Uszer-Szaja Halpern, at that time living at Swobody 9 in Bukhara, was one of many rabbis on the list.[270] By July of that year he had apparently relocated to Tolstogo 29; that was the address where Vaad Hatzala sent him one hundred dollars.[271] A list of rabbis and rabbinical students compiled by the World Jewish Congress has him at the same address in 1944.[272] When I interviewed Rabbi Halpern's son, who was old enough to have his bar mitzvah in Bukhara, he did not recall the family moving.[273] Yet the records indicate that a variety of organizations across the world were keeping close track of Rabbi Halpern's movements.

This collection and disbursement of the addresses of the Polish Jewish refugees in the USSR also made it possible for families to reconnect through letters. After their flight into Soviet territory, refugees kept in contact with their relatives who had stayed in the areas under German control. Even after the refugees were deported, they continued to write to, and often receive packages from, their friends and family members on both sides of what had been Poland. The German invasion of the Soviet Union put an end to this communication, but refugees in Soviet territory continued to keep in touch with one another. As the Soviet Union's relations with Western countries improved during the war, these refugees were also able to reestablish contact with relations who had escaped Europe before the war began.

Refugees had an overwhelmingly positive attitude toward these letters and the networks they represented. Nonetheless, they were also aware that their letters were not private. The Soviet censor was an unseen intermediary in their correspondence. Many of the refugees recall using fairly simple codes to share information that they believed would not pass the censor otherwise. Moshe Grossman and his friends signed their letters with common Yiddish names that also signaled emotions: "Klogman (lamentman), Weiman (woeman) and Brochman (calamityman) [and] occasionally Hoffman (hopeman) or Treistman (consoleman)." He adds, "In general we wrote these letters with many hints, references and other forms of concealment."[274]

Yet as the war progressed and Stalin began to plan for victory, he had less interest in positive relations with Western countries. In his memoir published in the midst of the Cold War, Abraham Kreusler discusses the NKVD's growing suspicion of foreigners and their contacts abroad in the final year of World War II. He mentions that some refugees were arrested for receiving packages from other countries, without providing many details.[275] L.L., interviewed right after the war, confirms Kreusler's impressions. He explains that the NKVD took a greater interest in the refugee population beginning in 1943, and that some individuals who had received packages from the Jewish Labor Committee were arrested.[276] However, relatively few of the refugees discuss these ominous policy changes.

Letters and packages from abroad provided evidence to the refugees that they had not been forgotten. The packages supplied necessary commodities, while letters allowed them to once again become part of a larger community. As the war came to an end, they also placed the refugees at the center of a nexus of family members trying mightily to find out what had happened to those left behind in Poland.

5

Nusekh Poyln, or *Yetsies Poyln?*

The Polish Way, or Exodus from Poland?

> *"Yetsies Poyln"* became the desire of almost all Polish Jews
> who were saved, and not only the Zionists.
> —DOVID SFARD

AS SOVIET FORCES advanced westward, Polish Jews in the Soviet interior learned gradually about the destruction in their native land. The details of what we now know as the Holocaust were only just emerging, and they pieced it together from multiple sources. Liberation brought horrific news, but it also afforded the refugees the opportunity to contact friends and relatives in Poland and around the world. In memoirs and oral testimonies, former refugees write of coming full circle and reflect on the shock of repatriation: in most cases, they found that the homes to which they returned no longer felt like home. The weary travelers thus faced yet another decision: should they stay in Poland and try to re-create what was lost, or once again decamp into unknown realms? Would it be possible to forge a Polish Jewish way, a *nusekh Poyln,* or were they fated to search for a way out, a *yetsies Poyln?*

Nusekh Poyln and *yetsies Poyln* are both hybrid constructions, combining the Germanic-origin word for Poland with a Hebrew modifier. Although the Yiddish language grew out of medieval German, approximately 10 percent of the Yiddish lexicon is borrowed, and in some cases reinterpreted, from Aramaic and Hebrew. These loan words usually describe uniquely Jewish religious or cultural features. Although they can also be used in alternative secular ways, the Semitic terms retain some of their ancient connotations, thus leading to double entendres and wordplay.

The Hebrew word *nusah*, rendered in Yiddish as *nusekh*, means custom or rite. It is traditionally accompanied by a geographic designation: Jews who lived in different locations developed variant rites of prayer and customs of religious observances, all of which could be described as *nusekh* in Yiddish. The term, and its religious connotations, was widely familiar to Yiddish speakers. When activists referred to the premise of postwar Jewish culture in Communist Poland as *nusekh Poyln,* they both nodded to the Jewish past and envisioned a novel socialist Yiddish culture.[1]

The significance of the term *yetsies Poyln* would also have been immediately apparent to Yiddish speakers. The exodus from Egypt, a seminal moment in Judaism's sacred history that appears frequently in its liturgy, is known as *yetsiat Mitsrayim* in Hebrew and *yetsies Mitsroyim* in Yiddish. The combination *yetsies Poyln* thus implicitly compared emigration from Poland with the biblical Exodus, thereby emphasizing its inevitability and necessity. This construction held particular appeal for Zionists, given that the original Exodus was followed, after a hiatus in the desert, by entry into the Land of Israel. In reality, however, leaving Poland again was neither an inevitable nor an imperative step for the Polish Jews who returned in the war's aftermath. Instead, the Jewish returnees weighed the relative potentialities of *nusekh Poyln* and *yetsies Poyln* within the chaotic context of postwar Poland. Even before encountering yet another consequential decision, the Polish Jews in the USSR learned about the Holocaust and awaited their opportunity to return to Poland.

News of the Holocaust

Polish Jews in the Soviet interior learned about the Holocaust gradually, and from multiple sources. In many cases, they had lived through the first weeks or months of the German occupation in 1939. They witnessed the brutality and terror of the German invasion, and the implementation of policies meant to divide the ethnic Poles from their Jewish neighbors. In some places the radical dispossession of the Jewish population was accompanied by violence and expulsion. In others it was more orderly. In all places, however, Polish Jews understood that they no longer had any civic standing.

Those who fled east to the Soviet territories in 1939 deliberated whether to return to the west or bring other family members to join them in the east. During this period of alliance between the Soviet Union and Nazi Germany, up until the summer of 1941, it was possible to send letters and parcels across the border through the regular post. From these communications, Polish Jews under Soviet occupation learned about the next steps in the genocide: expropriation, ghettoization, and the closure of educational institutions under the Nazis. Hanna Davidson Pankowsky remembers receiving disturbing news from her cousin, incarcerated in the Warsaw Ghetto. She and her family, who had accepted labor in the Soviet interior, were able to send her a package from Orsha.[2]

Many of the sources available come from well after the war and are thus subject to backshadowing. A few, however, come from during the war. Olga Kochanska, a non-Jewish Pole who was deported to Kazakhstan, published her book in 1941 after reaching the United States. She remembers one of her fellow deportees, a rabbi, reporting on a letter that he received from his relatives outside Warsaw. "This looks like an attempt at systematic extermination of a whole people," he said conclusively. "From the little we know, we can guess the rest. It is only beginning now."[3] In fact, it is not so easy to "guess the rest," given that the mass murder to follow was previously unimaginable. Nonetheless, news of the German suppression of Jewish life in Poland deeply concerned this exiled Polish Jew. After the German invasion of the USSR, Polish Jews in Soviet exile had to look elsewhere for news of home.

Scholars have shown that previous assumptions about the lack of coverage of the Holocaust in the Soviet press were greatly exaggerated. In fact, not only the Yiddish newspaper *Eynikayt* (Unity), but also Russian-language organs covered both German atrocities and Jewish heroism during the war. Although the ethnic background of the victims was sometimes masked, at other times it was stated unambiguously.[4] The Soviet Polish press also included articles about the Holocaust and the heroic ghetto fighters.[5] Nonetheless, Polish Jews who spent the war in the USSR do not report having learned about the Holocaust from Soviet media. Given their day-to-day struggles to survive, they were often unable to seek out such sources of information. Language barriers also hindered their access. In addition, they were frequently barred from residence in the larger cities where newspapers were more readily available.

In her diary written in Yakutsk, Pearl Minz chronicles some of these difficulties. In August 1942 they received a Soviet Polish newspaper but lamented that it contained no news from home. That December, from Russian-language news sources, Minz was cheered to hear good news from the front. In November 1943 Minz's son Bunek was able to bring home a newspaper from work. "You have to be made of steel to read the news," Minz writes. "If there is one percent of truth in it, it will still be very difficult to believe."[6] While her skepticism of Soviet propaganda is clear, it is difficult to know exactly what she means. Further reading of the diary, however, reveals that she had not grasped the Holocaust. In early September 1944 the Minz family and other Polish deportees were moved from Siberia closer to the western border. Minz rejoiced to be nearer to her beloved daughter back home in Krosno. Knowing that the liberation was proceeding, Minz sent her several letters and a telegram. Only in late September, when a Polish newspaper reached them on the Ukrainian sovkhoz, did she begin to worry in earnest, wondering if what she read could really be true. They did not know with certainty until the following year, when they were able to go home and confirm the truth.

Many other Polish Jews do not mention news reports at all, or, like the Minzes, refer to them as episodic and unreliable. While some Soviet-sponsored Polish-language periodicals became available later in the war, the Polish Jews do not describe finding news of the Holocaust there. Even if they had regular access to *Wolna Polska* (Free Poland) and *Nowe Widnokręgi*, (New Horizons) Ewa Koźmińska-Frejlak has demonstrated that they would have had to read between the lines very skillfully to recognize the uniquely Jewish tragedy amid the greater Polish tragedy.[7]

Far more frequently, the memoirs and testimonies describe learning about the Holocaust through the Red Army, which began liberating Soviet territory in 1943, followed by the rest of Eastern Europe. Red Army soldiers were the first outside observers to see the death camps, as well as the evidence of the "Holocaust by bullets." Oleg Budnitskii has written about the effect of these experiences on Soviet Jews among the soldiers, as well as apprehensions of the Holocaust among Soviet Jews more broadly.[8] The Red Army included Polish Jews from among the refugee population, in both the general units and the Polish division created in 1943. Mark Edele and Wanda Warlik suggest that between ten thousand and twenty thousand Polish Jews were recruited before the invasion and perhaps as many again afterward.[9] Given that Jews accepted into the Polish First Division, known as Berling's Army, were often encouraged to change their names, however, it is difficult to determine exact numbers.[10]

Jack Pomerantz was the youngest of eight children growing up in Radzyń, and one of only two who fled east in 1939. In 1944, as his unit of Berling's

Army moved westward in Ukrainian and Polish territory, he slowly gathered information about his family members. In Olyka (Pol. Ołyka), he learned that two of his sisters were shot, while a brother denounced for payment was sent to a death camp. The unit then reached Majdanek:

> When I closed my eyes, I saw those piles of small shoes, so many shoes, so many little children taken from their mothers. They took the children from their mothers, and killed them. And they kept the shoes. Even when I slept, I saw the shoes. It was unrelenting.

Not long afterward they camped outside Radzyń, and Pomerantz received permission to take a day off to visit his home. Only six Jews survived. From them and former neighbors, he learned of his parents' end. Throughout the liberation, Pomerantz kept in touch with his brother Moshe back in the USSR, communicating the news of their dear ones as he learned it.[11]

Bernard Ginsburg left Zamość with his parents and siblings in 1939. They resettled in Lutsk (Pol. Łuck), in the areas annexed by the USSR, but then separated for professional and educational reasons. Ginsburg moved deep into Soviet territory, while his parents and younger sister stayed behind in Lutsk. On January 11, 1945, Ginsburg learned from his brother Arthur, serving in the Red Army, that their parents and sister had not survived.[12]

Szymon Grajcar and his younger brother avoided mobilization into the Red Army because their work digging uranium in Uzbekistan was considered crucial to the war effort. However, they knew other Polish Jews who had been called up. In 1945, one of these acquaintances helped them to reestablish correspondence with their older brother Avrom, who had stayed in German-occupied Poland with his family and was serving in the Red Army. Szymon learned that Avrom had brought his carpenter's tools on the deportation train to Treblinka and had removed the window in the train car and jumped out. Although he escaped the guard's bullets with only a minor wound, his wife and daughter were not so lucky. No one else from their family survived.[13]

In these cases, as well as many more, Polish Jews serving in the Soviet forces passed their accounts of the devastation to larger networks of relatives, friends, and compatriots, including other Polish Jews in the Soviet interior. These accounts, which included specific information about hometowns and family members, were often far more convincing than newspaper articles. In her oral testimony, Tema Abel explains that she and other Polish Jews in Tashkent had read about the carnage in the Soviet papers but that no one wanted to believe it. Only the letter from her brother in the Red Army, recounting his visit with their janitor in Tomaszów (Mazowiecki), persuaded her.[14]

Brothers Gene and Mark Elsner learned about the genocide from their own close call with German forces. After their amnesty from a Soviet labor camp, they had settled in a Cossack village in the North Caucasus. Fortunately, while working with the locals, they had not revealed that they were Jews. This allowed them to continue passing as Poles when the Germans arrived in July 1942. They witnessed the separation and transport of the Jewish population, but only learned about the mass graves after they were mobilized into Berling's Army and sent to the front.[15]

Other sources of information included public events and early interactions with survivors. Simon Davidson attended a lecture offered by the Union of Polish Patriots in the USSR (Związek Patriotów Polskich w ZSRR, or ZPP) in Yoshkar-Ola (Mari Autonomous Soviet Socialist Republic, ASSR) in 1943, shortly before his son was mobilized into Berling's Army. He notes in his memoir that there were many Jews present and that this was the first they had heard about German atrocities against Polish Jews. In 1944, long before most of the other refugees, Davidson was allowed to move west. Working at a bank in Proskurov (Ukr. Khmelnytskyy), he met the handful of remaining Jews and heard their stories first-hand.[16]

Although his particular experiences are unique, Davidson is typical in gathering his information about the Holocaust from multiple sources and in assimilating it over time. Indeed, how could one—or even many—confirmed testimonies be sufficient to absorb the enormity of the loss? Many of the former refugees report, in their postwar writings and interviews, that it was not enough to read newspaper articles, or even to learn about the tragic deaths of their own family members. Only when their repatriation trains reentered Polish territory did they fully understand the scale of the loss. Włodzimierz Szer portrays this developing consciousness in his memoir. In September 1944, while serving in Berling's Army, he reconnected with some surviving friends on the outskirts of Warsaw. As he tells it,

> It was that evening that I found out about the Holocaust. I just read this sentence to myself and I do not think the shock of it really sank in at the time. I found out, but I still didn't know. I couldn't believe it. It was too horrifying. It didn't register that Karmelicka Street was no more, that neither Grandma nor Mum existed, that our friends and the world we lived in were gone.[17]

Lena Jedwab Rozenberg's diary also reflects her growing awareness. Rozenberg, an adolescent, was evacuated from Lithuania with her summer camp in June 1941. She could not even say goodbye to her parents. Already in December 1941 she wrote, "I no longer have any hope of seeing my parents again." Although similar sentiments pervade the diary, she was still awaiting news in August 1944:

> A sharp pain has pierced my innermost being. Fifteen days have passed since my numerous letters and cards went off to Bialystok with the first mail after the liberation of the city. . . . Instead of an answer, sensational articles in the newspaper about the death camp near Lublin. . . . After all this news, can I still have hope? . . . Are my loved ones still there? I am waiting for an answer. How long will I be able to endure? After so many days, to receive nothing. . . . With every passing day my hope dims. And the pain begins![18]

Rozenberg never learned her parents' exact fates. Shaul Shternfeld, who repatriated as late as April 1948, received a package of Passover foods from the Jewish community in Brest (Pol. Brześć, Yid. Brisk) at the border. He decided to save most of it for his sisters back in Sosnowiec, still believing they were awaiting his return.[19]

Many refugees followed the news of the Red Army's movements closely and tried to contact relatives in the newly liberated areas. Yet discovering the situation of their loved ones often proved surprisingly convoluted, as Avrom Zak's memoir illustrates. After none of his missives to Grodno were returned, in desperation, Zak turned to a Polish non-Jewish colleague in Ak-Bulak (Rus. Akbulak), who had received a letter from his own wife in Grodno. Zak asked permission to send this other man's wife a letter:

> So that's really how I did it. Writing the unfamiliar Polish woman a letter of request, giving her a whole list of addresses and begging her to ask around, inform herself from anyone she can in the area, from neighbors of the sought after, from surviving Jews, and by any other means.

Within a couple of weeks Zak received first a telegram, and then a letter and series of postcards from Hayele, the wife of his nephew, all alone in Grodno. After naming the many family members who had died, she wrote, "I do not know whether it was their destiny to have the good fortune to die, or mine—the misfortune to remain alive, to live in pain." Paralyzed by his own pain, and mourning for his mother, sister, and other relatives, Zak still held out hope that his wife and child in Warsaw might yet live. Not long afterward, he received a letter that dashed that fragile hope. Dorota Sheyn-feld, a painter from Warsaw who had fled to Bukhara with her mother, wrote to him that she had managed to contact her sister Liuba through the Central Committee of Jews in Poland (Centralny Komitet Żydów w Polsce, CKŻP). Liuba was a close friend of Zak's wife Mania. She asked Dorota to tell him that his son had been killed in Lublin and his wife in Majdanek.[20]

The Union of Polish Patriots and Repatriation

As Włodzimierz Szer relates, "It was May 1945. The nightmare was over. Over? Mom had been murdered. Dad was in jail. What kind of end was it?"[21] For many of the refugees, the end of the war did not mean the end of their trials, only a new chapter. Polish citizens in the USSR could not simply return to their homes and pick up where they had left off. Relocation was not only prohibitively expensive for most refugees but also leaving one's employment or traveling by train required special permission in the Soviet Union. Additionally, the newly liberated areas were often lawless and particularly unsafe for Jews. In any case, many of the Poles had been designated Soviet citizens by fiat or intimidation.

Some of the testimonies make no mention of the war ending at all. Others, like Ruth Hohberg, chronicle a celebration of the demise of Nazi Germany but also note that their lives did not change appreciably.[22] Real change depended on the Soviet authorities. Although Joseph Stalin had decided early on to retain the annexed Polish territories, his plans for the rest of Poland had changed over the course of the war. In early 1943 he began to construct the building blocks for a future communist Poland. The Soviet government renewed contact with the communist underground fighting in Poland and called on trusted Polish communists in the Soviet Union to form both a Party structure and a more popular outreach organization.

The idea of a Soviet-sponsored Polish organization—a sort of central address for Polish issues in the USSR and a potential government in the wings—had surfaced previously but could only come to fruition in the right circumstances.[23] The Soviets had accepted the contractual obligations with the Polish government-in-exile only grudgingly, and had staunchly refused to agree to return the annexed territories after the war. The Soviet government also continued to obstruct the goals of the London Poles in other ways, by interfering in recruitment for Anders Army, cutting supplies, and forcing Soviet citizenship on nonethnic Poles. Relations between the two putative allies remained tense throughout their period of cooperation. In the early months of 1943, after the victory at Stalingrad (Rus. Volgograd) and the disclosure of the Katyn Massacre, the Soviets suspended relations with the Polish government-in-exile in order to pursue their own Polish future.

Even before the official rupture, the wheels were in motion. After a meeting held in Moscow in January 1943, planning for the launch of a Polish communist replacement organization began. On March 1 the first issue of its press organ *Wolna Polska* was published. Preparations for a Polish military unit of the Red Army were also underway.[24] In April 1943, after the Polish government-in-exile decried the news of the murdered Polish officers, the leftist writer Wanda Wasilewska announced on Soviet Polish radio that the Poles in London did not represent the Polish nation and that henceforth all ties with them were broken.[25] The ZPP held its inaugural congress in June.[26]

Wasilewska had impressed Stalin from the time of her flight into Soviet territory. She had leadership qualities, ideological purity, and lacked the association with the discredited prewar Polish Communist Party that doomed other Polish left-leaning intellectuals to imprisonment in the USSR. Additionally, her father's renown as a Polish patriot, political leader, and associate of Polish statesman Józef Piłsudski lent her standing.[27] As a result, she had been groomed for power and was ready to assume a public role in the pro-Soviet ZPP when the time came. While other prominent communist Poles, including some Jews, were also involved at the higher echelons, Wasilewska's name is always mentioned first in both historical and testimonial sources; she became the figurehead for the group.

Following the break in relations between the Soviet state and the London Poles, the NKVD (Narodnyi Komissariat Vnutrennikh Del, People's Commissariat for Internal Affairs) began closing Polish bureaus and arresting delegates. The ZPP took over many of the services formerly offered by the Polish government-in-exile. Simultaneously, the ZPP began to collect information about all of the Polish institutions. Thus, for example, based on a July 1943 meeting in Moscow, and a tentative listing of Polish schools and orphanages, telegrams and questionnaires were sent to Polish educational institutions in Kazakhstan. Once the ZPP received the data about numbers and staffing, it followed up with a set of rules for running a Polish school under Soviet auspices.[28]

This multipronged approach allowed the ZPP to form a demographic and geographic profile of Polish citizens in the USSR even as it took over con-

FIGURE 5.1. Tsivia Korenzyer (fourth from right) with her classmates in her Polish school in Bukhara, Uzbek Soviet Socialist Republic, circa 1945. United States Holocaust Memorial Museum, courtesy of Zvia Levy.

trol of Polish institutions and communities. Soon the ZPP had established committees and staff members in each region of significant Polish settlement and built an institutional structure not unlike that held previously by the Polish embassy and its delegates, although more centralized and efficient. Unlike the Delegatura, the ZPP had the full support of the government and operated in conjunction with Soviet bureaucracy, infrastructure, and local leadership.

Two reports sent from the Mari ASSR to the head office of the ZPP in Moscow in May 1945 illustrate the scope of the organization's activities and oversight. Signed by Regina Poniatowska, the president of the local ZPP board, the first report included a wide range of population statistics. The capital city of Yoshkar-Ola housed 1,356 Polish citizens, of whom 53 percent were ethnic Poles, 42 percent were Jews, and 5 percent were Ukrainians. Among them were 151 children below the age of seven and 149 between the ages of seven and sixteen. In the four quarters of 1944, the membership of the ZPP had grown from 124 to 236, to 391, and eventually to 428. Poniatowska also included information about cultural activities and participation in the Red Army, among other topics. Appended to this report was Dr. Zygmunt Mintz's account of exactly how much food and clothing had been given to Polish citizens in the region.[29]

The ZPP prioritized obtaining population figures in order to assess its own influence and prepare for a future repatriation. Local offices had to collect this information in addition to completing their other duties and send updates to the head office in Moscow. In April 1945 the Kuibyshev (Rus. Samara) office submitted a detailed chart of Polish citizens in the region. For each of the twenty areas within the region, Polish citizens were divided by sex, age, nationality, profession, membership in the ZPP, and number of sponsored institutions.

Unfortunately, this information is neither standard nor uniformly retained. Other areas broke down their data in different ways, and many of the reports no longer appear in the archival files. As settlement patterns differed greatly by region, it is not possible to extrapolate from the existing data. Nonetheless, the data yield important regional results. Of the roughly three thousand Polish citizens in the Kuibyshev region, about half were Jews. The other half split between ethnic Poles and Belorussians and Ukrainians. Men outnumbered women two to one, with children making up about 20 percent of the population. Less than 8 percent are classified as military families, although presumably this number includes only those serving in the Red Army. Apparently, the regional population was too small to qualify for more than a handful of Polish institutions. Nonetheless, it hosted a high number of ZPP committees and members.[30]

Certainly, the collection and analysis of population statistics remained opaque to most of the Polish citizens in the USSR. Before the repatriation, their interactions with the ZPP tended to be relatively brief unless they worked in a Polish institution. When Victor Zarnowitz arrived in Ili, Kazakhstan, in late 1942 he found a thriving Polish community there, including a school run by a Jewish woman from Warsaw. He began teaching in the school and formed a romantic relationship with its principal. According to Zarnowitz, the staff had to go to many meetings once the ZPP arrived.[31] Abraham Kreusler, also a teacher, describes the ZPP bringing aid and Polish culture to his refugee school and community in Belovodskoye (Kirghiz SSR), but also bringing propaganda and denunciations: "The Union became a laboratory in which methods of turning Poland into a satellite were worked out, and the subjugation of the country from within prepared."[32] Avrom Zak, who worked for the ZPP, attended a meeting in the regional capital of Chkalov (Rus. Orenburg). Any time one of the distinguished speakers mentioned Stalin's name, everyone on the dais had to rise and enthusiastically applaud. It occurred to him, he later wrote, that they were not human beings, "but dolls, marionettes, in which someone squeezed a mechanism—and they clapped, all in unison."[33]

Polish Yiddish actress Ida Kaminska presents a more positive picture. In 1944 she and her husband Mel (Marian Melman) were welcomed warmly by the members of the ZPP and the Jewish Anti-Fascist Committee (JAFC) in Moscow. They received excellent ration cards and housing, and Mel went to work as an announcer for Polish-language Soviet radio.[34] Both of them joined the Jewish Organizing Committee of the ZPP.[35] Shimon Redlich writes that they were among a group of privileged cultural figures invited to the capital and feted by members of the JAFC, but that their appreciation was often laced with ambivalence over what they witnessed.[36]

Those in less elevated positions had less direct exposure to Soviet control, but still had to live with compromise. Bernard Ginsburg, a photojournalist before the war, was thrilled to pick up freelance work through the ZPP in Kirghizia. His first set of photographs, which featured Polish citizens supporting the war effort through their labor in the mines, led to other commissions. Ginsburg, who had learned about the politics of the Soviet press after his flight into Soviet territory, knew that he was producing propaganda, but was glad for the added income.[37]

A collection of photographs from the Fergana region, taken between 1943 and 1946, shows the ZPP's priorities. Nearly half of the images display Polish citizens, male and female, engaged in skilled and unskilled labor. Men and women work in various types of agriculture. Men use specialized machinery and tools. Women dye and sew fabric. Approximately one-third of the photographs portray educational institutions. Children pose outside their schools; inside their classrooms, while performing calisthenics or folk dances; and relaxing in a sanatorium. Cultural projects make up the remainder of the photographs. Several images showcase an exhibition of Polish culture, including the traditional national costume, posters of important figures, and printed information. Also featured are a library, a dramatic society, and a number of public gatherings. Based on the Polish and Yiddish posters displayed in the background, one image appears to show a commemoration of the Warsaw Ghetto Uprising.[38]

A few Polish Jews played a role in the Jewish Organizing Committee, which contacted Polish Jews spread throughout the Soviet Union in order to encourage cultural activities and coordinate welfare. Dovid Sfard writes that when the prominent Polish Jewish communist Jakub Berman recruited him for a leadership position in the committee, he was told that American and British Jews preferred to send donations to a Jewish organization, although of course the goods would be distributed to all Polish citizens.[39] The committee membership also included both communist and noncommunist Polish Jews, in order to appeal to a broad array of Jews inside and outside the Soviet Union. In the event, the Jewish Organizing Committee's legitimacy was cemented with the addition of Emil Sommerstein.

A leading Zionist and longtime member of the Polish Sejm, Sommerstein had been languishing in a hospital after his prolonged incarceration. While the combined efforts of the Polish government-in-exile and the Yishuv in Palestine had not been able to help him, Polish communists managed to bring him to Moscow to serve on the committee.[40] When Sommerstein called for aid, Jewish communities and organizations around the world responded. The Federation of Polish Jews in Montreal wrote that his telegram "touched our heart" and offered to send clothing, medicine, food, and other assistance.[41]

Like the ZPP as a whole, the committee also oversaw cultural events for Polish citizens. Sfard recalls celebrations of Stalin, as well as literary evenings and concerts from the likes of Cantor Moshe Koussevitzky, formerly of the Great Synagogue of Warsaw.[42] Simon Davidson, who learned about the Holocaust at a ZPP-sponsored public lecture, is one of the few refugees to actually recall attending any of the activities.[43] In his postwar interview with the American Jewish Committee (AJC), J.S. noted that the ZPP organized Jewish cultural programs in Ushtobe (Kazakh SSR), but does not say whether he attended them.[44] There are occasional mentions of Polish song nights in various communities, although it is unclear whether these events resulted from local initiative or were organized by the ZPP. The photographs from Fergana, however posed and propagandistic, also show actual cultural events, even if they were rarely remembered.

More frequently the refugees write of receiving material aid and benefiting from the schools. Lena Jedwab Rozenberg, a nineteen-year-old orphan studying in Moscow in 1944, wrote in her diary about a heartwarming visit to the offices of the ZPP. There she not only received valuable used clothing but also met other Yiddish speakers of her age.[45] Jacob Halpern and his family received occasional supplies from the ZPP in Bukhara. His brother also attended their school.[46] Dr. R., who evacuated to Tashkent with his teenage son, recalls that the boy was the victim of antisemitism before he transferred to a ZPP school.[47]

Although the ZPP also oversaw the Soviet Polish Kosciuszko Division, or Berling's Army, its biggest responsibility—and the one most often mentioned in the postwar memoirs and testimonies—was undoubtedly the repatriation. As Soviet troops marched westward across Europe, Stalin's vision for the postwar world developed. In 1942 and early 1943 his agents had routinely prevented ethnically Belorussian, Jewish, and Ukrainian Poles from joining Anders Army, forcing them to take Soviet citizenship instead. By late 1943, however, these groups were accepted into Berling's Army. When it came time to register for repatriation, ethnic Poles and Jews, whether originally from eastern or western Poland, could register for return. Belorussians and Ukrainians, whatever their previous citizenship, had to stay in the Soviet Union.

At the time and afterward, people endeavored to understand Stalin's change of policy. Yosef Litvak cites Hersh Smolar, a prominent Jewish communist involved in the negotiations, as saying that Stalin believed that Polish Jews were more trustworthy than ethnic Poles in their commitment to communism. However, Smolar adds that Stalin was also acting on the advice of Politburo member Lazar Kaganovich, who was concerned that Polish Jews were a bad influence on Soviet society. Reading further into Smolar's depiction of events, Litvak raises the possibility that Stalin wished to proactively thwart Polish nationalism by forcing them to readmit Jews.[48] Hanna Shlomi, based on the testimonies of other Polish Jewish communists, argues that all parties understood that most of the returning Polish Jews would actually not stay in Poland but move on to the Jewish homeland in Palestine.[49] Attempting to explain the related question of why Stalin allowed so many Polish Jews to subsequently leave Poland, Albert Kaganovitch submits that Stalin believed that the arrival of Polish Jews in Palestine would both destabilize British control there and serve the interests of the USSR.[50]

The absence of documents showing Stalin's calculations makes assessing these theories challenging. Certainly, all are correct in understanding that Polish Jews were but a token in Stalin's negotiations with his allies and competitors. Given what they had experienced in the Soviet Union, it is hard to believe that anyone could have imagined them as a loyal bloc, either in Poland or Palestine. However, Stalin surrounded himself with staunch loyalists and may even have believed in the pedagogical potential of Soviet camps and prisons. Moreover, he was a canny strategist and willing to change course when he deemed it beneficial.

Unlike the flight, deportation, and much of the evacuation and migration of Polish Jews in the USSR, repatriation took place within a clear legal context. In September 1944 in Lublin, the recently formed Polish Committee of National Liberation (Polskii Komitet Wyzwolenia Narodowego), a provisional government sponsored by the Soviets, signed a series of population transfer agreements with the Soviet republics of Belorussia, Lithuania, and Ukraine. These accords provided permission and a legal structure for Catholic and Jewish Poles to resettle in recently liberated Polish lands and for members of the other ethnic groups to "return" to their territories in the USSR.[51] This was supplemented in July 1945 with a Polish-Soviet agreement establishing a procedure for the organized repatriation of ethnic Poles and Polish Jews from all Soviet territory.[52]

Even after the documents were signed, the policies of repatriation developed slowly due to the progress of the war and the enormous logistical challenges. While the ZPP painstakingly gathered data and awaited instructions from above, self-repatriation began. As Israel Gutman and Shmuel Krakowski point out, the first repatriates were the Polish soldiers serving in the Red Army. Soviet forces reached what had been eastern Poland in early 1944 and crossed the Bug River into what would become postwar Poland in July.[53] I. Lieberman's antitank unit arrived in Lublin in November 1944. In order to avoid punishment when the vehicle he was driving was damaged, he escaped, obtaining clothing and papers from local Jews.[54] Jack Pomerantz was on furlough in newly liberated territory, looking at a list of surviving Jews posted in a makeshift Jewish community center, when his surviving sister recognized him. The chance reunion strengthened his desire to desert. Soon afterward, as he was changing out of his uniform, a Soviet officer saw him and Pomerantz feared he was about to be arrested. Fortunately, the officer was also on his way back to Poland, and they left together.[55]

Włodzimierz Szer stayed with the military, but in other ways his experience mirrors those of other returning soldiers. He interacted with Jews who had experienced the war in Poland and searched for information about his family members. In January 1945, while convalescing in a military hospital in Lublin, Szer received a visit from his only surviving relative in Poland, an uncle who had lived on the so-called Aryan side, disguised as a deaf-mute. That spring, he went to visit the group of friends with whom he had been deported, and who had only then returned to Poland.[56] Helena Starkiewicz, a nurse, also returned with the Polish division of the Red Army.

She writes that Polish civilians told them about both the Warsaw Ghetto Uprising and the Warsaw Uprising, but that she remained unsure of the fate of her family.[57]

Some Polish Jews outside the military organized their own early repatriation. Betty Rich lived with a small group of young Polish Jews in Georgia throughout the war. When their homeland was liberated, the chief of police, with whom they had become friendly, suggested they return to Poland. Rich and some of her friends reached Lvov (Pol. Lwów, Ukr. Lviv, Yid. Lemberg) in May 1945 and settled in Łódź soon afterward. Others in their group, however, arrived only the following summer.[58] Rich mentions neither the ZPP nor any particular difficulties en route. Aleena Rieger, who was a child at the time, states in her memoir that her family and their friends in Dzhambul (Kaz. Taraz) rented an entire train to bring them back to the old border in June 1945.[59] While the exact details of the transaction may be lost to history, the story suggests that travel was possible for those with funds, permissions, or daring.

Abraham Bichler and his family had a harder time returning home. In the early fall of 1945, while living in Turkestan (Kaz. Turkistan) and longing for a way home, they saw an unguarded troop train heading west and paid off a lieutenant to allow them to board. Although they had packed food, the ride took over seven weeks and they ran out of provisions on the way. At one stop he and his aunt almost missed the train while trading for foodstuffs. Their presence on the train was an open secret. Although some of the troops wanted to expel them, they managed to stay on until Kovel (Pol. Kowel). Local Jews helped them find their way to Lvov, where more refugees congregated. They soon crossed the Bug to Lublin, where they encountered the Majdanek concentration camp and the magnitude of the Holocaust.[60]

Although most of the refugees—including Rich's and Szer's companions—returned to Poland only in 1946, the ZPP was actively registering and vetting Polish citizens long before then. The union worked closely with its Soviet sponsors. On the one hand, this meant they could count on the Soviet bureaucracy to help them to identify and reach Polish citizens. For example, a March 1944 letter from Wanda Wasilewska to the secretary of the Kazakh Communist Party, with a copy sent to Minister of Foreign Affairs Vyacheslav Molotov, authorized her to demand that Polish citizens be given work on kolkhozy, while also letting him know they would soon be evacuating.[61] On the other hand, the Soviet authorities' involvement in evacuation perturbed some Polish citizens, and made it difficult for others to prove their status.

Zyga Elton became involved in the ZPP while living in Bukhara. Soon he had a job providing aid and recreational activities for local Polish citizens. He notes, however, that many members of Bukhara's large expatriate Polish community did not trust the organization, whose leadership was composed largely of Jews and communists. After the war, when registration for repatriation began, Elton had to review each applicant's documents with representatives of the NKVD. He tried to give the benefit of the doubt to legitimate Polish citizens lacking proper papers but was not always able to convince his Soviet colleagues. Elton did manage to place his future father-in-law on a repatriation train in March 1946, despite the fact that the older man was officially still under investigation and should not have been allowed to leave.[62]

Sarah K. worked for the ZPP in Kiev beginning in 1944. She recalls in her testimony that Jews who reached them often had no documents, after all they had been through. The Soviet members of their joint review board, however, were unsympathetic.[63] In his oral testimony, Yankl Saler describes being rejected by the ZPP committee in Leninsk (Uzb. Asaka) because he and his family had accepted Soviet passports. He adds that bribery got them added to the list.[64] The Saler family had actually crossed the border from Hrubieszów in 1939, but the Soviet authorities had legitimate reason to be concerned about longstanding Soviet citizens trying to get out with the Poles.

According to Z. Vagner, Hasidic Jews were particularly eager to escape the strictures on Jewish life in the USSR. Dov Vilenkin's family paid for falsified papers but were unable to use them because the High Holy Days and the death of a grandfather intervened.[65] Shalom Duber Levin, the official chronicler of the Chabad Lubavitch movement, claims that some orphans from religious Soviet families were able to evacuate with Polish Jewish families whose own children had died.[66] Soviet Jewish cultural activists also sought means of escape. In his memoir published in New York in 1950, Yiddish writer Herschel Weinrauch (Grigory Vinokur) describes the growing fears of Yiddish cultural figures as antisemitism increased in the USSR. Many of them, like himself, used the flow of refugees to depart.[67]

A young Soviet Jewish woman, identified in her postwar AJC interview only as Id. Lib., left Soviet territory with the Red Army. Born near Kiev and raised in Kharkov (Ukr. Kharkiv), she had fled the latter in 1941 and completed her medical studies in Frunze (Kir. Bishkek). She was then sent to a military surgery course, and then to the front, where she mentions that antisemitism had increased. In the autumn of 1944, Id. Lib.'s hospital relocated to Polish areas, where the staff was augmented with Polish Jews and non-Jews. When Soviet staff were recalled at the end of the war, Id. Lib. elected to stay in Bydgoscz. She later traveled to a displaced persons camp and then to the United States. When asked about her religious life, Id. Lib. expresses embarrassment over her ignorance of Jewish practice.[68] While she appears to have avoided passing through border control, and certainly did not rely on the ZPP, her story illustrates that Soviet Jews of diverse backgrounds took advantage of opportunities to start new lives outside the USSR.

The ZPP made a great effort not to leave Polish citizens behind in the USSR, although it clearly did not want to allow others to leave with them. Because Polish citizens were spread out across the country, getting word to all of them was a major task. Henry Skorr read about the plans for repatriation in the ZPP newspaper *Wolna Polska*.[69] In 1946 Szymon Grajcar had a job traveling to outlying collective farms searching for Polish citizens. He was even given a bicycle for the purpose, although he determined he was safer from the local dogs on foot.[70]

In addition to gathering adults, the ZPP also pursued underage Polish citizens in institutions. This painstaking process involved cooperation with Soviet authorities, as well as private initiative. The files of the body overseeing orphanages in the Kazakh Republic, for example, contain an abundance of correspondence about Polish children. A report on the number of children in orphanages in the Merki district of the Dzhambul region in August 1946 is followed by a listing of Polish children evacuated.[71] Irene Rogers, born in 1935 in Warsaw, had been placed in a Polish orphanage in Andizhan by her older sister after the mobilization of their brother and death of their parents. In 1946 her orphanage, along with two others from Kokland and Samarkand, evacuated on the same train and reopened in Bielsko, Poland. Rogers's sister repatriated separately, and it took time to reunite what remained of their family.[72]

The archives and testimonies contain numerous other stories of families separated and reunited in the process of repatriation. The Regional Executive of the Communist Party of the Bukharan Region holds a collection of letters from forlorn parents trying to ascertain the projected repatriation dates of their children's orphanages and join the same transports. Regina Barber wrote that her own ill health had forced her to place her children in an orphanage. She begged to be allowed to evacuate with their institution, as they were all she had.[73]

Rabbi Moshe Nachum Kaner was born in Poland in 1938, and his first memory is of life in a Russian children's house. After his parents disembarked from the deportation train to seek medical help for his sister Sarah, Moshe Nachum and his other four siblings stayed with their grandparents. In their special settlement, the authorities determined that the grandparents were not able to care for the children properly and divided them into institutions by age. Remarkably, after the war, the oldest two siblings traveled around the region and found the others. Kaner was pleased to find he had living relatives, although he no longer remembered how to speak Yiddish.[74] His exceptional reunion story stands for others like it, although many families did not have the good fortune to locate missing members.

And even before the repatriation could proceed, there was an effort to round up some Poles from the farthest reaches of the country. This process is reflected in Pearl Minz's diary. In early May 1944 the Polish community in Yakutsk received the heartening news that they would soon be transported to the Caucasus as a prelude to returning to their homes. They began selling off their possessions immediately. Registration and checking of documents took place in June, followed by more waiting. In July, as she was preparing food for the road, Minz received word that her family would be sent to a city rather than a kolkhoz. She describes the first part of their trip as being like a vacation; they were even allowed to leave the boat and sightsee along the route. After a few weeks, however, the insects, unsanitary conditions, and low food supplies began to take their toll. On August 10 the group reached Makarovka (Ger. Merkel) in the former Volga German ASSR. Many were ill by that point, and others suffered in an anti-Jewish riot instigated by returning soldiers. They moved into barracks and awaited further direction.

In September the displaced Poles were divided up into smaller groups and sent to communal farms in the area. Minz and her family had a room to themselves on a sovkhoz previously populated by ethnic Germans, but other families did not. There was neither work nor food, and soon scarlet fever spread through the community. Finally, in November, the Minz family was allowed to move to Saratov, where they worked and lived until repatriation.[75]

Ezra Zynger and his wife Felicia also experienced a partial return, moving west to Kherson in 1944. In his interview with the Shoah Foundation, Zynger suggests that Soviet authorities may have allowed them to move westward because they had refused to take Soviet passports during their period in the Komi ASSR. The Zyngers had their first child while living in Kherson, after the war ended but before their repatriation. Simcha Shafran was released from a settlement outside Novosibirsk in 1944, along with a group of students from his yeshiva and their rabbi. They were all transferred to a kolkhoz in the Caucasus. In his memoir he states that the Polish government secured both their release and transfer.[76] As the Polish government-in-exile no longer had diplomatic relations with the USSR by 1944, it is more likely that he understood the ZPP as part of a Soviet-Polish administration.

In the absence of information about their transfer partway home, both Zynger and Shafran created explanations. Mordechai Altshuler, later a distinguished scholar of Soviet Jewish life, was a child during the war. In his oral testimony, he explains that although he could not be sure of the actual reasons, his mother understood that they were sent from the Sverdlovsk Oblast to the relatively rich areas in Ukraine from which the ethnic Germans had been deported in 1944 in order to fatten them up.[77] They surmised that the Soviet state wished to avoid the poor optics of sending thousands of emaciated and weak Polish citizens back to their country. Given that the program affected only a small portion of the Polish Jewish refugees, this seems unlikely. It does appear that at least some of the refugees transferred within Soviet territory came from distant Siberian locations. The transfer westward may simply have been a means of concentrating the Polish citizens in preparation for repatriation.

During this same period, news of the liberation of Belorussian and Ukrainian territory induced a small number of Polish Jewish refugees to move westward on their own—with or without permission. Dovid Feinzeig and his family were so hungry on the kolkhoz in the Chkalov Oblast that when their travel permit arrived in the fall of 1944 they accepted transport on the Jewish holiday of Sukkot rather than risk missing their chance to leave altogether. As Orthodox Jews, they justified their decision as a matter of life and death, which always outweighs other religious obligations. Resettling in Gorodnia (Ukr. Horodnia) turned out to have great benefits. They not only found it possible to earn a living on the black market but were able to live among other religious Jews for the first time in several years.[78] Most of the Polish Jews, however, remained in the places they had settled after the amnesty until repatriation.

As the Red Army pushed the German forces westward, the ZPP registered Polish citizens for return. Some of the refugees recall a long wait in between registration and repatriation. Others do not even mention registration, only the moment they boarded the trains to go home. Notification frequently came suddenly, leaving the refugees little time to prepare for departure. Often they did not know when the transports would leave. According to an article in *Wolna Polska,* the first trains of repatriates left from Ukrainian territory in January 1946.[79]

Tema Abel and her husband traveled from Tashkent to Turkestan, having heard that the groups from there would be leaving earlier. She was pregnant and hoped to have her child back in Poland. However, the train was delayed. Abel gave birth in November in a medical wagon with snow drifting through the slats. They had neither diapers nor clothing for the baby and were not able to bathe or circumcise him until they reached Poland.[80]

The organizers of the massive transfer faced not only the daunting task of locating all of the Polish citizens in the USSR but also the challenges of arranging transportation and coordination with organizations back in Poland. In September 1945 the ZPP organized a conference on repatriation in Sverdlovsk (Rus. Yekaterinburg). According to a conference report, the major issues for discussion included the economic and political situations in Poland, as well as the necessity of preparation on both sides. The ZPP activists expressed confidence that the many deported Poles in the building trades could be put to work immediately in Poland.[81]

Despite the efforts of the ZPP and individual families, some Polish Jews could not be located. The climactic scene of the 2018 documentary film *Rosja* involves the rediscovery of the whereabouts of a Polish Jewish adolescent who had stepped off of a deportation train to look for her brother and completely disappeared. Soviet officials had taken her to an orphanage and insisted that she change her name and age. While this made her more attractive to potential adoptive families, it also made it impossible for her family to trace her. Not long after her adoption, she married a neighbor and assimilated into the local Muslim culture.[82] Even if she had wanted to leave, she had no access to the Polish press, and no one would have found her.

Some Polish Jews who wanted to leave the Soviet Union hesitated due to fear. Simon Davidson writes that during his time working for the ZPP, some Polish Jews refused to put their names on the registration lists. Given their previous experience with Soviet deportation, they did not want to tempt fate by once again signaling a desire to leave.[83] Davidson's daughter, in her own memoir, echoes this sentiment. Having registered to depart and filed their paperwork, the family boarded a train in February 1946. "Until the last minute," she writes, "we were not sure whether we'd be moving west toward Poland or east toward Siberia."[84]

Others were prevented from returning home by Red Army service. Chaim Ajzen had stayed in Hrubieszów and fought with the partisans. In late 1943 his ragtag group merged with a Soviet unit, officially joining the Red Army in April 1944. By 1945 Ajzen was stationed in the interior and learned of the repatriation from other Polish Jews. He requested permission to evacuate with them, only to be told that he owed the state an additional six years of service. Ajzen traveled to Moscow to seek the help of the ZPP but found them unsympathetic. According to his memoir, he managed to escape and reach Poland on his own.[85] Some Polish Jews serving in the Red Army, however, chose to follow orders even when these orders did not allow them to stay in or return to Poland. After discovering that a brother and sister had survived and were living in Wrocław, Moshe Erlich requested permission to leave the military and join them. His request was not granted. By the time he was released three years later, the repatriation had long since ended. Obtaining authorization to return to Poland took him an additional three years.[86]

Incarceration also kept some Polish citizens from repatriating on time. Their experiences were especially difficult, as they endured both terrible conditions and uncertainty as to whether they would ever be allowed to leave. Jane Lipski entered Soviet territory after serving in the anti-Nazi resistance, and was arrested immediately. She soon discovered that she was pregnant. In June 1945 she gave birth to a son. For the next two and a half years, Lipski struggled to keep her son Eddie alive and with her while moving around various prisons and camps. She chronicles dire diseases and inhumane officials, but also help from friends and strangers on the way. She reached Poland in early 1948 and emigrated to Israel in 1950.[87] For Ruth Turkow Kaminska, the pain of separation from her daughter Erika was far worse than the miserable prison conditions. After six months in prison, she declared a hunger strike until she had news of her daughter. Her daughter's caregiver, Doba, an old friend of Kaminska's mother, was then given permission to visit periodically and bring updates. Two years later, after Kaminska's sentencing and exile, Doba brought Erika to Kaminska's exile settlement in northern Kazakhstan. Kaminska finished her five-year sentence in 1952 but was only able to return to Poland in 1956.[88]

The official repatriation peaked in the summer of 1946 and finished soon afterward. By the end of the year the ZPP closed down as well. Polish citizens in the Soviet Union who still wished to return now had to find other ways.[89] Kaminska, a well-known entertainer in her own right, as well as the daughter of the beloved Ida Kaminska, counted on connections in Poland, the USSR, and elsewhere. The same was true for the imprisoned Yiddish writer Moyshe Broderzon. According to a *New York Times* article published on his return to Poland in August 1956, Broderzon had been freed from prison after Stalin's death, and the Socio-Cultural Association of Jews in Poland (Towarzystwo Społeczno-Kulturalne Żydów w Polsce, TSKŻ), under the leadership of Hersh Smolar, had organized his repatriation.[90] Broderzon's obituary appeared in the paper two weeks later.[91] Sheyne Miriam Broderzon, his widow, chronicled his suffering in the USSR, as well as her own, in her 1960 memoir.[92]

Obtaining permission for repatriation was even more arduous for those who lacked connections. After her release from prison in the fall of 1947, Jane Lipski traveled with her toddler son to meet with Polish government representatives in Moscow. She spent the next few months journeying back and forth between Moscow and a now almost empty repatriation camp in Grodno—with and without her child—trying to secure their release from the USSR. Finally, in January 1948, they boarded a train bound for Łódź.[93]

Taking advantage of the period known as the Thaw after Stalin's death, Poland was able to negotiate a second, smaller repatriation beginning in 1956. This repatriation allowed Polish citizens newly released from prison or exile, as well as those who had stayed for ideological reasons and come to regret their decision, to return to Poland in a more orderly and efficient manner. As Gennady Estraikh has shown, it was also an opportunity for other Soviet citizens to seek egress. He estimates that up to 15 percent of the so-called repatriates may never have been Polish citizens to start. They included Soviet Jews, especially those from the Baltic states. Having apparently underestimated the strong motivation to leave, Soviet premier Nikita Khrushchev soon began limiting the numbers.[94]

In the course of this research, I was contacted by a woman seeking to understand the life story of her great-uncle. He had crossed into Soviet territory in 1939 and never been heard from again. Yet her grandfather, who survived the Holocaust in Poland, never gave up hope that his brother was alive. Fulfilling his dying wish, she had recently made contact, via Facebook, with her cousin, the son of her grandfather's brother. She wanted me to explain how her great-uncle had ended up in Siberia, why he might have married a local woman and changed his last name to hers, why his children only discovered he was Jewish after his death, and why he never tried to contact his family outside the USSR. Others have also told me about long-lost relatives who fled east and then disappeared. It is likely that most of these people died in prisons, work camps, the Red Army, or from hunger and disease during the war. Yet the story of the rediscovered Siberian cousin alerts us to the many stories we will never know. While most of the Polish Jews repatriated, some number—for reasons we can only guess at—stayed behind.

At least a few must have remained in the USSR by chance. In their testimonies, many of the refugees refer to near misses. Dina Gabel's mother was so ill that a doctor warned Gabel not to try to transport her. Yet the alternative was so daunting that Gabel showed up at that station anyway with her invalid mother. Fearing contagion, no one would let them board the train cars. Eventually someone helped Gabel and her mother to find a place.[95] Adela Sherman's daughter was at the bazaar when the transport arrived to bring them to the station. Although the driver refused to wait, he discovered that he needed to change his tire before departing. Commenting on this serendipity in her oral testimony, Sherman, who had already lost two children and her husband to disease, said, "God is a little good to me."[96]

While Iakov Khonigsman never entirely explains his decision to stay in the Soviet Union, it would appear from his testimony for the Shoah Foundation that he married a Soviet citizen. Born in 1922 and raised in Lublin, Khonigsman fled to Soviet territory in late October 1939. Over the next few years he moved frequently, served in the Red Army, and started the university education he had longed for in Poland. After graduating from Kiev University, he and his wife settled in Lvov, where their daughter was born. As antisemitism increased and he feared arrest, Khonigsman considered escaping to Poland, but says that his heart would not allow him to leave his daughter behind.[97] Later in life Khonigsman wrote several books about Jewish history.[98] Khonigsman's testimony also highlights the importance of location in some people's calculations. The city that became Ukrainian Lvov had belonged to Poland before the war and retained architectural and other reminders of its past. One former Polish Jew who stayed in the USSR after the war stated that he chose Lvov because it was closest to Poland.[99] There may well have been other Polish Jews from that region who elected to return to their hometowns rather than repatriate to foreign areas.

FIGURE 5.2. Polish Jews in Kazakhstan wait to board a repatriation train, 1946. Seated in the center are Doba (Cymerman) and Moshe Yermus with their sons Sam (next to mother) and Aaron (second row, second from left). United States Holocaust Memorial Museum, courtesy of Aaron Yermus.

A biography of the prominent Soviet composer Mieczysław Weinberg does not mention repatriation at all. Although he focuses primarily on Weinberg's voluminous body of work, biographer David Fanning also describes many other aspects of Weinberg's personal experiences. The book chronicles his flight from Warsaw, his continuing musical education in Minsk, and his self-evacuation to Tashkent, where he married Natalia Vovsi, the daughter of Yiddish theater impresario and JAFC head Solomon Mikhoels. It also covers Weinberg's move to Moscow in 1943, as well as his postwar experiences in the Soviet Union, including a relatively brief period of imprisonment. There is no discussion of Weinberg deciding not to return to Poland, and it is possible that Fanning may even have been unaware of the repatriation.[100] We can only surmise the reasons that Weinberg had for staying: his marriage to a Soviet citizen, his father-in-law's position, the knowledge that his entire family back in Poland had been murdered, and the opportunities he had as a composer in the USSR among them.

Indeed, the USSR did offer enticing educational and professional advantages—especially for young people who had already benefited from the Soviet educational system, and who knew they had no family remaining back home. Khonigsman and Weinberg took advantage of such opportunities, although their stories are known only because they achieved postwar acclaim. Other Polish Jews also married locals, integrated into Soviet culture, and benefited from educational and professional offerings. Most of these people are not typically included in the history of Polish Jews in the wartime USSR. In declining—or missing the chance—to return to Poland, they disappeared from the larger narrative.

Overall, more than one million Polish citizens took part in the repatriation. Most of these were ethnic Poles who had lived in their homes under German occupation and now had to relocate to leave the USSR. Included in this group was a small number of Jews who survived the Holocaust in occupied Soviet territory. Kaganovitch estimates this group to have numbered about fifty-five thousand.[101] Most of these would have been residents of the areas, and a smaller number refugees who accepted Soviet citizenship.

Official numbers for the repatriates from the Soviet interior show just over two hundred thousand Polish citizens, of whom about 136,000 were Jews.[102] On top of this were the refugees able to self-repatriate earlier or later. Mark Edele and Wanda Warlik estimate that this included between two thousand and twenty thousand soldiers in Berling's Army or other Red Army units and six thousand who came on their own. Their total of 144,600–162,600 is slightly lower than the roughly two hundred thousand Polish Jewish repatriates by the end of 1946 that is assumed by some other scholars.[103] Over eighteen thousand more came with the second repatriation in the late 1950s.[104] These figures are, of course, incomplete. Even with a fairly accurate count of official repatriates, there can be no exact accounting for Polish Jews in the Red Army and those who returned illegally. Given that so many Polish Jews stole across the border in 1939, it is not surprising that some did so again after 1944. The chance to finally return home was bittersweet for Polish citizens. As Ann Szedlecki explains in her memoir, they were not the same as when they had left:

> My luggage consisted of a bag of suchary, which is dried bread rusks, a jar of melted butter, very little clothing, a pair of size twelve boots and nothing else. I took very little away with me but I left behind what should have been

the best years of my life and a young brother buried in an unmarked grave, dead of tuberculosis at the age of twenty-three. I hadn't accumulated much in my six and a half years in the Soviet Union. I was traumatized and scarred, but I left Russia with my life. Under the circumstances, I couldn't ask for more.[105]

And, as they would soon learn, their homes, too, had changed inexorably.

Return and Rebuilding

Poland had been ravaged by the war. After the initial invasions in 1939, the uprisings in 1943 and 1944, and the Soviet liberation, not even ruins stood in much of Warsaw. Most of the country was not so unrecognizable, but destruction, dislocation, and poverty were widespread. The borders had also dramatically changed. The repatriation agreements allowed ethnic Poles and Polish Jews from what had previously been eastern Poland, even though they had been given automatic Soviet citizenship, to resettle in the newly reconstituted Polish state. This included the new territory in western Poland recently taken from Germany and in need of Polish settlement. Additionally, Soviet-style communism was being gradually imposed.[106] Thus, in Jaff Schatz's memorable formulation, "on the new geographic map of Europe, Poland was moved one hundred fifty miles west, while on the political map, it was moved radically to the east."[107]

Poland's demographics had also changed definitively. The Germans had decimated the Jewish population of over three million. While the survival rate typically given is just over 10 percent, this figure includes returnees from the Soviet Union and elsewhere in Europe. For Jews who remained in Polish territory, the rate is closer to 4 percent.[108] Due to territorial change and population transfer, neither its once sizable Ukrainian population nor its smaller Belorussian and Lithuanian populations were to be part of postwar Poland. All of these groups, as well as others, were in motion. As Krystyna Kersten has shown, the repatriation of Polish citizens from the USSR must be contextualized within larger migratory patterns in postwar Poland.[109]

All of these changes bewildered the returning Polish Jews, who had left six to seven years earlier. Yet the first, and strongest, impression that most of the Jewish repatriates recorded was the virulence of the antisemitism that greeted them. Of course, the country they fled in 1939 had not always been friendly toward its Jewish citizens. In a moving 1946 article about returning to his hometown of Kielce, Y. Shmulevitsh even hints at a certain comfort in seeing the familiar faces of the "Endeks" (members of the antisemitic National Democratic Party) alongside the town drunks and prostitutes when he arrived at the train station.[110] Yet the repatriates could not have predicted the augmented fear and hatred awaiting them on their return.

Some returnees noticed this change while still on the repatriation trains. When Tema Abel gave birth to her son on the train, she did not have clothing, diapers, or food for him. Thrilled to finally enter home territory, she requested milk from the first stationmaster on the Polish side of the border. When he instead threatened their lives, her expectations began to change.[111] Dorothy Zanker Abend, suffering from malaria, could not sit up to look out of the train windows. Nonetheless, she heard the antisemitic chants as they passed into Polish territory.[112] Zyga Elton tried to describe what these scenes meant for the returnees:

> The scenery changed somehow when we reached the border between Poland and the Ukraine. Wherever we stopped on the Polish side, we attracted the local population who stared at us, taunting and jeering, exhorting us to go back from whence we had come. It was painful to see the faces full of hatred, not yet satiated by the havoc brought upon our people: faces still burning with a merciless desire to destroy the wretched remnants. They went on with undiminished fervor, cursing and attacking the newly returned exiles. This welcome did not augur a bearable sojourn in the country of our birth, where for generations our forefathers had lived and toiled. We realized that our troubles were not yet over.[113]

Yiddish writer Dovid Sfard portrayed this same vengeful gaze as both familiar and novel: "In them [the eyes of the Polish non-Jews] was the old hatred and contempt but hidden behind it a sort of bitterness and schadenfreude that shocked the heart."[114]

Non-Jewish Poles returning from the Soviet Union were also often taken aback by the transformation of their compatriots in their absence. Ewa Koźmińska-Frejlak quotes in full Halina Jodko-Kamińska's disturbing description of her repatriation train's layover in Biała Podlaska. When she got out to stretch her legs, passersby asked her to identify the carriages in which the Jews were traveling. She was initially puzzled by the request: "We were in exile together, we are returning together. And why are you asking?" She understood when young men appeared with iron rods and began attacking the Jews outside of the wagons. At the next stop, people shouted for Jews to be thrown off the train and she heard shots and cries. In Jodko-Kamińska's retelling, the Catholic returnees protected the Jews from assault.[115]

A number of Polish Jewish returnees refer to hearing rumors of antisemitic violence on the repatriation trains.[116] While hearsay cannot be relied upon for facts, it certainly illuminates their concerns. Dovid Feinzeig and his family, however, actually had a positive experience of return: "We were greeted at the station by a band playing Russian and Polish songs and by a number of Polish dignitaries who delivered welcoming addresses in our honor." Nonetheless, having heard about the growing threat of antisemitism, Feinzeig notes that his family did not speak Yiddish at any of the stations where the train stopped.[117]

Although antisemitism appears frequently in the testimonial literature, it was certainly not the only concern of the returnees. Now refugees once again, they focused on finding safe places to stay and seeking information about their loved ones. While a few describe returning directly to their hometowns, most arrived either in Łódź or in the formerly German areas to be incorporated into Poland, especially Lower Silesia. With the destruction of Warsaw, Łódź had become a hub of postwar Jewish life. Polish authorities were eager to lay claim to the new regions and tried to steer returnees to settle there—especially Polish citizens who had given up their homes and property in the eastern regions incorporated by the Soviet Union. As Bożena Szaynok has demonstrated, the emerging Jewish community and Polish state organs also agreed that Jews would be safer in this area, without the possibility of violence over property disputes.[118] Katharina Friedla shows, however, that the relative hospitality toward Polish Jews did not extend to German Jews returning to their homes in the region.[119]

While the ZPP had overseen the repatriation, its authority stopped at the Soviet border. The Polish government in formation had to help the new arrivals, supported by the reconstituted Jewish community and charitable organizations. Files from the Society for Safeguarding the Health of the Jewish Population (Towarzystwo Ochrony Zdrowia Ludności Żydowskiej, TOZ) show that the veteran public health organization had already set up committees and clinics in Lower Silesia. Founded in 1922 as a breakaway from a similar society that had functioned in prerevolutionary Russia, TOZ served the health needs of the Jewish poor in Poland throughout the interwar period.[120] With funding from the American Jewish Joint Distribution Committee (JDC), TOZ continued to operate in several ghettos until lack of personnel, medicine, and money put an end to its work.[121] After the war, TOZ reformed under the auspices of the CKŻP, which also supervised the reception of Jewish repatriates.[122]

In June 1946 a Dr. Szpindel in Dzierżoniów (Ger. Reichenbach) submitted a report on the recent arrival of a transport from Bukhara. Each of the train's forty wagons contained between thirty and thirty-five people. A nurse and two doctors from TOZ met the train to offer immediate medical help. According to Dr. Szpindel's report, those in need included two-day-old twins and their mother, a forty-three-year old man with advanced typhus, another man who injured his leg jumping out of the wagon, and many children suffering from dyspepsia and anemia.[123]

Despite their careful records and efforts, it would appear that other trains arrived to a less organized welcome. Jacob Pat, a Polish Jew who had immigrated to the United States before the war, returned soon afterward as a representative of the Jewish Labor Committee. His fast-moving memoir chronicles the scenes that he witnessed in various cities across the country. As he met with the local Jewish community in Częstochowa, nine hundred hungry Jews from "Deep Russia" arrived at the train station. The members of the Jewish committee had to scrape together funds to feed them before their train departed for Lower Silesia.[124]

The repatriates' destinations and the timing of their arrival could also play a role in the sort of reception they received. Dovid Feinzeig, the returnee whose train was greeted with music and speeches instead of jeers and taunts, repatriated fairly early. His family had relocated from Central Asia to Ukraine toward the end of 1944. They were thus among the first to return, arriving on February 1, 1946. Although he was already a teenager, Feinzeig writes that the staff of the Jewish community in Łódź were thrilled to see a child.[125] Both Jewish children and the elderly had become endangered species due to the Holocaust. Jacob Pat recalls that Emil Sommerstein, who also repatriated on the early side, found himself surrounded by children pointing excitedly at his white beard. He had been planning to shave after the long journey but vowed to keep the whiskers if it gave the few surviving Jewish children joy.[126]

While the self-repatriates and early repatriation trains trickled in, by the spring and summer of 1946, the number of repatriates overwhelmed the numbers and capacities of the Polish Jews already in place. A report on Jewish life in Lower Silesia on January 15, 1946, listed 3,873 Jews, of whom 877 had returned from the USSR.[127] Six months later, as of July 1, 82,840 repatriates had arrived in Lower Silesia. By the end of July, the culmination of the repatriation, the number had reached 90,700.[128] On a local level, this meant that by November 1946, there were 8,632 repatriates in Dzierżoniów alone. They made up over half of the 13,114 Jews registered there.[129] In the smaller community of Lubań (Ger. Lauban), repatriates were 62 out of the 77 registered Jews.[130] Throughout this period, the CKŻP and its local affiliates expended great energy keeping track of the repatriates and their needs.

Like many other repatriates, Ezra Zynger and his family were taken directly to the western regions of the country—in their case, to Dzierżoniów. Although they had originally fled from Warsaw and wanted to find out about relatives left behind there, they understood that it would be easier to live in the formerly German areas. From their new home base they could trace news of their family members.[131]

The search for the living and facts about the dead consumed many of the repatriates. Dina Gabel and her mother settled in Szczecin (Ger. Stettin), where they found a small apartment abandoned by its former German inhabitants. In their first months back, she writes,

> the days were spent in the streets around the Joint Committee. Strangers stopped each other, constantly inquiring, "Where have you been? Did you hear about so and so? Did you meet someone by the name of . . . ?" Constantly looking, eyes searching, asking, hoping to hear what was never destined to be heard.[132]

In addition to word of mouth, the survivors relied on the lists that were centrally posted in communities across Poland. These lists were grassroots efforts to facilitate family reunions, and people often put their names on multiple lists. If they knew that they would be moving on, they might leave a note of their planned destination and contact information. Jack Pomerantz's surviving sister recognized him while he was checking the list in Łódź.[133] Over time, organizations like the JDC, the Red Cross, and the United Nations Relief and Rehabilitation Administration (UNRRA) would attempt to create central databases for this information. The CKŻP also kept a list of returning Polish Jews.

Yet even finding a familiar name did not necessarily result in an instantaneous reunion. Moshe Erlich took his first leave from the Red Army soon after the end of the war. He traveled to Warsaw and, finding no trace of his family, left his name and address on a list. Three months later Erlich re-

FIGURE 5.3. Armed guard in front of the Jewish Committee in Wałbrzych, Poland, c. 1946; note the Yiddish newspapers on display. American Jewish Joint Distribution Committee Archives.

ceived a letter from his brother, recently liberated from a German labor camp and residing in Wrocław (Ger. Breslau). However, by the time Erlich could secure another leave to visit, his brother was no longer at the address he had sent. In his disappointment, Erlich checked the list at the local Jewish community building and found his sister's name. She and her child had survived in the Soviet Union. Armed with this cheering news, Erlich had to return to his unit. On his third leave, the three siblings finally reunited and shared their stories.[134] Betty Rich describes the emotional impact of the lists in a retrospective analogy: "Many years later, when I visited Israel and stood at the Wailing Wall in Jerusalem, I was struck by the memory that I had been at a wailing wall once before—the wall covered with the long lists of only survivors."[135]

While searching for information and relatives, the returnees also had to reorganize their lives in these new settings. The postwar Polish Yiddish newspaper *Dos Naye Lebn* (The New Life, 1945–1950) contains numerous articles on the attempt to reestablish Jewish life in Poland, particularly in the so-called Recovered Territories (Ziemie Odzyskane). Some of the articles about these new communities sound more like communist propaganda or travel pieces than balanced journalism. Describing his new home in Zgorzelec (Ger. Görlitz), on the German border, Mikhael Rubinovitsh waxed eloquent about the modern houses with gas and electricity. The only drawback, he teased his readers, was the profusion of gardens and fruit trees.[136] An article filed from Szczecin profiled problems establishing new communities in the region, but also great energy. The author, Y. Fogtlman, acknowledged that war had destroyed much of the housing stock and that the arrival of the repatriates had exacerbated this problem. He also pointed to a lack of economic opportunities. Fogtlman ended his piece on a positive note, describing the potential of new cooperative crafts and agricultural initiatives.[137]

A 1947 book and film also showcase the remarkable optimism of at least a portion of the Jewish settlers in Lower Silesia. Jacob Egit's *Tsu a nay lebn (tsvey yor in Yidisher yishev in Nidershlezie)* (To a New Life (Two Years in the Jewish Settlement in Lower Silesia)) is a celebration of the achievements of the Jewish communal and economic life rising out of the ashes.[138] The short film combines the same themes with dramatic music, an upbeat Yiddish voiceover, and footage of the beautiful scenery, new factories, and religious, cultural, and educational institutions and events.[139] Egit, who had resided in the section of Poland annexed by the Soviets in 1939, was mobilized into the Red Army and returned as a liberator. He fell in love with the idea of building an autonomous and creative new Jewish life in Lower Silesia and quickly became a leader there. Even in the book written later in his life, *Grand Illusion,* chronicling the failure of the experiment, Egit still recognized the power of the idea: "For those Jews and many others who would return from Siberia and other parts of Russia, Lower Silesia could be the first stop on the road to rehabilitation, here Jews could regain their strength and self-respect by reasserting their identity."[140]

While the depictions of these contemporaneous boosters tend to focus on economic accomplishments, when describing this period of time in retrospect, the returnees themselves focus more on Jewish cultural life. Yiddish theater impresario Ida Kaminska was asked to lead the State Yiddish Theater in Łódź soon after her repatriation in late 1946. Later she succeeded in moving it back to Warsaw.[141] Comic actors Shimon Dzigan and Israel Schumacher also returned to Łódź, although, having been in prison in the USSR, they had a much harder time getting out. Dzigan complains that the lowliest street dog in Lvov lived better than they did at that point. The Jewish community welcomed them warmly on their return to Poland in July 1947, and they threw themselves into work, including the film *Undzere kinder* (Our Children). The Surviving Remnant of Polish Jewry eagerly attended their performances even if, according to Dzigan, many in the audience silently cried through the shows.[142]

Many Jewish writers and artists returned as well, both from the Soviet Union and from camps, hiding, and service in the partisans. A number of scholars have written about the challenge and promise of their position.[143] The new communist government offered regular employment, but only to those willing to embrace its tenets. According to Joanna Nalewajko-Kulikov and Magdalena Ruta, "From the outset, the best-known and most talented survivors wanted to leave Poland. Those who stayed supported the political changes underway, although few of them were true creative personalities."[144] Kaminska stayed, although Dzigan and Schumacher decamped to Israel soon after the completion of the film.

Survivors and returnees also created their own cultural activities, especially under the auspices of the newly revived Zionist youth movements. On his return, Zev Katz expressed wonderment at the vitality of the Zionist movement in postwar Poland. "The whole thing looked as if the Germans and the Holocaust, camps in Siberia, years in Central Asia had never happened—all those terrible, eventful years each of which seemed like an entire epoch."[145] For the youth, this brief cultural flowering was particularly important. Janka Goldberger, age fifteen when her family returned to Kraków, joined the Zionist youth group Szomer. She contrasts her own and her peers' joy and freedom with their parents' planning and mourning.[146] Shimon Redlich also reflects on the robust political activism and the joy of youth in a book about postwar Łódź that is part memoir and part historical research. Redlich and his mother survived the war in hiding in eastern Poland. After the war he interacted with repatriates and others in the bustling center of postwar Polish Jewish life. He describes Bundists, Zionists, and communists vying for control of the Jewish street, but also the pleasure and hope of a return to life.[147]

Even Jewish religious life in Poland experienced a rebirth after the war. Dovid Feinzeig and his mother and siblings repatriated early, in February 1946. They immediately presented themselves at the Jewish community complex in Łódź, where they received help with clothing, housing, and kosher food. In the coming months Feinzieg watched numerous important rabbis arrive from Soviet exile. The growing concentration of Orthodox leaders meant greater opportunities for young Dovid and his

FIGURE 5.4. Helena Storch, who survived the war in Kazakhstan with her mother, joins other Polish Jews in commemorating the anniversary of the Warsaw Ghetto Uprising in Szczecin, April 19, 1947. United States Holocaust Memorial Museum, courtesy Helena Jacobs.

siblings to continue their religious education. Later he even worked for the Agudah (Agudath Yisrael), an Orthodox organization that existed before the war, providing aid to other Jewish refugees and helping to establish religious institutions.[148]

Jewish religious life began to flourish elsewhere as well, particularly in Lower Silesia. When Yitzhak Meir Safronovitch and his family arrived in Ziębice (Ger. Müsterberg), they promptly involved themselves in the synagogue and Jewish school.[149] Many such institutions received funding from the Joint, as the JDC was known. According to August Grabski and Albert Stankowski, the JDC provided subsidies to thirty-eight synagogues, a larger number of prayer houses, three yeshivas, thirty-six Talmud Torahs, thirty-four daycare centers, fifteen kosher kitchens, seventeen ritual baths, sixty-seven cemeteries, and twenty-two rabbis between 1945 and 1949. They also note that many more communal structures certainly functioned without JDC aid.[150]

Of course, the revivals of Jewish culture, politics, and religion during this period were entwined. Zvi Faier and his siblings, for example, repatriated to Poland with their orphanage. Their father was serving in the Red Army and their mother returned alone. When Zionists came to recruit them in the orphanage, Faier explained that they had parents and would wait for them before making any decisions. The family eventually reunited in Szczecin, where Faier attended a Jewish school, had his bar mitzvah, joined the Orthodox Zionist youth group Hashomer Hadati, and sang in a choir. Faier recalls everyone in the audience crying during their version of Psalm 137 on the Jewish fast day of the Ninth of Av. Later the choir traveled to Warsaw to perform at the dedication of the Warsaw Ghetto Uprising Monument.[151]

In addition to pursuing cultural activities, the youth pursued education with great enthusiasm. Janina Bauman, who had survived in German-occupied Poland, took a position as a tutor for repatriated children in an orphanage. In her memoir she describes the uphill battle they faced:

> Nearly all these children had spent most of their lives in exile, wandering across the Soviet Union, until they were finally sent to a home in Uzbekistan. Although they had on and off attended local schools they had not learnt much. When the home with its director and his wife was repatriated to Poland, the children found themselves lost in Polish schools: they knew very little about Polish history and literature, they had never learnt Latin or French, and they could hardly write in Polish.

Later Bauman herself, while active in a Zionist group and working part-time for the CKŻP, started a degree in journalism.[152] Both within the Jewish community and outside it, postwar Poland offered many educational opportunities.

While the high concentration of others like themselves led the majority of postwar Polish Jews to settle in Łódź and Lower Silesia, some returned to their hometowns. Even those who had chosen to reside in the new Jewish centers were inexorably drawn to their former homes, whether by the pull of nostalgia, the desire to recover their property, or hopes of information about missing family members. Most of the repatriates made at least one trip to their homes of origin, where they personally confronted the repercussions of the German genocide. Here, where they knew the streets and their former residents, the loss could not be abstract. Shalom Omri, along with many others, recalls in his video testimony the pain of returning to a hometown paved with Jewish tombstones.[153] Scholars have noted the common trope of survivors referring to postwar Poland as a Jewish graveyard.[154]

This description captures not only the knowledge that millions of European Jews had met their deaths there but also the visible reality that the German occupiers had destroyed Jewish cemeteries and repurposed the tombstones.

Confronted with the agonizing physical legacy of the German occupation, Jews who returned to their homes also faced antisemitism from the local population. From strangers, and even from acquaintances, the newly arrived Polish Jews heard appreciation for the genocide and distress that they had returned. In a casual conversation on the tram in Kraków after the war, Janka Goldberger recalls a passenger declaring, "Ah, but it was bad here during the war. You can't imagine how bad. In fact there is only one good thing that Hitler ever did, and for that he ought to be given a golden monument. He got rid of the Jews."[155]

Many other returnees record comparable remarks. One young man began dating a non-Jewish woman he met soon after his return. He reports that he broke off the relationship as soon as she voiced a similar sentiment.[156] A variation, generally expressed by neighbors, was surprise mixed with distaste at the Jews' survival and return. Sara Bergman describes running into an old girlfriend, Halina, soon after her joyous return to Poland. "How come they did not kill you?" Halina asked. Bergman adds that while she was emaciated and bedraggled, Halina looked hale and healthy.[157]

These sorts of welcomes were at times paired with threats of violence. In her relatively gentle story, Ruth Hohberg recalls being turned away rudely from the home they had left behind in Bielsko. Her father's subsequent effort to retrieve their possessions led to accusations and threats.[158] Szymon Grajcar was still in Uzbekistan with his younger brother when their older brother Avrom, in the Red Army, asked them to send the paperwork that would allow him to reclaim their family property in Ryki. They did so, but when Avrom attempted to submit the legal documentation, he was told that it would seal his death sentence, and he thus fled for his life.[159]

Postwar antisemitism in Poland also manifested in actual violence. Drawing on the work of Jan Gross and Irena Grudzińska-Gross,[160] Łukasz Krzyżanowski emphasizes the connections—and causality—among these forms of antisemitism. The violence was often occasioned and exacerbated by Jews' attempts to reassert their legal standing, which had been stripped away by German practices during the occupation and held in abeyance by the Polish state's aggressive policies of nationalization afterward. After the war, many Polish non-Jews no longer saw Jews as legitimate Polish citizens.[161] To highlight this point, Krzyżanowski refers to the Jews throughout his book as "ghost citizens." In this he echoes the sentiment of Isaiah Trunk, a repatriate who became an important historian of the Holocaust: "We've learned that Jew-hatred does not require the presence of a single Jew! Polish anti-Semites made war against ghosts; there were no Jews."[162] Local violence against Jewish property seekers soon spiraled, leading to spasms of anti-Jewish violence motivated by more general anti-Jewish sentiment in postwar Poland.

Jonas Landesman related a particularly gruesome tale in October 1945. After his release from a penal camp in Arkhangelsk in December 1944, Landesman had returned to Rzeszów in the hopes of finding his family. On discovering that neither his wife and baby nor his parents or his many siblings and in-laws had survived, he moved in with several other lone Jewish men. In June 1945 they were all arrested and accused of conducting a ritual murder on a Polish child. As word—and violence—spread, the other men left town immediately upon their release the next day. Landesman stayed to take care of some business and as a result spent the next few months in jail, where he endured constant beatings from guards and other prisoners. At the time he gave his testimony, he had been allowed out but still awaited trial.[163]

The disinterest, or even participation, of local officials in antisemitic actions is a motif in many Jewish accounts. This hostility was not lost on the governing powers. Natalia Aleksiun reproduces two reports prepared by the NKVD and delivered to the highest levels of the Soviet state apparatus in August and October 1945. Both detail a range of antisemitic incidents, participants, local responses, and potential explanations.[164] Polish officials also monitored the situation closely. Of course, the safety of Jews was of prime concern to the CKŻP. As Bożena Szaynok notes, "News came in almost daily of attacks on Jews, or robberies and murders."[165] Jews also brought their complaints to the central authorities. Jan Gross cites numerous examples of Jews raising charges against local officials.[166]

Jews increasingly chose to live in the safety of Poland's larger Jewish communities but remained vulnerable in transit. Polish trains, in particular, became a peril. Irving Badner was returning to Kraków from a visit with friends in Wrocław when the train stopped and a band of people began pulling Jews out of the cars. He could hear shooting and was petrified. To his immense relief, the rioters did not reach his car, and his fellow passengers did not point him out to them. Nevertheless, the close call convinced him that he could not stay in Poland.[167]

As Gross has shown, anti-Jewish violence became normalized as a result of the Holocaust. Even the majority of Polish non-Jews, who did not take part in killing and looting, came to see Jews as deserving victims. As Alina Skibińska wrote of the war as a whole, "Indifference of the majority remained the prevailing attitude, and distance turned into hate."[168] From this perspective, Jews caught and murdered in isolated villages or on train cars were themselves worthy of blame, and should have known better than to travel or visit small towns alone.[169] Andrzej Żbikowski cites a figure of 650–750 corroborated murders of Jews in Poland after the Holocaust, although he emphasizes the impossibility of an exact count due to the furtive and local nature of most of the crimes.[170]

The postwar violence culminated in the Kielce Pogrom of July 1946. A great deal has been written about the lead up to the outbreak of violence, as well as its aftermath.[171] Motivated by vague rumors that a local boy had been abducted by Jews, a mob converged on an apartment building that housed most of the survivors in Kielce and began beating them to death. Local authorities proved unable to stop the violence, which soon spread to the train station as well. Forty people were murdered, yet there was neither public outcry nor legal justice in response to the shocking violence. Many Church leaders justified the event as a reprisal for Jewish involvement in the ascendant communist regime. Survivors of the Holocaust and Soviet exile saw the monstrous violence and abandonment by both sides of the political spectrum as a clarion call to leave Poland. Kielce marked a turning point in Jewish emigration.

Although the Polish Jewish repatriates found the antisemitism in postwar Poland harder to fathom than did Polish Jews who had spent the war years in Poland, both responded with equal shock to the grisly events in Kielce. It could have been any one of them. Yocheved Zamari's father had hoped to travel back to their hometown soon after their arrival in Lower Silesia. However, as she was still recovering from appendicitis and her father did not want to leave her alone, he let a friend go without him. According to Zamari's testimony, the friend was murdered in Kielce on his way.[172]

Moshe Kaner, only nineteen when he fled Hrubieszów, traveled to Bukhara after the amnesty because he had heard that his friend from home, Barukh, was there. Kaner moved in with Barukh's relatives and joined their illegal trading business. In 1945 he married a woman named Raya and their daughter was born. After repatriating to western Poland in 1946, Kaner, his cousin, and Barukh returned to Hrubieszów to search for traces of their families or possessions. On the way back, in July 1946, their train was stopped in Kielce, and Barukh and Kaner's cousin got off to investigate the problem. Kaner waited on board until a group of local Poles came into the car and asked the passengers whether there were any Jews among them. They all pointed to Kaner. The men dragged him off the train and forced him to stand against the wall of the station. According to his testimony for Yad Vashem, Kaner was fortunate to be standing next to a window: the shooter wanted to avoid killing any of the non-Jewish Poles inside the station and as a result Kaner was not gravely wounded.

At the hospital Kaner was able to help other victims. Later he located his cousin, but neither of them could find Barukh, even in the morgue. Kaner stayed for the mass funeral service and to testify to the police. He assumes that his friend Barukh was murdered that day in Kielce when he himself only narrowly escaped death.[173] Kaner's traumatic experience, and dramatic escape, makes for compelling testimony. Indeed, his Yad Vashem interviewer seemed far more interested in his brush with the aftermath of the Holocaust than his time in the USSR. His subsequent decisions to leave Poland and settle in the Jewish state also make sense. Yet what came to be known as the Kielce Pogrom appears not just in testimonies of those who witnessed or eluded it but in most of the sources produced by Polish Jewish repatriates after the war. In the words of Zev Katz, "Kielce gave us the last push."[174]

As they tried to make sense of virulent antisemitism and to reconstruct at least a semblance of Poland's once vibrant Jewish civilization, the returnees also had to contend with the state's ongoing political transformation. At the Yalta Conference in February 1945, President Franklin Roosevelt and Prime Minister Winston Churchill exacted a promise of free and fair elections in Poland from Stalin. The Soviet definition of elections, however, turned out to be very different from that of the other Allies. Poland, along with the rest of Eastern Europe, gradually came under communist domination despite the opposition of the majority of the population.

In Poland the imposition of communist rule met with active political resistance and ongoing violence. Repatriates from the Soviet Union had firsthand experience with Soviet communism. Poland's transition presented a great opportunity for the small minority who had joined the Communist Party before the war or worked with communist organizations such as the ZPP during the war. It led to profound anxiety for the majority, who had never embraced communist ideology and had suffered in the USSR.

As Krystyna Kersten shows in *The Establishment of Communist Rule in Poland*, the Soviet campaign in Poland was characterized by numerous contradictions: "On the one hand, they [the communist authorities] urgently attempted to win a minimum of social acceptance; on the other hand, knowing the majority of society was against them, they broke all opposition and suppressed all actions threatening their monopoly." The Soviet authorities moved cautiously in dealing with the cultural sphere, hoping to incorporate this useful element of Polish society.[175]

Jewish cultural institutions began forming even before the war ended and gradually came under increasing state supervision. As Natalia Aleksiun demonstrates, the Central Jewish Historical Commission (Centralna Żydowski Komisja Historyczna) formed in Lublin only one month after liberation in late 1944. In the next few years it was remarkably productive in forming new branches, publishing books, collecting material, conducting interviews, and contributing to historical investigations and judicial proceedings. Yet, by October 1947, the now streamlined organization came under the auspices of the Jewish Historical Institute (Żydowski Instytut Historyczny, ŻIH) in Warsaw and under Communist Party control oversight.[176]

Other Jewish cultural, political, and religious organizations were also brought into conformity. The CKŻP, formed in 1944 to serve the needs of the emerging postwar Jewish community, originally functioned pluralistically, with communists, Bundists, and Zionists serving together. It was very active in helping the repatriates upon their arrival in Poland. In 1949, the CKŻP came under Communist Party control, and by 1950 it no longer existed.[177] The TSKŻ, which replaced it, had a far narrower purview and functioned as an arm of the state.

In November 1945 the CKŻP established a Department of Care for Young People to oversee the patchwork of emerging Jewish schools trying to meet the needs of Polish Jewish children and adolescents. The schools under its oversight grew in number and student bodies over the next year. Even after the wave of emigration in late 1946, thirty schools in twenty-nine locations served nearly three thousand students. Religious and Zionist schools thrived separately, and with significant financial support from abroad. While waves of repatriation briefly swelled the classrooms of all of these schools, waves of emigration would soon make many of them superfluous. The nationalization of Jewish schools in 1948 put an end to officially sanctioned Hebrew and Orthodox schooling, but a handful of secular Polish Jewish schools remained until 1968.[178]

The lively Yiddish cultural institutions that grew up after the war were threatened by emigration even before the imposition of communist orthodoxy. Joanna Nalewajko-Kulikov and Magdalena Ruta refer to the period from 1944 to 1949 as "Salvage Culture" and the period from 1950 to 1958 as "Culture in the Service of Ideology."[179] With the installation of the TSKŻ, the remaining Yiddish writers had to content themselves with one official newspaper.[180] The state-sponsored Yiddish theater also came under close supervision.[181]

Beginning in 1946, Orthodox institutions faced pressure to come under the auspices of the CKŻP. This led to the formation of the Religious Union of the Mosaic Faith in Poland (Związek Religijny Wyznania Mojżeszowego w Polsce) in 1949. Although the Union endured legal limbo, public attacks, state-sponsored secularization, and ongoing emigration, it continued to function and fulfill its members' religious needs on a small scale.[182]

In 1950 all Jewish activities and institutions were merged under the TSKŻ. Together with the expulsion of the JDC in 1949, this transition effectively signaled the end of pluralism and autonomy in the Jewish community. As Audrey Kichelewski has written, "This was but the application in the 'Jewish Street' of the same process going on in the country as a whole."[183] After a relatively gradual period of transition, the Soviet Union demanded adherence to its strict Stalinist dictates. Kamil Kijek explains that Jews could only build their institutions by endorsing the communist project. Paradoxically, the escalation of that project necessitated the destruction of their cultural creations.[184]

In the early years of the communist experiment in postwar Poland, activists believed that they could improve upon the Soviet model. They tried to convince themselves and others that they could create a "Polish way" that would select the best parts of communism without its Stalinist excess and with room for uniquely Polish character. In a parallel manner, some Jewish activists advocated for a *nusekh Poyln:* a Polish-Jewish-socialist culture that would marry the best of Jewish traditional modes with cutting-edge socialist theory and praxis. Joanna Nalewajko-Kulikov, Magdalena Ruta, Jaff Schatz, Marci Shore, and others have written about the painful reckoning of this generation of believers.[185]

If 1946 and the Kielce Pogrom was the turning point for those who chose to leave the country, 1950 and the sovietization of Jewish life was a turning point for those who chose to stay. The closure and restriction of cultural, religious, political, and even charitable institutions signaled the end of a dream. The cultural activists realized that *nusekh Poyln* was not to be. Ordinary Polish Jews saw their hopes for re-creating a vibrant and pluralistic Poland replaced with an all too familiar Soviet hegemony. The activists continued to produce positive and patriotic depictions of their situation while in Poland. Those who later left then wrote critical retrospective analyses. There is relatively little testimonial literature on how the contraction of postwar Jewish life affected those who were less involved. Undoubtedly, this is primarily because of the relatively small numbers who stayed and the fact that few of them produced memoirs or testimonies. Additionally, they were more engaged with building new families and lives than with politics and ideology.

Polish Jews were also blamed for the imposition of Soviet-style communism in an echo of the accusations that Jews had welcomed the Soviet invaders in 1939. This remains a sensitive issue in Jewish and Polish relations today. In fact, the two discussions are often mistakenly merged, with anachronistic assumptions transferred from one set of historical circumstances to the other. The Soviets delivered decrees and established order in post-liberation Poland through a set of handpicked loyal communist Poles, most of whom had been in the USSR during the war. This group included Jews, although they were generally not at the very top. Nonetheless, the very presence of Jewish names, or even of polonized names hiding those known to be of Jewish background, allowed some among the fiercely anticommunist and nationalist Polish camp to impugn the entire enterprise as a foreign imposition. As Schatz points out, "It was not the actual number of Jews on the regime's side but their visibility that reinforced this Jewish stereotype. The new social prominence won by a group of top politicians of Jewish origin stood in shocking contrast to the inferior status ascribed Jews in their traditional image."[186] The potency of existing antisemitism could be used to amplify anticommunism, and vice versa.

Drawing on prewar antisemitic stereotypes and familiar Nazi wartime propaganda, opponents of the new regime exploited the myth of the *żydokomuna* and instrumentalized antisemitism against communism. This, of course, affected the political alliances of Polish Jews. Natalia Aleksiun writes of a "vicious circle" whereby Jews were pushed into association with the communists by the very anticommunist—and antisemitic—opposition that accused them of association with the communists.[187] As Michael Steinlauf notes, there were also other reasons that at least some Polish Jews worked with the communists:

The kernel of truth in such accusations was related to the vast difference between the situation of Poles and Jews in the new Poland. Because so many Jews owed their survival to having spent the war years in the Soviet Union and because the postwar Polish government seemed the only force capable of defending Jewish rights and safeguarding Jewish life and property after the war, most Jews in Poland and throughout the world, although not without many reservations, supported the new government.[188]

While Steinlauf may be correct that most Polish Jews wished for the success of the communist-led government, this does not mean that they agitated, or even voted, on its behalf. Perhaps even more importantly, as Feliks Tych writes, "Any objective observer of the historical process knows full well that communism would have been introduced in Poland by Stalin irrespective of whether Jews had access to the ruling Communist Party hierarchy or not."[189] Tych refers specifically to antisemitic accusations about the overly Jewish makeup of the leadership, but he makes an important point regarding the trajectory of postwar Poland overall.

Whether or not they voted for the communists, most of the Surviving Remnant of Polish Jewry, wherever they survived the war, decided to leave Poland after the war. As Koźmińska-Frejlak observes, "emigration can be considered as a form of plebiscite or test."[190] Indeed, the postwar period was one of rapid and continuous decline in the Polish Jewish community. Of a postwar Polish Jewish population of slightly over three hundred thousand, it is estimated that at most one-third survived in camps or hiding in Poland. Over two-thirds lived out the war in the unoccupied regions of the Soviet Union and came back afterward. According to figures compiled by Dariusz Stola, between thirty thousand and eighty thousand Polish Jews left before the repatriation, leading to a postwar population height of 220,000 registered Jews in June 1946. "From 1946 until the end of the communist regime in 1989, Poland's Jewish population was in constant decline."[191] As many as seventy thousand left between the time of the Kielce Pogrom and February 1947, when it became harder to do so. The number of Polish Jews remained steady at around one hundred thousand for the next few years. It is not possible to distinguish between Holocaust survivors and repatriates in these figures.

A number of scholars have tried to understand this exodus. While they may differ over the relative size of the emigration, all agree on the major contributing factors. Tych and Monika Adamczyk-Garbowska describe these factors in the introduction to their outstanding volume of articles about the postwar period:

> Some could not imagine living in their loved ones' cemetery; others did not feel safe after the wave of pogroms, especially after the Kielce Pogrom in 1946, and the hidden murder of Jews. Still others did not want to stay in postwar Poland because of the Communist system imposed there. Many left Poland because they wanted to contribute to building the Jewish State in Palestine. Besides, with each passing year, especially since the late 1940s, the Communist authorities withdrew more and more of the broad cultural and political autonomy granted to Jews between 1944 and 1947.[192]

By far the reason most frequently stated in the memoirs and testimonies of flight survivors is the Kielce Pogrom. On the one hand, this can be read as a statement of generalized insecurity. The events in Kielce were but a symptom of the rampant antisemitism and lawlessness of the period and would not have been so decisive had they not been part of a larger pattern. The brutal murders, and the public indifference to them, convinced Polish Jews that the hostility they faced and the rumors of antisemitic violence they heard were the new reality in their homeland.

On the other hand, Kielce also becomes a sort of cliché in both the scholarship and the testimonies. Decades after the events in question, historians and witnesses face the challenge of articulating Polish Jews' lengthy and complicated decision-making processes in a couple of sentences. Thus, everyone left because of Kielce, but in truth they also left because everyone else was leaving. Jewish life in Poland could only be rebuilt with the active participation of Polish Jews. As more departed, those who remained had to reconsider their own options and the viability of their fragile communal structures. The Kielce Pogrom is an easily justifiable metonym for a host of reasons that are too difficult and convoluted to untangle.

This is particularly true for the official repatriates. While survivors of camps and those hiding on the "Aryan" side returned as early as 1944, followed by Red Army soldiers and self-repatriates, the trains carrying Polish Jews from the depths of the USSR began arriving only in February 1946 and culminated in July of that year. In the intervening time, these people had been able to contact relatives in Poland and abroad. Even if they had not yet fully registered the scope of the Holocaust, they realized that the Poland to which they would be returning was vastly different from the one they had left. Zionists among them had reestablished their organizational networks and received support from the Yishuv. Thus, many of the Polish Jewish refugees had made plans to leave Poland even before they returned.

Additionally, it is hard to imagine how repatriates who had not intended to leave again could have changed their plans so drastically after just a few weeks or months back in Poland. The repatriates needed time to trace missing family members, visit sites of personal significance, and, where possible, liquidate assets. If and when they decided to depart, they also needed to identify a destination and plan transportation. Jews who returned in June 1946 could hardly have done all of this within a matter of weeks. Accordingly, even when they name the Kielce Pogrom as the decisive moment in their path to emigration, the repatriates likely quit the country only months later and after considering a variety of other factors.

A poignant set of letters gathered in Szczecin helps to illustrate how Polish Jewish repatriates from the Soviet Union attempted to contact relatives abroad. None of the missives in this collection reached their addressees, as they all ended up in the possession of the local branch of the CKŻP. However, it is probable that family members on both ends expected missed connections and continued to try to reach one another. Presumably, the preserved letters are fairly representative of the types of correspondence that recent returnees sent and received.

Writing in Yiddish to an uncle in New York in May 1946, one woman prefaced her letter with a somber statement: "Of course [you] will not know from whom you could receive a letter from Poland." She went on to explain that she had just returned from Russia with her children, and asked him for help: "They are already people [*gantse mentchn*] but I have for them nothing that anyone needs."[193] In a postcard returned from France, a young man who introduced himself as the son of Freidl Müller wrote that he was the sole survivor of his family. Only his flight to Russia, he clarified, had saved him from being murdered in Treblinka.[194]

On August 7, 1946, Lieutenant Feiwel Szafran, stationed in Scotland with the Polish Armed Forces, wrote in Polish to his brother and sister-in-law in Szczecin. He had received their address from their daughter Hana in Palestine. "Hana writes to me that all day and night she cries for you," Szafran wrote, adding that he had written to them several times in Russia, but now understood that they had not received his letters. "Do you have any news of [our] relatives?" From context it would appear that they had all been in the USSR, but only the child Hana and Szafran had been fortunate enough to evacuate with Anders Army. He had then lost touch with his brother and been unable to find out information about their family members back in Poland. Now he promised to stay in close contact and to help in any way he could.[195]

The Jewish Social Service Bureau of Detroit wrote to Jakob Rubin in Szczecin in August 1946 with the good news that they had located his cousin, Hyman Ginsberg. "He and his wife were very glad to hear of your survival and are willing to do all they can to help you." The Ginsbergs' address was included.[196] Most of the letters from abroad contained addresses. Relatives who were not in a position to offer financial or immigration support, as well as those who could, sent the contact information for other family members. They also frequently requested information about other relatives in Poland. The information—about the living and the dead—was the currency of these epistolary transactions.

Although all of the Jews in postwar Poland may well have contemplated leaving, their ability to do so often was dictated by conditions only partly within their control. The returnees contacted relatives abroad out of love and longing, but also in a pragmatic search for options. As Anna Cichopek-Gajraj points out in her book on postwar Poland and Slovakia, aptly titled *Beyond Violence,* emigration was not a foregone conclusion. Scholars have adopted a paradigm of "violence and emigration" from the testimonies, but these are retrospective. Moreover, they heavily privilege those who left Poland. In fact, even after Kielce, approximately one hundred thousand Jews remained in Poland. While some were exploring exit routes, others were trying to build lives there.[197] To ignore the choices of these Polish Jews is to tell only part of the postwar story.

Gabriel and Hanna Temkin saw the increase in antisemitism and felt the pain of living so close to the former ghetto in Łódź where their relatives had suffered and died. Yet after years of dislocation, they also recognized the rare opportunity they had to complete their education. Hanna was pregnant, they received subsidized housing in a dormitory financed by the Joint, and university education was free. The Temkins elected to stay in their native country.[198] Włodzimierz Szer's deliberations also included both personal and familial concerns:

> Two reasons were keeping me here: the possibility of continuing my education in Poland and Dad still in a Soviet gulag. Leaving for the west with the aim of going to the States, Canada, Australia, or perhaps Palestine would have been then, for me, a complete break up with my dad. It was an extremely difficult decision, which I was unable to make.[199]

He and his wife stayed in Poland, and after more than ten years, were able to help his father emigrate first to Poland, and then to Israel and the United States.

Family also figured prominently in Moshe Erlich's deliberations. While serving in the Red Army in 1946, Erlich discovered that a sister and brother had also survived the war. Once he received permission, he reunited with his sister in Wrocław. As a trained violinist, he joined the orchestra of the opera. Erlich does not mention whether he considered leaving Poland at that point, but clearly the presence of his siblings made a difference.[200]

Janina and Zygmunt Bauman present an instructive case study for the interplay between family and ideology. They met at Warsaw University after the war. Janina, who had survived in the Warsaw Ghetto and by hiding in the countryside, was part of the Gordonia youth movement and planned to move to Israel after she finished her education. Zygmunt (referred to as Konrad throughout her memoir), however, had returned as a captain in the Red Army, committed to the new Poland:

> Unflinching in his faith, yet sound and clear in his reasoning, Konrad explained that there would be no room for anti-Semitism, or any other racial hatred, under Communism—this fairest of social systems, which would guarantee full equality between human beings regardless of language, race or creed. We were particularly lucky, he stressed, to have been born at the right time and in the right place to become active fighters for this noblest cause. The greatest of historical changes was happening before our eyes, here and now. To stand by as idle witnesses would be to miss a unique opportunity. Running away would be a betrayal.[201]

By marrying Zygmunt, Janina tied her fate to his, and to the great experiment of the Polish People's Republic. Both had sisters who moved to Israel, and parents who later followed, but due to Zygmunt Bauman's sense of purpose, they stayed and worked for the future there.

Polish Jews did actually benefit from improved security after Kielce, although this was due to the increasing entrenchment of the communist system rather than outrage over the killings. By the end of 1946 the Polish Communist Party had already staged a successful referendum and was preparing for elections. A campaign of terror against armed resistance fighters, intense propaganda against political opponents, and increasing surveillance of daily life had significantly narrowed the range of viable options and of people's sense of autonomy. As Kersten underscores, "Let us repeat: one of the basic functions the elections were to accomplish was to deprive society of the feeling of its own importance and dignity, to force it to surrender."[202] Nevertheless, the police state did provide added security.

The year 1947 was a period of "stabilization" in Poland as a whole, and for its Jewish community.[203] As both repatriation and emigration declined, according to Koźmińska-Frejlak, "Jewish organizations, which initially focused on providing the survivors with short-term relief, were able to undertake activities with expected long-term results, in accordance with their ideological guidelines."[204] While the Polish communist state continued to tighten its hold on all aspects of society, as well as to encourage polonization and secularization, survivors and repatriates could finally settle down, take permanent jobs, pursue their educational goals, raise families, and take part in a circumscribed Polish Jewish culture.

Stalin's death in early 1953 led to a gradual loosening of the most extreme strictures in the Soviet Union, as well as in other Eastern Bloc countries. This process sped up after Nikita Khrushchev, the new Soviet premier, denounced Stalin's cult of personality in his famous "Secret Speech" of 1956. For Poland as a whole, the ascendancy of Władysław Gomułka in 1956 seemed to augur liberalization. Polish citizens found it easier to contact relatives in the Soviet Union, easing the second repatriation. Gennady Estraikh suggests that the return of prisoners of war was meant to curry favor with frustrated Poles and distract them from the open wound left by the Katyn Massacre.[205] Among the approximately quarter of a million Poles who returned between 1955 and 1959 were about eighteen thousand Jews.[206]

A number of prominent cultural figures were among the first to be released, and the organized Jewish community in Poland hoped that this would revitalize the institutions weakened by earlier emigration. However, many of the new arrivals soon departed for Israel. This prompted some concern over the potentially negative influence of these "nationalist" elements within the Jewish community, as well as in fomenting antisemitism.[207]

In fact, antisemitism was a prominent feature of the Thaw in Poland, although not due to the influx of repatriates. The reckoning occasioned by the end of Stalinism required Polish leaders to appease the people by punishing those responsible for the worst transgressions of the previous era. Drawing on Soviet models, and on well-rehearsed Polish cultural tropes, it was expedient to blame Jews in the Communist Party. This attitude was then adopted more widely, spreading to the general public as well. Yet some Party leaders did counsel restraint, as Grzegorz Berendt emphasizes, which limited the scope of the popular response.[208] Somewhat ironically, the combination of growing antisemitism and liberalization engendered by the transitions at the top helped to loosen emigration strictures and made possible the next wave of Jewish emigration from Poland.

In what has been called the Gomułka Aliyah, around fifty-one thousand Jews left Poland, including approximately fourteen thousand of the eighteen thousand recent repatriates from the USSR.[209] The departure of just about half of the remaining Jews in the course of a few years could only have devastating effects on the few Jewish cultural, religious, and educational institutions still functioning in the country. This, of course, encouraged further emigration, especially of those most committed to Jewish life. On the other hand, the readmission of the JDC after 1956, to help with repatriation and emigration and to combat outside perceptions of antisemitism, meant that the Jewish institutions still holding on had expanded support.[210]

Mayer Galler repatriated in 1959. During the first repatriation, he had been a political prisoner. Although he had been released in 1952, he was not able to pursue an exoneration in order to have his record cleared until after Stalin's death. In 1957, with a clean passport at last, he applied to return to Poland and received permission two years later. Galler spent about a year living in Warsaw. He worked there, but mainly focused on renewing contact with relatives abroad in order to emigrate. As he had been unable to correspond with the outside world during his long incarceration, everyone in his family assumed that he had died. In his 1989 oral testimony, Galler says that after his lengthy imprisonment for a crime he did not commit, and knowing that Poland was really under Soviet control, he did not feel safe remaining there. He left as soon as he found a place to go.[211]

For some who chose to leave at this juncture, it was a relatively simple decision. They had meant to emigrate earlier but missed their chance for a variety of reasons. For Shaul Shternfeld, timing seems to have played a key role. Because he had been in prison, Shternfeld repatriated only in the spring of 1948. An active Zionist before and during the war, he had every intention of making Aliyah. However, in the time it took him to visit his home, gather information about the death of his parents, and discover two surviving sisters in Germany, Poland became a communist country and he could no longer leave. Shternfeld found work, married, and started a family. When an opening presented itself in 1957, he and his family moved to Israel.[212]

As with the earlier wave of emigration, some left mainly because many other people were doing so. Moshe Erlich, who had decided to stay in Wrocław with his sister, watched the arrival and departure of the second repatriates with some trepidation. In 1957, even though his brother and sister had no plans of leaving Poland, he elected to join the Aliyah to Israel, saying that he did not want to live among only non-Jews.[213] Like many others, Erlich did not want to be among the last Jews left in Poland.

By the end of the 1950s the Jewish population in Poland consisted of people who were committed to the communist vision, who had married non-Jewish Poles, retained their "Aryan" identities or assimilated fully into Polish culture, or who could not, for one reason or another, leave. Looking back on his youthful decision to stay in Poland after the war, Mietek Sieradzki describes a mixture of skepticism and hope: "And yet I drifted into Poland's communist service rather than taking a conscious decision to join it. Like thousands of others, I was swept along by the events and circumstances. The choices were made for me."[214] Sieradzki's father had died in the Warsaw Ghetto. His mother and brother, who survived with him in the Soviet Union, emigrated to France and Israel, respectively. He remained in Poland, where he put the language training he had received in Moscow to use in the foreign service.

Most of the twenty-five thousand to thirty thousand Jews who remained in Poland by the 1960s were highly acculturated. Quite a few worked for the government or lived in mixed Jewish and non-Jewish families. They were often also distinguished by their level of education and prominence. These were people deeply entrenched in Polish life and culture. In her innovative microhistory of the postwar Jewish residents of a particular building in Warsaw, Karen Auerbach calls attention to generational differences in this cohort. Of the children born after the war, she writes, "They grew up in homes where Polish culture filled the gaps resulting from their parents' suppression of the Jewish past."[215]

These young people would have to confront their Jewish identity for perhaps the first time, and their parents face old questions once again, in the wake of the next shockwave to hit the Jews of Poland in 1968. What came to be known as the Anti-Zionist Campaign began after the 1967 Six-Day War in Israel, with a reversal of foreign policy, but turned aggressively against Jews in Poland only following the March 1968 student protests. Dariusz Stola has outlined the campaign's three main objectives: to stop the protests, to keep them from spreading to other sectors of the population, and to initiate changes in the Party leadership: "Crushing any real Zionists was probably among the least important."[216] Nonetheless, with the encouragement of the state, Jews throughout Poland were dismissed from their jobs, socially isolated, and encouraged to depart the country based on vague and unsubstantiated accusations of Zionism. The eruption of antisemitism, promoted by the communist system they had supported, shocked the tiny community of Jews still in Poland. Close to thirteen thousand left the country in the wake of 1968.[217]

Among those who left was Suzanna Eibuszyc, born in Poland after the war to parents who had survived in the USSR. During their stay there, her father had contracted pneumonia, which then left him susceptible to tuberculosis. His tuberculosis advanced to such a stage that the family could not obtain immigration papers for any country, and thus they remained in Poland. Eibuszyc remembers that in the early 1950s there was a synagogue and Jewish community center in Ziębice, the town in Lower Silesia in which they had been placed. Later these institutions closed. She also recalls her mother lighting candles on Friday evenings behind closed curtains: "Surrounded by the hostile environment of the Catholic Church, the Communist Polish government, and her own post-traumatic stress, she found some degree of comfort in the rituals from her childhood; that was the only thing she had left of her murdered family."[218] Yet even after her father's death in 1961, they left Poland only as the situation for Jews deteriorated, and they did so with great ambivalence.

Mietek Sieradzki had been somewhat shielded from the realities of life in Communist Poland by his career in the foreign service. At first, he thought official anti-Zionism was just a high-level power struggle. As it spread, he became concerned that he might be executed on trumped-up charges. He and his wife Krysia, a non-Jewish Pole, immigrated to England with their teenage son. Jewish organizations helped them with travel costs, documents, and settling in. Eventually Sieradzki obtained a position at the British Broadcasting Company that called upon his knowledge and skills.[219]

In her memoir, Janina Bauman chronicles the fall from grace of her once prominent and committed family and their entire social circle. Bauman watched friends who had supported communism against Zionism lose their jobs under false accusations. When students in Warsaw, including her daughter, protested government overreach, they were met with overwhelming force and antisemitism. Bauman resigned her Party membership. She eventually lost her high-level position at the Polish Film Institute, as did her husband, a world-famous sociologist. At school and on the street, their younger children faced humiliations and even physical attacks. The only way to leave the country was to resign their Polish citizenship and then apply for permission to immigrate to Israel via the Dutch embassy, which was then representing Israel in Poland.[220] Their eldest daughter remained in Israel, while the rest of the family settled in England.

Those who left in 1968 had been the most committed to the communist path and had often also, in many cases, joined the Party and worked for the system. As Stola notes, "None seems to have calculated the human capital loss due to the post-March emigration. It was the best-educated wave of emigrants from Poland ever. Several thousand members of the Polish intelligentsia, including many outstanding scientists, artists and writers, left the country."[221] This group included a number of Yiddish cultural figures. Despite its many deficits, the Polish People's Republic had offered a place for artists willing to toe the line. Ida Kaminska watched the growing antisemitism and authoritarianism with alarm but was able to tour the world with her Yiddish theater ensemble. When she left in 1968, despite her fame and popularity, there was no guarantee that she would ever be able to work in her field again.[222] From their new homes, writers who had devoted their lives to rebuilding Jewish life in Poland wrote with a mix of bitterness and nostalgia. Two years after arriving in Israel, Dovid Sfard, once a central figure in postwar Polish Jewish cultural life, wrote in the poem "Benkshaft" (Longing), "Every night the Vistula flows to me."[223]

The departure of this substantial group of cultural figures meant the end of organized Jewish life in Poland. Most of the country's remaining Jewish cultural institutions did not survive the antisemitic campaign of 1968. Although the TSKŻ continued to exist, funding from the Joint was once again cut off, hastening the decline of religious and cultural life.[224] Having witnessed and experienced the purge, the remaining five thousand to ten thousand or so Jews mostly kept a low profile.[225]

Displaced Persons

The repatriates who left Poland soon after their return were transformed into the new postwar category of displaced persons (DPs). In popular consciousness, DPs and Holocaust survivors are essentially synonymous. According to numerous films, novels, journalistic portrayals, and scholarly accounts, the DP camps were peopled by those who emerged from the concentration camps, partisans, and hiding and passing. Yet the DP population overall included millions of non-Jews displaced by the war, while the Jewish DP population was composed predominantly of people who had spent the war in the unoccupied regions of the Soviet Union. Since Polish Jewish repatriates constituted almost three-fourths of the postwar Polish Jewish population, and Polish Jews were the largest group in the Jewish DP camps, this group accounted for up to two-thirds of the Jewish DPs overall.[226] However, they were also relative latecomers.

Although DP camps began opening in mid-1945, most of the Polish Jews in the Soviet Union only succeeded in repatriating nearly a year later. Many spent time in Poland before leaving once again. By the time they began arriving in the DP camps in late 1946, the camps had become functioning societies with well-established norms and administrations. As Tamar Lewinsky and Laura Jockusch have shown, this affected the Polish Jewish refugees' modes of integration into the memorial culture of the camps.[227] Margarete Myers Feinstein has compared the DP camps to the shtetlach that once characterized East European Jewish life: concentrated Jewish communities, permeable to outside forces.[228] Earlier arrivals had shaped the camps in this way through their activism and engagement.

Insofar as the Allies had considered the plight of civilians displaced by the war, they expected that these civilians would return to their homes once the fighting stopped. In late 1943 UNRRA was formed to oversee and aid this process. However, the scale of the problem stretched the capacities of the new organization. Moreover, the Allies had not realized that many Jews, as well as others from countries coming under the yoke of communism, had no intention of repatriating. Ad hoc holding centers were established, often on the sites of recently liberated concentration camps. Surrounded by guards and barbed wire, and shared with their persecutors, these centers were not safe spaces for the Jewish survivors. The survivors formed organizations to advocate for their rights.[229] Jews were granted separate camps and conditions improved, but life was not easy. As one popular witticism put it,

Question: What was the status of Adam and Eve?
Answer: Certainly they were displaced persons. They had no clothes,
    nothing to eat but an apple and lived in Paradise.[230]

Yet in 1946 the DP camps looked increasingly attractive to recent repatriates in Poland who were eager to escape the growing violence and live in communities of other Jews. The Allied authorities, already overwhelmed by those who had come before, resented these later arrivals and referred to them as infiltrees. Concerned about how many would attempt to reach Palestine, the British camps even refused to accept them. This placed further strain on the American camps, and on the Jewish nongovernmental organizations that supported them.[231] According to the 1953 memoir of Leo Schwarz, an American Jew stationed in Germany who stayed to work for the JDC, "Hardly a day passed without some new complication caused by the arrival of those who were leaving Poland, out of discouragement or fear, and seeking asylum in the American Zone."[232] Nonetheless, Polish Jewish repatriates continued to infiltrate the camps.

While none of the testimonies that I have seen describe difficulties entering the camps, the repatriates did face numerous problems in reaching the American zone. Until 1947, Polish authorities were generally well disposed toward allowing the Jewish exodus. Yet this approval was more tacit than legal, and it decreased over time. The refugees also had to pass through less open jurisdictions along the way. The Saler family paid smugglers to get them into Czechoslovakia. Mendel had to carry his mother, whose health had deteriorated due to their trials. The smugglers abandoned them at the train station, but fortunately the conductor did not look too closely at their documents. In Bratislava, local Jews gave them money and helped them to reach Prague. The Jewish community there provided them with false documents and cash to bribe the border guards. They reached the Feldafing Displaced Persons Camp at the end of 1948.[233]

On arrival the refugees began to assimilate into the camp culture. They continued to search for survivors and information about the dead. Aleena Rieger's description of her parents reflects the whole culture of the camps: "They networked frantically. They posted messages on bulletin boards, on walls, in newspapers. Letters were dispatched, crossed, forwarded from one to another: "Did you know . . . ? Have you heard . . . ? Did you see . . . ?"[234] Dorothy Zanker Abend was thrilled to learn through UNRRA that her brother Roman had survived. Roman, who had evacuated with Anders Army in 1943, subsequently helped Abend and her husband Oscar to leave the DP camp in Germany for a nicer one in Italy.[235]

In the DP camps, repatriates also continued to memorialize and chronicle what would later be known as the Holocaust.[236] According to Gabriel Finder, Jewish refugees in Germany's DP camps engaged in four types of memorialization: burial and reburial of the dead, memorial assemblies, writing memorial books, and holding days of commemoration.[237] Of the *troyer akademeyen* (mourning academies) formed to mark and mourn individual locations, Feinstein writes, "Thus they provided a forum in which those who had survived the war years in the Soviet Union and who had arrived later in the DP camps could share in their grief with others from their hometowns and become integrated into the preexisting DP society."[238]

A photograph of Alexander Contract, shared with the Shoah Foundation, shows him standing with other survivors from the same town beside a monument to their lost families and communities.[239] Many other early postwar photographs show flight survivors next to similar monuments. At the end of his testimony, Szymon Grajcar read aloud in Yiddish the entry he had contributed to the Ryki memorial book about the deaths of his family members.[240] Hanna Davidson Pankowsky recalls a monument created to honor all of the six million dead in Babenhausen, the DP camp outside Frankfurt where she lived with her family.[241] As Koppel Pinson, an American Jew and historian who worked with Jewish DPs in the American zone, wrote, "Every DP is a live documentation center and every DP camp has a historical commission."[242]

Once again beginning anew, many DPs immersed themselves fully into living in relative freedom at last. Some, like Bernard Ginsburg, were able to return to their old professions in the DP camps. He was a correspondent at the First Congress of Liberated Jews in January 1946.[243] Others trained in new professions. Many studied languages and other skills that they hoped would serve them in the future. Frumie Cohen and her family spent five years in DP camps, where she remembers the humiliation of the barbed wire and searches for contraband, but also the joy of beginning her formal Jewish education. Although the family had originally planned to go to Israel, her father changed his mind after hearing about conditions there. They were able to get an affidavit to immigrate to the United States, arriving in 1951.[244]

While Cohen finally had the opportunity to start her education in the DP camps, Victor Zarnowitz decided to complete his in Heidelberg. He recalls, "The disasters of 1939–1945—invasion, flight, war, partition, and defeat; threat of genocide and reality of deportation; loss of home, family, freedom, and everything but life—bordered on overwhelming. In the Gulag, so much concentration was required to survive from day to day, there had been little time to think about the future."[245] Zarnowitz completed his doctorate in Germany in 1951. He went on to become a prominent economist at the University of Chicago.

FIGURE 5.5. Wedding portrait of Eugenia Hochberg and Henryk Lanceter, July 1945, Lublin, Poland. Although both were raised in Brody, she survived the war under German occupation while he was mobilized into the Red Army. United States Holocaust Memorial Museum, courtesy Eugenia Hochberg Lanceter.

For others, a fresh beginning meant starting a new family. Helen Zuberman, after her repatriation from Kirghizia with her family, and several months in Poland, moved to a DP camp outside Linz, Austria. There she was involved with Zionist and theater groups and met her future husband. In her testimony for the Shoah Foundation, she refers to him as a refugee but does not specify his war experiences. They married in 1949 in a barrack with a rabbi. She then lived with him, his mother, and his sister until they all emigrated.[246] Irving Badner also married in an Austrian DP camp, although he, too, does not reveal where his wife spent the war. Trained as a dentist, Badner rented a chair at a Viennese dental office. Soon all of the DPs, including his future wife, came to him.[247]

For witnesses at the time, the visible presence of children and the elderly among the Polish Jews who survived in the USSR was this group's most noteworthy feature. As Na'ama Seri-Levi has demonstrated, it also changed the character of the DP camps. Many camp residents and staff commented on the unexpected family structures of the new arrivals, including the presence of intact nuclear families. Seri-Levi quotes a letter from a Zionist activist from the Yishuv, describing his visit to a camp in September 1946:

Their character is very different from what we have grown accustomed to in the camps. There are whole families, with many children who were born in Russia—that is to say, children between the ages of 1 and 5. It is the first camp in which the kindergarten has come to play an important role.[248]

Daniella Bell, only seven at the time, knew that she was unusual in having two parents who had survived the war. Her friends in the Austrian DP camp were not so lucky. Nonetheless, she resembled them in many other ways. In her interview with the Shoah Foundation, Bell describes her childhood as only beginning in the camp. She refers to it as a "rebirth." In the DP camp, she ate well, started school, learned about Judaism, joined clubs, and made friends. Yet although she had both of her parents, she had no other relatives. When her mother became pregnant, Bell was overjoyed that her small family circle would expand.[249] Bell's baby sister was named after her two grandmothers, the details of whose deaths they had only recently learned.

Many DPs married and began having children in the camps. In fact, camp administrators expressed concern about the rapid pace of relationships and the readiness of the DPs to care for children. In Atina Grossmann's words, "The quick marriages—'Hitler married us,' DPs wryly noted—promised some sense of comfort and stability to people who possessed neither."[250] Although the returnees from the USSR had not witnessed their relatives' deaths, they felt the overwhelming loss and desire to bring their family trees back to life.

Residents of the DP camps, which were always meant to be temporary, worked hard to find new homes. However, few countries were keen to absorb Jewish refugees. Even those countries willing to take in a small number of immigrants often required sponsors and enormous amounts of paperwork or money. In the DP camps the refugees continued their attempts to contact surviving relations in Europe, as well as relatives who had emigrated before the war, to probe the possibility of help. Ultimately, despite British policies and the ongoing Israeli War of Independence, approximately two-thirds of the Jewish war refugees immigrated to the Jewish homeland.[251] Some scholars have suggested that Zionism, a natural outgrowth of prolonged antisemitic persecution, made Israel the most obvious and desired destination. Others have countered that propaganda, pressure, and aid from representatives of the Yishuv tipped the scales. The remaining refugees chose their destinations based on availability and family. Australia, Canada, and parts of South America had relatively open policies toward migrants from Europe. For those with family members already there, or no other viable options, these locations proved acceptable. According to records from the Joint, as cited by Zeev Mankowitz, 1,217 Jewish DPs had moved to South American locations, eighty-two to Australia, and 310 to other European countries by the end of 1946. During this same period, 4,135 migrated to the United States, and ten thousand to Palestine.[252]

In all likelihood, more of the Jewish DPs would have liked to get to the United States, which offered stability, prosperity, and a large Jewish community. Most of the survivors also had relatives in the United States, to which many Eastern European Jews had immigrated in the late nineteenth and early twentieth centuries, followed by the smaller group of refugees able to gain entrance in the 1930s. Unfortunately, bureaucratic hurdles made the process nearly impossible for Jewish DPs. After the First World War, the United States had instituted immigration quotas that discriminated against Eastern Europeans. It maintained these quotas strictly in the lead-up to the Second World War. After the war there was some greater leniency, but still with rigorous requirements. At the beginning of the Cold War, the US government was also concerned about admitting possible Soviet spies. The Davidson family, despite the efforts of a relative in the United States, was denied entrance because of their time in the Soviet Union. In 1947 they immigrated to Mexico, although they later moved to the United States.[253]

Many of the DPs no longer had their personal documents, which often led to problems and delays but could occasionally prove convenient as well. A number of Polish Jews who had spent time in the USSR, having lost, or chosen to discard, their papers, reinvented their war histories in order to be admitted to the United States. Joseph Berger learned that he had been born in Russia only when he was about to graduate from college and needed to file paperwork to avoid the draft for the Vietnam War. He had previously believed that he was born in Lublin, as his parents had reported in their immigration file.[254] Aleena Rieger, on the other hand, knew the place of her birth but was forbidden from speaking about it. Both sets of parents sought to shield their children from the repercussions of choices made on their behalf. As Rieger puts it,

> My parents and uncles were in a bind. They had been forced to flee their homes, were incarcerated in labor camps, were forcibly taken to Siberia. They escaped Siberia; they escaped the Soviet Union; they could have lost their

lives many times over. Now there was a possibility that they would not be allowed into the United States.

They could not take the chance. Once again, in nightly sessions, they planned and plotted. They didn't think about long-term effects. They had become accustomed to doing whatever was necessary to survive.[255]

It is impossible even to estimate the number of refugees who obscured their past in order to enter the United States. Unlike former Nazis who lied in order to gain permission to immigrate, the Polish Jewish refugees had no criminal activities to hide. On the contrary, most had never even been communists. Even those who had once supported the Communist Party had mostly lost their faith in it after years of living in the Soviet Union. Nonetheless, it behooved them to erase any association with the growing red menace, and the subject remained taboo. Berger and Rieger's confessions are unusual. A colleague of mine shared a similar story with me, and even showed me her grandmother's contradictory documents; her family members would not allow me to use their names or publish the documents. Cold War concerns spread to other countries as well. Israel Feldman notes with regret that he threw all of his Red Army medals overboard on the way to Canada in order to avoid any trouble there.[256]

While the barriers to immigration to the United States were largely bureaucratic, reaching Palestine required overcoming major logistical hurdles. Even as Zionism held great appeal, the British resolutely attempted to avoid conflict in their colonial holdings and sought to limit immigration. After the enormous human and financial costs of the war, the United Kingdom had no appetite for policing the Middle East. It hoped that restricting the number of Jewish arrivals would discourage Arab revolts. As a result, Jewish refugees who wished to settle in their biblical homeland had to either agree to wait for a coveted certificate or seek extralegal means.

For those who followed this latter path, the turmoil of the war continued. Their testimonies and memoirs reflect an ongoing sense of tension and conflict. Yocheved Zamari, as she recalls in her testimony for Yad Vashem, first had difficulties leaving Bukhara due to appendicitis. Shortly thereafter she faced a harrowing walk across the Alps in winter with Hashomer Hatsair. After a brief hiatus in Italy, they boarded an overcrowded fishing boat and survived a storm at sea, only to be captured and sent to camps in Cyprus. When she reached Palestine in early 1948, the youth group sent her to a kibbutz in the Golan Heights that was soon overrun by the Syrian Army.[257] Zamari's war experience included Israel's War of Independence.

Zionist activists who had spent the war as partisan and ghetto fighters were already on Polish territory as the war ended. They initiated what came to be known as the Bricha, the illegal efforts to smuggle surviving Jews out of Europe and into Palestine. They often began by helping Jews in Poland reach and "infiltrate" DP camps. Repatriates joined them as soon as they could. According to Yehuda Bauer,

> They were much more of a closely-knit group than even the partisans; their loyalty to each other and to their movement had withstood the test of illegality in the Soviet Union. They returned to Poland with the very clear idea that all they wanted was to get out and go to Palestine, and to settle on a kibbutz once they got there.[258]

Bauer adds that they had also developed a far more pervasive skepticism toward the Soviet Union than had the other groups, and that they were more interested in action than in negotiations.

With the help of emissaries from Palestine and Jewish Brigade soldiers, the Polish Zionists immediately began establishing escape routes, relying on multiple agents, numerous bribes, and some creative and audacious gambits. In one early effort, refugees traveled south by pretending to be displaced Greeks. They destroyed all personal documents and spoke only Hebrew, assuming that it could pass for Greek to any local customs officials along the way.[259] Yocheved Zamari was sorry to leave her photographs behind, but made it safely to Austria.[260] Shalom Omri claims that his transport across the Czech border was so convincing that an actual Greek national was removed from the train for not speaking "Greek." Omri reached Palestine, and after several months in jail in Atlit, was released and joined the Haganah.[261] By the time that Aleena Rieger and her family tried to cross into Czechoslovakia with the Bricha, the guards were suspicious enough to separate her, at age four, and try to determine whether she spoke Russian. Fortunately, she had been prepared and pronounced only the word "Mama."[262]

In a particularly striking example, Rachela Tytelman Wygodzki, who had trained as a nurse in Chimkent (Kaz. Shymkent) after her amnesty from forced labor in the Arkhangelsk region, boarded an illegal boat bound for Palestine that would garner world attention. When the *Exodus 1947* neared the Port of Haifa in July 1947, the British Navy engaged, inadvertently killing several of the DPs on board. The passengers were then forcibly transported back to France, where they refused to disembark. The entire episode exposed British policies in Palestine to opprobrium and focused attention on the plight of the Surviving Remnant.[263] Wygodzki finally arrived in Israel the following July and volunteered her services in a military hospital.[264]

Some of the other would-be immigrants, like Zamari, were sent to Cyprus. Bob Golan's parents placed him and his brother Moshe in a Polish orphanage in the USSR in 1942. In 1943 the boys reached Palestine as so-called Teheran Children and managed to reestablish contact with their parents back in the Soviet Union. They maintained contact as their parents repatriated and tried to reach them after the war, but their reunion was delayed when the parents' illegal boat was detained and sent to Cyprus.[265] Natan Degani, the youngest of four surviving children, fled across the Bug River with his family in 1939. Born in 1934, he did not recall exact locations or dates in his oral testimony for Yad Vashem. After amnesty from a labor installation, the family moved to Uzbekistan. In 1942 Degani's father disappeared. The rest of the family was forced onto a kolkhoz near Turkestan. Back in Poland after the war, the family separated temporarily when the Jewish Agency offered to take the children to Palestine. Degani enjoyed the ride, especially on deck, but did not like Cyprus or the jails to which they were sent. He remembers civil disobedience there.[266]

Like the attack on the *Exodus*, the decision to send Jewish refugees to internment camps in Cyprus turned public opinion against the British and emboldened the Zionists. At an August 1946 demonstration outside the British embassy in Washington, DC, protesters called attention to the cruel irony of interning Holocaust survivors, with signs that read "From Dachau to Cyprus" and "Neither Nazi nor British concentration camps."[267] Although neither the press nor the protesters acknowledged Polish Jews who had spent time in Soviet camps and prisons, they, too, were pained to be locked up once again.

While committed Zionists—especially the young among them—pursued daring escapes and risked further captivity to settle in the Promised Land, most of the refugees waited in the DP camps for permission to reach their destinations legally. The wait was often long, and complicated in some cases by the desire to keep families together. After returning to Poland, Szymon Grajcar and his brother reunited with two siblings who had survived there. The reconstituted family moved across Czechoslovakia and into a DP camp. Grajcar married there and stayed for three years. Only in 1949, when the

International Ladies' Garment Workers' Union in Montreal sent out a request for tailors, did he move to Canada. He and his sister, who had also settled in Canada, were later able to bring over their two brothers from France and Israel.[268] Although he does not say so explicitly, it would appear that an eagerness to keep his remaining family together for as long as possible contributed to Grajcar's relatively late migration.

By 1951 the remaining Jewish DPs had been concentrated in a single camp. The Föhrenwald Displaced Persons Camp contained the "hard cases," as they were called by the aid workers and administrators. Due to medical or other reasons, these refugees could not gain admittance to any country. About 3,500 returnees also lived there. The latter had immigrated, usually to Israel, only to find their way back to the DP camps. Föhrenwald closed in 1957.[269]

Strangers in Strange Lands

The Polish Jewish survivors of the war in the unoccupied regions of the USSR and of the Holocaust in Poland were largely indistinguishable as refugees in the new countries in which they settled after the war. After years of suffering and dislocation, they had to start again from nothing. Even for those who had familial or institutional help, the transition was always difficult. Often, they arrived together, having formed new families along the way. Even when they did not, they tended to live in proximity or at least form communities with one another. The examples of rebuilding given here come from flight survivors but could just as easily have been taken from camp survivors. Family played a major role in many of the refugees' experiences of their new homes.

In March 1947, while still in Poland, Betty Rich, who had fled as an adolescent, married David, a man she had met in the Soviet Union. He had a brother in Canada and was awaiting immigration paperwork. When the documents arrived, in 1949, they had to sneak out of the country. In Germany they had barely enough to live on until boarding their ship. After a harrowing journey, they were greeted warmly in Toronto. David's relatives held a shower and gifted the young couple with household goods. Rich was deeply impressed by his family's generosity and warmth. She and her husband worked in factories during the day and took English classes in the evenings. Over time they had two children, moved into a larger apartment, and continued to gather with his relatives for celebrations.[270]

Irving Badner had originally hoped to settle in Israel, but his relatives there did not respond to his letters. Instead, his wife's uncle in America agreed to sponsor them. Her relatives welcomed them, and even helped Badner find his first job. Nonetheless, the first years were trying. From his perspective, only with the birth of their first child did his luck change and their lives begin to improve.[271]

While some of the refugees had family to help them on arrival, others relied on Jewish organizations. Ezra Zynger had trained as a pharmacist in Warsaw but worked as an accountant in the Komi ASSR and subsequently in Kherson, Ukraine. When a commission from Montreal looking for furriers approached him in an Austrian DP camp, he was eager to go. He and his family thus received guidance with their paperwork, transport, and finding work on arrival.[272] Daniella Bell's father, a chemist by training, also took advantage of the need for furriers in Canada. In her recollection, however, they were given only ten dollars on arrival and struggled to establish themselves.[273]

While the JDC was the main organization helping Jews in Europe, in the New World many relied on the Hebrew Immigrant Aid Society (HIAS). For Joseph Berger, born in Russia and raised in the United States by refugee parents, HIAS was so much a part of his existence that it took him until adulthood to realize that it was an English acronym rather than a Yiddish word.[274] HIAS placed Helen Zuberman and her husband in a hotel in Brooklyn, New York, with communal meals. Later, they received help moving to an apartment of their own. She found the situation somewhat humiliating, but eventually, through hard work, they and their children made their way in America.[275]

Herman Taube arrived in New York City with his wife Suzy and two small children in April 1947. HIAS put them up in a hotel before they could travel to Suzy's father in Baltimore. HIAS also gave them some cash and helped them to find a room to rent in Baltimore. In his oral testimony Taube also recalls receiving a very generous payment for an article he wrote in Yiddish from a journalist who interviewed them in New York. When he stepped into a Jewish-owned bakery to shop for food soon after they reached Baltimore, the proprietor took a look at him and asked in Yiddish, "A grine?" (Are you a newcomer?) before handing him a full bag of day-old bread and offering him a job.[276]

Tema Abel, on the other hand, remembers a less friendly welcome. Given a ticket from Montreal to Toronto from the Jewish community, she and her husband and small son were taken off the train in the middle of the night. Without food or money, and unable to speak English, they eventually made their way to Toronto. The Jews there, she says, were not interested in their stories and had little patience for refugees. They gave them money, but never invited them for coffee. Both of the Abels worked in tailor shops, and by saving money, they were eventually able to purchase one of their own.[277]

Given all they had lived through, a surprising number record further crossings of borders. This was particularly true for those who had settled initially in Israel.[278] The early years of the new state were difficult, with great sacrifices demanded of its residents. Boris Baum and his wife chose to move to Israel because she had uncles there. The skills Boris had developed working on the black market in the Soviet Union and in the DP camp served him well there. After two years in a refugee camp, he was able to purchase an apartment in Ramat Gan. Yet life was hard, and the climate proved difficult for his wife. When he discovered a cousin in Canada in 1952, Baum requested an invitation. In Montreal he had to start from scratch as a peddler, but he eventually made a good living.[279] Similarly, Bronia Zisfain lived in a tent with her husband and two small children for her first nine months in Israel. Subsequently they received an apartment that was so new that the electricity and water had not yet been installed. Nonetheless, the family adjusted and enjoyed helping to build the Jewish state. Ultimately, however, a combination of lack of occupational prospects for their children and the knowledge that they had relatives in the United States led them to relocate in 1962.[280]

Family played a major role in Sara Bergman's decision as well. She and her husband Shalom had worked for the Bricha before settling in Israel with their young daughter Anne. Shalom had learned Hebrew at the Tachkemoni School in Warsaw and found work through contacts of his father's. Sara thought she had no surviving family until she discovered around 1950 that her brother and four of her sisters were alive in Melbourne. Two of her sisters were living in an orphanage, so she decided to visit and try to help them. The Bergmans left everything behind in Israel, planning to return, but Shalom became ill and they ended up staying in Australia with Sara's family. Neither knew English, and Shalom could no longer work as a journalist, so they started again with a small business and slowly worked their way up.[281]

For some, the decision to leave Israel was painful. Having arrived as Zionists, they wanted to contribute to the collective Jewish endeavor. Others, as we have seen, moved to Israel because they had relatives there, or because no other country would take them. Without a commitment to the ideal, life in the new Jewish state could be terribly difficult. Marcos Silber has written about the unexpected phenomenon of Polish Jews seeking to return to Poland in the 1950s. Mixed Jewish and non-Jewish families made up a high percentage of those who applied, and a particularly high percentage of those whose applications for return were accepted by both Israeli and Polish officials. The vast majority did not receive permission to return to Poland and could either redouble their efforts to settle into Israeli society or leave for other destinations.[282]

Wherever they ended up, children often had smoother transitions than adults. Daniella Bell spoke seven languages by the time her family settled in Canada. However, English was not one of them. She had a rough time in school at first, but soon adjusted.[283] Celia Balavram, born in 1936, lost her father in Kazakhstan and her mother in a German DP camp. She would have been sent to Palestine with other war orphans, but a cousin happened to see an article that mentioned her name in the Yiddish daily *Forverts,* and her grandparents in New York brought her to them. She recalls happily going home with the relatives who met her at Ellis Island and catching up in school quickly.[284]

While testimonies recorded by the Jewish historical commissions or other postwar organizations still have a certain raw quality, by the time that survivors sat down with the Shoah Foundation in the 1990s, they had lived long lives and had decades to reflect back on their choices. Sitting in their living rooms, surrounded by evidence of their material success, they told stories with happy endings. As Sharon Kangisser Cohen writes in her study of Holocaust survivors, "It might be argued that because these testimonies are taken sixty years later, they reveal more about the way survivors have made sense of their pasts than about their decisions themselves."[285]

In their testimonies and memoirs, many discuss social and institutional connections with other refugees and survivors. In particular, they engaged in Holocaust commemoration. Hasia Diner, among others, has demonstrated that the Jewish community in the United States paid far greater attention to the Holocaust in the decades after the war than had previously been acknowledged.[286] Much has also been written about the place of the Holocaust in Israeli society.[287] The refugees' involvement in Holocaust commemoration, however, was not focused as much on large public events as it was on the creation of physical and literary memorials to their lost towns. As

Mark L. Smith points out, much of their written legacy was not even legible to others, as it appeared in Yiddish.[288]

In their new homes, the Polish Jews who had survived the war in the unoccupied regions of the USSR blended together with Polish Jews who survived under the Germans. Together refugees and survivors built families, homes, and communities in their new homelands. They worked hard to provide for their children, and learned the languages, culture, and customs of their new homes. Yet they also always carried their stories, memories, losses, and longing with them. The choice of *yetsies Poyln* continued to reverberate in their lives. Arnold Zable evokes this lingering sense in his novel based on interviews at a Melbourne café frequented by survivors:

> To this day, I no longer have a centre of gravity. I feel rootless. I will always feel rootless. I have been stripped of everything. Of the scent of my youth, my known way of life. And there is a certain advantage in this, a certain freedom. Even today, though I have lived in Melbourne for over fifty years, I have no sense of belonging. I am acutely aware that everything is temporary in life, a mere bridge. One does not build a house on a bridge. Instead I find my true home inside. I escape inside and I can go wherever my fancy takes me.[289]

Conclusion

Expanding the Compass of Survival

> This is a tale of maps, both old and new. Maps with shifting
> borders, obsolete before the ink could dry. Maps that created
> bands of nomads, stateless refugees. Maps criss-crossed by
> trains shunting their cargoes of uprooted wanderers thou-
> sands of kilometres east, on a nine-week journey, over glacial
> plains and snow-capped ranges, through white nights and
> broken days, an interminable journey that came to an abrupt
> halt at a remote station.
>
> —ARNOLD ZABLE

WHILE THIS IS certainly a book about literal, physical maps, per Arnold
Zable's insight regarding his own semifictional foray into the experiences
of Polish Jews who survived World War II in the interior regions of the Soviet Union, it is also about the ways in which knowledge is mapped. Telling
a story requires temporal and geographic boundaries. Yet these boundaries
also necessitate leaving out other stories. In narrating a marginal story, this
book thus encourages a reexamination of existing maps of the war and the
Holocaust—expanding the compass of survival.

Primarily however, even before considering these larger questions, the
goal of this book has been to tell the story of the wartime experiences of a
particular set of Polish Jews. Despite the fact that the majority of Polish Jews
fortunate enough to see the end of the war did so in the Soviet interior, little
is known about their experiences. This applies not only to the general public
but even to the former refugees themselves and their kin. Of course, they

know what happened to themselves or their family members, but often they have no context within which to understand these exotic and implausible occurrences.

In the absence of historical context, people naturally adjust stories to make more sense or fill in reasons for apparently random acts. Descendants of Polish Jewish refugees from the USSR whom I chance to meet, for example, frequently tell me the cause of their family's deportation. A grandfather told a joke about Joseph Stalin. A grandmother got into a fight in a bread line. A cousin's plan to steal across the Lithuanian border was discovered. All these events are highly likely. Plenty of refugees and residents of the annexed areas worked out their anxiety through the use of humor, had trouble adjusting to the regimen of waiting in line, and considered border crossing. However, it is unlikely that these acts led to their deportation. The Soviet state deported entire categories of the Polish population in an orderly manner, just as they had previously deported large groups of their own citizens. Only with this background about forced population movements and the treatment of Polish citizens as a whole do the individual stories become part of a larger history.

Others not only often tell me stories of their family's survival of the Second World War that include conjectures like those above but they also frame their story as utterly unique. This is the case especially when I have just introduced my subject of study. Elevator pitches cannot be too detailed, and once I have mentioned the broad outlines of this work, they will proceed to share with me stories that in their minds fall outside any preordained story line or historical avenue. Someone might tell me, for example, that while no other Jews were allowed to do so, her great-uncle talked his way into the Polish Army and miraculously reached Palestine in 1943. People have told me excitedly about their families' harrowing flight into Soviet territory or chancy return to Poland, as if only their families had the audacity or luck to pursue such a course.

By no means do I seek to belittle the experiences of any individual or family. On the contrary, each story is important. Nor do I advocate a sort of homogenization that would eschew personal remembrances in favor of a single dominant narrative. I hope that I have amply demonstrated this by including the voices of hundreds of former refugees in this text. Just as each person is an individual, so too is each experience unique and worthy of attention. In addition, however, historical context will help individuals and families to better understand their own family stories. It is worth knowing how their particular stories fit within the larger narrative of Polish Jewish survival in the vast and distant unoccupied realms of the Soviet Union.

This book is an exercise in mapping. The narrative opens in Poland and traces the resources Polish Jews had in evaluating their options after the Second World War began in September 1939. It looks at how much they knew about Nazi rhetoric and practices in the preceding years, as well as how they approached the question of flight. The action then moves into what had been eastern Poland and became the Soviet republics of Western Belorussia and Western Ukraine. A small number of refugees managed to reach Lithuania, and an even smaller number to exit Europe from there. Sovietization affected everyone who stayed, but the extreme aspects of passportization and deportation played out differently among the resident and refugee Jews.

Deportation requires expanding the map even further. The unprepared Polish Jews were banished in the northern Arkhangelsk region, the mountainous Ural region, the steppes of northern Kazakhstan, and the Siberian taiga. Everything about these areas was foreign, and the combination of the labor and climate made life precarious. Amnesty saw a minority remain in the frozen north, and most embarked on a journey southward that often entailed many temporary stops and starts. The refugees were joined in Central Asia by millions of evacuated Soviet citizens, as well as some additional Polish Jews able to escape ahead of the German forces.

It was during this period that a small number of the Polish Jews evacuated the USSR with Anders Army. The children, and many of the adults, stayed in Palestine while some went on to fight in Italy and elsewhere. Another group was mobilized in the Red Army and became some of the first witnesses to the devastation of the Holocaust. Most of the refugees remained in Central Asia until repatriation in 1946 brought them full circle. However, the home they returned to was not the one they had left six or seven years earlier, and after an initial period of consideration, most left postwar Poland. Their subsequent travels took them first to Germany or Palestine and then to entirely new sectors of the globe. Writing from the survivor community in Melbourne, Zable was correct to focus on maps.

Just describing the immensely convoluted journey of the Polish Jews in the Soviet Union during the war has taken many pages. In addition to telling the story of their peregrinations in a clear and clarifying manner, this book has also sought to uncover and explain aspects of their experiences. Some of these, such as the topic of Jewish and Polish relations, have received scholarly attention in the past. Contextualizing the moments of tension within the larger story should help to illuminate not only the incidents, but how their memory has been shaped by postwar realities.

Other topics have received less academic analysis but loom large in the memories of the flight survivors. Utilizing their sources has thus led the narrative toward such areas as deportation trains, religious observances, Siberian exile, and encounters with Soviet Jews. To be sure, the book relies on archival sources as well, but firsthand accounts surfaced as the most thorough and thoughtful depictions of the life of the Polish Jewish refugee in the USSR.

Like the analysis of testimonies, other topics and insights have arisen out of this research. The importance of the family was a constant throughout the war and in its aftermath. Families played a major role in decisions to flee—leading to both separation and reunion. Relatives who remained apart kept in touch by letter and sent one another packages until 1941. After 1941, family packages began to arrive in the USSR from the United States, Palestine, and other locations outside of Europe, via Iran. And then, after the war, family networks were crucial in passing on information, sending goods, and aiding immigration. Despite the dislocation and death occasioned by the war, the Polish Jews took great pains to retain contact with their relatives across the globe.

Another overarching theme to emerge regards the role of human agency. In their testimonial literature, many survivors of exile in the Soviet Union reflect on the contingency of their survival. They use different words and concepts to describe it, and attribute varying amounts of importance to diverse turning points, but they are keenly aware that active choice divided their lives from those of most of the members of their prewar communities. To one degree or another, all of their postwar musings have to confront the moments when they left the beaten track and headed out on their own. These choices are most starkly realized in Chapters 1 and 2. Although decisions continued unabated, the initial choice to flee in 1939, as well as choices about registration, passports, labor in the interior, and flight in 1941, turned out to have life-and-death consequences.

All of this, the story of the survival of well over one hundred thousand Polish Jews in the Soviet interior and the insights to be gleaned from learning about it, deserves to be known more widely. Yet, for a variety of reasons, it has been overshadowed by the Holocaust and never fully integrated into the history and memory of the Second World War. As Mark

Edele, Sheila Fitzpatrick, John Goldlust, and Atina Grossmann write, "Neither historians of the Soviet Union nor Holocaust scholars, let alone historians of Poland, considered themselves 'in charge' of this history, which, at best, is pushed to the margins and, at worst, forgotten altogether."[1] How, then, might it be possible to better integrate this story, and what would be the results?

History and Memory

On a trip to Warsaw, standing at the foot of Nathan Rapoport's imposing and iconic Monument to the Ghetto Heroes, I was reminded that the sculptor survived the Second World War in the Soviet Union. He heard about the Warsaw Ghetto Uprising while in Novosibirsk, and immediately began to think about how to commemorate this momentous event. Back in Warsaw after his 1946 repatriation, Rapoport received permission to create what would become the first major Holocaust monument in 1948.[2] A great deal has been written about the Soviet heroic style of the larger-than-life ghetto fighters and the symbolic role of the massive monument over the years. The less prominent relief on the back, often referred to as the Last March, has received less attention. Echoing the Arch of Titus with its timeless exiles marching into the unknown, it represents a more traditional artistic style and Jewish response to suffering. On this occasion, I wondered if these figures might not also gesture toward refugees like Rapoport, whose period of Soviet exile placed them just beyond the frame of the trauma—and valor—of the Warsaw Ghetto.

It is difficult to disaggregate the experiences of the flight survivors from those of Holocaust survivors. They began the war together, and often ended up together again after the war. Additionally, throughout the book, I have had occasion to note that the Polish Jewish refugees were treated as Polish citizens in the USSR. Deportation, amnesty, and repatriation swept up thousands of Poles, regardless of religion and background. And the movement of this population, both voluntary and forced, took place amid expanding war and evacuation in the Soviet Union. Polish citizens experienced all of this alongside the panoply of Soviet citizens. Notwithstanding the important ways in which the Polish Jewish refugees were part of all of these stories, they have largely fallen through the cracks of history and memory. Expanding the compass of survival requires examining how they fit into these established stories and what their inclusion would mean.

The Holocaust

One of the most popular sights on the Mount of Remembrance on the Yad Vashem campus in Jerusalem is the Garden of the Righteous among the Nations. Since its dedication in 1962, requests have come in from Jews around the world to honor the individuals who risked their own safety to save Jews during a time of great danger. Following the Talmudic dictum that saving one human life is akin to saving the world, a tree has been planted for each of the recognized rescuers. Today there are over twenty thousand trees.[3] Visitors can stroll through areas dedicated to rescuers from different countries and contemplate the names of the Jews who survived and the non-Jews who saved them. It is a beautiful physical commemoration of the best side of human nature during a dark time. A space dedicated to non-Jews, it is also profoundly Jewish, representing an Israeli and Jewish response to the memory of the Holocaust.

When speaking about Polish Jewish survival in the USSR to a group of Jewish educators several years ago, I suggested that perhaps a particularly large tree should be planted for Joseph Stalin. This received quite a laugh. Even setting aside Stalin's murderous regime and the fact that Yad Vashem has strict criteria for recognizing Righteous Gentiles, it is entirely clear that the deportation of Polish Jewish refugees was not meant to save them from Adolf Hitler. On the contrary, the deportees were absorbed into a brutal and exploitative system of forced labor wherein individual lives and liberties had no value. Clearly, then, Stalin does not belong among the recognized rescuers. Yet the fact remains that the savage policies of the Soviet Union paradoxically enabled the survival of thousands of Polish Jews.

If not among the rescued, the Polish Jews who fled east certainly fall under the category of Holocaust refugees. Yet even that does not guarantee them a place in the narrative. In the words of Debórah Dwork, "Oddly, the exclusion of those who flee from discussion or analysis of genocide appears to be unique to the Holocaust." She is quite right in emphasizing that every war and genocide creates refugees. Population movement is integral to war, even when policies of "ethnic cleansing" are not enacted. In this case, some of the Polish Jews living west of the Bug and San Rivers were forced out of their homes. German forces expelled entire Jewish communities in 1939. Other Polish Jews fled of their own free will, but all of them left as a direct result of the German invasion. Dwork goes on to offer a reasoned plea for their inclusion: "Fleeing does not write refugees out of the story; it simply takes the story elsewhere. Indeed, it takes it everywhere."[4] One option is thus to write a history of the Holocaust that takes into account the enormous number of Jewish refugees who fled all over the world.

Thanks to scholars such as Marion Kaplan, the efforts of German and Austrian Jews to find refuge, and the conditions they faced at home and abroad in the process, have entered Holocaust history.[5] The third edition of Doris Bergen's *War and Genocide,* for example, discusses emigration in a section entitled "German Jewish Responses." Would-be emigrants come up again in a subsequent chapter in the consecutive sections "Far-Flung Destinations: Safety and Isolation," "The Voyage of the St. Louis," and "The Kindertransport."[6] Once the narrative leaves Germany and the war begins, however, there is considerably less space devoted to refugees.

Bergen includes many individual stories within her narrative. In one, from the early days of the war, the reader learns of Adina Blady Szwajger and her husband's decision to escape Warsaw for the Soviet zone of occupation. Bergen mentions that most of the other refugees "ended up in one of the deadly Soviet labor camps known as Gulags," but Szwajger returned to Warsaw where she served as an underground courier. There is more information a couple of pages later, in the section entitled "Division and Dual Occupation." Here Bergen explains the context for flight and the conditions in both areas: "Anyone who welcomed the Soviets in 1939 would be disappointed, too." Later, after the German invasion of the USSR in 1941, a vignette about Nelly Toll demonstrates how interethnic tensions during the Soviet period led to violence when the Germans arrived. From there the Polish Jewish refugees disappear, only to reappear somewhat suddenly at the end of the book. On the final page of the final chapter, amid the terrible reckoning of the dead, Bergen inserts a photograph of Jewish refugees from Poland observing Passover in Uzbekistan and remarks upon the continuation of Jewish family life and tradition.[7]

Bergen's up-to-date and exceedingly thoughtfully organized text thus follows trends in scholarship that include refugees deliberately when discussing German and Austrian Jews and more incidentally with regard to the Polish Jewish flight eastward. It is interesting to note that all of this coverage has expanded since the second edition.[8] The inclusion of more personal stories led Bergen to have to explain the multiple border crossings and threat of Soviet deportation in greater depth. It is possible that the increasing scholarly attention to this field will encourage Bergen and others to incorporate additional information in future works on the Holocaust. Beyond the

present volume, and the many works cited within, there are also other related projects in preparation.

On the one hand, Bergen's textbook demonstrates the impracticability of
excluding the Polish Jewish refugees entirely. Once you start looking at the
survival experiences of Polish Jews, it becomes clear that the border between
the two halves of what had been their country was somewhat imaginary for
them. Many crossed back and forth, but even those who lived or stayed in
the eastern regions soon found that the Germans could still reach them. The
stories of those who did manage to evade the Germans, deep in Soviet territory, are in fact intimately linked with those caught up in the killing.

On the other hand, Bergen's book also highlights the logistical challenges
of including the story. The typical narrative used in teaching and writing
about the Holocaust begins in Germany, with the rise of Nazism, and then
follows the German forces around Europe as they conquer territory and
develop their genocidal programs. There is thus time and space to discuss
the evolving responses of the German Jewish community to their ever-
worsening situation. Once the narrative reaches Poland, however, the war
has begun, the Germans' genocidal methods have accelerated, and pursuing their momentum requires moving into ghettoization and the conquest
of western Europe. Trying to insert more than something like Bergen's section "Division and Dual Occupation" would disrupt the narrative flow and
sequence. Yet the reemergence of these survivors at the end of the war is
necessarily abrupt.

As this case study of a leading textbook on the Holocaust should make
clear, incorporating the Polish Jewish refugees into Holocaust history is not
a matter of comparing—much less equating—the experiences of those who
fled east with those who faced the full wrath of the German genocide. Despite the use of deportation, camps, trains, and various forms of torture, the
two experiences are not commensurate. Even aside from the enormously
divergent rates of survival, Jews in the unoccupied regions of the USSR were
not persecuted as Jews. Nor were the considerable resources of a powerful
state devoted to their murder. Rather, this textbook illustrates the complexities of either including or excluding Polish Jewish refugees in the broader
narrative of the Holocaust. They are an inseparable part of the Holocaust
in Poland and the USSR. Yet our models for teaching and writing about the
Holocaust do not make room for them.

Truly integrating the Polish Jewish refugees into Holocaust history, and
thus memory, would necessitate rethinking the paradigm. A victim-centered

chronology, as opposed to the conventional perpetrator-driven one, would go a long way toward enabling this transformation. New trends in scholarly thinking about periodization will also prove relevant.[9] We have come to realize that the war and the Holocaust ended at different times, depending on location. Liberation arrived earlier and later, and in some cases led directly into civil wars and partisan violence. Additionally, from the perspective of trauma theory, it is possible to say that genocide never really ends. The growth of what has been called aftermath studies follows the integration of the repatriates. As has been noted in Chapter 5, back in Poland, in DP camps, and in new communities outside Europe, the flight survivors seamlessly joined the Surviving Remnant of Polish Jewry.

Another scholarly trend that bodes well for rescuing this story is the exponential growth in research about the Holocaust in the Soviet Union since the fall of communism. Before the 1990s the Holocaust was taught in the west according to a model that viewed Poland as quintessential. Ghettoization and death camps defined the Holocaust. In the USSR itself, the Holocaust was not a separate subject of study. Since then a flurry of research both within and outside the former Soviet states has contributed greatly to our collective understanding of the stages of the genocide. Paying close attention to conditions in Soviet territory, to interactions between Jews and their neighbors, and to the agency of Soviet Jews, opens up space for including the experiences of those passing through as well.

This constant mobility, which so defines the experience of Polish Jews who fled eastward, is both an opportunity and a challenge in terms of placing their story. It means that they defy national historical boundaries, making it difficult to figure out where they belong. At the same time, they represent a larger group of refugees, survivors, and victims whose Holocaust story is transnational. While there were, of course, many European Jews who had no ability to avoid or delay their deaths, there were also many—especially in areas where deportation happened relatively late in the war—who managed to move around the continent in their quest to stay out of the reach of the Nazis. This did not always save them, but it is part of the story of the Holocaust.[10] Emphasizing one such story, and especially one that affected a relatively large number of Jews, calls attention to the importance of studying the global Holocaust.

As in this case of mobility, focusing on this lesser-known and less-contested area may also make it easier to explore some of the more fraught topics relating to the Holocaust. Examining issues surrounding choice, resistance,

Orthodox Jews and other groups of testimonies in this population, for example, can shed light and offer methodological models for related questions regarding the Holocaust.[11] And just as there are clear challenges—as well as potential gains—to including the Polish Jewish refugees in Holocaust history, so too is there a benefit in the expanding scholarship on Soviet wartime history.

The War in the USSR

Research on the Holocaust in the USSR has of course been accompanied by a far more nuanced discussion of the Great Patriotic War, Stalinism, and other aspects of Soviet history than had been possible previously. In Russia one can visit large museums devoted to the history of the Gulag—in Moscow and in a former camp outside of Perm.[12] There are also smaller local museums and exhibitions in other camps spread out across the Russian hinterland. However, as Masha Gessen and several news outlets have noted, these places currently face increasing political pressure to display a more favorable picture of the Stalinist era.[13]

Notwithstanding such setbacks (and the fact that many security service files are still not publicly available), inside Russia, in former Soviet countries, and in the West, ongoing research is painting a more complex picture of the war and accompanying events. The process and effects of evacuation, deportations and deprivations during the war, the Siege of Leningrad, and the involvement of civilians, paramilitaries, and prisoners of war in genocide have all garnered attention.[14] The ways in which war and Holocaust are entangled in post-Soviet memory and history creates an opening for integrating the Polish Jewish refugees. The tremendous civilian and military deaths in the USSR place the Holocaust in a different perspective and make integrating other experiences more feasible.

Even in Soviet Jewish memory, the Holocaust, or Katastrofa, holds a less singular place. The twentieth century was a challenging one for all Soviet citizens. Although the Holocaust put the nail in the coffin of Jewish communal life, it had been under siege since the Bolshevik Revolution. Additionally, state-sponsored antisemitism after the war meant that one period of danger led to another. As Anna Shternshis writes, "The war was understandably the most important historical event that each of these people had witnessed." Yet she adds that the war meant army service, evacuation, and partisan fighting as well as ghettos and death.[15]

In terms of periodization and geography, the exiled Polish Jews' experiences dovetail with Soviet history and memory. Regarding nationality and ethnicity, however, the fit is less assured. They were, after all, temporary visitors. Nevertheless, they offer valuable insights on the process of sovietization, as was seen in Chapter 2. In this their voices represent other Polish and Baltic citizens incorporated into the USSR in 1939 and 1940. These people had not lived through the revolution. Their nations' interwar trajectories were entirely different from the Soviet way until the outbreak of war led to their occupation and annexation. Many of these people stayed in Soviet territory, or the Soviet sphere, after the war as well, and were thus unable to write about these transformations. The Polish citizens who fled or were incorporated in the USSR and then repatriated afterward provide firsthand testimony of the rapid imposition of Soviet norms and laws in new areas.

In a similar vein, their impressions of Soviet life in the interior are invaluable. Just as they provide a rare account of sovietization in action, so too do the Polish Jewish refugees witness the workings of the Soviet system as a whole, and of various sectors of the population, during a time of great upheaval. As we have seen in Chapter 4, in their testimonies many evince fascination with the diverse peoples with whom they interacted in Soviet Central Asia. The native population, in particular, is portrayed as navigating traditional folkways and Soviet practices simultaneously. They describe the role of the security services in everyday life, Soviet bureaucracies and hierarchies, illegal economic activities, and communist believers with notable interest. All of this is part of Soviet history, but from an unusual perspective.

On a more speculative plane, one cannot help but wonder what sort of influence these refugees had on Soviet spaces and peoples. That the Polish Jews took with them both trauma and newfound knowledge from their years in the USSR is beyond question, but what did they leave behind? Although they were tiny in number compared to the evacuated Soviet population, the refugees nonetheless tended to concentrate in certain areas where, logically, their imprint should have been greater. For a resident or visitor to those areas today, the only obvious relics are the graves. In cemeteries across Central Asia, one finds individual tombstones, or sometimes entire sections, of people who died in the 1940s and whose place of birth is a Polish city. Surely some of the local people tending to their family graves must be curious about the men and women, young and old, born in Kraków, Łódź, and Warsaw who are buried in Almaty, Bukhara, and Samarkand.

FIGURE C.1. Headstone of Bernard Klapholz, originally of Kraków, who was laid to rest in the Jewish cemetery in Bukhara, Uzbekistan, 2016. The Hebrew text contains the unusual descriptor that he was a "Polish refugee." Photo courtesy Rachel Friedberg.

The story these tombstones tell is an ambivalent one. On the one hand their deaths, often far too young, evince the raging diseases and hunger of the period. On the other hand, while German forces mercilessly tracked down and murdered their relatives back in Poland, these refugees were allowed to live and die relatively freely. My attempt to use this latter reasoning to convince the director of an archive in Kazakhstan to grant me access to NKVD (Narodnyi Komissariat Vnutrennikh Del, People's Commissariat for Internal Affairs) files from the period was not successful. He appreciated my evocation of the storied hospitality of the Kazakh people but was undoubtedly still too concerned about the revelations contained within the security service documents to let me see them. Polish Jewish refugees left behind not only their dead but also, as we have seen, some of their own who chose to stay or were not allowed to leave. The graves, the stories, and the people form part of the history of those regions as well.

Several of the former refugees submit, in later testimonies, that in addition to learning from Soviet Jews about the limits and possibilities of Jewish life in the USSR they also passed along to them ideas about Judaism, Zionism, and other aspects of Jewish culture that the state had largely eradicated. Yehoshua Gilboa writes of a Jewish awakening occasioned by news of the Holocaust and the relative laxity of state supervision during the war:

> To all this was added the fertile influence of encounters between Russian Jews—after years of being cut off—and Jews from the republics annexed to the Soviet Union or with Jews from Poland who had fled to the USSR as war refugees. These were meetings with Jewish communities rooted in tradition and national culture, dynamic, active communities, and such a confrontation once more revived in the hearts of Russian Jews the latent yearning for a more abundant, richer, and more dynamic Jewish life.[16]

Similarly, the Polish Yiddish writer Dovid Sfard describes the excitement engendered in Soviet Yiddish writers by the many cultural activities hosted by the Union of Polish Patriots in the USSR (ZPP). He rejoiced at seeing their authentic Yiddish *geyst* (spirit) and reflected on their longing for *yidishkeyt* (Jewish culture).[17]

On the other hand, these perspectives may say more about the perceived cultural superiority of the Polish Jews, in addition to their Cold War attitudes, than about their actual influence. A number of scholars have argued that Jewish life in the USSR was not nearly as depleted as had been previously assumed, especially in the provinces.[18] Shternshis adds that applying Western models and definitions of Jewish life and practice to Soviet Jews is misleading.[19] That said, however, the suggestion of a Polish Jewish contribution to Soviet Jewish identity and practice remains intriguing.

Moreover, notwithstanding elements of continuity, a brief Jewish resurgence after the war and a more sustained one beginning in the 1960s are well documented.[20] A couple of scholars have hinted at a causal relationship. Regarding the Jewish Anti-Fascist Committee and its legacy, Shimon Redlich writes, "Jewish cultural nationalism in the USSR was influenced considerably by the close and intensive contacts maintained between the JAC, its Soviet Yiddish writers and Jewish refugee writers from Poland, Rumania and the Baltic States."[21] Benjamin Pinkus, writing about postwar Jewish reconstruction, makes a similar point.[22] All of this is difficult to prove, particularly for the later period. Nonetheless, it is equally difficult to dismiss. It stands to reason that the presence of tens of thousands of foreigners would leave lasting effects on a society.

Sheila Fitzpatrick suggests a more pernicious legacy. She agrees with the scholarly consensus that antisemitism increased during the war as a result of Nazi propaganda.[23] She writes, "Yet, from the nature of the antisemitic comments of the early war months, particularly in the panic of October 1941 when Moscow nearly fell to the Germans, it is hard to avoid the sense that flight and evacuation of Jews from the western regions eastward into the Soviet hinterland after the German attack was a key issue."[24] Fitzpatrick shows how the overrepresentation of Jews among evacuees was seen as cowardice rather than a rational response to the German threat. The additional presence of the Polish Jewish refugees only enhanced the assumption that Jews were not contributing their fair share in the military. The problem—and problematic presumption—escalated as the war ebbed and Jews began to return to their hometowns and attempt to reclaim their homes.

Thus, the presence of the Polish Jewish refugees may well have left a lasting impression on both Soviet Jews and Soviet society as a whole. Certainly Soviet cultural and political norms forever changed the life trajectories of the Polish Jews who had fled German aggression. Albeit inadvertently, Stalin's Soviet Union saved them. More intentionally, it also tried to reeducate them, eventually sending them back to Poland with their new ideological training. Although most of the Polish Jews quickly abandoned not only Soviet communism but also postwar Poland, others dedicated themselves to attempting to establish a Jewish future in communist Poland. In all of these ways their war story is entwined with the history and memory of the Great Patriotic War in the USSR. We will see that they are also part and parcel of the Polish story of the war.

Poland

On a busy intersection in Warsaw today stands a somber monument to the enormous hardship and losses of this period. The Monument to the Fallen and Murdered in the East, more frequently called Mothers' Square or the Golgotha of the East, begins with a row of large horizontal blocks, representing railway ties, named, in Polish, for some of the regions and camps from which and to which Poles were deported, including Achangielsk, Katyń, Murmansk, and Syberia. At the head is a dilapidated railway flatcar, the sort used to bring Polish citizens to the unsettled areas where they were forced to labor; but instead of people, it is filled with crosses. The crosses vary in size and stand tall, clearly visible from the traffic below. Amid the many large metal Catholic crosses are a few Orthodox ones, as well as a couple of Jewish and Muslim headstones. From the Polish perspective, Stalin's deportation was a national tragedy affecting mostly ethnic Poles, with some other Polish citizens dragged along as well. Throughout the long period of postwar Soviet hegemony, it was not possible to speak or write about this travesty in Poland. The monument, unveiled on September 17, 1995, is just the most graphic illustration of the ways in which contemporary Poland has constructed a national memory of Soviet deportation.

For the Poles, deportation was an unmitigated disaster, even an "ethnic cleansing." Its evils are encapsulated in the massacre of over twenty thousand Polish officers and other leaders at Katyn in 1940. The cruel, unjust, and illegal deportations, and especially the horrific executions, remain a flash point in Polish society and in Polish and Russian relations. This was only exacerbated by the fatal crash of a plane carrying Poland's top civilian and military leaders to an event marking the seventieth anniversary of the killings in 2010. At the same time, there is a recognition that not only ethnic Poles were swept up in the maelstrom. The monument in Warsaw includes stylized Jewish headstones. The narrative is a Polish one, although Jews can be subsumed within it.

As we have seen, however, the Jewish narrative of deportation and exile is very different. From a Jewish perspective, although the deportation was certainly punishing and terrible, it was also an unexpected and unplanned salvation. Those Polish Jews not deported perished at the hands of the Nazis and their local collaborators. Of course, the testimonies of Polish Jews also contain the shock and betrayal of being caught up in a forced population movement, the indignities of slave labor, severe hunger, physical breakdown,

FIGURE C.2. The death cart of the Monument to the Fallen and Murdered in the East, Warsaw, 2015. Author photo.

disease, and the sorrow of losses within the family. These are all a part of the story but, ultimately, any Jewish testimony composed after the encounter with the reality of the Holocaust can only be one of deliverance.

A 2007 documentary film about the Jewish experience carries the ironic title *Saved by Deportation.* Whereas the Monument to the Fallen and Murdered in the East lists places of deportation in funereal solemnity, one child of a flight survivor remembers her father singing her to sleep with some of these same names. He had composed a lullaby made up of the colorful and curious-sounding names of all of the places he passed through in order to get back to his native Poland.[25] Thus the two narratives, while overlapping in significant ways, have diverged, and while the monument in Warsaw gestures toward Jewish inclusion, it is fundamentally a Polish monument.

Elżbieta Janicka goes further in differentiating the two narratives, as well as the role of the Warsaw monument. In her *Festung Warschau* she questions the placement of the dramatic death cart, making the important point that the Soviet deportation of Polish citizens did not take place in Warsaw. Moreover, the majority of Polish citizens of all faiths survived Soviet exile whereas the Umschlagplatz, just up the street, was actually the place from which Polish Jews did not return. For Janicka, locating the Polish monument on a prominent corner within what had been the Warsaw

Ghetto creates an unjustified symmetry between the Holocaust and Soviet deportation.[26]

Lidia Zessin-Jurek explains how this situation of competing memories came about. Although the memory of Soviet deportation was suppressed under communism, it did not actually flourish in 1990s Poland. Zessin-Jurek described the Holocaust as a "hot" memory in this era while the distant Gulag was a "cold" memory. Over time, however, and with the European Union's focus on totalitarianism and a growing scholarly interest in documenting complicity, collaboration, and perpetration among local populations, deportation has come to serve as a bulwark: "The Gulag—the experience of Stalinist labor camps, common to many states with victims in the millions—has been assigned the role of a symbol of Stalinist/communist crimes, a counterpart of the Holocaust and, as discussions have become increasingly dramatic and tempers frayed—its competitor."[27]

Thus, whereas in regard to the history and memory of the Holocaust and the Great Patriotic War in the USSR, the Polish Jewish refugees are simply missing; in the Polish case their story is well known but reinterpreted. In an oral testimony recorded in 2010, Rabbi Avraham Steinberg states that although he found the name of his uncle, Rabbi Major Baruch Steinberg, the chief rabbi of the Polish armed forces, on a commemorative wall of Katyn victims in a church in Kraków, he was distressed to see a cross next to his name.[28] In fact, there is no cross on the individual plaque, but it is part of an installation inside a Catholic Church, and there are certainly many crosses present.[29] In the large outdoor monument in Warsaw, as in the intimate religious memorial in Kraków and in hundreds of others across Poland, the memory of the Polish citizens deported and killed in the Soviet Union is prominent. The occasional Jewish name and symbol even appears in these monuments, but the Jewish story of deportation and survival has yet to be heard.

Of course, the most jarring difference between the two narratives is the relative danger of the two occupying powers to the various Polish citizens. Polish Catholics suffered greatly under both regimes, but while one of them was eventually defeated, the other not only held onto the territories it had annexed but also extended its oppressive political system over all of Poland after the war. Throughout the communist period, Poles could only speak publicly about Nazi crimes and anti-Nazi resistance. The reckoning with Soviet crimes and anti-Soviet resistance is a later phenomenon, and one still developing. For Polish Jews, on the other hand, the brutal efficiency of the

Holocaust in Poland has meant that there can be no comparison between the two experiences. Bob Golan's retrospective analysis is fairly typical:

> Although many hardships lay ahead for us, we were in fact very fortunate. Had we moved to Uman in the Ukraine as we were ordered to do by the NKVD, or had we stayed in Lubomel, or had the Germans agreed to take back the Polish refugees from the U.S.S.R., my family and I would almost certainly have been murdered by the SS mobile killing-squads or sent to a death camp. That was the virtually inevitable fate of the Jews who remained in Poland, or who got caught up in the German invasion of the western part of the Soviet Union in 1941.[30]

Introducing this Jewish perspective into the Polish narrative of Soviet exile has the potential to unsettle a number of accepted tropes. First, it demands an honest appraisal of the wartime destruction caused by the Germans and the Soviets. Jews were an integral part of interwar Poland: 10 percent of the population. The almost complete annihilation of this community of over three million souls amputated part of the Polish nation. While many Polish citizens languished and died during the war, the genocide perpetrated against the Jews was unprecedented. Deportation, imprisonment, and even execution by the Soviets were dire and cruel circumstances which did not threaten the very existence of the Polish people.

Second, Soviet policies affected all Polish citizens. Belorussians, Jews, ethnic Poles, and Ukrainians faced the panoply of Soviet administrative behavior. Jews, because of their escape from the Germans, were overrepresented among Polish deportees. Neither during the war, in the decisions and materials of the Polish government-in-exile, nor afterward, in collective memory, has this matter been fully assimilated. Notwithstanding the inclusion of an exceptional Jewish name or image in commemorative memorials or activities, the context remains Catholic and Polish. A deeper grasp of the significance of the Jewish presence would require not just inviting a rabbi to stand on the dais now and then but examining the variety of experiences of exile.

Indeed, the narrative of Soviet suppression of Catholicism, for example, would be enriched by a discussion of the ways in which Soviet antireligious policies impacted Judaism as well. The special settlements in which many Jewish refugee families labored expands the picture of Soviet deportation of Polish citizens. A number of organizations collect testimonies from Poles deported by the Soviets—also known as Sybiraks because of the time they spent in "Siberia."[31] Many of these include the voices of ex-patriots evacuated with Anders Army and subsequently settled around the globe. Here again the experiences of Polish Jews, far less likely to evacuate and thus in the USSR through the end of the war, add to the picture of Soviet exile. As we saw in Chapter 4, in terms of both passportization and mobilization, at times Soviet authorities treated Jewish Poles differently from Catholic Poles. In these and other ways, the Jewish experience fills in aspects of the greater Polish experience.

Another corollary would be interethnic Polish relations in exile. Katherine Jolluck has written about this in a sensitive manner, but as Zessin-Jurek notes, Jolluck's English-language scholarship has had little influence in Poland.[32] The memoirs and testimonies of Polish Jews provide an important counterpoint to the wartime narrative put forth by the Polish government in London, which has largely been adopted in post-communist Polish collective memory. We have seen that Polish Jews' experiences ranged from solidarity through exclusion, depending on individual circumstance as well as time and place. This, too, is part of the Polish exile story.

This discussion leads necessarily to the postwar period and the imposition of communism in Poland. One strand of Polish nationalist thought has consistently sought to blame this turn of events on Jewish repatriates. The conflation between postwar Soviet communism and the welcome that Soviet troops received from Polish Jews in September 1939 came out in Chapter 2. In Chapter 5 the ways in which Church and other leaders justified postwar violence against the tiny Jewish community by Jewish involvement with the new regime revealed another facet of the pernicious myth of the *żydokomuna*. A more nuanced examination of the situation in Poland after the war, hopefully possible after the passage of so many years, would recognize the complex of reasons that led some Poles—both Catholic and Jewish—to embrace communism. Some factors, such as coercion, greed, and genuine faith, were commonly held. Others, such as fear of antisemitism and the belief that the only viable Jewish future lay in communism, were particular to Jewish adherents.

Especially in the early years of the Polish People's Republic, Jews in general, and repatriated Jews in particular, were overrepresented in the ranks of the new ruling elite. While this is beyond question, excavating the reasons is crucial. Moreover, the prominence of Jewish names should not detract from the equally unimpeachable fact that the majority of Party members and cadres were ethnic Poles. At times antisemitism becomes a fig leaf covering more difficult issues. With the passage of several decades since the end of communism, and new information about Jewish Sybiraks, a more complex picture of communist activism may emerge.

At the time of writing, political pressures in Poland mitigate against an honest reckoning with the past. Yet despite the political climate, Polish scholars are actively engaged in delving into all aspects of the Polish and Jewish past, and excellent work about the Holocaust comes out yearly.[33] Such work will add to the substantial Polish-language scholarship about Soviet deportation. In time it may lead to a broadening conversation about the wartime experience of Polish citizens in the USSR.

It is clear that further scholarship and public awareness of the plight of Polish Jews who fled or were deported into the Soviet interior during World War II can significantly enrich the history and memory of the Holocaust, the Second World War in the USSR, and Polish exile in the Soviet Union. In and of itself this is a worthy and ambitious endeavor, and this book will have been successful if it can contribute in some way toward that goal. Perhaps an even weightier, and more distant, objective would be if increased focus on this area might also be able to integrate all of these historiographies and landscapes of memory.

Integration

Vasily Grossman's epic World War II novel *Life and Fate* opens with a description of a camp. The air is heavy, and railway tracks and fences fill the scenery: "This was a world of straight lines: a grid of rectangles and parallelograms imposed on the autumn sky, on the mist and on the earth itself." There is a generic quality to the barracks, and even to the blurred faces of those arriving: "Their very uniformity was an expression of the inhuman character of this vast camp." Grossman goes on to underline his point. The paragraph following the dreary introduction calls on the reader to witness the unnatural quality of the camp:

> Among a million Russian huts you will never find even two that are exactly the same. Everything that lives is unique. It is unimaginable that two people, or two briar-roses, should be identical. . . . If you attempt to erase the peculiarities and individuality of life by violence, then life itself must suffocate.[34]

Grossman's focus on this insight, one of the central themes of his book, almost obscures a more subtle point that is equally fundamental to his concerns in the novel, although perhaps more difficult to put into words.

Because only after the editorial insertion quoted above do we learn that the unnamed camp is in the Soviet Union. Two train conductors pass and converse briefly, and suddenly the reader has a context. Up until that point, the Soviet camp could easily have been mistaken for one of the infamous camps of its enemy. Indeed, the next chapter takes place among Soviet prisoners of war in a German camp. Grossman thus implicitly juxtaposes the camps of the two totalitarian systems. Even as his magnum opus exposes both heroism and perfidy in the Soviet Union, Grossman is loath to compare it directly to Nazi Germany. Yet the ambiguity of the opening image and the proximity of descriptions of the two camps are suggestive.

Grossman wrote his book in the Soviet Union. While he did not succeed in having it published there during his lifetime, there is every reason to believe that he had hoped to do so. According to his biographers, he submitted the manuscript in 1960.[35] Thus, although *Life and Fate* is a devastating critique of the excesses of the Stalin era, it was also written in an attempt to pass through the official state censors. Grossman tried to stay within the boundaries of what was acceptable during the period of the Thaw.

Yet by 1962, with his manuscript essentially under arrest and no response from the many prominent figures he approached to seek its release, Grossman had lost hope. In addition, he was dying of cancer. At this point, with nothing left to lose, he revised his masterpiece to reflect the radical nature of his views.[36] Katarina Clark suggests that it was not so much the changed circumstances as the full development of his outlook on the Soviet Union that allowed for the final revisions.[37] In either case, there was no room for a comparison of Nazi and Soviet policies in the Soviet Union. *Life and Fate* was first published in the West in 1980 and returned to the Soviet Union only during perestroika.

The Second World War and the Holocaust, while often taught and written about in separate classes and monographs, make up parts of the same historical event. Hitler chose to pursue genocide and war simultaneously, and the developments in each area had consequences on the other. Jews and others across Europe also often experienced the results of both war and genocide. Similarly, it is almost impossible to discuss either the war or the Holocaust in Poland and the USSR separately. Not only did a large part of Poland become part of the USSR, but soon the whole area came under

German occupation. This story of voluntary and forced migration—in which Jews from Warsaw relocated to Lvov, were taken to Kotlas, and then moved temporarily to the Fergana Valley—traces a route through and beyond geographic boundaries. It can provide a model for conceptualizing the war and Holocaust as integrated.

Over the years, some thinkers and writers, like Grossman, have addressed the two great authoritarian regimes of twentieth century Europe as connected. Most famously, Hannah Arendt's *The Origins of Totalitarianism*, first published in 1951, charted the various factors that enabled the rise of Nazism and Stalinism in tandem. Arendt does not seek to streamline the two systems, and in fact focuses more on Nazi Germany than on the Soviet Union. The book culminates in one of the earliest scholarly treatments of the German camps in English.[38] Although, like any work on such disputed topics, it has received its fair share of criticism, it is also still read and assigned.

Terrence Des Pres's book *The Survivor: An Anatomy of Life in the Death Camps* won the National Jewish Book Award in the Holocaust field in 1978.[39] Yet while it focuses mainly on reports from German camps, Des Pres also frequently juxtaposes similar material from Soviet camps. His interest lies in the people who managed to live through conditions of extremity, and for that purpose he is willing to cast a wide net. Des Pres notes commonalities across the two systems of camps; concentration camps, death camps, and Soviet labor camps all fall within his purview. He also points to differences:

> And what, really, is the difference if Buchenwald was not classified as an extermination camp and had no gas chamber, but had special rooms for mass shooting and a level of privation so severe that prisoners died in hundreds every day? Starvation claimed victims by the thousands everywhere. Apart from that, Nazi victims were usually gassed or shot, whereas Soviet prisoners died mainly of exhaustion and sickness. There was likewise a difference in atmosphere; horror and dread were overwhelming in the Nazi camps, while in Soviet camps the predominant mood was a blend of rage and hopelessness.[40]

Even Primo Levi, while averring that he can only write as a witness of German camps, nonetheless explores the overlaps between German and Soviet camps in the "Afterword" to his 1986 reissue of *The Reawakening*. "The principal difference lies in the finality," writes Levi. "From this fundamental difference, the others arise." Chief among these other distinctions is the level of humanity accorded to prisoners: "The relationships between guards and prisoners are less inhuman in the Soviet Union. They all belong to the same nation, speak the same language, are not labeled 'Supermen' and 'Non-men' as they were under Nazism."[41] As we have seen, Soviet prison camps often contained people of many national groups and speaking a variety of languages. Certainly, however, even with resulting interethnic tensions, there was no strict racial hierarchy enforced.

In the fields of literature and political philosophy, as well as in fictional and essay writing, analogies and correlations are acceptable. Historians shy away from comparisons, preferring to tell individual stories. There have, however, been some attempts to write an integrated history of the Second World War. One of the strands of the *Historikerstreit* controversy that broke out in Germany in the 1980s involved normalizing the Third Reich by showcasing its common elements and origins with other regimes. At the end of an essay comparing Hitler's Germany to just about every other imperial power and highlighting the dangers of communism, Ernst Nolte recommends a radical revision of historical writing: "Auschwitz is not primarily a result of traditional anti-semitism. It was in its core not merely a 'genocide' but was above all a reaction born out of the anxiety of the annihilating occurrences of the Russian Revolution."[42] As Dominick LaCapra points out, Nolte's reasoning not only recapitulates Nazi tropes in justifying preemptive war, but also in racializing the Soviets. In this essay and others, Nolte removes the blame for the Holocaust from the "Aryans" and places it on the purportedly more brutal "Asiatics."[43] Thus, some revisionist historians have sought to support ideological viewpoints by constructing a particular relationship between the two regimes.

Is it possible to create a responsible historical narrative about the interplay between totalitarian systems in the twentieth century? Timothy Snyder's *Bloodlands* is an ambitious attempt to do just that. Snyder centers his account on the Baltic, Belorussian, Polish, and Ukrainian borderlands and the unfathomable violence that took place there between 1933 and 1945. As he states, national histories are insufficient for understanding the area:

> Perfect knowledge of the Ukrainian past will not produce the causes of the famine. Following the history of Poland is not the best way to understand why so many Poles were killed in the Great Terror. No amount of Belarusian

history can make sense of the prisoner-of-war camps and the anti-partisan campaigns that killed so many Belarusians. A description of Jewish life can include the Holocaust, but not explain it.[44]

Released in 2010, it was one of the rare books written by an academic that received both popular and serious scholarly attention. Indeed, it would not be possible to discuss all of the responses here. Amid general praise for the sweep and scope, as well as the written style of the book, many reviewers have analyzed its synthetic approach. Most germane to our interests is the discussion of how the Holocaust fits into Snyder's bloodlands.

Mark Roseman, a scholar of German history and the Holocaust, notes that the comparative framework allows Snyder to demonstrate, for example, the joint German and Soviet assault on the Polish nation: "It is an unusual perspective for Holocaust scholars to see the Nazis as somewhat amateurish in terror." Yet he also finds the geographical focus limiting:

> After all, one of the distinctive characteristics of the Nazi's [sic] Final Solution is indeed that it was so global, or at least so continental, in its reach. It is true that because the killing centres were established in the areas of highest concentration of Jews, even Jews from western and southern Europe were brought to be killed there. The bloodlands were soaked with their blood too. But the geography of killing centres is a lesser matter than the reach of killing policies. The volume's regional focus should not be allowed to obscure the distinctive continental ambitions of the Nazis' Jewish policy.[45]

Mark Mazower likewise notes the impressive findings of the comparative approach but raises concerns about the temporal as well as the geographic scope. Violence in the area started before 1933 and included a broader swath of territory, he avers.[46]

In his review of *Bloodlands* Dan Diner touches upon some of these same questions but ultimately problematizes the very comparative framework within which the Holocaust has been placed—the epistemological distinction, in his words, between "death and death." He writes,

> It is perfectly clear that the suffering of a Ukrainian child dying of starvation cannot be distinguished in any way, in terms of individual suffering, from that of a Jewish child in the ghetto, or facing the gas chamber. Yet not *all* Ukrainians were put to death simply for being Ukrainian, and certainly not *everywhere*. By contrast, for the Jews death was the rule. In the face of this murderous consistency, survival was the exception. Of course, Timothy

Snyder is well aware of these and other distinctions that led to this extreme situation. He also expresses them repeatedly in this book. Yet their meaning is in the nature of a severability clause: they are actually inconsequential for the overarching narrative he constructs.[47]

These readers do not impugn any insidious significance to the weaknesses in the book. They find much to acclaim in Snyder's presentation, but also point out when his conceptual structure inhibits comprehensive interpretation.

Some scholars have gone further in critiquing the underlying assumptions and how they might be misused. Dan Michman shows that in Snyder's framework, "the Holocaust" and "the murder of the Jews" are equated. This ignores the other critical steps in the genocide, beginning in Germany in 1933.[48] On his website, in academic forums, and in the press, Dovid Katz has called attention to the ways that nationalist politicians in the Baltic states have instrumentalized some of Snyder's arguments for their own purposes:

> Snyder, turning to the important point of local collective memory, happens to be in concord with the Baltic ultra-nationalists who want the Molotov-Ribbentrop pact, rather than the genocide of the Holocaust, to be the psychologically central sin of the century; to be sure, the master historian and the local nationalist hijackers of history are coming to it with altogether different tools and motives.[49]

Katz decries the ease with which far-right political leaders across Eastern Europe have embraced *Bloodlands* as justification for their own equation of the German and Soviet terrors.

Snyder's intervention is an important and necessary one. Despite somewhat overstating the novelty of the insight, he is certainly correct that a transnational approach to the Holocaust, World War II, and the violence in the region yields crucial connections. Yet who could really master the languages, cultures, histories, and historiographies of all of the nations and peoples in the "bloodlands"? His reviewers point to specific misinterpretations, and also to larger problems with the comparative framework and specific chronological and geographic boundaries. At the same time, the concept of the bloodlands has already entered mainstream historical conversation. Still, many question his delineation of that time and place, as well as the results of the subsuming of the Holocaust within other incidents of death and violence.

Snyder's study offers one model for integrating war and Holocaust across borders. Rather than comparing numbers or finding common origins, it demonstrates how the Holocaust itself was a multifaceted experience and set in motion other related events. And all of these occurred within the larger frame of the Second World War. In his review of *Bloodlands*, Roseman even refers to the anomaly of the Polish Jewish refugees as an example of the surprising results of juxtaposing the actions of the two regimes:

> Occasionally, of course the brutality of one regime could actually protect groups from the ruthlessness of the other. Jewish refugees from Western Poland who had flown into Soviet occupied territory in 1939 found themselves the target of Stalin's paranoid resettlement policies, because they refused Soviet passports, fearing this might bar them from return to their homeland after the war.[50]

Studying the war and the Holocaust, and the interplay of German and Soviet policies, reveals the unintended consequences. This revelation, in turn, provides affirmation of the complexity and precariousness of survival.

The refugees themselves, as well as the historical factors that compelled them, determine the boundaries of this study. The temporal boundaries are mainly the war and its aftermath. As we have seen, the duration and conclusion of the aftermath depended greatly on location. For those who left Poland, Kielce is the caesura. For those who stayed, 1947, 1949, 1956, or even 1968 might provide the bookend for their journey. Refugees who reached the Land of Israel often include its fight for independence as part of their war experience. This book reflects all of their perspectives, as well as reflecting upon them.

To return once again to the topic of maps, the same is true for the geographical scope of this work. Even had I set out to focus on a certain area, such as the borders of interwar Poland or the USSR, it would not have been possible to remain inside of it. The refugees, by chance and per force, spread at first slowly and incrementally into Soviet territory and then much farther and much faster. While the main narrative has followed those who were deported into the Soviet interior and then relocated to Central Asia, we have also noted smaller groups who reached Lithuania and emigrated from there to Shanghai and elsewhere, some who stayed in Siberia rather than move south after the amnesty, and others who evacuated via Iran and reached Palestine and other Middle Eastern destinations. After the war, the compass of survival expands still further as many of the Polish Jews became refugees again, first in Germany and then across the globe. All of this was a direct result of the war and the Holocaust.

The story of the immense and arduous journeys of the largest surviving group of Polish Jews should be told on its own merits. It is a fascinating and largely unknown tale. In various formats, and under a variety of circumstances, the refugees themselves have been telling their story ever since the war, yet it has not reached a wide audience. Thus, first and foremost, this book exists to compile the many sources of information into a coherent narrative. It will serve to fill in gaps in memory and speculation in the firsthand testimonies of the survivors, to provide background and context to their relatives, and to educate others about the experience.

In addition, it is hoped that this book will move the story from the margins of the history of the Holocaust, and of the Second World War in Poland and the USSR, to a more salient position. Doing so not only illuminates an important story within all of these cultures of history and memory but offers a path toward greater integration. Refugees are a part of the Holocaust story, necessitating further consideration of survival and the global repercussions of the genocide. Further, the Polish Jewish story of deportation and survival offers a productive contrast to the Polish national construction of the same experience. Reading and listening to testimonies of refugee life in the Soviet interior during the war provides a contradictory picture of the everyday brutality of Stalinism, the varied responses of a diverse population, and the ultimate survival of a significant number of Polish Jews.

This story of maps and migrations expands the borders of the war, the Holocaust, and the history and memory of Polish deportation and the wartime Soviet Union. In doing so it highlights the ways in which all of these stories are connected. It is not possible to write about the Polish Jewish refugees without crossing into all of these territories, and thereby showing the linkages between them. Perhaps, over time, it will be possible to envision some sort of physical monument that marks and commemorates the experiences of the Polish Jewish refugees amid these complicated and complicating contexts. For the present, this book will have to suffice.

Notes

Dedication

Rokhl Korn, "Home," translated by Shulamis Yelin and Rachel Korn, in *Generations: Selected Poems*, ed. Seymour Mayne (Oakville, Ontario: Mosaic Press, 1982), 41.

Introduction

Epigraph: Peretz Opoczynski, "House No. 21," in *Voices from the Warsaw Ghetto: Writing Our History*, ed. David Roskies (New Haven, CT: Yale University Press, 2019), 92.

1. Opoczynski, "House No. 21," 95.
2. Peretz Opoczynski, "s'Hoiz nomer 21," in *Reportazshn fun Varshever geto*, Ber Mark, ed. (Warsaw: Yidish-bukh, 1954), 9–24.
3. Meir Korzen, "Problems Arising out of Research into the History of Jewish Refugees in the USSR during the Second World War," *Yad Washem Studies* 3 (1959): 119.
4. Nora Levin, *The Jews in the Soviet Union since 1917: Paradox of Survival*, vol. 1 (New York: New York University Press, 1988), 348.
5. Saul Friedländer, *Nazi Germany and the Jews, 1933–1945*, abridged by Orna Kenan (New York: Harper Perennial, 2009), 163.
6. Zeev W. Mankowitz, *Life between Memory and Hope: The Survivors of the Holocaust in Occupied Germany* (Cambridge: Cambridge University Press, 2002), 19.
7. Dina Porat, *Israeli Society, the Holocaust and its Survivors* (London and Portland, OR: Vallentine Mitchell, 2008), 344–345.

8. Olga Medvedeva-Nathoo, "Certificate of Birth, Certificate of Survival (From the Cycle 'Scraps of Lives: Polish Jews in Central Asia during the Second World War')" (unpublished manuscript, n.d., trans. Marta Daria Olynyk), in American Association for Polish-Jewish Studies, "New Views," http://www.aapjstudies.org/manager/external/ckfinder/userfiles/files/Medvedeva-Nathoo(1).pdf, 2–3.

9. Atina Grossmann, "Jewish Refugees in Soviet Central Asia, Iran, and India: Lost Memories of Displacement, Trauma, and Rescue," in *Shelter from the Holocaust: Rethinking Jewish Survival in the Soviet Union,* ed. Mark Edele, Sheila Fitzpatrick, and Atina Grossmann (Detroit: Wayne State University Press, 2017), 187.

10. I first heard this term used by Hannah Pollin-Galay, who pointed me to Dovid Katz's website as her source; see Defending History, http://defendinghistory.com.

11. Chaim Grade, *My Mother's Sabbath Days: A Memoir,* trans. Channa Kleinerman Goldstein and Inna Hecker Grade (New York: Schocken Books, 1987); Esther Hautzig, *The Endless Steppe: Growing Up in Siberia* (New York: HarperCollins, 1987).

12. Jan T. Gross, *Neighbors: The Destruction of the Jewish Community in Jedwabne Poland* (Princeton, NJ: Princeton University Press, 2001), 21–22.

13. Yosef Litvak, *Pelitim Yehudim mi-Polin be-Verit-ha-Mo'atsot, 1939–1946* (Jerusalem: Hebrew University Press, 1988). While Litvak's is the only academic work devoted to the topic, there are a few popular or literary books. See, for example, Henryk Grynberg, *Children of Zion,* trans. Jacqueline Mitchell (Evanston, IL: Northwestern University Press, 1997), which is also available in Polish and Hebrew; and Dorit Bader Whiteman, *Escape via Siberia: A Jewish Child's Odyssey of Survival* (New York: Holmes and Meier, 1999). A new work came out in German as this book was going to press; see Markus Nesselrodt, *Dem Holocaust entkommen. Polnische Juden in der Sowjetunion, 1939–1946* (Berlin: De Gruyter Oldenbourg, 2019).

14. Kate Brown, *Dispatches from Dystopia: Histories of Places Not Yet Forgotten* (Chicago: University of Chicago Press, 2015), 2.

15. Sonja Luehrmann, *Religion in Secular Archives: Soviet Atheism and Historical Knowledge* (Oxford: Oxford University Press, 2015), 31.

16. Daria Khubova, Andrej Ivankiev, and Tonia Sharova, "After Glasnost: Oral History in the Soviet Union," in *International Yearbook of Oral History and Life Stories,* vol. 1, *Memory and Totalitarianism,* ed. Luisa Passerini (Oxford: Oxford University Press, 1992), 95–96, quoted in Jehanne M.

Gheith and Katherine R. Jolluck, eds., *Gulag Voices: Oral Histories of Soviet Incarceration and Exile* (New York: Palgrave Macmillan, 2011), 8.

17. Joanna B. Michlic, "What Does a Child Remember? Recollections of the War and the Early Postwar Period among Child Survivors from Poland," in *Jewish Families in Europe, 1939–Present: History, Representation, and Memory,* ed. Joanna Beata Michlic (Waltham, MA: Brandeis University Press, 2017), 153.

18. Yehuda Bauer, *American Jewry and the Holocaust: The American Jewish Joint Distribution Committee, 1939–1945* (Detroit: Wayne State University Press, 1981), chap. 12; Atina Grossmann, "Remapping Relief and Rescue: Flight, Displacement, and International Aid for Jewish Refugees during World War II," *New German Critique* 39, no. 3, 117 (2012): 61–79; Shlomo Kless, "Pe'ilut tsionit shel pelitim Yehudim be-Verit-ha-Moa'tsot be-shanim 1941–1945 ve-kesher ha-Yishuv ha-Yehudi be-Erets Yisra'el 'imahem" (Ph.D. diss., Hebrew University of Jerusalem, 1985), chap. 6; Litvak, *Pelitim,* 294–306 and passim; Keith Sword, "The Welfare of Polish-Jewish Refugees in the USSR, 1941–43: Relief Supplies and Their Distribution," in *Jews in Eastern Poland and the USSR, 1939–46,* ed. Norman Davies and Antony Polonsky (New York: St. Martin's, 1991), 145–158.

19. See for example, Eliyana R. Adler, "Singing Their Way Home," *Polin* 32 (2020): 411–428; Eliyana R. Adler, "The Miracle of Hanukkah and Other Orthodox Tales of Survival in Soviet Exile During World War II," *Dapim* 32:3 (2018): 155–171; Eliyana R. Adler, "Crossing Over: Exploring the Borders of Holocaust Testimony," *Yad Vashem Studies* 43, no. 2 (2015): 83–108; Eliyana R. Adler, "Hrubieszów at the Crossroads: Polish Jews Navigate the German and Soviet Occupations," *Holocaust and Genocide Studies* 28, no. 1 (2014): 1–30.

20. Zoë Vania Waxman, *Writing the Holocaust: Identity, Testimony, Representation* (Oxford: Oxford University Press, 2006), 2. See also Hannah Pollin-Galay, *Ecologies of Witnessing: Language, Place, and Holocaust Testimony* (New Haven, CT: Yale University Press, 2018).

21. Noah Shenker, *Reframing Holocaust Testimony* (Bloomington: Indiana University Press, 2015), 192.

22. Henry Greenspan, *On Listening to Holocaust Survivors: Beyond Testimony* (St. Paul, MN: Paragon House, 2010), 42, 45.

23. Pascale Rachel Bos, "Women and the Holocaust: Analyzing Gender Difference," in *Experience and Expression: Women, the Nazis, and the Holocaust,* ed. Elizabeth R. Baer and Myrna Goldenberg (Detroit: Wayne State University Press, 2003), 32.

24. On responses to the Soviet invasion and subsequent occupation, see, for example, Ben Cion Pinchuk, "Facing Hitler and Stalin: On the Subject of Jewish 'Collaboration' in Soviet-Occupied Eastern Poland, 1939–1941," in *Contested Memories: Poles and Jews during the Holocaust and Its Aftermath,* ed. Joshua D. Zimmerman (New Brunswick, NJ: Rutgers University Press, 2003), 61–68; Andrzej Żbikowski, "Polish Jews under Soviet Occupation, 1939–1941," in Zimmerman, ed., *Contested Memories,* 54–60; Marek Wierzbicki, "Polish-Jewish Relations in Vilna and the Region of Western Vilna under Soviet Occupation, 1939–1941," *Polin* 19 (2006): 487–516; Marek Wierzbicki, "Western Belarus in September 1939: Revisiting Polish-Jewish Relations in the *Kresy,*" in *Shared History—Divided Memory: Jews and Others in Soviet-Occupied Poland, 1939–1941,* ed. Elazar Barkan, Elizabeth A. Cole, and Kai Struve (Leipzig: Leipziger Universitats-verlag, 2007), 135–145; Joanna B. Michlic, "Anti-Polish and Pro-Soviet? 1939–1941 and the Stereotyping of the Jew in Polish Historiography," in Barkan, Cole, and Struve, eds., *Shared History—Divided Memory,* 67–101; Alexander Brakel, "Was There a 'Jewish Collaboration' under Soviet Occupation? A Case Study from the Baranowicze Region," in Barkan, Cole, and Struve, eds., *Shared History—Divided Memory,* 225–237; and Christoph Mick, "Incompatible Experiences: Poles, Ukrainians and Jews in Lviv under Soviet and German Occupation, 1939–44," *Journal of Contemporary History* 46, no. 2 (2011): 336–363. Articles about Jewish reception in various Polish fighting units include Israel Gutman, "Jews in General Anders' Army in the Soviet Union," *Yad Vashem Studies* 13 (1977): 231–296; Ryszard Terlecki, "The Jewish Issue in the Polish Army in the USSR and the Near East, 1941–1944," in Davies and Polonsky, eds., *Jews in Eastern Poland and the USSR,* 161–170; and Klemens Nussbaum, "Jews in the Kosciuszko Division and the First Polish Army," in Davies and Polonsky, eds., *Jews in Eastern Poland and the USSR,* 183–208.

25. This topic appears in memoranda from the period, in numerous books about Jewish life in the Soviet Union, and in David Engel, "The Polish Government-in-Exile and the Erlich-Alter Affair," in Davies and Polonsky, eds., *Jews in Eastern Poland and the USSR,* 172–180.

26. In English, see Na'ama Seri-Levi, "'These people are unique': The Repatriates in the Displaced Persons Camps," *Moreshet* 14 (2017): 49–100; Edele, Fitzpatrick, and Grossmann, eds., *Shelter from the Holocaust;* John Goldlust, "A Different Silence: The Survival of More than 200,000 Polish Jews in the Soviet Union during World War II as a Case Study in Cultural Amnesia," *Journal of the Australian Jewish Historical Society* 21, no. 1 (2012): 29–94; Atina Grossmann, "Remapping Relief and Rescue: Flight,

Displacement, and International Aid for Jewish Refugees during World War II," *New German Critique* 39, no. 3 (2012): 61–79; Albert Kaganovitch, "Jewish Refugees and Soviet Authorities during World War II," *Yad Vashem Studies* 38, no. 2 (2010): 85–121; Albert Kaganovitch, "Stalin's Great Power Politics, the Return of Jewish Refugees to Poland, and Continued Migration to Palestine, 1944–1946," *Holocaust and Genocide Studies* 26, no. 1 (2012): 59–94; Laura Jockusch and Tamar Lewinsky, "Paradise Lost? Postwar Memory of Polish Jewish Survival in the Soviet Union," *Holocaust and Genocide Studies* 24, no. 3 (2010): 373–399.

27. Timothy Snyder, *Bloodlands: Europe between Hitler and Stalin* (New York: Basic Books, 2010).

1. Esau or Laban?

Epigraph: Bogdan Wojdowski, "A Little Person, a Songless Bird, a Cage, and the World," in *Contemporary Jewish Writing in Poland: An Anthology,* ed. Antony Polonsky and Monika Adamczyk-Garbowska (Lincoln: University of Nebraska Press, 2001), 240.

1. On the use of Esau as a literary trope, see Gerson D. Cohen, "Esau as Symbol in Early Medieval Thought," in *Studies in the Variety of Rabbinic Cultures* (Philadelphia: Jewish Publication Society, 1991), 243–261. Carol Bakhos has argued for a less overly determined and more multivalent reading of Esau, yet she also finds the biblical character used as a stand-in for both specific and more amorphous others. See Carol Bakhos, "Figuring (Out) Esau: The Rabbis and Their Others," *Journal of Jewish Studies* 58, no. 2 (Autumn 2007): 250–262.

2. "Memoirs of Hendel Family: Genealogy," in *Bene ha-ʿayarah mesaprim,* ed. Eliezer Tsvi Cohen (Bnei Brak, Israel: Yots'e Horodlo be-Erets Yisra'el, 2000), 89–90.

3. Krystyna Chiger and Daniel Paisner, *The Girl in the Green Sweater: A Life in Holocaust's Shadow* (New York: St. Martin's, 2008), 17.

4. Omer Bartov, *Germany's War and the Holocaust: Disputed Histories* (Ithaca, NY: Cornell University Press, 2003), 33.

5. Norman Davies, *God's Playground: A History of Poland,* vol. 2, *1795 to the Present* (New York: Columbia University Press, 1982), 437.

6. Halik Kochanski, *The Eagle Unbowed: Poland and the Poles in the Second World War* (Cambridge, MA: Harvard University Press, 2012), 57.

7. Davies, *God's Playground,* 438.

8. Kochanski, *The Eagle Unbowed,* 82.

9. Julien Bryan, *Siege* (New York: Doubleday, Doran, 1940), 54.

10. Jan Karski, *Story of a Secret State: My Report to the World* (1944; Washington, DC: Georgetown University Press, 2013), 7.

11. Anna Landau-Czajka, "Polish Press Reporting about the Nazi Germans' Anti-Jewish Policy, 1933–1939," in *Why Didn't the Press Shout? American & International Journalism during the Holocaust*, ed. Robert Moses Shapiro (Jersey City, NJ: Yeshiva University/Ktav, 2003), 411–428.

12. Shalom Omri, University of Southern California Shoah Foundation, Visual History Archive (hereafter VHA), Interview 41743, Holon, Israel, March 1, 1998, tape 2, minutes 1–15.

13. Moshe Ben-Asher, VHA Interview 47417, London, August 19, 1998, tape 2, minutes 23–25.

14. Jerzy Tomaszewski, "The Polish Right-Wing Press, the Expulsion of Polish Jews from Germany, and the Deportees in Zbąszyń, 1938–1939," *Gal-Ed* 18 (2002): 90–92.

15. Zyga Elton, *Destination Buchara* (Ripponlea, Australia: Dizal Nominees, 1996), 46; Shaul Shternfeld, *Halom ben gederot* (Tel Aviv: Halonot, 1999), 22.

16. Ann Szedlecki, *Album of My Life* (Toronto: Azrieli Foundation, 2010), 35–37.

17. Boruch B. Frusztajer, *From Siberia to America: A Story of Survival and Success* (Scranton, PA: University of Scranton Press, 2008), 37.

18. Simon Davidson, *My War Years, 1939–1945*, trans. Marie Morgens (San Antonio: University of Texas, 1981), 7.

19. Moshe Etzion (Atsmon), VHA Interview 28297, Kibbutz Nirim, Israel, October 3, 1997, tape 1, minute 11.

20. Henry Orenstein, *I Shall Live: Surviving the Holocaust, 1939–1945* (New York: Oxford University Press, 1990), 34.

21. Israel Ignac Feldman, *The Lost Dream* (Toronto: Lorne Miller and Associates, 2007), 41–49.

22. Larry Wenig, *From Nazi Inferno to Soviet Hell* (Hoboken, NJ: Ktav, 2000), 52.

23. "Secret Additional Protocol to the Treaty of Non-Aggression between Germany and the USSR concerning Delimitation of German and Soviet Spheres of Interest in Eastern Europe," in General Sikorski Historical Institute, *Documents on Polish-Soviet Relations, 1939–1945*, vol. 1, *1939–1943* (London: Heinemann, 1961), 40.

24. John Erickson suggests that the Soviets were not, in fact, ready for the invasion, but the speed of the German advance forced their hand. See John Erickson, "The Red Army's March into Poland, September 1939," in *The Soviet Takeover of the Polish Eastern Provinces, 1939–41*, ed. Keith Sword (New York: St. Martin's, 1991), 9–10.

25. Kochanski, *The Eagle Unbowed*, 102, 129. For more on the experiences of Polish prisoners of war, see Jan T. Gross, "Polish POW Camps in Soviet-

Occupied Western Ukraine," in Sword, ed., *The Soviet Takeover of the Polish Eastern Provinces,* 44–56.

26. Doris L. Bergen, *War and Genocide: A Concise History of the Holocaust,* 2nd ed. (Lanham, MD: Rowman & Littlefield, 2009), 103; Davies, *God's Playground,* 439.

27. Kochanski, *The Eagle Unbowed,* 96.

28. Maciej Siekierski, "The Jews in Soviet-Occupied Eastern Poland at the End of 1939: Numbers and Distribution," in *Jews in Eastern Poland and the USSR, 1939–46,* ed. Norman Davies and Antony Polonsky (New York: St. Martin's, 1991), 112. There were 3.1 million Jews in Poland according to the 1931 census. Emigration in the following years was more than matched by natural increase. Estimates of the Jewish population in 1939 range from 3.2 to 3.4 million. Of these, approximately 1.3 million lived in the eastern territories before the war. Andrzej Żbikowski, "Polish Jews under Soviet Occupation, 1939–1941," in *Contested Memories: Poles and Jews during the Holocaust and Its Aftermath,* ed. Joshua D. Zimmerman (New Brunswick, NJ: Rutgers University Press, 2003), 54–55. Mordechai Altshuler estimates the number of Polish Jews in Soviet territory to have been between 1.440 and 1.442 million, including the refugees. See Mordechai Altshuler, *Soviet Jewry on the Eve of the Holocaust: A Social and Demographic Profile* (Jerusalem: Hebrew University Press/Yad Vashem, 1998), 9.

29. Jerzy Tomaszewski, *Ojczyzna nie tylko Polaków: mniejszości narodowe w Polsce w latach 1918–1939* (Warsaw: Młodzieżowa Agencja Wydawnicza, 1985), 50.

30. "German-Soviet Boundary and Friendship Treaty," in General Sikorski Historical Institute, *Documents on Polish-Soviet Relations,* 1:42. See also "Supplementary Protocol to the German-Soviet Boundary and Friendship Treaty of September 28, 1939, on the Delineation of the Frontiers between Germany and the USSR," in General Sikorski Historical Institute, *Documents on Polish-Soviet Relations,* 1:57–61.

31. For a discussion of this decision in one town, see Eliyana R. Adler, "Hrubieszów at the Crossroads: Polish Jews Navigate the German and Soviet Occupations," *Holocaust and Genocide Studies* 28, no. 2 (2014): 1–30.

32. Testimony of Sacher Grünbaum, Archiwum Żydowskiego Instytutu Historycznego w Warszawie, Record Group 301, file 4534, 2. English translation included in the file.

33. Testimony of Yosef Rozenberg, Ganzach Kiddush Hashem, Flinker Collection, 45941 (Protocol 65), 2.

34. Avraham Blander, Interview Video Testimony (hereafter VT) 6066, Yad Vashem Archives (hereafter YVA), O.3 Oral Testimonies, Afula, Israel, February 5, 2007, tape 1, minutes 31–38.

35. Martin Kaner, VHA Interview 05304, South Fallsburg, NY, August 8, 1995, tape 1, minute 18.

36. Tsiporah Horvits, *Tutim asurim* (Tel Aviv: Moreshet, 2009), 39.

37. Elton, *Destination Buchara*, 113.

38. Moshe, "Meyne iberlebenishn," YVA, M.10 AR1 Ringelblum Archives, 1045, 1.

39. Gerda Weissmann Klein, *All But My Life* (New York: Hill and Wang, 1996), 6.

40. Sara Selver-Urbach, *Through the Window of My Home: Recollections from the Lodz Ghetto*, trans. Siona Bodansky (Jerusalem: Yad Vashem, 1986), 33.

41. Yankl Saler, VHA Interview 41969, Melbourne, March 18, 1998, tape 1, minutes 9–12.

42. Mendel Saler, VHA Interview 45281, Melbourne, June 24, 1998, tape 2, minutes 4–6.

43. Isabelle Choko, "My First Life," in Isabelle Choko, Frances Irwin, Lotti Kahana-Aufleger, Margit Raab Kalina, and Jane Lipski, *Stolen Youth: Five Women's Survival in the Holocaust* (New York: Yad Vashem/Holocaust Survivors' Memoirs Project, 2005), 21.

44. Jack Pomerantz and Lyric Wallwork Winik, *Run East: Flight from the Holocaust* (Urbana: University of Illinois Press, 1997), 14–22.

45. Helena Starkiewicz, *Blades of Grass between the Stones* (Melbourne: H. Starkiewicz, 1998), 46.

46. Meyer Megdal, *My Holocaust Testimony* (n.p.: M. Megdal, 1994), 7.

47. Boris Baum, VHA Interview 11354, Hallandale, FL, January 25, 1996, tape 1, minute 10.

48. Omri interview, tape 2, minute 19.

49. Chaim Ajzen, *Chaim Ajzen Remembers* (Melbourne: C. Ajzen, 2001), 27.

50. Matla (Kleiner) Blander, Interview VT 6065, YVA, O.3, Afula, Israel, February 4, 2007, tape 1, minutes 30–33.

51. Aleksandra (Oleńka) Alexander, *To My Dear Daughters Inka and Nana: Tracing the Past* (n.p.: A. Alexander, n.d.), 7.

52. Megdal, *My Holocaust Testimony*, 6–7.

53. Matla Blander interview, tape 1, minutes 31–32.

54. Josef Scher, VHA Interview 35210, New York, November 6, 1997, tape 1, minutes 22–23.

55. Avraham Ayzen, "Khronologye fun khurbn Hrubyeshov," in *Pinkes Hrubyeshov: tsum 20-tn yortog nakh dem groyzamen khurbn fun undzer*

gevezener heym, ed. Barukh Kaplinski (Tel Aviv: Irgun yoytse Hrubye-shov in Yisroel un in di Fareynikte Shtatn mit der hilf fun di Hrubye-shover landsmanshaftn in gor der velt, 1962), 601.

56. Rachel Auerbach, *Varshaver tsavoes: bagegenishn, aktivitetn, goyrlos, 1933–1943* (Tel Aviv: Yisroel Bukh, 1974), 40.

57. Selver-Urbach, *Through the Window of My Home*, 30.

58. See, for example, Yisrael [Israel] Gutman, *ha-Yehudim be-Polin ahare milhemet-ha-'olam ha-sheniyah* (Jerusalem: Zalman Shazar Center, 1985), 12; Yosef Litvak, *Pelitim Yehudim mi-Polin be-Verit ha-Mo'atsot, 1939–1946* (Jerusalem: Hebrew University Press, 1988), 353–359; Norman Davies and Antony Polonsky, "Introduction," in Davies and Polonsky, eds., *Jews in Eastern Poland and the USSR* (New York: St. Martin's, 1991), 3; Dov Levin, *The Lesser of Two Evils: Eastern European Jewry under Soviet Rule, 1939–1941* (Philadelphia: Jewish Publication Society, 1995), 180; Feliks Tych, "Polish Jews—Prisoners of Soviet Camps," in *Widziałem Anioła Śmierci: Losy deportowanych Żydów polskich w ZSRR w latach II wojny światowej*, ed. Maciej Siekierski and Feliks Tych (Warsaw: Rosner i Wspólnicy, 2006), 16; and Yehuda Bauer, *The Death of the Shtetl* (New Haven, CT: Yale University Press, 2009), 33.

59. See, for example, Altshuler, *Soviet Jewry on the Eve of the Holocaust*, 9, and the calculations in the appendix, 323–326; Grzegorz Hryciuk, "Victims 1939–1941: The Soviet Repressions in Eastern Poland," in *Shared History—Divided Memory: Jews and Others in Soviet-Occupied Poland, 1939–1941*, ed. Elazar Barkan, Elizabeth A. Cole, and Kai Struve (Leipzig: Leipziger Universitätsverlag, 2007), 195; and Albert Kaganovitch, "Jewish Refugees and Soviet Authorities during WWII," *Yad Vashem Studies* 38, no. 2 (2010): 98–100.

60. Katherine R. Jolluck, *Exile and Identity: Polish Women in the Soviet Union during World War II* (Pittsburgh: University of Pittsburgh Press, 2002), 10–11.

61. Mark Edele and Wanda Warlik, "Saved by Stalin? Trajectories of Polish Jews in the Soviet Second World War," in *Shelter from the Holocaust: Rethinking Jewish Survival in the Soviet Union*, ed. Mark Edele, Sheila Fitzpatrick, and Atina Grossmann (Detroit: Wayne State University Press, 2017), 98.

62. Litvak, *Pelitim Yehudim*, 24.

63. Kochanski, *The Eagle Unbowed*, 57.

64. Marian Feldman, *From Warsaw, through Łuck, Siberia, and Back to Warsaw* (Morrisville, NC: LuLu, 2009), 58–59.

65. Natan Gross, *Who Are You, Mr. Grymek?* (London: Vallentine Mitchell, 2001), 123–124.

66. Orenstein, *I Shall Live,* 39–40.

67. Wenig, *From Nazi Inferno to Soviet Hell,* 68.

68. Zorach Warhaftig, *Refugee and Survivor: Rescue Efforts during the Holocaust* (Jerusalem: Yad Vashem/World Zionist Organization, 1988), 32.

69. Ajzen, *Chaim Ajzen Remembers,* 23.

70. Victor Zarnowitz, *Fleeing the Nazis, Surviving the Gulag, and Arriving in the Free World: My Life and Times* (Westport, CT: Praeger, 2008), 32–33.

71. Frida Zerubavel, *Hayiti plitah* (Tel Aviv: Davar, 1941), 8–9.

72. Michal Unger, "The Status and Plight of Women in the Lodz Ghetto," in *Women in the Holocaust,* ed. Dalia Ofer and Lenore J. Weitzman (New Haven, CT: Yale University Press, 1998), 123–124.

73. Dalia Ofer, "Gender Issues in Diaries and Testimonies of the Ghetto: The Case of Warsaw," in Ofer and Weitzman, eds., *Women in the Holocaust,* 145.

74. Edele and Warlik, "Saved by Stalin?," 111.

75. Kitty Hart, *Return to Auschwitz: The Remarkable Life of a Girl Who Survived the Holocaust* (London: Sidgwick and Jackson, 1981), 30.

76. Moshe Brener, Interview VT 9992, YVA, O.3, Israel, December 28, 1994, tape 1, minutes 2–5.

77. Helen Zuberman, VHA Interview 47875, Bronx, NY, December 1, 1998, tape 1, minute 28.

78. Alexander Donat, *The Holocaust Kingdom: A Memoir* (New York: Holt, Rinehart and Winston, 1963), 4.

79. Henry Skorr with Ivan Sokolov, *Through Blood and Tears: Surviving Hitler and Stalin* (London: Vallentine Mitchell, 2006), 92–107, 132.

80. Irving Beada, VHA Interview 13383, Boynton Beach, FL, March 18, 1996, tape 1, minutes 16–17.

81. Sally Alban, VHA Interview 4102, Toronto, July 19, 1995, tape 1, minutes 15–19.

82. Hanna Davidson Pankowsky, *East of the Storm: Outrunning the Holocaust in Russia* (Lubbock: Texas Tech University Press, 1999), 13–27.

83. Alban interview, tape 1, minutes 15–19.

84. Hart, *Return to Auschwitz,* 30–36.

85. Feldman, *From Warsaw,* 66.

86. Adam Boren, *Journey through the Inferno* (Washington, DC: United States Holocaust Memorial Museum/Holocaust Survivors' Memoirs Project, 2004), 10.

87. Zvi Faier, Interview VT 6929, YVA, O.3, Israel, August 3, 2007, tape 1, minutes 19–27.

88. Marion Kaplan, *Between Dignity and Despair: Jewish Life in Nazi Germany* (New York: Oxford University Press, 1998).

89. See, for example, Sara Bender, *The Jews of Bialystok during World War II and the Holocaust*, trans. Yaffa Murciano (Waltham, MA: Brandeis University Press, 2008), 53.

90. Jan Dvořák and Adam Hradilek highlight the importance of proximity in Czechoslovak Jews' decisions to cross into Soviet territory. See Jan Dvořák and Adam Hradilek, "The Persecution of Czechoslovak Jews in the Soviet Union during World War II," in *Jewish Studies in the 21st Century: Prague—Europe—World,* ed. Marcela Zoufala (Weisbaden: Harrassowitz Verlag, 2014), 199.

91. Yitzhak Erlichson, *My Four Years in Soviet Russia*, trans. Maurice Wolfthal (Boston: Academic Studies Press, 2013), 9.

92. Yankl Saler interview, tape 1, minute 9, through tape 2, minute 1.

93. Alexander, *To My Dear Daughters Inka and Nana,* 70.

94. Rabbi Jacob Halpern, interview with the author, September 28, 2010, Silver Spring, MD.

95. Selver-Urbach, *Through the Window of My Home,* 33.

96. Janka Goldberger, *Stalin's Little Guest* (London: Janus, 1995), 3–9.

97. Klara Samuels, *God Does Play Dice: The Autobiography of a Holocaust Survivor* (Philadelphia: Bainbridge Books, 1999), chap. 4.

98. Matla Blander interview, tape 1, minutes 31–32.

99. Eliyana R. Adler and Natalia Aleksiun, "Seeking Relative Safety: The Flight of Polish Jews East in the Autumn of 1939," *Yad Vashem Studies* 46, no. 1 (2018): 53–60.

100. Yehoshua A. Gilboa, *Confess! Confess! Eight Years in Soviet Prisons,* trans. Dov Ben Aba (Boston: Little, Brown, 1968), 8.

101. See, for example, Christopher R. Browning, *Remembering Survival: Inside a Nazi Slave-Labor Camp* (New York: W. W. Norton, 2010); Rochelle Saidel, *Mielec, Poland: The Shtetl That Became a Nazi Concentration Camp* (Jerusalem: Gefen, 2012); Shimon Redlich, *Together and Apart in Brzezany: Poles, Jews, and Ukrainians, 1919–1945* (Bloomington: Indiana University Press, 2002); Bauer, *The Death of the Shtetl;* and David Silberklang, *Gates of Tears: The Holocaust in the Lublin District* (Jerusalem: Yad Vashem, 2013).

102. Chaim A. Kaplan, *Scroll of Agony: The Warsaw Diary of Chaim A. Kaplan,* ed. and trans. Abraham I. Katsh (New York: Macmillan, 1965), 49–50.

103. Erlichson, *My Four Years in Soviet Russia,* 29.

104. Levin, *The Lesser of Two Evils,* 180–183.

105. Litvak, *Pelitim Yehudim,* 360.

106. The text of the secret protocol is reprinted in Izidors Vizulis, "The Division of Europe into Spheres of Influence," in *The Molotov-Ribbentrop Pact of 1939: The Baltic Case* (New York: Praeger, 1990), 16–17.

107. "Telegram from Ambassador Schulenburg to the German Ministry for Foreign Affairs concerning M. Stalin's Proposal to Erase Poland as a State and Fix the New Frontier on the River Bug," in General Sikorski Historical Institute, *Documents on Polish-Soviet Relations*, 1:51–52.

108. "German-Soviet Boundary and Friendship Treaty," 1:52; "Supplementary Protocol to the German-Soviet Boundary and Friendship Treaty," in *Documents on Polish-Soviet Relations*, 1:57–60.

109. Betty Rich, *Little Girl Lost* (Toronto: Azrieli Foundation, 2011), 42–43.

110. Moshe, "Meyne iberlebenishn," 6.

111. Zarnowitz, *Fleeing the Nazis*, 29, 31–45.

112. Harry Berkelhammer, VHA Interview 14300, Toronto, April 16, 1996, tape 1, minute 24, through tape 2, minute 2.

113. Orenstein, *I Shall Live*, 34–40.

114. Rozenberg testimony, 3.

115. Leybish Frost, "In di ershte milkhome vokhn," in Kaplinski, *Pinkes Hrubyeshov*, 610–612.

116. Donat, *The Holocaust Kingdom*, 4–5.

117. Yosef Goldkorn, *Navenad iber di shlyakhn fun Rusland* (Tel Aviv: H. Leivik, 1998), 22–31.

118. Kaplan, *Scroll of Agony*, 70–71.

119. Testimony of Roza Hirsz, Hoover Institution Archives, Poland, Ministerstwo Informacji i Dokumentacj, Box 123, File 6, 123-6, Protocol 85, 1–2.

120. "Bialystok un svive," YVA, M.10 AR 1, 433, 37.

121. Kaplan, *Scroll of Agony*, 70.

122. Sara Bergman, VHA Interview 30068, Melbourne, April 6, 1997, tape 2, minutes 0–3.

123. Eve Silver, VHA Interview 18512, Atlanta, August 12, 1996, tape 2, minutes 1–2.

124. Mietek Sieradzki, *By Twist of History: The Three Lives of a Polish Jew* (London: Vallentine Mitchell, 2002), 17.

125. "[Early Days—Course of Events 1939–1940]," ARII/129, in *To Live with Honor and Die with Honor! Selected Documents from the Warsaw Ghetto Underground Archives "O. S."["Oneg Shabbath"]*, ed. Joseph Kermish (Jerusalem: Yad Vashem, 1986), 140.

126. Szymon Grajcar, VHA Interview 16434, Toronto, June 24, 1996, tape 3, minutes 1–2.

127. Adam Boren, *Journey through the Inferno* (Washington, DC: United States Holocaust Memorial Museum/Holocaust Survivors' Memoirs Project, 2004), 13.

128. "Fun yene zeyt," YVA, M.10 AR1, 450-1, 4. The Polish translation of this testimony lists the unidentified refugee interviewed as St. Aau ("Z tamtej

strony," *Archiwum Ringelbluma: Konspiracyjne Archiwum Getta Warszawy*, Vol. 3, *Relacje z Kresów*, ed. Andrzej Żbikowski (Warsaw: Żydowski Instytut Historyczny, 2000), no. 43, 886.

129. "Bialystok un svive," YVA, M.10 AR1, 433, 39–40.

130. Zerubavel, *Hayiti plitah*, 63–64.

131. Jan Karski, "An Early Account of Polish Jewry under Nazi and Soviet Occupation Presented to the Polish Government-in-Exile, February 1940," trans. David Engel, in Davies and Polonsky, eds., *Jews in Eastern Poland and the USSR*, 263.

132. David Silberklang, "The Holocaust in the Lublin District" (Ph.D. diss., Hebrew University of Jerusalem, 2003), 60. Silberklang's work was later published in book form as *Gates of Tears: The Holocaust in the Lublin District* (Jerusalem: Yad Vashem, 2013).

133. For more on the death march, see Ariel Hurwitz, "Mits'ad ha-mavet shel Yehude Helm ve-Hrubyeshov le-'ever ha-nahar Bug be-Detsember 1939," *Yalkut Moreshet* 68 (October 1999): 51–68; and Adler, "Hrubieszów at the Crossroads."

134. Chaim Zemel, VHA Interview 26622, Chicago, February 23, 1997, tape 2, minute 5, through tape 4, minute 8.

135. "Soviet Refusal to Accept Jewish Refugees Who Flee from Polish Territory Occupied by Germany," Documents on German Foreign Policy, 1918–1945 (hereafter DGFP), vol. 8, doc. 419, 489, cited in Yosef Govrin, *The Jewish Factor in the Relations between Nazi Germany and the Soviet Union 1933–1941* (London: Vallentine Mitchell, 2009), 132.

136. "Continued Soviet Refusal to Accept Jewish Refugees Who Flee from Polish Territory Occupied by Germany," DGFP, vol. 8, doc. 477, 560–561, cited in Govrin, *The Jewish Factor*, 133.

137. Horvits, *Tutim asurim*, 42.

138. Hart, *Return to Auschwitz*, 29–36.

139. Omri interview, tape 2, minutes 17–22.

140. Yochewed Deutch, VHA Interview 46608, Kiryat Bialik, Israel, September 7, 1997, tape 1, minutes 10–12.

141. Judith Gerson notes a similar trend in German Jewish testimonies regarding the last train or ship out of the country. See Judith Gerson, "Family Matters: German Jewish Masculinities among Nazi Era Refugees," in *Jewish Masculinities: German Jews, Gender, and History*, ed. Benjamin Maria Baader, Sharon Gillerman, and Paul Lerner (Bloomington: Indiana University Press, 2012), 222–223.

142. Rachela Tytelman Wygodzki, *The End and the Beginning (August 1939–July 1948)* (n.p.: R.T. Wygodzki, 1998), 6–16.

143. Danna J. Azrieli, *One Step Ahead: David J. Azrieli (Azrylewicz), Memoirs: 1939–1950* (Jerusalem: Yad Vashem, 2001), 46–54.

144. Samuel D. Kassow, *Who Will Write Our History? Emanuel Ringelblum, the Warsaw Ghetto, and the Oyneg Shabes Archive* (Bloomington: Indiana University Press, 2007), 226–227. The questionnaire can be viewed in the Ringelblum archival materials, YVA, M.10 AR1, 142; or as published in Żbikowski, *Relacje z Kresów*, 39–42, 43–45, 45–47.

145. "Fun Varshe keyn Vitebsk un tsurik: mayn 'kurikulum vite'," YVA, M.10 AR1, 456, JM3489 21, 44–46.

146. "Bialystok un svive," YVA, M.10 AR1, 433, 59.

147. Donat, *The Holocaust Kingdom*, 4.

148. Baum interview, tape 1, minutes 12–15.

149. Elton, *Destination Buchara*, 112.

150. Azrieli, *One Step Ahead*, 27.

151. Tema Abel, VHA Interview 14584, Toronto, April 26, 1996, tape 2, minutes 12–15.

152. Moshe Erlich, VHA Interview 10029, Jerusalem, December 13, 1995, tape 2, minutes 26–27.

153. Włodzimierz Szer, *To Our Children: Memoirs of Displacement. A Jewish Journey of Hope and Survival in Twentieth-Century Poland and Beyond* (Boston: Academic Studies Press, 2016), 2.

154. Chaim Shapiro, *Go, My Son: A Young Jewish Refugee's Story of Survival* (Jerusalem: Feldheim, 1989), 37–38, 69–84.

155. Nechama Tec, VHA Interview 43812, Westport, CT, July 6, 1998, tape 2, minutes 21–27.

156. Nechama Tec, *Dry Tears: The Story of a Lost Childhood* (New York: Oxford University Press, 1984), 60–62.

157. Zoë Vania Waxman, *Writing the Holocaust: Identity, Testimony, Representation* (Oxford: Oxford University Press, 2006), 125.

158. Correspondence between Lawrence Langer and Michael Berenbaum, cited in Noah Shenker, *Reframing Holocaust Testimony* (Bloomington: Indiana University Press, 2015), 25.

159. Browning, *Remembering Survival*, 11.

160. Browning, *Remembering Survival*, 11.

161. Marianne Hirsch introduced the concept of "postmemory" to discuss the ways in which children of Holocaust survivors are profoundly influenced by the memories and experiences of their parents. She has elaborated on it in a number of works. See Marianne Hirsch, *Family Frames: Photography, Narrative, and Postmemory* (Cambridge, MA: Harvard University Press, 1997); Marianne Hirsch, *The Generation of Postmemory: Writing*

and Visual Culture after the Holocaust (New York: Columbia University Press, 2012); and Marianne Hirsch and Leo Spitzer, *Ghosts of Home: The Afterlife of Czernowitz in Jewish Memory* (Berkeley: University of California Press, 2010). Other examples of collective or collaborative memoirs between parents and children include Joseph Berger, *Displaced Persons: Growing Up American after the Holocaust* (New York: Scribner, 2001); Mayer Kirshenblatt and Barbara Kirshenblatt-Gimblett, *They Called Me Mayer July: Painted Memories of a Jewish Childhood in Poland before the Holocaust* (Berkeley: University of California Press, 2007); Kaja Finkler and Golda Finkler, *Lives Lived and Lost: East European History before, during, and after World War II as Experienced by an Anthropologist and Her Mother* (Boston: Academic Studies Press, 2012); Regina Grol, *Saving the Tremors of Past Lives: A Cross-Generational Holocaust Memoir* (Boston: Academic Studies Press, 2014); and Meri-Jane Rochelson, *Eli's Story: A Twentieth-Century Jewish Life* (Detroit: Wayne State University Press, 2018).

162. Suzanna Eibuszyc, *Memory Is Our Home: Loss and Remembering: Three Generations in Poland and Russia 1917–1960s* (Stuttgart: ibidem-Verlag, 2015), 20.

163. Ida Kaminska, *My Life, My Theater*, ed. and trans. Curt Leviant (New York: Macmillan, 1973), 100. Kaminska's fairly upbeat description is belied by that of Roza Hirsz, recorded in 1943 for the Polish government-in-exile in Palestine. According to Hirsz, the Germans beat Kaminska and stole her karakul coat, dresses, and lingerie before demanding that she play a role for them. See Hirsz, Protocol 85, 2.

2. If a Man Did Flee from a Lion, and a Bear Met Him

Epigraph: Peretz Markish, "To a Jewish Dancer," in *Inheritance (Yerushe)*, ed. Mary Schulman, Joan Braman, and David Weintraub, trans. Mary Schulman (Toronto: TSAR, 2007), 33–34. This work contains a bilingual version of the entire poem. A bilingual excerpt, translated by Leonard Wolf, is available in *The Penguin Book of Modern Yiddish Verse*, ed. Irving Howe, Ruth R. Wisse, and Khone Shmeruk (New York: Viking Penguin, 1987), 376. Wolf's arguably more poetic translation captures the chaos of the flight while obscuring the reality that many refugees slept in synagogue buildings.

1. For more on Markish, see Joseph Sherman, Gennady Estraikh, Jordan Finkin, and David Shneer, eds., *A Captive of the Dawn: The Life and Work of Peretz Markish (1895–1952)* (London: Legenda, 2011). Although

written in 1940, the poem was only published later. See Ben-Cion
Pinchuk, *Shtetl Jews under Soviet Rule: Eastern Poland on the Eve of the
Holocaust* (Oxford: Basil Blackwell, 1990), 138.

2. Alexander Brakel, "Was There a 'Jewish Collaboration' under Soviet
Occupation? A Case Study from the Baranowicze Region," in *Shared
History—Divided Memory: Jews and Others in Soviet-Occupied Poland,
1939–1941*, ed. Elazar Barkan, Elizabeth A. Cole, and Kai Struve
(Leipzig: Leipziger Universitatsverlag, 2007), 226.

3. Marek Wierzbicki, "Western Belarus in September 1939: Revisiting
Polish-Jewish Relations in the *Kresy*," in Barkan, Cole, and Struve, eds.,
Shared History—Divided Memory, 137.

4. Joanna B. Michlic, "Anti-Polish and Pro-Soviet? 1939–1941 and the
Stereotyping of the Jews in Polish Historiography," in Barkan, Cole, and
Struve, eds., *Shared History—Divided Memory*, 97.

5. Jan Karski, "An Early Account of Polish Jewry under Nazi and Soviet
Occupation Presented to the Polish Government-in-Exile," trans. David
Engel, in *Jews in Eastern Poland and the USSR, 1939–46*, ed. Norman
Davies and Antony Polonsky (New York: St. Martin's, 1991), 265–266, 264.

6. David Engel, *In the Shadow of Auschwitz: The Polish Government-in-
Exile and the Jews, 1939–1942* (Chapel Hill: University of North Carolina
Press, 1987), 61.

7. "Lemberg," Yad Vashem Archives (hereafter YVA), M10 AR1, Ringelblum
Archives, 1042, 3–4.

8. Documents collected by the underground archive, Oneg Shabbes, show
that reports of Polish accusations about Jews reached the Warsaw Ghetto.
See, for example, "Polish-Jewish Relations in Occupied Warsaw," AR I/91,
in *To Live with Honor and Die with Honor! Selected Documents from the
Warsaw Ghetto Underground Archives "O. S." ["Oneg Shabbath"]*, ed.
Joseph Kermish (Jerusalem: Yad Vashem, 1986), 613–614. Samuel Kassow,
in his treatment of the archive and its founder, also notes that the inter-
viewers in the ghetto were sensitive to these issues. See Samuel D.
Kassow, *Who Will Write Our History? Emanuel Ringelblum, the Warsaw
Ghetto, and the Oyneg Shabes Archive* (Bloomington: Indiana University
Press, 2007), 227.

9. Katherine R. Jolluck, *Exile and Identity: Polish Women in the Soviet
Union during World War II* (Pittsburgh: University of Pittsburgh Press,
2002), 199, 205, 213.

10. Yehuda Bauer, *The Death of the Shtetl* (New Haven, CT: Yale University
Press, 2009), 36.

11. Baruch Milch, *Can Heaven Be Void?*, ed. Shosh Milch-Avigal (Jerusalem:
Yad Vashem, 2003), 58–59. For the original Polish, see Baruch Milch,

Testament z Archiwum Żydowskiego Instytutu Historycznego (Warsaw: Ośrodek KARTA, 2001), 79. The English translation, based on a heavily redacted Hebrew version, does not always match the Polish version but expresses the same ideas.

12. Andrzej Żbikowski, "Polish Jews under Soviet Occupation, 1939–1941," in *Contested Memories: Poles and Jews during the Holocaust and Its Aftermath,* ed. Joshua D. Zimmerman (New Brunswick, NJ: Rutgers University Press, 2003), 59.

13. See Jan T. Gross, *Neighbors: The Destruction of the Jewish Community in Jedwabne, Poland* (Princeton, NJ: Princeton University Press, 2001), the chapter entitled "Collaboration" and passim.

14. See Antony Polonsky and Joanna B. Michlic, eds., *The Neighbors Respond: The Controversy over the Jedwabne Massacre in Poland* (Princeton, NJ: Princeton University Press, 2004), especially Polonsky and Michlic's thorough introduction.

15. Ben-Cion Pinchuk, "Facing Hitler and Stalin: On the Subject of Jewish 'Collaboration' in Soviet-Occupied Eastern Poland, 1939–1941," in Zimmerman, ed., *Contested Memories,* 67.

16. Michlic, "Anti-Polish and Pro-Soviet?," 68.

17. Tarik Cyril Amar, *The Paradox of Ukrainian Lviv: A Borderland City between Stalinists, Nazis, and Nationalists* (Ithaca, NY: Cornell University Press, 2015), 45, emphasis in the original.

18. Abraham A. Kreusler, *A Teacher's Experiences in the Soviet Union* (Leiden: E. J. Brill, 1965), 12.

19. Symcha Burstin, University of Southern California Shoah Foundation, Visual History Archive (hereafter VHA), Interview 31555, Melbourne, July 22, 1997, tape 2, minutes 10–13.

20. Ann Szedlecki, *Album of My Life* (Toronto: Azrieli Foundation, 2010), 66.

21. "Lemberg," YVA, M.10 AR1,1042, 5.

22. Shaul Shternfeld, *Halom ben gederot* (Tel Aviv: Halonot, 1999), 76.

23. Iakov Khonigsman, VHA Interview 45050, Lviv, Ukraine, June 6, 1998, tape 2, minutes 15–16.

24. Dov Levin, *The Lesser of Two Evils: Eastern European Jewry under Soviet Rule, 1939–1941* (Philadelphia: Jewish Publication Society, 1995), 184.

25. Emanuel Goldberg, "'Ayara 'erev ha-Shoah: Svislots tahat shilton ha-Sovetim 1939–1941," Yerahmiel Lifshits, *Sefer Svislots B* (Netanya, Israel: Irgun yots'e Svislots be-Yisra'el, 1984), 64.

26. Betty Rich, *Little Girl Lost* (Toronto: Azrieli Foundation, 2011), 47.

27. Zyga Elton, *Destination Buchara* (Ripponlea, Australia: Dizal Nominees, 1996), 118.

28. SL, interview no. 17, in Rachel Erlich, *Interviews with Polish and Russian Jewish DP's in DP Camps on Their Observations of Jewish Life in Soviet Russia* (New York: American Jewish Committee, 1948), 1.

29. "File on the Activities of the Commission Organizing Help for Refugees and the Unemployed," October 2–December 21, 1939, Derzhavnii Arkhiv L'vivskoi Oblasti (hereafter DALO), fond P-300, opis 01, delo. 1, 1–64.

30. Daniel Boćkowski, "Losy żydowkich uchodźców z centralnej i zachodniej Polski (bieżeńców) przebywających na terenie obwodu białystockiego w latach 1939–1941," *Studia Podlaskie* 16 (2006): 95.

31. See, for example, "Bialystok and Environs," 365; "From the Other Side," 388; and Salomea L., "Notebook Two," 401, in Shimon Huberband, *Kiddush Hashem: Jewish Religious and Cultural Life in Poland during the Holocaust*, trans. David E. Fishman, ed. Jeffrey S. Gurock and Robert S. Hirt (Hoboken, NJ: Ktav, 1987).

32. Irving Badner, VHA Interview 02742, Little Neck, NY, May 14, 1995, tape 1, minutes 14–15.

33. Mike Weinreich, VHA Interview 10011, Toronto, December 12, 1995, tape 1, minutes 25–26.

34. Zorach Warhaftig, *Refugee and Survivor: Rescue Efforts during the Holocaust* (Jerusalem: Yad Vashem/World Zionist Organization, 1988), 35–37.

35. According to Jan Gross, the very ubiquity of this phrase suggests that the troops were in fact primed beforehand. See Jan T. Gross, *Revolution from Abroad: The Soviet Conquest of Poland's Western Ukraine and Western Belorussia* (Princeton, NJ: Princeton University Press, 1988), 28.

36. Baruch Minz, "Introduction," in Pearl Minz, *Surviving the Holocaust in Siberia: The Diary of Pearl Minz*, trans. Alexander B. White (Goodyear, AZ: D. de Frain, 2010), 17.

37. A. Reisfeld, *To Run for Life from Swastika and Red Star* (Bloomington, IN: Xlibris, 2002).

38. Frida Zerubavel, *Hayiti plitah* (Tel Aviv: Davar, 1941), 55–71.

39. For abridged English translations, see "Soviet-Lithuanian Agreement," in Republic of Poland, Ministry of Foreign Affairs, *Official Documents concerning Polish-German and Polish-Soviet Relations 1933–1939* (New York: Roy, 1940), 193; and "Extract from the Soviet-Lithuanian Agreement," General Sikorski Historical Institute, *Documents on Polish-Soviet Relations 1939–1945*, vol. 1, *1939–1943* (London: Heinemann, 1961), 62–63.

40. Sarunas Liekis, "The Transfer of Vilna District into Lithuania, 1939," *Polin* 14 (2001): 212–222.

41. Herman Kruk, *The Last Days of the Jerusalem of Lithuania: Chronicles from the Vilna Ghetto and the Camps, 1939–1944,* ed. Benjamin Harshav, trans. Barbara Harshav (New Haven, CT: Yale University Press, 2002), 28.
42. Zerubavel, *Hayiti plitah,* 78–91.
43. Shternfeld, *Halom ben gederot,* 80–90.
44. Testimony of Leib Novik, Ganzach Kiddush Hashem (hereafter GKH), Flinker Collection, 45590 (Protocol 24), 2–5.
45. Klara Samuels, *God Does Play Dice: The Autobiography of a Holocaust Survivor* (Philadelphia: Bainbridge Books, 1999), 59.
46. Testimony of Szlomo Zdrojowicz, Hoover Institution Archives (hereafter HIA), Poland, Ministerstwo Informacji i Dokumentacji, Box 123, File 6, Protocol 82, 2.
47. Zekharia Chesno, *Kol ha-neharot zormot le-Yarden: zikhronot* (Jerusalem: Philobiblion, 2008), 14.
48. Dina Porat, "Nesibot ve-sibot le-matan vizot-maʻavar sovetiot le-plite Polin ha-Yehudim be-Vilna be-shanim 1940–1941," *Shvut* 6 (1978): 54.
49. Porat, "Nesibot ve-sibot le-matan," 54.
50. Liekis, "The Transfer of Vilna District to Lithuania," 216.
51. Sarunas Liekis, *1939: The Year That Changed Everything in Lithuania's History* (Amsterdam: Rodopi, 2010), 282.
52. Testimony of Menachem Mendl Grossman, GKH, Flinker Collection, 45584 (Protocol 16), 1–3.
53. Rabbi Simcha Shafran with Avi Shafran, *Fire, Ice, Air: A Polish Jew's Memoir of Yeshiva, Siberia, America* (New York: Hashgachapress, 2010), 33–43. "Eating days" are an old Jewish custom whereby a local Jewish community provides support to its yeshiva by offering to feed students in individual homes according to a weekly schedule.
54. Shlomo Kless, "Peʻilut tsionit shel pelitim Yehudim be-Verit-ha-Moʻatsot be-shanim 1941–1945 ve-kesher ha-yishuv ha-Yehudi be-Erets Yisraʼel ʻimahem" (Ph.D. diss., Hebrew University, 1985), v–xi.
55. [Rachela Zilberberg], "Der khurbn fun di kehilos oyf di nay farnumener stokhim, zumer 1941," YVA, M.10 AR1, 433, 2–16. The published Polish translation lists the witness as likely Rachela Zilberberg ("Zagłada gmin na terenach zajętych latem 1941 roku"), *Archiwum Ringelbluma: Konspiracyjne Archiwum Getta Warszawy,* Vol. 3, *Relacje z Kresów,* ed. Andrzej Żbikowski (Warsaw: Żydowski Instytut Historyczny, 2000), no. 21, 326.
56. Kruk, *The Last Days of the Jerusalem of Lithuania,* 29–40.
57. Yehuda Bauer, *American Jewry and the Holocaust: The American Jewish Joint Distribution Committee, 1939–1945* (Detroit: Wayne State University Press, 1981), 112.

58. M. W. Beckelman, "Memorandum re Expulsions over the Lithuanian German Border," November 8, 1939, American Joint Distribution Committee Archives, 1933–1944 New York Collection: Selected Documents, Poland: Administration, General, 1939 (Oct.–Dec.), 3. For more on the situation, see, for example, Michal Frankl, "'Exhausted, Frozen and Only Half Alive': The Suwałki No Man's Land," We Refugees, https://en .we-refugees-archive.org/chapters/the-suwalki-no-mans-land/.

59. Bauer, *American Jewry*, 113.

60. For more on this organization, see Efraim Zuroff, *The Response of Orthodox Jewry in the United States to the Holocaust: The Activities of the Vaad Ha-Hatzala Rescue Committee, 1939–1945* (Hoboken, NJ: Ktav, 2000).

61. Liekis, *1939: The Year That Changed Everything*, 281.

62. Warhaftig, *Refugee and Survivor*, chaps. 5–8.

63. Dina Porat, "Rikuz ha-pelitim ha-Yehudim be-Vilna ba-shanim 1939–1941," (Ph.D. diss., Tel Aviv University, 1973), 35–36.

64. Warhaftig, *Refugee and Survivor*, 72.

65. Dov B. Lederman, *These Children Are Mine: A Story of Rescue and Survival* (Jerusalem: Feldheim, 2002), 35–55.

66. Zerubavel, *Hayiti plitah*, 107–127.

67. Zerubavel, *Hayiti plitah*, 98.

68. Chesno, *Kol ha-neharot zormot le-Yarden*, 15.

69. Of course, the arrest and demotion of some can create opportunities for others. Kalman Weiser discusses how the refugee Polish activist and writer Noah Prylucki came to occupy the first chair of Yiddish in Vilna after the Soviet occupation. See Kalman Weiser, *Jewish People, Jewish Nation: Noah Prylucki and the Folkists in Poland* (Toronto: University of Toronto Press, 2011), 226–259.

70. Levin, *The Lesser of Two Evils*, 208, 217.

71. Porat, "Nesibot ve-sibot," 60–61.

72. Porat, "Nesibot ve-sibot," 59–60.

73. Letter from Vilnius to Yokohama, December 11, 1940, YVA, P.20, Dr. Zorach Warhaftig Collection, File 24, Letters Requesting Visas Sent by Refugees, 1940–1941, 34–35.

74. Porat, "Nesibot ve-sibot," 62–64. A good deal has been written about Japanese consul Chiune Sugihara and his heroic rescue efforts. He was aided by other diplomats, including Dutch consul Jan Zwardendijk and Polish consul Tadeusz Romer in Shanghai. For more on their efforts, as well as the refugee Jewish community in Shanghai during the war, see, for example, Hillel Levine, *In Search of Sugihara: The Elusive Japanese Diplomat Who Risked His Life to Rescue 10,000 Jews from the Holocaust*

(New York: Free Press, 1996); and Meron Medzini, *Under the Shadow of the Rising Sun: Japan and the Jews during the Holocaust Era* (Boston: Academic Studies Press, 2016).

75. Rabbi Yisrael Gerber, Interview, GKH, Testimonies and Interviews, Israel, May 2, 2008.

76. Sam Roberts, "Masha Leon, Columnist Who Fled Nazis, Dies at 86," *New York Times,* April 10, 2017. See also Masha Leon, "How Shirley Temple Helped Me Come to America," *Jewish Forward,* February 11, 2014, https://forward.com/schmooze/192605/how-shirley-temple-helped-me -come-to-america/. On Leon's father, see Martyna Rusiniak-Karwat, "Bundists under the Soviet Occupation: The Case of Matwiej Bernstein," *Studia Polityczne* 45, no. 3 (2017): 143–153.

77. Chaim Grade, *My Mother's Sabbath Days: A Memoir,* trans. Channa Kleinderman Goldstein and Inna Hecker Grade (New York: Schocken, 1987), 240.

78. Israel Ignac Feldman, *The Lost Dream* (Toronto: Lorne Miller and Associates, 2007), 59.

79. Amar, *The Paradox of Ukrainian Lviv,* 50.

80. Sheila Fitzpatrick, *Everyday Stalinism: Ordinary Life in Extraordinary Times: Soviet Russia in the 1930s* (New York: Oxford University Press, 1999), 6.

81. "Fun Varshe keyn Vitebsk un tsurik: meyn 'kurikulum vite'," YVA, M.10 456 AR1, 32.

82. Szymon Grajcar, VHA Interview 16434, Toronto, June 24, 1996, tape 3, minutes 5–10. Grajcar claims to have arrived in Soviet territory in November 1940 and been deported in the summer of 1941. This is most likely a mistake.

83. Rabbi Dr. Jacob Halpern, interview with the author, Silver Spring, MD, September 28, 2010.

84. Helen Zuberman, VHA Interview 47875, Bronx, NY, December 1, 1998, tape 2, minutes 0–2.

85. Yocheved (Hei) Zamari, Interview VT 6026, YVA, O.3 Oral Testimonies, Israel, December 21, 2006, tape 1, minutes 14–17.

86. Volodymyr Muzychenko, *Jewish Ludmir: The History and Tragedy of the Jewish Community of Volodymyr-Volynsky* (Boston: Academic Studies Press, 2016), 116. Muzychenko mentions only that the area was overrun with refugees, but testimonies by Jews from Hrubieszów often refer to Ludmir as a destination.

87. Yankl Saler, VHA Interview 41969, Melbourne, March 18, 1998, tape 2, minutes 1–4. See also Mendel Saler, VHA Interview 45281, Melbourne, June 24, 1998, tape 2, minutes 5–6.

88. "Bialystok un svive," YVA, M.10 AR1 433, 41–42.

89. Feldman, *The Lost Dream*, 54, 61.

90. Testimony of Mikhael Berlovitch, GKH, Flinker Collection, 45586 (Protocol 18), 1–2.

91. Adam Boren, *Journey through the Inferno*, trans. Menachem Z. Rosensaft (Washington, DC: United States Holocaust Memorial Museum/Holocaust Survivors' Memoirs Project, 2004), 25–27.

92. Testimony of Khanina Teitel, GKH, Flinker Collection, 45591 (Protocol 26), 1. For more on Teitel, who became Hannan Dekel, see the book by his daughter: Mikhal Dekel, *Tehran Children: A Holocaust Refugee Odyssey* (New York: W.W. Norton and Company, 2019).

93. Harry Berkelhammer, VHA Interview 14300, Toronto, April 16, 1996, tape 2, minutes 1–4.

94. Testimony of Shmuel Burshtein, GKH, Flinker Collection, 45585 (Protocol 17), 3–4.

95. Testimony of Nachman Elbojm, HIA, Poland, Ministerstwo Informacji i Dokumentacji, Box 123, File 5, Protocol 55, 3.

96. Boren, *Journey through the Inferno*, 27.

97. Elton, *Destination Buchara*, 117–150.

98. Chawa Kestenbojm, Protocol 41, trans. David Engel, in "Documents," in Davies and Polonsky, eds., *Jews in Eastern Poland and the USSR, 1939–46* (New York: St. Martin's, 1991), 229–230.

99. Eliyana R. Adler and Natalia Aleksiun, "Seeking Relative Safety: Polish Jews' Flight East in the Fall of 1939," *Yad Vashem Studies* 461 (2018): 53–60.

100. Yaffa Margulies-Shnitzer, *I Survived Belzec Crematories* (Tel Aviv: Parnass, 1991), 13–14.

101. Adler and Aleksiun, "Seeking Relative Safety," 53–60.

102. Żbikowski, "Polish Jews under Soviet Occupation," 59.

103. Bernard L. Ginsburg, *A Wayfarer in a World of Upheaval* (San Bernardino, CA: Borgo, 1993), 21–22.

104. Danna J. Azrieli, *One Step Ahead: David J. Azrieli (Azrylewicz), Memoirs: 1939–1950* (Jerusalem: Yad Vashem, 2001), 46–56.

105. Marian Feldman, *From Warsaw, through Łuck, Siberia, and Back to Warsaw* (Morrisville, NC: LuLu, 2009), 67–74.

106. Moshe Erlich, VHA Interview 10029, Jerusalem, December 13, 1995, tape 3, minute 27 through tape 4, minute 9.

107. Testimony of Malka Rozenblat, HIA, Poland, Ministerstwo Informacji i Dokumentacji, Box 6, File 123, Protocol 84, 1.

108. Bob Golan, *A Long Way Home: The Story of a Jewish Youth, 1939–1949*, ed. Jacob Howland (Lanham, MD: University Press of America, 2005), 26, 17–19.

109. Samuels, *God Does Play Dice*, 55–56.
110. Testimony of Yosef Rozenberg, GKH, Flinker Collection, 45941 (Protocol 65), 4–5.
111. Weinreich interview, tape 1, minutes 25–29.
112. Testimony of Yehudis Patash, GKH, Flinker Collection, 45629 (Protocol 37), 3.
113. Samuels, *God Does Play Dice*, 73–74.
114. Zerubavel, *Hayiti plitah*, 48–49.
115. On the brief run of the paper, see Sara Bender, *The Jews of Bialystok during World War II and the Holocaust*, trans. Yaffa Murciano (Waltham, MA: Brandeis University Press, 2008), 73–75.
116. *Der Bialystoker Shtern* 6, January 8, 1940.
117. *Der Bialystoker Shtern* 26, February 10, 1940.
118. Feldman, *From Warsaw*, 58–62.
119. Alexander Donat, *The Holocaust Kingdom: A Memoir* (New York: Holt, Rinehart and Winston, 1963), 4.
120. Amar, *The Paradox of Ukrainian Lviv*, 47.
121. One resident, home sick with a fever on the day of the plebiscite, at first believed that the officers who arrived at his door had come to take him to the hospital. Instead they forced him out of bed and to the polling station. Testimony of Leon Klajman, HIA, Poland, Ministerstwo Informacji i Dokumentacji, Box 123, File 5, Protocol 38, 4.
122. Some memoirists, and a few scholars, refer to the plebiscite and resulting representatives in quotation marks, in order to emphasize the undemocratic nature of the enterprise. I follow the lead of most scholars who do not, while still accurately describing the conditions.
123. For a Polish protest against the vote, the incorporation documents, and the text of the citizenship decree, see General Sikorski Historical Institute, *Documents on Polish-Soviet Relations*, vol. 1, documents 64, 67, 68, and 71.
124. Amar, *The Paradox of Ukrainian Lviv*, 10–11.
125. Gross, *Revolution from Abroad*, 226, 229, 230–231.
126. Pinchuk, *Shtetl Jews under Soviet Rule*, 8.
127. "Moshe Kleinbaum's Report on Issues in the Former Eastern Polish Territories, 12 March 1940," trans. David Engel, in Davies and Polonsky, eds., *Jews in Eastern Poland and the USSR*, 281.
128. Margulies-Shnitzer, *I Survived Belzec Crematories*, 13.
129. "Fun Varshe keyn Vitebsk un tsurik," 16.
130. Dov Levin, "The Jews of Vilna under Soviet Rule, 19 September–28 October 1939," *Polin* 9 (1996): 122.
131. Ola Hnatiuk, *Courage and Fear* (Boston: Academic Studies Press, 2019), 8.
132. Janka Goldberger, *Stalin's Little Guest* (London: Janus, 1995), 30.

133. Hanna Davidson Pankowsky, *East of the Storm: Outrunning the Holocaust in Russia* (Lubbock: Texas Tech University Press, 1999), 44.

134. Chaim Shapiro, *Go, My Son: A Young Jewish Refugee's Story of Survival* (Jerusalem: Feldheim, 1989), 24–25.

135. "Fun Varshe keyn Vitebsk un tsurik," 17.

136. On jokes in the USSR, see, for example, David Brandenberger, ed., *Political Humor under Stalin: An Anthology of Unofficial Jokes and Anecdotes* (Bloomington, IN: Slavica, 2009).

137. Krystyna Chiger and Daniel Paisner, *The Girl in the Green Sweater: A Life in Holocaust's Shadow* (New York: St. Martin's, 2008), 20.

138. Testimony of Aharon Fish, GKH, Flinker Collection, 45588 (Protocol 20), 1.

139. Warhaftig, *Refugee and Survivor,* 118. Another version of this joke is relayed in Moshe Kleinbaum, "Report on Issues in the Former Eastern Polish Territories," March 12, 1940, trans. David Engel, in Davies and Polonsky, eds., *Jews in Eastern Poland and the USSR,* 280.

140. "From the Other Side (Recorded from Wanderers)," Notebook One, interview with St. Am., cited in Huberband, *Kiddush Hashem,* 396.

141. Boruch B. Frusztajer, *From Siberia to America: A Story of Survival and Success* (Scranton, PA: University of Scranton Press, 2008), 53.

142. Milch, *Can Heaven Be Void?,* 61.

143. Feldman, *From Warsaw,* 71–72.

144. "Iber a grenets," YVA, M10, AR1, 1046, 24.

145. Gennady Estraikh, "The Missing Years: Yiddish Writers in Soviet Bialystok, 1939–41," *East European Jewish Affairs* 46, no. 2 (2016): 180.

146. Zerubavel, *Hayiti plitah,* 52.

147. Chone Szmeruk, "Yiddish Publications in the U.S.S.R.: From the Late Thirties to 1948," *Yad Vashem Studies on the European Jewish Catastrophe and Resistance* 4 (1960): 112.

148. Quoted in Awrom Zbar, "The Rise and Fall of Bialystok," in *Der Bialystoker yizkor buch,* ed. I. Shmulewitz (New York: Bialystoker Center, 1982), English section, 54.

149. Estraikh, "The Missing Years," 179.

150. Hersh Smolar, *Vu bistu khaver Sidorov?* (Tel Aviv: Y. L. Perets Farlag, 1975), 161.

151. Joseph Rubinstein, "In Bergelson's shtub," in *Megilath Russland: Scroll of Woe of a Polish Jew in Russia* (New York: CYCO, 1960), 30–68.

152. Itzhak Yasanowicz, *Mit Yidishe shrayber in Rusland* (Buenos Aires: Kiyum, 1959), 153.

153. Yehoshua A. Gilboa, *The Black Years of Soviet Jewry: 1939–1953,* trans. Yosef Schachter and Dov Ben-Abba (Boston: Little, Brown, 1971), 27.

154. Tania Fuks, *A vanderung iber okupirte gebitn* (Buenos Aires: Tsentral Farband fun Poylishe Yidn in Argentine, 1947), 98.

155. Pinchuk, *Shtetl Jews under Soviet Rule,* 137.

156. Gilboa, *The Black Years of Soviet Jewry,* 23.

157. Bogdan Czaykowski, "Soviet Policies in the Literary Sphere: Their Effects and Implications," in *The Soviet Takeover of the Polish Eastern Provinces,* ed. Keith Sword (New York: St. Martin's, 1991), 118–119.

158. Mieczysław Inglot, "The Socio-political Role of the Polish Literary Tradition in the Cultural Life of Lwow: The Example of Adam Mickiewicz's Work," in Sword, ed., *The Soviet Takeover of the Polish Eastern Provinces,* 131–145.

159. Szmeruk, "Yiddish Publications," 111–113.

160. In her memoir, journalist Tania Fuks discusses a project to open a second Yiddish paper in Lvov in the spring of 1941. See Fuks, *A vanderung,* 104–105. Dov Levin suggests that this new paper may have been meant to focus on the more recently annexed areas of Bessarabia and Northern Bukovina. See Levin, *The Lesser of Two Evils,* 120.

161. Fish testimony, 4.

162. Ginsburg, *A Wayfarer,* 21–24.

163. Ida Kaminska, *My Life, My Theater,* ed. and trans. Curt Leviant (New York: Macmillan, 1973), 113–117.

164. Aleksander Wat, "Nowy Teatr," *Czerwony Sztandar* 77, December 24, 1939.

165. Advertisement for Teatr Żydowski's "Wuj Tom," *Czerwony Sztandar* 73, December 20, 1939.

166. Advertisement for Teatr Żydowski's "Mój Syn," *Czerwony Sztandar* 90, January 9, 1940.

167. P. Stark, "Matka revolucjonisty," *Czerwony Sztandar* 91, January 10, 1940.

168. P. Stark, "Owcze Źródło," *Czerwony Sztandar* 159, March 30, 1940.

169. See also Mirosława M. Bułat, "The Polish Press and the Yiddish Theater in Poland (1947–1956)—Screens of a Dialogue, Part 1: Excerpts from the World of Appearances," in *Under the Red Banner: Yiddish Culture in the Communist Countries in the Postwar Era,* ed. Elvira Grözinger and Magdalena Ruta (Wiesbaden: Harrassowitz Verlag, 2008), 66.

170. Shimon Dzigan, *Der koyekh fun Yidishn humor* (Tel Aviv: Orli, 1974), 160.

171. Bender, *The Jews of Bialystok,* 82.

172. See, for example Salomea L., "Notebook Two," 64.

173. Zerubavel, *Hayiti plitah,* 50.

174. "Lemberg," YVA, Ringelblum Archives, M10 AR1 1042, 15.

175. [Stanisław Różycki], "Lwów: Szkolnictwo 1939-41," YVA, M.10 ARI 75, 1–6. The published version lists the author as probably Różycki (see Żbikowski, *Relacje z Kresów,* no. 42, 792).

176. Zerubavel, *Hayiti plitah,* 60.

177. "Lwów," 8–13.

178. See, for example, "Documents relating to Polish schools," DALO, f. P-163, op. 1, 3–6.

179. "Lists of teachers for Lvov, Stanislav and Tarnopol," DALO, f. P-163, op. 1, 26–30.

180. "Materials for the reorganization of schools," DALO, f. P-163, op. 1, 10–14 ob, 17 ob, 111.

181. "Lwow," 23–49, 53–57.

182. Kreusler, *A Teacher's Experiences,* 18–27.

183. Yosef Halperin, *Ne'urim be-azikim: be-Polin u-ve-Belarus ba-milhemet-ha-'olam ha-sheniyah* (Tel Aviv: Moreshet, 2002), 31–41.

184. Frusztajer, *From Siberia to America,* 55–56.

185. Pankowsky, *East of the Storm,* 40.

186. On the history and practice of the ritual, see Ivan G. Marcus, *Rituals of Childhood: Jewish Acculturation in Medieval Europe* (New Haven, CT: Yale University Press, 1996), chap. 2. Gross shows that the Soviets employed this spectacle with non-Jewish, as well as Jewish, Polish children. See Gross, *Revolution from Abroad,* 131.

187. All educational systems seek to inculcate particular ideas and ideals into young minds. There is a rich literature on this process in the Soviet Union. On schools as agents of sovietization, see, for example, Lisa A. Kirschenbaum, *Small Comrades: Revolutionizing Childhood in Soviet Russia, 1917–1932* (New York: RoutledgeFalmer, 2001). On the role of the Komsomol in Soviet life, see Matthias Neumann, *The Communist Youth League and the Transformation of the Soviet Union* (New York: Routledge, 2011). For an examination of sovietization among Jews, see Anna Shternshis, *Soviet and Kosher: Jewish Popular Culture in the Soviet Union, 1923–1939* (Bloomington: Indiana University Press, 2006).

188. "In undzere shuln: antireligyeze dertsiung in der shul," *Der Bialystoker Shtern* 19, January 29, 1940.

189. S. Gortman, "Dos shtetl oyfgelebt," *Der Bialystoker Shtern* 5, January 6, 1940.

190. "Bialystok un svive," YVA, M.10 AR1, 433, 45.

191. Ahron Blenkitni, *Goyrl: iberlebungen fun a Yidisher mishpokhe in der tsveyter velt-milkhome* (Tel Aviv: Y. L. Perets, 1968), 76.

192. "Bialystok un svive," 42–43.

193. "Secret Report," Belorussia, YVA, M.41 Archives in Belarus, 2583, 1–33.

194. Levin, *The Lesser of Two Evils,* 156.

195. Testimony of Shmuel Labin, GKH, Flinker Collection, 45587 (Protocol 19), 5–6.

196. "Bialystok un svive," 43.

197. Michael Maik, *Deliverance: The Diary of Michael Maik, A True Story*, ed. Avigdor Ben-Dov, trans. Laia Ben-Dov (Kedumim, Israel: Keterpress, 2004), 17. This text, taken from a memorial book, appears to be more of a memoir than a diary.

198. Labin, Flinker Collection, GKH, 6.

199. Shapiro, *Go, My Son*, 74–75.

200. Pinchuk, *Shtetl Jews under Soviet Rule*, 93–101.

201. Margulies-Shnitzer, *I Survived Belzec Crematories*, 26.

202. Goldberg, "'Ayara 'erev ha-Shoah," 55. For a translation by Goldberg's son Mel Shalev, see "A Shtetl on the Eve of Its Destruction: Svisloch under Soviet Rule, 1939–1941," JewishGen, http://kehilalinks.jewishgen.org /Svisloch/EmanuelGoldberg.htm.

203. Yuli Margolin, quoted in Yosef Litvak, "The Plight of Refugees from the German-Occupied Territories," in Sword, ed. *The Soviet Takeover of the Polish Eastern Provinces*, 66.

204. Keith Sword, "Soviet Economic Policy in the Annexed Areas," in Sword, ed., *The Soviet Takeover of the Polish Eastern Provinces*, 98.

205. Amar, *The Paradox of Ukrainian Lviv*, 49–50.

206. Pinchuk, *Shtetl Jews under Soviet Rule*, 41.

207. "From the Other Side (Recorded from Wanderers)," in Huberband, *Kiddush Hashem*, 389, 395.

208. Testimony of Chawa Kestenbojm, HIA, Ministerstwo Informacji i Dokumentacji, Box 5, File 123, Protocol 41, 2.

209. Ann Benjamin-Goldberg, VHA Interview 11455, Huntington, NY, December 14, 1995, tape 1, minutes 1–10.

210. Rich, *Little Girl Lost*, 50–51.

211. See for example, Simon Davidson, *My War Years, 1939–1945*, trans. Marie Morgens (San Antonio: University of Texas, 1981), 72; and Shternfeld, *Halom ben gederot*, 78.

212. Jolluck, *Exile and Identity*, 260–265.

213. Documents of the NKVD, January–February 1940, Natsionalny arkhiv respubliki Belarus, Minsk, 4-21-2075, YVA, M.41 2428, 2–24.

214. "Rutki," YVA, M.10 AR1, Ringelblum Archives, 899, 1–2.

215. "Surowe kary na spekulantów i sabatażystów," *Czerwony Sztandar* 19, October 14, 1939.

216. See, for example, *Czerwony Sztandar* 52, November 24, 1939; 54, November 26, 1939; 60, December 3, 1939; 63, December 8, 1939.

217. "In kamf kegn spekulantn," *Der Bialystoker Shtern* 7, January 9, 1940.

218. "Samuel Rengler, Markus Kal'bauer, speculation," April 5–May 10, 1940, DALO, f. R-239, op. 1, d. 22, 1–4.

219. "Secret list of accused speculators submitted to the secretary of the Belarus Obkom," January 2–September 5, 1940, Gosudarstvenny Arkhiv Grodenskoy oblasti-Belarus, Grodno 6195-1-90, YVA, M.41, 3096, 19–23.

220. Evgenii Rozenblat, "'Contact Zones' in Interethnic Relations—The Case of Western Belarus, 1939–1941," in Barkan, Cole, and Struve, eds., *Shared History—Divided Memory*, 217.

221. Evgenii S. Rozenblat, "'Chuzhdyi element': evreiskie bezhentsy v Zapadnoi Belorussii (1939–1941)," in *Istorii I kul'tura rossiiskogo i vostochnoevropeiskogo evreistva: novye istochniki, novye podkhody,* ed. Oleg V. Budnitskii (Moscow: Dom evreiskoi knigi, 2004), 334. I follow Estraikh, "The Missing Years," in the translation of the terms.

222. Rozenblat, "'Chuzhdyi element,'" 338.

223. Zerubavel, *Hayiti plitah,* 61.

224. "Fun Varshe keyn Vitebsk un tsurik," 20, 24–27.

225. David Brandshpigel, *Hisardut: sipur hayehem shel ha-Yehudim bi-Verit ha-Mo'atsot bi-zeman milhemet ha-'olam ha-sheniyah* (Holon: D. Brandshpigel, 1998), 55–65.

226. Dora Drescher, VHA Interview 25544, Plantation, FL, February 6, 1997, tape 1, minutes 18–20.

227. Dmitrii Tolochko, "Polish Refugees in Eastern Belorussia, 1939–1941," *Jews in Russia and Eastern Europe* 1, no. 56 (2006): 14.

228. Shternfeld, *Halom ben gederot,* 94–95.

229. Dovid Feinzeig, *Faith & Flight: A Young Boy's Memories of the Prewar Shtetl, Shavuos in Ger, a Family's Travels through Russia, Rebuilding in Postwar Poland and France* (Lakewood, NJ: Israel Bookshop Publications, 2013), 127.

230. Levin, *The Lesser of Two Evils,* 190. Mark Edele and Wanda Warlik provide of range of forty thousand to fifty-three thousand volunteers. See Mark Edele and Wanda Warlik, "Saved by Stalin? Trajectories of Polish Jews in the Soviet Second World War," in *Shelter from the Holocaust: Rethinking Jewish Survival in the Soviet Union,* ed. Mark Edele, Sheila Fitzpatrick, and Atina Grossmann (Detroit: Wayne State University Press, 2017), 103.

231. Rozenblat, "'Chuzhdyi element,'" 340.

232. "February 1, 1940, Resolution of the Executive Committee of the Council of Workers' Delegates regarding the Situation of Polish Refugees," *Dokumenty i materiały do historii stosunków polsko-radzieckich,* vol. 7, *Styczeń 1939–grudzień 1943* (Warsaw: Książka i wiedza, 1973), 207–8.

233. Yosef Goldkorn, *Navenad iber di shlyakhn fun Rusland* (Tel Aviv: H. Leivik, 1998), 44–49.

234. Szedlecki, *Album of My Life*, 66–67.

235. Dovid Brenner, "Mir zaynen gliklekh!" *Der Bialystoker Shtern* 22, February 4, 1940.

236. Markus Zwerling, "List z Donbasu," *Czerwony Sztandar* 118, February 12, 1940.

237. Bender, *The Jews of Bialystok*, 58.

238. Davidson, *My War Years*, 62–85.

239. "Iberegistratsye fun pleytim," *Der Bialystoker Shtern* 23, February 5, 1940.

240. Pinchuk, *Shtetl Jews under Soviet Rule*, 112.

241. Mordechai Altshuler, *Soviet Jewry on the Eve of the Holocaust: A Social and Demographic Profile* (Jerusalem: Yad Vashem, 1998), 326. Rozenblat reaches a figure of fifty thousand for the Belorussian territories alone. See Rozenblat, "'Chuzhdyi element,'" 356–357.

242. "[Early Days—Course of Events 1939–1940]," ARII/129 in Kermish, ed., *To Live with Honor*, 140.

243. "Fun Varshe keyn Vitebsk un tsurik," 38.

244. Chaim A. Kaplan, *Scroll of Agony: The Warsaw Diary of Chaim A. Kaplan*, ed. and trans. Abraham I. Katsh (New York: Macmillan, 1965), 148.

245. [St. Aau.], "Fun yene zeyt," YVA, M.10 AR1 450-1, 17.

246. See, for example, Milch, *Can Heaven Be Void?*, 64–70.

247. Rich, *Little Girl Lost*, 53–55.

248. Fuks, *A vanderung*, 81.

249. Amar, *The Paradox of Ukrainian Lviv*, 59–60.

250. Nikita Khrushchev, *Khrushchev Remembers*, ed. Strobe Talbott (Boston: Little, Brown, 1970), 141.

251. Yosef Litvak, *Pelitim Yehudim mi-Polin be-Verit ha-Mo'atsot, 1939–1946* (Jerusalem: Hebrew University Press, 1988), 361.

252. Gross, *Revolution from Abroad*, 206.

253. Jan T. Gross, "A Tangled Web: Confronting Stereotypes concerning Relations between Poles, Germans, Jews, and Communists," in *The Politics of Retribution in Europe: World War II and Its Aftermath*, ed. Isvan Deak, Jan T. Gross, and Tony Judt (Princeton, NJ: Princeton University Press, 2000), 92–99.

254. Żbikowski, "Polish Jews under Soviet Occupation," 56.

255. Testimony of Chana Gelernter, HIA, Poland, Ministerstwo Informacji i Dokumentacji, Box 123, File 5, Protocol 56, 3.

256. Shternfeld, *Halom ben gederot*, 129–130.

257. Halperin, *Ne'urim be-azikim*, 27.

258. Elton, *Destination Buchara*, 132–148.

259. Victor Zarnowitz, *Fleeing the Nazis, Surviving the Gulag, and Arriving in the Free World: My Life and Times* (Westport, CT: Praeger, 2008), 47.

260. Halpern interview.

261. Margulies-Shnitzer, *I Survived Belzec Crematories,* 15.

262. Menachem Ben-Moshe, "Metsukat-gerush, derekh golim ve-yesure galut," in *Sanok: Sefer zikharon le-kehilat Sanok ve-ha-sevivah,* ed. Elazar Sharvit (Jerusalem: Irgun yots'e Sanok ve-ha-sevivah be-Yisra'el, 1970), 395.

263. Zamari Interview, tape 1, minutes 16–19.

264. Eva G. Gregoratos, *An Unintended Odyssey: From War Torn Europe to America* (Bloomington, IN: AuthorHouse, 2008), 37–43.

265. On the deaths of cultural figures in Lvov, see Philip Friedman, "The Destruction of the Jews of Lwów, 1941–1944," in Philip Friedman, *Roads to Extinction: Essays on the Holocaust,* ed. Ada June Friedman (New York: Conference on Jewish Social Studies/Jewish Publication Society of America, 1980), 290–294.

266. Jaff Schatz, *The Generation: The Rise and Fall of Jewish Communists in Poland* (Berkeley: University of California Press, 1991), 157.

267. Hersh Smolar, *The Minsk Ghetto: Soviet-Jewish Partisans against the Nazis* (New York: Holocaust Library, 1989), 7–8.

268. Goldkorn, *Navenad iber di shlyakhn,* 72–88, 111–113.

269. "Fun Varshe keyn Vitebsk un tsurik," 30–33.

270. Blenkitni, *Goyrl,* 64–70.

271. Ben-Moshe, "Metsukat-gerush," 396.

272. Azrieli, *One Step Ahead,* 56–65. For more on relief packages sent between Polish Jews, see Eliyana R. Adler, "Ties that Bind: Packages as a Means of Transnational Support and Solidarity for Polish Jews in the USSR during World War II," in *More than Parcels: Wartime Relief for Jews in Nazi Camps and Ghettos,* ed. Jan Láníček and Jan Lambertz (forthcoming).

273. Davidson, *My War Years,* 115–140.

274. Elton, *Destination Buchara,* 161.

275. Michael (Teichholz) Sherwood, *Odyssey* (n.p.: M. Sherwood, 2007), 49.

276. Brandshpigel, *Hisardut,* 94–142.

277. Halperin, *Ne'urim be-azikim,* 44–46.

278. Solomon M. Schwarz, *The Jews in the Soviet Union* (Syracuse, NY: Syracuse University Press, 1951), 222.

279. Leybish Frost, "Hrubyeshaver in di Tutaner vald," in *Pinkes Hrubyeshov: tsum 20-tn yortog nakh dem groyzamen khurbn fun undzer gevezener heym,* ed. Barukh Kaplinski (Tel Aviv: Irgun yoytse Hrubyeshov in Yisroel un in di Fareynikte Shtatn mit der hilf fun di Hrubyeshover landsman-shaftn in gor der velt, 1962), 697.

280. The findings of Dov Levin support this conclusion. See Dov Levin, "The Fateful Decision: The Flight of Jews into the Soviet Interior in the Summer of 1941," *Yad Vashem Studies* 20 (1990): 130–133.

281. Henry Orenstein, *I Shall Live: Surviving the Holocaust, 1939–1945* (New York: Oxford University Press, 1990), 41–62.

282. Samuels, *God Does Play Dice,* 87.

283. Boren, *Journey through the Inferno,* 46–58.

284. For more on the historiography regarding this issue, as well as a strong statement on the policies, see Dov Levin, "The Attitude of the Soviet Union to the Rescue of Jews," in *Rescue Attempts during the Holocaust: Proceedings of the Second Yad Vashem International Historical Conference,* ed. Israel Gutman and Efraim Zuroff (Jerusalem: Yad Vashem, 1977), 225–236, as well as the "Debate" that follows (237–246).

285. On the policies and process of evacuation, see Rebecca Manley, *To the Tashkent Station: Evacuation and Survival in the Soviet Union at War* (Ithaca, NY: Cornell University Press, 2009); and Vadim Dubson, "On the Problem of the Evacuation of Soviet Jews in 1941 (New Archival Sources)," *Jews in Eastern Europe* 3, no. 40 (1999): 37–55.

286. Pinchuk, *Shtetl Jews under Soviet Rule,* 74.

287. Several scholars have explored this question in regard to Soviet Jews, and their conclusions are relevant to Polish Jews as well. See Levin, "The Fateful Decision"; Mordechai Altshuler, "Escape and Evacuation of Soviet Jews at the Time of the Nazi Invasion: Policies and Realities," in *The Holocaust in the Soviet Union: Studies and Sources on the Destruction of Jews in the Nazi-Occupied Territories of the USSR, 1941–1945,* ed. Lucjan Dobroszycki and Jeffrey S. Gurock (Armonk, NY: M. E. Sharpe, 1993), 77–104; and Anna Shternshis, "Between Life and Death: Why Some Soviet Jews Decided to Leave and Others to Stay in 1941," *Kritika* 15, no. 3 (2014): 477–504. For an examination of the fate of Jews from the western territories, see Albert Kaganovitch, "Jewish Refugees and Soviet Authorities during World War II," *Yad Vashem Studies* 38, no. 2 (2010): 85–121.

288. Bauer, *The Death of the Shtetl,* 154.

289. Rozenblat, "'Contact Zones.'"

290. Father Patrick Desbois, *The Holocaust by Bullets: A Priest's Journey to Uncover the Truth behind the Murder of 1.5 Million Jews* (New York: Palgrave Macmillan, 2008).

291. Yitzhak Arad, *The Holocaust in the Soviet Union* (Lincoln: University of Nebraska Press/Yad Vashem, 2009), 524.

3. Jewish Luck

Epigraph: Janka Goldberger, *Stalin's Little Guest* (London: Janus, 1995), 29.

1. Max Weinreich, "*Yidishkayt* and Yiddish: On the Impact of Religion on Language in Ashkenazic Jewry," in *Mordecai M. Kaplan Jubilee Volume on the Occasion of His Seventieth Birthday*, ed. Moshe David, vol. 1, English section (New York: Jewish Theological Seminary of America, 1952), 504. I am grateful to Beatrice Brukhe Lang Caplan for sending me this source.

2. Goldberger, *Stalin's Little Guest*, 60–61, 27.

3. For more on the development of the system from one regime to the other, see, for example, Galina Mikhailovna Ivanova, *Labor Camp Socialism: The Gulag in the Soviet Totalitarian System* (Armonk, NY: M. E. Sharpe, 2000), preface.

4. Pavel Polian, *Against Their Will: The History and Geography of Forced Migrations in the USSR* (Budapest: Central European University Press, 2004), 17.

5. Kate Brown, *A Biography of No Place: From Ethnic Borderland to Soviet Heartland* (Cambridge, MA: Harvard University Press, 2004), 114.

6. Polian, *Against Their Will*, 23, 43.

7. The Great Famine perpetrated in Ukraine has received increasing scholarly attention since the collapse of the USSR. See, for example, Anne Applebaum, *Red Famine: Stalin's War on Ukraine* (New York: Doubleday, 2017); and Michael Ellman, "Ellman on Applebaum, 'Red Famine: Stalin's War on Ukraine,'" H-Diplo, April 2018, https://networks.h-net.org/node /28443/reviews/1713560/ellman-applebaum-red-famine-stalins-war -ukraine.

8. Brown, *A Biography of No Place*, 128.

9. A great deal has been written about this topic. For a readable treatment, see Mark Edele, *Stalinist Society 1928–1953* (New York: Oxford University Press, 2011), chap. 2 and passim.

10. Lynne Viola, *The Unknown Gulag: The Lost World of Stalin's Special Settlements* (New York: Oxford University Press, 2007), 168.

11. Yaacov Ro'i, "The Transformation of Historiography of the 'Punished Peoples,'" *History and Memory* 21, no. 2 (2009): 151 and passim.

12. Alexander Statiev, "Soviet Ethnic Deportations: Intent versus Outcome," *Journal of Genocide Research* 11, nos. 2–3 (2009): 246.

13. Halik Kochanski, *The Eagle Unbowed: Poland and the Poles in the Second World War* (Cambridge, MA: Harvard University Press, 2012), 102, 129.

14. Bronislaw Kusnierz, *Stalin and the Poles: An Indictment of the Soviet Leaders* (London: Hollis and Carter, 1949), 90; Natalia S. Lebedeva, "The Deportation of the Polish Population in the USSR, 1939–1941," *Journal of Communist Studies and Transition Politics* 16, nos. 1–2 (2000): 30.

15. Grzegorz Hryciuk, "Victims 1939–1941: The Soviet Repressions in Eastern Poland," in *Shared History—Divided Memory. Jews and Others in Soviet-Occupied Poland, 1939–1941,* ed. Elazar Barkan, Elizabeth A. Cole, and Kai Struve (Leipzig: Leipziger Universitatsverlag, 2007), 180.

16. Jan Gross provides a chart of POW camps in Western Ukraine, but also notes that similar camps probably existed in Western Belorussia. See Jan T. Gross, "Polish POW Camps in the Soviet-Occupied Western Ukraine," in *The Soviet Takeover of the Polish Eastern Provinces, 1939–41,* ed. Keith Sword (New York: St. Martin's, 1991), 45, 53–54.

17. Lebedeva, "The Deportation of the Polish Population," 32.

18. Herman Taube, oral history interview, February 15, 2010, United States Holocaust Memorial Museum, RG-50.106*0182 Oral Testimonies, Part 1, tape 2, minutes 4–19.

19. Keith Sword, *Deportation and Exile: Poles in the Soviet Union, 1939–48* (Hampshire, England: St. Martin's, 1994), 3.

20. Joseph Czapski, *The Inhuman Land,* trans. Gerald Hopkins (London: Polish Cultural Foundation, 1987), 7–8.

21. Kusnierz, *Stalin and the Poles,* 99.

22. In addition to numerous monuments and commemorations, there is a rich scholarly literature about the events in Polish. In English, see, for example, Kusnierz, *Stalin and the Poles;* and Anna M. Cienciala, Natalia S. Lebedeva, and Wojciech Materski, eds., *Katyn: A Crime without Punishment,* trans. Marian Schwartz with Anna M. Cienciala and Maia A. Kipp (New Haven, CT: Yale University Press, 2007).

23. Maria Hadow, *Paying Guest in Siberia* (London: Harvill, 1959), 21–23. Two former refugees claim to have been witnesses to aspects of the massacre, but their testimonies are questionable in certain aspects. See Alexander Contract, University of Southern California Shoah Foundation Visual History Archive (hereafter VHA) Interview 36559, King of Prussia, PA, November 7, 1997; and Yitshak (Jerzy) Edison, *Mayne fir yor in Soviet-Rusland* (Paris: Gelbard, 1953), translated as Yitzhak Erlichson, *My Four Years in Soviet Russia,* trans. Maurice Wolfthal (Boston: Academic Studies Press, 2013).

24. Rabbi Avraham Steinberg, Interview, Ganzach Kiddush Hashem Archives (hereafter GKH), Testimonies and Interviews, Israel, August 29, 2010, disc 1, minutes 42–44.

25. Natalia Aleksiun, "As Citizens and Soldiers: Military Rabbis in the Second Polish Republic," *Jahrbuch des Simon-Dubnow-Institute*=Simon Dubnow Institute Yearbook 12 (2013): 221.

26. Erlichson, *My Four Years in Soviet Russia*, 35–57.

27. Helena Starkiewicz, *Blades of Grass between the Stones* (Melbourne: H. Starkiewicz, 1998), 47–81.

28. For more on the circumstances of the event, see Ariel Hurwitz, "Mits'ad ha-mavet shel Yehude Helm ve-Hrubyeshov le-'ever ha nahar Bug be-Detsember 1939," *Yalkut Moreshet* 68 (1999): 51–68.

29. Moshe Kaner, Interview VT 6426, Yad Vashem Archives (hereafter YVA), O.3, Kiryat Haim, Israel, September 26, 2006, tape 1, minute 44, through tape 2, minute 3.

30. Testimony of Maria Rudnicka, Hoover Institution Archives (hereafter HIA), Poland, Ministerstwo Informacji i Dokumentacji, Box 123, File 5, Protocol 47, 1–2.

31. Klara Samuels, *God Does Play Dice: The Autobiography of a Holocaust Survivor* (Philadelphia: Bainbridge Books, 1999), 69–75, 82.

32. Edele, *Stalinist Society*, 46–47.

33. Testimony of Leib Novik, GKH, Flinker Collection, 45590 (Protocol 24), 1–7.

34. Garri S. Urban, *Tovarisch, I Am Not Dead*, 2nd ed. (London: Cyclops Vision, 2006), 6–26.

35. Danna J. Azrieli, *One Step Ahead: David J. Azrieli (Azrylewicz), Memoirs: 1939–1950* (Jerusalem: Yad Vashem, 2001), 56–57.

36. Ester Luft to the Polish government-in-exile, July 20, 1942, HIA, Ambassada, Box 18, Folder 107.

37. Israel Ignac Feldman, *The Lost Dream* (Toronto: Lorne Miller and Associates, 2007), 55–57.

38. Hryciuk, "Victims 1939–1941," 182. Mark Edele and Wanda Warlik's figure of 23,600 conforms with this estimate. See Mark Edele and Wanda Warlik, "Saved by Stalin? Trajectories of Polish Jews in the Soviet Second World War," in *Shelter from the Holocaust: Rethinking Jewish Survival in the Soviet Union*, ed. Mark Edele, Sheila Fitzpatrick, and Atina Grossmann (Detroit: Wayne State University Press, 2017), 105.

39. Aleksander Wat, *My Century: The Odyssey of a Polish Intellectual*, ed. and trans. Richard Lourie (Berkeley: University of California Press, 1988), 111, 126.

40. Yehoshua A. Gilboa, *Confess! Confess! Eight Years in Soviet Prisons*, trans. Dov Ben Aba (Boston: Little, Brown, 1968), 19.

41. Starkiewicz, *Blades of Grass*, 64.

42. Jane Lipski, "My Escape into Prison and Other Memoirs of a Stolen Youth, 1939–1948," in Isabelle Choko, Frances Irwin, Lotti Kahana-

Aufleger, Margit Raab Kalina and Jane Lipski, *Stolen Youth: Five Women's Survival in the Holocaust* (New York: Yad Vashem/Holocaust Survivors' Memoirs Project, 2005), 271–278.

43. Moshe Grossman, *In the Enchanted Land: My Seven Years in Soviet Russia* (Tel Aviv: Rachel, 1960), 34.

44. Novik testimony, 2.

45. For more on the tragic imprisonment and death of Rabbi Schorr, see Grażyna Pawlak, Daniel Grinberg, and Maciej Sadowski, eds., *Professor Moses Schorr: Last Rabbi of the Great Synagogue* (Warsaw: Prof. Moses Schorr Foundation, 2016).

46. Testimony of Edmund Finkler, GKH, Flinker Collection, 45637 (Protocol 45), 4–7.

47. Edison, *Mayne fir yor in Soviet-Rusland,* 52–53.

48. Grossman, *In the Enchanted Land,* 66–76.

49. Terry Martin, "Stalinist Forced Relocation Policies: Patterns, Causes, Consequences," in *Demography and National Security,* ed. Myron Weiner and Sharon Stanton Russell (New York: Berghahn Books, 2001), 308.

50. Sword, *Deportation and Exile,* 15–18.

51. Katherine R. Jolluck, *Exile and Identity: Polish Women in the Soviet Union during World War II* (Pittsburgh: University of Pittsburgh Press, 2002), 13.

52. For more on the prewar deportation of ethnic Poles in the USSR, see Brown, *A Biography of No Place,* chap. 4.

53. Piotr J. Wróbel, "Class War or Ethnic Cleansing? Soviet Deportations of Polish Citizens from the Eastern Provinces of Poland, 1939–1941," *Polish Review* 59, no. 2 (2014): 40.

54. Jan T. Gross, *Revolution from Abroad: The Soviet Conquest of Poland's Western Ukraine and Western Belorussia* (Princeton, NJ: Princeton University Press, 1988), 199.

55. See, for example, Stanisław Ciesielski, Grzegorz Hryciuk, and Aleksander Srebrakowski, *Masowe Deportacje radzieckie w okresie II wojny światowej,* 2nd ed. (Wrocław: Prace Historyczne, 1994); and Stanisław Ciesielski, Wojciech Materski, and Andrzej Paczkowski, *Represje sowieckie wobec Polaków i obywateli polskich* (Warsaw: Ośrodek KARTA, 2002).

56. Ciesielski, Materski, and Paczkowski, *Represje sowieckie wobec Polaków i obywateli polskich,* 33; Jolluck, *Exile and Identity,* 13.

57. Hryciuk, "Victims 1939–1941," 190–191, 195.

58. Edele and Warlik, "Saved by Stalin?," 105.

59. Gulag, originally an acronym for Stalin's Glavnoe Upravlenie Lagerei (Main Camp Administration), has become a proper noun referring to the

entire Soviet system of mass imprisonment and forced labor. In practice, defining the scope of the Gulag can be tricky. Edwin Bacon contends that some forced labor fell outside the "Gulag umbrella" but that the Polish special settlers did not. See Edwin Bacon, *The Gulag at War: Stalin's Forced Labor System in Light of the Archives* (New York: New York University Press, 1994), 29–30. Oxana Klimkova describes the special settlements as "adjacent to labor camps," yet she adds that their "isolation from the Gulag system was only partial." See Oxana Klimkova, "Special Settlements in Soviet Russia in the 1930s–50s," *Kritika* 8, no. 1 (2007): 138.

60. Lebedeva, "The Deportation of the Polish Population," 42.

61. Menachem Begin, *White Nights: The Story of a Prisoner in Russia,* trans. Katie Kaplan (New York: Harper and Row, 1977), 16.

62. Martyna Rusiniak-Karwat, "Bundists under the Soviet Occupation: The Case of Matwiej Bernstein," *Studia Polityczne* 45, no. 3 (2017): 146, 150.

63. Marian Pretzel, *Portrait of a Young Forger: An Incredible True Story of Triumph over the Third Reich* (New York: Knightsbridge, 1989), 36.

64. Frumie Cohen, VHA Interview 47312, Brooklyn, NY, November 23, 1998, tape 2, minutes 6–9.

65. "Basic Instructions on Deportations, Order No. 00123," in *Report of the Select Committee to Investigate Communist Aggression and the Forced Incorporation of the Baltic States Into the U.S.S.R.: Third Interim Report of the Select Committee on Communist Aggression,* 82nd Cong., 2nd Sess., 464–468, in Sword, ed., *The Soviet Takeover,* 301–306.

66. "Instruktsiia NKVD SSSR 'O poriadke pereseleniia pol'skikh osadnikov iz zapadnykh oblastei USSR I BSSR' 29 Dekabria 1939," in *Stalinskie deportatsii, 1928–1953,* ed. N. L. Pobol' and P. M. Polian (Moscow: Materik, 2005), 111–112.

67. Testimony of Dora Werker, HIA, Poland, Ministerstwo Informacji i Dokumentacji, Box 123, File 5, Protocol 7, 2.

68. Steinberg interview, tape 1, minutes 34–35.

69. The participation of local residents in the process of deportation has been viewed, in some quarters, as a form of anti-Polish collaboration perpetrated by Jews and Ukrainians. See, for example, Tadeusz Piotrowski, ed., *The Polish Deportees of World War II: Recollections of Removal to the Soviet Union and Dispersal throughout the World* (Jefferson, NC: McFarland, 2008), 6–7. It is worth noting that these assumptions rely on a selective, decontextualized, and noncritical reading of memoirs.

70. Testimony of Moshe Bunem Gliksberg, GKH, Flinker Collection, 45664 (Protocol 76), 3–4.

71. Rachela Tytelman Wygodzki, *The End and the Beginning (August 1939– July 1948)* (n.p.: R.T. Wygodzki., 1998), 13–16.

72. Goldberger, *Stalin's Little Guest*, 16.

73. Menahem Ben-Moshe, "Metsukat-gerush, derekh-golim ve-yesure galut," in *Sanok: Sefer zikharon le-kehilat Sanok ve-ha-sevivah*, ed. Elazar Sharvit (Jerusalem: Irgun yots'e Sanok ve-ha-sevivah be-Yisra'el, 1970), 396.

74. Rabbi Yisrael Orlansky, Interview, GKH, Testimonies and Interviews, Israel, July 31, 2008, disc 3, minutes 20–50.

75. Orlansky interview, disc 3, minute 28.

76. Esther Hautzig, *The Endless Steppe: Growing Up in Siberia* (New York: HarperCollins, 1987), 17–18.

77. Writing about Soviet POW camps for Polish soldiers, Jan Gross also emphasizes the unique experience of transport, focusing especially on the high death rate. See Gross, "Polish POW Camps," 46.

78. Harry Berkelhammer, VHA Interview 14300, Toronto, April 16, 1996, tape 2, minutes 5–10.

79. Shalom Omri, VHA Interview 41743, Holon, Israel, March 1, 1998, tape 4, minutes 1–4.

80. Sally Alban, VHA Interview 4102, Toronto, July 19, 1995, tape 1, minutes 19–21.

81. Szymon Grajcar, VHA Interview 16434, Toronto, June 24, 1996, tape 3, minutes 11–15.

82. Samuel Honig, *From Poland to Russia and Back, 1939–1946* (Windsor, ON: Black Moss, 1996), 80–82.

83. Omri interview, tape 4, minutes 2–4.

84. Ruzena Berler, VHA Interview 01207, Beverly Hills, CA, March 7, 1995, tape 2, minutes 27–29.

85. Symcha Burstin, VHA Interview 31555, Melbourne, July 22, 1997, tape 3, minutes 24–26.

86. Berler interview, tape 2, minute 27.

87. Dorothy Zanker Abend, VHA Interview 08317, Tucson, AZ, November 4, 1995, tape 3, minutes 6–7.

88. David Shadkhanovich, *Zikhronot me-ha-mas'a ha-gadol* (Tel Aviv: D. Shadkhanovich, 1996), 16–18.

89. Testimony of Menachem Mendl Grossman, GKH, Flinker Collection, 45584 (Protocol 16), 6.

90. Włodzimierz Szer, *To Our Children: Memories of Displacement. A Jewish Journey of Hope and Survival in Twentieth-Century Poland and Beyond*, trans. Bronisława Karst (Boston: Academic Studies Press, 2016), 67.

91. Yankl Saler, VHA Interview 41969, Melbourne, March 18, 1998, tape 2, minutes 14–18.

92. Pearl Minz, *Surviving the Holocaust in Siberia, 1940–1945: The Diary of Pearl Minz,* trans. Alexander B. White (Goodyear, AZ: D. de Frain, 2010), 23.

93. Helen Zuberman, VHA Interview 47875, Bronx, NY, December 1, 1998, tape 2, minutes 10–11.

94. Goldberger, *Stalin's Little Guest,* 27.

95. Yitzchok Perlov, *The Adventures of One Yitzchok* (New York: Award Books, 1967), 72.

96. Testimony of Leon Klajman, HIA, Poland, Ministerstwo Informacji i Dokumentacji, Box 123, File 5, Protocol 38, 5.

97. Minz, *Surviving the Holocaust,* 26.

98. Anonymous, personal correspondence with the author, October 20, 2017.

99. Tarik Cyril Amar, *The Paradox of Ukrainian Lviv: A Borderland City between Stalinists, Nazis, and Nationalists* (Ithaca, NY: Cornell University Press, 2015), 55.

100. Begin, *White Nights,* 146–153.

101. "Instruktsiia Narkoma NKVD L. P. Berii 'O vyselenii iz zapadnykh oblastei USSR i BSSR lits, ukazannykh v postanovlenii SNK Soiuza SSR ot 2 Marta 1940 g. za no. 287–127 cc,'" in N. L. Pobol' and P. M. Polian, eds., *Stalinskie deportatsii: 1928–1953* (Moscow: Materik, 2005), 138–140.

102. Berler interview, tape 2, minutes 13–26.

103. Testimony of Chawa Kestenbojm, HIA, Poland, Ministerstwo Informacji i Dokumentacji, Box 123, File 5, Protocol 41, 1–3.

104. Dina Gabel, *Behind the Ice Curtain* (New York: CIS, 1992), 87–119.

105. Burstin interview, tape 3, minutes 26–28.

106. For more on the inclusion of maps, see Eliyana R. Adler, "I Became a Nomad in the Land of Nomadic Tribes: Polish Jewish Refugees in Central Asia and Perceptions of the Other," in *Jews and Non-Jews in the USSR during the Second World War,* ed. Christoph Dieckmann and Arkadi Zeltser (Jerusalem: Yad Vashem, forthcoming).

107. Burstin interview, tape 3, minute 26, through tape 4, minute 3.

108. Ann Szedlecki, *Album of My Life* (Toronto: Azrieli Foundation, 2010), 69.

109. Lilian T. Mowrer, *Arrest and Exile: The True Story of an American Woman in Poland and Siberia, 1940–41* (New York: William Morrow, 1941), 47–49.

110. Gabel, *Behind the Ice Curtain,* 118.

111. Bob Golan, *A Long Way Home: The Story of a Jewish Youth, 1939–1949,* ed. Jacob Howland (Lanham, MD: University Press of America, 2005), 39.

112. Grajcar interview, tape 3, minutes 14–16.

113. Klajman testimony, 5.

114. Kate Brown, *Dispatches from Dystopia: Histories of Places Not Yet Forgotten* (Chicago: University of Chicago Press, 2015), 4.

115. See Mark Bassin, "Russia between Europe and Asia: The Ideological Construction of Geographical Space," *Slavic Review* 50, no. 1 (1991): 1–17.

116. Yuri Slezkine, "Introduction: Siberia as History," in *Between Heaven and Hell: The Myth of Siberia in Russian Culture,* ed. Galya Diment and Yuri Slezkine (New York: St. Martin's, 1993), 1.

117. Goldberger, *Stalin's Little Guest,* 27.

118. For more on this concept, see, for example, Mark Bassin, Christopher Ely, and Melissa K. Stockdale, "Introduction: Russian Space," in *Space, Place and Power in Modern Russia: Essays in the New Spatial History,* ed. Mark Bassin, Christopher Ely, and Melissa K. Stockdale (DeKalb: Northern Illinois University Press, 2010), 8.

119. A formative text in this regard is Yi-Fu Tuan, *Space and Place: The Perspective of Experience* (Minneapolis: University of Minnesota Press, 1977).

120. Zuberman interview, tape 2.

121. Testimony of Khanina Teitel, GKH, Flinker Collection 45591 (Protocol 26), 3.

122. Testimony of Roza Buchman, HIA, Poland, Ministerstwo Informacji i Dokumentacji, Box 5, File 123, Protocol 69, 4.

123. Abraham Bichler, *Little Miracles: A Story of Courage, Faith and Survival* (Raleigh, NC: Ivy House, 2004), 23.

124. Slezkine, "Introduction," 4.

125. A. Zak, "Tshibiu," in *Yorn fun vandern* (Buenos Aires: Tsentral Farband fun Poylishe Yidn in Argentine, 1949), 40–41, cited and translated in Magdalena Ruta, *Without Jews? Yiddish Literature in the People's Republic of Poland on the Holocaust, Poland and Communism* (Kraków: Jagiellonian University Press, 2017), 44–45.

126. Golan, *A Long Way Home,* 43.

127. Boruch B. Frusztajer, *From Siberia to America: A Story of Survival and Success* (Scranton, PA: University of Scranton Press, 2008), 15.

128. Goldberger, *Stalin's Little Guest,* 38.

129. Moshe Etzion, VHA Interview 28297, Kibutz Nirim, Israel, March 10, 1997, tape 2, minute 4.

130. Yosef Shvarts, "Yorn fun na-ve-nad," in *Pinkes Hrubyeshov: tsum 20-tn yortog nakh dem groyzamen khurbn fun undzer gevezener heym,* ed. Barukh Kaplinski (Tel Aviv: Irgun yoytse Hrubyeshov in Yisroel un in di Fareynikte Shtatn mit der hilf fun di Hrubyeshover landsmanshaftn in gor der velt, 1962), 771.

131. Etzion interview, tape 2, minutes 4–6.

132. Gliksberg testimony, 6.

133. Starkiewicz, *Blades of Grass,* 79.

134. "Decree," November 23, 1940, Arkhiv Prezidenta Respubliki Kazakhstan, Tsentral'nyi komitet Kommunisticheskoi Partii (Bol'shevikov) Kazakhstana, Alma Ata, f. 708, op. 4/1, d. 199, l. 118.

135. See, for example, Viola, *The Unknown Gulag,* 168.

136. Testimony of Shmuel Zifberfeyn, GKH, Flinker Collection, 45940 (Protocol 64), 9.

137. Rudnicka testimony, 4.

138. Azriel Regenbogen, "Mi-zikhronot palit be-Rusya," in Sharvit, ed., *Sanok,* 399–400.

139. Saler interview, tape 2, minute 25, through tape 3, minute 3.

140. Testimony of Shmuel Labin, GKH, Flinker Collection, 45587 (Protocol 19).

141. Novik testimony, 7–8.

142. Testimony of Z. Elsan, HIA, Poland, Ministerstwo Informancji i Dokumentacji 123-5, protocol 36, 2–3. Elsan's first name is incomplete in the written testimony.

143. Testimony of Shmuel Burshtein, GKH, Flinker Collection, 45585 (Protocol 17), 5, 11.

144. Rabbanit Chava Chaya Frenkel, Interview, GKH, Testimonies and Interviews, Israel, 28 November 2010, disc 1, minutes 58–60.

145. Testimony of Jozef Zgudnicki, HIA, Poland, Ministerstwo Informacji i Dokumentacji, Box 7, File 123, Protocol 149, 3.

146. Finkler testimony, HIA, 5–6.

147. Berler interview, tape 3, minutes 12–22.

148. Kestenbojm testimony, 3–5.

149. Testimony of Emma Lewinowna, HIA, Poland, Ministerstwo Informacji i Dokumentacji, Box 123, File 5, Protocol 68, 1–3.

150. Etzion interview, tape 2, minutes 8–12.

151. Testimony of Rojza Lauterbach, HIA, Poland, Ministerstwo Informacji i Dokumentacji, Box 123, File 5, Protocol 39, 4–6.

152. Cohen interview, tape 2, minutes 16–18.

153. Lauterbach testimony, 4.

154. Frenkel interview, tape 1, minute 60.

155. Dora Drescher, VHA Interview 25544, Plantation, FL, February 6, 1997, tape 1, minutes 23–30.

156. K. Segal, "A mayse vegn Gots nisim," in *Vu shmeterlingn shvebn* (Tel Aviv: Farlag Y. L. Perets, 1981), 109–110, quoted and translated in Ruta, *Without Jews?,* 46–47.

157. Omri interview, tape 4, minutes 10–12.

158. Etzion interview, tape 2, minutes 12–14.

159. Zuberman interview, tape 2, minutes 21–28.

160. Alban interview, tape 1, minutes 22–24.

161. Daniella Bell, VHA Interview 19812, Montreal, September 17, 1996, tape 1, minutes 15–17.

162. Abend interview, tape 3, minutes 9–10.

163. Moshe Ben-Asher, VHA Interview 47417, London, August 19, 1998, tape 3, minutes 19–21.

164. Frusztajer, *From Siberia to America*, 70.

165. Teitel testimony, 6.

166. Diana Ackerman, VHA Interview 02418, Chicago, May 4, 1995, tape 1, minutes 12–14.

167. Emilia Koustova, "Equalizing Misery, Differentiating Objects: The Material World of the Stalinist Exile," in *Material Culture in Russia and the USSR: Things, Values, Identities*, ed. Graham H. Roberts (London: Bloomsbury Academic, 2017).

168. Etzion interview, tape 2, minutes 10–12.

169. Ben-Asher interview, tape 3, minutes 22–24.

170. Frusztajer, *From Siberia to America*, 66.

171. Azrieli, *One Step Ahead*, 56–64.

172. Testimony of Yosef Rozenberg, GKH, Flinker Collection, 45941 (Protocol 65), 8.

173. Testimony of Dina Stahl, Protocol 110, in *Widziałem Anioła Śmierci: Losy deportowanych Żydów polskich w ZSRR w latach II wojny światowej*, ed. Maciej Siekierski and Feliks Tych (Warsaw: Rosner i Wspólnicy, 2006), 222.

174. Starkiewicz, *Blades of Grass*, 82.

175. Berkelhammer interview.

176. Dov B. Lederman, *These Children Are Mine: A Story of Rescue and Survival* (Jerusalem: Feldheim, 2002), 80.

177. Goldberger, *Stalin's Little Guest*, 73.

178. Testimony of Naftali Zylbersztejn, HIA, Poland, Ministerstwo Informacji i Dokumentacji, Box 123, File 6, Protocol 101, 5.

179. Gilboa, *Confess!*, 62.

180. Ruth L. Hohberg, *Getting Here: Ruth's Story, 1935–1949* (Baltimore: Publish America, 2002), 29.

181. Minz, *Surviving the Holocaust*, 25–28.

182. Cohen interview, tape 1, minute 27, through tape 2, minute 17.

183. Testimony of Yehudis Patash, GKH, Flinker Collection, 45629 (Protocol 37), 5.

184. Novik testimony, 6–9.

185. Urban, *Tovarisch, I Am Not Dead,* 50–51.

186. David Shmietanke, "In der tsveyter velt milkhome," in *Sefer Yadov (Jadow) Yadov-bukh,* ed. Wolf Jasni (Jerusalem: Entsiklopediah shel galuyot, 1966), 351.

187. Finkler testimony, GKH, 11.

188. Zylbersztejn testimony, 6.

189. Lebedeva, "The Deportation of the Polish Population," 35; Jolluck, *Exile and Identity,* 144.

190. Albert Kaganovitch, "Jewish Refugees and Soviet Authorities during World War II," *Yad Vashem Studies* 38, no. 2 (2010): 100; Jolluck, *Exile and Identity,* 144.

191. Rozenberg testimony, 7.

192. Shaul Shternfeld, *Halom ben gederot* (Tel Aviv: Halonot, 1999), 148–156.

193. Elsan testimony, 4.

194. Werker testimony, 3.

195. Irving Beada, VHA Interview 13383, Boynton Beach, FL, March 18, 1996, tape 2, minutes 1–11.

196. Stahl, *Widziałem,* 222.

197. Rozenberg testimony, 6.

198. M. Buchwajc, "Żydzi Polscy pod władzą sowiecką," May 25, 1944, HIA, Wladyslaw Anders Collection, Box 72, Doc. No. 556, 15.

199. Grajcar interview, tape 3, minutes 28–29.

200. Honig, *From Poland to Russia,* 106.

201. Rivka Agron, VHA Interview 22887, Jerusalem, November 11, 1996, tape 3, minutes 4–11.

202. Zuberman interview, tape 3, minutes 2–3.

203. Lewinowna testimony, 4.

204. Bichler, *Little Miracles,* 36.

205. Testimony of Mordechai Altschuler [Altshuler], September 29, 1992–January 9, 1993, Oral History Division, Hebrew University of Jerusalem, Project 101, 3491, transcript, 41.

206. Mowrer, *Arrest and Exile,* 182.

207. Burshtein testimony, 8.

208. Agron interview, tape 2, minute 27–tape 3, minute 5.

209. Golan, *A Long Way Home,* 52–55.

210. Szer, *To Our Children,* 68–75.

211. Azriel Regenbogen, "Mi-zikhronot palit be-Rusya," in Sharvit, ed., *Sanok,* 401–402.

212. Ackerman interview, tape 1, minutes 13–14.

213. Frusztajer, *From Siberia to America,* 75.

214. Adina Lahav, "Me-'arvot Sibir le-erets-Yisra'el," in Kaplinski, ed., *Pinkes Hrubyeshov,* 765.

215. Steinberg interview, tape 1, minutes 49–53.

216. Gilboa, *Confess!,* 87.

217. Novik testimony, 8.

218. Gilboa, *Confess!,* 97.

219. Testimony of Dr. Moshe Zolenfreind, Moreshet Archives, A.1488/11, Testimonies, Tel Aviv, March 25, 1981, transcript, 10.

220. Testimony of Shlomo Gevirtz, YVA, O.17 YIVO Testimonies Collection, file 62, 4–6 (YIVO RG 104, Series 2, box 6, 1954).

221. "Memoirs of Hendel Family: Genealogy," in *Bene ha-'ayarah mesaprim,* ed. Eliezer Tsvi Cohen (Bnei Brak, Israel: Yots'e Horodlo be-Erets Yisra'el, 2000), 100–101.

222. Testimony of Gitla Rabinowicz, Protocol 77, *Widziałem,* 182.

223. Testimony of Ludwik Pechster, HIA, Poland, Ministerstwo Informacji i Dokumentacji, Box 123, File 7, Protocol 170, 5.

224. Rabbi Nasan Tvi Baron, Interview, GKH, Testimonies and Interviews, Israel, April 10, 2011, disc 1, minute 56, through disc 2, minute 2.

225. Bichler, *Little Miracles,* 37–38.

226. Juda Ari Wohlgemuth, *Pesah 5702 be-Novosibirsk: Pesach 1942 in Novosibirsk (Siberia)* (London: G. J. George, 1963), 16.

227. Gliksberg testimony, 3–9.

228. Rabbi Jacob Halpern, interview with the author, September 28, 2010, Silver Spring, MD.

229. Minz, *Surviving the Holocaust,* 64.

230. Patash testimony, 5.

231. See, for example, Rabbi Shlomo Vakshtok, Interview, GKH, Testimonies and Interviews, Israel, December 1, 2010, minutes 20–21.

232. Orlansky interview, disc 2, minute 57 through disc 3, minute 6.

233. Grossman testimony, 12–14.

234. Golan, *A Long Way Home,* 50.

235. Bronia Zisfain, VHA Interview 06910, N. Miami Beach, FL, September 19, 1995, tape 1, minutes 23–25.

236. Testimony of Jechiel Tennenblum, HIA, Poland, Ministerstwo Informacji i Dokumentacji, Box 123, File 5, Protocol 70, 5–6.

237. Burshtein testimony, 11–12.

238. Szer, *To Our Children,* 71.

239. Gabel, *Behind the Ice Curtain,* 217.

240. Many works about this period capitalize the word Amnesty to signal their reference to a particular collective and formal amnesty for a large group of people rather than the freeing of any single individual. Some Polish

scholars refer to "amnesty" in quotation marks in order to highlight the fact that most of the Polish citizens freed had not even been accused, let alone convicted, of any crime. The quotation marks emphasize that there was no real amnesty, and that the word just gave the Soviets cover for their illegal deportation and incarceration of Polish citizens. This work, for the sake of clarity, convenience, and compromise, will take the middle ground of neither capitalizing nor using quotations.

241. For the text of the agreement, see "Polish-Soviet Agreement Annulling the Soviet-German Treaties of 1939 Relating to Poland, Restoring Mutual Diplomatic Relations, Undertaking Mutual Aid and Support in the Present War and Formation of a Polish Army on the Territory of the USSR. Additional Protocol on an Amnesty to Be Granted to All Polish Citizens on the Territory of the USSR Deprived of Their Freedom," London, July 30, 1941, in General Sikorski Historical Institute, *Documents on Polish-Soviet Relations 1939–1945*, vol. 1, *1939–1943* (London: Heinemann, 1961), 141–142. On aspects of its negotiation, see Anna M. Cienciala, "General Sikorski and the Conclusion of the Polish-Soviet Agreement of July 30, 1941: A Reassessment," *Polish Review* 41, no. 4 (1996): 401–434.

242. Patash testimony, 7–8.

243. Victor Zarnowitz, *Fleeing the Nazis, Surviving the Gulag, and Arriving in the Free World: My Life and Times* (Westport, CT: Praeger, 2008), 56–58.

244. Goldberger, *Stalin's Little Guest*, 76.

245. Alan Elsner, *Guarded by Angels: How My Father and Uncle Survived Hitler and Cheated Stalin* (New York: Yad Vashem/Holocaust Survivors' Memoirs Project, 2005), 95–99.

246. Shternfeld, *Halom ben gederot*, 164–183.

247. Olga Adamova-Sliozberg, "My Journey," in *Till My Tale Is Told: Women's Memoirs of the Gulag*, ed. Simeon Vilensky (Bloomington: Indiana University Press, 1999), 62.

248. Testimony of Maria Mandelbrot, HIA, Poland, Ministerstwo Informacji i Dokumentacji, Box 123, File 5, Protocol 49, 1–6.

249. Hautzig, *The Endless Steppe*, 226.

250. Testimony of Aharon Fish, GKH, Flinker Collection, 45588 (Protocol 20), 13.

251. "Memo," YVA, M.27, Public Records Office, London, file 33, 00030.

252. Dov Levin, *Baltic Jews under the Soviets, 1940–1946* (Jerusalem: Hebrew University, 1994), 112.

253. Violeta Davoliūtė, "A 'Forgotten' History of Soviet Deportation: The Case of Lithuanian Jews," in *Population Displacement in Lithuania in the*

Twentieth Century: Experiences, Identities and Legacies, ed. Tomas
Balkelis and Violeta Davoliūtė (Leiden: Brill Rodopi, 2016), 179–210. See
also Anton Weiss-Wendt, *On the Margins: Essays on the History of Jews
in Estonia* (Budapest: Central European University Press, 2017), 108–109;
and Eliyana R. Adler, "Exile and Survival: Lithuanian Jewish Deportees
in the Soviet Union," in *ha-Kayits ha-norah ha-hu: 70 shana le-
hashmadat ha-kehilot ha-Yehudiot be-'are ha-sadeh be-Lita,* ed. Michal
Ben Ya'akov, Gershon Greenberg, and Sigalit Rosmarin (Jerusalem: Efrata
College, 2013): 27–49.

254. Violeta Davoliūtė, "Multidirectional Memory and the Deportation of
Lithuanian Jews," *Ethnicity Studies* 2 (2015): 134.

255. See, for example, Dalia Kuodytė and Rokas Tracevskis, *Siberia: Mass
Deportations from Lithuania to the USSR* (Vilnius: Genocide and
Resistance Centre of Lithuania, 2004).

256. Rachel Rachlin and Israel Rachlin, *Sixteen Years in Siberia: Memoirs of
Rachel and Israel Rachlin,* trans. Birgitte M. de Weille (Tuscaloosa:
University of Alabama Press, 1988), 27.

4. City of Want

Epigraph: Alexander Neweroff, *City of Bread* (New York: George H.
Doran Company, 1927), 235.

1. For the English translation, see Neweroff, *City of Bread.*

2. Rebecca Manley, *To the Tashkent Station: Evacuation and Survival in the
Soviet Union at War* (Ithaca, NY: Cornell University Press, 2009), 141.

3. Yitzchok Perlov, *The Adventures of One Yitzchok* (New York: Award
Books, 1967), 64–65.

4. See, for example. the Polish consular memo from November 10, 1941,
preserved in *Dokumenty i materialy po instorii sovetsko-pol'skikh
otnoshenii,* vol. 7 (Moscow: Izdatel'stvo "Nauka," 1973), 240–241.

5. Yosef Litvak, *Pelitim Yehudim mi-Polin be-Verit-ha-Mo'atsot, 1939–1946*
(Jerusalem: Hebrew University Press, 1988), 205–211.

6. Lewis H. Siegelbaum and Leslie Page Moch, "Evacuation as Migration:
The Soviet Experience during the Great Patriotic War," in *Migration and
Mobility in the Modern Age: Refugees, Travelers, and Traffickers in
Europe and Eurasia,* ed. Anika Walke, Jan Musekamp, and Nicole
Svobodny (Bloomington: Indiana University Press, 2017), 188–190.

7. Mark Edele, "The Second World War as a History of Displacement: The
Soviet Case," *History Australia* 12, no. 2 (2015): 17–40.

8. Testimony of Aharon Fish, Ganzach Kiddush Hashem Archives (hereafter
GKH), Flinker Collection, 45588 (Protocol 20), 14–15.

9. Testimony of Zeev F., Protocol 119, PGC/Box 131, cited in Irena Grudzińska-Gross and Jan Tomasz Gross, eds., *War through Children's Eyes: The Soviet Occupation of Poland and the Deportations, 1939–1941* (Stanford, CA: Hoover Institution Press, 1981), 232–233.

10. Testimony of Z. Elsan, Hoover Institution Archives (hereafter HIA), Poland, Ministersterstwo Informacji i Dokumentacji, Box 123, File 5, Protocol 36, 5. Her first name is not preseved in the file.

11. Testimony of Khanina Teitel, GKH, Flinker Collection, 45591 (Protocol 26), 17.

12. Symcha Burstin, University of Southern California Shoah Foundation Visual History Archive (hereafter VHA) Interview 31555, Melbourne, July 22, 1997, tape 4, minute 25, through tape 5, minute 1.

13. Shaul Shternfeld, *Halom ben gederot* (Tel Aviv: Halonot, 1999), 182–184.

14. Testimony of Leib Novik, GKH, Flinker Collection, 45590 (Protocol 24), 12.

15. Testimony of Shmuel Labin, GKH, Flinker Collection, 45587 (Protocol 19), 16–17.

16. Natalia S. Lebedeva, "The Deportation of the Polish Population in the USSR, 1939–1941," *Journal of Communist Studies and Transition Politics* 16, nos. 1–2 (2000): 43.

17. For official Soviet purposes, the Central Asian republics included the Kirghiz, Tajik, Turkmen and Uzbek SSR, but not the Kazakh SSR. Nonetheless, most of the former refugees include Kazakhstan in their understandings of Central Asia, as is now widely accepted. I will follow their lead in this manner.

18. Samuel Honig, *From Poland to Russia and Back, 1939–1946* (Windsor, ON: Black Moss, 1996), 134.

19. Ruth L. Hohberg, *Getting Here: Ruth's Story 1935–1949* (Baltimore: Publish America, 2002), 32.

20. Herman Taube, oral history interview, February 15, 2010, United States Holocaust Memorial Museum (hereafter USHMM), RG-50.106*0182, Part 2, minutes 26–28.

21. Rabbanit Chava Chaya Frenkel, Interview, GKH, Testimonies and Interviews, Israel, November 28, 2010, disc 2, minutes 6–11.

22. Rabbi Dr. Jacob Halpern, interview with the author, Silver Spring, MD, September 28, 2010.

23. Azriel Regenbogen, "Mi-zikhronot palit be-Rusya," in *Sanok: Sefer zikharon le-kehilat Sanok ve-ha-sevivah*, ed. Elazar Sharvit (Jerusalem: Irgun yots'e Sanok ve-ha-sevivah be-Yisrael, 1970), 402.

24. Shlomo Kless, "A Zionist Pioneer Underground in the Soviet Union (June 22, 1941–May 9, 1945)," in *Zionist Youth Movements during the*

Shoah, ed. Asher Cohen and Yehoyakim Cochavi (New York: Peter Lang, 1995), 329–330. See also Dov Levin, *Baltic Jews under the Soviets, 1940–1946* (Jerusalem: Hebrew University Press, 1994), 202–205.

25. Miriam Bar, *Lelot Tashkent* (Tel Aviv: Levin-Epshtein, 1970), 7–36.

26. Yehudi Lindeman, ed., *Shards of Memory: Narratives of Holocaust Survival* (Westport, CT: Praeger, 2007), 153–154.

27. Herman Taube, *Autumn Travels, Devious Paths: Poetry and Prose* (Washington, DC: Dryad, 1992), xv.

28. Keith Sword, *Deportation and Exile: Poles in the Soviet Union, 1939–48* (Hampshire, England: St. Martin's, 1994), 45–46.

29. Pearl Minz, *Surviving the Holocaust in Siberia, 1940–1945: The Diary of Pearl Minz,* trans. Alexander B. White (Goodyear, AZ: D. de Frain, 2010), 122.

30. Rabbi Simcha Shafran with Avi Shafran, *Fire, Ice, Air: A Polish Jew's Memoir of Yeshiva, Siberia, America* (New York: Hashgachapress, 2010), 78.

31. Ann Szedlecki, *Album of My Life* (Toronto: Azrieli Foundation, 2010), 161.

32. Janka Goldberger, *Stalin's Little Guest* (London: Janus, 1995), 80.

33. A number of scholars have explored how Soviet Jews decided whether or not to try to flee the German advance. See, for example, Dov Levin, "The Fateful Decision: The Flight of Jews into the Soviet Interiors in the Summer of 1941," *Yad Vashem Studies* 20 (1990): 115–142; Anna Shtern-shis, "Between Life and Death: Why Some Soviet Jews Decided to Leave and Others to Stay in 1941," *Kritika* 15, no. 3 (2014): 477–504; and Kiril Feferman, "To Flee or Not to Flee: The Conflicting Messages of Wartime Propaganda and the Holocaust, 1941," *Cahiers du monde russe* 56, no. 2 (2015): 517–542. Much of this would be relevant to Polish Jews as well, with the addition of their previous experience with the Germans in 1939.

34. For estimates of numbers, see Mordechai Altshuler, *Soviet Jewry on the Eve of the Holocaust: A Social and Demographic Profile* (Jerusalem: Yad Vashem, 1998), 323–326; and Yitzhak Arad, *The Holocaust in the Soviet Union* (Lincoln: University of Nebraska Press/Yad Vashem, 2009), 75–87.

35. Yankl Saler, VHA Interview 41969, Melbourne, March 18, 1998, tapes 2–4.

36. Eva G. Gregoratos, *An Unintended Odyssey: From War Torn Europe to America* (Bloomington, IN: AuthorHouse, 2008), 52.

37. Lena Jedwab Rozenberg, *Girl with Two Landscapes: The Wartime Diary of Lena Jedwab, 1941–1945,* trans. Solon Beinfeld (New York and London: Holmes and Meier, 2002), 18, 45–46.

38. Children, Deportation and Life in the USSR, Social Welfare Department, Poland Ambassada (Soviet Union), HIA, Box 24, Folders 5–6.

39. Yosef Goldkorn, *Navenad iber di shlyakhn fun Rusland* (Tel Aviv: H. Leivik, 1998), 20, 122–130.

40. Abraham A. Kreusler, *A Teacher's Experiences in the Soviet Union* (Leiden: E. J. Brill, 1965), 41.

41. Kreusler, *A Teacher's Experiences*, 94.

42. Manley, *To the Tashkent Station*, 1.

43. Xavier Pruszynski, *Russian Year: The Notebook of an Amateur Diplomat* (New York: Roy, 1944), 48.

44. Fish testimony, 14–16.

45. Shimon Dzigan, *Der koyekh fun Yidishn humor* (Tel Aviv: Orli, 1974), 178.

46. Bar, *Lelot Tashkent.*

47. John Barber and Mark Harrison, *The Soviet Home Front, 1941–1945: A Social and Economic History of the USSR in World War II* (London: Longman, 1991), 77.

48. On the Soviet experience of evacuation, see, for example, Manley, *To the Tashkent Station;* Natalie Belsky, "Encounters in the East: Evacuees in the Soviet Hinterland during the Second World War" (Ph.D. diss., University of Chicago, 2014); and Siegelbaum and Moch, "Evacuation as Migration."

49. Testimony of Yehudis Patash, GKH, Flinker Collection, 45629 (Protocol 37).

50. Burstin interview, tape 5, minutes 2–6.

51. Saler interview, tape 4, minutes 14–20.

52. Boris Baum, VHA Interview 11354, Hallandale, FL, January 25, 1996, tape 1, minutes 22–24.

53. Dzigan, *Der koyekh*, 245–246.

54. Moshe Grossman, *In the Enchanted Land: My Seven Years in Soviet Russia* (Tel Aviv: Rachel, 1960), 146–157.

55. Taube interview, Part 2, tape 1, minutes 30–32.

56. Herman Taube, *Kyzl Kishlak: Refugee Village* (Washington, DC: Olami Press, 1993), 68–183.

57. Rivka Agron, VHA Interview 22887, Jerusalem, November 11, 1996.

58. Testimony of Sarah K., in *Holocaust Memoirs: Jews in the Lwow Ghetto, the Janowski Concentration Camp, and as Deportees in Siberia*, ed. Joachim Schoenfeld (Hoboken, NJ: Ktav, 1985), 274–279.

59. Dov B. Lederman, *These Children Are Mine: A Story of Rescue and Survival* (Jerusalem: Feldheim, 2002), 118.

60. Sarah K. testimony, 275–278.

61. Burstin interview, tape 5, minutes 7–14.

62. Manley, *To the Tashkent Station*, chaps. 2–3.

63. Barber and Harrison, *The Soviet Home Front*, 80.

64. Kreusler, *A Teacher's Experiences,* 144.

65. K. Red, interview no. 8, in Rachel Erlich, *Interviews with Polish and Russian Jewish DP's in DP Camps on Their Observations of Jewish Life in Soviet Russia* (New York: American Jewish Committee, 1948), 8–10.

66. Alban interview, tape 2, minute 21, through tape 3, minute 4.

67. H., interview no. 14, in Erlich, *Interviews,* 9–10, 12–13.

68. Paul Stronski, *Tashkent: Forging a Soviet City, 1930–1966* (Pittsburgh: University of Pittsburgh Press, 2010), 96, 89.

69. Goldberger, *Stalin's Little Guest,* 93.

70. Esther Hautzig, *The Endless Steppe: Growing Up in Siberia* (New York: HarperCollins, 1987), 91.

71. Goldkorn, *Navenad iber di shlyakhn,* 234–235.

72. Agron interview, tape 3, minutes 27–29.

73. Frumie Cohen, VHA Interview 47321, Brooklyn, NY, November 23, 1998, tape 2, minutes 23–25.

74. Irene Rogers, VHA Interview 01754, Northbrook, IL, March 29, 1995, tape 1, minutes 14–17.

75. Dina Gabel, *Behind the Ice Curtain* (New York: CIS, 1992), 244.

76. Eva Blatt, VHA Interview 05884, Yonkers, NY, November 10, 1995, tape 2, minutes 15–19.

77. SL, interview no. 17, in Erlich, *Interviews,* 5.

78. Lederman, *These Children Are Mine,* 104–116.

79. Frenkel interview, tape 2, minutes 15–21.

80. Suzanna Eibuszyc, *Memory Is Our Home: Loss and Remembering: Three Generations in Poland and Russia 1917–1960s* (Stuttgart: ibidem-Verlag, 2015), 232.

81. Harry Berkelhammer, VHA Interview 14300, Toronto, April 16, 1996, tape 3, minutes 2–6.

82. Ann Benjamin-Goldberg, VHA Interview 11455, Huntington, NY, December 14, 1995.

83. Rozenberg, *Girl with Two Landscapes,* 145.

84. For more on Zionist groups, see Kless, "A Zionist Pioneer Underground," and Shlomo Kless, "Pe'ilut tsionit shel pelitim Yehudim be-Verit-ha-Mo'atsot be-shanim 1941–1945 ve-kesher ha-Yishuv ha-Yehudi be-Erets Yisra'el 'imahem" (Ph.D. diss., Hebrew University of Jerusalem, 1985).

85. Shternfeld, *Halom ben gederot,* 106–116.

86. For more on interethnic interactions, see Eliyana R. Adler, "I Became a Nomad in the Land of Nomadic Tribes: Polish Jewish Refugees in Central Asia and Perceptions of the Other," in *Jews and Non-Jews in the USSR during the Second World War,* ed. Christoph Dieckmann and Arkadi Zeltser (Jerusalem: Yad Vashem, forthcoming).

87. Yehoshua A. Gilboa, *Confess! Confess! Eight Years in Soviet Prisons,* trans. Dov Ben Aba (Boston: Little, Brown, 1968), 32.

88. Natalie Belsky, "Fraught Friendships: Soviet Jews and Polish Jews on the Soviet Home Front," in *Shelter from the Holocaust: Rethinking Jewish Survival in the Soviet Union,* ed. Mark Edele, Sheila Fitzpatrick, and Atina Grossmann (Detroit: Wayne State University Press, 2017), 175–176.

89. Betty Rich, *Little Girl Lost* (Toronto: Azrieli Foundation, 2011), 82.

90. Abel, tape 3, minutes 21–22.

91. Abraham Bichler, *Little Miracles: A Story of Courage, Faith and Survival* (Raleigh, NC: Ivy House Publishing Group, 2004), 46.

92. Hautzig, *The Endless Steppe,* 206.

93. Goldberger, *Stalin's Little Guest,* 151, 169.

94. Hanna Davidson Pankowsky, *East of the Storm: Outrunning the Holocaust in Russia* (Lubbock: Texas Tech University Press, 1999), 68–93.

95. See Simon Davidson, *My War Years, 1939–1945,* trans. Marie Morgens (San Antonio: University of Texas, 1981).

96. Zeev Levin, "Antisemitism and the Jewish Refugees in Soviet Kirgizia," *Jews in Russia and Eastern Europe* 50, no. 1 (2003): 191–203.

97. Oleg Leibovich, "Antisemitskie nastroeniia v sovetskom tyle," in *SSSR vo vtoroi mirovoi voine. Okkupatsiia. Kholokost. Stalinizm,* ed. Oleg Budnitskii and Liudmila Novikova (Moscow: ROSSPEN, 2014), 282.

98. Sheila Fitzpatrick, "Annexation, Evacuation, and Antisemitism in the Soviet Union, 1939–1946," in Edele, Fitzpatrick, and Grossmann, eds., *Shelter from the Holocaust,* 141–142.

99. See Rachel Erlich, *Summary Report of Eighteen Intensive Interviews with Jewish DPs from Poland and the Soviet Union* (New York: American Jewish Committee, 1949), especially 1, 11.

100. J.S., interview no. 6, in Erlich, *Interviews,* 3.

101. Barber and Harrison, *The Soviet Home Front,* 48.

102. Minz, *Surviving the Holocaust,* 110, 114.

103. Dr. R., interview no. 1, in Erlich, *Interviews,* 3.

104. Ida Kaminska, *My Life, My Theater,* ed. and trans. Curt Leviant (New York: Macmillan, 1973), 170.

105. Gabel, *Behind the Ice Curtain,* 282–283, 394.

106. Rabbi Yitzhak Meir Safronovitch, Interview, GKH, Testimonies and Interviews, Israel, March 22, 2011, disc 2, minutes 22–23.

107. Frenkel interview, disc 2, minutes 18–19.

108. Safronovitch interview, tape 2, minutes 19–20.

109. Testimony of Menachem Mendl Grossman, GKH, Flinker Collection, 45584 (Protocol 16), 23.

110. Chaim Shapiro, *Go, My Son: A Young Jewish Refugee's Story of Survival* (Jerusalem: Feldheim, 1989), 304–326.

111. J.S., interview no. 6, in Erlich, *Interviews*, 4.

112. Traitman, interview no. 4, in Erlich, *Interviews*, 3.

113. Shimon Redlich, *Propaganda and Nationalism in Wartime Russia: The Jewish Antifascist Committee in the USSR, 1941–1948* (Boulder, CO: East European Monographs, 1982), 1–7.

114. Arno Lustiger, *Stalin and the Jews: The Red Book: The Tragedy of the Jewish Anti-Fascist Committee and the Soviet Jews* (New York: Enigma Books, 2003), 119–123. See also Dov-Ber Kerler, "The Soviet Yiddish Press: Eynikayt During the War, 1942–1945," in *Why Didn't the Press Shout? American & International Journalism during the Holocaust*, ed. Robert Moses Shapiro (Hoboken: NJ: Yeshiva University/Ktav, 2003), 221–249.

115. Arkadi Zeltser, "How the Jewish Intelligentsia Created the Jewishness of the Jewish Hero: The Soviet Yiddish Press," in *Soviet Jews in World War II*, ed. Harriet Murav and Gennady Estraikh (Boston: Academic Studies Press, 2014), 111–116.

116. Zvi Gitelman, *A Century of Ambivalence: The Jews of Russia and the Soviet Union, 1881 to the Present*, 2nd ed. (Bloomington: Indiana University Press, 2001), 146–147.

117. B[er] Mark, "Yidishe pleytim ofn ern-tovl fun di beste erd-arbeter," *Eynikayt* 14, October 15, 1942.

118. Binem Heller, "Onshtot a viglid," *Eynikayt* 18, November 25, 1942, 3.

119. Rokhl Korn to Vilenski, October 1, 1942 and February 22, 1943, YIVO, RG 107, Letters, in *YIVO Encyclopedia of Jews in Eastern Europe*, https://yivoencyclopedia.org/search.aspx?query=korn%2C+rokhl.

120. Dr. R, interview no. 1, in Erlich, *Interviews*, 4; J.S., interview no. 6, in Erlich, *Interviews*, 4–5.

121. Shimon Redlich, *War, Holocaust and Stalinism: A Documented History of the Jewish Anti-Fascist Committee in the USSR* (Oxford: Harwood Academic, 1995), 9–15.

122. Redlich, *Propaganda and Nationalism*, 20–22.

123. Olga Medvedeva-Nathoo, "Certificate of Birth, Certificate of Survival (from the Cycle 'Scraps of Life: Polish Jews in Central Asia during the Second World War')" (unpublished manuscript, n.d., trans. Marta Daria Olynyk), in American Association for Polish-Jewish Studies, "New Views," http://www.aapjstudies.org/manager/external/ckfinder/userfiles/files/Medvedeva-Nathoo(1).pdf.

124. See, for example, Stanislaw Kot, *Conversations with the Kremlin and Dispatches from Russia* (London: Oxford University Press, 1963), 182; and

the reply to Simcha Sztern regarding his forced mobilization, July 10, 1942, HIA, Poland, Ambassada (USSR), Consular Legal Department, Polskie Siły Zbrojne, General 16-5.

125. Embassy reply, HIA, Poland, Ambassada, Consular Legal Department, Polskie Siły Zbrojne, General 16-5.

126. J. Otto Pohl, "Soviet Apartheid: Stalin's Ethnic Deportations, Special Settlement Restrictions, and the Labor Army: The Case of the Ethnic Germans in the USSR," *Human Rights Review* 13 (2012): 215–219.

127. Jack Pomerantz and Lyric Wallwork Winik, *Run East: Flight from the Holocaust* (Urbana: University of Illinois Press, 1997), 28–76.

128. Marian Feldman, *From Warsaw, through Łuck, Siberia, and Back to Warsaw* (Morrisville, NC: LuLu, 2009), 90–137.

129. Albert Kaganovitch, "Stalin's Great Power Politics, the Return of Jewish Refugees to Poland, and Continued Migration to Palestine, 1944–1946," *Holocaust and Genocide Studies* 26, no. 1 (2012): 65–66.

130. Minz, *Surviving the Holocaust,* 117–118.

131. Sara Bergman, VHA Interview 30068, Melbourne, April 6, 1997, tape 2, minutes 17–20.

132. Aleksander Wat, *My Century: The Odyssey of a Polish Intellectual,* ed. and trans. Richard Lourie (Berkeley: University of California Press, 1988), 358, 361–376.

133. Marci Shore, *Caviar and Ashes: A Warsaw Generation's Life and Death in Marxism, 1918–1968* (New Haven and London: Yale University Press, 2006), 243.

134. Moskwa Nr. 14, London 15/III/43, HIA, Poland, Ministerstwo Informacji i Dokumentacji, Box 46, File 7.

135. For more on Sommerstein's time in the USSR, see Yosef Litvak, "Korotav u-fe'iluto ha-tsiburit shel Emil Zomershtain [Sommerstein] bi-Verit ha-Mo'atsot be-milhemet ha-'olam ha-sheniyah," *Gal-Ed* 12 (1991): 135–162 (Hebrew pagination).

136. Klemens Nussbaum, "Jews in the Kosciuszko Division and the First Polish Army," in *Jews in Eastern Poland and the USSR, 1939–46,* ed. Norman Davies and Antony Polonsky (New York: St. Martin's, 1991), 183–184, 197–199.

137. Hersz-Harr Bimka (Bimko), VHA Interview 43830, Brooklyn, NY, May 18, 1998, tape 4, minutes 8–10.

138. Pomerantz and Winik, *Run East,* 107–148.

139. Letter 99, in Arkadi Zeltser, ed., *To Pour Out My Bitter Soul: Letters from Jews in the USSR, 1941–1945* (Jerusalem: Yad Vashem, 2015), 259–260.

140. See, for example, Norman Davies and Antony Polonsky, "Introduction," in Davies and Polonsky, eds., *Jews in Eastern Europe and the USSR,* 42; and

"The Proposal to Establish a 'Jewish Legion' within the Polish Army in the USSR: Two Documents," in Davies and Polonsky, eds., *Jews in Eastern Europe and the USSR*, 361–368.

141. M.K., interview no. 12, in Erlich, *Interviews*, 4.
142. Nussbaum, "Jews in the Kosciuszko Division," 188–195.
143. I. Lib. [Lieberman], interview no. 2, in Erlich, *Interviews*, 6.
144. Ruzena Berler, VHA Interview 01207, Beverly Hills, CA, March 7, 1995, tape 4.
145. Bernard L. Ginsburg, *A Wayfarer in a World of Upheaval* (San Bernadino, CA: Borgo, 1993), 76–79.
146. Hautzig, *The Endless Steppe*, 119.
147. SL, interview no. 17, in Erlich, *Interviews*, 8.
148. Interview with Sarah K., in Joachim Schoenfeld, *Holocaust Memoirs: Jews in the Lwow Ghetto, the Janowski Concentration Camp, and as Deportees in Siberia* (Hoboken, NJ: Ktav, 1985), 276–286.
149. Rich, *Little Girl Lost*, 89–90, 107–111.
150. Shternfeld, *Halom ben gederot*, 197–230.
151. Shternfeld, *Halom ben gederot*, 271–287.
152. Szedlecki, *Album of My Life*, 95.
153. Katherine R. Jolluck, *Exile and Identity: Polish Women in the Soviet Union during World War II* (Pittsburgh: University of Pittsburgh Press, 2002), 204–213.
154. Edward J. Jesko, *A Journey into Exile* (New York: iUniverse, 2006), 21.
155. Garri S. Urban, *Tovarisch, I Am Not Dead*, 2nd ed. (London: Cyclops Vision, 2006), 124.
156. Stuart Urban, dir., *Tovarisch, I Am Not Dead* (London: Cyclops Vision, 2008), DVD.
157. Halpern interview.
158. Zoë Vania Waxman, *Writing the Holocaust: Identity, Testimony, Representation* (Oxford: Oxford University Press, 2006), 150.
159. Jolluck, *Exile and Identity*, 234–237.
160. Joan Ringelheim, "The Split between Gender and the Holocaust," in *Women in the Holocaust*, ed. Dalia Ofer and Lenore J. Weitzman (New Haven, CT: Yale University Press, 1998), 342.
161. S. Rotstein, interview no. 13, in Erlich, *Interviews*, 4.
162. Szedlecki, *Album of My Life*, 68, 77, 147.
163. Pankowsky, *East of the Storm*, 126.
164. Helen Zuberman, VHA Interview 47875, Bronx, NY, December 1, 1998, tape 3, minutes 15–24.
165. Rachela Tytelman Wygodzki, *The End and the Beginning (August 1939–July 1948)* (n.p.: R.T. Wygodzki., 1998), 29.

166. Eibuszyc, *Memory Is Our Home*, 207.
167. Anna Hájková, "Sexual Barter in Times of Genocide: Negotiating the Sexual Economy of the Theresienstadt Ghetto," *Signs* 38, no. 3 (2013): 503–533.
168. Grossman, *In the Enchanted Land*, 172.
169. Erlichson, *My Four Years in Soviet Russia*, trans. Maurice Wolfthal (Boston: Academic Studies Press, 2013), 103–104.
170. Testimony of Szlomo Zdrojowicz, HIA, Poland, Ministersterstwo Informacji i Dokumentacji, Box 123, File 6, Protocol 82, 4.
171. Minz, *Surviving the Holocaust*, 83, 115.
172. Rogers interview, tape 1, minutes 22–23.
173. Jane Lipski, "My Escape into Prison and Other Memoirs of a Stolen Youth, 1939–1948," in Isabelle Choko, Frances Irwin, Lotti Kahana-Aufleger, Margit Raab Kalina, and Jane Lipski, *Stolen Youth: Five Women's Survival in the Holocaust* (New York: Yad Vashem/Holocaust Survivors' Memoirs Project, 2005), 283.
174. Pomerantz and Winik, *Run East*, 95–106.
175. Garri S. Urban, *Tovarisch, I Am Not Dead*, 56, 68.
176. Garri S. Urban, *Tovarisch, I Am Not Dead*, 82.
177. Eibuszyc, *Memory Is Our Home*, 206, 166.
178. Taube, *Kyzl Kishlak*, 291.
179. L. Witkowska, interview no. 3, in Erlich, *Interviews*, 1.
180. Testimony of Roza Buchman, HIA, Poland, Ministersterstwo Informacji i Dokumentacji, 123-5, Protocol 69, 6.
181. Helena Starkiewicz, *Blades of Grass between the Stones* (Melbourne: H. Starkiewicz, 1998), 111–112.
182. Berler interview, tape 4.
183. Erlichson, *My Four Years in Soviet Russia*, 84.
184. See, for example, Minz, *Surviving the Holocaust*, 115. Anna Shternshis discusses how Soviet Jews spoke about these sorts of wartime relationships in interviews fifty years later. See Anna Shternshis, *When Sonia Met Boris: An Oral History of Jewish Life under Stalin* (Oxford: Oxford University Press, 2017), 47–53.
185. Włodzimierz Szer, *To Our Children: Memoirs of Displacement. A Jewish Journey of Hope and Survival in Twentieth-Century Poland and Beyond* (Boston: Academic Studies Press, 2016), 81–82.
186. Szer, *To Our Children*, 172.
187. Szer, *To Our Children*, 175.
188. L.L., interview no. 5, in Erlich, *Interviews*, 3.
189. Rotstein, interview no. 13, in Erlich, *Interviews*, 4–5.

190. Joseph Berger, *Displaced Persons: Growing Up American after the Holocaust* (New York: Scribner, 2001).

191. Bronia Zisfain, VHA Interview 06910, N. Miami Beach, FL, September 19, 1995, tape 1, minutes 23–25.

192. For a contribution to this long scholarly conversation, see, for example, Kamil Kijek, "Between a Love of Poland, Symbolic Violence, and Antisemitism: The Idiosyncratic Effects of the State Education System on Young Jews in Interwar Poland," *Polin* 30 (2018): 237–264.

193. Lilian T. Mowrer, *Arrest and Exile: The True Story of an American Woman in Poland and Siberia 1940–41* (New York: William Morrow, 1941), 36, 244.

194. Testimony of Dora Werker, HIA, Ministersterstwo Informacji i Dokumentacji, Box 123, File 6, Protocol 27, 2–3.

195. "Polish-Soviet agreement annulling the Soviet-German treaties of 1939 relating to Poland, restoring mutual diplomatic relations, undertaking mutual aid and support in the present war and formation of a Polish Army on the territory of the USSR. Additional protocol on an amnesty to be granted to all Polish citizens on the territory of the USSR deprived of their freedom," July 10, 1941, General Sikorski Historical Institute, *Documents on Polish-Soviet Relations 1939–1945*, vol. 1, *1939–1943* (London: Heinemann, 1961), 141–142.

196. Kot, *Conversations with the Kremlin*, 153, 95, 141.

197. Davies and Polonsky, "Introduction," 40–42.

198. David Engel, *In the Shadow of Auschwitz: The Polish Government-in-Exile and the Jews, 1939–1942* (Chapel Hill: University of North Carolina Press, 1987), 132–147.

199. Engel, *In the Shadow of Auschwitz*, 146–147.

200. Gilboa, *Confess!*, 111.

201. Michael (Teichholz) Sherwood, *Odyssey* (n.p.: M. Sherwood, 2007), 82–85.

202. I. Lib. [Lieberman], interview no. 2, in Erlich, *Interviews*, 5.

203. Testimony of Abraham Frydman, Archiwum Żydowskiego Instytutu Historychnego w Warszawie (hereafter AŻIH), 301/6220, 5.V.1965, 2.

204. Danna J. Azrieli, *One Step Ahead: David J. Azrieli (Azrylewicz), Memoirs: 1939–1950* (Jerusalem: Yad Vashem, 2001), 91–94.

205. Testimony of Mikhael Berlovitch, GKH, Flinker Collection, 45586 (Protocol 18), 17.

206. Testimony of Roza Hirsz, HIA, Ministersterstwo Informacji i Dokumentacji, Box 123, File 6, Protocol 85, 1, 4.

207. Testimony of Celina Goldberg, AŻIH, 301/1341, 1.

208. Testimony of Helena Ajzenberg, HIA, Ministersterstwo Informacji i Dokumentacji, Box 124, File 6, Protocol 88, 4.

209. Dr. Jerzy G. Gliksman, "Jewish Exiles in Soviet Russia (1939–1943)," May 7, 1947, American Jewish Joint Committee Archives, part 2, 12.

210. Testimony of Leon Klajman, HIA, Ministersterstwo Informacji i Dokumentacji, Box 123, File 5, Protocol 38, 10.

211. Werker testimony, 5.

212. Testimony of Szmul Zyfberfajn, HIA, Ministersterstwo Informacji i Dokumentacji, Box 123, File 5, Protocol 64, 6.

213. For more on the experiences of these children see Eliyana R. Adler, "Children in Exile: Wartime Journeys of Polish Jewish Youth," in *Polish Jews in the Soviet Union (1939–1959). History and Memory of Deportation, Exile and Survival,* ed. Katharina Friedla and Markus Nesselrodt (Boston: Academic Studies Press, forthcoming).

214. Labin testimony, 21.

215. Testimony of Dina Stahl, Protocol 110, *Widziałem Anioła Śmierci: Losy deportowanych Żydów polskich w ZSRR w latach II wojny światowej,* ed. Maciej Siekierski and Feliks Tych (Warsaw: Rosner i Wspólnicy, 2006), 222.

216. Elsan testimony, 7.

217. Bob Golan, *A Long Way Home: The Story of a Jewish Youth, 1939–1949,* ed. Jacob Howland (Lanham, MD: University Press of America, 2005), 74–77, 90–93.

218. Testimony of Gitla Rabinowicz, Protocol 77, *Widziałem,* 183.

219. Testimony of Edmund Finkler, GKH, Flinker Collection, 45637 (Protocol 48), 12–13.

220. Testimony of Emma Lewinowna, HIA, Poland, Ministerstwo Informacji i Dokumentacji, Box 123, File 5, Protocol 68, 5–6.

221. L. Witkowska, interview no. 3, in Erlich, *Interviews,* 1, 3–4.

222. Beth Holmgren, "The Jews in the Band: The Anders Army's Special Troops," *Polin* 32 (2020): 177–199.

223. Testimony of Dawid Zylkiewicz, HIA, Ministerstwo Informacji i Dokumentacji, Box 123, File 5, Protocol 58, 2, 7.

224. Joseph Czapski, *The Inhuman Land,* trans. Gerald Hopkins (London: Polish Cultural Foundation, 1987), 202–203, 199.

225. See for example, "List of Activists in Russia," HIA, Poland, Ministerstwo Informacji i Dokumentacji, Box 123, File 3.

226. Testimony of Rabbi Joel Landau, HIA, Ministerstwo Informacji i Dokumentacji, Box 123, File 4, 5–6.

227. Testimony of Zeev F., 233.

228. Shapiro, *Go, My Son,* 231–251.

229. "Russia Charged with Hindering Emigration of Polish Jews to Palestine," *JTA Daily News Bulletin* 9, no. 116, May 24, 1942, Jewish Telegraphic Agency, http://pdfs.jta.org/1942/1942-05-24_116.pdf.

230. Testimony of Regina Treler, HIA, Poland Ministersterstwo Informacji i Dokumentacji, Box 123, File 5, Protocol 51, 6–7.

231. Testimony of Naftali Zylbersztejn, HIA, Ministersterstwo Informacji i Dokumentacji, Box 123, File 6, Protocol 101, 7.

232. Testimony of Jozef Zgudnicki, HIA, Poland, Ministersterstwo Informacji i Dokumentacji, Box 123, File 7, Protocol 149, 4–5.

233. Testimony of Chawa Kestenbojm, HIA, Poland, Ministersterstwo Informacji i Dokumentacji, Box 123, File 5, Protocol 41, 5–6.

234. Edward H. Herzbaum, *Lost between Worlds: A World War II Journey of Survival*, trans. Piotr Graff (Leicester, UK: Matador, 2010), front matter.

235. Herzbaum, *Lost between Worlds*, 133, 206.

236. "Treatment of Jews in Polish Army Will Be Discussed by Polish National Council," *JTA Daily News Bulletin* 9, no. 247, October 26, 1942, Jewish Telegraphic Agency, http://pdfs.jta.org/1942/1942-10-26_247.pdf.

237. Israel Gutman, "Jews in General Anders' Army in the Soviet Union," *Yad Vashem Studies* 12 (1977): 294.

238. See pages 4–32 in Polish Institute and Sikorski Museum Archive (hereafter PISM), A.11.E/149 Ministry of Foreign Affairs, Jews in the Polish Army.

239. "Polish Paper in Russia Charges Polish Army with Deliberate Anti-Jewish Acts," *JTA Daily News Bulletin* 9, no. 257, November 6, 1942, Jewish Telegraphic Agency, http://pdfs.jta.org/1942/1942-11-06_257.pdf.

240. Sword, *Deportation and Exile*, 81.

241. Gutman, "Jews in General Anders' Army in the Soviet Union," 285–286.

242. Pruszynski, *Russian Year*, 44, 62.

243. Grossman, *In the Enchanted Land*, 183.

244. Shternfeld, *Halom ben gederot*, 197.

245. Starkiewicz, *Blades of Grass*, 110, 115.

246. Ahron Blenkitni, *Goyrl: iberlebungen fun a Yidisher mishpokhe in der tsveyter velt-milkhome* (Tel Aviv: Y.L. Peretz, 1968), 215–216.

247. Testimony of Chana Gelernter, HIA, Poland, Ministersterstwo Informacji i Dokumentacji, Box 123, File 5, Protocol 56, 1, 5.

248. Dorothy Zanker Abend, VHA Interview 08317, Tucson, AZ, November 4, 1995, tape 4, minutes 14–19.

249. Testimony of Mikhael Berlovich, GKH, Flinker Collection, 45586 (Protocol 18), 14.

250. "Protect Poland's Population in the USSR," HIA, Poland, Ministersterstwo Informacji i Dokumentacji, Box 46, File 6.

251. "Report on the Relief Accorded to Polish Citizens by the Polish Embassy in the USSR with Special Reference to Polish Citizens of Jewish Nationality," September 1941–April 1943, PISM, A.7/307/40, Embassy of the Polish Republic in Moscow and Kuibyshev, 1941-1943.

252. "Kujbyszew Nr. 495," HIA, Poland, Ministersterstwo Informacji i Dokumentacji, Box 46, File 6.

253. Keith Sword, "The Welfare of Polish-Jewish Refugees in the USSR, 1941–43: Relief Supplies and Their Distribution," in *Jews in Eastern Poland and the USSR, 1939–46,* ed. Norman Davies and Antony Polonsky (New York: St. Martin's, 1991), 154–157; Engel, *In the Shadow of Auschwitz,* 127–129.

254. Moshe Ben-Asher, VHA Interview 47417, London, August 19, 1998, tape 4, minutes 5–11.

255. Lederman, *These Children Are Mine,* 138, 143.

256. Regenboign, "Mi-zikhronot palit be-Rusya," 404.

257. See David Engel, "The Polish Government-in-Exile and the Erlich-Alter Affair," in Davies and Polonsky, eds., *Jews in Eastern Poland and the USSR,* 172–180; Engel, *In the Shadow of Auschwitz;* and David Engel, *Facing a Holocaust: The Polish Government-in-Exile and the Jews, 1943–1945* (Chapel Hill: University of North Carolina Press, 1993), especially 211–212.

258. Although Jews were among those arrested, the staff of the Polish bureaus was a small group and very few Polish Jews expressed awareness about this in their testimonial materials. The Polish government-in-exile, of course, voiced its concern. See for example the letters, reports, and requests in Liquidation of the Delegatura: Internal Correspondence of the Polish Authorities, PISM, A.11.49/Sow/28 Ministry of Foreign Affairs, 42-3.

259. For more on the history of the JDC, see Yehuda Bauer, *My Brother's Keeper: A History of the American Jewish Joint Distribution Committee 1929–1939* (Philadelphia: Jewish Publication Society of America, 1974); Yehuda Bauer, *American Jewry and the Holocaust: The American Jewish Joint Distribution Committee, 1939–1945* (Detroit: Wayne State University Press, 1981); Tom Shachtman, *I Seek My Brethren: Ralph Goldman and "The Joint"* (New York: Newmarket, 2001); and Michael Beizer and Mikhail Mitsel, *The American Brother: The "Joint" in Russia, the USSR and the CIS* (New York: American Jewish Joint Distribution Committee, 2004).

260. Redlich, *War, Holocaust and Stalinism,* 74.

261. "Memorandum #2 of Luncheon Conference, at Hotel Gotham, 12 noon, September 27, 1943," American Jewish Joint Distribution Committee Archives (hereafter JDCA), File 1056, 1/3, 1.

262. Paul Baerwald to Dr. Judah L. Magnes, March 25, 1943, JDCA, File 1056 1/3, 1.

263. "J.D.C. Program in the USSR 1942–1943," July 17, 1944, JDCA, File 1056 2/3, 1.

264. Atina Grossmann, "Remapping Relief and Rescue: Flight, Displacement, and International Aid for Jewish Refugees during World War II," *New German Critique* 39, no. 3 (117) (2012): 62.

265. Cohen interview, tape 3, minutes 9–11.

266. Rabbi Avraham Steinberg, Interview, GKH, Testimonies and Interviews, Israel, August 29, 2010, disc 2, minute 41.

267. Feldman, *From Warsaw*, 117.

268. Gabel, *Behind the Ice Curtain*, 278, 398–402.

269. Mietek Sieradzki, *By Twist of History: The Three Lives of a Polish Jew* (London: Vallentine Mitchell, 2002), 30.

270. "List of Certificate Holders for Palestine," HIA, Polish Ambassada (USSR), Box 15, File 6, Consular Legal Department.

271. "List of Packages Sent to USSR through American Express, 1943," Yeshiva University Archives, Vaad Hatzala Collection, Box 11, folder 4.

272. "List of Rabbinical Students and Rabbis Refugees in U.S.S.R.," USHMM, RG 67.011, Records of the New York Office of the World Jewish Congress, Relief and Rescue Department, D57, file 3, 1.

273. Halpern interview.

274. Grossman, *In the Enchanted Land*, 178–179.

275. Kreusler, *A Teacher's Experiences*, 165–166.

276. L.L., interview no. 5, in Erlich, *Interviews*, 5.

5. Nusekh Poyln, or Yetsies Poyln?

Epigraph: Dovid Sfard, *Mit zikh un mit andere: oytobiografye un literarishe eseyen* (Jerusalem: Farlag "Yerusholaimer almanakh," 1984), 165–166.

1. For more on cultural and political uses of this concept, see Magdalena Ruta, *Without Jews? Yiddish Literature in the People's Republic of Poland on the Holocaust, Poland, and Communism* (Krakow: Jagiellonian University Press, 2017), 255–265; and Joanna Nalewajko-Kulikov, *Obywatel Jidyszlandu: rzecz o żydowskich komunistach w Polsce* (Warsaw: Neriton, 2009), 172–177.

2. Hanna Davidson Pankowsky, *East of the Storm: Outrunning the Holocaust in Russia* (Lubbock, Texas: Tech University Press, 1999), 44.

3. Lilian T. Mowrer, *Arrest and Exile: The True Story of an American Woman in Poland and Siberia 1940–41* (New York: William Morrow, 1941), 142–143.

4. Karel Berkhoff, "'Total Annihilation of the Jewish Population': The Holocaust in the Soviet Media, 1941–45," in *The Holocaust in the East: Local Perpetrators and Soviet Responses,* ed. Michael David-Fox, Peter Holquist, and Alexander M. Martin (Pittsburgh: University of Pittsburgh Press, 2014); Arkadi Zeltser, "How the Jewish Intelligentsia Created the Jewishness of the Jewish Hero: The Soviet Yiddish Press," in *Soviet Jews in World War II: Fighting, Witnessing, Remembering,* ed. Harriet Murav and Gennady Estraikh (Boston: Academic Studies Press, 2014).

5. See, for example, Emil Sommerstein, "W rocznicę bohaterskiej obrony getta warszawskiego" (k. 31), and Alexander Bardin, "Życie w bunkrze" (k. 120), *Wolna Polska,* 1944, United States Holocaust Memorial Museum (hereafter USHMM), RG-15.341 Union of Polish Patriots in the USSR, file 2259.

6. Pearl Minz, *Surviving the Holocaust in Siberia, 1940–1945: The Diary of Pearl Minz,* trans. Alexander B. White (Goodyear, AZ: D. de Frain, 2010), 122.

7. Ewa Koźmińska-Frejlak, "The Adaptation of Survivors to the Post-war Reality from 1944 to 1949," in *Jewish Presence in Absence: The Aftermath of the Holocaust in Poland, 1944–2010,* ed. Feliks Tych and Monika Adamczyk-Garbowska (Jerusalem: Yad Vashem, 2014), 139–144.

8. See, for example, Oleg Budnitskii, "Jews at War: Diaries from the Front," in Murav and Estraikh, eds., *Soviet Jews in World War II,* 57–84.

9. Mark Edele and Wanda Warlick, "Saved by Stalin? Trajectories of Polish Jews in the Soviet Second World War," in *Shelter from the Holocaust: Rethinking Jewish Survival in the Soviet Union,* ed. Mark Edele, Sheila Fitzpatrick, and Atina Grossmann (Detroit: Wayne State University Press, 2017), 105, 118.

10. As Klemens Nussbaum notes, "A special handicap is the fact that Jewish officers bore different names at different times. It is, indeed, difficult for instance to find out today that Col. Roman Garbowski, for many years commander of the 15th and 16th Divisions and commander of the Frontier Protection Units is none other than the former modest young Second Lieutenant, Rachmiel Garber, decorated after the first battle of Lenino." See Klemens Nussbaum, "Jews in the Polish Army in the USSR," *Soviet Jewish Affairs* 2, no. 1 (1972): 95.

11. Jack Pomerantz and Lyric Wallwork Winik, *Run East: Flight from the Holocaust* (Urbana: University of Illinois Press, 1997), 127–144.

12. Bernard L. Ginsburg, *A Wayfarer in a World of Upheaval* (San Bernadino, CA: Borgo, 1993), 68.

13. Szymon Grajcar, University of Southern California Shoah Foundation Visual History Archive (hereafter VHA) Interview 16434, Toronto, June 24, 1996, tape 4, minutes 25–29 and tape 5, minutes 3–6.

14. Tema Abel, VHA Interview 14584, Toronto, April 26, 1996, tape 3, minutes 26–28.

15. Alan Elsner, *Guarded by Angels: How My Father and Uncle Survived Hitler and Cheated Stalin* (New York: Yad Vashem/Holocaust Survivors' Memoirs Project, 2005), 156–218.

16. Simon Davidson, *My War Years, 1939–1945*, trans. Marie Morgens (San Antonio: University of Texas, 1981), 170–198.

17. Włodzimierz Szer, *To Our Children; Memoirs of Displacement. A Jewish Journey of Hope and Survival in Twentieth-Century Poland and Beyond*, trans. Bronisława Karst (Boston: Academic Studies Press, 2016), 113.

18. Lena Jedwab Rozenberg, *Girl with Two Landscapes: The Wartime Diaries of Lena Jedwab, 1941–1945*, trans. Solon Beinfeld (New York: Holmes and Meier, 2002), 46, 159–160.

19. Shaul Shternfeld, *Halom ben gederot* (Tel Aviv: Halonot, 1999), 290–291.

20. Avrom Zak, *Oyf shlyakhn fun hefker*, vol. 2 (Buenos Aires: Tsentral farband fun Poylishe Yidn in Argentine, 1958), 322, 323, 324.

21. Szer, *To Our Children*, 127.

22. Ruth L. Hohberg, *Getting Here: Ruth's Story 1935–1949* (Baltimore: Publish America, 2002).

23. Wlodzimierz Rozenbaum, "The Road to New Poland: Jewish Communists in the Soviet Union, 1939–46," in *Jews in Eastern Poland and the USSR, 1939–46*, ed. Norman Davies and Antony Polonsky (New York: St. Martin's, 1991), 215–219.

24. Krystyna Kersten, *The Establishment of Communist Rule in Poland, 1939–1948*, trans. John Micgiel and Michael H. Bernhard (Berkeley: University of California Press, 1991), 8–9.

25. Marci Shore, *Caviar and Ashes: A Warsaw Generation's Life and Death in Marxism, 1918–1968* (New Haven, CT: Yale University Press, 2006), 229.

26. Kersten, *The Establishment of Communist Rule*, 9.

27. For an analysis of Wasilewska's life choices and scholarship about her, see Agnieszka Mrozik, "Crossing Boundaries: The Case of Wanda Wasilewska and Polish Communism," *Aspasia* 11 (2017): 19–53.

28. Minutes of the Committee of Polish Orphanages and the Children in Them of the Kazakh SSR, 1943, Tsentral'nyi gosudarstvennyi arkhiv Respubliki Kazakhstan (hereafter TsGARK), f. 1692, d. 800, 19 II.

29. Report from Mari ASSR, Związek Patriotów Polskich w ZSRR, USHMM, RG-15.341, Archiwum Akt Nowych, 130, 1.14, 861, 50–54.

30. Chart of Polish Population for the Kuibyshev Region, April 1, 1945, USHMM, RG-15.341, Związek Patriotów Polskich w ZSRR, Archiwum Akt Nowych, 130, 1.14, 861, 107.

31. Victor Zarnowitz, *Fleeing the Nazis, Surviving the Gulag, and Arriving in the Free World: My Life and Times* (Westport, CT: Praeger, 2008), 68–74.

32. Abraham A. Kreusler, *A Teacher's Experiences in the Soviet Union* (Leiden: E. J. Brill, 1965), 189.

33. Zak, *Oyf shlyakhn fun hefker,* 2:320.

34. Ida Kaminska, *My Life, My Theater,* ed. and trans. Curt Leviant (New York: Macmillan, 1973), 184–187.

35. Sfard, *Mit zikh un mit andere,* 142.

36. Shimon Redlich, *Propaganda and Nationalism in Wartime Russia: The Jewish Antifascist Committee in the USSR, 1941–1948* (Boulder, CO: East European Monographs, 1982), 63.

37. Ginsburg, *A Wayfarer,* 22–24, 50–51.

38. Photographs from Fergana, 1943–1946, USHMM, RG-15.341, Związek Patriotów Polskich w ZSRR, Archiwum Akt Nowych, 130, 3.2, 2173.

39. Sfard, *Mit zikh un mit andere,* 142.

40. Yosef Litvak, "Korotav u-fe'iluto ha-tsiburit shel Emil Zomershtain [Sommerstein] be-Verit ha-Mo'atsot be-milhemet ha-'olam ha-sheniyah," *Gal-Ed* 12 (1991): 135–143.

41. Federation of Polish Jews, Montreal, to Dr. Emil Sommerstein, USHMM, RG-15.341, Związek Patriotów Polskich w ZSRR, Archiwum Akt Nowych, 130, 6, 2330, 16.

42. Sfard, *Mit zikh un mit andere,* 142–143.

43. Davidson, *My War Years,* 170.

44. J.S., interview no. 6, in Rachel Erlich, *Interviews with Polish and Russian Jewish DPs in Camps on Their Observations of Jewish life in Soviet Russia* (New York: American Jewish Committee, 1948), 4.

45. Rozenberg, *Girl with Two Landscapes,* 153–156.

46. Rabbi Dr. Jacob Halpern, interview with the author, Silver Spring, MD, September 28, 2010.

47. Dr. R., interview no. 1, in Erlich, *Interviews,* 7–8.

48. Yosef Litvak, "Polish-Jewish Refugees Repatriated from the Soviet Union to Poland at the End of the Second World War and Afterwards," in Davies and Polonsky, eds., *Jews in Eastern Poland and the USSR,* 228–230.

49. Hanna Shlomi, "The 'Jewish Organising Committee' in Moscow and the 'Jewish Central Committee' in Warsaw, June 1945–February 1946: Tackling Repatriation," in Davies and Polonsky, eds., *Jews in Eastern Poland and the USSR,* 240–241.

50. Albert Kaganovitch, "Stalin's Great Power Politics, the Return of Jewish Refugees to Poland, and Continued Migration to Palestine, 1944–1946," *Holocaust and Genocide Studies* 26, no. 1 (2012): 75–83.

51. See, for example, "Agreement between the Government of the Belarusian Soviet Socialist Republic and the Polish Committee of National Liberation regarding the Evacuation of the Belarusian Population from the Territory of Poland and Polish Citizens from the Territory of the BSSR," September 9, 1944, in *Dokumenty i materialy po istorii sovetsko-pol'skikh otnoshenii*, vol. 8, *January 1944–December 1945* (Moscow: Izdatel'stvo 'Nauka," 1974), 213–219.

52. "Agreement between the Government of the Union of Soviet Socialist Republics and the Provisional Government of the Republic of Poland on the Right of Withdrawal from Soviet Citizenship of Individuals of Polish and Jewish Nationality, Residing in the USSR, and for Their Evacuation to Poland, and on the Right of Withdrawal from Polish Citizenship of Individuals of Russian, Ukrainian, Belarusian, Ruthenian, or Lithuanian Nationality, Residing in the Territories of Poland, and Their Evacuation to the USSR," July 6, 1945, in *Dokumenty i materialy po istorii sovetsko-pol'skikh otnoshenii*, 467–471.

53. Israel Gutman and Shmuel Krakowski, *Unequal Victims: Poles and Jews during World War II* (New York: Holocaust Library, 1986), 360, 350.

54. I. Lib. [Lieberman], interview no. 2, in Erlich, *Interviews*, 7–8.

55. Pomerantz and Winik, *Run East*, 158–171.

56. Szer, *To Our Children*, 121, 140–141.

57. Helena Starkiewicz, *Blades of Grass between the Stones* (Melbourne: H. Starkiewicz, 1998), 140–155.

58. Betty Rich, *Little Girl Lost* (Toronto: Azrieli Foundation, 2011), 113–119, 131.

59. Aleena Rieger, *I Didn't Tell Them Anything: The Wartime Secrets of an American Girl* (New York: SunPetal Books, 2015), 82–88.

60. Abraham Bichler, *Little Miracles: A Story of Courage, Faith and Survival* (Raleigh, NC: Ivy House, 2004), 97–116.

61. Wanda Wasilewska to the Secretary of the Communist Party of Kazakhstan, March 10, 1944, Arkhiv Prezidenta Respubliki Kazakhstan, f. 708, op. 8, d. 156, 1.

62. Zyga Elton, *Destination Buchara* (Ripponlea, Victoria: Dizal Nominees, 1996), 237–258.

63. Joachim Schoenfeld, *Holocaust Memoirs: Jews in the Lwow Ghetto, the Janowski Concentration Camp, and as Deportees in Siberia* (Hoboken, NJ: Ktav, 1985), 279.

64. Yankl Saler, VHA Interview 41969, Melbourne, March 18, 1998, tape 6, minutes 23–27.

65. S. Vagner, *Vosemnadtsat'* (Jerusalem: Shamir, 1989), 33.

66. Shalom Duber Levin, ed., *Toldot Habad be-Rusya ha-Sovetit: ba-shanim 678–710* (Brooklyn, NY: Kehot, 1989), 338.

67. Herschel Weinrauch, *Blut oyf der zun: Yidn in Sovet-Rusland* (New York: Farlag "Mensh un Yid," 1950), 20–37.

68. Id. Lib., interview no. 9, in Erlich, *Interviews*. Although the text of the interview does not mention the circumstances, a note at the top states that at the time of the interview Id. Lib was married to I. Lib, a Polish Jew also interviewed (no. 2). It is not clear whether their relationship had anything to do with her decision to leave the USSR.

69. Henry Skorr with Ivan Sokolov, *Through Blood and Tears: Surviving Hitler and Stalin* (London: Vallentine Mitchell, 2006), 299.

70. Szymon Grajcar, VHA Interview 16434, Toronto, June 24, 1996, tape 4, minutes 19–22.

71. "Notes on the State of Children's Homes of the Republic, 25 Feb. 1946–20 Dec. 1946," TsGARK, f. 1692, op. 1, d. 1073, 67–79.

72. Irene Rogers, VHA Interview 01754, Northbrook, IL, March 29, 1995, tape 2.

73. Letter from Regina Barber, USHMM, State Archives of the Bukharan Region, Regional Executive Committee of the Communist Party, f. 1023, op. 1, d. 300, 88 (courtesy of Vadim Altskan).

74. Rabbi Moshe Nachum Kaner, Interview, Israel, December 29, 2010, Ganzach Kiddush Hashem Archives (hereafter GKH), Testimonies and Interviews, disc 1.

75. Minz, *Surviving the Holocaust*, 125–145.

76. Ezra Zynger, VHA Interview 05985, Montreal, August 24, 1995, tape 2, minutes 3–10.

77. Testimony of Mordechai Altschuler [Altshuler], February 27, 1993, Oral History Division, Hebrew University of Jerusalem, Project 101, 3491, tape 4, transcript, 64.

78. Dovid Feinzeig, *Faith & Flight: A Young Boy's Memories of the Prewar Shtetl, Shavuos in Ger, a Family's Travels through Russia, Rebuilding in Postwar Poland and France* (Lakewood, NJ: Israel Bookshop Publications, 2013), chaps. 11–12.

79. Dr. H. Wolpe, "Pierwsze transporty repatriantów wracają z ZSSR do Kraju," *Wolna Polska* 1, no. 137, January 10, 1946, USHMM, RG-15.341, Związek Patriotów Polskich w ZSRR, Archiwum Akt Nowych, 130, 3.4, 2261, 4.

80. Abel interview, tape 4, minutes 1–7.

81. Report on the Fourth Conference of the ZPP, September 14–16, 1945, USHMM, RG-15.341, Związek Patriotów Polskich w ZSRR, Archiwum Akt Nowych, 130, 1.5, 169, 93–97.

82. Ruth Lichtenstein and Gi Orman, dirs., *Rosja: Escaping Hitler Was Just the Beginning* (Brooklyn, NY: Project Witness, 2018), DVD.

83. Davidson, *My War Years*, 210.

84. Pankowsky, *East of the Storm*, 128.

85. Chaim Ajzen, *Chaim Ajzen Remembers* (Melbourne: C. Ajzen, 2001).

86. Moshe Erlich, VHA Interview 10029, Jerusalem, December 13, 1995, tape 5, minute 27—tape 6, minute 1.

87. Jane Lipski, "My Escape into Prison and Other Memoirs of a Stolen Youth, 1939–1948," in Isabelle Choko, Frances Irwin, Lotti Kahana-Aufleger, Margit Raab Kalina, and Jane Lipski, *Stolen Youth: Five Women's Survival in the Holocaust* (New York: Yad Vashem/Holocaust Survivors' Memoirs Project, 2005), 271–297.

88. Ruth Turkow Kaminska, *Mink Coats and Barbed Wire* (London: Collins and Harvill, 1979).

89. Grzegorz Berendt, "A New Life: Jewish Institutions and Organizations in Poland from 1944–1950," in Tych and Adamczyk-Garbowska, eds., *Jewish Presence in Absence*, 222.

90. Sydney Gruson, "Yiddish Poet Ends Ordeal in Soviet; Rehabilitated Writer Returns to Warsaw After Five Years of Imprisonment," *New York Times*, August 6, 1956.

91. "Moishe Broderzon, Yiddish Dramatist," *New York Times*, August 21, 1956.

92. Sheyne Miriam Broderzon, *Meyn laydns-veg mit Moyshe Broderzon* (Buenos Aires: Tsentral Farband fun Poylishe Yidn in Argentine, 1960).

93. Lipski, "My Escape," 289–295.

94. Gennady Estraikh, "Escape through Poland: Soviet Jewish Emigration in the 1950s," *Jewish History* 31, nos. 3–4 (2018): 12–16.

95. Dina Gabel, *Behind the Ice Curtain* (New York: CIS, 1992), 426–445.

96. Interview with Adela Sherman, March 15, 1986, Fortunoff Video Archive for Holocaust Testimonies 747, Dallas affiliated project, minutes 31–33.

97. Iakov Khonigsman, VHA Interview 45050, Lviv, Ukraine, June 6, 1998, tape 7, minutes 0–3.

98. See, for example, Ia. S. Khonigsman, *Katastrofa l'vovskogo evreistva* (Lviv, Ukraine: L'vovskoe obshchestvo evreiskoi kul'tury im. Sholom-Aleikhema, 1993); Ia. S. Khonigsman, *Evrei Ukrainy: kratkii ocherk istorii*, 2 vols. (Kiev: Ukrainsko-finskii in-t menedzhmenta i biznesa, 1992–1995); Ia. S. Khonigsman, *Katastrofa evreistva Zapadnoi Ukrainy: evrei vostochnoi Galitsii, zapadnoi Volyni, Bukoviny i Zakarpat'ia v 1933–1945 gg.* (Lviv, Ukraine: s.n. 1998); Ia. S. Khonigsman, *Bnei-Brit vo L'vov: istoricheskii ocherk* (Lviv, Ukraine: Bnei-Brit "Leopolis" im. Emilia Dombergera, 1999); and Ia. S. Khonigsman, *Blagotvoritel'nost' evreev Voltochnoi Galitsii* (Kiev: Instytut Iudaiky, 2002).

99. Catherine Wanner, *Burden of Dreams: History and Identity in Post-Soviet Ukraine* (University Park, PA: Penn State University Press, 1998), 196.

100. David Fanning, *Mieczysław Weinberg: In Search of Freedom* (Hofheim, Germany: Wolke Verlag, 2010).

101. Kaganovitch, "Stalin's Great Power Politics," 74.

102. Kaganovitch, "Stalin's Great Power Politics," 74; Edele and Warlik, "Saved by Stalin?," 121.

103. Edele and Warlik, "Saved by Stalin?," 118. Litvak counted 230,700 by 1949, with the caveat that some returnees may have registered in more than one location in Poland on their return thus inflating the number by as much as 10 percent. See Litvak, "Polish-Jewish Refugees," 235. Kaganovitch uses repatriation data to arrive at the figure of 202,000. See Kaganovitch, "Stalin's Great Power Politics," 75.

104. Ewa Węgrzyn, *Wyjeżdżamy! Wyjeżdżamy?! Alija gomułkowska 1956–1960* (Kraków: Wydawnictwo Austeria, 2016), 202; Estraikh, "Escape through Poland," 21. Litvak lists the considerably larger figure of thirty thousand; it is likely that he is also estimating unofficial repatriates during this period. See Yosef Litvak, *Pelitim Yehudim mi-Polin be-Verit ha-Mo'atsot, 1939–1946* (Jerusalem: Hebrew University Press, 1988), 351.

105. Ann Szedlecki, *Album of My Life* (Toronto: Azrieli Foundation, 2010), 146.

106. On this process, see Kersten, *The Establishment of Communist Rule*.

107. Jaff Schatz, *The Generation: The Rise and Fall of Jewish Communists in Poland* (Berkeley: University of California Press, 1991), 200.

108. Albert Stankowski, "How Many Polish Jews Survived the Holocaust?," in Tych and Adamczyk-Garbowska, eds., *Jewish Presence in Absence*, 215.

109. Krystyna Kersten, *Repatriacja ludności polskiej po II wojnie światowej* (Wrocław: Polska Akademia Nauk, 1974).

110. Y. Shmulevitsh, "Oyf di khurvos fun meyn heym-shtot Kelts," *Dos Naye Lebn* 24, no. 49, July 19, 1946.

111. Abel interview, tape 4, minutes 3–4.

112. Dorothy Zanker Abend, VHA Interview 08317, Tucson, AZ, November 4, 1995, tape 4, minutes 27–28.

113. Elton, *Destination Buchara*, 259.

114. Sfard, *Mit zikh un mit andere*, 160.

115. Koźmińska-Frejlak, "The Adaptation of Survivors," 148–149.

116. See, for example, Symcha Burstin, VHA Interview 31555, Melbourne, July 22, 1997, tape 5, minutes 20–21.

117. Feinzeig, *Faith & Flight*, 285, 288.

118. Bożena Szaynok, "The Beginnings of Jewish Settlement in Lower Silesia after World War II," *Acta Poloniae Historica* 76 (1997): 172–173.

119. Katharina Friedla, "Experiences of Stigmatization, Discrimination and Exclusion: German-Jewish Survivors in Wrocław, 1945–1947," *Leo Baeck Institute Yearbook* 62 (2017): 95–113.

120. Joseph Marcus, *Social and Political History of the Jews in Poland, 1919–1939* (Berlin: Mouton, 1983), 141–142.

121. Miri Freilich, "TOZ," in *The YIVO Encyclopedia of Jews in Eastern Europe*, ed. Gershon David Hundert (New Haven, CT: Yale University Press, 2008), 1891–1892.

122. Berendt, "A New Life," 227.

123. Dr. Szpindel, Sprawozdanie z przyjazdu transportu Żydów z Buchary, 1946, USHMM, RG-15-107M.

124. Jacob Pat, *Ashes and Fire* (New York: International Universities Press, 1947), 100–101.

125. Feinzeig, *Faith & Flight*, 296.

126. Pat, *Ashes and Fire*, 9–10.

127. "Report on aid, numbers, repatriates," January 15, 1946, Archiwum Panstwowe we Wroclawiu (hereafter APW), RG 324/III Jewish Provincial Committee for Lower Silesia, Vol. 5 Descriptive reports on the activities of the Jewish Provincial Committee, 20–24.

128. "Movement of repatriates," APW, RG 324/III, Vol. 5, 110.

129. "Collated answers to questionnaires for Dzierżoniów," APW, RG 324/III, Vol. 50 Committees' statistical reports-decadal questionnaire, 1946, 17.

130. "Collated answers to questionnaires for Lubań," APW, RG 324/III, Vol. 50, 68.

131. Zynger interview, tape 2, minutes 10–11.

132. Gabel, *Behind the Ice Curtain*, 459.

133. Pomerantz and Winik, *Run East*, 158.

134. Erlich interview, tape 5, minutes 16–25.

135. Rich, *Little Girl Lost*, 120.

136. Mikhael Rubinovitsh, "Oyfshteyg fun Yidishn lebn in Zgorzshelets," *Dos Naye Lebn* 25, no. 50, July 26, 1946.

137. Y. Fogtlman, "Problemen funem Yidishn yishev in Shtshetshin," *Dos Naye Lebn* 27, no. 52, August 9, 1946.

138. Jacob Egit, *Tsu a nay lebn (tsvey yor in Yidisher yishev in Nidershlezye)* (Wrocław: Wydawnictwo "Niderszlezje", 1947).

139. Natan Gross, *Der Yidisher yishev in Nidershlezye* (1947) (https://www.youtube.com/watch?v=5q82LKt7Zi0).

140. Jacob Egit, *Grand Illusion* (Toronto: Lugus Productions Ltd., 1991), 44.

141. Kaminska, *My Life, My Theater*, 216, 227.

142. Shimon Dzigan, *Der koyekh fun Yidishn humor* (Tel Aviv: Orli, 1974), 267–292.

143. Joanna Nalewajko-Kulikov and Magdalena Ruta, "Yiddish Culture in Poland after the Holocaust," in Tych and Adamczyk-Garbowska, eds., *Jewish Presence in Absence,* 327–351; Nathan Cohen, "Motives for the Emigration of Yiddish Writers from Poland (1944–1948)," in *Under the Red Banner: Yiddish Culture in the Communist Countries in the Postwar Era,* ed. Elvira Grözinger and Magdalena Ruta (Weisbaden: Harrassowitz Verlag, 2008), 157–164; Nathan Cohen, "The Renewed Association of Yiddish Writers and Journalists in Poland, 1945–1948," in *Yiddish after the Holocaust,* ed. Joseph Sherman (Oxford: Boulevard, 2004), 15-36.

144. Nalewajko-Kulikov and Ruta, "Yiddish Culture in Poland," 330.

145. Zev Katz, *From the Gestapo to the Gulags: One Jewish Life* (London: Vallentine Mitchell, 2004), 122.

146. Goldberger, *Stalin's Little Guest,* 187–194.

147. Shimon Redlich, *Life in Transit: Jews in Postwar Lodz, 1944–1950* (Boston: Academic Studies Press, 2010).

148. Feinzeig, *Faith & Flight,* chaps. 14–15.

149. Rabbi Yitzhak Meir Safronovitch, Interview, GKH, Testimonies and Interviews, Israel, March 22, 2011, disc 3, minutes 11–13.

150. August Grabski and Albert Stankowski, "Jewish Religious Life in Poland after the Holocaust," in Tych and Adamczyk-Garbowska, eds., *Jewish Presence in Absence,* 253.

151. Zvi Faier, Interview VT 6929, Yad Vashem Archives (hereafter YVA), O.3, Israel, March 8, 2007, tape 2, minutes 7–14.

152. Janina Bauman, *A Dream of Belonging: My Years in Postwar Poland* (London: Virago, 1988), 23, 30–31.

153. Shalom Omri, VHA Interview 41743, Holon, Israel, March 1, 1998, tape 5, minutes 5–6.

154. See, for example, Alina Skibińska, "The Return of Holocaust Survivors and the Reaction of the Polish Population," in Tych and Adamczyk-Garbowska, eds., *Jewish Presence in Absence,* 28; and Andrzej Żbikowski, "The Post-War Wave of Pogroms and Killings," in Tych and Adamczyk-Garbowska, eds., *Jewish Presence in Absence,* 72.

155. Janka Goldberger, *Stalin's Little Guest* (London: Janus, 1995), 173.

156. Shternfeld, *Halom ben gederot,* 290.

157. Sara Bergman, VHA Interview 30068, Melbourne, April 6, 1997, tape 3, minutes 4–6.

158. Hohberg, *Getting Here,* 72–73.

159. Grajcar interview, tape 5, minutes 6–9.

160. Jan T. Gross, *Fear: Anti-Semitism in Poland after Auschwitz* (New York: Random House, 2007); Jan Tomasz Gross with Irena Grudzińska-Gross,

Golden Harvest: Events at the Periphery of the Holocaust (Oxford: Oxford University Press, 2016).

161. Łukasz Krzyżanowski, *Dom, którego nie było: powroty ocalałych do powojennego miasta* (Warsaw: Wydawnictwo "Czarne," 2016), chap. 5.

162. Isaiah Trunk, "The Historian of the Holocaust at YIVO," in *Creators and Disturbers: Reminiscences by Jewish Intellectuals of New York,* ed. Bernard Rosenberg and Ernest Goldstein (New York: Columbia University Press, 1982), 65.

163. Testimony of Jonas Landesman, Kraków, October 5, 1945, Archiwum Żydowskiego Instytutu Historychnego w Warszawie (hereafter AŻIH), RG 301 Testimonies, file 1581, 1–4.

164. Natalia Aleksiun, "The Situation of the Jews in Poland as Seen by the Soviet Security Forces in 1945," *Jews in Eastern Europe* 3, no. 37 (1998): 52–68.

165. Bożena Szaynok, "The Role of Antisemitism in Postwar Polish-Jewish Relations," in *Antisemitism and Its Opponents in Modern Poland,* ed. Robert Blobaum (Ithaca, NY: Cornell University Press, 2005), 271.

166. Gross, *Fear,* 58–63.

167. Irving Badner, VHA Interview 02742, Little Neck, NY, May 14, 1995, tape 2, minutes 12–15.

168. Skibińska, "The Return of Holocaust Survivors," 27.

169. Gross, *Fear,* 36–38.

170. Żbikowski, "The Post-war Wave," 94.

171. See Gross, *Fear;* Żbikowski, "The Post-war Wave"; Krystyna Kersten, "The Pogrom of Jews in Kielce on July 4, 1946," *Acta Poloniae Historica* 76 (1997): 197–212; David Engel, "Patterns of Anti-Jewish Violence in Poland, 1944–1946," *Yad Vashem Studies* 26 (1998): 43–85; and Szaynok, "The Role of Antisemitism."

172. Yocheved (Hei) Zamari, Interview VT 6026, YVA, O.3, Israel, December 21, 2006, tape 2, minutes 9–14.

173. Moshe Kaner, Interview VT 6426, YVA, O.3, Kiryat Hayim, Israel, September 26, 2006, tape 2.

174. Katz, *From the Gestapo to the Gulags,* 141.

175. Kersten, *The Establishment of Communist Rule,* 142, 416.

176. Natalia Aleksiun, "The Central Jewish Historical Commission in Poland, 1944–1947," *Polin* 20 (2008): 74–97.

177. August Grabski, "Jews and Political Life in Poland from 1944–1949," in Tych and Adamczyk-Garbowska, eds., *Jewish Presence in Absence,* 185–188.

178. Anna Sommer Schneider, "The Survival of *Yidishkeyt:* The Impact of the American Jewish Joint Distribution Committee on Jewish Education in Poland, 1945–1989," *Polin* 30 (2018): 359–361, 365.

179. Nalewajko-Kulikov and Ruta, "Yiddish Culture in Poland," 328, 339.
180. Szaynok, "The Role of Antisemitism," 280.
181. Nalewajko-Kulikov and Ruta, "Yiddish Culture in Poland," 343.
182. Grabski and Stankowski, "Jewish Religious Life in Poland," 258–261.
183. Audrey Kichelewski, "Imaging 'the Jews' in Stalinist Poland: Nationalists or Cosmopolites?" *European Review of History / Revue européenne d'histoire* 17, no. 3 (2010): 509.
184. Kamil Kijek, "Aliens in the Land of the Piasts: The Polonization of Lower Silesia and Its Jewish Community in the Years 1945–1950," in *Jews and Germans in Eastern Europe,* ed. Tobias Grill (Berlin: De Gruyter, 2018), 250.
185. Schatz, *The Generation;* Shore, *Caviar and Ashes;* Ruta, *Without Jews?.*
186. Schatz, *The Generation,* 206.
187. Natalia Aleksiun, "The Vicious Circle: Jews in Communist Poland, 1944–1956," *Studies in Contemporary Jewry* 19 (2003): 157–158.
188. Michael Steinlauf, *Bondage to the Dead: Poland and the Memory of the Holocaust* (Syracuse, NY: Syracuse University Press, 1997), 50.
189. Feliks Tych, "The 'March '68' Antisemitic Campaign: Onset, Development, and Consequences," in Tych and Adamczyk-Garbowska, eds., *Jewish Presence in Absence,* 471.
190. Koźmińska-Frejlak, "The Adaptation of Survivors," 132.
191. Dariusz Stola, "Jewish Emigration from Communist Poland: The Decline of Polish Jewry in the Aftermath of the Holocaust," *East European Jewish Affairs* 47, nos. 2–3 (2017): 171.
192. Feliks Tych and Monika Adamczyk-Garbowska, "Introduction," in Tych and Adamczyk-Garbowska, eds., *Jewish Presence in Absence,* 15.
193. Letter from Ma. Abfajer, Szczecin, Poland, May 10, 1946, AŻIH, Centralny Komitet Żydów w Polsce, Wydział Ewidencji i Statystyki Centralnego Komitetu Żydów w Polsce, 1945–1950, Sygn. 303/V/984, 118–123.
194. Postcard from Szczecin, Poland, August 1946, AŻIH, Centralny Komitet Żydów w Polsce, Wydział Ewidencji i Statystyki Centralnego Komitetu Żydów w Polsce, 1945–1950, Sygn. 303/V/984, 176–177.
195. Letter from Ppor. Szafran Feiwel, Inveraray, Scotland, August 7, 1946, AŻIH, Centralny Komitet Żydów w Polsce, Wydział Ewidencji i Statystyki Centralnego Komitetu Żydów w Polsce, 1945–1950, Sygn. 303/V/984, 130–132.
196. Letter from Jewish Social Service Bureau, Detroit, August 12, 1946, AŻIH, Centralny Komitet Żydów w Polsce, Wydział Ewidencji i Statystyki Centralnego Komitetu Żydów w Polsce, 1945–1950, Sygn. 303/V/984, 302.
197. Anna Cichopek-Gajraj, *Beyond Violence: Jewish Survivors in Poland and Slovakia, 1944–1948* (Cambridge: Cambridge University Press, 2014), 7.

198. Gabriel Temkin, *My Just War: The Memoir of a Jewish Red Army Soldier in World War II* (Novato, CA: Presidio, 1998), 225.

199. Szer, *To Our Children*, 148.

200. Erlich interview, tape 5, minute 19, through tape 6, minute 5.

201. Bauman, *A Dream of Belonging*, 49. Bauman notes in the text that she changed the names of some of the people profiled. As she wrote the book in England while Communist Poland still stood, this makes sense. It is less clear why she changed the name of her husband, the prominent sociologist Zygmunt Bauman.

202. Kersten, *The Establishment of Communist Rule*, 338–339.

203. Kijek, "Aliens in the Lands of the Piasts," 243.

204. Koźmińska-Frejlak, "The Adaptation of Survivors," 129.

205. Estraikh, "Escape through Poland," 5.

206. Grzegorz Berendt, "The Impact of the 1956 Liberalization of Poland's Political System on the Jewish Population," in Tych and Adamczyk-Garbowska, eds., *Jewish Presence in Absence*, 438.

207. Estraikh, "Escape through Poland," 7–8, 17.

208. Berendt, "The Impact of the 1956 Liberalization," 423–439.

209. Stola, "Jewish Emigration from Communist Poland," 176–177.

210. Dariusz Stola, "Anti-Zionism as a Multipurpose Policy Instrument: The Anti-Zionist Campaign in Poland, 1967–1968," *Journal of Israeli History* 25, no. 1 (2006): 179–180.

211. Mayer Galler, oral history interview, San Francisco, California, December 13, 1989, Holocaust Oral History Project, USHMM, RG-50.477.0819, 28–33.

212. Shternfeld, *Halom ben gederot*, 290–301.

213. Erlich interview, tape 6, minutes 5–8.

214. Mietek Sieradzki, *By Twist of History: The Three Lives of a Polish Jew* (London: Vallentine Mitchell, 2002), 38.

215. Karen Auerbach, *The House at Ujazdowskie 16: Jewish Families in Warsaw after the Holocaust* (Bloomington: Indiana University Press, 2015), 6.

216. Stola, "Anti-Zionism as a Multipurpose Policy Instrument," 193–194.

217. Stola, "Jewish Emigration from Communist Poland," 180.

218. Suzanna Eibuszyc, *Memory Is Our Home: Loss and Remembering: Three Generations in Poland and Russia 1917–1960s* (Stuttgart: ibidem-Verlag, 2015), 155, 31.

219. Sieradzki, *By Twist of History*, 165–189.

220. Bauman, *A Dream of Belonging*, 168–197.

221. Stola, "Anti-Zionism as a Multipurpose Policy Instrument," 196.

222. Kaminska, *My Life, My Theater*, 255–287.

223. Ruta, *Without Jews?*, 251. On Sfard's life and thought, see Sfard, *Mit zikh un mit andere;* Dovid Sfard, *Shrayber un bikher* (Lodz, Poland: Farlag "Yiddish-Bukh," 1949); and Nalewajko-Kulikov, *Obywatel Jidyszlandu.*

224. Grabski and Stankowski, "Jewish Religious Life in Poland," 267–269; Nalewajko-Kulikov and Ruta, "Yiddish Culture in Poland," 349–350.

225. Steinlauf, *Bondage to the Dead,* chap. 6.

226. Arieh J. Kochavi, *Post-Holocaust Politics: Britain, the United States, and Jewish Refugees, 1945–1948* (Chapel Hill: University of North Carolina Press, 2001), 160; Zeev Mankowitz, *Life between Memory and Hope: The Survivors of the Holocaust in Occupied Germany* (Cambridge: Cambridge University Press, 2002), 19.

227. Laura Jockusch and Tamar Lewinsky, "Paradise Lost? Postwar Memory of Polish Jewish Survival in the Soviet Union," *Holocaust and Genocide Studies* 24, no. 3 (2010): 383–384.

228. Margarete Myers Feinstein, *Holocaust Survivors in Postwar Germany, 1945–1957* (Cambridge: Cambridge University Press, 2007), 302.

229. Feinstein, *Holocaust Survivors in Postwar Germany,* 15, 251–255.

230. Leo W. Schwarz, *The Redeemers: A Saga of the Years 1945–1952* (New York: Farrar, Straus and Young, 1953), 138.

231. Feinstein, *Holocaust Survivors in Postwar Germany,* 58.

232. Schwarz, *The Redeemers,* 76.

233. Mendel Saler, VHA Interview 45281, Melbourne, June 24, 1998, tape 3, minutes 5–9.

234. Rieger, *I Didn't Tell Them Anything,* 126.

235. Abend interview, tape 5.

236. Ada Schein, "'Everyone Can Hold a Pen': The Documentation Project in the DP Camps in Germany," in *Holocaust Historiography: Emergence, Challenges, Polemics and Achievements,* ed. David Bankier and Dan Michman (Jerusalem: Yad Vashem, 2008), 104.

237. Gabriel N. Finder, "Yizkor! Commemoration of the Dead by Jewish Displaced Persons in Postwar Germany," in *Between Mass Death and Individual Loss: The Place of the Dead in Twentieth-Century Germany,* ed. Alon Confino, Paul Betts, and Dirk Schumann (New York: Berghahn Books, 2008), 235.

238. Feinstein, *Holocaust Survivors in Postwar Germany,* 77.

239. Alexander Contract, VHA Interview 36559, King of Prussia, PA, November 7, 1997, tape 11.

240. Szymon Grajcar, VHA Interview 16434, Toronto, June 24, 1996, tape 6, minutes 20–25.

241. Pankowsky, *East of the Storm,* 166.

242. Koppel E. Pinson, "Jewish Life in Liberated Germany: A Study of Jewish DP's," *Jewish Social Studies* 9, no. 2 (1947): 109, quoted in Boaz Cohen, *Israeli Holocaust Research: Birth and Evolution* (London: Routledge, 2013), 29.

243. Ginsburg, *A Wayfarer,* 95–99.

244. Frumie Cohen, VHA Interview 47312, Brooklyn, NY, November 23, 1998, tape 3, minutes 19–29.

245. Zarnowitz, *Fleeing the Nazis,* 89.

246. Helen Zuberman, VHA Interview 47875, Bronx, NY, December 1, 1998, tape 4.

247. Badner interview, tape 2, minutes 15–17.

248. Na'ama Seri-Levi, "'These People Are Unique': The Repatriates in the Displaced Persons Camps, 1945–1946," *Moreshet* 14 (2017): 60.

249. Daniella Bell, VHA Interview 19812, Montreal, September 17, 1996, tape 2, minute 19, through tape 3, minute 2.

250. Atina Grossmann, *Jews, Germans, Allies: Close Encounters in Occupied Germany* (Princeton, NJ: Princeton University Press, 2007), 187.

251. Sharon Kangisser Cohen, "Choosing *A Heim:* Survivors of the Holocaust and Post-War Immigration," *European Judaism* 46, no. 2 (2013): 32–33.

252. Mankowitz, *Life between Memory and Hope,* 273.

253. Pankowsky, *East of the Storm,* 141, 178–196, 203–205.

254. Joseph Berger, *Displaced Persons: Growing Up American after the Holocaust* (New York: Scribner, 2001), 275–279.

255. Rieger, *I Didn't Tell Them Anything,* 135.

256. Israel Ignac Feldman, *The Lost Dream* (Toronto: Lorne Miller and Associates, 2007), 126.

257. Zamari interview, tape 2.

258. Yehuda Bauer, *Flight and Rescue: Brichah* (New York: Random House, 1970), 27.

259. Bauer, *Flight and Rescue,* 28–30.

260. Zamari interview, tape 2, minutes 16–17.

261. Omri interview, tape 5.

262. Rieger, *I Didn't Tell Them Anything,* 99–100.

263. See, for example, Ruth Gruber, *Exodus 1947: The Ship That Launched a Nation* (New York: Times Books, 1999).

264. Rachela Tytelman Wygodzki, *The End and the Beginning (August 1939–July 1948)* (n.p.: R.T. Wygodzki, 1998), 43–54.

265. Bob Golan, *A Long Way Home: The Story of a Jewish Youth, 1939–1949,* ed. Jacob Howland (Lanham, MD: University Press of America, 2005), 119.

266. Natan Degani, Interview 6522, YVA, O.3, Israel, November 1, 1991, tape 1.

267. "Pickets Demonstrate before British Embassy to Protest Deportation of Jews to Cyprus," *JTA Daily News Bulletin* 13, no. 189, August 16, 1946, Jewish Telegraphic Agency, http://pdfs.jta.org/1946/1946-08-16_189.pdf.

268. Grajcar interview, tape 5, minutes 11–29.

269. Feinstein, *Holocaust Survivors in Postwar Germany*, 295–297.

270. Rich, *Little Girl Lost*, 131–170.

271. Badner interview, tape 2, minutes 17–21.

272. Zynger interview, tape 2.

273. Bell interview, tape 3, minutes 3–5.

274. Berger, *Displaced Persons*, 26.

275. Zuberman interview, tape 4, minute 26, through tape 5, minute 8.

276. Herman Taube, oral history interview, February 15, 2010, USHMM, RG-50.106°0182, Part 3, minutes 29–44.

277. Abel interview, tape 4, minutes 10–18.

278. Cohen, "Choosing *A Heim*," 49.

279. Boris Baum, VHA Interview 11354, Hallandale, FL, January 25, 1996, tape 2, minutes 15–23.

280. Bronia Zisfain, VHA Interview 06910, North Miami Beach, FL, September 19, 1995, tape 2, minutes 9–12.

281. Bergman interview, tape 3, minutes 9–17.

282. Marcos Silber, "'Immigrants from Poland Want to Go Back': The Politics of Return Migration and Nation Building in 1950s Israel," *Journal of Israeli History* 27, no. 2 (2008): 209–211, 204.

283. Bell interview, tape 3, minutes 6–8.

284. Celia Balavram, VHA Interview 24371, Del Ray Beach, FL, December 20, 1996.

285. Cohen, "Choosing *A Heim*," 49.

286. Hasia Diner, *We Remember with Reverence and Love: American Jews and the Myth of Silence after the Holocaust, 1945–1962* (New York: New York University Press, 2009). See also David Cesarani and Eric J. Sundquist, eds., *After the Holocaust: Challenging the Myth of Silence* (London: Routledge, 2012); and Eliyana R. Adler and Sheila E. Jelen, eds., *Reconstructing the Old Country: American Jewry in the Post-Holocaust Decades* (Detroit: Wayne State University Press, 2017).

287. See, for example, Tom Segev, *The Seventh Million: The Israelis and the Holocaust* (New York: Hill and Wang, 1993); Roni Stauber, *The Holocaust in Israeli Public Debate in the 1950s: Ideology and Memory* (London: Vallentine Mitchell, 2007); Dina Porat, *Israeli Society, the Holocaust and its Survivors* (London: Vallentine Mitchell, 2008); and Boaz Cohen,

Israeli Holocaust Research: Birth and Evolution (New York: Routledge, 2013).

288. Mark L. Smith, "No Silence in Yiddish: Popular and Scholarly Writing about the Holocaust in the Early Postwar Years," in Cesarani and Sundquist, eds., *After the Holocaust*, 55.

289. Arnold Zable, *Cafe Scheherazade* (Melbourne: Text Publishing, 2001), 101.

Conclusion

Epigraph: Arnold Zable, *Cafe Scheherazade* (Melbourne: Text Publishing, 2001), 50.

1. Mark Edele, Sheila Fitzpatrick, John Goldlust, and Atina Grossmann, "Introduction," in *Shelter from the Holocaust: Rethinking Jewish Survival in the Soviet Union,* ed. Mark Edele, Sheila Fitzpatrick, and Atina Grossmann (Detroit: Wayne State University Press, 2017), 8.

2. James E. Young, "The Biography of a Memorial Icon: Nathan Rapoport's Warsaw Ghetto Monument," *Representations* 26 (1989): 75, 81.

3. More information about the program can be found at "About the Righteous," Yad Vashem, website: http://www.yadvashem.org/righteous/about -the-righteous. The citation exists in two versions: the Babylonian Talmud, Sanhedrin 37a, and the Jerusalem Talmud, Sanhedrin 4:1.

4. Debórah Dwork, "Refugee Jews and the Holocaust: Luck, Fortuitous Circumstances, and Timing," in *"Wer bleibt, opfert seine Jahre, vielleicht sein Leben": deutsche Juden 1938–1941,* ed. Susanne Heim, Beate Meyer, and Francis R. Nicosia (Göttingen: Wallstein Verlag, 2010), 281, 282.

5. See, for example, Marion A. Kaplan, *Between Dignity and Despair: Jewish Life in Nazi Germany* (Oxford: Oxford University Press, 1988); Marion A. Kaplan, *Dominican Haven: The Jewish Refugee Settlement in Sosúa, 1940–1945* (New York: Museum of Jewish Heritage, 2008); and Marion A. Kaplan, *Hitler's Jewish Refugees: Hope and Anxiety in Portugal* (New Haven, CT: Yale University Press, 2020).

6. Doris L. Bergen, *War and Genocide: A Concise History of the Holocaust,* third edition (Lanham, MD: Rowman and Littlefield, 2016), 79, 121–126.

7. Bergen, *War and Genocide,* 135, 192–194, 133, 295.

8. Doris L. Bergen, *War and Genocide: A Concise History of the Holocaust,* second edition (Lanham, MD: Rowman and Littlefield, 2009).

9. See, for example, Kobi Kabalek, "Edges of History and Memory: The 'Final Stage' of the Holocaust," *Dapim* 29, no. 3 (2015): 240–263.

10. For just one example among many, see Gabrielle Anderl and Walter Manoschek, *Gescheiterte Flucht—Der jüdische "Kladovo-Transport" auf*

dem Weg nach Palästina 1939–42 (Vienna: Verlag für Gesellschaftskritik, 1993).

11. For more on how these studies can be relevant, see, for example, Eliyana R. Adler, "Singing Their Way Home," *Polin* 32 (2019): 411–428; and Eliyana R. Adler, "The Miracle of Hanukkah and Other Orthodox Tales of Survival in Soviet Exile during World War II," *Dapim* 32, no. 3 (2018): 155–171.

12. See Gulag History Museum, website, https://gmig.ru/en/; and Gulag Museum at Perm-36, website: Мемориальный Музей-заповедник истории политических репрессий «Пермь-36» http://perm36.com.

13. Masha Gessen and Misha Friedman, *Never Remember: Searching for Stalin's Gulags in Putin's Russia* (New York: Columbia Global Reports, 2018). See also, "Revamped Perm-36 Museum Emphasizes Gulag's 'Contribution to Victory,'" July 25, 2015, Radio Free Europe / Radio Liberty, https://www.rferl.org/a/russia-perm-gulag-museum-takeover -contribution-to-victory/27152188.html.

14. Among other works in English, see Pavel Polian, *Against Their Will: The History and Geography of Forced Migrations in the USSR* (Budapest: Central European University Press, 2004); Lisa A. Kirschenbaum, *The Legacy of the Siege of Leningrad, 1941–1945: Myth, Memories, and Monuments* (Cambridge: Cambridge University Press, 2006); Rebecca Manley, *To the Tashkent Station: Evacuation and Survival in the Soviet Union at War* (Ithaca, NY: Cornell University Press, 2009); Paul Stronski, *Tashkent: Forging a Soviet City, 1930–1966* (Pittsburgh: University of Pittsburgh Press, 2010); Wendy Z. Goldman, *Hunger and War: Food Provisioning in the Soviet Union during World War II* (Bloomington: Indiana University Press, 2015); Tarik Cyril Amar, *The Paradox of Ukrainian Lviv: A Borderland City between Stalinists, Nazis, and Nationalists* (Ithaca, NY: Cornell University Press, 2015); Sergey Yarov, *Leningrad 1941–42: Morality in a City under Siege* (Cambridge: Polity, 2017); Larry E. Holmes, *Stalin's World War II Evacuations: Triumph and Troubles in Kirov* (Lawrence: University of Kansas Press, 2017); and Mark Edele, *Stalin's Defectors: How Red Army Soldiers Became Hitler's Collaborators, 1941–1945* (Oxford: Oxford University Press, 2017).

15. Anna Shternshis, *When Sonia Met Boris: An Oral History of Jewish Life under Stalin* (Oxford: Oxford University Press, 2017), 11.

16. Yehoshua A. Gilboa, *Confess! Confess! Eight Years in Soviet Prisons* (Boston: Little, Brown, 1968), 102.

17. Dovid Sfard, *Mit zich un mit andere: oytobiografye un literarishe eseyen* (Jerusalem: Farlag "Yerusholaimer almanakh," 1984), 143–145.

18. See, for example, Anna Shternshis, *Soviet and Kosher: Jewish Popular Culture in the Soviet Union, 1923–1939* (Bloomington: Indiana University Press, 2006); Elissa Bemporad, *Becoming Soviet Jews: The Bolshevik Experiment in Minsk* (Bloomington: Indiana University Press, 2013); Jeffrey Veidlinger, *In the Shadow of the Shtetl: Small-Town Jewish Life in Soviet Ukraine* (Bloomington: Indiana University Press, 2013); and Mordechai Altshuler, *Religion and Jewish Identity in the Soviet Union, 1941–1964* (Waltham, MA: Brandeis University Press, 2012).

19. Shternshis, *When Sonia Met Boris*, 192–193 and passim.

20. Veidlinger, *In the Shadow of the Shtetl*, chap. 9; Zvi Gitelman, *A Century of Ambivalence: The Jews of Russia and the Soviet Union, 1881 to the Present*, 2nd ed. (Bloomington: Indiana University Press, 2001), chap. 6; Yaacov Ro'i, "The Reconstruction of Jewish Communities in the USSR, 1944–1947," in *The Jews Are Coming Back: The Return of Jews to their Countries of Origin after WWII*, ed. David Bankier (Jerusalem: Yad Vashem, 2005); Yaacov Ro'i, "The Role of the Synagogue and Religion in the Jewish National Reawakening," in *Jewish Culture and Identity in the Soviet Union*, ed. Yaacov Ro'i and Avi Beker (New York: New York University Press, 1991).

21. Shimon Redlich, *Propaganda and Nationalism in Wartime Russia: The Jewish Antifascist Committee in the USSR, 1941–1948* (Boulder, CO: East European Monographs, 1982), 62.

22. Benjamin Pinkus, *The Jews of the Soviet Union: The History of a National Minority* (Cambridge: Cambridge University Press, 1988), 138.

23. Many scholars have noted this result of German occupation. In the introduction to her 1966 revised edition of *On the Origins of Totalitarianism*, Arendt suggests that German antisemitism even influenced Stalin in his postwar policies: "The open, unashamed adoption of what had become to the whole world the most prominent sign of Nazism was the last compliment Stalin paid to his late colleague and rival in total domination with whom, much to his chagrin, he had not been able to come to a lasting agreement." See Hannah Arendt, *The Origins of Totalitarianism*, rev. ed. (New York: Harcourt, Brace and World, 1966), xxiv.

24. Sheila Fitzpatrick, "Annexation, Evacuation, and Antisemitism in the Soviet Union, 1939–1946," in Edele, Fitzpatrick, and Grossmann, eds., *Shelter from the Holocaust*, 141.

25. This anecdote comes from a conversation with a woman who did not wish to be identified.

26. Elżbieta Janicka, *Festung Warschau* (Warsaw: Wydawnictwo Krytyki Politycznej, 2011), 83–93.

27. Lidia Zessin-Jurek, "The Rise of an East European Community of Memory? On Lobbying for the Gulag Memory via Brussels," in *Memory*

and Change in Europe: Eastern Perspectives, ed. Małgorzata Pakier and Joanna Wawrzyniak (New York: Berghahn Books, 2016), 138, 143.

28. Rabbi Avraham Steinberg, Interview, Ganzach Kiddush Hashem Archives, Testimonies and Interviews, Israel, August 29, 2010, minutes 45–47.

29. The Parish of St. Agnes in Kraków is dedicated to the military and contains named plaques of high-ranking officers killed in the massacre, including the one reading "Mjr Rabin Baruch Steinberg, lat 43, Starobielsk."

30. Bob Golan, *A Long Way Home: The Story of a Jewish Youth, 1939–1949,* ed. Jacob Howland (Lanham, MD: University Press of America, 2005), 37.

31. Lidia Zessin-Jurek, "Forgotten Memory? Vicissitudes of the Gulag Remembrance in Poland," in *Life Writing and Politics of Memory in Eastern Europe,* ed. Simona Mitroiu (New York: Palgrave Macmillan, 2015), 59–61.

32. Zessin-Jurek, "Forgotten Memory?," 60.

33. For a collection of articles translated into Polish about the Jewish experience of Soviet exile, see Lidia Zessin-Jurek and Katharina Friedla, eds., *Syberiada Żydów polskich* (Warsaw: Wydawnictwo Żydowski Instytut Historyczny, forthcoming).

34. Vasily Grossman, *Life and Fate: A Novel,* trans. Robert Chandler (New York: Harper and Row, 1986), 19.

35. John Garrard and Carol Garrard, *The Bones of Berdichev: The Life and Fate of Vasily Grossman* (New York: Free Press, 1996), 259.

36. Garrard and Garrard, *The Bones of Berdichev,* 291.

37. Katarina Clark, "Ehrenburg and Grossman: Two Cosmopolitan Jewish Writers Reflect on Nazi Germany at War," *Kritika* 10, no. 3 (2009): 626.

38. Arendt, *The Origins of Totalitarianism.*

39. Jewish Book Council, "National Jewish Book Awards: Past Winners, 1978," https://www.jewishbookcouncil.org/awards/national-jewish-book -awards/past-winners?year=1978.

40. Terrence Des Pres, *The Survivor: An Anatomy of Life in the Death Camps* (New York: Washington Square, 1976), 133.

41. Primo Levi, *The Reawakening* (New York: Collier Books, 1993), 222–223.

42. Ernst Nolte, "Between Myth and Revisionism? The Third Reich in the Perspective of the 1980s," in *Aspects of the Third Reich,* ed. H. W. Koch (London: Macmillan, 1985), 36.

43. Dominick LaCapra, "Representing the Holocaust: Reflections on the Historians' Debate," in *Probing the Limits of Representation: Nazism and the "Final Solution,"* ed. Saul Friedländer (Cambridge, MA: Harvard University Press, 1992), 113.

44. Timothy Snyder, *Bloodlands: Europe between Hitler and Stalin* (New York: Basic Books, 2010), xix.

45. Mark Roseman, "Timothy Snyder, *Bloodlands: Europe between Hitler and Stalin*" (review), *Journal of Genocide Research* 13, no. 3 (2011): 323, 325.

46. Mark Mazower, "Timothy Snyder's Bloodlands," *Contemporary European History* 21, no. 2 (2012): 120–121.

47. Dan Diner, "Topography of Interpretation: Reviewing Timothy Snyder's *Bloodlands*," *Contemporary European History* 21, no. 2 (2012): 130, 131.

48. Dan Michman, "*Bloodlands* and the Holocaust: Some Reflections on Terminology, Conceptualization and Their Consequences," *Journal of Modern European History / Zeitschrift für moderne europäische Geschichte / Revue d'histoire européenne contemporaine* 10, no. 4 (2012): 443–444.

49. Dovid Katz, "Why Red Is Not Brown in the Baltics," *Guardian*, September 30, 2010, https://www.theguardian.com/commentisfree/cifamerica/2010/sep/30/baltic-nazi-soviet-snyder. See also the articles at Dovid Katz, "Respectfully Disagreeing with Professor Timothy Snyder," Defending History, http://defendinghistory.com/30081/30081.

50. Roseman, "Timothy Snyder, *Bloodlands*," 324.

Bibliography

Readers who wish to consult a full bibliography, including secondary sources, are invited to visit openpublishing.psu.edu/survivalmargins

Archival Collections

AJCA   American Jewish Committee Archives, New York, http://ajcarchives
       .org/main.php
APRK   Arkhiv Prezidenta Respubliki Kazakhstan (Archive of the Presi-
       dent of the Republic of Kazakhstan), Almaty, Kazakhstan
       Fond 8 Alma-Ata Regional Committee of the Communist Party of
           Kazakhstan
       Fond 12 Communist Party of the Talgar District of the Republic of
           Kazakhstan
       Fond 708 Central Committee of the Communist Party of Kazakh-
           stan in the city of Alma-Ata
APW   Archiwum Panstwowe we Wroclawiu (State Archive of Wrocław),
       Wrocław, Poland
       41/III Provincial Office in Wrocław
       324/III Jewish Provincial Committee for Lower Silesia
AŻIH   Archiwum Żydowskiego Instytutu Historychnego w Warszawie
       (Archive of the Jewish Historical Institute of Warsaw), Warsaw
       RG 301 Testimonies
       RG 303/V/984 Central Committee of the Jews of Poland, Depart-
           ment of Statistics 1945–1950
       RG S/333 Bernard Mark Collection

DALO Derzhavnii Arkhiv L'vivskoi Oblasti (State Archive of Lviv Oblast), Lviv, Ukraine
Fond P-119 Lviv University
Fond P-163 Educational Authority, 1939
Fond P-238 Lviv Prosecutor, 1939
Fond P-300 Temporary Authority for the City of Lvov, 1939

FVA Fortunoff Video Archive for Holocaust Testimonies, Yale University Library

GKH Ganzach Kiddush Hashem Archives, Bnei Brak, Israel
Flinker Collection
Testimonies and Interviews

HIA Hoover Institution Archives, Stanford University
Poland, Ambassada (Soviet Union)
Poland, Ministerstwo Informacji i Dokumentacji
Wladyslaw Anders Collection

JDCA American Jewish Joint Distribution Committee Archives, New York and Jerusalem

JTA Jewish Telegraphic Agency Archive, New York, https://www.jta.org/archive

Moreshet Archives Mordechai Anielevich Memorial Holocaust Study and Research Center, Givat Haviva, Israel
A.1488 Testimonies
C.54 Shlomo Kless Archive
D.1 Kushta Collection (Constantinople)

OHD Oral History Division, Avraham Harman Institute of Contemporary Jewry, Hebrew University of Jerusalem, http://multimedia.huji.ac.il/oralhistory/eng/about-en.html
Project 101 Jews from the Areas Annexed to the USSR in World War II
Project 170 Rescue of Soviet Jewry via Teheran
Project 220 Anders' Army Defectors in Eretz Israel

PISM Polish Institute and Sikorski Museum Archive, London
A.7 Embassy of the Polish Republic in Moscow and Kuybyshev, 1941–1943
A.11 Ministry of Foreign Affairs

TsDIAL Tsentral'nii derzhavnii istorichnii arkhiv Ukraini, Lviv (Central State Historical Archives of Ukraine in Lviv), Lviv, Ukraine

TsGARK Tsentral'nyi gosudarstvennyi arkhiv Respubliki Kazakhstan (Central State Archive of the Republic of Kazakhstan), Almaty, Kazakhstan

Fond R-1125 Kazakh Central Committee for International
Aid to Fighters for the Revolution of the Kazakh
SSR

Fond R-1137 Council of the Ministers of the Kazakh SSR

Fond R-1146 Military Commission of the Kazakh SSR

Fond R-1692 Ministry of Education of the Kazakh SSR

USHMM   United States Holocaust Memorial Museum, Washington, DC
Photo Archives

RG-10.055°01 Herman Taube Collection

RG-15.107M Society for Safeguarding the Health of the Jewish
Population in Poland (TOZ)

RG-15.341 Union of Polish Patriots in the USSR (ZPP)

RG-50 Oral Testimonies

RG-67.011 Records of the New York Office of the World Jewish
Congress

VHA   University of Southern California Shoah Foundation Visual History
Archive, Los Angeles

YUA   Yeshiva University Archives, New York
Vaad Hatzala Collection

YVA   Yad Vashem Archives, Jerusalem

M.10 ARI Ringelblum Archives

M.27 Public Record Office, London: Documentation Pertaining to
Jewish Matters

M.41 Archives in Belarus

M.52 Documentation from Regional Archives in the Ukraine

O.3 Oral Testimonies

O.17 YIVO Testimonies Collection

O.32 Soviet Union Collection

O.33 Letters and Diaries

O.54 JM/10005 National and Provincial Archives in Poland

P.20 Dr. Zorach Warhaftig Collection

Published Documentary Collections

Abylkhozhin, B. Zh., L. D. Degitaeva, E. M. Zulkasheva, and M. U. Maskeev, eds. *Iz istorii Poliakov v Kazakhstane (1936–1956 gg.): Sbornik dokumentov.* Almaty, Kazakhstan: "Qazaqstan," 2000.

Afans'ev, Iu. N., and V. P. Kozlov. eds. *Istoriia stalinskogo Gulaga.* Vol. 4, *Naselenie Gulaga: chislennost' i usloviia soderzhaniia.* Vol. 5, *Spetspereselentsy v SSSR.* Moscow: ROSSPEN, 2004.

Arad, Yitzhak, Israel Gutman, and Abraham Margaliot, eds. *Documents on the Holocaust: Selected Sources on the Destruction of the Jews of Germany and Austria, Poland and the Soviet Union.* 8th ed. Lincoln: University of Nebraska Press/Yad Vashem, 1999.

Beizer, Michael, and Mikhail Mitsel. *The American Brother: The "Joint" in Russia, the USSR and the CIS.* New York: American Jewish Joint Distribution Committee, 2004.

Cienciala, Anna M., Natalia S. Lebedeva, and Wojciech Materski, eds. *Katyn: A Crime without Punishment.* Translated by Marian Schwartz with Anna M. Cienciala and Maia Kipp. New Haven, CT: Yale University Press, 2007.

Dokumenty i Materiały do Historii Stosunków Polsko-Radzieckich. Vol. 7. Warsaw: Książka i Wiedza, 1973.

Dokumenty i materialy po istorii sovetsko-pol'skikh otnoshenii. Vol. 7. Moscow: Izdantel'stvo "Nauka," 1973.

Formakov, Arsenii. *Gulag Letters.* Edited and translated by Emily D. Johnson. New Haven, CT: Yale University Press, 2017.

General Sikorski Historical Institute. *Documents on Polish-Soviet Relations, 1933–1945.* Vol. 1, *1933–1943.* London: Heinemann, 1961.

Grudzinska-Gross, Irena, and Jan Tomasz Gross, eds. *War through Children's Eyes: The Soviet Occupation of Poland and the Deportations, 1939–1941.* Stanford, CA: Hoover Institution Press, 1981.

Grynberg, Henryk. *Children of Zion.* Translated by Jacqueline Mitchell. Evanston, IL: Northwestern University Press, 1997.

Huberband, Rabbi Shimon. *Kiddush Hashem: Jewish Religious and Cultural Life in Poland During the Holocaust.* Edited by Jeffrey S. Gurrock and Robert S. Hirt. Translated by David E. Fishman. Hoboken, NJ: Ktav, 1987.

Jarausch, Konrad H., ed. *Reluctant Accomplice: A Wehrmacht Soldier's Letters from the Eastern Front.* Princeton, NJ: Princeton University Press, 2011.

Jasni, A. Volf. *Sefer Yadov: Yadov-bukh.* Jerusalem: Ensiklopediah shel galuyot, 1966.

Kermish, Joseph, ed. *To Live with Honor and Die with Honor! Selected Documents from the Warsaw Ghetto Underground Archives "O. S." (Oneg Shabbath).* Jerusalem: Yad Vashem, 1986.

Kot, Stanislaw. *Conversations with the Kremlin and Dispatches from Russia.* London: Oxford University Press, 1963.

Kugelmass, Jack, and Jonathan Boyarin, eds. *From a Ruined Garden: The Memorial Books of Polish Jewry.* 2nd ed. Bloomington: Indiana University Press, 1998.

Levin, Dov. *Historian's Testimony: A Collection of Oral History Abstracts.* Jerusalem: Hebrew University Magnes Press, 2013.

Levin, Shalom Duber, ed. *Toldot Habad be-Rusya ha-Sovetit: ba-shanim 678–710.* Brooklyn, NY: Kehot, 1989.

Niewyk, Donald L. *Fresh Wounds: Early Narratives of Holocaust Survival.* Chapel Hill: University of North Carolina Press, 1998.

Pobol', N. L., and P. M. Polian, eds. *Stalinskie deportatsii: 1928–1953.* Moscow: Materik, 2005.

Polish Embassy in Washington. *Polish-Soviet Relations 1918–1943: Official Documents Issued by the Polish Embassy in Washington by Authority of the Government of the Republic of Poland.* Washington, DC: Polish Embassy in Washington, 1943.

Prais, Lea, ed. *Ba-'arafel ha-nedudim: asufat 'eduyot shel plitim Yehudim me-arkhion 'oneg shabat, 1939–1942.* Translated by Shoshana Ronen. Jerusalem: Yad Vashem: 2014.

Redlich, Shimon, ed. *War, Holocaust and Stalinism: A Documentary Study of the Jewish Anti-Fascist Committee in the USSR.* Oxford: Harwood Academic Publishing, 1995.

Republic of Poland, Ministry of Foreign Affairs, *Official Documents Concerning Polish-German and Polish-Soviet Relations 1933–1939.* New York: Roy, 1940.

Schneersohn, Joseph Isaac. *Igrot-kodesh.* 18 vols. Brooklyn, NY: Kehot, 1982–1985.

Shlomi, Hana. *Asupat mehkarim le-toldot she'erit ha-pletah ha-Yehudit be-Polin, 1944–1950.* Tel Aviv: Tel Aviv University, 2001.

Siekierski, Maciej, and Feliks Tych, eds. *Widziałem Anioła Śmierci: losy deportowanych Żydów polskich w ZSRR w latach II wojny światowej.* Warsaw: Rosner i Wspólnicy, 2006.

The Tragedy of Polish Jewry. Jerusalem: Joint Committee for the Aid of the Jews of Poland, 1940. Reprint, South Deerfield, MA: Schoen Books, 2005.

Tułacze Dzieci = Exiled Children. Warsaw: Fundacja Archiwum Fotograficzne Tułacze, 1995.

Wohlgemuth, Juda Ari. *Pesah 5702 be-Novosibirsk: Pesach 1942 in Nobosibirsk (Siberia).* London: G. J. George, 1963.

Wróbel, Janusz, and Joanna Żelazko, eds. *Polskie dzieci na tułaczych szlakach 1939–1950.* Warsaw: Instytut Pamięci Narodowej, 2008.

Żbikowski, Andrzej. *Archiwum Ringelbluma: konspiracyjne Archiwum Getta Warszawy.* Vol. 3, *Relacje z Kresów.* Warsaw: Żydowski Instytut Historyczny, 2000.

Zeltser, Arkadi, ed. *To Pour Out My Bitter Soul: Letters of Jews from the USSR, 1941–1945.* Translated by Yisrael Elliot Cohen. Jerusalem: Yad Vashem, 2016.

Memorial Books

Apenszlak, Jacob, ed. *The Black Book of Polish Jewry: An Account of the Martyrdom of Polish Jewry under the Nazi Occupation (1943).* Edited by Arno Lustiger. Frankfurt, Germany: Syndikat Buchgesellschaft, 1995.

Bernstein, Mordechai, ed. *Pinkes Zamoshtsh: yizker-bukh tsum fuftsntn yortsayt (1942–1957) nokh der ershter shihite fun di Zamoshtsher Yidn.* Buenos Aires: Tsentral-Komitet far Pinkes Zamoshtsh, 1957.

Cohen, Eliezer Tsvi. *Bene ha-'ayarah mesaprim.* Bnei Brak, Israel: Yots'e Horodlo be-erets Yisra'el, 2000.

Der Bialystoker yizkor buch. New York: Bialystoker Center, 1982.

Flinker, Dovid. *Varshe.* In *'Arim ve-imahot be-Yisra'el: matsevet kodesh li-kehilot Yisra'el she-nehrevu bi-yede 'aritsim ve-temaim ba-milhemet ha-'olam ha-aharonah,* vol. 3, edited by Ha-rav Y. L. ha-Kohen Fishman. Jerusalem: Mosad ha-Rav Kook, 1946.

Jasni, Wolf, ed. *Sefer Yadov (Jadow) Yadov-bukh.* Jerusalem: Ensiklopediah shel galuyot, 1966.

Kanc, Shimon. *Sefer zikaron Otvotsk, Karts'ev.* Tel Aviv: Irgun yots'e Otvotsk be-Yisra'el, 1968.

Kaplinski, Barukh. *Pinkes Hrubyeshov: tsum 20-tn yortog nakh dem groyzamen khurbn fun unzer gevezener heym.* Tel Aviv: Irgun yoytse Hrubyeshov in Yisroel un in di Fareynikte Shtatn mit der hilf fun di Hrubyeshover landsmanshaftn in gor der velt, 1962.

Kronenberg, Avraham, ed. *Khurbn Bilgoraj.* Tel Aviv: Irgun yots'e Bilgoray, 1956.

Lifshits, Yerahmiel, ed. *Sefer Svislots B: mikets te'ude, perakim nivharim, reshimat bate-av, ma'amarim, 'eduyot, temunut, u-masmakhim.* Netanya, Israel: Irgun yots'e Svislots be-Yisra'el, 1984.

Our Roots = Shorashim Shelanu: In Memory to the Victims of the Holocaust, 1939–1945. Tel Aviv: Einat, 1992.

Porat, Eliyahu, ed. *Sefer Kotsk.* Tel Aviv: Va'ad irgun yots'e Kotsk be-Yisra'el, 1961.

Sharvit, Elazar. *Sanok: sefer zikharon le-kehilat Sanok ve-ha-sevivah.* Jerusalem: Irgun yots'e Sanok ve-ha-sevivah be-Yisra'el, 1970.

Tchorsh, Katriel Fishel, and Meir Korzen, eds. *Vlotslavek un umgegnt: yizker-bukh.* Tel Aviv: Irgun yots'e Velotslavek ve-ha-sevivah be-Yisrael uve-Artsot ha-Brit, 1967.

Literary Sources

Broderzon, Moyshe. *Dos letste lid.* Tel Aviv: I. L. Peretz, 1974.

Frajlich, Anna. *Between Dawn and the Wind.* Translated by Regina Grol. Austin, TX: Host Publications, 2006.

Grossman, Vasily. *Life and Fate: A Novel.* Translated by Robert Chandler. New York: Harper and Row, 1986.

Grynberg, Henryk. *Children of Zion.* Translated by Jacqueline Mitchell. Evanston, IL: Northwestern University Press, 1997.

———. *The Jewish War and the Victory.* Translated by Henryk Grynberg, Richard Lourie, and Celina Wieniewska. Evanston, IL: Northwestern University Press, 2001.

Heller, Binem. *Zey veln oyfshteyn.* Tel Aviv: I. L. Peretz Farlag, 1984.

Howe, Irving, Ruth R. Wisse, and Khone Shmeruk, eds. *The Penguin Book of Modern Yiddish Verse.* New York: Viking Penguin, 1987.

Kassow, Samuel D., and David Suchoff, eds. *In Those Nightmarish Days: The Ghetto Reportage of Peretz Opoczynski and Josef Zelkowicz.* Translated by David Suchoff. New Haven, CT: Yale University Press, 2015.

Klepfisz, Irena. *A Few Words in the Mother Tongue: Poems Selected and New (1971–1990).* Portland, OR: Eighth Mountain, 1990.

Korn, Rachel. *Generations: Selected Poems.* Edited by Seymour Mayne. Oakville, Ontario: Mosaic Press, 1982.

———. *Paper Roses.* Translated by Seymour Levitan. Toronto: Aya, 1985.

Korn, Rokhl H. *Bashertkeyt: lider 1928–1948.* Montreal: R. Korn, 1949.

Kviatkovski-Pinchasik, Rivka. *In zikhere hent.* Haifa: Farlag, 1965.

Mann, Mendel. *At the Gates of Moscow.* Translated by Christopher Derrick and I. M. Lask. London: Macmillan, 1963.

———. *Seeds in the Desert.* Translated by Heather Valencia. Amherst, MA: Yiddish Book Center, 2019.

Markish, Peretz. *Inheritance (Yerushe).* Edited by Mary Schulman, Joan Braman, and David Weintraub. Translated by Mary Schulman. Toronto: TSAR, 2007.

Neweroff, Alexander. *City of Bread.* New York: George H. Doran Company, 1927.

Opoczynski, Peretz. *Reportazhshn fun Varshaver geto.* Edited by Ber Mark. Warsaw: Yidish-bukh, 1954.

Polonsky, Antony, and Monika Adamczyk-Garbowska, eds. *Contemporary Jewish Writing in Poland: An Anthology.* Lincoln: University of Nebraska Press, 2001.

Roskies, David G., ed. *Voices from the Warsaw Ghetto: Writing Our History.* New Haven, CT: Yale University Press, 2019.

Ruta, Magdalena, ed. *Nisht bay di taykhn fun bovl: antologye fun der Yidisher poezye in nokhmilhomedikn Poyln = Nie nad rzekami Babilonu: antologia poezji jidysz w powojennej Polsce.* Kraków: Księgarnia Akademicka, 2012.

Shulevitz, Uri. *How I Learned Geography.* New York: Farrar, Straus and Giroux, 2008.

Taube, Herman. *Autumn Travels: Devious Paths: Poetry and Prose.* Washington, DC: Dryad, 1992.

———. *Kyzl Kishlak: Refugee Village.* Washington, DC: Olami, 1993.

———. *Looking Back, Going Forward: New and Selected Poems.* Takoma Park, MD: Dryad, 2002.

Zable, Arnold. *Cafe Scheherazade.* Melbourne: Text Publishing, 2001.

Audiovisual Media

Alberstein, Chava, and the Klezmatics. *The Well.* Nashville: Xenophile Records, 1998, CD.

Gross, Natan, dir. *Der Yidisher yishev in Nidershleyze,* 1947. YouTube, https://www.youtube.com/watch?v=5q82LKt7Zi0.

———, and Shaul Goskind, dirs. *Unzere kinder,* 1948. Rerelease, Waltham, MA: National Center for Jewish Film, 1991, DVD.

Grunberg, Slawomir, and Robert Podgursky, dirs. *Saved by Deportation: An Unknown Odyssey of Polish Jews.* Los Angeles: Seventh Art Releasing, 2007, DVD.

Lichtenstein, Ruth, and Gi Orman, dirs. *Rosja: Escaping Hitler Was Only the Beginning.* Brooklyn, NY: Project Witness, 2018, DVD.

Seltmann, Gabriela von, and Uwe von Seltmann, dirs. *Boris Dorfman: A Mentsh.* Yonkers, NY: LOGTV Ltd., 2014, DVD.

Sinai, Khosrow, dir. *The Lost Requiem.* Tehran: CMI, 1983, DVD.

Urban, Stuart, dir. *Tovarisch, I Am Not Dead.* London: Cyclops Vision, 2008, DVD.

Diaries, Memoirs, Autobiographies, and Anthologies

Ajzen, Chaim. *Chaim Ajzen Remembers.* Melbourne: C. Ajzen, 2001.

Alexander, Aleksandra (Oleńka). *To My Dear Daughters Inka and Nana: Tracing the Past.* N.p.: A. Alexander, n.d.

Applebaum, Anne. *Gulag Voices: An Anthology.* New Haven, CT: Yale University Press, 2011.

Auerbach, Rachel. *Varshaver tsavoes: bagegenishn, aktivitetn, goyrlos, 1933–1943.* Tel Aviv: Yisroel Bukh, 1974.

Azrieli, Danna J. *One Step Ahead: David J. Azrieli (Azrylewicz), Memoirs: 1939–1950.* Jerusalem: Yad Vashem, 2001.

Bar, Miriam. *Lelot Tashkent.* Tel Aviv: Levin-Epshtein, 1970.

Bauman, Janina. *A Dream of Belonging: My Years in Postwar Poland.* London: Virago, 1988.

Beever, Antony, and Luba Vinogradova, eds. and trans. *A Writer at War: Vasily Grossman with the Red Army 1941–1945.* New York: Pantheon Books, 2005.

Begin, Menachem. *White Nights: The Story of a Prisoner in Russia.* Translated by Katie Kaplan. New York: Harper and Row, 1977.

Berger, Joseph. *Displaced Persons: Growing Up American after the Holocaust.* New York: Scribner, 2001.

Bichler, Abraham. *Little Miracles: A Story of Courage, Faith and Survival.* Raleigh, NC: Ivy House, 2004.

Blenkitni, Ahron. *Goyrl: iberlebungen fun a Yidisher mishpokhe in der tsveyter velt-milkhome.* Tel Aviv: I. L. Peretz, 1968.

Boder, David P. *I Did Not Interview the Dead.* Urbana: University of Illinois Press, 1949.

Boren, Adam. *Journey through the Inferno.* Washington, DC: United States Holocaust Memorial Museum/Holocaust Survivors' Memoirs Project, 2004.

Brandshpigel, David. *Hisardut: sipur hayehem shel ha-Yehudim bi-Vrit ha-Moʻatsot bi-zeman milhemet ha-ʻolam ha-sheniyah.* Holon: D. Brandshpigel, 1998.

Broderzon, Sheyne-Miriam. *Mayn laydns-veg mit Moyshe Broderzon.* Buenos Aires: Tsentral farband fun Poylishe Yidn in Argentine, 1960.

Bryan, Julien. *Siege.* New York: Doubleday, Doran, 1940.

Carmi, Krystyna. *The Strange Ways of Providence in My Life.* North Charleston, SC: CreateSpace Independent Publishing Platform, 2015.

Chesno, Zekharia. *Kol ha-neharot zormot le-Yarden: zikhronot.* Jerusalem: Philobiblion, 2008.

Chiger, Krystyna, and Daniel Paisner. *The Girl in the Green Sweater: A Life in Holocaust's Shadow.* New York: St. Martin's, 2008.

Choko, Isabelle, Frances Irwin, Lotti Kahana-Aufleger, Margit Raab Kalina, and Jane Lipski. *Stolen Youth: Five Women's Survival in the Holocaust.* New York: Yad Vashem/Holocaust Survivors' Memoirs Project, 2005.

Cywiak, Rabbi Samuel, with Jeff Swesky. *Flight from Fear: A Rabbi's Holocaust Survival Story.* Palm Coast, FL: Jeff Swesky, 2010.

Czapski, Joseph. *The Inhuman Land.* Translated by Gerald Hopkins. London: Polish Cultural Foundation, 1987.

Davidson, Simon. *My War Years, 1939–1945.* Translated by Marie Morgens. San Antonio: University of Texas, 1981.

Dawidowicz, Lucy S. *From That Place and Time: A Memoir, 1938–1947.* New York: W. W. Norton, 1989.

Dekel, Mikhal. *Tehran Children: A Holocaust Refugee Odyssey.* New York: W. W. Norton, 2019.

Donat, Alexander. *The Holocaust Kingdom: A Memoir.* New York: Holt, Rinehart, and Winston, 1963.

Dunaevsky, Dov. *Be-hoshekh efshar rak la-halom.* Pardes Hanah-Karkur: Muzah, 2008.

Dzigan, Shimon. *Der koyekh fun Yidishn humor.* Tel Aviv: Orli, 1974.

Edison, Yitshak (Jerzy). *Mayne fir yor in Soviet-Rusland.* Paris: Gelbard, 1953.

Efron, Georgii. *The Diary of Georgy Efron, August 1942–August 1943 (the Tashkent Period).* Translated by Olga Zaslavsky. Lewiston, NY: Edwin Mellen Press, 2010.

Egit, Jacob. *Grand Illusion.* Toronto: Lugus, 1991.

———. *Tsu a nay lebn (tsvey yor Yidisher yishev in Nidershlezye).* Wrocław: Wydawnictwo "Niderszlezje", 1947.

Eibuszyc, Suzanna. *Memory Is Our Home: Loss and Remembering: Three Generations in Poland and Russia 1917–1960s.* Stuttgart: idedem-Verlag, 2015.

Elsner, Alan. *Guarded by Angels: How My Father and Uncle Survived Hitler and Cheated Stalin.* New York: Yad Vashem/Holocaust Survivors' Memoirs Project, 2005.

Elton, Zyga. *Destination Buchara.* Ripponlea, Australia: Dizal Nominees, 1996.

Erlichson, Yitzhak. *My Four Years in Soviet Russia.* Translated by Maurice Wolfthal. Boston: Academic Studies Press, 2013.

Farbstein, Esther. *The Forgotten Memoirs: Moving Personal Accounts from Rabbis Who Survived the Holocaust.* Brooklyn, NY: Shaar, 2011.

———, ed. *Mi-telz 'ad telz: yomano shel ha-rav Hayim Shtein T'Sh-TSh'D 1940–1944.* Jerusalem: Holocaust Research Center, 2015.

Feinzeig, Dovid. *Faith & Flight: A Young Boy's Memoir of the Prewar Shtetl, Shavuos in Ger, A Family's Travels through Russia, Rebuilding in Postwar Poland and France.* Lakewood, NJ: Israel Bookshop Publications, 2013.

Feldman, Israel Ignac. *The Lost Dream.* Toronto: Lorne Miller and Associates, 2007.

Feldman, Marian. *From Warsaw, through Łuck, Siberia, and Back to Warsaw.* Morrisville, NC: LuLu, 2009.

Friedman, Ellen G. *The Seven: A Family Holocaust Story.* Detroit: Wayne State University Press, 2017.

Frusztajer, Boruch B. *From Siberia to America: A Story of Survival and Success.* Scranton, PA: University of Scranton Press, 2008.

Fuks, Tania. *A vanderung iber okupirte gebitn.* Buenos Aires: Central farband fun Polishe Yidn in Argentine, 1947.

Gabel, Dina. *Behind the Ice Curtain.* New York: CIS, 1992.

Gheith, Jehanne M., and Katherine R. Jolluck, eds. *Gulag Voices: Oral Histories of Soviet Incarceration and Exile.* New York: Palgrave Macmillan, 2011.

Gilboa, Yehoshua A. *Confess! Confess! Eight Years in Soviet Prisons.* Translated by Dov Ben Aba. Boston: Little, Brown, 1968.

Ginsburg, Bernard L. *A Wayfarer in a World of Upheaval.* San Bernadino, CA: Borgo Press, 1993.

Golan, Bob. *A Long Way Home: The Story of a Jewish Youth, 1939–1949.* Edited by Jacob Howland. Lanham, MD: University Press of America, 2005.

Gold, Betty, with Mark Hodermarsky. *Beyond Trochenbrod: The Betty Gold Story.* Kent, OH: Kent State University Press, 2014.

Goldberger, Janka. *Stalin's Little Guest.* London: Janus, 1995.

Goldkorn, Yosef. *Navenad iber di shlyakhn fun Rusland.* Tel Aviv: H. Leivik, 1998.

Grade, Chaim. *My Mother's Sabbath Days: A Memoir.* Translated by Channa Kleinerman Goldstein and Inna Hecker Grade. New York: Schocken Books, 1987.

Gregoratos, Eva G. *An Unintended Odyssey: From War Torn Europe to America.* Bloomington, IN: AuthorHouse, 2008.

Grim, P. [Moshe Grossman]. *In Farkishuftn land fun legendarn Dzshugashvili: meyne zibn yor lebn in Ratnfarband—1939–1946.* Vol. 1. 2nd ed. Paris: Emes un frayhayt, 1950.

———. *In Farkishuftn land fun legendarn Dzshugashvili: meyne zibn yor lebn in Ratnfarband—1939–1946.* Vol. 2. Paris: "Emes un frayhayt, 1949.

Gross, Natan. *Who Are You, Mr. Grymek?* London: Vallentine Mitchell, 2001.

Grossman, Moshe. *In the Enchanted Land: My Seven Years in Soviet Russia.* Tel Aviv: Rachel, 1960.

Hadow, Maria. *Paying Guest in Siberia.* London: Harvill, 1959.

Halperin, Yosef. *Ne'urim be-azikim: be-Polin, u-ve-Belarus ba-milhemet-ha-olam-ha-sheniyah.* Tel Aviv: Moreshet, 2002.

Halpern, Ada. *Liberation—Russian Style.* London: Maxlove, 1945.

Hart, Kitty. *Return to Auschwitz: The Remarkable Life of a Girl Who Survived the Holocaust.* London: Sidgwick and Jackson, 1981.

Hartglas, Apolinary. *Na pograniczu dwóch światów.* Edited by Jolanta Żyndul. Warsaw: Oficyna Wydawnicza, 1996.

Hautzig, Esther. *The Endless Steppe: Growing Up in Siberia.* New York: HarperCollins, 1987.

Heler, Yehoshu'a Heshil. *Avo bi-gevurot: korot hayim u-firke zikhronot mi-Teshin (Polin) 'ad Bene Berak derekh 'arvot Sibir.* Bnei Brak, Israel: Y. H. Heller, 2009.

Heller, Binem. "Togbukh oyf tsurik." *Di Goldene Keyt* 123 (1987): 93–102.

Heller, Fanya Gottesfeld. *Love in a World of Sorrow: A Teenage Girl's Holocaust Memoirs.* Jerusalem: Geffen, 2015.

Herzbaum, Edward H. *Lost between Worlds: A World War II Journey of Survival.* Translated by Piotr Graff. Leicester, UK: Matador, 2010.

Hoffman, Eva. *Lost in Translation: A Life in a New Language.* New York: E. P. Dutton, 1989.

Hohberg, Ruth L. *Getting Here: Ruth's Story 1935–1949.* Baltimore: Publish America, 2002.

Honig, Samuel. *From Poland to Russia and Back, 1939–1946.* Windsor, ON: Black Moss, 1996.

Horvits, Tsiporah. *Tutim asurim.* Tel Aviv: Moreshet, 2009.

Jesko, Edward J. *A Journey into Exile.* New York: iUniverse, 2006.

Kahana, David. *Ahare ha-mabul.* Jerusalem: Mossad Harav Kook, 1981.

Kaminska, Ida. *My Life, My Theater.* Edited and translated by Curt Leviant. New York: Macmillan, 1973.

Kaminska, Ruth Turkow. *Mink Coats and Barbed Wire.* London: Collins and Harvill, 1979.

Kaplan, Chaim A. *Scroll of Agony: The Warsaw Diary of Chaim A. Kaplan.* Edited and translated by Abraham I. Katsh. New York: Macmillan, 1965.

Karski, Jan. *Story of a Secret State: My Report to the World,* 1944. Reprint, Washington, DC: Georgetown University Press, 2013.

Katz, Zev. *From the Gestapo to the Gulag: One Jewish Life.* London: Vallentine Mitchell, 2004.

Kawecka, Zdzisława-Krystyna. *Do Anglii przez Syberię.* Wrocław, Poland: Polskie Towarzystwo Ludoznawcze, 1994.

Kesler, Michael G. *Shards of War: Fleeing to & from Uzbekistan.* Durham, CT: Strategic Book Group, 2010.

Khrushchev, Nikita. *Khrushchev Remembers.* Edited by Strobe Talbott. Boston: Little, Brown, 1970.

Klein, Gerda Weissmann. *All But My Life.* New York: Hill and Wang, 1996.

Kozhina, Elena. *Through the Burning Steppe: A Wartime Memoir.* Translated by Vadim Mahmoudov. New York: Riverhead Books, 2000.

Kreusler, Abraham A. *A Teacher's Experiences in the Soviet Union.* Leiden: E. J. Brill, 1965.

Kruk, Herman. *The Last Days of the Jerusalem of Lithuania: Chronicles from the Vilna Ghetto and the Camps, 1939–1944.* Edited by Benjamin Harshav. Translated by Barbara Harshav. New Haven, NJ: Yale University Press and the YIVO Institute for Jewish Research, 2002.

Lane, Arthur Bliss. *I Saw Poland Betrayed: An American Ambassador Reports to the American People.* Indianapolis: Bobbs-Merrill, 1948.

Lanir, David. *Urus.* Israel: Beit Lochamei Hagettaot, 1988.

Lederman, Dov B. *These Children Are Mine: A Story of Rescue and Survival.* Jerusalem: Feldheim, 2002.

Levi, Primo. *The Reawakening.* Translated by Stuart Woolf. New York: Collier Books, 1993.

Libeskind, Daniel. *Breaking Ground: An Immigrant's Journey from Poland to Ground Zero.* New York: Riverhead Books, 2004.

Lindeman, Yehudi, ed. *Shards of Memory: Narratives of Holocaust Survival.* Westport, CT: Praeger, 2007.

Lipiner, Lucy. *Long Journey Home: A Young Girl's Memoir of Surviving the Holocaust.* Bloomington, IN: iUniverse, 2013.

Lubetkin, Zivia. *In the Days of Destruction and Revolt.* Translated by Ishai Tubbin. Tel Aviv: Hakibbutz Hameuchad, 1981.

Maik, Michael. *Deliverance: The Diary of Michael Maik, A True Story.* Edited by Avigdor Ben-Dov. Translated by Laia Ben-Dov. Kedumim, Israel: Keterpress Enterprises, 2004.

Margulies-Shnitzer, Yaffa. *I Survived Belzec Crematories.* Tel Aviv: Parnass, 1991.

Milch, Baruch. *Can Heaven Be Void?* Edited by Shosh Milch-Avigal. Jerusalem: Yad Vashem, 2003.

————. *Testament z Archiwum Żydowskiego Instytutu Historycznego.* Warsaw: Ośrodek KARTA, 2001.

————. *Ve-ulai ha-shamayim rekim.* Edited and translated by Shosh Milch-Avigal and Ephraim F. Sten. Jerusalem: Yad Vashem, 1999.

Minz, Pearl. *Surviving the Holocaust in Siberia: The Diary of Pearl Minz.* Edited by Baruch Minz. Translated by Alexander B. White. Goodyear, AZ: D. de Frain, 2010.

Mowrer, Lilian T. *Arrest and Exile: The True Story of an American Woman in Poland and Siberia 1940–41.* New York: William Morrow, 1941.

Niewyk, Donald L. *Fresh Wounds: Early Narratives of Holocaust Survival.* Chapel Hill: University of North Carolina Press, 1998.

Nomberg-Przytyk, Sara. *Auschwitz: True Tales from a Grotesque Land.* Chapel Hill: University of North Carolina Press, 1985.

————. *Kolumny Samsona.* Lublin, Poland: Wydawnictwo Lubelskie, 1966.

Orenstein, Henry. *I Shall Live: Surviving the Holocaust, 1939–1945.* New York: Oxford University Press, 1990.

Pankowsky, Hanna Davidson. *East of the Storm: Outrunning the Holocaust in Russia.* Lubbock: Texas Tech University Press, 1999.

Pat, Jacob. *Ashes and Fire.* New York: International Universities Press, 1947.

Perel, Solomon. *Europa, Europa.* Translated by Margot Bettauer Dembo. New York: John Wiley and Sons, 1997.

Perlov, Yitzchok. *The Adventures of One Yitzchok.* New York: Award Books, 1967.

Piotrowski, Tadeusz. *The Polish Deportees of World War II: Recollections of Removal to the Soviet Union and Dispersal throughout the World.* Jefferson, NC: McFarland, 2008.

Pomerantz, Jack, and Lyric Wallwork Winik. *Run East: Flight from the Holocaust*. Urbana: University of Illinois Press, 1997.

Pretzel, Marian. *Portrait of a Young Forger: An Incredible Story of Triumph over the Third Reich*. New York: Knightsbridge, 1989.

Pruszynski, Xavier. *Russian Year: The Notebook of an Amateur Diplomat*. New York: Roy, 1944.

Rachlin, Rachel, and Israel Rachlin. *Sixteen Years in Siberia: Memoirs of Rachel and Israel Rachlin*. Translated by Birgitte M. de Weille. Tuscaloosa: University of Alabama Press, 1988.

Reisfeld, A. *To Run for Life from Swastika and Red Star*. USA: Xlibris, 2002.

Rich, Betty. *Little Girl Lost*. Toronto: Azrieli Foundation, 2011.

Rieger, Aleena. *I Didn't Tell Them Anything: The Wartime Secrets of an American Girl*. New York: SunPetal Books, 2015.

Rozenberg, Lena Jedwab. *Girl with Two Landscapes: The Wartime Diary of Lena Jedwab, 1941–1945*. Translated by Solon Beinfeld. New York: Holmes and Meier, 2002.

Rubinstein, Joseph. *Megilath Russland: Scroll of a Polish Jew in Russia*. New York: CYCO, 1960.

Samuels, Klara. *God Does Play Dice: The Autobiography of a Holocaust Survivor*. Philadelphia: Bainbridge Books, 1999.

Schoenfeld, Joachim. *Holocaust Memoirs: Jews in the Lwow Ghetto, the Janowski Concentration Camp, and as Deportees in Siberia*. Hoboken, NJ: Ktav, 1985.

Schwarz, Leo W. *The Redeemers: A Saga of the Years 1945–1952*. New York: Farrar, Straus and Young, 1953.

Selver-Urbach, Sara. *Through the Window of My Home: Recollections from the Lodz Ghetto*. Translated by Siona Bodansky. Jerusalem: Yad Vashem, 1986.

Sendyk, Helen. *The End of Days*. Syracuse, NY: Syracuse University Press, 2000.

Sfard, Dovid. *Mit zikh un mit andere: oytobiografye un literarishe eseyen*. Jerusalem: Farlag "Yerusholaimer almanakh," 1984.

Shadkhanovich, David. *Zikhronot me-ha-mas'a ha-gadol*. Tel Aviv: D. Shadkhanovich, 1996.

Shafran, Rabbi Simcha, with Avi Shafran. *Fire, Ice, Air: A Polish Jew's Memoir of Yeshiva, Siberia, America*. New York: Hashgachapress, 2010.

Shapiro, Chaim. *Go, My Son: A Young Jewish Refugee's Story of Survival*. Jerusalem: Feldheim, 1989.

Sherwood, Michael (Teichholz). *Odyssey*. n.p: M. Sherwood, 2007.

Shternfeld, Shaul. *Halom ben gederot*. Tel Aviv: Halonot, 1999.

Sieradzki, Mietek. *By a Twist of History: The Three Lives of a Polish Jew*. London: Vallentine Mitchell, 2002.

Sikorska, Helena. *The Dark Side of the Moon*. New York: Charles Scribner's Sons, 1947.

Skorr, Henry, with Ivan Sokolov. *Through Blood and Tears: Surviving Hitler and Stalin.* London: Vallentine Mitchell, 2006.

Smolar, Hersh. *The Minsk Ghetto: Soviet-Jewish Partisans against the Nazis.* New York: Holocaust Library, 1989.

———. *Vu bistu khaver Sidorov?* Tel Aviv: Farlag Y. L. Perets, 1975.

Spiegel, Renia. *Renia's Diary.* New York: St. Martin's, 2019.

Starkiewicz, Helena. *Blades of Grass between the Stones.* Melbourne: H. Starkiewicz, 1998.

Szedlecki, Ann. *Album of My Life.* Toronto: Azrieli Foundation, 2010.

Szer, Włodzimierz. *To Our Children: Memoirs of Displacement. A Jewish Journey of Hope and Survival in Twentieth-Century Poland and Beyond.* Translated by Bronisława Karst. Boston: Academic Studies Press, 2016.

Szwajger, Adina Blady. *I Remember Nothing More: The Warsaw Children's Hospital and the Jewish Resistance.* Translated by Tasja Darowska and Danusia Stok. New York: Pantheon Books, 1989.

Szwarc, Szmul. *Unter royte himlen.* Melbourne: York, 1981.

Tec, Nechama. *Dry Tears: The Story of a Lost Childhood.* New York: Oxford University Press, 1984.

Temkin, Gabriel. "Flight from Poland—1968," *Midstream* XV:4 (April 1969): 3–12.

———. *My Just War: The Memoir of a Jewish Red Army Soldier in World War II.* Novato, CA: Presidio, 1998.

Temkin, Hanna. *My Involuntary Journeys: A Memoir.* Jerusalem: Yad Vashem, forthcoming.

Trunk, Isaiah. "The Historian of the Holocaust at YIVO." In *Creators and Disturbers: Reminiscences by Jewish Intellectuals of New York,* edited by Bernard Rosenberg and Ernest Goldstein, 61–74. New York: Columbia University Press, 1982.

Urban, Garri S. *Tovarisch, I Am Not Dead.* 2nd ed. London: Cyclops Vision, 2006.

Vida, George. *From Doom to Dawn: A Jewish Chaplain's Story of Displaced Persons.* New York: Jonathan David, 1967.

Vilensky, Simeon, ed. *Till My Tale Is Told: Women's Memoirs of the Gulag.* Translated by John Crowfood, Marjorie Farquharson, Catriona Kelly, Sally Laird, and Cathy Porter. Bloomington: Indiana University Press, 1999.

Wachtel, Joseph H., and Sylvia Chayat. *Escape from the Hounds of Hell.* West Palm Beach, FL: Oceanco, 1993.

Warhaftig, Zorach. *Refugee and Survivor: Rescue Efforts during the Holocaust.* Jerusalem: Yad Vashem/World Zionist Organization, 1988.

Wat, Aleksander. *My Century: The Odyssey of a Polish Intellectual.* Edited and translated by Richard Lourie. Berkeley: University of California Press, 1988.

We Sang through Tears: Stories of Survival in Siberia. Riga: Jānis Roze, 1999.

Weinrauch, Herschel (Grigory Vinokur). *Blut af der zun: Yidn in Sovet-Rusland*. Brooklyn, NY: Farlag "Mensh un Yid," 1950.

Wenig. Larry. *From Nazi Inferno to Soviet Hell*. Hoboken, NJ: Ktav, 2000.

Wielhorski, Władysław. *Wspomnienia z przeżyć w niewoli sowieckiej*. London: Orbis, 1965.

Wygodzki, Rachela Tytelman. *The End and the Beginning (August 1939– July 1948)*. n.p.: R. T. Wygodzki, 1998.

Yasanowicz, Itzhak. *Mit Yidishe shrayber in Rusland*. Buenos Aires: Kiyum, 1959.

Yafeh, Aryeh. *Yoman milhamah 'Ivri: Berit ha-Mo'atsot, 1941–1945*. Edited by Avivah Ufaz. Tel Aviv: Moreshet, 2009.

Zak, Avrom. *Knekht zenen mir geven*. 2 vols. Buenos Aires: Tsentral Farband fun Poylishe Yidn in Argentine, 1956.

———. *Oyf shlyakhn fun hefker*. 2 vols. Buenos Aires: Tsentral Farband fun Poylishe Yidn in Argentine, 1958.

———. *Yorn fun vandern*. Buenos Aires: Tsentral Farband fun Poylishe Yidn in Argentine, 1940.

Zarnowitz, Victor. *Fleeing the Nazis, Surviving the Gulag, and Arriving in the Free World: My Life and Times*. Westport, CT: Praeger, 2008.

Zerubavel, Frida. *Hayiti plitah*. Tel Aviv: Davar, 1941.

Acknowledgments

I am deeply grateful for the confluence of fate, family, and fortune that has allowed me to pursue a career as an academic. It is a true privilege to be able to follow one's interests from one project to the next. This book emerged from what had originally been envisioned as an article. Through its development, I have had the opportunity to learn a new language, meet many generous and hardworking scholars, and visit places I never imagined going.

Heartfelt thanks go to the institutions that believed in the importance of this project. I held the Sosland Foundation Fellowship at the Center for Advanced Holocaust Studies of the United States Holocaust Memorial Museum (USHMM) for the 2010–2011 academic year. The following year I was the Baron Friedrich Carl von Oppenheim Chair for the Study of Racism, Antisemitism, and the Holocaust Post-Doctoral Fellow at the International Institute for Holocaust Research at Yad Vashem. For the summers of 2013 and 2015, I received the Families, Children, and the Holocaust Research Award of the Hadassah-Brandeis Institute and the Short-Term Travel Grant of the International Research and Exchange Board. I was granted a research fellowship at the German Historical Institute of Warsaw in the spring of 2017, and at the Humanities Institute of the Pennsylvania State University in the fall of 2017.

At all of these institutions, as well as in the many libraries and archives that I visited, I have benefited from the attention of the academic and professional staff. I cannot possibly name all of them, but I would be remiss in not mentioning those where I have spent the most time or ordered the most material. Special thanks go to Vadim Altskan, Judith Cohen, Ron Coleman, Megan Lewis, and Vincent Slatt at the USHMM. Rabbi David Skulski and the staff of Ganzakh Kiddush Hashem have been kind enough to send me documents when needed. The Interlibrary

Loan department at Penn State has been heroic and Eric Novotny is always responsive and helpful.

We tell our students—and it is true—that you will not survive as a scholar if you cannot abide solitude. Sometimes, while working intensely at an archive in another country, I have noted with some alarm that over twenty-four hours has passed since I last spoke to another human being. Yet it is also true that all of our work improves with consultation and collaboration with others. I learned this lesson well in chasing down a story this large.

Over the past few years I have attended and presented parts of this work at more conferences than I can possibly mention. I am grateful for the opportunity to pilot content and approaches and learn from other scholars in the many fields that this book touches upon. While I cannot thank them all by name, I would like to call attention to the Dr. Jan Randa Aftermath Workshop in Holocaust and Genocide Studies at Monash University and the Jewish Holocaust Centre, Melbourne organized by John Goldlust (and with a resulting volume edited by Mark Edele, Atina Grossmann, and Sheila Fitzpatrick). I am also grateful to Andrzej Kamiński and the staff of the Foundation for Civic Space and Public Policy for inviting me to attend the manuscript workshop "Recovering Forgotten History" and to Katharina Friedla and Markus Nesselrodt for the workshop "Deported, Exiled, Saved. History and Memory of Polish Jews in the Soviet Union" at the Polin Museum (with its own forthcoming volume).

Many colleagues have offered advice and encouragement over the course of this project. In particular I would like to thank Rachel Feldhay Brenner, Kateřina Čapková, Boaz Cohen, Michael David-Fox, Mikhal Dekel, Havi Dreyfus, Esther Farbstein, Kiril Feferman, Steven Feldman, Olga Gershenson, Emil Kerenji, Zeev Levin, Dan Michman, Eliot Nidam-Orvieto, Iael Nidam-Orvieto, Shimon Redlich, Mark Roseman, Marla Segol, Anna Shternshis, David Silberklang, David Slucki, and Asaf Yedidya. My doctoral adviser, Antony Polonsky, remains an inspiration and a source of much support. After sharing numerous panels and discussions with Natalie Belsky and Atina Grossmann over nearly a decade, I am sometimes no longer sure whether certain insights are my own or theirs. I thank them both for their many contributions.

The manuscript profited greatly from the generosity of colleagues willing to offer comments on individual chapters. My thanks go to Natalia Aleksiun, Natalie Belsky, Grzegorz Berendt, Anna Cichopek-Gajraj, Mark Edele, Gennady Estraikh, Gabriel Finder, John Goldlust, Łukasz Kamiński, Kamil Kijek, Łukasz Krzyżanowski, Katarzina Person, Bożena Szaynok, Polly Zavadivker, Andriy Zayarnyuk, and Arkadi Zeltser.

After many years as a contingent faculty member, and several as an independent scholar, I had the somewhat unlikely good fortune in 2014 to join the faculty of the Pennsylvania State University. Both the Department of History and the Jewish Studies Program have offered supportive environments for completing this book, and I would like to thank Michael Kulikowski and Benjamin Schreier for their leadership. Among my many distinguished colleagues, my work and equilibrium have benefited especially from conversations with Michelle Baker, Tobias Brinkmann, Daniel Falk, Eric Fleisch, Lori Ginsburg, Pearl Gluck, Tawny Holm, Kobi Kabalek, Lior Sternfeld, Catherine Wanner, and Ran Zwigenberg.

Kathleen McDermott became an early booster of this manuscript and helped to usher it through the review and publication process. Her expertise and experience have helped to make the process run smoothly. Thanks also to the rest of the highly professional staff at Harvard University Press, and to Emily Silk for excellent editing. Professional mapmaker Isabelle Lewis has been extremely patient with this amateur. Tomasz Frydel was kind enough to check over my Polish translations. It goes without saying that all of the errors that remain in the book are my own responsibility.

My family has lived with this project for a long time now. I hope that in some ways it has been enriching. It has been particularly gratifying to watch my older daughters Maya and Rana enter college and grow into their own research in the course of these years. In talks about sources, content, and footnotes, we now share these interests. I am grateful to my younger daughter Selah for wholeheartedly adopting the Soviet method of the "norm" to govern my progress. My partner Stephen Bickel has been my patron and my interlocutor, and is endlessly patient and supportive. This book is dedicated to him, as well as to all of the Polish Jews who wandered through the USSR during the Second World War.

Index

Note: Figures are indexed in italic. Page numbers followed by *t* refer to tables.

284; 38; and German-Soviet border in Poland, 21, 37; Red Army crossing of, 226; refugees' crossing of, 32, 35, 37, 40–41, 44, 50, 65, 98, 273; Soviet liberation, 226, 227; Soviet retreat behind, 16

Bukhara: as destination for amnestied Poles, 159; graves of Polish Jews in, 289, 290; Polish Jewish refugees in, 5, 161, 166, 184, 210, 219, 250; Polish school in, 221; repatriated Jews from, 241, 271; ZPP in, 224, 228

Bukharan Jews, 169

Bukharan Region, efforts to reunite separated families in, 229

Bukhovina, migration from, after Soviet annexation, 36

Bund. *See* Jewish Labor Bund

Burshtein, Shmuel, 65, 129, 142

Burstin, Symcha, 41, 54, 118, 121, 152, 160, 163

Canada, Jewish migration to, 63, 258, 269, 271, 274, 275–276, 277

Catholic Church, in postwar Poland, 250, 263, 297

Caucasus, Poles resettled in, prior to repatriation, 230

Cemeteries, Jewish, Nazi desecration of, 248

Central Asia, amnestied Poles in, 2, 8, 281; contact with unfamiliar ethnic groups, 168; daily life in exile, 165–174; graves of, 289–290, 290; value of reports by, 289; views on local people and cultures, 169–170. *See also* Amnestied Polish Jews

Central Asian republics, *xiv–xv*, 152, 352n17. *See also* Kazakh SSR (Kazakhstan); Kirghiz SSR (Kirghizia); Tajik SSR (Tajikistan); Uzbek SSR (Uzbekistan)

Central Committee of Jews in Poland (Centralny Komitet Żydów w Polsce. *See* CKŻP

Central Jewish Historical Commission (Centralna Żydowski Komisja Historyczna), 9–10, 252. *See also* ŻIH (Jewish Historical Institute, Żydowski Instytut Historyczny)

Certificates, for immigration to Palestine, 61, 62, 163, 198, 210, 271

Chabad Lubavitch movement, 228

Chełm, death march and executions of Jewish youth in, 43, 106

Chelyabinsk Oblast, number of deportees to, 112t

Chesno, Zekharia, 59, 62

Chiger, Krystyna, 16, 73

Chkalov (Orenburg), ZPP in, 222

Chkalov Oblast, collective farm in, 231

Choice, 7, 213, 277, 288; flight decisions in 1939, 2, 16, 19, 22–27, 27–35, 45, 46–47, 48–49, 81, 90, 156, 282, 285; flight in 1941, 156, 157, 282; to leave Poland after repatriation, 212, 251, 261, 278; to lie for immigration purposes, 270–71; to migrate after immigration, 276–77; to move within the USSR after amnesty, 231; registration in 1940, 13, 45, 82, 90, 91, 93–94, 100; in relationships, 188; to remain in north after amnesty, 154, 155; to remain in Poland after repatriation, 212, 258, 262; to return to German-occupied territories, 46, 98; vis a vis Soviet policies, 82, 114, 142, 144; to stay in the USSR, 234, 235; to travel to Central Asia after amnesty, 150, 152;

Churchill, Winston, 144, 251

Citizenship, Polish: of Polish Jews in Soviet Union, 4; Soviet efforts to exclude Belorussians, Jews, and Ukrainians from, 27–28, 150; Soviet's postamnesty redefinition of, 150, 177, 225, 238

Citizenship, Soviet: as automatic for residents of annexed Polish territories, 70, 90, 150, 237; and engagement in Soviet politics, 82; forcing of Polish Jews' acceptance of, 4, 150, 193, 219, 225; Jews jailed for refusing, 178–179. *See also* Passportization drive (1940)

Citizenship, Soviet, Polish Jews accepting: ability to remain in place, 91, 94, 96, 156, 157, 177; avoiding deportation, 132, 194; choice, 93–94; as concern to Polish officials, 193, 197, 201; flight of, 158; mass deaths of, 100; motives of,

11-8-21